D0985072

Việt Nam

OTHER BOOKS BY BEN KIERNAN

How Pol Pot Came to Power: Colonialism, Nationalism, and Communism in Cambodia, 1930–1975

The Pol Pot Regime: Race, Power, and Genocide in Cambodia under the Khmer Rouge, 1975–1979

Blood and Soil: A World History of Genocide and Extermination from Sparta to Darfur

Genocide and Resistance in Southeast Asia: Documentation, Denial, and Justice in Cambodia and East Timor

Việt Nam

A History from Earliest Times to the Present

Ben Kiernan

OXFORD
UNIVERSITY PRESS

OXFORD
UNIVERSITY PRESS

Oxford University Press is a department of the University of Oxford.
It furthers the University's objective of excellence in research, scholarship,
and education by publishing worldwide. Oxford is a registered trade mark of
Oxford University Press in the UK and certain other countries.

Published in the United States of America by Oxford University Press
198 Madison Avenue, New York, NY 10016, United States of America.

Library of Congress Cataloging-in-Publication Data

Names: Kiernan, Ben, author.
Title: Việt Nam : a history from earliest times to the present / Ben Kiernan.
Other titles: Việt Nam, a history from earliest times to the present
Description: New York City : Oxford University Press, [2017] |
Includes bibliographical references and index.
Identifiers: LCCN 2016035618 (print) | LCCN 2016036923 (ebook) |
ISBN 9780195160765 (hardcover : alk. paper) | ISBN 9780190627294 (Updf) |
ISBN 9780190627300 (Epub)
Subjects: LCSH: Vietnam—History.
Classification: LCC DS556.5 .K53 2017 (print) | LCC DS556.5 (ebook) |
DDC 959.7 dc23
LC record available at https://lccn.loc.gov/2016035618

1 3 5 7 9 8 6 4 2

Printed by Edwards Brothers Malloy, United States of America

Published with the assistance of the Frederick W. Hilles Publication Fund of Yale University,
the Whitney and Betty MacMillan Center for International and Area Studies at Yale,
and the Yale Council on Southeast Asia Studies.

for Glenda, Mia-lia, Derry, and Miles

CONTENTS

ABBREVIATIONS

ANCL	*An Nam chí lược* (Brief annals of Annam, 1307)
ANOM	Archives Nationales d'Outre-Mer (Aix-en-Provence, France)
ARVN	Army of the Republic of [South] Việt Nam
Bajaraka	Political movement of Bahnar, Rhadé, Jarai, and Koho (Cơ Ho) ethnic groups
BEFEO	*Bulletin de l'Ecole Française d'Extrême-Orient*
CC	Central Committee
Ch.	Chinese language
CIDG	Civilian Irregular Defense Groups (South Việt Nam)
COSVN	Central Office for South Việt Nam (communist)
DNTL	*Đại Nam thực lục* (Veritable records of Đại Nam), 1811–
DVSK	*Đại Việt sử ký* (Record of the history of Đại Việt, 1272)
DVSKTT	*Đại Việt sử ký toàn thư* (Complete historical records of Đại Việt, 1479)
DRV	Democratic Republic of Việt Nam, 1945–76 (North Việt Nam)
FBIS-APA	Foreign Broadcast Information Service, Daily Report, Asia and Pacific
FEER	*Far Eastern Economic Review*
FULRO	Front Unifié de la Lutte des Races Opprimés
GBA	General Buddhist Association of Việt Nam
GGI	Gouvernement-Général de l'Indochine (ANOM).
GVN	Government of Việt Nam, 1954–75 (South Việt Nam)
ICP	Indochina Communist Party (Đông Dương Cộng Sản Đảng), 1930–51
MAAG	(U.S.) Military Assistance Advisory Group, 1955–62
MACV	(U.S.) Military Assistance Command, Vietnam, 1962–73
MOS	(CIA) Military Operations Section
NLF	National Liberation Front of [South] Việt Nam (Việt Cộng)
NYT	*New York Times*
PAVN	People's Army of [North] Việt Nam

PLAF	People's Liberation Armed Forces of South Việt Nam
PMS	Pays Montagnards du Sud
PRG	Provisional Revolutionary Government of South Việt Nam, 1969–75
PSA	(U.S.) Province Senior Adviser
RSA	Résidence Supérieure en Annam (ANOM)
RST (NF)	Résidence Supérieure au Tonkin (Nouveaux Fonds), (ANOM)
RVN	Republic of [South] Việt Nam, 1955–75
Sources	*Sources of Vietnamese Tradition*, ed. George E. Dutton, Jayne S. Werner, and John K. Whitmore (New York, Columbia University Press, 2012)
SVN	State of Việt Nam, 1949–55
SRV	Socialist Republic of Việt Nam, 1976–
V.	Vietnamese language
VC	Việt Cộng
VCI	Viet Cong Infrastructure
VCP	Việt Nam Communist Party, 1976–
VDLT	*Việt điện u linh tập* (Departed spirits of the Việt Realm, 1329)
VNQDD	Việt Nam Nationalist Party (Việt Nam Quốc Dân Đảng, or VNQDĐ)
VSL	*Việt sử lược* (Brief history of Việt, c. 1350)
VWP	Việt Nam Workers Party, 1951–76

Weights and Measures

ha	hectare(s); 1 hectare = 2.47 acres
kg	kilogram; 1 kilogram = 2.2 lbs.
km	kilometer(s); 1 kilometer = 0.62 miles
m	meter(s); 1 meter = 1.09 yards
picul	133 lbs.
quan	a string of hundreds of cash coins
quan tiền	a string of six hundred cash coins
thăng	2 liters, or 2.67 kg (5.89 lbs.) of grain

NOTE ON SPELLING

In the case of Việt Nam and other proper names, I have used Vietnamese spelling with diacritics, except for the cities of Saigon (Sài Gòn) and Hanoi (Hà Nội), while making a distinction in chapter 7 between the city of Hanoi and rural Hà Nội province. For Chăm and Khmer names, I have generally not used diacritics, except where indicated in the sources.

For Chinese terms, I have used Pinyin except for other forms of romanization where the original characters were undetermined. Tonal marks are used sparingly, mainly for clarity, as in "Yuè."

In quotations, I have preserved the original spellings.

PREFACE

I first visited Việt Nam as a student, three months before the American-Vietnamese war ended in 1975. Early that January, communist forces had just overrun the southern town of Phước Bình, capital of Phước Long province. But then a month of apparent calm preceded their final military campaign of March and April. Public buses running regularly from Saigon took me north to the Central Highlands, to the southeast coast, and west through the Mekong delta to the Gulf of Siam. Even in wartime, and without speaking Vietnamese or being able to visit central or northern Việt Nam, I was struck by the country's diversity and its long multiethnic and pluri-religious history. I talked with Vietnamese Catholic university students in the hill town of Đà Lạt, photographed medieval Cham Hindu temples by the sea, and watched ethnic Khmer children play in the grounds of a Buddhist wat in the delta. In Long Xuyên province, leaders of the anti-communist Hòa Hảo Buddhist sect welcomed me to their historic headquarters, and in the west-coast town of Rạch Gía I met a former resident of a longtime communist-held zone in the U Minh forest. Back on the sidewalks of Saigon, I admired the Chinese calligraphy of an elderly scholar trained in the classical Confucian tradition. And I interviewed a Buddhist neutralist senator who would soon briefly become the last prime minister of the Republic of Việt Nam.[1] I took away a strong impression of Việt Nam's variety, not only culturally and politically but across space and time as well.

This book owes a debt to three prolific and pioneering Vietnamese scholars who worked in New Haven, Paris, and Hanoi, respectively. Huỳnh Sanh Thông (1926–2008), founder of Vietnamese studies in the United States, translator into English of a vast corpus of Vietnamese literature including a masterful rendering of *The Tale of Kiều*, and publisher of *Vietnam Forum* and *Vietnam Review*, was an innovative thinker, gifted writer, inspiring teacher, and treasured friend. He is sadly missed.[2] Likewise, I can only marvel at the scholarly range and productivity of Lê Thành Khôi (born in 1923), author of a dozen books from his pathbreaking *Le Viêt-nam, histoire et civilization*

(1955) to his *Histoire et anthologie de la littérature vietnamienne* (2008), and also at the lifelong contribution of Nguyễn Khắc Viện (1913–97), founding editor of *Vietnamese Studies* from 1964 to 1983, translator and editor of the three-volume *Anthologie de la littérature vietnamienne* (1972), and author of *Histoire du Vietnam* (1974). Like most of their compatriots, these three extraordinary people agreed and disagreed on many things. But my debt to the work of all of them will be clear in the pages that follow, and I am grateful that I had the opportunity to meet them, on four continents. I am fortunate to have the memory, as a graduate student in 1979, of driving Nguyễn Khắc Viện around the waterfront streets of Stockholm in my kombi van, and then tracking him down in his office in Hanoi a year later.

Only a quarter century afterward did I turn to writing this history of their country. I could not have done so without benefiting from the superb scholarship on early and modern Vietnamese history, epitomized by the work of the late Oliver Wolters and many others. David P. Chandler, John D. Legge, Merle C. Ricklefs, and Jamie Mackie at Monash University, along with Ian D. Black and John Ingleson at the University of New South Wales, all started me off in Southeast Asian history. At Yale University Paul M. Kennedy, Dori Laub, Gaddis Smith, Robin W. Winks, and Jay M. Winter taught me most of what I know about international history. Abbas Amanat and Jonathan D. Spence expanded my interest in Asia. John Merriman and James C. Scott encouraged me to delve into rural social history. Ramsay MacMullen and Paul Freedman rekindled my interest in ancient and medieval history; Howard Lamar and John Mack Faragher deepened my understanding of the history of frontiers.

I am also fortunate to have had the opportunity to work with former and current Yale graduate students, especially Haydon Cherry, Charles Keith, Conor Lauesen, Mark A. Lawrence, Tram Luong, Emily Nguyen, Lien-Hang T. Nguyen, Kim N. B. Ninh, Lorraine Paterson, Charles Wheeler, Brian Turner, and Sam C. Vong, who are all making important contributions to the study of Vietnamese history and have taught me much about Việt Nam along the way.

Haydon Cherry, George Dutton, Charles Keith, Alexander B. Woodside, my OUP editor Susan Ferber, and an anonymous reviewer all read the entire manuscript in draft and generously provided extensive, invaluable feedback and helpful suggestions for improvement. Nayan Chanda, Glenda E. Gilmore, Val Noone, C. Michele Thompson, and Joanna Waley-Cohen kindly read and offered comments on various chapters. Joanna Waley-Cohen also provided transliterations of Chinese terms. Brian Turner sent notices of new work that otherwise I might have missed. Eric Henry generously sent me his translations of early Chinese texts and writings on early Vietnamese historical subjects. Bích-Ngọc Turner provided me with her full English translation of *Việt sử lược*, and Mai Bui Dieu Linh with hers of *Chính Sách Khuyến Nông Dưới Thời Minh Mạng*. Drs. Quang Phú Văn and Trần Đức Anh Sơn kindly assisted me with archaic Vietnamese titles, Chăm family names, and several other issues. My Yale research assistants Van Nguyen, Don Phan, Vy Vu, Helen Pho, Mitchell Tan, Michael Thornton, and Jinping Wang were all unfailingly efficient. Classroom interactions with the students who have taken my seminars on Vietnamese history for the past three decades at the University of Wollongong and Yale University gave me many new insights and helped clarify my understanding.

Over the years I have benefited from innumerable discussions of Vietnamese history with Nina Adams, Melanie Beresford, David Biggs, Đỗ Ngọc Bích, Nayan Chanda, David P. Chandler, Bradley Davis, Dan Duffy, George Dutton, Olga Dror, David W. P. Elliott, Christopher E. Goscha, Erik Harms, Judith Henchy, Eric Henry, David Hunt, George McT. Kahin, Christian Lentz, Greg Lockhart, Fredrik Logevall, David G. Marr, Edward Miller, Edwin E. Moïse, Ngo Vinh Long, Nguyễn Phạm Điền, Lien-Hang T. Nguyen, Nguyen Thi Thu, Nhung Tuyet Tran, Kim N. B. Ninh, Val Noone, Don Oberdorfer, Milton E. Osborne, Kristin Pelzer, D. Gareth Porter, Quang Phú Văn, Sophie Quinn-Judge, Jonathan Schell, James C. Scott, Keith W. Taylor, C. Michele Thompson, Trần Đức Anh Sơn, Esta Ungar, Thaveeporn Vasavakul, Joanna Waley-Cohen, Jayne S. Werner, Wynn Wilcox, Alexander B. Woodside, and Peter Zinoman.

I have been the fortunate recipient of sabbaticals, research grants, and visiting fellowships that have given me the time and facilities I needed to write this book. I wish to thank the National Humanities Center in Research Triangle Park, North Carolina; the University of Sydney; the Camargo Foundation in Cassis, France; the Long Room Hub at Trinity College, Dublin; the American Council of Learned Societies; the Rockefeller Foundation for a fellowship at Bellagio, Italy; the Bogliasco Foundation for a fellowship at the Liguria Study Center for the Arts and Humanities; and the Shelby Cullom Davis Center for Historical Studies, Princeton University. I would particularly like to thank Philip Nord, Katja Guenther, and my fellow fellows at the Davis Center during the spring semester of 2014. Their helpful feedback on drafts of chapters 4 and 5 is much appreciated. Over many years my wonderful literary agent, Lisa Adams, has been unfailingly supportive. The ever capable Heather Salome drew the twelve custom maps (figs. 1.1, 2.1, 4.1, 4.3, 5.1, 6.1, 8.1, 8.3, 10.1–3, and 11.1). Daniel Judt flattened fig. 8.2. Dana Lee commanded the cloud.

Finally, I am deeply indebted to my Yale colleague Dr. Quang Phú Văn, who in addition to his expertise on Vietnamese philosophy was the best language teacher I have ever experienced in the classroom.

None of these scholars are responsible for any faults in this book, which are mine alone.

Throughout the research and writing of this book, my wife, Glenda, has made my life a joy.

—The Sailor's Bar, Killaha West, July 2016

Việt Nam

Introduction

"The mountains are like the bones of the earth. Water is its blood," wrote a Vietnamese geographer in 1820.[1] Lowland Việt Nam is aquatic, but it is also multiregional and polyethnic. The country's three historic lowland regions are bounded by extensive uplands, all linked by interrelated landscapes, economies, and cultures. Throughout the plains, water plays a key role in the economy and communications. In the north and south, the Red River and the Mekong River form wide deltas and flow into the South China Sea. Linking the two deltas is the central region, many hundreds of miles of curving coastline, broken every twenty miles or so by river mouths and port towns.

Central Việt Nam, once known as Champa, is a long, narrow coastal plain that Vietnamese often picture as a thin bamboo pole, at whose ends are suspended two bulky rice baskets, the northern and southern deltas of the Red River and the Mekong.[2] In the past three millennia, these three lowland regions have nourished unique wet-rice civilizations, speaking primarily forms of the Vietnamese, Cham, and Cambodian languages, respectively. Overlooking the lowlands, and descending very close to the coast along the narrow central plain, forested ranges and hills ("the bones of the earth") serve as the watersheds of the country's many rivers, occupy three-quarters of its territory, and are home to over fifty more ethnic minority groups speaking as many languages.

In one sense, this polyethnic culture helped usher in the first use of the name "Việt Nam." That term first appeared early in the nineteenth century after the consolidation of all these regions under a new dynasty that had been founded by a multicultural military force. In the late eighteenth century a long civil war had wracked the divided lands then known as Đại Việt

(Great Việt). The ultimately victorious Nguyễn armies, largely composed of ethnic Vietnamese, also received aid from an army raised by a Cambodian former palace slave, a Cham chief and his followers, fleets commanded by a Siamese rebel and a Chinese pirate, twenty thousand Siamese royal troops, and units of French and other European forces. Some five thousand Cambodians marched with Nguyễn troops as they advanced north in 1800.[3] Two years after conquering the entire country in 1802, the triumphant Nguyễn dynasty gave it a new name, Việt Nam (Southern Việt). The name change did not, however, reflect the kingdom's multiethnic composition.

Although its long history includes civil wars, Chinese and French invasions, and the colossal American-Vietnamese conflict, Việt Nam has always been much more than a war. Looking back and seeing only "the Vietnam War" might capture that conflict, but it misses the multidimensional character of the country, its culture, and its history. Conceiving of it only as an American war can erase more. "Vietnam" was America's first televised war, and U.S. discussion of it has often conveyed an impression of distance from the actual events in Việt Nam. As historian David Elliott put it, "Vietnam has come to represent a national American trauma rather than a real place with real people."[4]

Perhaps this is unsurprising. The myths of the American war are legion and long-lived. Ten years after its end an American boxer, limbering up for a title fight in Sydney, Australia, predicted he would win "like Rambo did in Vietnam" (he didn't say "in the movie").[5] The American became mired in a fifteen-round defeat. Two decades later the George W. Bush administration also seemed to recall the Vietnam War as a military victory, lacking only its final triumph, which was supposedly blocked by weak politicians or denied by antiwar media. Bush's father had proclaimed in 1991 after winning the first Gulf War, "We've kicked the Vietnam Syndrome" and "slain the ghost of Vietnam at last."[6] Conversely, in 2007, a critic of America's second war in Iraq called that U.S. invasion "a Vietnam replay."[7] Seven years later the *New York Times* was asking "Will Syria be Obama's Vietnam?" and concluded that "The Vietnam War Still Sets Off a Battle in America."[8] A columnist compared "ISIS and Vietnam," or rather, present and past U.S. policies toward them, as "loosely akin." Then the *Times* editorialized: "Vietnam has emerged as a major player in America's plans to build a regional counterweight to China, despite the trauma of the Vietnam War."[9] Visiting Hanoi in May 2016, President Obama told the Vietnamese government:

> In the South China Sea, the US is not a claimant in current disputes, but we will stand with our partners in upholding key principles like freedom of navigation....

> Vietnam will have greater access to the equipment you need to improve your security.... Nations are sovereign and no matter how large or small a nation may be, its territory should be respected.... Big nations should not bully smaller ones.[10]

"Vietnam" has become many things—an American experience, a slippery slope, a military model, a mortal ghost, a replayable disc, a recyclable ally. But the real country has even more variety than the projected one. Not only its recent past and contemporary international symbolism but also centuries of its own disputed histories all yield important insights about the making of both the premodern and the modern worlds, from the rise of chiefdoms to the role of empires and the creation of states. Such a history merits a long-range view.

Take again the name "Việt Nam." First introduced in the early nineteenth century, the country's contemporary name came into widespread use only in the mid-twentieth, under French colonial rule, after two millennia of documented history of the territory and its inhabitants. The ancient form *Nam Việt*, "the Việt South," first appears (in Chinese as *Nán Yuè*) as far back as 207 BCE. Its written Vietnamese version dates from 973 CE.[11] The first use of the reversed modern form, "Việt Nam" (*Yuè Nán* in Chinese) came eight centuries later—in 1804.[12] And that very brief appearance resulted only from Middle Kingdom officials overruling the new Nguyễn monarch's proposal to resurrect the name Nam Việt, which for the suzerain self-image of imperial China too closely recalled the aspirations to autonomy of an ancient southern kingdom.[13] A long history lay behind these modern decisions.

Over the past century modern Vietnamese nationalism, manifested in local opposition first to French colonial rule and then to American intervention, has influenced the writing of the country's history both at home and abroad. Retrospectively, nationalism has written a new past, projecting backward a sense of long-term continuity. But this rewritten history masks the dramatic changes that nationalism itself has quite recently wrought.

Moreover the record of earlier changes is also incontrovertible: a survey of the political history of the land of Việt Nam might neatly identify three quite discontinuous, distinct eras, marked by their very different forms of governance: indigenous chiefdoms of the first millennium BCE, imperial Chinese rule in the first millennium CE, and in the second, independent Vietnamese kingdoms followed by a century of French colonialism and a new independence. Conversely, an ethnic history might focus on three or four of its geographic regions and their different cultures and experiences, instead of treating the entire area as a single nation.

An accurate history needs to refrain from backdating modern geographical conceptions of territorial polities and from applying them to the prehistoric, classical, or even medieval eras. For instance, premodern "Việt Nam" and "China" (even when those names were used) each comprised different territories and included more cultural and often political variety than their contemporary names suggest. Moreover their common frontier was much less sharply defined, with people in both realms sharing many social, cultural, and economic beliefs and practices. Though the modern Vietnamese state occupies a lengthy contiguous territory, scholars dispute not just how long that territory has hosted a "nation," but whether its ethnic Vietnamese inhabitants even possess a single continuous political history. In different eras its "Chinese" and "Vietnamese" authorities gave the country different names. In the first millennium a succession of classical imperial and local rulers of what is now the northern region of Việt Nam formally named it Nán Yuè, Jiaozhi, Jiao, An Nan, and Đại Cồ Việt. Second-millennium kingdoms and governments have in turn named the entire country Đại Việt, Đại Ngu, Jiaozhi (again), An Nan (again), Yuè Nán, Đại Nam, Annam, and finally Việt Nam.

Competing frameworks for the past have made dating Vietnamese nationhood a political as well as a historical issue. After independence from France, the Catholic nationalist Nguyễn Mạnh Hà wrote: "We are a nation that has existed for twenty-five centuries."[14] Hồ Chí Minh and the Vietnamese Marxist historian Trần Huy Liệu located "the origins of the nation" in the first millennium BCE. At that time, they proclaimed, the "Hùng kings," an otherwise unnamed and undocumented line of legendary monarchs, had "built the country" before China conquered Nán Yuè in 111 BCE.[15] Three decades later a U.S. historian, Keith W. Taylor, partially agreed that "the story begins" before that conquest, but he dated "the final phase" of "the birth of Vietnam" to the tenth century CE, "when Vietnamese leaders drew a political frontier between themselves and the Chinese."[16] He doubts that "pre-tenth century people" may be termed Vietnamese by any modern definition.[17] Another American scholar of the country, Stephen O'Harrow, has dated the rise of a Vietnamese "nation" as beginning somewhat earlier, perhaps when "the first Vietnamese" lived in the third century CE, but reaching its completion later, with the advent of the powerful Lê dynasty in the early fifteenth century.[18] Meanwhile leading Vietnamese scholars in the United States argued that at least by the time the French began to conquer it in 1858, Việt Nam was "already a nation" with "a unified tradition, culture and language, and an effective political and economic system."[19] Yet others have dated it even later, after the French conquest, locating the birth of the Vietnamese "nation" only in the first half or even the middle of the twentieth century.[20] Writing a history of Việt Nam as a nation is a fraught enterprise.

Thus the rich tapestry of Vietnamese history cannot be reduced to a national story, an unchanging ethnic identity, or an enduring ancient polity—any more than the country can be reduced to a singular twentieth-century war. What is known today as Việt Nam is a land shared and contested by many peoples and cultures for several thousand years.

This book treats Việt Nam over the millennia primarily as a place, a series of homelands that have become a shared territory, a changing land and common home rather than a continuous culture or a developing polity. It focuses not on the origins of Vietnamese nationhood or the persistence of a political identity but on documenting and narrating the experiences of the variety of peoples who have inhabited the country's different regions since earliest recorded times, as well as their interactions with their natural environments and with neighboring countries.[21] The focus is on much more than the political history of a geographical area defined by the modern state's contemporary boundaries. Rather, a history of the different regions within those boundaries helps to integrate the multiethnic nature of its people's histories and their cultural relationships with the lands where they have lived.

The book therefore departs in several ways from previous Western-language histories of Việt Nam. Its multiethnic coverage, its inclusion of non-Vietnamese premodern geographic settings, and its historical organization are all distinct. Most histories have focused on the story of the ethnic Vietnamese, often commencing with their emergence in the north and then pursuing their intermittent "march to the south."[22] Here attention is given not only to the history of the modern Vietnamese majority but also to the extensive historical record of the Cham and Khmer peoples who have long populated the central and southern lowlands, and to the smaller ethnic groups of the northern uplands and Central Highlands. The histories of these central, southern, and upland regions and their inhabitants are presented here as significant in themselves, not simply for the part they played in Vietnamese settlement in those regions, though the shared history of their interethnic relations is equally important.[23]

Many earlier works have also focused on specific eras of the country's history, determined by the ethnicity or political system of its rulers: the Chinese imperial period in the first millennium CE, or that of Vietnamese monarchies in the second; the era before the first French conquests in 1859, or the era that followed; the period up to the 1945 communist revolution, or the postwar era. Previous works have also divided the history of independent Việt Nam (like that of imperial China) into successive, implicitly cyclical eras based on the rise and fall of the kingdom's ruling families or dynasties, for example the Lý, Trần, Lê, and Nguyễn. In contrast, this book attempts a long-range view that includes in one narrative the diverse people and peoples of all these different eras from prehistory to the present. Its chapters periodize Việt Nam's past on the basis of broader historical themes—not only political but also cultural, economic, and environmental changes. Some chapters, for instance, are divided on the basis of climate eras.

While this book is not a "deep history" of Việt Nam in the sense of covering forty thousand years of the country's human habitation, nonetheless "thinking far back," integrating its prehistory into its history, represents one goal of this survey of the last three millennia there. It seeks to uncover some of the "vibrations of deeper time" that can be detected more easily through a wide-angle view over what historians call the *longue durée*: "horizons longer—usually much longer—than a generation, a human lifetime, or the other roughly biological time-spans that have defined most recent historical writing." As historians Jo Guldi and David Armitage argue, "Micro-history and macro-history—short-term analysis and the long-term overview—should work together" by fusing close study of individual eras into "big picture work . . . woven from a broad range of sources" to pursue the search for "crucial pivots, turning points" and achieve an understanding of multiple causality over time.[24] A long-range narrative should enable readers to assess the changes and continuities, the themes and variations, the similarities and differences between historical eras, as well as among the peoples who inhabited the land.

On a transnational level, this book further departs from other histories by assessing Việt Nam not only in terms of its long political and cultural relationships with China but also in the contexts of Southeast Asian and global history, including environmental history. The fact that the name "Việt Nam" became widely used only in the twentieth century was far from unique in Southeast Asia. Siam changed its name to Thailand in 1939, emphasizing its own ethnic majority, and the names "Indonesia" and "Malaysia" are also twentieth-century neologisms. To go back to the early modern era, the formation of the "geo-body" of Việt Nam resembles much more closely those of Burma and Siam than the vast inland empire of China. The long, thin coastal regions of southern Việt Nam, Burma, and Siam all betray their common historical experience of north-south, partly seaborne expansion at the expense of other Southeast Asian realms. For instance, Việt Nam's incorporation of Champa and of Cambodia's Mekong delta from the fifteenth to the nineteenth centuries roughly parallels the Upper Burman kingdom's conquest of the Lower Burman kingdom of Pegu, which was independent up to 1539 and again in 1740–57, and of the coastal kingdom of Arakan.

In addition, the impact on Việt Nam of what a nineteenth-century Vietnamese thinker termed "world trends" is important. Factors such as colonialism, along with climate changes and other global patterns such as the spread of the Latin alphabet to Việt Nam and other maritime countries of Southeast Asia—the Philippines, Indonesia, and Malaysia—all merit close study along with the local lifeways they transformed.

A long history of such a rich place brings to the forefront themes of continuity and disruption. This book identifies ten major themes of Vietnamese history, three of which appear to have a rather continuous influence and seven are transformative and often recurrent. Over three millennia, these themes have marked the lives of the people of the region.

Three perennial themes—ecological, linguistic, and genealogical—have permeated the long histories of these lands and their inhabitants. First is the importance of the natural environment, including both the landscape and climate, themselves varying over the different geographical spaces within this territory and changing over time as heavy rains swept silt downstream and new sea levels transformed coastlines. Second is the history of languages spoken in the region. From the first millennium BCE onward, people in parts of this territory spoke Proto-Vietic and Vietic languages, early but scientifically recognizable linguistic ancestors of the dialects of modern Vietnamese. And third, while individuals and groups often migrated and could learn and switch languages over time, some of their genealogical heritage and cultural affinities just as easily persisted.

If nations, states, and sea levels rise and fall, some elements of the regional ecology and climate have proved enduring influences on cultural life in Việt Nam. The country has long possessed an aquatic culture. In his study "Live by Water, Die for Water (*Sống vì nước, chết vì nước*)," Huỳnh Sanh Thông, a scholar of the Vietnamese language and culture, documented and analyzed the frequent use, from earliest times to the present, of aquatic metaphors in poetry, writing, and folklore. He wrote: "The ancestors of the Vietnamese attached far more importance to 'water' than to either 'hills' or 'land' in their idea of a homeland." Aquatic metaphors recurred in nineteenth- and twentieth-century poetry.[25] In Vietnamese literature, water could represent far more than just the idea of a homeland. "The sea and streams, ponds and lakes, water plants and beasts, barges and bridges, fisherfolk and boaters, all serve as graphic metaphors to embody harsh facts or base desires as well as noble truths or deep thoughts." Huỳnh Sanh Thông characterized "the Vietnamese worldview" itself as "Water, water everywhere."[26]

The crucial role of water across the land has long struck foreign observers too.[27] "Elephants can actually swim," marveled a Chinese border official peering southward in the twelfth century.[28] Samuel Baron, probably the first Westerner born and raised in Việt Nam, wrote in the seventeenth century that in the northern region from March to May, "the great rains" caused floods to descend down the Red River "with that incredible rapidity . . . as threatens banks and dams with destruction . . . drowning thereby whole provinces." Baron likened the "low and flat" Red River plain to the Netherlands, "especially for its moats and banks." For most of the year, the river's many branches irrigated vast areas of "wet ground," creating "infinite ponds" and flowing into the sea through "eight or nine mouths, most of them navigable for vessels of small draught." These rivers, he added, "swarm with boats and large barks."[29]

Not long afterward, but during the dry season, the English buccaneer William Dampier reached northern Việt Nam. He described its landscape as he headed inland up the Red River in July 1688, "sometimes rowing, sometimes sailing" through its low-lying, irrigated delta. Dampier found "a delightful prospect over a large level fruitful country. It was generally either pasture or rice-fields, and void of trees, except only about the villages, which stood thick, and appeared mighty pleasant at a distance." He reported: "Every house has a small gate or stile to enter into the garden first. . . . In the gardens every man has his own fruit trees, as oranges, limes, betel; his pumpkins, melons, pineapples and a great many herbs."[30] But as months passed and the rains returned, Dampier discovered that during the wet season these northern delta villages looked very different: "All the land about them is under water, two or three foot deep," like "so many duck-houses." People could not "pass from one village to another, but mid-leg or to their knees in water, unless sometimes in boats, which they keep."[31]

The landscape was different farther south, in the hill country and narrow coastal strip that today comprise central Việt Nam. A Chinese admiral visiting the Hindu realm of Champa in 1433 remarked on its tropical weather and flora, different from those in China: "The climate is pleasantly hot, without frost or snow. . . . The plants and trees are always green."[32] In 1686 a Portuguese Jesuit described the winds off the South China Sea that often drove ships against Champa's coasts, where mountains and forests descended almost to the shore and a passing Indian mariner could count the individual branches of trees. "No one can pass by Champa without seeing and hearing the birds in its trees."[33]

Here, by the seventeenth century, Vietnamese governments and settlers had expanded southward from the Red River delta and gradually conquered most of the land of Champa. Although the lay of its land was very different and the monsoons reversed, the aquatic environment and lifestyle there also struck foreign observers. From 1618 to 1622, the Italian Jesuit Christoforo Borri lived at Qui Nhơn on the central coast. Perhaps the first Westerner to reside in Việt Nam, Borri wrote of "the continual rains" from September to November over the nearby mountains, "whence the waters running down in abundance do so flood the kingdom, that meeting with the sea, they seem to be all of a piece." And here too the local population, "very often when they do not think of it at night, ... find themselves the next morning surrounded with water; so that they cannot go out of their houses." Nevertheless, "the country being all navigable" and its commodities "very easily convey'd from one city to another," the wet season saw "the greatest fairs and markets," and "greater concourse of people than at any other time in the year." Borri remarked how the locals, their boats loaded with wood from the mountains, would row them "into the very houses, built for this purpose on high pillars." Between the stilts of their homes, the residents placed only loose boards, removable to "leave free a passage for the water and boats." Throughout the rest of the year, the proximity of the South China Sea was equally important. Borri recorded that in this central region, a narrow coastal plain "lying all along upon the sea, there are so many boats that go out a fishing, and they bring in so much fish to all parts of the kingdom, that it is really very remarkable to see the long rows of people continually carrying fish from the shore to the mountains, which is duly done every day, for four hours before sun-rising."[34]

In the far south lay the Mekong delta, part of Cambodia until the nineteenth century. The Mekong's slow flow through its low-lying, wide basin built up one of the world's flattest deltas, where marine tides can wash sixty miles inland.[35] In 1686 the Portuguese Jesuit wrote that a traveler heading south from Champa down the coast to Cambodia would see people "collecting wood in its forests."[36] One of the very first Vietnamese descriptions of the Mekong delta, written in 1776, noted the "many rivers" that made travel on foot difficult there. "Waterways were so numerous that they resembled a net over the land."[37] By 1820 a more familiar and settled portrayal of the region had emerged: "Water is like a system of blood vessels for the land." Living on its rivers and islands, "nine people out of ten are good swimmers and know something about piloting boats. They like to eat salted fish." Moreover, "there are boats everywhere. People use boats as their homes or to go to market or to visit their relatives [and to] transport firewood and rice or engage in itinerant commerce.... The boats fill the rivers both day and night."[38] A modern description of the Mekong delta province of Bến Tre ("bamboo port," from its original Khmer name Kompong Russei) notes that its three main islands were "created over the years by the alluvial deposits of the four main branches of the Mekong River as they poured their way down into the South China Sea. The province, therefore, is completely surrounded by water and has about 65 kilometers of coastline. The three main islands are further divided into many smaller ones by scores of other rivers, major canals, and waterways which crisscross the main islands like veins in a human body."[39]

This historical survey includes all three of the ancient lands—north, center, and south—that fall within Việt Nam's contemporary frontiers drawn in the twentieth century. In considering these territories as a whole, it attempts to integrate their climate, water, and landscapes into the histories of their different inhabitants. The historian of medieval Việt Nam Oliver W. Wolters remarked on the need to take account of the impact of "ecological considerations" on the country's development, a gap this book aims to help fill.[40]

While cultural and political history tends to focus on change, some environmental issues are perennial. Rhinoceros horn has long been a component of Sino-Vietnamese traditional medicine and a part of the transnational trade in items of the region's ecology that began millennia ago, long before the "age of commerce" of the early modern era.[41] Around 1620, Christoforo Borri had witnessed a rhinoceros hunt near Qui Nhơn: "A hundred men, some a foot, and some a horseback, and eight or ten elephants" confronted the creature as it emerged from a wood near Borri's house. The fearless rhino "furiously encountered them all; who opened and making a lane, let the rhinoceros run through." There in the rear, the Vietnamese governor of Qui Nhơn sat "a-top of his elephant, waiting to kill it; the elephant endeavors to lay hold with his trunk, but could not by reason of the rhinoceros's swiftness and leaping" and its "striving to wound the elephant with its horn." The governor held back "till leaping it laid open the naked place, and casting a dart, [he] dexterously struck it through from side to side." The excited "multitude of spectators" quickly laid the animal's carcass "upon a great pile of wood, and setting fire to it, leap'd and danc'd about" as they roasted, sliced, and ate the flesh. From high ground the governor surveyed his subjects, enjoyed "a more dainty dish" of the heart, liver, and brain, and presented the hoofs to Borri, who reported that "the horn is good against poison," but added skeptically, "as is the unicorn's."[42] In the Central Highlands in the late nineteenth century, a rhino horn was worth no fewer than eight water buffalo.[43] The trade continued and accelerated from the 1980s on.

Just as the environment set contours from early history, a second long-range continuity is the country's Proto-Vietic linguistic heritage and its evolution. Yet linguistic diversity has an equally long history. The oldest surviving text in any Southeast Asian language was composed in the fourth century in a southern region now part of Việt Nam. Its author wrote not in any form of Vietnamese but in the Malayo-Polynesian language and Indic script of the Cham people.[44] By contrast the first extant Vietnamese-language historical sources date only from the fourteenth century, a millennium later.[45]

To write the country's history exclusively from contemporaneous Vietnamese texts would be to conceive of it as beginning only in northern Việt Nam and as recently as the second millennium.[46] Any traces of preexisting cultures there and farther south must be found in other kinds of evidence. Chapter 1 takes up the rich archaeological record from before the Common Era to survey the prehistory of the lands that became Việt Nam. As chapters 2–4 show, the first thirteen centuries of the Common Era are documented in Chinese-language sources, in inscriptional texts in Southeast Asian languages such as Cham and Khmer, and, at least for the post-939 period, in fourteenth- and fifteenth-century Vietnamese histories.

These sources reveal the development in the north over several millennia of complex local communities speaking precursor Vietic languages and dialects that borrowed heavily from their neighbors, slowly transformed into modern Vietnamese, and spread to the center and south.[47] These early inhabitants have been termed "Proto-Vietnamese," but only in limited linguistic and geographic senses.[48] It would be misleading to see their languages (or cultures or polities) as stages in a teleological "progression" toward modern Vietnamese nationhood, just as it would be tenuous to rely on prehistory for the origins even of a medieval Vietnamese state. The evidence for that emerges only much later, during a millennium of imperial rule.

A history that includes the ancient Việt, Cham, and Khmer lands of what we know as northern, central, and southern Việt Nam necessarily encompasses a range of ethnic groups, a succession of realms and polities, and, even among ethnic Vietnamese, a mosaic of regions and cultures, competing monarchies, successive dynasties, and finally contending republics. Yet over more than two millennia of human history in a single but extensive geographical space, the longevity there of a detectable ethnolinguistic family of Proto-Vietic and later modern Vietnamese dialects does provide, along with the ecologies of the three regions, an element of narrative continuity. That theme projects back into the past a statement of the early twentieth-century Vietnamese scholar Phạm Quỳnh: "As long as our language lasts, our country will last."[49] If his measure is extended back to include archaic linguistic ancestors of modern Vietnamese, the history of northern Việt Nam has lasted more than two millennia, and that of the Cham and Khmer communities, whose languages are still spoken in the country's southerly regions, possibly even longer.

A third long-term continuity is the importance most Vietnamese attach to family life and extended clan affiliations. At least as early as the first century CE, regional families dominated social organization. A millennium of imperial influence brought little change in that regard; in China too clan loyalty and "ancestor worship" were features of everyday life. After independence in the tenth century, the Red River delta briefly dissolved into nearly a dozen fiefdoms. Many Vietnamese families have kept records of their ancestors going back for many generations; wealth was often displayed in elaborate ancestral tombs and shrines. The identities of many Vietnamese are deeply rooted in the very land where their ancestors lie buried.

Vietnamese clan loyalties may have outstripped Chinese ones. As late as the 1930s, eight out of ten Vietnamese in Bắc Ninh province were found to belong to one of twelve surname groups, or lineage clans.[50] Officials vainly tried to prevent people from marrying members of the same clan. Possibly half of Việt Nam's population today bears the single surname Nguyễn. Genealogical continuity, however, is not necessarily genetic. Centuries of ethnic Chinese immigration has contributed significantly to the modern Vietnamese gene pool, still detectable in DNA. Likewise, in modern southern Việt Nam the DNA of Cham speakers reveals their assimilation of numerous indigenous Mon-Khmer speakers who long ago adopted the Cham language.[51] The genealogical records of some central Vietnamese families trace back as far as their Cham forbears.[52] In the Huế area family names such as Chế have recognizably Cham origins, as do others in Quảng Nam and Quảng Ngãi provinces (Ông, Trà, Ma).[53] Among ethnic Cambodians in the Mekong delta, unlike in Cambodia itself, a few Khmer family names (Son, Thach, Chau) are very common and identify their bearers as hailing from Kampuchea Krom (Lower Cambodia).

Against these continuous themes of ecology, language, and genealogy, this book argues for seven transformative historical forces. Vietnamese history is punctuated by these transformations and discontinuities, ranging from imperial conquest to climate change to transregional migration, seaborne commerce, ethnic and religious diversification, and regional and political confrontations from north to south, as well as increasingly important interactions between Vietnamese and the world outside—not only in what became China and Southeast Asia but also elsewhere across the globe.

A first transformative influence on Vietnamese history was the Chinese imperial conquest of the early first millennium CE. This conquest was followed by colonization and the local adoption of what became a shared classical high culture that outlived nine centuries of northern political domination and weathered the storms of subsequent imperial invasions and occupations. Chinese political models and vocabulary and China's writing system and literary canon all helped shape Vietnamese culture.

A second major external influence has been climate change. The young kingdom of Đại Việt, separated from imperial China in the tenth century, benefited from the Medieval Warm Period, several centuries of higher rainfall that raised crop yields in the wet-rice economies of mainland Southeast Asia and their neighbors and favored the development of agrarian states. As historian Victor Lieberman has shown, the "charter state" of early Đại Việt, like those of Burma and Siam, commenced what became many centuries of fitful economic expansion and slow, intermittent administrative and cultural integration.[54] Even after the end of the Medieval Warm Period, Đại Việt had gained sufficient strength to overcome invasions from Champa and Ming China and also launch new southward territorial expansion.

Third, transregional migration has long played a role in Vietnamese history. Especially from the late fifteenth century onward, Đại Việt military colonies and then Vietnamese civilian settlers moved south into the Cham territories, in some cases intermarrying there and in many cases adopting southern customs while also bringing with them their strong attachments to the cults of their northern ancestral shrines. Conversely, conquered Cham communities, often driven north and resettled in the Vietnamese heartland, slowly switched languages but sometimes retained distinctive cultural traits traceable to their Hindu past. An "island" of three Cham villages forcibly relocated north to Nghệ An in the 1250s was still identifiable to a French scholar seven centuries later.[55] Eighteenth- and nineteenth-century Vietnamese settlers in the flat, waterlogged landscape of the Mekong delta borrowed heavily from its Khmer inhabitants, not only by propitiating their local spirits (*neak ta*) but also by adopting their fast-growing "floating rice" varieties, their agricultural techniques and tools, and their species of draft animals, which worked more effectively in the marshy soils.[56] A new Vietnamese society was emerging based on migration and a sense of genealogical connection to one's origins while adapting to a new southern environment.

Fourth, the new environment meant that Việt Nam was increasingly a seaborne economy. Champa and the sinuous coastline of eastern mainland Southeast Asia, narrow and infertile compared with "the riches that mountains and sea offered," had long been a hub of transregional and transoceanic commerce. After Đại Việt's conquest of most of Champa in 1471, the Cham ports near river mouths strung out along the shore continued to serve as entrepôts of trade with China, Japan, Southeast Asia, India, and the Middle East. Vietnamese settlers moving south from the riverine world of the wide northern delta, historian Charles Wheeler writes, "entered a coastal stream that merged with one of the largest thoroughfares for oceanic shipping in Asia." Here, "riparian, coastal, and overseas crosscurrents converged, somewhere between the sea and the lagoons." Central Việt Nam was a multiethnic littoral society, clustered around a series of port towns integrated into the "archipelagic" world of the South China Sea and beyond.[57]

Fifth, as Vietnamese settlers moved farther south they tempered but also partly reproduced the longstanding regional differentiations along the extended coast of the eastern mainland. The three major contemporary Vietnamese dialects vary greatly in the country's three lowland regions, partly as a result of the fact that their inhabitants once spoke different languages: Vietnamese, Cham, and Khmer.

Language was not the only factor that influenced regional diversity. For many centuries, Cham speakers of the central coast and Khmer speakers of the southern delta, before becoming ethnic minorities within Việt Nam late in the second millennium, inhabited a variety of successive, sometimes even contemporaneous and conflicting, indigenous polities. The ancient and medieval kingdoms of Linyi and Champa occupied and contested the land that comprises central Việt Nam today. For much of its history Champa was not only multiethnic but also politically divided into several kingdoms along the central coastline.[58] As for the Mekong delta region, classical Chinese writers knew it first as the kingdom of Funan and then as part of "Water Chenla." It belonged to the Khmer kingdom of Cambodia until the final Vietnamese conquest of the delta in the early nineteenth century. Khmers in modern Cambodia still often call that region Kampuchea Krom. During the period from the fifteenth to nineteenth centuries, as Vietnamese states incorporated most of the Cham territories and then the Khmer-speaking Mekong delta, Taylor identifies no fewer than five discrete geographical and cultural/political regions stretching down the length of Việt Nam.[59] Ethnolinguistic and environmental diversity settled uneasily into a Vietnamese state framework.

A sixth recurring theme has been the persistent historical and political differences that have long divided ethnic Vietnamese and often overlapped with regional divisions. For instance, in the seventeenth and eighteenth centuries, competing Vietnamese kingdoms occupied the northern and central regions. In the nineteenth and twentieth centuries, the French ruled the far south as a separate colony (Cochinchina) and the center and

Table 0.1 THREE HISTORIC LANDS OF VIỆT NAM: CHANGING NAMES FOR THE NORTH, CENTER, AND SOUTH

Era	North	Center	South
BCE	Âu Lạc/ (*Ch.* Wu-lo)		
3rd–2nd cent. BCE	part of Lingnan part of Nán Yuè		
1st cent. BCE–1st cent. CE	Jiaozhi	Jiuzhen	
1st–5th centuries CE	Jiaozhi; Jiao	Jiuzhen, Rinan Linyi (from c. 220)	"Funan" (to c. 640)
6th–10th centuries	Jiao Annam	Linyi (to 793) Huanwang (9th cent.) Champa (from c. 650)	"Chenla" (from c. 616) "Water Chenla" (from c. 710)
10th cent.	Đại Cồ Việt	Champa kingdoms (Chiêm Thành)	Kampuchea Krom (Lower Cambodia)
11th–14th centuries	Đại Việt	Champa; Pāṇḍuraṅga	Kampuchea Krom
1400–1407	Đại Ngu	Champa; Pāṇḍuraṅga	Kampuchea Krom
1407–1428	Jiaozhi	Champa; Pāṇḍuraṅga	Kampuchea Krom
1428–1471	Đại Việt	Champa; Pāṇḍuraṅga	Kampuchea Krom
1471–c. 1600	Đại Việt	Đại Việt Thuận Quảng, Hóa Anh, Nam Bàn; Rump Champa kingdom: Pāṇḍuraṅga	Kampuchea Krom
c. 1600–1800	Đại Việt Đàng Ngoài ("Tongking")	Đại Việt (to c. 1750) Đàng Trong ("Cochinchina") Champa/Pāṇḍuraṅga/ Prădară (to 1835)	Kampuchea Krom Đồng Nai
1804–13: Việt Nam/*Ch.* Yuè Nán			Kampuchea Krom
1813–38: Đại Việt			Kampuchea Krom
1838–84: Đại Nam			
1859–1884	Đại Nam	Đại Nam	French Cochinchina
1884–1945			
(French)	Tonkin	Annam	Cochinchina
(V.)	Bắc Kỳ	Trung Kỳ	Nam Kỳ
1897–54: French Indochina			
1945–: Việt Nam	Bắc Bộ	Trung Bộ	Nam Bộ

north as protectorates (Annam and Tonkin). Then from 1954 to 1975, the center was divided between Vietnamese regimes based in the north and south. Historians take these political regionalisms seriously. John K. Whitmore stresses "the variety of media and messages available to us from the lands we call Vietnam." Taylor urges us to hear these "many voices that undermine the idea of a single Vietnamese past" and to disregard "the strangling obsession with identity and continuity." Of course these plural histories may not disaggregate the country, while others may transcend its borders.[60]

The seventh key theme is the globalization of Việt Nam's economy, culture, and politics, especially in the twentieth and twenty-first centuries. This noticeably began in the early modern era with seaborne international trade; the arrival of European ideas, scripts, and technology; and by the mid-nineteenth century the increasingly thoughtful responses of Vietnamese to the challenges these posed.

Each chapter that follows addresses some or all of these ten themes as keys to understanding Vietnamese history. The more continuous themes of an aquatic society, linguistic continuity and change, and the importance of family genealogies and ancestral sites appear continually throughout the book. The relationship with China also emerges very early. The Medieval Warm Period, with its boost to the rain-fed wet-rice economy and the agrarian state, represents another distinct transformation that propelled new forces for change: mobility and migration, the seaborne political economy especially in the center and south, a polyethnic culture, regional differences, and global influences.

The narrative of the book is divided into six chronological parts on the basis of broad political formations that have predominated in the country's three major regions in different eras of their histories: chiefdoms, provinces, kingdoms, regions, colonies, and republics. These polities and periods are of course neither singular nor mutually exclusive. Succeeding historical eras shared many of the same political and cultural institutions, while a single period could exhibit divergent or contesting regimes. For instance, each of the early modern northern and southern kingdoms that divided between them most of the territories now comprising modern Việt Nam was regional and monarchical. Yet for most of that era these rival regional royalties both proclaimed their fealty to the same figurehead emperor of Đại Việt. Vietnamese histories are decidedly plural, presenting alternative forms of national unification even when there was consensus on that concept. If some cultural and ecological features have proved enduring, political change has been as persistent as continuity. And that change was hardly continuous or cumulative: the six successive political eras represent no linear progressive evolution, or developmental phases, of statehood.

Readers might equally view the chronological chapters of this book as arranged geographically, with chapters 1–4 focusing mostly on the northern region up to the fourteenth century, chapters 5–6 on both the north and center in the early modern era, and chapters 7–11 on all three regions—north, center and south—in the period since the eighteenth century. Yet this history does not privilege the formation of a Vietnamese nation-state, but attempts from the outset to integrate all three regions, just as it seeks to integrate environmental and economic changes into both political and cultural narratives. While some chapters are defined in part by the arrival of a new climate era, each includes (when possible) voices of Vietnamese and other actors from different political and ethnic groups, geographic regions, cultural currents, and socioeconomic sectors.

Part 1, "Chiefdoms," introduces what is known of the prehistory of the disparate lands that became Việt Nam, especially their Neolithic and Bronze Age archaeology. It examines modern scholarship on the archaic origins of what eventually evolved into the Vietnamese language and the heterogeneous cultures of the early inhabitants of those territories, including "Proto-Vietnamese," ancient Chams and Khmers, and newly arrived northern "Yuè" refugees fleeing China's imperial expansion.

Part 2, "Provinces," analyzes the impact on these lands of more than a millennium of imperial rule as Chinese provinces, up to 939 CE. The slow spread of literacy in Chinese, the varying influences of Confucianism, Buddhism, and Daoism, and the evolution in the Red River delta of a provincial administrative bureaucracy were also accompanied by the rise and fall of imperial dynastic power, sporadic secessionist or other revolts, and conflicts and exchanges with both upland groups and more southerly neighboring peoples and their different cultures and polities, including Linyi, Champa, and the early Khmer coastal and inland kingdoms.

Part 3, "Kingdoms," 940–1570, charts the end of imperial administration and the emergence and incremental, discontinuous development of Vietnamese monarchical rule and territorial consolidation, retreat, and expansion. Several centuries of improved climate conditions brought economic prosperity and also saw the ascendancy of Vietnamese Buddhism and a flourishing cultural and literary life, despite intermittent warfare with kingdoms of neighboring Champa and repeated brief but traumatic Chinese invasions. Then after 1340, multiple decades of severe droughts and military incursions from Champa fostered a new intellectual and political transformation among the Vietnamese elite. Defeat and occupation by Ming armies were followed by recovery, victory, seventy-five years of higher rainfall, southern territorial expansion, the imposition of a Neo-Confucian administration, and the composition of an eclectic legal code. But the sixteenth century brought fluctuating extreme weather patterns, political crises, and dynastic and regional divisions.

Part 4, "Regions," 1570–1860, covers the divergence, separation, conflict, and unification of the northern and southern Vietnamese kingdoms known respectively as Đàng Ngoài (the Outer Region) and Đàng Trong (the Inner Region). From the sixteenth to the eighteenth centuries a combination of climate crises, agrarian pressures, north-south migration, failures of governance, and new international commercial and religious influences fueled three major sociopolitical breakdowns. The last, the thirty-year nationwide Tây Sơn rebellion, ended in 1802 with its defeat and the unification of an expanded Vietnamese state. While regional issues persisted, a reimposition of Confucian orthodoxy under the Nguyễn dynasty managed to hold the new kingdom together until the first landing of French colonial forces at Saigon in 1859.

In Part 5, "Colonies," the powerful impact of global historical trends included both European colonial conquest and a major deterioration in worldwide climatic conditions. Starting in the south, the progressive French defeat and division of Việt Nam challenged the worldviews of the Huế court, Confucian scholars, and peasants alike. The piecemeal colonial conquest also relied on significant Vietnamese collaboration, exposed rivalries between different French interests, accentuated divergences between south, center, and north, and provoked varying Vietnamese responses. The first half of the twentieth century brought an internationalization of Vietnamese culture, the economy, and political life. Colonial adoption of the *quốc ngữ* romanized script fostered an explosion in Vietnamese written and printed culture, while political subjugation, rapid economic change, and the ruptures of the Great Depression and World War II all sparked a major upsurge in anticolonial activism that propelled a successful war of independence.

Part 6, "Republics," charts the north-south division of Việt Nam from 1954 to 1975 and its subsequent reunification. Chapter 10 covers the outbreak of a civil war and insurgency in the South, the involvement of the communist regime in the North, the large-scale U.S. intervention, and the three theaters of the American-Vietnamese conflict: the guerrilla war in the agrarian southern lowlands, the conventional "big-unit" ground battles in the forested Central Highlands and remote border areas, and the air war over the North. Chapter 11 examines the history of postwar Việt Nam, including its economic stagnation and recovery, the wars with Cambodia and China, the continuing confrontation in the South China Sea, and the nature of contemporary political and cultural life in a one-party state.

Over three millennia, the country's three main regions have seen dramatic changes in their climate, landscapes, ruling powers, populations, and politics. They have been home to scores of ethnolinguistic groups and most of the world's major religious traditions, and have experienced dozens of political formations from chiefdoms to provinces, tributary kingdoms, independent monarchies, colonies, and republics. The lasting outcome of the "Vietnam War" was the unification of Việt Nam's two republics and three multiethnic geographic regions. The country's democratic future in the fast-changing Southeast Asian and global environment remains unclear.

In a new era of global warming, with droughts and upstream dams restricting the flow of water in the Mekong River, while sea levels rise and a new conflict heats up in the South China Sea, water is still the life blood of Việt Nam.[61]

PART ONE

Chiefdoms

Rugged uplands of northern Việt Nam, view from Thiên Túc, 1930s. Archives nationales d'outre-mer (ANOM), Aix-en-Provence, France: FR ANOM 3502 COL 4923 (FM INDO NF 4923)—"Tournée d'inspection forestière de M. Consigny," 1939.

Limestone hill country of Van Linh, northern Việt Nam, 1930s. Archives nationales d'outre-mer (ANOM), Aix-en-Provence, France: FR ANOM 3502 COL 4923 (FM INDO NF 4923)—"Tournée d'inspection forestière de M. Consigny," 1939.

Raft on the fast-flowing Chảy (Clear) River, northern Việt Nam, 1939. Archives nationales d'outre-mer (ANOM), Aix-en-Provence, France: FR ANOM 3502 COL 4923 (FM INDO NF 4923)—"Tournée d'inspection forestière de M. Consigny," 1939.

Swidden fields beneath limestone hills, northern Việt Nam, 1939. Archives nationales d'outre-mer (ANOM), Aix-en-Provence, France: FR ANOM 3502 COL 4923 (FM INDO NF 4923)—"Tournée d'inspection forestière de M. Consigny," 1939.

Wet-rice fields bunded for cultivation, northern Việt Nam, 1939. Archives nationales d'outre-mer (ANOM), Aix-en-Provence, France: FR ANOM 3502 COL 4923 (FM INDO NF 4923)—"Tournée d'inspection forestière de M. Consigny," 1939.

View from the hills overlooking the Red River delta plain, 1939. Archives nationales d'outre-mer (ANOM), Aix-en-Provence, France: FR ANOM 3502 COL 4923 (FM INDO NF 4923)—"Tournée d'inspection forestière de M. Consigny," 1939.

Upland valleys covered with ricefields, northern Việt Nam, 1939. Archives nationales d'outre-mer (ANOM), Aix-en-Provence, France: FR ANOM 3502 COL 4923 (FM INDO NF 4923)—" Tournée d'inspection forestière de M. Consigny," 1939.

Bamboo rafts at Tiên Yên, northern Việt Nam, 1939. Archives nationales d'outre-mer (ANOM), Aix-en-Provence, France: FR ANOM 3502 COL 4923 (FM INDO NF 4923)—"Tournée d'inspection forestière de M. Consigny," 1939.

Riverbank in Tonkin, c. 1930. From Henri Gourdon, *L'Indochine* (Paris: Larousse, c. 1931).

The narrow coastal plain of central Việt Nam, hemmed between hills and sea. Photo by Ben Kiernan, January 1975.

On the south-central coast, thirteenth-century Cham towers survey the arid landscape. Photo by Ben Kiernan, January 1975.

The broad Mekong basin in southern Việt Nam, January 1975. Photo by Ben Kiernan.

Lush Mekong delta scene, January 1975. Photo by Ben Kiernan.

Canal in the upper Mekong delta, January 1975. Photo by Ben Kiernan.

Village in the upper Mekong delta, January 1975. Photo by Ben Kiernan.

CHAPTER 1

Water, Rice, and Bronze

PREHISTORIC VIỆT NAM

How is it possible to narrate undocumented histories, or even to understand an ancient land's preliterate inhabitants without reading anything they could have written? Without hearing their voices, as the historian Fernand Braudel put it, "how are we to imagine their life, their legends, their religions?"[1] During the millennia of prehistory before the Common Era, no documents are known to have been composed in any form of Vietnamese or other local languages. No such texts survive even from the first millennium of early history; the earliest extant Vietnamese text is from 1282 CE.[2] Scattered Chinese-language commentaries begin in the late first millennium BCE. Before that, the study of prehistoric Việt Nam requires an assembly of nontextual evidence. It is important to do this because, as Braudel insisted, prehistory is integral to understanding the past.[3]

This chapter, a prehistory of the first occupants of the land now known as Việt Nam, draws mainly on the rich early archaeological record found there, the modern field of historical linguistics, and anthropological research among neighboring communities and in adjacent areas of Southeast Asia. The few contemporary documents composed by ancient Chinese officials coming from the north who described this southern territory and the people living there in the first millennium BCE also cast light on those first communities.

In the first millennium BCE, the Hồng (Red River) delta of what is today northern Việt Nam became the meeting point of two cultural influences, from areas now known as Southeast Asia and China. From the south arrived early ancestors of the Vietnamese ethnolinguistic group, speakers of an ancient Austroasiatic language known as "Proto-Vietic," who became dominant in the delta over local speakers of other Austroasiatic and Southeast Asian languages. From the north, fleeing Chinese southward expansion, came speakers of one or more different Austroasiatic or Tai languages who were bearers of the ethnonym Yuè. As these two groups met and merged, the delta's initially polyglot but mostly fellow Austroasiatic-speaking residents eventually adopted the term Yuè as their own name for themselves. In Vietnamese this was pronounced "Việt."

These early inhabitants experienced three other important external developments in this late prehistoric era. These were the rise of the Southeast Asian sea trade with India, the landing on the central Vietnamese coast of Austronesian-speaking settlers from the Southeast Asian islands, and, finally, the first approaches of imperial armies and officials from the Chinese mainland to the north.

Meanwhile the indigenous inhabitants adapted to the ecology of the Red River delta, situated near the intersection of Asia's tropical and subtropical zones.[4] They developed rice agriculture and metalwork. The structures and artifacts they created suggest several themes: the significance of water in their environment, an artistic preoccupation with aquatic creatures and motifs, and the important role of women and fertility in their rulership and ritual. These linked sociocultural themes are not uncommon in archaic societies.[5] They would long mark Vietnamese thought and language. The same scholar of Vietnamese culture and literature who summed up the Vietnamese worldview as "Water, water everywhere" also noted that the Vietnamese words for "woman" (*nữ*) and "water" (*nước*) are related.[6]

THE ENVIRONMENT AND FIRST INHABITANTS

Before the melting of Ice Age glaciers ten thousand years ago, worldwide sea levels were much lower than at present, and mainland Southeast Asia was a larger landmass. It was geographically very diverse, with both extensive uplands and "a vast region of low-lying marshy land across which snaked several major rivers and numerous tributaries."[7] One of these, the Red River, continued much further east than today, traversing what prehistorians call "Nanhailand," a broad coastal plain that extended one hundred miles beyond the modern coastline, fifty meters below the current sea level. But from about 6000–4000 BCE, the water level rose sharply. It first inundated Nanhailand, which became the Gulf of Tonkin. From 5000 BCE, the sea washed even further inland to submerge what is now the Red River plain, which temporarily became a shallow bay. Then from about 2000 BCE, the shoreline began to recede again. As the fast-flowing Red River plunged steeply out of the surrounding hills, prone to flash-flooding and carrying downstream a kilogram of silt per cubic meter, its alluvial deposits gradually rebuilt the delta. They then began to once more extend the coastline eastward, back out into the Gulf of Tonkin, an ongoing process.[8]

Even on the central coast, where the rivers are smaller, the process of streams depositing silt and reclaiming flooded coastal land is detectable from historic times. In the fifteenth century a coastal lagoon in Nghệ An was recorded as containing oysters, clams, and mussels. By the early nineteenth century it had become a freshwater pond, marooned two kilometers inland and separated from the sea by dunes several meters high. The land reclamation represented four centuries of work on the part of the Cả River.[9] Similarly in the south, around 4000–3000 BCE the Mekong delta region was almost entirely underwater. Remnants of coral reefs and sand dunes from the former coastline have been found forty miles inland. Even two millennia ago, much of the Mekong delta (like the lower Red River delta) was still submerged.[10]

Some of the northern delta remained below river beds until modern times. The inland Đỗ-động river flowed as recently as the fourteenth century, when it was mentioned in historical chronicles, but has since dried up.[11] The first French official to take charge of Sơn Tây province after the colonial conquest reported in 1886 that the Red River too could change course: "At each bend in its path, the river strikes with the speed of its waters against the concave bank. The bank barely resists, crumbles, and falls into the current which carries it away." But across the river on the convex bank, eddies form, and the water stills. "This slowing and swirling of the river water laden with suspended matter produces deposits which soon appear at the surface." Mudflats form, then a new riverbank. "The river is thus laterally displaced," while retaining its width.[12]

Downstream, where the river reaches the coast, its massive silt deposits annually reclaim more than fifty meters of offshore shallows, creating each century an average of 1.2 miles of new land. Parts of the Red River delta now extend from ten to fifty miles out to sea beyond the ancient coastline.[13] The Thần-phù estuary, "once superstitiously dreaded for its choppy waters which sent many boats to the bottom, has now silted up and become part of the mainland, miles away from the seacoast."[14] In the interior of Nam Định and Thái Bình provinces, now landlocked dunes and sand ridges mark the former shore.[15] In 1886 the French official wrote that in Nam Định and Ninh Bình "many villages which are today rather far inland were, barely two hundred years ago, close to the shore." Diggings there uncovered the roots of trees that grow only in brackish coastal waters.[16]

Yet the sea retains sway over this reclaimed land. As the rivers extended into the ocean, the sea continued to wash upriver. When the English buccaneer William Dampier sailed to the Tonkin coast in 1688 he docked near the river mouth. For the trip upstream to Hanoi, he boarded a local boat "with the tide of flood, and anchored in the ebb; for the tide runs strong for thirty or forty miles" inland.[17] Two centuries later the French official from Sơn Tây reported that the ocean also plays a part in the extension of the delta: "The enormous volume of soil in suspension carried downriver during the high water season... is pushed back by the sea onto the shoreline, all the more because that season also brings the S.E. winds which carry sea sand to the shore."[18]

The region's shifting coastline and aquatic environment, along with the volume and speed of its rivers and tides, demanded that its inhabitants give special attention to water and water control. The Red River delta's extensive network of natural waterways gives ready access across a wide fertile plain, situated between mountains in the north and west and coastal swamplands in the south and east.[19] Further west, the more precipitous Đà (Black) River cascades down through (according to folk tradition) three hundred waterfalls and rapids, to join the Red River at the edge of the plain.[20] It then flows into the Chảy (Clear) River. But the waters soon divide again and fan out, criss-crossing the low-lying delta with interconnecting branches and canals that multiply toward the coast. The delta's communities and cultures emerged from the water.[21] Vietnamese came to call their homeland *non nước*, their "mountains and waters," or even just *nước* (waters).[22]

Hunter-gatherer communities appear in the archaeological record of the Red River delta region as early as thirty thousand years ago. In rock shelters overlooking the southern edges of the plain, beginning about 14,000 BCE, people belonging to a culture now known as Hoabinhian (named after Hòa Bình, where it was first identified, west of modern Hanoi) ate wild cattle, water buffalo, rhinoceros, forest birds, turtles, tortoise, shellfish, and uncultivated, or "wild," rice. These people soon began to grind and polish stone tools, including "almond-shaped" axes. They occupied more than 120 caves and shelters, mostly located about thirty feet above the valley floors.[23] Then, around 9000 BCE in the limestone hills north of the Red River delta, a culture labeled Bacsonian (for Bắc Sơn in modern Lạng Sơn province) emerged, distinctive for its characteristic edge-ground axes. Bacsonians settled at more than fifty sites and made the earliest pottery found in northern Việt Nam, "black, thick, coarse pottery decorated by beating with a cord-wrapped paddle," a technique also developing in southern China. Bacsonian stone art includes possibly human forms and "groups of figures incised in clay slabs."[24] After 6000 BCE, as the sea level progressively rose, these upland peoples came into contact with coastal communities retreating inland.[25] Cord-marked pottery vessels became common by the fifth millennium BCE, when sea levels reached their peak.[26]

From about this time in what became northern Việt Nam, as the saltwater gradually rose, riverbank and maritime cultures may have slowly merged. Archaeologists note the development there of "riverine-, estuarine-, and later, marine-oriented foraging communities" in the mid-Holocene era, especially the Da But culture, which is dated to between 4500 and 2700 BCE.[27]

There was little local evidence of agriculture. The world's earliest known sites of rice cultivation and horticulture are dated to around 7000 BCE in what is now south-central China, where rice was first cultivated, and in the New Guinea highlands, where people drained swamps for taro cultivation so that by c. 3500 BCE, "true agriculture was supporting permanent villages in forest clearings."[28] It is hard to know how quickly such techniques spread to mainland Southeast Asia. The permanent submersion of its offshore continental shelf (Nanhailand) from 6000 BCE wiped out any preexisting coastal or lowland settlements there, along with evidence of their technology. Even in the inland areas of the Red River plain that were submerged only from about 5000 to 2000 BCE, during that interval the river's continuing silt deposits buried forever any coastal settlements established there earlier.[29]

To the south along the coast, the shorter, smaller Mã River carries and deposits less silt. Its lower delta has preserved five sites inhabited during the period 4500–2700 BCE. There people made paddle-beaten pottery in basketry molds with a distinctive coarse sand temper, and they fashioned stone and clay fishing tools such as net sinkers with grooves for cordage. As sea levels fell, they grew vegetables and tubers in the Mã River delta and fished in streams and offshore. Similar pottery also became common in the coastal plains farther south, modern Nghệ An and Hà Tĩnh provinces, in twenty-one sites dating from the last three millennia BCE.[30]

Pottery appeared north of the Red River delta, too. Near the modern Chinese border, coastal and offshore island dwellers produced low-fired, handmade objects from sandy clay. They too fished the sea with nets. By the third millennium BCE, people in Hạ Long Bay had learned to grind, saw, drill, and polish stone, and they were making pottery that archaeologists consider of high quality. In inland foothills farther west, by the early second millennium hunter-gatherers who kept cattle, buffalo, pigs, and dogs were producing abundant thin-walled pottery of "fine clay, sometimes coated with a red slip." Twenty sites have yielded bowls decorated with rosettes, bell-mouthed vessels, and ring-footed vases.[31]

The waters of the South China Sea receded after 2000 BCE, again exposing the Red River plain. People came down from the uplands and foothills to reoccupy the delta. They gained subsistence mostly from the encroaching lowland forest, the reemerging rivers and tributaries, and the sea. It may have been at this point that people adopted a form of shifting agriculture known as swidden, or "slash-and-burn," rice cultivation. In at least the northeastern part of the delta and the surrounding hills, the first farmers cleared fields from the forest, burned off the remaining vegetation, and planted rice in the fertile ashes, which gave the soil several seasons of high productivity. When yields fell, these farmers fired new jungle clearings for "dry-field," rain-fed cultivation. Perhaps they had learned this agricultural method from upland peoples in the hills to their northwest.[32] Or both groups may have emerged from a wider culture, since prehistoric polished stone hoes found in northern Việt Nam closely resemble others found in Cambodia and even some that uplanders of southern Việt Nam still used in the twentieth century.[33]

However, the Neolithic inhabitants of the Red River delta were more fortunate than their western or southern neighbors, because unlike the highlands and Cambodia the rich alluvial Red River plain enjoyed an unusual climate of two annual monsoons. This ecological region proved especially suitable for settled agriculture. It was also "the only lowland corridor" from the mountains of Tibet to the South China Sea and was centrally located on the East Asian littoral. As sea levels receded, on newly exposed coastlines "pot-making maritime settlements appeared all the way down from Taiwan to central Vietnam."[34] Among these regions, the Red River delta was ecologically favored, with its broad, accessible, and fertile hinterland. Soon after 2000 BCE, a new culture began to emerge in the upper delta. Inland rice-farming village communities raised domestic animals and made polished stone hoe tips and axes, and pottery thrown on the wheel and fired in kilns at 800° F.[35]

During the early second millennium BCE, communities known as the Phùng Nguyên culture inhabited more than fifty locations in the mid-Red River valley west of the delta near the junctions with the Black and Clear Rivers. Phùng Nguyên habitations covered large areas, with relatively little social differentiation among gravesites, indicating a pattern of fairly close communal settlement.[36] Their inhabitants used harpoons, spearheads, halberds, and barbed arrowheads and made ceramic cooking pots, jars, and "fruit stands," which they decorated symmetrically with triangles, circles, and rows of S curves. This pottery was thin-walled, its polished surfaces varying in color from a dark to a light rose or brown.[37] Phùng Nguyên people adorned themselves with fashioned stone rings, bracelets, and beautiful blue nephrite bangles with flared ends.[38] Their rings and bracelets were carefully polished, with ribs and flanges. Their sites reveal early transregional influences on this late Neolithic culture that are reminiscent of the third millennium's more advanced regions to the north, which later became part of south-central China. The Phùng Nguyên burial practice of extended inhumation and the incised and cord-marked pottery found at these sites resemble the earlier examples from further north. Their stone adze blades and bracelets of nephrite, amphibolite, quartzite, and jasper are equally impressive.[39] Jade blades excavated in Phùng Nguyên gravesites, too, resemble those found in China dating from the third millennium BCE.[40] While Phùng Nguyên pottery styles and motifs also suggest continuing links with nearby coastal communities, long-grain rice preserved at these sites points to the emergence of agriculture in Phùng Nguyên habitations, a further innovation that had spread there from south-central China.[41] Yet another involved textile production, using a distinctive biconical spindle whorl of a type identifiable in earlier sites in southeast China, which also suggests some immigration from that region and as far south as modern Thanh Hóa.[42]

In the mid-second millennium BCE, inhabitants of the Red and Black River valleys and the Mã River valley farther south began to smelt copper, and then to cast bronze, which has been found at late Phùng Nguyên sites.[43] Metal artifacts soon appeared in the Đồng Dậu period beginning around 1500 BCE in the same area of the Red River valley, but also extending downriver toward the delta.[44] Settlers were following the receding coastline. Đồng Dậu communities produced heavier, thicker pottery decorated with waves, spirals, "interwoven ropes," and horizontal S shapes, along with many bronze tools, including rectangular axes, spearheads, and fishhooks, dating from c. 1500–1350 BCE.[45] They made these with a true bronze alloy of tin and copper. Farmers began to harvest their crops with bronze-bladed sickles.[46]

Like the late Neolithic, Việt Nam's Bronze Age began later than in China or Mesopotamia, where the first evidence for bronze casting dates from 3000–2800 BCE, or in Egypt and Europe (2200–2000). Similar metallurgical advances in what is now central Thailand (1500–1400) were contemporaneous with those occurring in the Red River plain. Perhaps the earliest locally produced metal artifact excavated in northern Việt Nam was a bronze statue of a chicken, made about 1000 BCE.[47] Over the next five centuries, people of this region produced numerous bronze wedge-shaped axes, scythes, socketed spears, fishhooks, and bronze strings.[48] Building on the Đồng Dậu bronze culture, the successor Gò Mun communities began to mix tin and copper in varying proportions to suit individual requirements of their tools.[49]

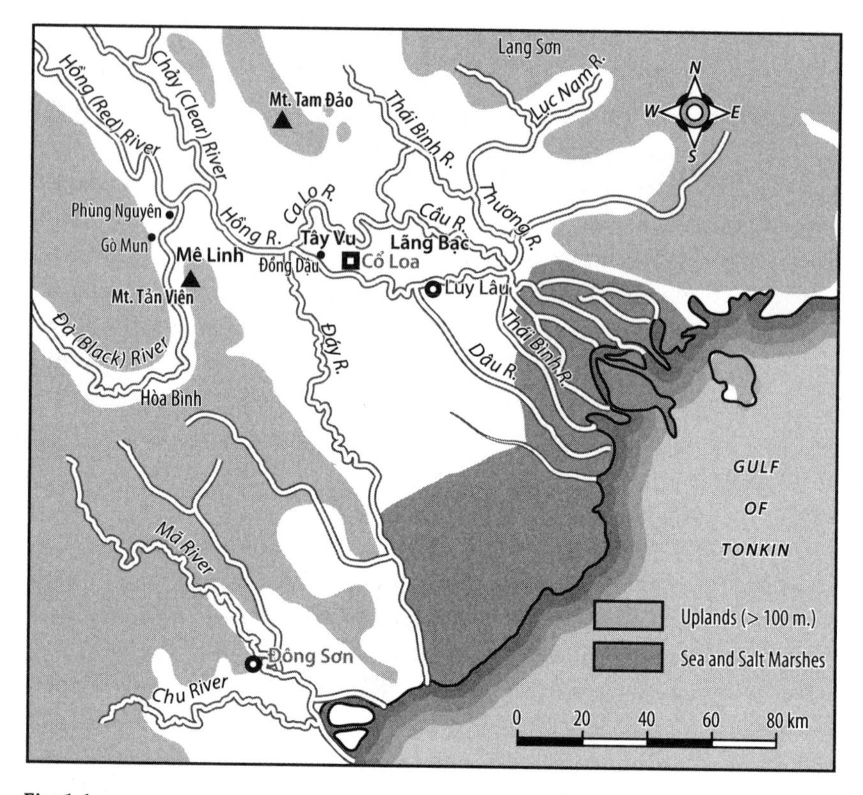

Fig. 1.1
Waterways of the Red River plain in northern Việt Nam: first millennium BCE.

This newly flourishing metallurgy accompanied a major agricultural development. By the turn of the first millennium, if not earlier, inhabitants of northern Việt Nam had begun producing "wet rice," the staple that has since characterized the country's civilization and culture. Farmers improved on dry-field shifting rice cultivation by taking advantage of the delta's dual monsoon (May–September and January–April) and its extensive alluvial plain. By raising low earth boundaries to enclose level paddy fields and allowing the July–August heavy rainfall to flood them to a controlled depth, they fabricated a shallow "aquarium" of water-fed nutrients for the rice shoots.[50] Yields became more stable and fields more permanent. Agricultural intensification also involved the use of the plow and draft animals, as well as double-cropping, which took advantage of northern Việt Nam's January–April light rain, or "drizzle," brought by the South China Sea monsoon.[51] On a small scale, farmers may also have harnessed the substantial Red River tidal flows to irrigate rice fields in cases of inadequate rainfall. This intensive wet-rice agriculture based on carefully flooded fields produced a grain surplus that fostered the rise of a series of indigenous chiefdoms.

ĐÔNG SƠN CULTURE

Further south, the Mã and Chu Rivers meet in a narrowing plain, forming their deltas in more rugged, uneven country, less fertile than the open, expansive Red River plain. Relatively early dense settlement of this constricted area might have led quickly to the next cultural era. From 1000 to 700 BCE inhabitants used sandstone molds and crucibles to cast bronze socketed axes, spearheads, arrowheads, chisels, hammers, awls, bracelets, and necklaces. Grave goods included small pottery replicas and large pots in a distinctive drum shape.[52]

These pottery prototypes prefigured the large bronze "drums" that would characterize the emerging Đông Sơn culture, named for one of its richest sites, on the southern bank of the Mã River. From the seventh century BCE, several regions of the Red and Mã River valleys composed a larger cultural zone. Over one hundred archaeological sites near rivers, in deltas, coastal areas, and mountains, testify to flourishing new Bronze Age communities. The Đông Sơn district on the Mã River contains all five of the culture's known workshop sites for stone ornaments. Greater centralization of weapons manufacture and storage is noticeable too. A single site contained an arsenal of ten thousand bronze arrowheads.[53] In the prehistory of mainland Southeast Asia, Đông Sơn culture is considered "the best-known expression of the transition to the centralized chiefdom."[54]

That political transition probably benefited from mutual exchanges with inland Dian cultures in upper reaches of the Red River that are now part of southwest China, but it was also fairly independent of northern influence.[55] To copper and tin, Đông Sơn bronze metallurgists added lead to reduce the melting point of the alloy and facilitate the casting of large objects with delicate decoration.[56] Their bronzes contain around 20 percent lead, significantly higher than contemporary Chinese bronzes, and much less tin than elsewhere.[57] The forms of the artifacts also suggest the culture's local roots. Not only does the shape of the new Đông Sơn bronze drums resemble earlier locally made pottery, but the new bronze bracelets are also similar to the polished Phùng Nguyên stone bracelets with their projecting flanges, while the bronze pediform ax depicted in Đông Sơn art resembles the earlier rectangular stone ax.[58]

The new range of technical and artistic complexity reflected increased internal social stratification, in contrast to the extensive communal life evident at the earlier Phùng Nguyên sites. Đông Sơn communities produced enough wealth to bury some members with "considerable show."[59] Lavish tombs were packed with "high-value bronze artifacts," near "more numerous poor ones containing no or just a few pots."[60] Intriguingly, the new pottery was of inferior quality than before. Such regression had also occurred in early Bronze Age Europe, when ceramics became simpler, more utilitarian, and "less highly decorated." Archaeologists speculate that the display of "group identity" had been transferred to bronze ornaments and weapons.[61] Similarly in Việt Nam, though the Bronze Age culture had developed advanced kilns capable of high firing temperatures, pottery found in the cemetery at Đông Sơn is "very poorly decorated" compared with earlier periods. Pottery "no longer served as a vehicle for artistic expression."[62] Instead, from 1000 to 500 BCE, Đông Sơn artists specialized in bronze axes, spearheads, and knives, their handles cast as figures "with long hair gathered at the nape of the neck, a breech cloth, circular breasts, and hands on the hips."[63]

The Đông Sơn culture's signature artifact was the large ornamental bronze "drum"—technically a gong. The technology and art of these drums suggest the development of ranked, complex societies with large populations.[64] None of the drums bear dates, and very few have inscriptions, but their artistic styles and carbon-14 dating suggest rough estimates of their age. Most were produced from c. 500 BCE to the first century CE. The oldest

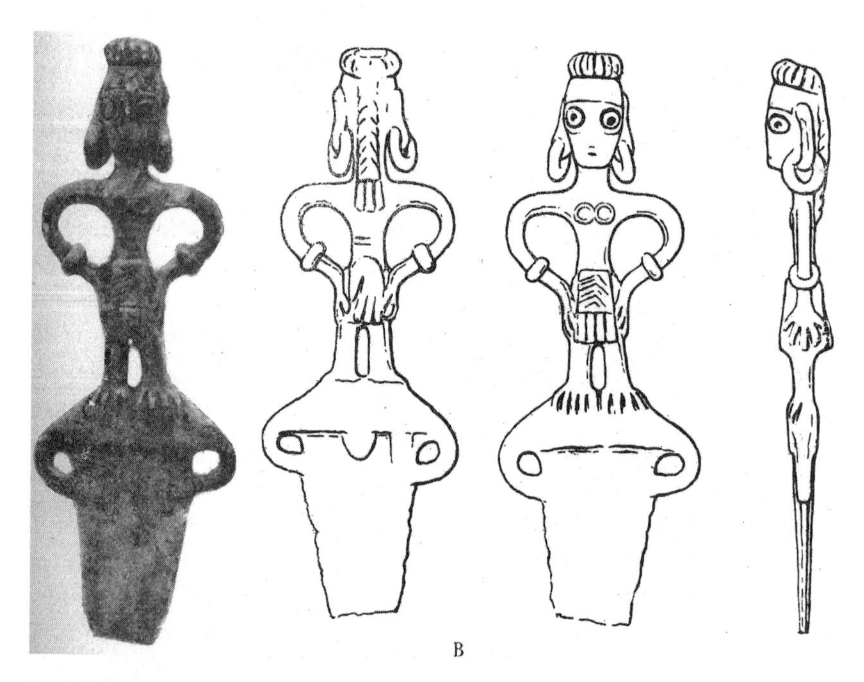

Fig. 1.2
Đông Sơn decorated bronze dagger hilt (National Museum of Vietnamese History, Hanoi). From Victor Goloubew, "L'Âge du Bronze au Tonkin et dans le Nord-Annam," *Bulletin de l'École Française d'Extrême-Orient* 29 (1929): plate 19.

styles are found in what is now northern Việt Nam and nearby inland southwest China.[65] Some 250–300 Đông Sơn–era drums have been found in Việt Nam alone. At least 140 more, along with various ornate items in the Đông Sơn style, were transported soon after their casting, some upriver into southwest China, others inland to what is now Cambodia, Thailand, and Burma, and others by sea across Southeast Asia even as far away as New Guinea. More than fifty Đông Sơn–era drums cast in northern Việt Nam from the third century BCE to the first century CE have been found in western Indonesia alone.[66]

The drums' practical use remains elusive. One scholar has argued that they were "directly associated with war and the power of a ruler" and were linked to the power of water. "This can be seen in the functional use of the drums as instruments of rain-making, in the frog motifs they contain, and in the association of the ruler with thunder and the *jiao* 'dragon,' or crocodile."[67] Archaeologists see in the drums and their ornamentation "an interest in ritual and ceremony" and note both Đông Sơn motifs that seem derived from previous periods and new ones such as "stylized human pictures done in feathers, aquatic birds, deer, and especially ritualistic scenes of the ancient people's activities."[68]

Fig. 1.3
Sông Đà bronze drum. From *Dong Son Drums in Viet Nam* (Hanoi: Viet Nam Social Science Publishing House, 1990), 10.

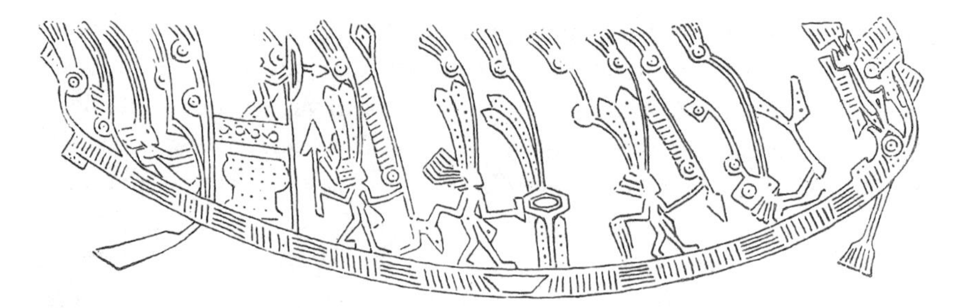

Fig. 1.4
Art from the Ngọc Lũ bronze drum. From Victor Goloubew, "L'Âge du Bronze au Tonkin et dans le Nord-Annam," *Bulletin de l'École Française d'Extrême-Orient* 29 (1929): plate 27.

From 500 BCE, Đông Sơn communities produced a much greater range of bronze artifacts, including daggers and swords, while making drums that reveal major technological capacities.

Late in this bronze era, the Đông Sơn civilization produced what was probably the first indigenous kingdom. The fortress of Cổ Loa on the Red river plain ten miles north of modern Hanoi, became a major ritual and military center.[69] Clearing of the site probably commenced in the fourth century BCE, and much of an earthen rampart (more than four miles long, thirty feet high, and sixty feet wide) was completed during the third century. Construction continued for several centuries. The second of Cổ Loa's three sets of concentric earthen ramparts, the outermost, stands up to ten feet high, thirty-five to sixty feet wide, and five miles in length, and encloses an area of nearly 1,500 acres (600 ha). Two concentric oval moats fed by the Red River skirt these outer and middle ramparts. Much of the third inner, rectangular rampart was also completed in the second century (its bastions were probably added after the Chinese conquest). To build the two outer fortifications around the same time as the first series of barriers far to the north that later became the Great Wall of China, laborers had to move one to two million cubic meters of earth.[70]

Cổ Loa was an amphibious defense complex. Its wide outer moat is ten to thirty meters across, "with some places wider," such as in the south where it joins the Hoàng River. From the east, it also flows into the inner moat, then passes through what were apparently water gates in the middle rampart, and inside it "divides into five channels, like the fingers on a hand." Two of these water channels curve around the remains of a ship dockyard.[71] Cổ Loa was both military fort and naval port.

The impressively large Cổ Loa bronze drum, apparently buried in the first century CE near the center of the earthen fortifications where it was

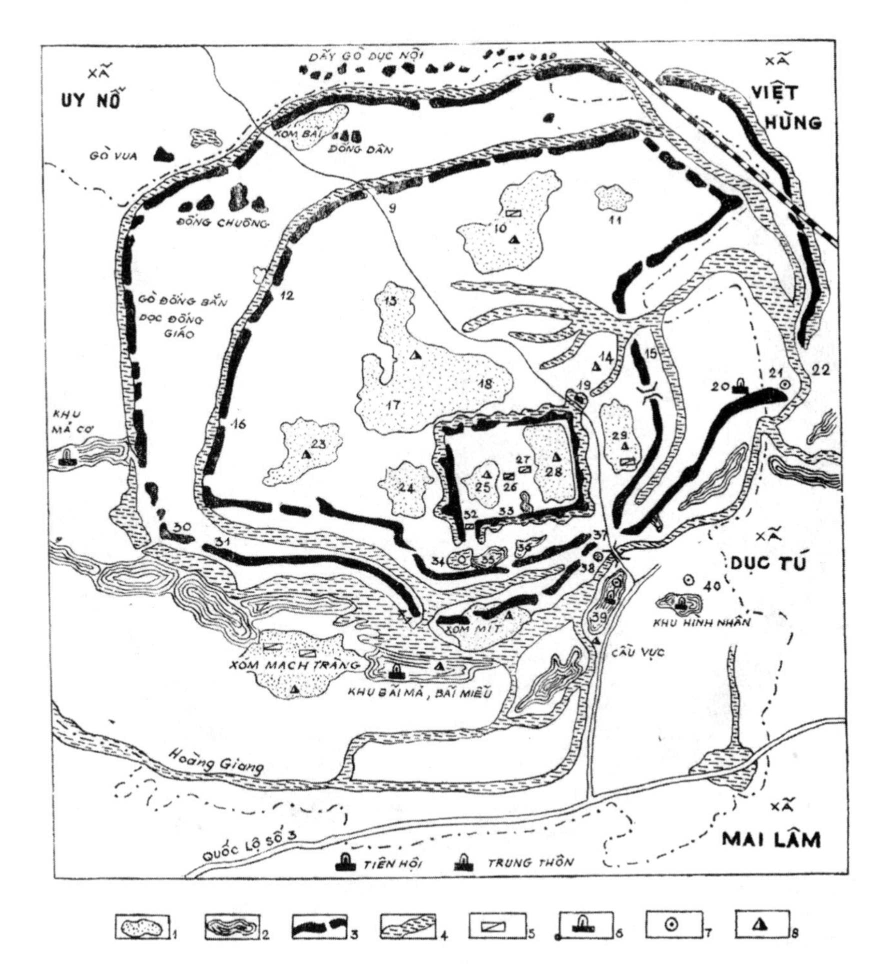

Fig. 1.5
Map of Cổ Loa citadel by archaeologist Trần Quốc Vượng. Source: Khảo Cổ Học Việt Nam, Tập III, Khảo Cổ Học Lịch Sử, NXB KHXH 2002, 445. Legend (Trần Quốc Vượng): *1*. Modern residential areas; *2*. Small hills; *3*. Ramparts; *4*. Rivers, marshes, moats; *5*. Temples and pagodas; *6*. Old tombs; *7*. Archaeological sites; *8*. Small objects discovered; *9*. North gate; *12*. Northwest gate; *14*. Naval docking area; *15*. Outer and central moat juncture; *16*. Southwest gate; *19*. Imperial reviewing stand; *20*. Citadel garrison area; *21*. Footpath; *22*. East gate; *25*. Chùa (Buddhist pagoda) hamlet; *26*. Mỵ Châu's pagoda; *27*. Location of the royal palace; *28*. Hamlet market; *30, 31*. Fortifications; *32*. South gate; *33*. King An Dương's pagoda.

excavated in 1982, is 57 cm high and 73 cm across. It weighs 72 kg and required the smelting of well over a ton of copper ore, possibly as much as seven tons.[72] A Chinese coin dated to 200 BCE was found inside the Cổ Loa drum, whose inner mantel was also inscribed with Chinese characters recording its weight and contents.[73] All this indicates a degree of centralized political and technological development, military power, and transnational

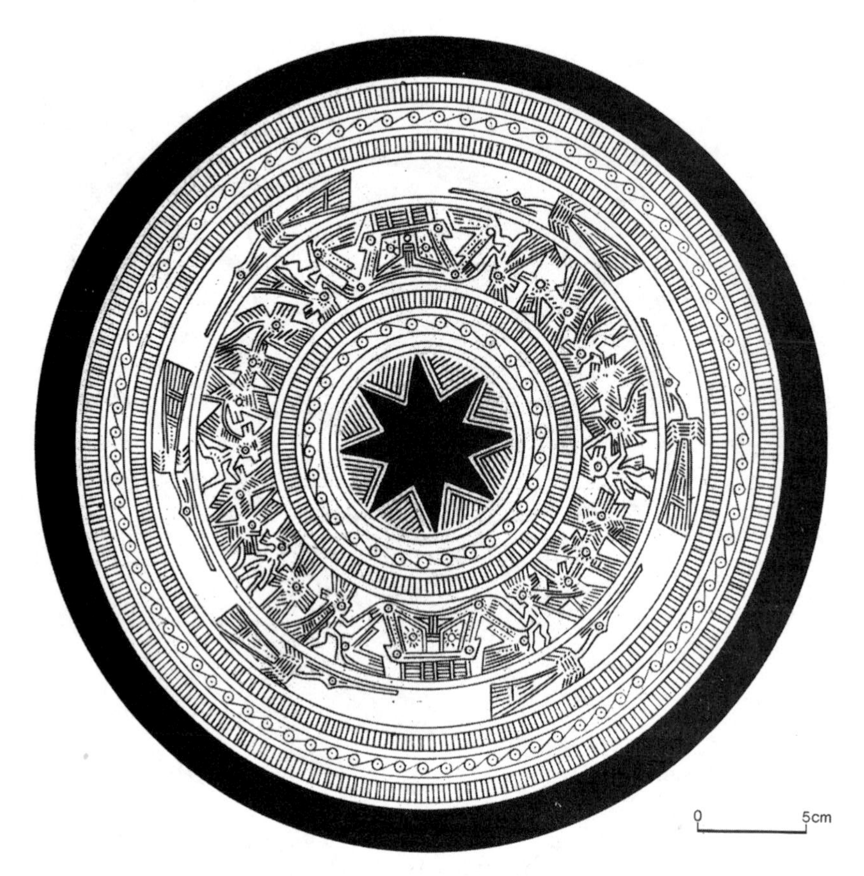

Fig. 1.6
Tympanum of the Quảng Xương bronze drum. From *Dong Son Drums in Viet Nam*, (Hanoi: Viet Nam Social Science Publishing House, 1990), 45.

connections, all beyond the capacity of a local chiefdom. Archaeologists have concluded that "a local and indigenous state-like polity" had appeared in the Red River plain.[74]

There is yet little local evidence of the forging or casting of iron, a technology that in China had first developed in the period 650–500 BCE and in what is now central Thailand around 600–500 BCE.[75] It is plausible that this also happened in the Red River plain, but the evidence for such early dates is unclear. The technology may have spread there via sea trade from China. On the coast of what is now central Việt Nam late in the first millennium BCE, there is evidence of the use of iron along with imported glass and exotic stoneware. Archaeologists have found iron weapons in burial sites, along with imported jewelry and "beautifully worked" burial urns. Domestication of draft animals may also have facilitated the use of iron plowshares, heavier than those made of bronze.[76]

Flourishing communities required more intensive agriculture. Rice cultivation became the basis of this entire Bronze Age civilization. Đông Sơn culture produced its first bronze plows, in four types, "apparently for use in different soils."[77] The Cổ Loa drum contained ninety-six socketed bronze plowshares, six hoes, and a chisel. These agricultural tools in the Cổ Loa trove far outnumbered weapons (sixteen spearheads, eight arrowheads, and a dagger), unlike in other Đông Sơn sites where half the bronze implements were weapons.[78] Cultivation, given its key role in supporting greater political centralization, may also have acquired a new importance in high-level ritual.

Water motifs pervaded the material culture as wet-rice cultivation combined with important riverine and maritime activity. Land and water mingled. The characteristic rounded pediform bronze axes from the Đông Sơn site on the Mã River depict pairs of "snake bodied crocodile-dragon motifs with coiled tails" facing one another above motifs of "feathered-men."[79] Seaborne trade, too, brought an increasing display of local wealth that highlighted the developing culture. Nearer the South China Sea coast, Đông Sơn–era communities buried their dead in cemeteries that included "opulent" boat tombs. One of these is a hollowed-out tree trunk more than fourteen feet long, containing more than a hundred artifacts dating from 500–300 BCE, including bronze weapons, drums, bells, a painted wooden box, and Chinese metal objects. Another coastal site yielded eight boat coffins with bronze axes and spearheads. The art on Đông Sơn drums portrays long, sleek wooden boats decked with cabins and raised platforms manned by plumed warriors and crews of paddlers, along with other maritime scenes of boats with seabirds and amphibians.[80]

The Đông Sơn culture illustrates the combination of "mountains and waters" (*non nước*) by which Vietnamese came to define their homeland. The drums depict houses on stilts above ground level, similar to those whose archaeological vestiges were found at Đông Sơn.[81] Like the dwellings still preferred in lowland Cambodia today, raised houses protected residents from flooding, snakes, and wild animals. The stilt houses may stem from an early cultural experience, when former coastal lowland communities had moved inland to escape fast-rising sea levels, which fostered cultural exchanges as "sedentary coastal peoples rushed back past each other." Aquatic "dragons," too, might even represent a memory of saltwater crocodiles that had swum inland and first infested the coastal plain as the encroaching ocean turned it into salt marshes.[82] In Chinese, the phrase "raise the crocodiles" (*jiao*) means "deluges" or "disastrous floods."[83] Or the memory may be more recent. Two Vietnamese archaeologists have concluded: "From the decorations on the bronze implements, we suggest that this culture was originally from the hills, and only later did it move to the plains and then coastal areas."[84] As the sea receded again, Đông Sơn settlements may indeed have expanded into the new coastal wetlands, encountering the estuarine crocodiles and other reptiles that appear on Đông Sơn drums and bronze situlas from the Red River valley.[85]

Crocodiles must have been a frequent sight in prehistoric Việt Nam. Historian Edward Schafer has speculated that the first Chinese name for the region, Jiao, may be the same word as *jiao* (crocodile, dragon).[86] The estuarine or saltwater crocodile, the world's largest living reptile, often reaching twenty-three feet in length, prefers coastal waters and river mouths like those of the Red River, but can also live inland in freshwater streams, swamps, and lakes. It was common in central and southern Vietnam until recent times, as was the freshwater Siamese crocodile.[87] Under the warmer conditions and higher sea levels of several millennia ago, substantial crocodile populations also inhabited northern Vietnam and southern China, where they were numerous in Guangdong until medieval times.[88] A large freshwater species is believed to have survived in China until the eleventh century, and the saltwater crocodile until the twelfth.[89] They were likely more numerous in Việt Nam, where a crocodile was reported in the Red River in the thirteenth century.[90] Later reports from Guangdong of

Fig. 1.7
Crocodiles on the Hòa Bình bronze drum (detail). From *Dong Son Drums in Viet Nam*, (Hanoi: Viet Nam Social Science Publishing House, 1990), 23.

Fig. 1.8
Boats, crocodiles, turtle, and aquatic birds on a Đông Sơn bronze vessel, 300–100 BCE. Yale University Art Gallery, object on loan from Thomas Jaffe.

crocodiles, "sea dragons," and coastal "alligators" suggest the presence of saltwater crocodiles in offshore waters bordering northern Việt Nam until as late as the nineteenth century.[91]

Clearly some of the roots of Vietnamese culture lie in the Red River plain and coastline.[92] Who, then, were those people who arrived there from the mountains?

TAI AND VIETICS IN PREHISTORIC VIỆT NAM

One source of information on prehistoric Vietnam that vaguely resembles a text is the Vietnamese language itself, which is like a constantly shifting kaleidoscope of sounds and concepts. A language does partly resemble an extant ancient document in the way it has been copied and recopied, both daily and from one generation to the next, memorized instead of written but passed on from parents to children in powerfully intimate ways and constantly checked and reconfirmed by family, friends, and strangers alike. An aural text, many of whose words have been lost in transmission, replaced by new borrowings, and supplemented by conceptual accretions, the Vietnamese language still undoubtedly preserves valuable information about a distant, undocumented past.

Modern Vietnamese belongs to the Mon-Khmer language group, but it includes "a smattering of Tai loanwords and a heavy layer of Chinese lexical and some structural influence."[93] Of seven words for "rice" in Vietnamese, three seem to share a common origin with Khmer terms, while one appears to have been borrowed later from Tai and one (probably later again) from Chinese.[94] Of the 150 Mon-Khmer languages, Vietnamese is "the remotest from its origin."[95] Scholarly recognition of its membership in that group came only in the 1960s, as shown in the linguist Heinz-Jürgen Pinnow's 1959 map (fig. 1.9), which still excluded Vietnamese not only from the Mon-Khmer group but even from its larger language family, Austroasiatic.[96] Tai languages, including modern Thai and Lao, belong to a separate family, Tai-Kadai. No relationship has been demonstrated between these two ancient language families. "Mon-Khmer history remains very mysterious," writes the historical linguist Gérard Diffloth.[97]

It is now clear that the common origins of Vietnamese and other Mon-Khmer languages lie in upland societies that cultivated rice but had yet to adopt wet-rice agriculture. By studying a variety of Austroasiatic languages and identifying words sharing a common origin (cognates), Diffloth reconstructed vocabulary from what must once have been their common language, which scholars call Proto-Austroasiatic. These original words include eleven key terms in rice agriculture: words for the rice plant, grain, husks, and bran, as well as terms for techniques of preparing rice, such as mortar, pestle, and winnow, and for food that is eaten with rice. However, this early vocabulary excludes terms specific to wet-rice agriculture, so Diffloth believes the first Austroasiatic or Mon-Khmer speakers grew dry rice in the hills. Even today (as fig. 1.9 shows), the upland areas host the greatest diversity of Austroasiatic languages, which indicates that their speakers probably originated in the hills, with some colonizing the plains only "at a later stage in their expansion."[98]

The vocabulary bequeathed by the first farmers of the plains of northern Việt Nam may thus reflect developmental phases of their agriculture. After "Proto-Vietic" had separated from other Mon-Khmer languages, Tai influence possibly followed with settled cultivation, perhaps wet-rice farming. Many Tai loanwords in Vietnamese refer to that form of agriculture, terms such as "ditch/canal" (*mương*), "fields" (*đồng ruộng*), or terms for related aquatic aspects of farm husbandry—for instance, "duck" (*vịt*).[99]

Yet other Vietnamese words associated with wet-rice agriculture may be older than those borrowed from Tai. Some are linked to Vietnamese origins and even to Vietnamese identity itself. Indeed, "the earliest recorded name

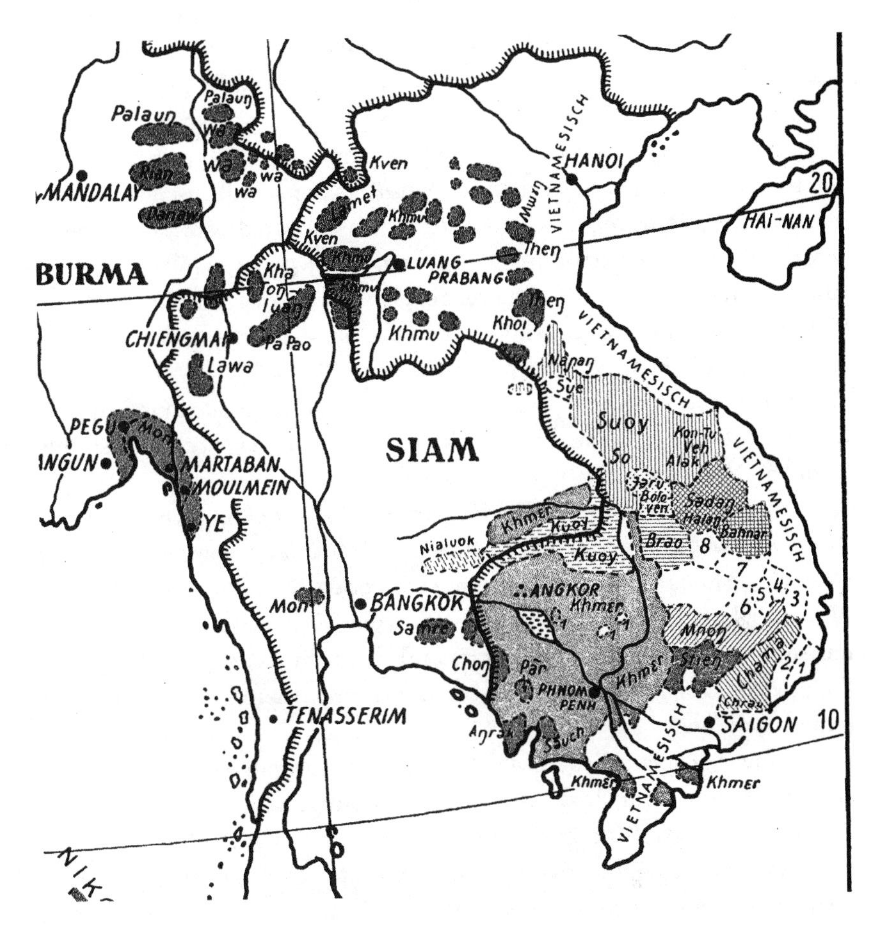

Fig. 1.9
Map of Austroasiatic linguistic groups of mainland Southeast Asia. From Heinz-Jürgen Pinnow, *Versuch einer historischen Lautlehre der Kharia-Sprache* (Wiesbaden, Germany: O. Harrassowitz, 1959).

for the Vietnamese people" is *Lạc*, a word meaning an aquatic, otter-like creature, which appears in the name of the mythical hero Lạc Long Quân ("otter dragon lord"), who came from the sea and purportedly introduced the Vietnamese to agriculture.[100] Japanese scholars have suggested that the name Lạc "derives from the Vietnamese word *lạch* or *rạch*," meaning "ditch, canal, waterway," and that farming in the Red River delta must have involved the draining of swampland.[101] Huỳnh Sanh Thông argued that *lạc* is "a variant of *nác*, an archaic or dialectal form of *nước*, or 'water,'" and that many other Vietnamese words denoting water or its qualities "sound very much like *lạc*."[102]

The first appearance of "Lạc" in any extant written record comes in a Chinese statement directly linking aquatic agriculture to Lạc ethnic identity (in its Chinese form, *Luo* or *Lo*) in the Red River plain, which the Chinese called Jiaozhi. A description of the region in the lost third- or fourth-century text *Jiaozhou waiyu ji* (a record of a region beyond Jiao prefecture) is quoted in the sixth-century *Shui Jing Shu* (Commentary on the waterways classic): "At the time when prefectures and counties were still not established in Jiaozhi, there were Lo [Lạc] Fields, which appeared or disappeared in accordance with the flooding of the tide. Local people reclaimed these lands and lived on them. Therefore, people there were called Lo people."[103] If Huỳnh Sanh Thông's etymology is correct, the Vietnamese were then the "water people," those who cultivated the "water fields."

Yet it is uncertain that the Vietnamese ethnic term *Lạc* long predates Chinese influence. Because extant Vietnamese-language texts date only from the thirteenth century CE, prior use of the indigenous ethnonym *Lạc* is unattested.[104] Even its Chinese form *Luo* appears no earlier than the third century CE. The fourth- or fifth-century *Guang zhou ji* mentions only former "Luo lords." Both texts refer back to a period no earlier than 111 BCE.[105] Whatever languages people spoke in the Red River delta in the mid-first millennium BCE, there is no contemporary written record that they called themselves "Lạc." Any names they then used for themselves or their language remain unknown.

Moreover, scholars dispute who these Luo/Lạc people were, if indeed this ancient Chinese term identified a single ethnolinguistic group. Speakers of Tai languages have lived in the hills of northern Việt Nam for more than four thousand years. Vietnamese archaeologists have identified ethnic Tai occupation of an upland site from the third millennium BCE, near the border with China.[106] One historical linguist argues that even the Lạc people of the Red River plain were Tai speakers who "originally occupied a north to south continuum which included the delta."[107]

If Tai speakers had preceded the other inhabitants of northern Việt Nam, by ancient times they were not alone there. Mon-Khmer and other Austroasiatic language groups also lived both north and south of the Red River delta, in ancient central Việt Nam and southern China.[108] By then, speakers of Mon-Khmer languages already occupied large areas farther north, even "far into the present borders of China," some linguists have argued. Inhabitants of parts of southern China whom the preclassical Chinese called "Yuè" (or Yüeh) already used some words of Austroasiatic origin resembling that of other Mon-Khmer languages, especially Vietnamese. A second-century Chinese commentator recorded the sound of the word that, as he put it, "the Yüeh people call 'to die.'" He wrote the character for the Old Chinese verb **tset*. Its pronunciation, two linguists assert, was very close to the Proto-Mon-Khmer form of the word "to die," *kcet*, and similar to the modern Vietnamese *chết*. Another second-century Chinese source recorded the sound for what "Nan-yüeh [southern Yuè] calls 'dog,'" *sio*, also similar to the Vietnamese equivalent *chó*. Ancient Chinese also borrowed terms from languages they called Yuè that resemble even modern Vietnamese words. Mon-Khmer loan words in Old Chinese and southern Chinese dialects were used especially for characteristically aquatic and tropical items, such as "river," "wet," "bubbles," "duckweed," and "crab," but also basic words for "child," "housefly," "ivory," "crossbow," "shaman," and the verb "know."[109]

Who, then, were the Yuè? And how did distinctively Mon-Khmer, even Proto-Vietnamese vocabulary find its way so far north? By the time of the classical Chinese contact with northern Việt Nam, the early ethnolinguistic pattern there had been transformed by two external influences from the south and north, from mainland Southeast Asia and southeast China. First, a new ethnic group migrated into northern Việt Nam from the highlands to the south. They were speakers of the Mon-Khmer language scholars call Proto-Vietic, the linguistic ancestor of Vietnamese. Arriving in the northern delta, these "Vietic" people joined and eventually supplanted the resident speakers of other Mon-Khmer languages and Tai. Meanwhile from the north, deep in what is now Chinese territory, came the new ethnonym "Yuè." In the first millennium BCE, China adopted the term "Yuè" as a northern imperial description first of the peoples living in southeast China and, later, those in northern Việt Nam as well.[110] This non-Sinitic word, possibly also of Mon-Khmer origin, passed into the Vietic and modern Vietnamese languages as "Việt," providing the mixed community in the Red River delta with a new identity marker that eventually replaced Lạc. There seems every reason, then, why Vietnamese vocabulary might derive from Tai and Chinese as well as from Mon-Khmer terms.

But first came the migration from the south of the early Proto-Vietic linguistic group into what is now northern Việt Nam. These speakers of an ancestral Vietnamese tongue originated from the southwest, in the uplands of what are now the north-central Vietnamese provinces of Nghệ An and Quảng Bình, and an adjacent inland region of east-central Laos, especially Kham Keut district of Borikhamxay province and Khammouane province.[111] There today the most diverse of the Vietic languages (seventeen of about twenty-six in the group) are still spoken, indicating this area as their original linguistic homeland.[112]

The twenty-six Vietic languages, of which modern Vietnamese and Mường are the most widely spoken, form one of a dozen subgroups in the Mon-Khmer branch of Austroasiatic languages.[113] Vietnamese only later acquired tones, became monosyllabic, and was written with Chinese characters, while most other Mon-Khmer languages remained atonal and polysyllabic, and

Fig. 1.10
Map of Vietic linguistic groups. Courtesy of Paul Sidwell.

several adopted Indic or Indic-derived alphabets. But dozens of basic Vietnamese words still resemble even their modern Khmer counterparts.[114] Across the length of the Austroasiatic linguistic world, over several millennia from ancient southeast China to modern Việt Nam and Cambodia, the words for "child" are recognizably similar: *con* in ancient Yuè and modern Vietnamese, *koun* in modern Khmer.[115] The word for "grandchild" is also *chau* in both Khmer and Vietnamese. Basic numerals, too, are close in sound, despite the very different scripts traditionally used to transcribe them:

Table 1.1 VIETNAMESE AND KHMER NUMERALS

English	Vietnamese ***(quốc ngữ)***	Khmer	in traditional Vietnamese script ***(chữ nôm)***	in Khmer script
One	**một**	*muoi*	沒	១
Two	**hai**	*pir*	𠄩	២
Three	**ba**	*bei*	𠀧	៣
Four	**bốn**	*buon*	𦊚	៤
Five	**năm**	*pram*	𠄼	៥

Also of Mon-Khmer origin are other Vietnamese words for basic things such as *nước* (water), *củi* (firewood), *lá* (leaf), *rễ* (root), and *chim* (bird).[116] The word for "hand" or "arm" in Vietnamese is *tay*—in Khmer, *dai*. Other cognates include words for "neck," "tail," "leg," "sun," "mountain," and "tiger."[117]

Precisely when Vietic speakers left their hilly southern homeland might be answered by determining how long ago Vietic languages diverged from the other Mon-Khmer languages. One indication may be the number of remaining cognates, which diminish over time, as all languages adopt new vocabulary. Across all Mon-Khmer subgroups today, cognates comprise only about one-quarter of each vocabulary. Three-quarters are presumably words adopted since these languages diverged. However, slow changes in vocabulary and pronunciation provide only an extremely rough method of measuring elapsed time, and estimates vary widely. Glottochronology, a technique some historical linguists use for language dating, suggests that "the grand splitting up" of the Mon-Khmer language groups occurred as recently as the second millennium BCE, possibly in "a mass dispersal" that could have been "the result of some major catastrophe."[118] But one writer identifies a much earlier event, the postglacial sea flood that drowned the Southeast Asian continental shelf in 6000–5000 BCE, causing a dispersal of the inhabitants. Such an early date is possible because in Southeast Asian languages the measurable linguistic changes occur much more slowly than elsewhere.[119] If so, the massive sixth-millennium BCE sea flood may suggest an approximate date for population displacements that caused the first separation of Proto-Vietic from other Mon-Khmer languages.

The extent of the variety among the seventeen Vietic languages that today remain concentrated in part of east-central Laos suggests that Vietic languages were first spoken there at least 2,000–2,500 years ago. From this homeland in the upland Annamite Cordillera, north and east of the modern Lao-Cambodian border, some of the Vietic populations moved east and northeast down out of the hills into the lowlands of central Việt Nam. It was there that the Proto-Vietnamese language emerged among them, its local longevity demonstrated by the fact that central Việt Nam now hosts the greatest diversity of modern Vietnamese dialects.[120] Some of these Proto-Vietnamese speakers then moved on north into the Red River plain.

The date of the Vietics' arrival in the north is disputed. Some linguists argue that Vietic speakers supplanted Tai speakers in the Red River Delta as early as the second millennium BCE.[121] One suggests a date late in the first millennium CE.[122] The truth may lie somewhere between. The adoption into Vietnamese of some early Chinese vocabulary, including the word for "paper," is dated phonologically to the era of the Han dynasty (206 BCE–220 CE).[123] Another Han-era loanword is the Vietnamese term for "census register" (*bộ*).[124] The Han conducted an extensive census in the Red River delta in 2 CE (another was attempted in 140 CE). To be in such contact with Chinese by then, many speakers of Proto-Vietnamese must already have reached at least that far north. By the late first millennium BCE, not only Tai speakers but also Mon-Khmer linguistic groups, latterly including Vietic speakers, occupied a continuum that stretched north from what is now east Laos to southeast China and must have included the northern Vietnamese delta.[125]

Beyond that the historical linguistic evidence remains too imprecise to date the arrival of speakers of Proto-Vietnamese from the southern uplands into the plains of northern Việt Nam, or to know whether their arrival preceded, provoked, accompanied, or followed the local transition to the more centralized Đông Sơn chiefdoms with their advanced metalwork. But these processes may have converged around the middle of the first millennium BCE. Proto-Vietic diverged first from Khmeric languages around 2500 BCE, then from Katuic around 1000 BCE.[126] Then Proto-Vietic itself split when the Thavưng linguistic subgroup separated from Proto-Việt-Mường, possibly as early as the third century BCE.[127] The northward movement of speakers of Proto-Việt-Mường may have occasioned this divergence. By "two millennia ago," according to a recent linguistic survey, speakers of Việt-Mường or Proto-Vietnamese had spread as far north as what is now southern China and made contact with Tai peoples there as well as in northern Vietnam. As they migrated northward, Vietic-speaking swidden farmers "were developing a more sophisticated civilization," and they "gained from the Tai concepts and associated words for wet-rice agriculture and animal husbandry," practices that "may have allowed further development of the early Vietnamese civilization." Speakers of Proto-Vietnamese probably first arrived in the Red River delta region around the mid-first millennium BCE, stimulating or joining the development of Đông Sơn culture. Following this came contact between Proto-Vietnamese and Chinese, which began in the third century BCE.[128]

YUÈ AND CHINESE

The earliest form of Chinese writing, the oracle bone inscriptions of the late Shang dynasty (1300–1046 BCE), mention a people of southeastern China with a name whose pronunciation in ancient Chinese modern scholars have reconstructed as **ywet*, pronounced in modern Mandarin as Yuè and in Vietnamese as "Việt."[129] The East Asia scholar Eric Henry notes the early Chinese character used for "Yuè": "a distinctive, hooked, Yuè axe," which apparently represents the shouldered ax associated with Austroasiatic speakers. These first Chinese texts record short, uneasy questions about that community and the loyalty of its rulers, asking, "Will Yuè be made to come?" and "Will Yuè be obtained?" Between 2000 and 300 BCE, the Yuè region of coastal southeast China, criss-crossed by watercourses like the Red River delta, was the homeland of a non-Sinitic culture that constructed as many as twenty thousand burial mounds.[130] Moving further south as early as the second millennium BCE, Yuè emigrants to the Red River plain likely brought the characteristic spindle whorls excavated in Phùng Nguyên sites there.[131]

Chinese-language texts suggest that late in the first millennium BCE, Yuè refugees fleeing imperial Chinese conquests once again traversed what is now southern China and this time carried the term "Yuè" southward. The ethnonym that eventually became "Việt" reached northern Việt Nam in the centuries BCE, or earlier.[132] Sometime later, the indigenous people of southeast China and north Việt Nam, the new subjects and neighbors of these Nán Yuè ("Southern Yuè") immigrants, adopted the exiles' ethnic name.

The peoples of these regions inhabited a shared cultural world, in which, as elsewhere in ancient times, ethnic identity and even linguistic adherence were fluid. Tai and Mon-Khmer speakers in the delta, in merging with the Vietics arriving from the south, not only adopted the Proto-Vietnamese language that had originated in eastern Laos and central Việt Nam but eventually also assumed the ethnic name Yuè that became that of the Vietnamese people, Việt.[133]

They are not the only linguistic groups to have adopted the name or identity of others. In France, the early ethnonym "Frank" derived from a Germanic-speaking group. And in Britain, indigenous Celts adopted both the name and the language of their Anglo-Saxon conquerors, slowly becoming "English." In what became northern Việt Nam, the Proto-Vietic language and the ethnonym Việt arrived there from opposite directions. In this case, too, most indigenous people may have stayed where they were. Studies in the physical anthropology of human remains found at northern Vietnamese sites ranging from prehistoric to contemporary show a "remarkable continuity."[134] The major changes were probably linguistic, cultural, and political.

Ethnic reidentification was probably slow and less significant than the political impact of the Yuè leaders who also brought new institutions. The story may have begun as early as the ninth century BCE, after the kingdom of Chu emerged in the area now comprising China's Hunan and Hubei provinces. A Chu monarch marched an army down the Yangzi and conquered the east-coast Yang Yuè region, in modern Zhejiang province. Leading Chu families, members of the Mi royal clan, moved downriver to settle there, launching a new polity. That became the site of the earliest autonomous Yuè kingdom, first mentioned in Chinese chronicles of the seventh century BCE. Later, Yuè is recorded as having established its capital at Kuaiji on the lower Yangzi in 510 BCE. The Chinese considered it "a state with a ruler and officers."[135] Preparing to invade the neighboring state of Wu, a Yuè prince is said to have motivated his troops by assembling their women on what became "the Mountain of Lone Ladies."[136] In the fifth century BCE, the Yuè kingdom, using advanced cargo vessels, played a role in the first documented sea trade between the mouth of the Yangzi and northern Chinese cities. It was "a great power on the southeastern coasts of China."[137]

This Yuè realm had much in common with that of the Lạc Việt. One Chinese account said that King Gou Jian of Yuè (r. 496–465 BCE) "lived in a country located on the shores of the eastern sea and governed a people of barbarians with tattooed bodies." A third-century Chinese text recounts the introduction of agriculture to Yuè during Gou Jian's reign by a figure named Tai-fu Chung whose role resembled that of the mythical Vietnamese founder, "otter dragon lord" Lạc Long Quân: "For the king of Yüeh, Tai-fu Chung opened the prairies to tilling and settled cities on them; he widened the lands and sowed them to grain."[138] This account of events in the early fifth century BCE possibly traveled south with Yuè refugees as later Chinese advances sent them fleeing (likely by ship as well as overland) toward the land of the Lạc, whose story of agriculture incorporated a similar local legend of an "otter dragon lord" arriving from the sea. Controversially, a French scholar even identified the early Yuè kingdom in coastal Zhejiang as sharing "the same ethnicity: Yueh; the same clan name: Mi, and the same customs" as the people then inhabiting northern Việt Nam. More likely, it was a defeat suffered by the Yuè kingdom at the hands of Chu in 333 BCE that drove members of the Yuè ruling elite southward with their followers, in "bands of armed fugitives."[139] The "Southern Yuè" (Nán-Yuè) are mentioned in Chinese records of the fourth and third centuries BCE.[140]

Scholars are divided on which linguistic group(s) the Yuè belonged to, but at least some of the evidence suggests the Mon-Khmer branch of Austroasiatic. Linguists in mainland China and elsewhere have argued that the various peoples known as Bai Yuè ("Many Yuè" or "Hundred Yuè") in ancient southeast China were all or mostly speakers of Tai-Kadai languages, though others including speakers of Austroasiatic languages lived there too.[141] Some scholars have even suggested that, like the Proto-Vietnamese, all the Yuè peoples were Austroasiatic speakers.[142] At the least, in archaic times Mon-Khmer as well as Tai languages were spoken both north and south of the Red River delta. But if people inhabiting the delta already used the term *Yuè* for themselves too, no early local record of it survives, just as none survives of *Lạc*.

Yuè exiles moving south carried with them a culture quite different from that which became identifiably Chinese. Even the rump Yuè kingdom that long survived in the Zhejiang region of southeast China remained "thoroughly non-sinitic" to its end.[143] The people of Yuè, Eric Henry writes, differed from their northern neighbors "in language, music, folklore, religion, diet, village layout, boat construction, weapons, terrain preferences (mountain tops), domestic architecture (stilt houses), coiffure (short), personal adornment (tattooing), funerary behavior," and in the serpentine characters of their script. In their warmer southern climate, the Yuè went barefoot in short sleeves and short trouser legs. Yuè military practices ranged from river-borne assaults to the beating of "deep-throated copper wardrums." Were these Yuè equivalents of Đông Sơn drums? A Chinese chronicle lists Yuè as one of the four most warlike kingdoms of the Warring States period (403–221 BCE). Its soldiers fought best on water: "Yuè often had the upper hand in its skirmishes with Chu, because the eastward flowing streams in the south made retreats difficult for Chu but easy for Yuè." Other Chinese chronicles record that in 312 BCE, the Yuè king sent "300 boats" including a large ship named the *Shi Wang*, to help an ally against Chu, along with five million arrows, bales of silk, rhinoceros horns, and ivory. Yuè culture was also distinct from the Chinese in its practice of naming boats and swords.[144] A Chinese text described the Yuè as a people who "used boats as their carriages and oars as their horses."[145] All this resembles Đông Sơn and Lạc culture further south, in the Red River delta.

The aquatic landscape was also similar. *The Book of the Prince of Huainan*, a compendium on natural history compiled around 120 BCE, described regions to the south as "places where the bright-positive aethers accumulate, being warm and moist... with land well suited to rice, and having numerous rhinoceroses and elephants."[146] This also applied to parts of coastal east China where the Yuè first appeared and where, even in the mid-twentieth century, the countryside was "so full of water that one [had] the feeling of swimming in water rather than standing on firm ground." And the ancient mythology of the region was similar, too. The early state of Yuè "considered itself a descendant of Yü," a mythical progenitor and apparently the son of a water creature. Yü was "the regulator of the waters, the builder of canals, and, thereby, the man who made wet-field agriculture possible." He was linked with other water creatures, including the dragon. According to myths of south China, "Yü busied himself with canal work for eight years," drained the land, and "became an earth god."[147] Like the mythical Yuè founder Tai-fu Chung, Yü bears a striking comparison with the "otter dragon lord" who introduced agriculture to the Lạc Việt.[148] And the Tan "boat people" of China's southern coasts and estuaries, snake-worshipping communities of fishers and divers thought to be descendants of the ancient Yuè, were known to medieval Chinese as "dragon house-holders," while Tan women and children were "otters."[149]

Rituals in the ancient Yuè regions of south and southeast China also resembled those of the Lạc. Bronze drums were common among the Yuè, including a "thunder drum," and these too were linked to water animals. The first millennium BCE *Shih Ching* (Book of songs) mentions a drum with a tympanum made from the skin of a *tuo*, a "typically southern" water creature resembling a crocodile. The *tuo* appears in classical texts in combination with *jiao* dragons; it can produce thunder, lightning, and rain. Like water, use of the *tuo* drum at weddings brought fertility. Drum decorations depicted ships, and tales of "copper ships" were common in South China "including also Annam," that is, modern northern Việt Nam.[150] Dragon boat festivals are still found throughout south China, with no northern Chinese counterpart.[151] In 1855, a Sinologist witnessed a festival in Guangdong that recalled accounts "over a thousand years earlier."

> Two boats, long and slender, each built to represent a dragon, the head of which rose high and formed the prow. A man sat upon it with a flag in each hand, which

> he waved to direct the movements of the crew, and with his face turned towards the helmsman who stood near the stern. Midway in the boats were two men beating with all their might, one a gong, the other a drum.[152]

This could almost describe the scene depicted on the Đông Sơn drum of Ngọc Lũ (fig. 1.4).

THE LẠC VIỆT

As they moved south, ancient Yuè exiles and Chinese advancing from the north encountered "a stable, structured, productive, populous, and relatively sophisticated society." The number of excavated sites and the size of ancient dikes and other earthworks in the delta indicates a relatively dense population in an area stretching from northern to north-central Việt Nam.[153]

Yuè and Lạc communities shared other common features distinct from Chinese culture, especially an aquatic life involving boats and water creatures. Intriguingly, given the link between water and fertility, early Yuè water deities were female, as were Yuè shamans, who were "very often connected with water cults."[154] Was this an ancient matriarchal society, whose leaders took multiple husbands?[155] Polyandry might once have existed among the Lạc. An early third-century Chinese account described the ancient Việt practice of levirate marriage: "The younger brother always marries his sister-in-law; this is a widespread custom."[156] Perhaps this practice had originated as polyandry or, more likely, a widow's right to a new husband. Yet its persistence may have also guaranteed a new right, that of the younger brother to a leader's widow and property. At the time of Chinese contact, Lạc society might have been undergoing a transition from an earlier more matriarchal community, or a bilateral one of significant gender equality, to one of increasing male status.[157] If the levirate was an innovation designed to keep land holdings in the same male family, it also reflected an earlier tradition of female authority and protection of widows' interests.

Linguistic vestiges of female status corroborate this view. Huỳnh Sanh Thông identified no fewer than thirty-two Vietnamese words for "mother" or "woman," including seven archaic and twelve modern terms for "mother." These also carry important other meanings, involving fertility, water, agriculture, and bronze drums. The words for water (*nác/nước*) and "country" (*nước*) derive from one of the archaic Vietnamese terms for woman (*nàng*), while another, *nương*, is also used to describe an upland field or swidden. Of two Vietnamese words for "witch, female medium," one (*bóng*) also means a type of drum. The other (*đồng*), a homonym for both "bronze" and "a field in the country," combines with an archaic term for "mother" (*áng*) to form *đồng áng* ("ricefields; the countryside").[158] All this suggests a possible Earth Mother cult and rituals associating water and fertility with bronze drums and female shamans.

High female status, the levirate, bronze drums, and a Mon-Khmer language were cultural features that early Việt society shared with other ethnic groups in mainland Southeast Asia. All societies of that region lack historical documentation for the first millennium BCE, but modern anthropologists' studies of small upland regional communities have found linguistic affinities to ancient Vietic speakers and similar cultural and economic activity even in modern times.[159] Small contemporary communities are not necessarily "static" ethnic holdovers from long-gone eras, but neither can evidence of long-term continuity be dismissed. For instance, as late as the 1930s the Lamet, a Mon-Khmer ethnolinguistic group of 3,800 shifting cultivators in the hills of western Laos, practiced levirate marriage.[160] Intriguingly, the Lamet also considered themselves "the earliest inhabitants" of that region, descended from mythical siblings who had survived a prehistoric deluge by making a large drum and living inside it. According to their origin myth, "When the earth was free of all the water, the brother and sister came out of the drum. They were the only two human beings left on earth." If there is a kernel of truth to this myth, it may represent an archaic Proto-Mon-Khmer memory of the maximum sea levels of 5000–2000 BCE. The siblings' first offspring were the Lamet, followed by the Mien (Yao) and the Thai. In the 1930s, Lamet would pay four buffalo for a bronze drum, the most valuable item of their culture. One man had accumulated more than a hundred.[161]

Twentieth-century inhabitants of the remote valleys of the Vietnamese Central Highlands, too, played bronze gongs from Tonkin, China, or Cambodia at all kinds of occasions.[162] The wooden longhouses of the Rhadé featured pairs of wooden sculptures that resemble Đông Sơn bronze drums, placed in key ritual locations such as the main entrance.[163] In the hills of northeast Cambodia, bronze gongs remain important in the twenty-first century: "People will still trade up to seven buffalo for one gong—the equivalent of four motorcycles—and then hold a two day celebration to inaugurate the gong." A Jarai man from upland central Việt Nam brought a polished bronze gong "newly refurbished with a 2003 Vietnamese coin welded into the back."[164] All this proves little about the early antecedents of the Rhadé, Jarai, or Lamet, or about the Vietics. What is striking is a continuing association of the levirate and bronze gongs with ancient and modern Mon-Khmer groups.

It remains difficult to date the prehistoric transition from Lạc chiefdoms to more complex social institutions like monarchy and literacy. The construction of the Cổ Loa center suggests that the first was present in the Lạc region from the third century BCE. After Chinese imperial forces arrived there in 111 BCE, they recognized not only Lạc lords but a "Lạc king" and a "King of Tây Vu," and they asserted that local officials possessed written records.[165] There is more scholarly agreement on the existence of Lạc kingship than on the names of any historical rulers. Early kings of indigenous realms are known only from much later sources. A lost Chinese text from around 300 CE, briefly cited in a fifth-century document, mentioned a "Hùng" dynasty of monarchs, who had supposedly, from a millennium earlier, ruled the kingdom of Yü Lo (*V.* Âu Lạc).[166] However, the French scholar Henri Maspero dismissed the name "Hùng" as a Chinese scribal error: "There were never any Hung kings, only Lac kings."[167] Similarly, a supposed ancient name for their kingdom, "Văn-lang," dates only from Tang sources of the seventh through ninth centuries CE. The first Vietnamese chronicles, from the fourteenth century, also mention a conquest of "Văn-lang," usually dated to 258 BCE, by a king who took the name An Dương. Keith Taylor has termed An Dương "the first authentic historical figure in Vietnam," whereas Maspero wrote him off: "A legend is a legend." Evidence predating the medieval Vietnamese sources at least indicates that both An Dương and his successor were of northern, non-Lạc origin. The first extant account, citing An Dương by his Chinese name, Anyang, comes in a Chin text of the third or fourth century CE, *Guang zhou ji*. It describes An Dương as a prince of the kingdom of Chu, who "with an army defeated the Lo lords, took the title of King [An Dương] and established himself at the prefecture of Fong-k'i." But his reign was brief. Soon Zhào Tuó, "king of Nan-yuè, defeated king [An Dương]."[168]

All this occurred within what is now China. It was Zhào Tuó (*V.* Triệu Đà), not his predecessor, who subsequently took over the Lạc regions to the south, within modern Việt Nam. By the late third century BCE, Chinese sources record four Yuè realms among the Bai Yuè (Hundred Yuè), all within the borders of modern China. These kingdoms were, from north to south: Eastern Ou in Zhejiang, the original east-coast Yuè heartland; Min Yuè in coastal Fujian; Western Ou, further inland; and Zhào Tuó's kingdom of Nan Yuè on the south China coast.[169] This suggests continuing Yuè dispersal and southern migration of northern exiles, some of whom had probably reached the Red River delta. But the Chinese sources do not yet tell us about developments there or further south.

KHMERS AND CHAMS

Early in the first millennium BCE, mainland Southeast Asia "would have been linguistically a solid Mon-Khmer block."[170] The exception was some Tai speakers in the north of what is now Việt Nam. Probably by the mid-first millennium BCE, early Vietic speakers were joining them and fellow Mon-Khmer groups in the northern coastal plains and delta, while speakers of early Khmer dialects, probably already inhabited the Mekong delta on the southern coast. Between these northern and southern deltas, other Mon-Khmer linguistic groups occupied both the long narrow central Vietnamese coastline and the Central Highlands. Here Neolithic cultures had emerged in the mid-second millennium BCE. On the north-central coastal plains near Nghệ An, they left a score of sites in riverside dunes, mounds on low hills, and accumulated piles of discarded shells known as middens. These sites contained shouldered axes and highly standardized pottery, some of it cord-marked, painted red.[171]

Further south are the Central Highlands, described by a French explorer in the 1890s: "This whole country is extremely rugged. Here are the highest peaks of the Annamite chain and the thickest massifs; the foothills intersect in all directions and cover an inextricable maze of watercourses. The valleys are mostly, especially toward the great ridge, only deep cuttings, tortuous corridors to the bottom of which plunge the torrents.... This region is covered with an immense forest, interrupted only by the sinuous river courses and by the crops of the indigenes on the intermediate slopes, around the villages."[172]

The first farmers in these well-watered uplands took up agriculture on the red soils beside rivers and lakes. On the Pleiku Plateau they also used potter's wheels to produce and decorate sand-tempered pottery, firing it at high temperatures. In the Kontum Basin they made "small thin and fine wares for domestic use, decorated with beautiful patterns." People of the Dắc Lắc highland region also produced wheel-turned, sand-tempered pottery. On the southern coast more advanced Neolithic pottery has been found, dating from the turn of the first millennium BCE. These early distinct cultures in what is now southeastern Việt Nam initially produced stone hoes, sickles, and chisels, and later wholly polished axes, some very large, but becoming smaller and more refined. However, none of these southern sites contained bronze artifacts.[173]

Then, in the first millennium BCE, three new commercial, demographic, and political developments began to complicate the Mon-Khmer territorial dominance of the east coast of the mainland. These were the rise of Southeast Asian maritime trade with India to the west, the arrival of ancestors of the

Cham people on the coast of central Việt Nam from the Malay Archipelago to the east, and the advance of Chinese power from the north. New influences from all three directions forged new relations between the outside world and the eastern mainland of Southeast Asia.

During the first millennium BCE, a new world emerged on the margins of the South China Sea. It developed, according to maritime historian Pierre-Yves Manguin, during a thousand years of "steady exchanges with India, in which certain populations of Southeast Asia, who were beginning to organize themselves within political systems of increasing complexity, played a decisive role, particularly in the setting up of seafaring merchant networks exporting gold and tin."[174] Southeast Asian sailors and shipbuilders became masters of the South China Sea. They carried Đông Sơn artifacts throughout the region, probably on boats like those depicted on the bronze drums. They also traveled north and obtained Chinese silks and manufactured goods in exchange for southern tropical products—ivory, rhinoceros horn, pearls, tortoise shell, kingfisher and peacock feathers, cinnamon, and scented woods.[175] Until at least as late as the sixth century CE, Chinese travelers venturing south of the central Vietnamese coast had to board ships coming from Southeast Asia.[176]

The Chams were one of the most active of these Southeast Asian maritime communities. Austronesian-speaking linguistic cousins of the Malays and the Acehnese of Sumatra, the Chams have been called "one of the great navigator peoples of prehistoric Southeast Asia." Probably before 1000 BCE, the first Chams set out from the west coast of the island of Borneo. Sailing northwest across the South China Sea, they probably made their initial landfall south of modern Huế in central Việt Nam.[177] To this new home they brought their Cham language, which today still preserves its ancient word for "sunset," meaning "sun plunge into sea," a vivid memory of their former home on Borneo's west coast.[178] Later voyages brought more Cham settlers to other parts of the central coast. Some moved inland and up into the Central Highlands, probably for trade.

Archaeological remains at the central Vietnamese coastal site of Sa Huỳnh are thought to be the first physical evidence of the Chams' arrival on the Southeast Asian mainland. Large pottery burial jars found in sand dunes there resemble others found across the South China Sea, on Borneo's west coast and in the Philippines. From the mid-second millennium BCE, writes prehistorian Dougald O'Reilly, "Sa Huynh people interred their dead in painted jars with stone tools. Near the end of the second millennium BCE, the style of painting changes and bronze tools begin to appear." Sa Huỳnh nephrite two-headed animals and globular earrings have been found in Đông Sơn burial sites to the north and at sites in modern Indonesia, the Philippines, and Thailand. By the mid- to late first millennium BCE, Sa Huỳnh people traded in semiprecious stones and glass beads with regions possibly as distant as India. Their jar burial sites have been unearthed all along Việt Nam's central coast.[179] Sixty-three were excavated in 2002–4 alone, the jars containing a total of ten thousand beads, including one thousand made of carnelian and more than one hundred gold beads and earrings. By the end of the last century BCE, Chinese Han dynasty bronze vessels began to appear in the south, in what is now central Việt Nam and Cambodia.[180] Some of the later Sa Huỳnh sites contained Han mirrors of the first century BCE, and a site in the far south, near Hồ Chí Minh City, has yielded a Chinese sword with possible traces of silk.[181]

Linguistic borrowing proceeded apace. The Austronesian Chamic languages spoken by the descendants of the first Sa Huỳnh settlers began to adopt some of the characteristics of neighboring Chinese and Mon-Khmer languages. In the northernmost Cham colony, on the island of Hainan, nontonal Cham eventually became fully tonal like Chinese languages.[182] In what is now central Việt Nam, Mon-Khmer forms soon came to influence about 10 percent of the ancient Chamic lexicon and phonology, revealing "intense and intimate" early contacts including bilingualism and intermarriage. On the coast, the disyllabic Cham language became more monosyllabic (as did Vietnamese) and developed vowel registers (like Khmer).[183] In the Central Highlands, Chams dominated and mixed with ancestors of some of the modern upland ethnic groups, including the Jarai, Rhadé, Chru and Roglai, whose languages today retain some of their early Mon-Khmer vocabulary and structure despite a dominant Chamic overlay.[184]

In the far south, archeological work in the Mekong delta region has revealed evidence of human occupation "from at least 2,000 BCE," and evidence of "extensive habitation of the delta after 500 BCE."[185] Excavations at the site of Angkor Borei, a Cambodian village near the modern border with Việt Nam, uncovered a very early settlement that was occupied from the start of the fourth century BCE and the remains of a brick-walled city with a double moat, as well as a cemetery that came into use long before the fifth century CE.[186] These were the origins of a Khmer-speaking kingdom in the Mekong delta that the Chinese would come to know as Funan. At least by the late first millennium BCE, inhabitants of the Mekong delta were probably already engaged in trade with parts of India.[187] The destiny of the northern Red River delta, however, was more closely linked to that of China, which itself was increasingly attracted by the South China Sea and India trade.

Over thousands of years, prehistoric communities developed in Việt Nam's rich aquatic and maritime environments. After the Ice Age, the fertile river valleys and plains, partly encircled by hills in the west, were subject to encroachment from the east by rising sea levels. As the sea receded again, the northern delta coastline gradually reemerged, and the alluvial plain created by the Red River's heavy cargo of silt slowly expanded further eastward. Hunter-gatherers and swidden farmers moved down from the hills, and many took up wet-rice cultivation. They also fished in the rivers and offshore, fashioned stone implements, and decorated pottery. In the first millennium BCE, they cast increasingly sophisticated bronze artifacts that partly reflected the importance of water and fertility in their environment. From the hills of eastern Laos, the first speakers of the archaic Proto-Vietnamese language also moved down the river valleys into the coastal plains and then northward into the Red River delta, joining its earlier inhabitants, who spoke other Mon-Khmer languages and Tai. Meanwhile, from the north, groups displaced by pre-imperial Chinese expansion also arrived in the Red River plain, bearing the ethnic name Yuè that indigenous southerners would adopt in something close to its original pronunciation, Việt. Without the benefit of literacy but with a rich language and culture, the first indigenous polity emerged in what would become the country of the "southern Việt."

PART TWO

Provinces

CHAPTER 2

Calming the Waves

Imperial Conquest and Indigenization, 221 BCE to 540 CE

The earliest document to describe people living in what is now Việt Nam appears to be a Chinese text dating from the 220s BCE. Reporting "unorthodox customs" of the Yuè in a part of the Lạc Việt region, it states: "To crop the hair, decorate the body, rub pigment into arms and fasten garments on the left side is the way of the Bakviet. In the country of Tai-wu [*V.* Tây Vu; see ch. 1] the habit is to blacken teeth, scar cheeks and wear caps of sheat [catfish] skin stitched crudely with an awl."[1]

In the late third century BCE, these people of the Lạc Việt region stood on the threshold of a new era, one of imperial subjugation, bitter resistance, flourishing trade, and mutual cultural accommodations on the part of both invaders and indigenes. By the sixth century CE, these changes had transformed both Lạc Việt society and its Chinese colonists. A complex new society emerged in the southern reaches of a northern empire.

That emerging empire commenced its conquest of the Yuè and Lạc regions in 221 BCE. Its expansion south of the mountain passes overlooking lowland south China into the plains and coastal areas that Chinese called Lingnan ("south of the ridges" or "passes"), continued to propel Yuè refugees southward into the Lạc Việt territory. It also for the first time brought the new northern empire into direct contact with the lucrative trade networks of the South China Sea.[2] The founding emperor of the Qin dynasty (255–206 BCE), Qin Shi Huangdi, coveted "the round and irregular pearls of Yuè," as well as its rhinoceros horn, elephant tusks, and kingfisher plumes.[3] Only the south could supply these tropical items, not only from the Yuè and Lạc Việt regions but also other Mon-Khmer and Cham realms, whose river ports served the eastern mainland of Southeast Asia and the north-south maritime trade that thrived along its coastline.

Conquest of the northern coast of the South China Sea only strengthened the imperial temptation to take control of this commerce. A rising domestic Chinese market for these luxury goods made the trade profitable, not only to the empire and visiting foreign merchants but also to imperial officials on southern appointments. Indeed, the latter's private acquisition of wealth would often disrupt the stability of northern rule. Along with imperial domination and official corruption, persistent cultural differences between Chinese and Lạc Việt eventually provoked a succession of serious revolts. Yet, over seven centuries of Chinese administrative imposition, the empire's cultural influence also penetrated the indigenous population, which demonstrated an openness to some features of northern society. Meanwhile the new Sinic ruling class put down local roots and retained power even when imperial political controls eventually began to loosen. Periods of full Chinese authority became intermittent and progressively briefer.[4] By the sixth century CE, the imperial outpost of Jiaozhi was demonstrating local administrative capacity as well as fulfilling its commercial potential.

QIN AND YUÈ

During its fast rise and brief reign, the Qin dynasty's conquests set the southern boundaries of classical and eventually of modern China. It imposed central control first over the inland kingdom of Chu in 223 BCE, and then moved on the Yuè realms of the south. On the east coast the next year, Qin forces overran the rump Yuè polity in Zhejiang. Finally, in successive campaigns from 221 to 214, they stormed south across the five mountain passes into Lingnan. The Qin conquered the Min-Yuè kingdom and overran other areas inhabited by the "Hundred Yuè" (Bai Yuè) across what would soon become south China. These conquests drove another stream of Yuè refugees further southward.

Yuè cultural differences were more difficult to uproot. Along with the institutions of kingship, one or more of the Yuè polities may have already developed writing systems to record their own languages in Chinese characters. If so, historian C. Michele Thompson writes, Qin officials would have moved to destroy most such texts. In 213 BCE Qin Shi Huangdi ordered the destruction of all books on the histories of states other than the Qin, as well as all their historical records and metal inscriptions. Rebels who overthrew the Qin in 206 burned many more documents. Until 191 BCE, criminal laws of the succeeding Han dynasty banned private ownership of books on most subjects other than medicine, pharmacy, and agriculture. The imperial library was again destroyed during the Han interregnum of 9 to 24 CE.[5]

As a result, Yuè texts of any kind survived only in earlier tombs. Modern archaeological finds at Yuè sites include bronze swords bearing inscriptions using Chinese characters to record Yuè names and, Thompson writes, "inscriptions on ritual bronzes, long and complex for such a medium."[6] Even Yuè texts written on perishable materials like wood, bamboo, and silk have come to light. Maps dated between 207 and 168 BCE were found during excavations of a classical tomb in south China.[7] Also in that tomb was the largest collection of ancient documents ever excavated in China, including fourteen medical texts, dating from as early as 300 to 168 BCE.[8] These were written in a nonstandard Chinese script emphasizing phonetic representation that apparently reflected local Yuè pronunciations. Thompson argues that this shows the presence of literacy among Yuè people "closely connected by legend, history and archaeology to the people of the Red River Delta." People of Yuè and some of their neighbors, she concludes, employed the script "not only to write Chinese but also to transcribe personal and place names in their own languages." Thus, "the written form of Yüeh/Viet appears to have been but one part of the indigenous culture" that was later "driven underground by the Chinese imposition of direct rule."[9] In the Lạc Việt region itself, the earliest indications of writing are an imperial report of population records compiled locally in an unidentified script sometime before 111 BCE and a short Chinese inscription on the Cổ Loa bronze drum from the early first century CE.[10]

More exotic Yuè cultural differences made a greater impression on the Chinese. A mid-third-century Qin text commented that the people of Chu fear ghosts "but the people of Yue seek blessings from them."[11] Chinese writers noted the Yuè preoccupation with aquatic life. One text, the *Huai nan zi*, stated in 135 BCE that in Nán Yuè ("Southern Yuè"), which then included the Red River delta, "people carry out few occupations on land and many on water." The inhabitants even cut their hair and "tattoo their bodies in order to resemble the scaly-skinned aquatic animals."[12] With their pervasive sense of cultural superiority, or perhaps a more general paternalism, Chinese who ventured south may have found a more complex society than they anticipated.

THE QIN CONQUEST OF YUÈ

A second-century BCE Chinese account describes Qin Shi Huangdi's campaigns against the Yuè. In 221 BCE he sent the military governor of a commandery, a commissioner (*wei*) named Tu Ju, "at the head of five hundred thousand men, divided into five armies."

> For three years [221–219 BCE], men wore their armor and held crossbows at the ready. The superintendent Lu, sent [by the Qin], lacking the means to effectively transport supplies, then had his troops dig a canal, and the grain was delivered by that route. Thus it was possible to make war on the people of Yuè. [Yi Xu Song], the lord of Western Âu, was killed. So all the Yuè people took to the forest and lived there with the animals; none agreed to be a slave of the Chinese. [The Yuè] chose courageous men from their ranks, and made them their leaders. Then they attacked the Chinese by night, inflicting on them a great defeat and killing the commissioner [Tu Ju]. The dead and wounded were very many.[13]

Resistance continued. The Chinese complained: "The people of Yuè having fled deep into the mountains and thick forests; it was impossible to fight them. The troops were kept in garrisons to watch over these abandoned territories. This went on for a long time. The troops became tired. The Yuè then came out and attacked them."[14] In their isolated garrisons, the Chinese faced a strong military challenge: "The sick could not be treated, and the dead could not be buried."[15]

Eventually northern numbers carried the day. The invasion was demographic as well as military. First, in 214, Qin Shi Huangdi sent reinforcements, "criminals, banished men, social parasites, and merchants," to "maintain the garrisons to defend against the people of Yuè." With difficulty, Qin forces occupied the lands that now became China's three southern commanderies.[16] The emperor's prestige "made the four oceans tremble. In the South, he occupied the territories of the Hundred Yuè" and renamed them Guilin and Xiang. A Chinese source records the humiliating defeat of these local leaders: "The princes of the Hundred Yuè, their heads bowed and ropes around their necks, delivered their fate into the hands of subordinate officers."[17]

To stabilize the military occupation, the Qin dispatched a new commissioner from north China, Zhào Tuó (*V.* Triệu Đà), who requested that thirty thousand maidens and widows be sent south for his men to marry.[18] Zhào Tuó later took up a post in the third new commandery, Nanhai (South Sea), headquartered at Panyu, modern Guangzhou (Canton). The empire had reached the South China Sea and intended to stay. It now held the entire coastline of modern China.[19]

In half a century, the Qin dynasty had forcefully unified China, incorporating into its new empire many former refugees from the north and indigenous peoples of the south. Further south, the Lạc Việt lands faced the same threat of conquest and incorporation into an expanding trade network as a key commercial outpost. However the Qin armies stopped short of the Lạc Việt region and penetrated no farther south in the Yuè lands.[20] Instead, possibly under the weight of its own expansionist campaigns as well as widespread internal revolts from 209 BCE, Qin authority disintegrated. The first imperial dynasty came to an early end in 206.[21]

NAN YUÈ

During the Qin collapse, the empire's southernmost commandery, Nanhai, transformed itself into a new Yuè kingdom. The ailing Qin commander at Panyu advised his lieutenant, the former imperial commissioner Zhào Tuó: "The Middle Kingdom is in turmoil.... Nanhai is remote, but I fear that bandit soldiers will raid this far. I wish to raise troops and block up the new roads, in preparation.... Panyu occupies a strategic mountainous location. Relying upon Nanhai, east and west for several thousand *li* [roughly six hundred miles] we have the support of many people from the Middle Kingdom. This [place and its commander] is also the lord of a region, and can be used to establish a kingdom."[22]

Zhào Tuó founded that independent kingdom in Nanhai in 207 BCE, after his commandant died and just before the final Qin collapse. The imperial grip on the Yuè lands had proved transitory. Zhào Tuó's new polity occupied the far south of China, and he renamed it the kingdom of Nán Yuè. Nán Yuè was based in the coastal region around Panyu. It was not far northeast of the Red River delta, but did not yet include it, nor all of the Hundred Yuè to the west.

In the north, China's new Han dynasty established itself the next year. It viewed this new southern kingdom, Nán Yuè, with concern. But the founding Hàn emperor, Han Gaozu (r. 206–195 BCE), was prudently circumspect toward the Yuè peoples and apparently sought first to divide them by winning some over. In a 202 edict rewarding those who had helped him overthrow the Qin, Han Gaozu restored to his throne in Fujian the king of Min-Yuè, who "for a generation has been perpetuating the ancestral sacrifices of Yüeh." And for leading "the troops of the many Yüeh" to perform "very signal service" against the Qin, the emperor appointed another former Yuè monarch as king of Changsha, a territory once part of Chu, and additionally granted him, on paper, authority over "Xiang Commandery,

Guilin, and Nanhai"—that is, over all of southern China including Zhào Tuó's realm of Nán Yuè.[23] The Han Empire had not relinquished its claim to the Yuè territory, but it was not yet prepared to renew that claim by force.

At this stage the imperial policy sought diplomatic incorporation. Emperor Han Gaozu quickly recognized the autonomy of three Yuè kingdoms: Min Yuè in 202, Nán Yuè in 196, and Dong Ou in southern Zhejiang in 192.[24] Acknowledging Zhào Tuó as king of Nán Yuè, the emperor proclaimed:

> According to the customs of the people of Yüeh, they like to attack each other. At a previous time, [the Qin] moved [Chinese] people from the central prefectures to the three commanderies of the southern quarter, and sent them to live intermixed with the many [tribes of] the Yüeh. It happened that when the world punished [the Qin], the Commandant of Nan-hai [Zhào Tuó] was living in the southern quarter and ruling it as its chieftain. He has made an excellent arrangement [of his government, so that] the people from the central prefectures have hence not diminished [in number] and the custom of the people of Yüeh to attack each other is progressively ceasing. For all [this, the region] is in debt to his ability. Now We establish [Zhào Tuó] as King of Nan-Yüeh.

The emperor then sent an ambassador to Zhào Tuó to "transmit his kingly seal."[25] He chose a hard-talking emissary, Lu Jia, who hailed from the defunct kingdom of Chu. Lu noted condescendingly that Zhào Tuó received him with his hair in a bun, "squatting, with his legs spread wide."[26]

A Chinese account of Lu Jia's meeting with Zhào Tuó at Panyu in 196 BCE records the imperial combination of cultural superiority, diplomacy, and threat. Lu began by softening up the king of Nán Yuè, reminding him how far he had fallen. The Han envoy sniffed that "your people number no more than a few hundred thousand, and they are all southern savages."[27] By contrast, he added, "You sir, are a man of the central states, and the graves of both the senior and cadet branches of your family are in Zhending. But now you have abandoned the qualities instilled in you by Heaven, have cast aside your cap and sash, and want to use this little place called Yuè to make yourself the equal and the rival of the Son of Heaven. Disaster will befall you!" Later in their conversation, Lu again accused Zhào Tuó of wanting "to use this newly created and still unformed land of Yuè to live in belligerent disobedience." But China could threaten war: "If the ruler of Han were to hear of this, he would dig up and burn the graves of your lordship's ancestors. He would wipe out your clan, and he would have a general lead a hundred thousand troops right up to the borders of Yuè, and the people of Yuè would kill you in order to have a means of surrendering to Han."

The admonishment worked: "*Wei* Tuó suddenly sat up straight and apologized to Master Lu." He replied contritely: "I have lived long among the southern savages, and have become extremely negligent in my observance of the rites."

Yet Zhào Tuó stood his ground. He still insisted on asking, "How do I compare to the Emperor? Am I as worthy?" And when Lu responded, "Sitting astride an area between the mountains and the sea, you rule a land that might be likened to a single Han commandery," Tuó laughed. He even retorted, "If I had lived in the central area, how could I not be as great as the ruler of Han?" Having asserted his claim, Tuó switched to effective diplomacy. He "showed the greatest affability" to Lu and "entertained him at drinking banquets for several months." The king confided in Lu: "Here in Yuè, there is no one worth talking to. Now that you have come, I hear new things every day." Tuó also showed his potential value to China by presenting Lu with "a thousand gold pieces" and goods of equal value. The envoy returned to the imperial court, having prevailed upon Zhào Tuó to "proclaim himself a loyal vassal"—but only after Lu had confirmed him in the post of "King of Nan Yuè, bowing to him as he did."[28]

Despite this diplomatic modus vivendi, Han China's relations with Nán Yuè and the other Yuè polities remained turbulent. In 195 the emperor again anointed a Yuè rival claimant to Zhào Tuó's throne: "The Marquis of Nan-wu, Chih, is also a descendant of Yüeh; We establish him as King of Nan-hai." But Han Gaozu died that year, and Zhào Tuó seized his chance. The Han historian Ban Gu recorded that in 192, once again, "The King of Nan-yüeh, Zhào Tuó, pronounced himself a subject and presented tribute." Yet Han dominion over Nán Yuè was tenuous. In 185 the Han empress dowager, perhaps viewing it as a potential rival power, banned the export of iron, gold, weapons, horses, and cattle to Zhào Tuó's kingdom. He responded by declaring himself no mere king but now emperor of Nán Yuè. In 181 he marched north on Changsha, ruled by another Yuè rival. The empress dowager sent troops to repel the Nán Yuè invaders.[29] Maps sealed in the tomb of a Han official who died after helping fortify Changsha against Zhào Tuó's attack document its defenses.[30] Zhào Tuó had to abandon his northern offensive and relinquish his title of emperor, but apparently "continued to use it locally."[31] He now turned south.

NÁN YUÈ INCORPORATES THE LẠC VIỆT REGION

In 180 BCE, Zhào Tuó brought the Lạc Việt region of the Red and Mã River deltas under the suzerainty of his Nán Yuè realm.[32] He was Chinese, but his

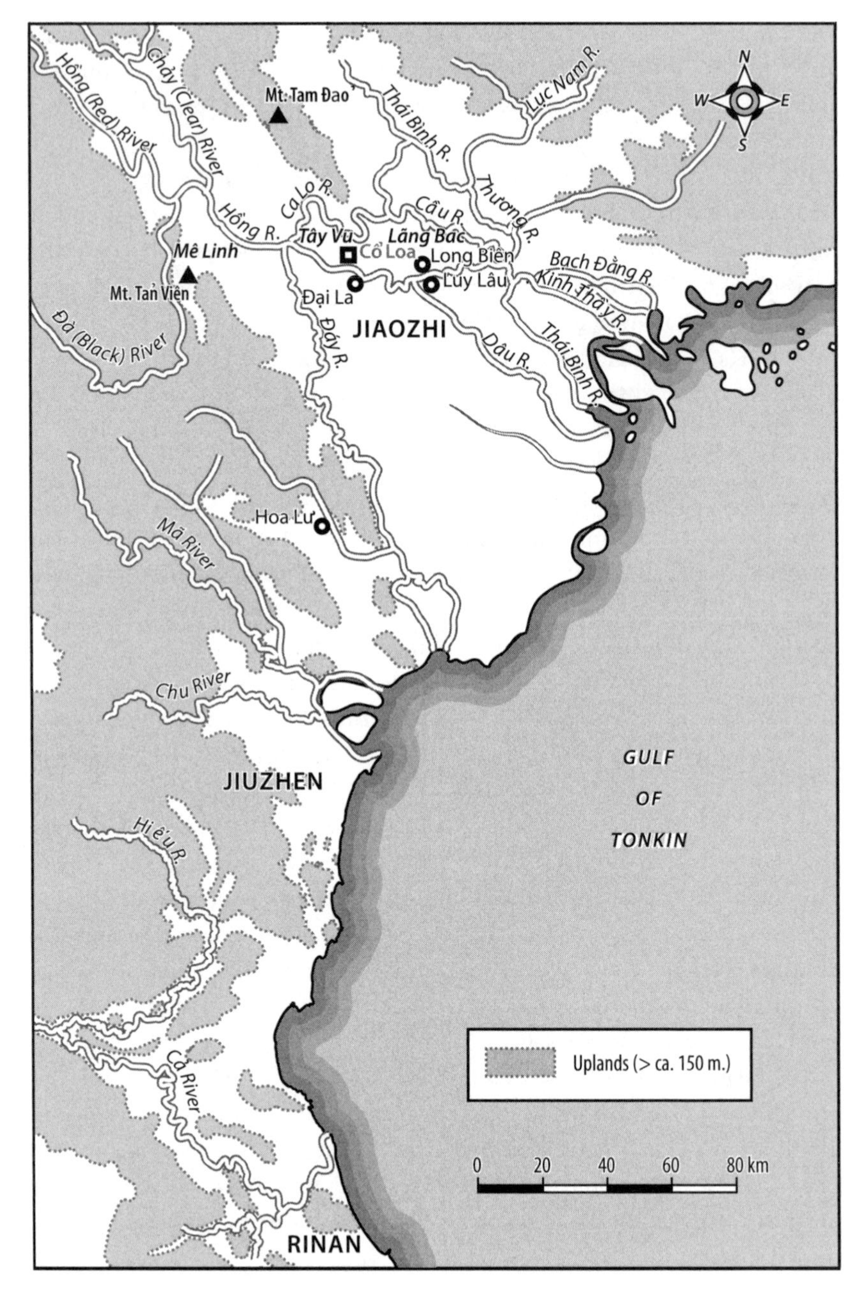

Fig. 2.1
Northern Việt Nam in the Imperial Era: first millennium CE.

actions followed the earlier pattern of Yuè emigrés who had provided new leadership to their southern ethnolinguistic cousins in south China and among the Lạc people. Zhào Tuó appointed "two legates to administer the two commanderies ... which comprise [Wu-lo, *V.* Âu-Lạc]."[33] These were the regions of Jiaozhi, modern Tonkin (or Tongking), including the Red River delta, and Jiuzhen, modern north-central Việt Nam. This southward extension of Nán Yuè's authority into what Zhào Tuó called the "country of the naked people"[34] gave his kingdom control of the entire region beyond the "Five Passes," Lingnan. For the first time, the Lạc Việt region formed part of a polity headed by a Chinese ruler.

Zhào Tuó gained access to new resources to lure China into yet another diplomatic reconciliation with Nán Yuè. In 179, he sent the Han court a cargo of exotic southern tribute: "A pair of white jades, 1,000 kingfishers' feathers, ten rhinoceros horns, 500 purple-striped cowries, a vessel of cinnamon insects [a delicacy eaten soaked in honey], forty pairs of live kingfishers and two pairs of peacocks."[35] Relations with the north improved. In 157, Emperor Xiao-Wen "summoned and honored Tuó's older and younger cousins and enveloped them with his goodness." Writing to the emperor, Tuó once again "declared himself his subject."[36]

But in the face of northern power, the other Yuè states began to disintegrate in warring rivalries. In 154, the Dong Ou kingdom joined that of Wu in an anti-Han revolt, then switched back to the imperial side, forcing the king of Wu to flee to another Yuè kingdom, Min Yuè. In 138, Min Yuè besieged Dong Ou, whose king asked China for help. The emperor sent a "Palace Grandee" to mobilize an army. He "rescued" the king of Dong Ou, expelling the Min-Yuè forces.[37] But for their future safety, the Yuè people of Dong Ou supposedly "requested" relocation from their homeland. China evacuated forty thousand of them to Anhui province. The Dong Ou kingdom disappeared.[38]

By contrast Zhào Tuó, after incorporating the Lạc Việt region into his Nán Yuè kingdom, seems to have left its indigenous chiefs in place, both in the Red River delta (Jiaozhi to the Chinese) and in Jiuzhen further south on the coast. In the eastern delta of the Red River in 179, Zhào Tuó founded a port township at Luy Lâu, which later became Jiaozhi's capital and market center. But a Lạc royal court continued to function at the major bronze age complex of Cổ Loa, north of modern Hanoi.[39]

From his palace surrounded by four rivers at Panyu, Zhào Tuó reigned over Nán Yuè for sixty-seven years, including forty-three years as overlord of the Lạc regions Jiaozhi and Juizhen. He died in 137, aged 102.[40] Unlike the Yuè kingdom of Dong Ou, Zhào Tuó's regime, even with its inconsistent professions of loyalty, had benefited from an imperial policy that loyal

Yuè deserved protection despite their strange inferior lifestyle, as a Han official argued at the court in 138 BCE. Otherwise, the courtier added, "How could we treat the myriad kingdoms as our children?"[41] Three years later Zhào Tuó's grandson and successor, Zhào Mei, enlisted Chinese aid in the defense of his kingdom against invading forces from Min Yuè. The Han emperor's uncle opposed any imperial intervention, arguing in more conventional terms: "Yuè is a land beyond this world, with a people who shear their hair and tattoo their bodies. It cannot be regulated by the laws of civilized countries."[42] Ban Gu tells us that the emperor disagreed and sent troops to aid Nán Yuè; the chastened people of Min Yué quickly killed their own king and surrendered to the Han.[43] Nán Yuè was saved, but China's power had increased. Zhào Yīngqí, who ascended the Nán Yuè throne in 122, fathered two sons, by Chinese and Việt consorts, respectively. Like the Yuè more generally, the Nán Yuè court soon split into pro- and anti-Chinese factions. In turn Zhào Tuó's two great-great-grandsons each ruled briefly. They were to be the last kings of Nán Yuè.[44]

THE HAN CONQUEST OF NÁN YUÈ AND THE LẠC VIỆT REGIONS

The emperor Han Wudi (r. 140–87 BCE) presided over a period of Chinese commercial expansion. In the lucrative southern trading zone, Yuè merchants owned the main ships plying the China coast and may have ventured as far south as the Gulf of Siam. The Chinese knew of rich trading kingdoms even farther south—probably in the Malay Archipelago. Like Qin Shi Huangdi in 221, Han Wudi likely weighed the commercial power that political domination of the south would bring.[45] In 112, he sent Chinese armies on a "punitive expedition" to conquer Nán Yuè. Within a year, imperial forces led by commander Lu Bode occupied most of the southern kingdom and stormed Panyu. The king of Nán Yuè got word to his "emissaries" ruling Jiaozhi and Jiuzhen, instructing them how best to surrender.[46] Nán Yuè collapsed. "The king and his chief ministers escaped by sea with a few hundred men," sailing southwest along the coast toward Jiaozhi. But the Chinese "put together a fleet at Canton and pursued them to the Gulf of Tongking where they were all captured."[47] The southward exodus of the Yuè had come to an end.

Sensing the imperial threat, the Min Yuè kingdom preemptively invaded China's Jiangxi province. Han Wudi ordered the forcible deportation of Min Yuè's population to Anhui. Like Dong Ou, Min Yuè was emptied of its population. The last Yuè kingdom vanished.[48] Only Nán Yuè's southernmost region remained unoccupied. Like the earlier Qin conquerors of south

China, Lu Bode's armies apparently stopped short of the Red River Delta in 111 BCE.

To preserve their autonomy, local Lạc rulers, just as they had under Zhào Tuó, bent with the northern wind.[49] According to the sixth-century Chinese author Li Daoyuan, Nán Yuè's "emissaries" governing its Jiaozhi and Jiuzhen prefectures quickly presented themselves at the border port of Hepu. "When General Lu arrived at Hepu, the King of Yuè ordered the two emissaries to offer the general one hundred cattle, one thousand *zhong* of wine, and the house registers of the two prefectures." Proffering these Lạc census records was a formal token of submission that satisfied the emperor: "The Han court [re-]appointed the two Lạc emissaries to be prefects of Jiaozhi and Jiuzhen."[50]

Other Lạc leaders seized the chance to play their new imperial rulers against the traditional monarch. In a different act of submission, a local Lạc commander, Huang Tong, a "General of the Left of Old Âu Lạc," showed his new loyalty by beheading his ruler, a Nán Yuè vassal, the indigenous "King of Xiyu" (*V.* Tây-Vu). Thus perished the last Lạc monarch to reign at Cổ Loa. In 110 BCE, the emperor rewarded Huang Tong by giving him the elevated title of marquis.[51]

Otherwise, the imperial intervention was indirect. At first, China's policy was to rule the Lạc Việt without interfering in their "barbarian" way of life. The king of Xiyu's large domain remained intact as Xiyu County.[52] Further upriver, Mê Linh, the home of another Lạc lord, became the capital of Jiaozhi prefecture.[53] Administration of the delta's inhabitants was left in the hands of their local chieftains, as it had been under Zhào Tuó and was elsewhere in the empire during the Former Han dynasty (206 BCE–9 CE). Chinese sources record that, as before, "Lạc Kings and Lạc Marquises were established to govern local prefectures and counties. Those who governed counties were often called Lạc lords, who used copper seals with blue ribbons." Equipped with these seals of Han authority, "the Lạc lords would govern local people as usual."[54] This pattern continued even after the Han began to reorganize local prefectures and districts in 106 BCE.[55] As late as 77 BCE, the son of one of the two Lạc marquis who had surrendered in 110 BCE still headed one of the Lạc Việt commanderies.[56] Han forces had "wiped out the kingdom" of Nán Yuè, as the Chinese historian Sima Qian wrote around that time: "On the southern border, from [Panyu] on the coast to the south . . . , seventeen new provinces were set up." However, "These were governed in accordance with the old customs of the inhabitants and were not required to pay taxes." The tax exemption applied even to surrendered Yuè populations who still inhabited districts of Hunan province, now well inside China proper.[57]

This arms-length policy made sense because, while claiming sovereignty over Jiaozhi, China saw the territory more as an opening to the southern seas—indeed, as the empire's key trading zone. All imperial ports of embarkation were on the Tonkin Gulf. Foreign diplomatic missions bringing trade goods, which China often termed "tribute," all came by sea via Jiaozhi. That region's importance became clear when Hán renamed the entire former Nán Yuè kingdom "Jiaozhi circuit." This comprised all seven commanderies of the south (Lingnan) and now included three in the Lạc Việt region alone: Jiaozhi, Jiuzhen, and a newly established Rinan commandery on the far south coast (modern central Việt Nam). Jiaozhi commandery even became the central seat of the imperial inspector-general of the larger Jiaozhi circuit.[58] However, the empire did not yet trust its many new subjects and maintained an embargo on the export to Jiaozhi of certain Chinese products, most importantly iron.

China considered its tropical south exotic, lush, and undeveloped. The classical term for south China, *Xiang*, meant "land of elephants." A ninth-century Chinese official wrote that Chao County in Guangdong had been "from the first named 'Tide' (*Chao*)," implying that its name derived from the ebb and flow of the sea.[59] As for *Jiaozhi*, the Han term for northern Việt Nam, scholars have suggested that the Chinese characters variously used to write it may be translated as "land of crocodiles" or "the territories occupied by the peoples who worshipped the *Kiao long* (the crocodile-dragon totem)."[60] The term has also been translated as "land at the foot of the mountains" or even "intertwined feet," supposedly describing a habit of southern barbarian groups to sleep with their feet close together and their bodies radiating outward.[61] For its part, the name of the new commandery of Rinan (south of the sun) conveyed a sense of remoteness.

The local populations lived off the land in ways unfamiliar to Chinese. Their agricultural practices struck northern observers as inefficient and unproductive. Early in the first century BCE, Sima Qian wrote:

> in the territories of Chu and Yuè, land was broad and the population sparse. For their food they had rice, and for their soup they had fish. Some of them tilled with fire and weeded with water, and the fruit and shellfish were sufficient without need to purchase them in markets. The land is by nature abundant with things to eat, and there is no danger of famine or death. For this reason, even those who are weak or ill can manage to survive, there is no occasion to store up goods, and many of the people remain poor. . . . [Unlike in north China,] south of the Yangxi and the Huai, there are no people cold or hungry, but there are also no families with as much as a thousand catties of gold.[62]

A later text specified how the Lạc Việt "tilled with fire." They practiced swidden farming, growing cereals that they "planted by burning down forests first and later sowing seeds. They neither fertilize nor irrigate the fields."[63]

Chinese found the bronze-age Lạc Việt region even more exotic than the rest of the south: "The whole territory of the Au Lac people is covered with dense forests, ponds and lakes. There are a lot of wild animals like elephants, rhinoceros and tigers. The natives earn their living by hunting and fishing. They eat the meat of boa constrictors, snakes and wild animals which they kill with bows propelling bone-headed arrows.... In fighting, they use bows propelling poisoned arrows. The process of making poison for arrows is a secret which they swear never to disclose to anyone. They know how to cast copper implements and pointed arrowheads. The natives tattoo themselves, wear chignon and turbans. They chew betel nuts and blacken their teeth."[64]

Even in the lush environment of the empire's southern provinces, the Lạc Việt region was exceptional, and the empire considered it the most important. The commercial windfalls obtainable in Jiaozhi tempted its officials, who required close imperial supervision and harsh exemplary punishment. The son of a Yuè marquis who had surrendered in 111 BCE became the only Nán Yuè native promoted to head of a commandery, but he was executed in 77 BCE for "having dealt in the slave trade and having earned illegally more than one million cash."[65] Later in the first century BCE, the imperial court appointed northern "grand administrators" to run both the Jiaozhi and Jiuzhen commanderies.

As Han officials gradually took up positions of authority in Lạc regions, they interacted with the local culture. A key Đông Sơn site in Jiuzhen remained in use and also contains ten large Han tombs dating from the late first century BCE. Their grave goods included characteristic Han artifacts such as bronze mirrors, models of furnaces, and coins, but Đông Sơn–style ceramics were also buried in one of these Han tombs, while a separate, presumably Việt tomb contained Han goods.[66]

The rich land of the Red River delta and the sea trade that passed through its river-mouth ports supported a large Lạc Việt population. The Han census of 2 CE counted 981,735 people living in the three commanderies (Jiaozhi, Jiuzhen, and Rinan), dwelling in 143,643 households. Jiaozhi, supporting 92,440 households, was "the most densely populated area in the Empire" south of the Yangzi. Its population alone (746,237 people) far outnumbered the total inhabitants of all four commanderies in what is now southern China (390,555). And Jiuzhen, with its 166,013 people living in 35,743 households, was the second most populous of the seven southern commanderies. Families in Jiaozhi were much larger than in the

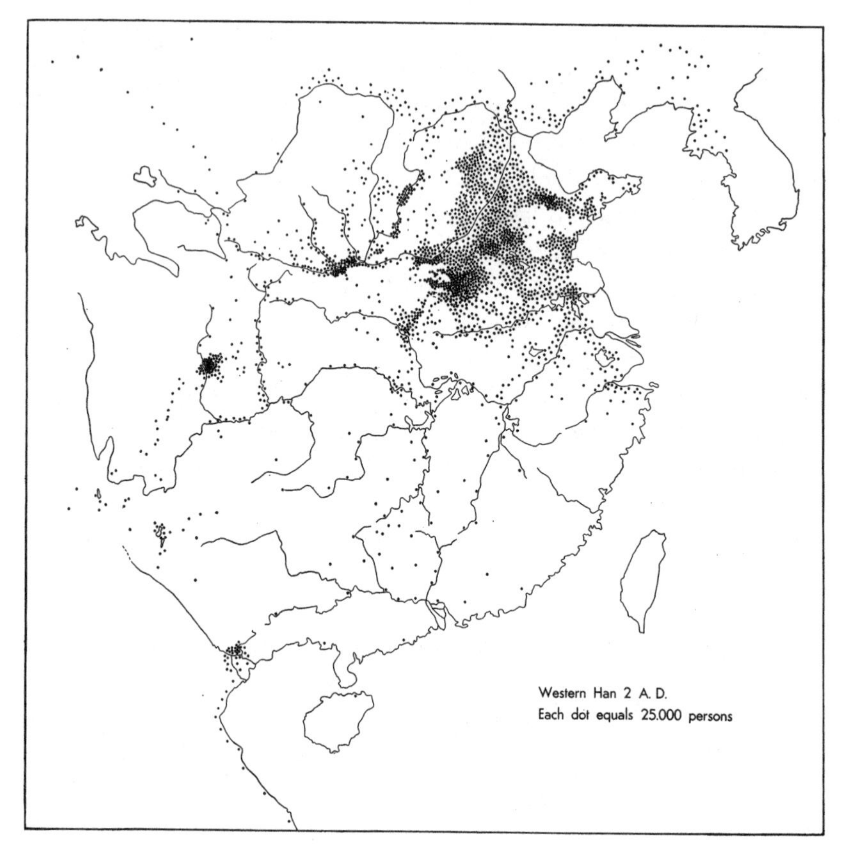

Fig. 2.2
Results of the Han Dynasty population census of 2 CE. From Hans Bielenstein, "The Census of China during the Period 2–742 A.D.," *Bulletin of the Museum of Far Eastern Antiquities* 19 (1948): 125–63, plate 2.

empire as a whole. In the Red River delta the average household exceeded eight members, compared with 4.7 for all China. Lạc Việt culture involved closer, communal life.[67] Unmarried couples often lived together.

This relatively open family structure contrasted with most of Chinese society, which was based increasingly though not solely on Confucian notions of the patriarchal family, in particular "filial piety," which also provided a model for imperial government. Just as sons were expected to be obedient to their fathers, and subjects to rulers, so wives had to be loyal to their husbands. Confucianism assigned women, like sons and subjects, subordinate roles. The obedience of inferiors, combined with the wise benevolence of superiors, was the prescription for a successful family unit, but also for social order, stability, and peace within an empire. Confucius (551–479 BCE) reputedly described the challenge: "Women and people of low birth are difficult to deal with. They become insolent if you treat them well, and resentful if you keep your distance with them."[68]

Lạc Việt people organized themselves along less strict, nonnuclear lines, giving authority to women as well as men. They formed matrilocal clans: couples after marriage would often go to live with the wife's family (as many still do in parts of southern China and also in Cambodia).[69] This matrilocal custom kept sisters together and gave married women key roles in social communication, and some were regarded as at least the equals of men. Việt society was not matriarchal, or female-ruled, but in an indigenous family unit, if anyone was an outsider, it was usually the husband. Other distinct Việt traditions in this period probably included annual fertility rites focusing on female sexuality and postponement of marriage until a first child was born. Confucian imperial administrators tended to consider these Lạc Việt customs problematic, if not immoral.

More compatible with local southern culture were the metaphysical and spirit-oriented practices of Chinese Daoism, which were also influential in the empire and may have made its rule seem more familiar. At least for a century and a half after the Han conquest of 111 BCE, the Lạc Việt and other Yuè peoples "inhabiting a broad belt along the southeast coast from [Zhejiang] to Indo-China" were all, one historian has written, "docile" imperial subjects. Lạc Việt society even incorporated the conquering Han general Lu Bode, who joined local mythical heroes as an appropriately southern aquatic spirit, "the General Who Calms the Waves."[70]

But as the waters of resistance stilled, cultural differences persisted, and the role of Lạc Việt women continued to appall many northerners. It is clear from the Han census of 2 CE (fig. 2.2) that imperial officers ruled only the Red River delta population and other riverine and coastal settlements. Much of the rural and upland Lạc region, like inland south China, remained beyond the empire's direct administration.

CHINA'S CIVILIZING MISSION

Early in the first century CE, Han grand administrators began to intervene more directly in the south. Contemporary Chinese texts suggest both negative and positive reasons for this. One was culturally dismissive, arguing that the southern environment fostered unappealing human traits that needed to be brought under control:

> The fiery air of the sun regularly produces poison. This air is hot. The people living in the land of the sun are impetuous. The mouths and tongues of these

> impetuous people become venomous. Thus the inhabitants of Chu and Yuè are impetuous and passionate. When they talk with others, and a drop of their saliva strikes their interlocutors, the arteries of the latter begin to swell and ulcerate. The southern commanderies are a very hot region. When the people there curse a tree, it withers, and when they spit on a bird it drops down dead.[71]

Despite these supposed climatic determinants, another Chinese writer believed that with the right "polishing," southerners could yet become civilized. It was a matter of habit, not habitat. He argued that "the people of cities and countries are all comfortable in and used to their own customs. Dwelling...in Yue one becomes a person of Yue....This is not inborn nature, but caused by accumulation and polishing. Thus, if a man is able to carefully focus on his actions, to be cautious against growing habituated to customs, and to greatly accumulate and polish, then he will become a gentleman."[72]

Soon after their completion of the census of 2 CE, the grand administrators of Jiaozhi and Jiuzhen launched systematic attempts to "civilize the barbarians" who lived there. The focus was on farming and gender relations. Jiuzhen's grand administrator, Ren Yan, introduced its hunting and fishing population to the ox-drawn plow and encouraged them to make iron tools.[73] He recommended near-continuous cultivation: "When the land has been plowed, sow white rice in the fifth month, and harvest in the tenth; for red rice, sow in the twelfth month, and harvest in the fourth."[74] Ren Yan "ordered the recasting of agricultural implements, and taught the people land reclamation. Year by year the amount of arable land increased and the common people were provided for."[75]

Ren also determined to restructure the family in Jiuzhen commandery. He "sent out letters to all dependent prefectures commanding them to have married all men between 20 and 50 years of age and all women between 15 and 40 years. The poor being without betrothal gifts, he ordered all officials to put aside a portion of their salaries to help them. Over 2,000 people were married." That year's good harvest linked agricultural prosperity to the Confucian family: "For the first time couples who had children recognized them as their own. Everyone said, 'It is Mr. Ren who has given these children to us,' and there were many who named their children Ren." The similar "civilizing" policies of Ren's counterpart, Xi Guang, who presided over the Red River delta as grand administrator of Jiaozhi commandery from about 1 BCE to 30 CE, earned praise in a fifth-century biography: "He gradually instructed the barbarians in feelings of respect and morality. His reputation in government was like that of [Ren Yan]." Xi Guang's biographer saw this as a model for all south China: "The civilization of Lingnan began with these two men."[76] Jiaozhi and Jiuzhen were clearly considered the key commanderies of the south.

Xi Guang attempted to "transform the people by rites and justice" and to change the marriage household system into a patrilocal one. He and Ren Yan not only "taught the people agriculture" but also "introduced hats and sandals," as well as schools, mainly for the immigrant Chinese. They also fostered "correct betrothal and marriage procedures" and attempted to instill "feelings of respect and morality."[77]

By contrast, disorder wracked the north at this time. The imperial usurper Wang Mang seized power in 9 CE, and the Former Han Dynasty collapsed. Most of the empire experienced fifteen years of war and instability. Lingnan's seven southern commanderies, however, were less troubled.[78] Large numbers of northern refugees, many of them educated people, fled to south China and further, into the Red River plain. Local Chinese officials in Jiaozhi had to call for help in settling these new arrivals. Assistance arrived after the establishment of the Later Han Dynasty in 25 CE.

All this led to problems with native Lạc Việt, who for the first time were seeing large-scale settlement and more direct Chinese involvement in their affairs. Some could have been moved from their land to make way for the newcomers. Indeed, the grand administrators' agricultural improvement policies may have been spurred by the need to feed these new arrivals and also to supply the increasing numbers of Chinese ships sailing the southern coasts seeking luxury items such as pearls. Jiaozhi soon became a major provider of grain to southern China. Local Lạc chiefs gradually lost whatever control they once had over their people's surplus production.[79] The effect on the lives of the peasantry is unknown, but the living standards and prestige of the old Lạc lords probably fell. They may also have been taxed for the first time. In Hunan to the north, the incoming Later Han authorities revoked the exemptions that the Former Han had given to local Yuè populations, now requiring them to make regular tax payments.[80] Whether this also happened in the far south is less clear. In 36 CE, Chinese annals assert, "a vulgar barbarian" from beyond the Jiuzhen border, "admiring the cultivation [of China], led his tribesmen to submit to the court. He was bestowed the title of 'Village Leader of [Those] Submitting to Han.'" The next year, "barbarians from regions outside the border of Nan Yuè offered white pheasants and white rabbits as tribute."[81]

By 29 CE, the new Later Han emperor Guangwu was flexing his imperial muscles. His brother-in-law was inspector-general of Jiaozhi circuit, and that southern region "fell easily into his hands."[82] Seeking yet closer control, the emperor made "a show of arms" and forced the "voluntary surrender" to the Later Han of all seven southern commanderies, including the Lạc regions. The emperor then formally reappointed their administrators, giving each the title of "marquis." But once "bought off" and neutralized, these local luminaries were soon displaced and disappeared from the historical record.[83] Xi Guang may have been one of them: he held office as grand administrator of Jiaozhi until at least 30 CE, then departed (it is unclear when). In 37 a new grand administrator, Su Ding, arrived to rule Jiaozhi.[84] The imperial grip on the Lạc Việt tightened.

THE TRƯNG SISTERS' REVOLT

One result was a briefly successful but traumatic Lạc rebellion in 39–43 CE. No contemporary indigenous view of these events survive, only Chinese accounts. Imperial annals report that the revolt was led by two sisters of the Cheng (*Việt.* Trưng) family, daughters of the Lạc lord of Mê Linh, a county in the western delta and capital of Jiaozhi prefecture.[85] These were scions of a very prominent Lạc family. The sisters, Trưng Trắc (*Ch.* Zheng Ce) and Trưng Nhị (Zheng Er), were both married to the same husband, Thi Sách (Shi Suo), who was a son of the Lạc lord of Chu Diên, a less important figure in the rebellion.[86] A Chinese source, the *Hou Han Shu*, implies that Su Ding, the grand administrator who took over Jiaozhi in 37, had provoked Trưng Trắc into revolt: "Su Ding used the laws with which to entangle her."[87] Though her husband Thi Sách possessed "a fierce temperament," it was Trưng Trắc who led the rebellion.[88]

Trưng Trắc and Trưng Nhị raised their armies in their home district of Mê Linh. Two of their generals were also reputedly female (Vietnamese texts a millennium later named them as Nguyệt Thai and Nguyệt Độ), as were many of the other fifty rebel commanders.[89] According to the sixth-century Chinese writer Li Daoyuan, "Trac was courageous and fearless. She led her husband Thi to rebel."[90] The revolt began in Mê Linh in the spring of 39. Downriver, the rebels enlisted support from Thi's prefecture of Chu Diên and marched on the commandery capital, Luy Lâu, the river port east of modern Hanoi. A Chinese account attributed their successes to Grand Administrator Su Ding's indecision. Not merely provocative but also avaricious and incompetent, Su Ding had "opened his eyes to money but closed them when it came to punishing rebels. He feared to go out and attack them." As the rebellion gathered force in the spring of 40, Su Ding fled back to China.[91]

The revolt quickly spread both south and north from Jiaozhi, stirring up all three Lạc Việt regions and most of Lingnan. According to the fifth-century Chinese annalist Fan Ye, "Barbarians from Jiuzhen, Rinan, and Hepu ['Sea Gate,' in coastal south China] joined the uprising. After the bandits conquered about sixty cities beyond the Ridges, Trắc enthroned herself as a queen."[92] Another text says she "conquered sixty-five cities," probably meaning fortified places.[93] Li Daoyuan adds that Trưng Trắc and her husband "conquered prefectures and made all Lạc lords submit to them. Those Lạc lords, therefore, all enthroned Trắc as the Queen. Trắc established her court at [Mê Linh] county and obtained [adjusted?] two years' taxes from Jiaozhi and Jiuzhen residents." Historian Keith Taylor has suggested, rather, that Trắc abolished the Chinese taxation system in these two commanderies.[94]

After driving the Chinese out of Jiaozhi commandery, the Trưng sisters established their court upriver at the prefecture capital of their home county, Mê Linh, rather than in the commandery capital, Luy Lâu, nearer the coast. And to the south in Jiuzhen, lesser-known local leaders held sway, including Du Yang and, in the Yufa district, Zhu Bo.[95] Việt society was still organized around local clans. Trưng Trắc's support was fragile beyond Mê Linh and Chu Diên, and she refrained from establishing an independent Lạc kingdom with wide regional authority.[96] This Lạc Việt political weakness sowed eventual defeat.

The empire struck back in the summer of 41. The Han court ordered an invasion of Jiaozhi by land and sea. "In the fourth month," the *Hou Han shu* informs us, "the Emperor sent Wave-Calming General Ma Yuan to direct Towered-Ship General Duan Zhi and others to attack Trưng Trắc and her followers in Jiaozhi." The generals were ordered "to lead more than ten thousand soldiers from Changsha, Guiyang, Lingling, and Cangwu to embark on a punitive expedition against the rebels."[97] Additional forces marched from as far afield as Sichuan in China's west.[98] However, Admiral Duan Zhi died of disease soon after the troops reached the southern border port of Hepu. The fifty-six-year-old veteran commander, General Ma Yuan (14 BCE–49 CE), took charge of both armies. China also had to win back local support. The emperor "re-granted" the title marquis to Liu Long, former marquis of Fule County, even naming him "Leader of Court Gentlemen." Liu Long now became "Ma Yuan's lieutenant in the attack on Jiaozhi's barbarians led by Trưng Trắc."[99] This defection reinforced the lack of internal cohesion that plagued her revolt.

The expeditionary force marched south along the Jiaozhi coast. Ma Yuan later reported: "I cautiously led 20,000 people—which combined the great army and 12,000 picked soldiers of Jiaozhi—as well as 2,000 towered ships of various sizes."[100] He then quickly cut inland to the west, to occupy the hills east of Cổ Loa, dominating the delta.[101] In the spring of 42, the imperial army reached high ground at Lãng Bạc, in the Tiên Du mountains of what is now Bắc Ninh province. There Ma Yuan stationed his forces, "fought with the bandits and eventually defeated them." In these battles he captured and beheaded "several thousand of Trưng Trắc's partisans," while "more than ten thousand surrendered" to him. But armed opposition persisted, and Ma Yuan pressed farther westward. He later recalled the difficulties of the local climate: "When I was between Lãng Bạc and Tây Vu and the rebels were not yet subdued, rain fell, vapors rose, there were pestilential emanations, and the heat was unbearable; I even saw a sparrowhawk fall into the water and drown." At Cổ Loa, local resistance initially blocked Yuan's forces.[102]

However, the Chinese general pushed on to victory. During the campaign he explained in a letter to his nephews how "greatly" he detested "groundless criticism of proper authority."[103] "Yuan pursued Trưng Trắc and her retainers to Jinxi [Tản Viên] and defeated them several times. The bandits, therefore, scattered and fled."[104] Yuan captured both sisters in early 43. Trắc's husband, Thi Sách, escaped to Mê Linh, "ran to a place called Jinxijiu and was not captured until three years later."[105] In one of these battles, Ma Yuan may have depended on local units commanded by his lieutenant, the reinstated marquis Liu Long. The *Hou Han shu* records: "Long alone defeated the rebels at Jinxikou [in Mê Linh County] and captured their leader Trưng Nhị. More than one thousand rebels were beheaded and more than twenty thousand surrendered."[106] Soon after their capture, in the first month of 43, Ma Yuan "decapitated Trưng Trắc and Trưng Nhị, and sent their heads to the Han court at Luoyang." He beheaded their retainers too.[107] A memorial from Ma Yuan, presumably accompanied by the sisters' severed heads, reached the Emperor in the ninth month of 43. Yuan reported his victories, and added: "Since I came to Jiaozhi, the current troop has been the most magnificent."[108]

The rebels in Jiuzhen still held out. Yuan decided to attack Jiuzhen by sea, sailing south along the coast. He "led his two thousand big and small towered ships with more than twenty thousand soldiers to attack Du Yang and others, who were remaining confederates of Trưng Trắc." Then in late 43, "in the tenth month, Yuan led his troops south into Jiuzhen and obtained the surrender of enemy chiefs at Wugong County."[109] As his forces advanced on the Mã River, the inhabitants of the Đông Sơn settlement scattered, permanently abandoning the iconic Bronze Age site. Ma Yuan also "attacked Du Yang and other bandits in Jiuzhen, defeating them and making them surrender."[110] But here the southern terrain, a narrow coastal strip dominated by hill tracts, favored resistance. Fighting took place in four counties and districts. "When Yuan entered Yufa [County?], Zhu Bo, a chief leader of the enemy, abandoned the prefecture and fled into remote mountains and immense lakes." These redoubts were hard to pacify. In Wugong, "rhinoceros and elephants gathered, and a herd of cattle numbered in the thousands. At that time people often saw a herd of elephants that numbered in tens of thousands. Yuan dispatched some of his soldiers to Wubian County.... When Yuan's troops entered Jufeng County, the enemy leader refused to surrender. Yuan therefore decapitated hundreds of enemies and eventually pacified Jiuzhen."[111] In all, "from Wugong County to Jufeng County, Yuan's army killed and captured more than five thousand enemies and finally pacified the Qiaonan area." The *Hou Han shu* indicates that Yuan also deported "more than three hundred rebel heads [of families?]" to the north. "The region beyond the Ridges [Lingnan] was therefore pacified."[112]

Word came south that the delighted emperor had appointed Ma Yuan as "Xinxi Marquis with a fief of three thousand households." Yuan "butchered cattle and filtered liquor to reward his soldiers." He told them: "I have received the grand favor and humbly carried a gold official seal with a purple ribbon attached to it before you men. I feel happy yet ashamed." At that, "all officers and soldiers bent over and yelled, 'Long live.'" But they had paid a high price in lives: nearly half the imperial expeditionary force was lost. "Four or five-tenths of the officers and soldiers in Yuan's army died of miasma and epidemic diseases."[113]

In their reconquest of Jiaozhi and Jiuzhen, Han forces also appear to have massacred most of the Lạc Việt aristocracy, beheading five to ten thousand people and deporting several hundred families to China.[114] In perhaps an even more devastating cultural blow, Ma Yuan also rounded up many of the Lạc Việt bronze drums and confiscated them. Future local leaders would emerge in a different social milieu, more heavily influenced by imperial culture and methods of government. Yet the outcome was far from certain. In Ma Yuan's letter to his nephews while campaigning in Jiaozhi, he quoted a Chinese saying: "If you do not succeed in sculpting a swan, the result will still look like a duck."[115]

Yuan now sculpted his swan by subjecting the Lạc Việt to close administrative control. One obstacle was the large size of the lands that had formerly belonged to the Lạc monarch of Cổ Loa, beheaded in 111 BCE. In a memorial to the throne, Yuan informed the emperor that "Xiyu [Tây Vu] County contained 32,000 households," more than a third of Jiaozhi's population, which he considered too many for optimal supervision. Counties in the upland southwest were way too large: "The remotest county border was more than one thousand *li* [c. 250 miles] distant from the seat of the county government." Yuan asked permission "to divide Xiyu County into Fengxi

County and Wanghai County." The emperor agreed.[116] So the domain of the last king of Cổ Loa was broken up. Yuan also emphasized Lạc Việt cultural differences and Han civilization. His biographer wrote:

> Wherever he passed, Yuan promptly established prefectures and counties, constructed or repaired city walls, and dug ditches to irrigate fields in order to benefit the people living in those places. Yuan reported [to the emperor] more than ten discrepancies between Viet laws and Han laws, item by item. He clearly explained the old [Han] regulations to the Viet people in order to bind them. From that time on, the Lac Viet carried on what had been established by General Ma.

In the fall of 44, Ma Yuan completed his mission. He "reorganized the troops and led them back to the capital," where he received his reward. "The emperor granted Yuan a chariot and promoted him to be one of the Nine Ministers." Yuan also brought the emperor gifts, made from melting down some of the Lạc bronze drums he had confiscated. "Yuan liked riding and was good at recognizing rare horses. He obtained Lạc Việt copper drums when he was in Jiaozhi and used them to found models of steeds." He presented these equine bronzes to the emperor.[117] Dramatically, Ma Yuan had Sinicized the Lạc Việt drums.

Nonetheless, an ongoing Lạc/Han cultural osmosis seeped in both directions, as well as back and forth in time. Perhaps to preserve it from destruction, surviving Lạc Việt leaders filled the large Cổ Loa bronze drum with culturally resonant items, including ninety-six bronze plowshares, and buried it at the fortress site—inscribed with a Chinese-language inscription detailing those contents.[118] In legends that soon spread across south China, Ma Yuan joined Lu Bode of the Former Han, both now remembered as "Generals Who Calm the Waves," for their conquests of Jiaozhi, in 111 BCE and 43 CE, respectively. In local myths, the two commanders later "fused into one," with Yuan the dominant figure. Yet a memory of Lạc material culture persisted in its own specific form: "The leitmotif in these legends is bronze: bronze drums, bronze boats, bronze arrows, bronze columns, and even a bronze ox."[119]

Centuries later, Chinese and Vietnamese texts recalling Yuan's conquest added a new reflection of this furthest southern reach of imperial power: "Ma Yuan then erected bronze pillars to indicate the Han border."[120] These included one at Anning, far up in the hills to the northwest of Jiaozhi, and five bronze pillars at Linyi, on the remote southern border of Jiuzhen.[121] The general had culturally transformed the bronze drums of the Lạc Việt, their symbols of indigenous governance, not only into very Chinese equine statuettes but literally into markers of imperial authority. A millennium later, a Vietnamese official would still call his country "the land of the bronze column."[122]

If Ma Yuan's border demarcation indicates an anachronistically modern conception of territorial statehood, other Chinese sources suggest that the cultural tide also submerged indigenous memory. Việt tradition incorporated Ma Yuan not merely as a "General Who Calms the Waves" but eventually even as the inventor and original caster of the bronze drums. Chinese control over the sources of Lạc Việt power—water and bronze—now seemed assured. So was the conquest, perhaps, of Việt female authority, when Yuan, executioner of the Trưng sisters, himself passed into legend as a water spirit.[123] Yet that reincarnation also marked an acknowledgement of continuing indigenous legitimacy. Bronze drums and aquatic figures retained their spiritual power.

IMPOSITION AND RELAXATION OF CHINESE RULE

The center of Chinese administration shifted west, to the region of modern Hanoi, south of Cổ Loa. The empire became capable of close supervision of the Việt as far as the western limits of the land they inhabited. Similar more centralized controls were emerging throughout China. The Later Han Dynasty was replacing local chiefs with its own bureaucracy, and in this it treated Jiaozhi as a part of China. In place of Jiaozhi circuit, the court established Jiao province (Jiaozhou), which still included all of Lingnan: the three Lạc commanderies of Jiaozhi, Jiuzhen, and Rinan and four in what is now south China (Hepu, Yulin, Cangwu, and Nanhai).[124]

Ma Yuan ended the Chinese embargo on the export of iron and domestic animals to Jiaozhi. Along with the construction of irrigation canals, iron plows increased rice production. And the roads that Yuan ordered built no doubt helped develop the economy, while local officials gained experience in organizing labor. The Chinese also retained their mercantile interest in Jiaozhi's exotica, as this passage in Ma Yuan's biography implies: "When Yuan was in Jiaozhi, he often ate the fruit of [the plant] Job's tears, which could help to make the body spry and light, to decrease the desire, and to overcome malaria. In the south, the fruit of Job's tears was large. Yuan thought to use them as seed, so when he led the army back to the court, he carried one cartload of it. His contemporaries thought the southern land produced precious and strange things, and influential officials all expected to have them." But later one official accused Yuan of having profited from importing "pearls and rhinoceros horns with veins."[125] That such a corruption charge was plausible suggests the wealth of products emanating from Jiaozhi.

The total crushing of Lạc Việt resistance in 43 had removed Chinese fears of being ousted and, according to one scholar, led to "a relatively relaxed atmosphere of social and political accommodation."[126] There was now less Chinese immigration to worry local farmers, whom their rulers increasingly registered as "Chinese." They adopted Chinese agricultural technology like the ox-drawn plow. Some indigenous couples presumably married in time for the birth of their children. There were no serious uprisings for sixty years.

Chinese records tell us little about social or economic developments in Jiaozhi and Jiuzhen for the next two centuries or more. What they do suggest is that Han officials and their families slowly became more indigenized, adopting certain elements of Việt culture.[127] Whereas first-century CE Đông Sơn–style graves and local Han-style tombs both contain Han objects, including bronze mirrors, models of barns and furnaces, coins, and Han vessels, by the second and third centuries local sites and artifacts often combine Việt and Han forms, including both Han-style brick tombs and Đông Sơn objects, such as a bronze drum, bronze basins, and terracotta trays.[128]

Jiaozhi's role in imperial foreign trade expanded. What is now the Hanoi region replaced Panyu and the south China pearling centers as the main port at the northern end of the Nanhai ("South Seas") transnational commercial network. Still more important was the long-established domestic trade along the Chinese coast. Jiaozhi became the focus of commerce from Rinan in the extreme south to as far north as the mouth of the Yangzi. It benefited from its southerly location and from two sources of wealth: its own products, including rice, and those of the exotic Nanhai trade. The population of Jiao province (most of whom lived in Jiaozhi) may have nearly doubled between the censuses of 2 and 140 CE.[129]

THE SOUTHERN FRONTIER

The sea trade also enriched others even farther south. After China sent "generous gifts" to an Indian kingdom, a reciprocal mission in 2 CE had delivered a live rhinoceros as tribute. This first recorded foreign embassy to reach China via the South China Sea accompanied envoys from four other kingdoms of the south. The increase in the passing international trade benefited many inhabitants of what later became the central or southern Vietnamese coasts. Chinese records first describe them in 85 CE as "barbarians from beyond the frontier" of Rinan.[130] Prehistorian Dougald O'Reilly writes that around the start of the first millennium, the distinctive jar burial sites along what is now the central Vietnamese coast, known as the prehistoric Sa Huỳnh culture, began to include new artifacts: "Iron and glass began to accompany the carnelian and agate beads in Sa Huynh burials." Some of these products came from India or were copies of Indian originals. Graves also contained Chinese coins dating from as early as 9–23 CE.[131] During that turbulent northern interregnum between the Former and Later Han, trade had continued with the far south, enriching local leaders.

Political integration of this southern frontier into China's Rinan commandery was fraught. After a peaceful period of initial interaction, by the end of the first century trouble loomed in Rinan and even Jiuzhen. There a similar cultural chasm existed as in Jiaozhi earlier. Frontier regions, Taylor writes, became "a chronic source of disaffection" from the empire, partly because officials it sent there "were often already disaffected" and disinclined to pursue imperial interests. The first frontier unrest broke out in 100, with a revolt in Rinan's extreme southern district, near modern Huế.[132] The Chinese had attempted to impose taxes on this district, which they named "Elephant Forest" (Xianglin, *V.* Tượng Lâm). In response, "more than two thousand" inhabitants of Tượng Lâm "attacked, plundered, and burned the Han centers." Deploying an army raised in more northerly districts, the Chinese put down the revolt and beheaded its leaders, then granted Tượng Lâm district a two-year tax respite. The combination of stick and carrot worked at first. In 124, officials obtained the surrender of a group of "barbarians from beyond the frontier," probably natives of Rinan who had escaped Chinese rule.[133]

But security deteriorated again in 136–37, and imperial administrators faced successive military challenges. The *Hou Han shu*, compiled beginning in the next century, records another rebellion in 136 by "barbarians of Rinan," thousands of whom came from "beyond the frontier," again burning down Han centers and killing officials in Tượng Lâm. Then, when the Chinese attempted to send northern troops south to repress the revolt, imperial "armies in Jiuzhen and Jiaozhi Prefectures" mutinied, destroying Han offices there too. Wang Gungwu writes that this "caused such alarm at the court that a conference of ministers and northern generals was called to discuss it. In the long debate, it became clear that the empire could not resort to the old solution of sending a massive force."[134] In midyear, the prefects of Jiuzhen and Jiaozhi somehow "lured" the Rinan rebels into surrender. The court then considered Lingnan "pacified," but seven years later, in 144, once more "Rinan barbarians attacked and burned down cities and towns." Again revolts erupted in Jiaozhi and Jiuzhen, and yet again Jiaozhi's prefect "lured them to surrender" with "enticing words."[135] After all this instability, any statistics collected in Jiaozhi in 140 are missing from the results of that year's census (fig. 2.3).[136]

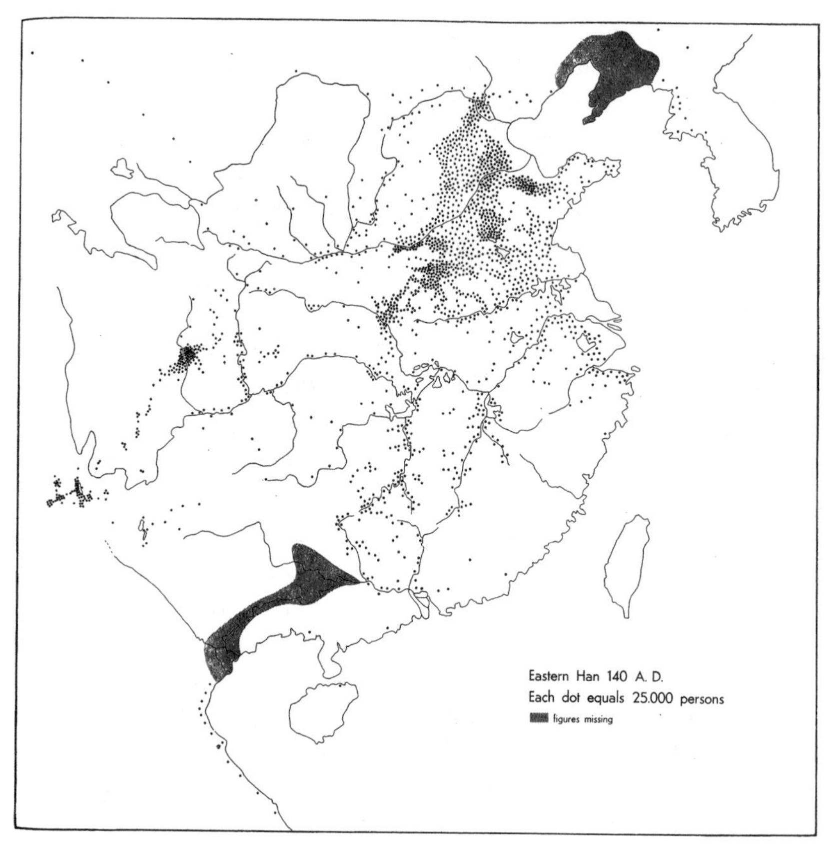

Fig. 2.3
Extant results of the Han Dynasty population census of 140 CE. From Hans Bielenstein, "The Census of China During the Period 2–742 A.D.," *Bulletin of the Museum of Far Eastern Antiquities* 19 (1948): 125–63, plate 2.

In 142–43, under the threat of revolt, the Han governor moved Jiaozhi's capital from the market town of Luy Lâu, across the Đuống River to the riverbank site of Long Yuan ("Dragon Pool").[137] And in Rinan and Jiuzhen, new rebellions followed in 157 and 160.[138]

Part of the problem was that the transnational Nanhai trade continued to strengthen chiefdoms on or beyond the southern frontier, enabling them to become or remain independent of China and contest its local authority. In 166, a trade mission arrived in Jiaozhi from distant Daqin (the Chinese name for the eastern Roman Empire), bringing tribute of "elephant tusks, rhinoceros horns and tortoise-shells"—probable local purchases.[139] The likely suppliers, whether residents of Rinan or emerging chiefdoms farther south down the coast, were enriching themselves and increasingly tempted to challenge Chinese rule.

Rinan's far southern border area seceded in 192. Ou Lian (*V.* Âu Liên), son of a district official in Tượng Lâm, assassinated the imperial district magistrate and seized power. By the 220s China was referring to this newly independent realm as Linyi.[140] The empire never reclaimed it.

UNREST IN JIAOZHI

To the north, official corruption amid the burgeoning maritime trade provoked new unrest in late second-century Jiaozhi. The *Hou Han shu* recorded that little had changed:

> [As of] old, Jiaozhi has many valuable products like pearls, kingfisher feathers, rhinoceros [horns], elephant [tusks], tortoise shells, various scented woods and beautiful timbers. Most of the governors, one after another, have been corrupt. While on the one hand they presented gifts to the noble and the influential, on the other they accumulated wealth by accepting bribes. [And when] they find their wealth sufficient, they quickly seek to be replaced and transferred elsewhere. For this reason the junior officials and the people [merchants] are very angry and [often] rebel in protest.[141]

Jiaozhi proved so lucrative that on occasions when rebels took it out of central control, the emperor would pay large sums and accord rich favors to officials who could restore imperial rule.

Another problem arose inland, in the hills to the north and west of the delta. Around 178, "the tribal peoples of Jiaozhi rebelled all together."[142] The "Wuhu barbarians" there, wrote the eleventh-century historian Sima Guang, "had long been making trouble." Their original homeland was in highland areas of Yulin, a neighboring commandery in south China, but they also lived in both Jiaozhi and Hepu.[143] The rebellion found fertile ground in Jiaozhi. The *Hou Han shu* records: "The governor was so incapable and weak that he could not prevent it." Even the head of Jiaozhi commandery joined the rebels.[144] In 178–79, the Wuhu revolt spread along both sides of the border, into Hepu as well. It also destabilized the far south, where rebels "attracted support from the people of Jiuzhen and Rinan." They "lured" people there "to attack and conquer prefectures and counties" and successfully "destroyed commandery and county offices."[145] For three years "the provincial and commandery administrators could do nothing to control them." Unrest escalated in 181. "Liang Long and other men of Jiaozhi also made a rebellion, and they attacked and occupied several commanderies and prefectures." This movement, too, spread back across the border into south

China's Nanhai commandery. Under Liang Long's leadership, more than ten thousand Jiaozhi residents "joined the uprising led by Kong Zhi—the Prefect of Nanhai—to attack and occupy prefectures and counties."[146]

This combination of revolts threatened Chinese rule across the south. An imperial edict dispatched a prefect, Zhu Jun, to take over as inspector of Jiaozhi. The *Hou Han shu* takes up the story: "Jun was ordered to recruit manservants when passing through his hometown and to lead them together with soldiers dispatched by the court—numbering five thousand in all—to enter Jiaozhi by two routes. When they arrived at the border of Jiaozhi Prefecture, Jun did not throw the army into battle. Instead he first sent emissaries to the Prefecture so that they could spy on the actual condition of the bandits and propagate the force and virtue of the court, in order to shake the rebels' minds." Then Jun gathered "troops from seven prefectures" for the assault.[147]

In April 181, Jun "attacked the Wuhu barbarians and destroyed them."[148] Next, "he attacked Liang Long and beheaded him; he captured several tens of thousands of men, and in a few weeks everything was settled." The emperor made Zhu Jun a marquis and summoned him to court as "Grandee Remonstrant and Consultant."[149] Jun received ten pounds of gold and a fief of 1,500 households. His son Zhu Fu became governor of Jiaozhi. Once more the waves calmed. In 183, "states beyond the border of Rinan came to present tributes again."[150]

The emperor's relief was obvious, but brief. Just a year later, Jiaozhi erupted again, and again the trouble spread north. During a mutiny in mid-184, "troops stationed at Jiaozhi captured the Prefect and the Prefect of Hepu." The mutineers named their leader "General Who is Pillar of Heaven."[151] Chronicler Sima Guang explained that "the officers and people were angry and made a rebellion." In response, he added,

> The central administration sent the Prefect of Ching, Chia Tsung of Tung commandery, to be Inspector of Jiaozhi. When Tsung reached his province, he enquired about the reasons for the rebellion. Everyone told him: "The taxation requirements are far too heavy and they took everything the people had. The capital is a long way away and there is no one to hear their complaints. The people had nothing to live on and that's why they have gathered together as rebels." Then Tsung sent around a proclamation saying that everyone was to carry on his own occupation in peace, and he received in comfort the homeless refugees and remitted the taxes and the corvée services. The only people to be executed were the ringleaders who had caused the most trouble. He made careful examination and chose the best officers to show their ability as heads of prefectures. Within a year, the disturbance was settled, and all the people were at peace.

Sima Guang asserted that a popular song now rang out "in the streets and alley-ways" of Jiaozhi. It went:

> Father Chia came too late,
> Or we would never have made rebellion.
> Now all is peace and content,
> And officials dare not feed at our expense.[152]

Within two years, the Later Han Dynasty was disintegrating in the north. After a century and a half of close imperial supervision and repression, Jiaozhi and Jiuzhen enjoyed a period of autonomy from 187 to 226 CE. The political stability there and an influx of scholars fleeing the new troubles in China enabled a Confucian tradition of scholarship to develop peacefully in Jiaozhi, even in contest with Daoism. Around 200 a future Buddhist convert put it this way: "Only Jiao province was relatively calm, and unusual men from the North came to live there. Many occupied themselves with the worship of gods and spirits, abstinence from cereals, and immortality. Many people of that time devoted themselves to these studies. Mou Bo unceasingly proposed objections based on the Five Classics; none of the Daoists and spiritualists dared argue with him."[153]

The major grand administrator in this period, Shi Xie, was a distinguished Confucian whose scholar ancestors had fled south in the early first century. A sixth-generation resident of Jiaozhi imbued with Chinese culture, son of the grand administrator of Rinan commandery, Shi Xie became prefect of Jiaozhi in 177. He was to see it through a turbulent turn of the century and into the post-Han era of the Three Kingdoms (221–277).[154] His late third-century biography depicts Shi Xie as an exemplary Confucian administrator: "Many scholars from the Central Kingdom went to rely on him [for protection]. He was extremely fond of the *Spring and Autumn Annals* and annotated them." A contemporary report submitted to the imperial secretariat observed that Shi Xie "has vast knowledge and excels at executing administrative matters.... When taking a break from official matters, he reads texts." He was "also versed in the *Classic of Documents*, and knows all the ancient and current explanations."[155]

In 196, "rebel barbarians" killed Zhu Jun's son, Zhu Fu, who had become the inspector of Jiao province. Quickly "the province and commanderies fell into disorder." As Jiaozhi's prefect, Shi Xie seized the opportunity to empower his own family, and "recommended his younger brothers for office." He had one sibling appointed grand administrator of Jiuzhen, while other brothers took over Hepu and Nanhai. Sima Guang informs us that Shi Xie "was a tolerant and generous man, and many of the gentry from central China came to him. The whole province, ten thousand *li* [2,500 m] from the court, was under his dominance, and he had no rivals. As time went by, his authority and the soldiers under his command steadily increased, and all the barbarians trembled and served him." Later the court awarded Shi Xie "a sealed commission as General of the Gentlemen of the Household Who Comforts the South, to govern the seven commanderies" of Jiao, while allowing him to retain his post as grand administrator of Jiaozhi.[156]

Shi Xie achieved stability in part by appealing to local customs. He relocated Jiaozhi's capital back to Luy Lâu, the river market town Zhào Tuó had founded in 179 BCE, which soon became "celebrated for its trading prosperity."[157] In a letter to the imperial court in 207, an observer wrote of Shi Xie: "Whenever he leaves or comes into the citadel, he is greeted with great pomp amid the sounds of flutes, pipes, bells and gongs."[158] Shi Xie even responded to the omen of a crocodile sighting by renaming the former capital of Long Yuan, which means "Dragon Pool": in 218, according to a tradition recorded in the sixth century, "dragons were seen entwining each other at the South and North Ferries," between the banks of two rivers in the central Jiaozhi plain. Shi Xie renamed Long Yuan county "Long Biên," or "Dragons Entwined."[159]

Throughout this period Shi Xie had to move cautiously to deal with the persistent instability that prevailed elsewhere in the south, where other imperial officials, in order to sustain their authority, felt even more obliged to fall back on indigenous Việt customs or to emphasize compatible metaphysical expressions of Daoism, which merged more easily with local religious practices than did Confucianism. Around 200, according to Sima Guang, "The court sent Zhang Jin of Nanyang to be inspector of Jiao province," Shi Xie's immediate superior. "Zhang Jin believed in spirits and worshipped demons. He always wore a purple-red turban, he played drums and flutes, he burnt incense, he read Daoist books; and he said all this would help his rule." But in 203 or 204 one of his officers assassinated him, sparking top-level turmoil in Jiao. Zhang's successor Lai Gong fell out with the new grand administrator of Cangwu commandery, Wu Ju, who "raised troops to drive Lai Gong out." Lai fled. His replacement, Bu Zhi, "had Wu Ju come to him, then cut his head off." Now Bu "made everyone tremble." In Jiaozhi, Shi Xie received promotion to "General of the Left," but had to deliver his son "as hostage." Then in 220, as China itself split into three rival kingdoms, Sun Quan, inaugural ruler of the Wu dynasty (220–280 CE), established his court in the southern capital, Nanjing, and took control of Jiao province, comprising all of Lingnan.[160]

Jiaozhi commandery remained a lucrative source of important exotic commerce. Whenever Shi Xie sent messengers to Sun Quan, they presented the Wu court with "varied types of incense, fine cloth, and always several thousand pearls, great cowries, porcelain, blue kingfisher feathers, tortoise shell, rhinoceros horn, and elephant tusk." Shi Xie's emissaries also brought "strange animals and curiosities, coconuts, bananas, and longans. Not a year went by without the arrival of a tribute mission." At one point Shi's brother Yi sent hundreds of horses. Sun Quan responded well. He would "invariably" dispatch letters to Shi and his family "greatly increasing their honours in order to keep their allegiance and make them happy."[161] Trade through Jiaozhi prospered. More emissaries arrived from the eastern Roman Empire, in 226 and again in 284.[162]

The south's trade and treasure attracted imperial power. After Shi Xie's death in 226, the Wu court at Nanjing reasserted direct Chinese control over Jiaozhi. An army of three thousand set out from Nanhai and sailed up the Red River. The Wu general summoned Xie's son, Xie Hui, with his five brothers and sons, and beheaded them all. Having conquered Jiaozhi, Wu forces also stormed Jiuzhen, killing or capturing ten thousand people, along with surviving members of Shi Xie's family. Yet resistance continued, and in 231, the Wu court had to send another general to Jiuzhen to "exterminate and pacify the barbarous Yuè" there.[163]

GENDER AND RELIGION

Even after three hundred years and fifty years of imperial rule in Jiaozhi and Jiuzhen, and even as Confucianism took root among the emerging elite, the Chinese were still able to rule much of the countryside only indirectly, if at all.[164] Việt customs and gender relations persisted. A Chinese scholar who took refuge in Jiaozhi under Shi Xie found its people "incorrigible" and complained: "Southern barbarian women are untrustworthy and promiscuously wander about."[165] A Wu official in Jiao wrote that "men and women beguiled each other, coupled hastily (*pen-sui*), and produced children whose fathers could not be ascertained." A memorial submitted to Sun Quan in 231 stated that the practice of levirate marriage persisted in old Lạc Việt strongholds: "In the two districts of Mi-leng [Mê Linh] in Jiaozhi and Tu-p'ang in Jiuzhen, it is usual for a younger brother to marry the widow of an older brother. Even the local officials cannot prevent it." The author recommended: "Give local chief officials strong authority to rectify this."[166]

Women also remained prominent in indigenous religious rites, including water rituals. Local worship of the *Chư vị*, or Spirits of the Three Worlds—Heaven, Earth, and Water—was still popular. Most of the priests or spirit mediums involved in this were women.[167] Indigenous aquatic motifs also persisted in the Vietnamese word *nước* ("waters") for "land, country." This contraction of *non nước*, "mountains and waters," is closer to the meaning of the Khmer equivalent *tik dei*, "water and land" than to the Chinese term for country, *guo jia*, "territory and family." Two lines in a traditional Vietnamese poem—"What your father has done (for you) is like Mt. Tai / what you owe to your mother is like water flowing out from a source"—convey a syncretic, dual message: a Chinese respect for the sacred Mount Tai and a Vietnamese association of the female gender with fertility and water.[168]

A new trade route opened up in maritime Southeast Asia. From the late second to the sixth century, at least twenty-seven large Đông Sơn bronze drums found their way as far as eastern Indonesia, including the Moluccas and Papua. They may have moved in a network of inter-island exchanges involving cloves and other Moluccan spices, for which a demand had arisen in both Jiaozhi and southwest China during this period of imperial expansion. A drum found on the Moluccan island of Kur was cast with a Chinese inscription containing an apparent Buddhist allusion to the "Triple World" (*san chieh*). These later, Han-Việt bronze drums are notable for their continuing representations of aquatic and marine motifs, including three-dimensional toads and boats with a bird-shaped prow or "water-serpent-like head" and rudder.[169]

Along with Confucianism and Daoism, Indian religious thought penetrated Jiaozhi and Jiuzhen. Buddhists from India, known to Chinese as Hu, had arrived by sea possibly as early as the first century and made many converts. Buddhism flourished under Shi Xie, who built monasteries and patronized monks. An observer told the court in 207: "Wherever he goes, he is escorted by a good many horsemen and his coach is surrounded by dozens of *Hu* holding burning joss sticks in their hands."[170] A Buddhist devotee from the Mekong delta moved north and settled in Jiaozhi, where he became known as Man ("the barbarian") and his daughter as Man Nương ("barbarian lady"). An Indian monk then taught Man Nương about both Buddhism and rainmaking. When a storm toppled a big tree at the gate of Shi Xie's palace, she alone possessed the power to move it. Shi Xie had its timber carved into four Buddha images and used them to found temples of clouds, rain, thunder, and lightning. The popular attractions of Buddhism included its power to tame nature and foster agriculture in ways that exhibited the continuing prominence of selected Việt women.[171] In addition,

Huỳnh Sanh Thông has argued that in contrast to Confucianism, "Buddhism sank deep roots in the Vietnamese psyche because all its metaphors had to do with water." Among other examples he cites the Buddhist image of being carried in the boat of "supreme wisdom" to "the yonder shore" and the Vietnamese saying, "Give a bowl of water and earn merit as high as a hill."[172]

Jiaozhi was an important region for Buddhism. At Luy Lâu in the late second century, a Chinese monk named Mâu Tử wrote *Lý Hoặc Luận* (Truth-illusion-metaphysics), one of the first Buddhist texts to be composed in Chinese. He recorded that Vietnamese monks, following Indian style, "wear clothes made of red material and do not follow Confucian rites in their relationships with other people." Mâu Tử complained of corruption among Jiaozhi's local and foreign monks, who "drink alcohol, take wives, hoard money and jewels, and love to deceive others."[173]

In a more positive vein, a later Vietnamese text records a sixth-century Chinese Buddhist monk describing this era to the emperor: "The area of Jiaozhou has long been in communication with India. Early on, when the Buddha-Dharma came to China and still had not been established, yet in Luy Lâu more than twenty precious temples were built, more than five hundred monks were ordained, and fifteen volumes of scriptures were translated."[174] An Indian Buddhist of Sogdian descent, the son of merchants who had settled in Jiaozhou, grew up there and was ordained as a monk, later becoming known to Vietnamese as Khương Tăng Hội (200–247 CE). It was probably at Luy Lâu that he made his Chinese translation of the *Aṣṭasāhasrikā Prajñāpāramitā* (Perfection of wisdom in eight thousand lines), one of the oldest sutras of Mahayana Buddhism. Khương Tăng Hội then moved farther north into China and in 247 converted its ruler Sun Quan to Buddhism. A Sri Lankan monk sailed to the Mekong delta and then walked northward along the coast displaying "supernatural power."[175] In 255–56, the Vietnamese monk Đạo Thanh coauthored one of the first translations of the Mahayana sutra entitled *The Saddharmapandarika* (V. *Pháp Hoa Tam Muội*), or *Lotus of Good Faith*. This was a famous text of the cult of Avalokiteśvara, an emergent Buddha or Bodhisattva, who represented mercy and compassion and was increasingly assuming a female form.[176] She became known to Chinese as Guanyin.

A new wave of foreign Buddhist influences reached Jiaozhou in the fifth century. The Chinese monk Tanhong moved there from Guangdong, established himself in the Tiên Sơn temple, and introduced the Amitabha, or Pure Land, sect of Buddhism to Jiaozhou. He immolated himself there in 455.[177] Half a century later, an Indian bonze named Dharmadeva (V. Đạt Ma Đề Bà) arrived in Jiaozhou and became a mentor of the Vietnamese monk Huệ Thắng. In the words of a sixth-century text, "A native of Jiaozhou,

Thích Huệ Thắng lived at the pagoda of Tiên Châu Sơn. He loved life as a recluse and recited the book *Pháp Hoa* once a day for several consecutive years. He was modestly clothed and accepted only what was strictly necessary. He learned Buddhist doctrine from the foreign bonze Đạt Ma Đề Bà, and each time he practiced meditation he continued till the end of the day." Invited north by the imperial court, Huệ Thắng moved to China and died there at the age of seventy.[178]

For many centuries Buddhist scholars in what is now Việt Nam probably outnumbered those with a Confucian education, with some overlap. But for most of the millennium of imperial rule the official ideology was Confucianism, grounded in the classical Chinese texts of Confucius and Mencius. The functioning of government thus required that Jiaozhi and Jiuzhen adopt the Chinese writing system. Local scholars may also have used it to record Vietnamese words or proper names, but they could read and write Buddhist texts only in Sanskrit or Chinese.

LINYI, FUNAN, AND THE CHAM REGIONS, SECOND TO FIFTH CENTURIES

The central and southern coasts of what is now Việt Nam also flourished in a diverse region of cultural exchange and commerce. In 1999–2010 in modern Khánh Hòa province on the south-central coast, archaeologists uncovered fifty burial jars dating from the last century BCE to the second century CE. One contained two Chinese coins of the Wu Zhu type first minted during that period, and another twenty gold beads from farther south.[179] The secession from Jiaozhi in 192 CE of the southern border kingdom of Linyi did not interrupt trade in either direction. Linyi, which sent six missions to China during the third and fourth centuries, flourished on coastal commerce, rice cultivation, and Indian cultural influence.[180] At Trà Kiệu in the Thu Bồn valley, a site founded in the first century CE in what is now Quảng Nam province, excavations in the 1990s uncovered third-century earthenware jars modeled on Chinese styles and locally produced tiles depicting human faces with nose and eyebrows "moulded in the form of a tree"—central Việt Nam's first figurative art. Hundreds of miles farther south, also in the third century, another new coastal polity produced Southeast Asia's earliest extant writing, an inscription in Sanskrit. A local Cham ruler was the likely sponsor of this text, found near Nha Trang.[181] Many Southeast Asian courts would soon adapt such Indic scripts to write their own languages.

Whether Linyi's indigenous population was linguistically Mon-Khmer or Chamic is uncertain. Chinese accounts refer to its language as "Kunlun." But they list most Linyi rulers as bearing the title *fan*, written with the same Chinese character as the common Vietnamese surname Phạm, which also resembles the early Khmer regional title *poñ*.[182] This suggests a Mon-Khmer language, related to Proto-Vietnamese.

The first Khmer civilization was emerging near the Mekong delta in the far south. Archaeological excavations undertaken from 1993 to 2005 at two coastal sites south of Hồ Chí Minh City uncovered more than four hundred burials, thirty-two of which contained a total of 250 gold beads and earrings, and three gold masks, dating from the period 100 BCE–100 CE.[183] In the late 240s CE, Chinese envoys made their first visit to a Mekong delta kingdom they called "Funan," which was probably Khmer. This Southeast Asian entrepôt polity was built on a millennium of trading contacts with regions in India.[184] Observers described Funan's ships as nearly one hundred Chinese feet long and six across, "with their bows and sterns like fishes.... The large ones carry a hundred men, each man carrying a long or short oar, or a boat-pole." Their hulls were made of layered wooden planks, caulked with tree resin and sewn together with twine made from coconut husk.[185] Local seafaring genius and skilled workmanship forged far-reaching economic and cultural contacts. Modern excavations at the earliest Funan site, the upper delta port of Óc Eo, have uncovered stone and brick architecture, "characteristic" tin and gold jewelry resembling the gold beads found farther north in Khánh Hòa, "uncountable" pearls, distinctive pottery, and even ancient Roman gold and bronze medallions minted under the emperors Antoninus Pius (152 CE) and Marcus Aurelius (c. 161–80).[186] The coins probably came via India, to whose cultural influence Funan became quite receptive in the second century.[187]

In the third century, Funan's king "had great ships built," which sailed across the Gulf of Siam, "attacked more than ten kingdoms," and conquered a Mon polity on the Malay peninsula. Funan sent an envoy to India in the early 240s, and an Indian monarch dispatched an accompanying return mission. His ambassadors reached Funan at the same time as China's first envoys, who inquired directly of the Indians about their homeland.[188] Funan sent six missions to China in the third century, and in 357 it offered to supply China with "tame elephants." A century later, Chinese sources reported, a man who was "originally a Brahman from India" became king of Funan and "changed all the rules according to the ways of India." Two fifth-century inscriptions from Funan express devotion to the Hindu god Vishnu. Funan's rulers often used the Sanskrit title *varma* ("warrior"). In an attempt to claim suzerainty over their kingdom, the Chinese emperor awarded King Jayavarman a different title, "General of the Pacified South [Annam], king of Funan." His son Rudravarman (r. 514–40) sent six missions to China.[189]

Just as optimistically, China awarded the king of Linyi the same title, "General of the Pacified South."[190] These were China's first uses of the term *Annam* (later reserved for Việt Nam), though neither Funan nor Linyi was ever "pacified" in the sense of being incorporated into the empire. In fact, imperial rule never extended far down the central Vietnamese coast, inhabited mostly by Chams. Linyi and a series of Cham courts dominated the coastline from various ports at river mouths. Their rulers converted to Hinduism and Buddhism, which were spreading through Southeast Asia. Chams may have been the first people of the region to adopt a writing system for their own language. A fourth-century Cham-language inscription, written in an Indic alphabet and found in the central Vietnamese province of Quảng Nam in 1935, is the oldest surviving text in a Southeast Asian language (fig. 2.4).[191]

Unlike contemporaneous Chinese and later Vietnamese-language texts, the main purpose of Cham inscriptions was religious. Yet they also reflected social and political power. For instance, the third-century Sanskrit text from Nha Trang, accompanied by verse, recorded a donation made by "the joy of the family of the daughter of the grandson of the king Shri Mara," a formulation which suggests that the king's daughters and his wife's matrilineage inherited his wealth.[192] The fourth-century inscription in Cham reads: "Success! This is the king's holy naga [Sanskrit: serpent; Malay: dragon]. Whoever treats it well... [*kurun*, unidentified word] (will see) joys fall from the sky; whoever insults it... [*kurun*] (will suffer) for a thousand years in the hells with seven generations of his family."[193]

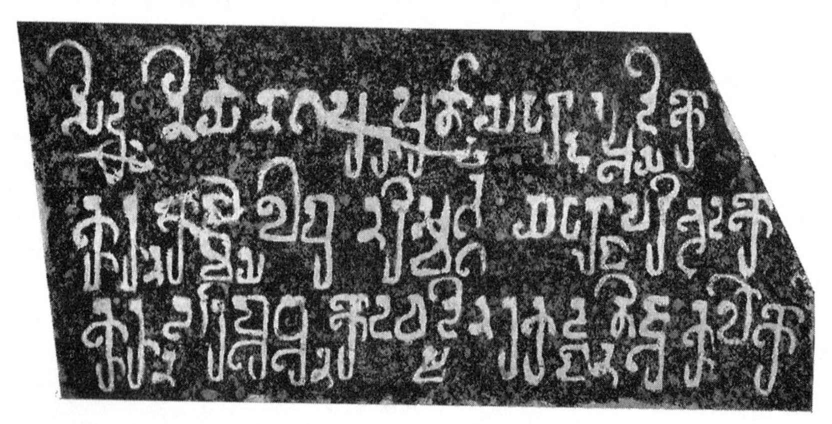

Fig. 2.4
The earliest extant text in a Southeast Asian language, the fourth-century Đông Yên Châu inscription in Cham. From George Coedès, "La plus ancienne inscription en langue cham," in, *A Volume of Eastern and Indian Studies Presented to Professor F. W. Thomas*, ed. S. M. Katre and P. K. Gode (Bombay: Karnatak, 1939), 46–49.

A subsequent pair of Sanskrit inscriptions documents the devotion to the Hindu god Siva on the part of the Cham monarch Bhadravarman I, who styled himself "Great King of the Law." These similar texts were inscribed two hundred miles apart, in Tuy Hoà and Quảng Nam, around the year 400.[194] A third inscription from Bhadravarman's reign, found in the same district of Quảng Nam, begins with praise for Siva and his consort, Uma, then adds: "to Brahma and to Vishnu! Homage to the Earth, to the Wind, to Space and . . . to Fire."[195] Indigenous earth cults obviously thrived alongside the new Indian deities. Indeed, Po Ino Nagar, the autochthonous Cham "Lady of the Land," eventually became identified as Uma herself.

For a thousand years, kingdoms of the coastal region later known as Champa rivaled one another and their Vietnamese and Khmer neighbors. They left inscriptions that throw light on events in Cham territories and the adjacent regions, including what became Việt Nam to the immediate north. Long predating the first extant texts in Vietnamese, more than 180 Cham inscriptions survive from the fourth to the thirteenth centuries.[196] Cham culture, music, and religion influenced Việt life, and there was a good deal of intermarriage.

AN EMERGING VIỆT ADMINISTRATION

Jiaozhi had become a major source of grain supply for south China, and its population was growing. The area of Việt and Chinese settlement was already becoming overcrowded. By the middle of the third century, farmers began moving out of the eastern part of the Red River delta toward the northeast, beyond the site of modern Hanoi. In the fifth century they also expanded to the southwest, taking up new lands that had emerged where the river's massive annual silt deposits were reclaiming the sea. So the imperial administration frequently had to move its headquarters and establish new prefectures to maintain control of its ever more dispersed and numerous subjects. In the third century, Wu officials increased the number of prefectural centers in Jiaozhi from about twelve to as many as twenty-six.[197]

The Wu regime was harsh. Turmoil plagued the southern commanderies by the late third century. In 248, Linyi forces invaded from the south, seized most of Rinan, and marched on into Jiuzhen, provoking major uprisings there and in Jiaozhi. One Jiaozhi rebel commanded thousands and invested several walled towns before Wu officials got him to surrender. In Jiuzhen, a hundred local commanders led fifty thousand families in revolt.[198] The leaders possibly included the last Lạc Việt woman rebel in the tradition of the Trưng sisters. Ignored in Chinese texts of the time, Triệu Ẩu (Lady Triệu) is named only in an early fourteenth-century text compiled by a Vietnamese exile in China, who described her, apparently on the basis of an earlier record, as married to Jun Ning Xian, who lived in Jiuzhen. Yet "she resolved very young to keep her virginity. Her breasts were three feet long; she carried them on her back. She wore shoes . . . and rode on an elephant to fight her enemies. She had assembled a force of brigands on Ju Shan mountain. Lu Yi, the governor of Jiaozhou put her to death."[199]

Meanwhile Wu forces fought more wars against Yuè "barbarians" in southern China. And in 263, another revolt in Jiaozhi and Jiuzhen launched a seventeen-year conflict there. The rebels handed the region over to Wu's rival, the northern Chinese kingdom of Jin. In 268 and 269, they held off large Wu armies and fleets, which eventually retook Jiaozhi's ports and main towns in 271. Fighting continued in the countryside until 280, when Jin destroyed Wu, reunifying China until a new and even longer period of division began in 313.[200]

The far south, however, prospered. A report reached the new Jin court stating that the king of Linyi "is in contact to the south with [the king of] Funan. Their tribes are numerous; their allied troops aid each other. Taking advantage of the ruggedness of their region, they do not submit [to China]."[201] The early Jin regime favored trade, and in 286 embassies arrived from Funan and twenty other southern kingdoms, including Xitu, probably a Cham polity, which reputedly dominated ten smaller realms near the central coast south of Linyi, and Quduqian, farther south again, possibly near modern Nha Trang.[202] Along with this brief peacetime "boom" in the southern trade, Jiaozhi and Jiuzhen enjoyed some autonomy from China until the 320s.[203] Linyi merchants "brought valuable goods by sea." Official corruption still plagued negotiations. According to a Chinese text, the governors of Jiaozhou and the prefects of Rinan "were very covetous and imposed a tax of 20 to 30 percent on their goods." Han Chi, the prefect of Rinan, "assessed their merchandise at less than half its value, and then [intimidated them] with his ships and war drums." The "various countries" from which the traders had come were "furious."[204]

Worse, from 312 a "chain of risings" broke out in south China. Rebel and imperial units fought each other with "ferocity" over Jiaozhi and Jiuzhen. Then, perhaps frustrated by the difficulty of trade, Linyi itself resorted from 323 to seaborne raids on northern ports, launching what became seventy-six years of southern incursions.[205] Local Việt defenders and Chinese reinforcements fought side by side against Linyi "barbarians." But with China again divided into "Northern" and "Southern" Dynasties (313–589 CE), its armies were less powerful than before. Fighting off decades of

Table 2.1 SHORTENING PERIODS OF FULL IMPERIAL CONTROL OF JIAOZHI AND JIUZHEN: FIRST TO FIFTH CENTURIES

Dates (CE)	Interval
43–187	144 years
226–269	43 years
427–454	27 years
485–494	9 years

Linyi attacks must have given local officials in Jiaozhi and Jiuzhen valuable experience in organizing defenses.

In the fourth century only four tribute missions reached China, from Funan and Linyi. Though defeated in 399, Linyi continued its raids on Jiaozhi and Jiuzhen for two decades. In 421 it recommenced sending tribute missions to China and persisted even after war resumed a decade later. Meanwhile a Chinese rebel army from Zhejiang briefly seized Jiaozhi's capital in 411. With the empire in turmoil, Jiaozhi and Jiuzhen experienced another period of semi-independence until 427. Periods of full Chinese control were becoming progressively shorter.[206]

China's southern challenges were transnational as well as domestic. After fifteen years of attacks from Linyi, imperial forces invaded it in 446. They met strong resistance. First they stormed the fortress of Qusu, which was defended by rectangular walls two kilometers long and ten meters high, topped by a wooden palisade and enclosing 2,100 houses. When the Chinese took the town, they slaughtered everyone over fifteen years old and then pushed south to Linyi's capital. This larger city, near modern Huế, comprised fifty blocks of closely packed houses, protected by four kilometers of walls. The victorious attackers plundered its eight temples and treasury, carrying off "100,000 pounds of gold." Yet again Linyi revived, flourishing on the ever more lucrative passing sea trade, described by a Chinese historian in 487 as "a chain of great and small ships" plying between China and Southeast Asia. Linyi also sold China its own produce: ivory, rhinoceros horns, gharu woods, tortoiseshell, amber, and gold and silver items. It sent fifteen trade missions to China between 455 and 540.[207]

Nor did China's victory over Linyi in 446 prevent another half century of "frequent troubles" in Jiaozhi and Jiuzhen: an uprising in 468, a period of independence in 479–85, and revolts in 505 and 516. The sea trade moved north, to modern Guangzhou. But once the "chain" of merchant ships resumed docking at Jiaozhi ports after 516, Jiaozhi profited from the flourishing commerce between China's Buddhist ruler Liang Wudi (r. 502–549) and Funan's

Rudravarman, whose realm supplied religious items such as gharu wood for incense, ivory and sandalwood stupas and statues, and glass vessels.[208]

From 250 to 550 CE, despite recurrent economic and military instability, important domestic developments had transformed Jiaozhi into a more self-administering imperial region. The dominance of Shi Xie in the early third century had prefigured the rise of a new Sino-Vietnamese governing class even though the Wu wiped out his lineage. Just four Jiaozhi-based family groups produced half of the twenty-four known imperial inspectors of Jiao province between 270 and 430. In these families, writes historian Jennifer Holmgren, the first member to hold the post did so until his death, and "in all but two cases these Inspectors were succeeded by a son or younger brother who in turn retained the post until his death and was himself succeeded by a close relative." Transitions proceeded "without objections or interference" from China. Leadership had become "a matter of local initiative." Under the Sung Dynasty (420–77), too, court-appointed officials did not curtail the power of Jiaozhi's dominant clans. Holmgren concludes that the first six centuries of Chinese rule in Jiaozhi saw more "Vietnamization" of local Chinese than Sinicization of indigenous Viets. Prominent Chinese clans "settled into, helped modify, and were finally absorbed into the social, economic and political environment in northern Vietnam." Beyond Jiaozhi's main Chinese-ruled urban centers of Luy Lâu, Long Biên, and Cổ Loa, most of the countryside remained indigenous, un-Sinicized. In Wang Gungwu's words, the whole Lingnan region was "still mainly populated by Chinese merchant-adventurers, foreign traders and the rebellious 'Mans and Laos,'" southern "barbarians." Expansion of Chinese rule from the growing merchant settlements of Guangzhou and Long Biên was "driving the 'barbarians' out of the fertile deltas of the West and Red rivers, or assimilating and sinicising them. But the area was still relatively undeveloped, and considered to be on the edge of the civilized world."[209]

Late in the fifth century, the imperial court detached Jiaozhou from south China, where it created a new province named Yuè. In the rump Jiao province, the former Lạc Việt region, the scene was set for the brief emergence of a new, separate kingdom. Its Confucian elite, imbued with Chinese culture and law, was capable of running its affairs and of challenging imperial control.[210] Over the ensuing centuries Jiao's population adopted more of the northern culture and system of government. They would also come to regard it as their own, adapt it to local conditions, and meld it with surviving indigenous traditions and with what they learned through contacts with their Indianized southern neighbors, Linyi, Funan, and Champa.

CHAPTER 3

Mountains and Rivers of the Southern Kingdom

Annam and Its Neighbors, Sixth to Tenth Centuries

In the second half of the first millennium, imperial power in Jiao province (modern northern Việt Nam) reached its height, with significant local acquiescence. Yet it also faced three kinds of challenges: a powerful Sinicized local elite, another series of indigenous revolts, and military threats from new or strengthened polities beyond the empire's borders to the west and south. Even Jiao's entrenched sociopolitical elite, which had emerged under five centuries of imperial supervision and proved itself competent at self-rule, posed an internal challenge to the northern empire. So did rebel leaders mobilizing Jiao's largely still un-Sinicized indigenous populations. Even in neighboring Yuè province of southern China, the empire still depended on the cooperation of indigenous Yuè leaders.

From the sixth century, Confucian ideology, Buddhist devotion, and Daoism all spread more widely in Jiao, yet they did not displace local cults and loyalties. The benefits of the increasingly effective imperial organization also served to enhance the local power of Jiao's provincial administrators. New commercial opportunities enriched indigenous, provincial, and imperial coffers, raising the stakes of economic power and encouraging stronger challenges even beyond the southern frontier. The neighboring kingdoms of Linyi and Chenla, and later Champa and Nanzhao, all threatened northern rule of Jiao. As the empire expanded under the Tang dynasty

(618–905 CE), it fought off each of these regional threats in turn but still faced a twofold internal challenge from the enhanced power of the Sinicized Jiao elite and the continuing strength of indigenous loyalties in parts of the lowlands but especially in the hills.

Over the centuries, as the Red River continued to spill silt into the sea, its delta slowly expanded, particularly in the east. In parts of the eastern and western delta, brackish coastal marshes formed and gradually gave way to more solid earth. Forests spread over the swampland. By the mid-first millennium, Jiao's hills and plains teemed with elephants, at least two species of rhinoceros, and several kinds of wild cattle.[1]

A NEW KINGDOM OF NAN YUÈ

Changing environmental conditions facilitated a successful revolt that broke out in 541 CE and overturned northern rule of Jiao for six decades. In the eastern delta, rebels launched surprise raids on imperial forces from a large swamp that had formed there over the previous three centuries, apparently unknown to the Chinese. A later Vietnamese source reported: "It is covered with thick forest and shrub and there is a hard base in the middle of it, around which there is nothing but mud and swamp. The place is hard to travel for humans and horses and can only be reached by canoes. But if one does not know the route he would still be lost and fall into the water and be bitten by worms or snakes and die."[2]

Armed with local knowledge, the new indigenized Jiao elite mounted their first major military challenge to northern domination. The extended rebellion has even been called "the first attempt at an independent Vietnam."[3] Its leader, Lý Bí, was a local secessionist who like other Jiao officeholders owed much of his cultural heritage to the empire. His ancestors had reportedly fled from north China to Jiaozhi around 15 CE. One had become a grand administrator there. Such Confucian families were a product of the autonomous transformation of Jiaozhi since the time of Shi Xie.[4] Bí's family maintained estates on the north bank of the Red River.[5] He had served at the court of the Liang dynasty, then returned south as imperial military commander in Jiuzhen, before taking up the cause of secession.[6] In that sense his career followed in the footsteps of Zhào Tuó in 207 BCE, another imperial appointee turned breakaway.

Lý Bí asserted that ancient legacy by restoring Zhào Tuó's name for the country, proclaiming himself "Emperor of Nán Yuè" in 544. Yet he also emphasized the future when he called his rebel kingdom Vạn Xuân (Ten Thousand Springs). Lý Bí's adoption of a literary name for his kingdom, like his use of the term "emperor" and of a reign title, *Thiên-đức* (Heavenly

Virtue), followed models from Chinese political culture.[7] He would not be the last to deploy these models to strengthen local autonomy from the empire.

"Ten Thousand Springs" was optimistic. But in declaring secession, the restored Nan Yuè followed the successful example of Linyi. Despite its defeat by imperial forces in 446, Linyi still fielded armies of more than forty thousand men and a thousand elephants.[8] When its king, Rudravarman, attacked Nán Yuè from the south in 543, Lý Bí had to fight off Linyi as well as combat two unsuccessful imperial expeditions in 542 and 544.[9] Despite the cultural differences that now separated it from Linyi, Jiao had briefly become a similar middle-ranking polity like others in the Southeast Asian region. Politically eclectic and located in a diverse region, it was now by no means certain that Jiao would always form part of a great northern empire.

At the peak of his career, Lý Bí commanded an army of twenty thousand. However, in 545–46 a third imperial army defeated him, and he fled west into the mountains above the Red River. In 548, Lao highlanders delivered Lý Bí's head to the Chinese. Two years later, however, his kinsmen and supporters vanquished the imperial army, which again withdrew, leaving Nán Yuè under an autonomous Lý dynasty for several decades.[10] During that time Lý Bí's heirs fought with another faction of his court. Although the secessionist leaders were better organized than the Trưng sisters five centuries earlier, as then, internecine divisions proved damaging in the face of the renewed northern attacks after 571. Lý Bí's successor, Lý Xuân, held on and ruled Jiao until 602, when armies of the new imperial Sui dynasty (589–618 CE) finally reconquered the province.[11]

Six centuries of imperial rule had also brought about long-term cultural changes. The influence of the tonal Chinese language on nontonal Vietic languages, primarily Proto-Việt-Mường, had led to the adoption of three tones. This process may have accelerated during the latter decades of the sixth century when for the first time Proto-Việt-Mường joined Chinese in official use, at the courts of Lý Bí and his successors.[12] Possibly another effect of the proximity of the two languages, ironically during this long period of autonomy from China, was the linguistic divergence of Việt-Mường from other Vietic languages such as Rục. Glottochronology dates that divergence vaguely to the mid-first millennium, possibly around the late sixth century.[13]

The kingdom of Ten Thousand Springs lasted less than fifty years, but ten times as long as the revolt of the Trưng sisters. With its solid, Sinicized administrative class, Jiao was no longer a Lạc Việt society those sisters could have recognized. And if their successor Triệu Ẩu (Lady Triệu) had in fact led the uprising of 248, she proved to be the last female warrior leader of that archaic society. Religious records of an extant shrine in Jiuzhen indicate that Lý Bí commemorated Triệu Ẩu by constructing the shrine there in her name.[14] But if he did see himself in her ethnic lineage, or even as tracing her footsteps, the political culture that had produced a series of Việt female commanders was no more.

CHINA'S YUÈ PROVINCE

The region that became southern China was a different matter. While the third-century Wu Dynasty was combating revolts in far-southern Jiaozhi and Jiuzhen, it had also fought wars against other Yuè "barbarians" in the empire's interior provinces of Kiangsi and Hunan.[15] Now, in sixth-century southern Guangdong near the border with Jiaozhi, a contemporary of Lý Bí known as "Lady Sinn" (Xian Furen, c. 512–602) rose to lead yet another group of Yuè. According to a seventh-century Chinese account, "The Sinn clan had for generations been leaders of the Nán Yuè. They stretched across the mountains and [valleys], and their tribe comprised in excess of 100,000 families."[16] Contemporaneous descriptions of these and other local groups in south China recall classical depictions of the Yuè. Chinese texts said the indigenous southerners' custom was "to cut their hair and decorate their bodies," and "they also cast bronze into large drums" that were key elements of their social organization. "When they sound these drums, people flood there." The owners of the drums "are selected by popular sentiment."[17] Women played a substantial role in agriculture and also conducted the slaughter of cattle, first ritually accusing the beast of "crimes": "I led you in season to plowing, but you would not go ahead: I rode you in season to cross the water, but then you would not move. Why should you escape death?"[18]

Lady Sinn's career in sixth-century Guangdong indicates a continuing key role of local female leadership. Here, though, a woman was instrumental not in resistance to China but in the political incorporation of the indigenous border populations into the empire, in stark contrast to earlier women rebels in Jiaozhi. Yet Lady Sinn's story also demonstrates several common cultural themes that pervaded most of these southern regions. She even calls to mind some attributes of the Trưng sisters as female military leaders.

Sixth-century administrators of southern Guangdong, like the imperial regional inspector Feng Rong and his family, "were people from another place," that is, from China's north, and they found it difficult to command local obedience. The south was also hard to govern because it was unstable: "The Yuè were, by custom, inured to attacking each other." Their channels of authority were also unfamiliar to Chinese. When Lady Sinn's elder brother "raided and attacked neighboring commanderies," Sinn alone wielded the authority to convince him to restore order. No doubt sensing this woman's indispensable prestige, Feng Rong prudently "proposed her betrothal in marriage to his son," Feng Bao. The two wed, and from then on, Lady Sinn helped the authorities calm or defeat local revolts against Chinese rule. When one rebellion erupted around 550, she disarmingly approached its leader, then "attacked him by surprise and achieved a great victory." After her husband died about 558, further unrest threatened, and Sinn's role became even more crucial to stability. She "cherished and gathered the Bai Yuè ['Hundred Yuè'], and several regions were brought to peace." The imperial court of the Chen dynasty (557–87) appointed her "Commandery Lady," and Sinn sent the emperor an unmistakably southern gift: "a staff made from Funan rhinoceros horn." After the Chen collapse in the 580s, during the turmoil in China before the rise of the Sui dynasty (589–618), Lady Sinn took regional control of the south under the title "Sacred Mother." Confronting another rebellion in 590, "the Lady herself donned armour, mounted her armour-clad steed, opened her brocaded parasol, and, leading her mounted archers, protected the imperial envoy." He in turn appointed her to "govern the tribes" on behalf of the Sui court. Another woman, Sinn's daughter-in-law, received command of a district.[19]

So the establishment of imperial control in the south (like its earlier rejection under the Trưng sisters) clearly depended on traditional Yuè female authority. Harnessing that authority helped form the empire, whose local grip at the time of Sinn's death in 602 remained so tenuous that during the Sui census seven years later, officials did not register the hundred thousand Yuè families ruled by her clan.[20] It may have been only her grandson and successor Feng Ang who completed the transition to more direct rule (and possibly taxation) of the Yuè people of Guangdong.

Significantly, similar conditions now prevailed in Jiao province to the south. The 609 population census there revealed the registration and imperial supervision of even fewer population centers than the Han census six centuries earlier had (compare fig. 3.1 on the next page with fig. 2.2). In contrast, what was becoming southern China exhibited slightly more registered settlements and imperial control than had existed there under the Han.[21]

Having overthrown the short-lived Sui, the new imperial Tang Dynasty (618–905) renamed Jiao province Jiaozhou. In 679, the Việt region became the Protectorate of Annam ("Pacified South"). This may have reflected imperial acknowledgement of Jiao's more recent unruliness; "Pacified South" was a name that China had previously applied only to breakaway Linyi and independent Funan.[22] But for centuries afterward, Annam failed to follow the path to autonomy traced by those kingdoms, and in the Tang era it fell more heavily under Chinese influence than ever before. The Tang court proactively commissioned its protector-general of Annam to supervise "the

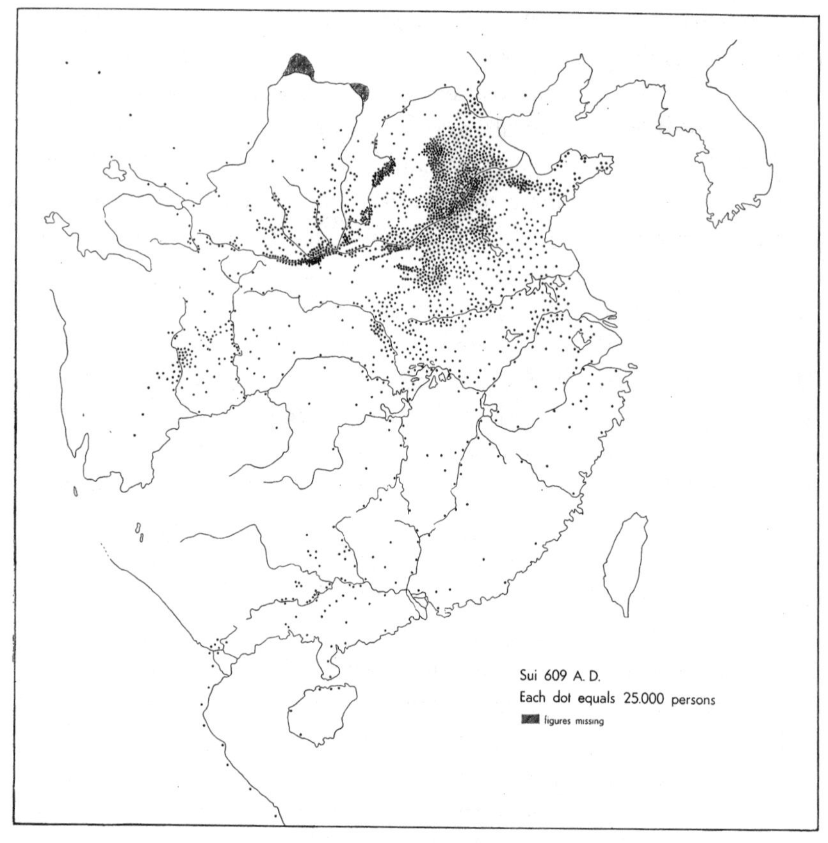

Fig. 3.1
Results of the Sui dynasty population census of 609 CE. From Hans Bielenstein, "The Census of China during the Period 2–742 A.D.," *Bulletin of the Museum of Far Eastern Antiquities* 19 (1948): plate 5.

pacification, subjugation, and patrol" of the non-Sinitic groups under his jurisdiction there.[23] This was initially successful. Local Confucian culture reached a peak, and from the seventh century it flourished at Annam's new capital, Đại La (the site of modern Hanoi).[24] This town was also known to Chinese as Jiaozhou city (from the province's former name). But unlike the other Yuè regions slowly incorporated into south China, Annam escaped eventual assimilation. Speakers of Proto-Việt-Mường languages managed to preserve them, while enhancing them mostly with borrowings from Chinese.

BUDDHISM

While drawing on elements of Chinese political culture, Lý Bí may also have been the first ruler of Jiao to employ Buddhist ideas and practices to strengthen local governance. He is reputed to have launched his reign with the construction of a temple containing the eight-foot stone image of a seated Amitabha Buddha, carved in a sculptural style influential in China at that time.[25] Other local accounts suggest that Buddha statues, as well as the chanting of sutras and belief in the magical powers of monks, were already common features of Jiao society. Late in the sixth century, a Chinese monk reputedly told the last Sui emperor: "Jiaozhou is no different than China. . . . There are already Buddhist teachers there; we do not have to go to convert them."[26] Vietnamese Buddhism had been fostered directly by Indian religious teachers, and by contacts with Champa as well as China. Jiao was home to an eclectic combination of the "northern" Mahayana school of Buddhism, the "southern" Theravada school, Tantric Buddhism, and even Hindu Brahmanical influences. However, the Pali Buddhist texts that eventually came to dominate the Theravada religious culture of the rest of mainland Southeast Asia (from Burma to Cambodia) never found a significant audience in Jiao.[27] After about 580 CE, as in China and Tibet, various sects of the Mahayana Buddhist school prevailed in Annam, slowly displacing Theravada influences.

One new Mahayana Buddhist sect was the meditational school known as Zen (*Ch.* Chan; *V.* Thiền).[28] An Indian monk named Bodidharma introduced this sect to China in 520. Four decades later, a Brahman from south India named Vinītaruci followed him to China, where he became the sect's fourth patriarch. But his predecessor told Vinītaruci: "Don't remain long here! Go rather to the south and mix with the people." So, around 580, Vinītaruci moved to Jiao and lived in the Pháp Vân pagoda near Luy Lâu, where he founded a Thiền order of monks. As Annam's first Thiền order, it retained much of the Indian influence characteristic of its origins, stressing meditation and contemplation more than textual study. Before he died in 594, Vinītaruci recited a *gatha* (strophe) portraying enlightenment as an understanding of the heart, not based on words or concepts but expressed in negations:

> The stamp of the spirit of the Buddhas
> Naturally does not lead to error,
> Nor is it perfect as nirvana,
> It is not in shortage nor in excess.
> It does not win nor does it lose
> It does not disappear nor does it become different
> It is not continuous nor is it interrupted.
> It has no place of birth
> And has no point of annihilation.[29]

Vinītaruci's successor Pháp Hiền, a native of Jiao, was reputedly "over seven feet tall." A fourteenth-century Buddhist text recorded that after Vinītaruci's death, Pháp Hiền "went directly to Mount Từ Sơn to practice meditation. He looked like a withered tree—things and self were both forgotten. Birds and beasts became tame and liked to linger around him." His virtuous reputation quickly attracted "countless" students. Pháp Hiền built a temple, whose monks "usually numbered over three hundred. The southern school of Zen [i.e., Vinītaruci's] has flourished ever since." He died in 626.[30]

The oldest inscription yet found in northern Việt Nam is a Buddhist stele dating from Pháp Hiền's lifetime. It was erected in the Đông Sơn district of Jiuzhen in 618 CE. Commissioned in praise of "Governor Lê," an officer of the Sui dynasty during its very last days, this Chinese-language text entitled "Inscription of the Temple of Precious Peace of Jiuzhen Commandery of the Great Sui" stresses the Buddhist concept of the illusory nature of the world. A local tradition records that Governor Lê and his son later fell in battle against the victorious Tang forces.[31]

Buddhism thrived in Annam throughout the Tang era (618–905 CE). Although Daoism became the dynasty's official religion, four prominent Tang poets praised Buddhist masters who hailed from the protectorate. A Chinese pilgrim in Jiuzhen dedicated these lines to the eminent local ascetic Vô Ngại Thượng Nhân, who had "built a temple at the foot of a mountain" in Rinan (V. Nhật Nam):

> Formerly the Buddha was born in India,
> Now he manifests himself here to convert the people of Nhật Nam...
> By the stream the fragrant branches are the standards,
> The boulders on the mountaintop become his home.
> Blue doves practice meditation,
> White monkeys listen to the *sutras*
> Creepers cover the cloud-high cliffs,
> Flowers rise above the pond at the foot of the mountain.
> The water in the streams is good for performing ritual,
> The trees let him hang his clothes on them.[32]

Not all Annam's Buddhists were reclusive. One of the Tang poets portrayed a monk from Rinan receiving "a visitor from the Southern Sea, asking in his barbaric tongue whose house this is?" Two senior Jiao monks known as masters of the dharma (Buddhist law) made the long journey north to the Tang court. There they delivered lectures on Buddhism and made strong impressions. Dharma Master Duy Giám inspired a Chinese poet to write:

Expounding the *sutras* in the royal palace
Flowers fly around the emperor's throne.
When did you leave the Southern Sea
Only to return to your homeland in old age?
Exposed to the wind the imperial seal loses its perfume.

And as Dharma Master Phụng Định departed the Chinese court, another Tang poet wrote:

Your native land is Nam Việt
Thousands of miles away beyond the snow-capped mountains
Bidding farewell to worldly discussions at court
You'll sail into the ocean of fragrant flowers...
Please think of the streets of Chang'an
Before you sound your night bell at Jiaozhou.[33]

At least six other monks from Jiao traveled to China in the Tang era. One spent ten years there and later lived as a layman in Srivijaya (in modern Sumatra). Four of these six were dharma masters who also traveled to Southeast Asia and on to India and Sri Lanka. Like many Jiaozhou monks, they were expert in Sanskrit and Central Asian languages.[34]

However, the Tang dynasty's official state religion, as noted, was Daoism. Tang Daoists sporadically persecuted Buddhism in China.[35] The only direct contemporary documentary record of Buddhism in Tang Annam is a lengthy Chinese-language text, dated 798 and inscribed on a large bronze bell discovered in 1986 buried in a sand bank of the Đáy River.[36] This is the oldest Buddhist bell found in northern Việt Nam. Its inscription lists the names of 243 members of a newly founded local Buddhist association (*she*), the first of this kind known in Annam, modeled on similar institutions that had appeared in China from the fifth century.[37] These *she*, initiated by monks but run by lay devotees, were affiliated to a temple and were responsible for the wider propagation of Buddhism as well as for conducting acts of piety, like casting bells and statues, sculpting Buddha images, copying and reciting sutras, acquiring religious paintings and banners, planning and running festivals, and holding funerals for *she* members. The name of this association in Annam is recorded on the bell as Suixi, the Chinese equivalent of a Sanskrit term for "the joy that follows the accomplishment of virtuous deeds." A poem incised on the bell begins: "We have turned our mind to the creation of blessings, / And together have made a far-reaching peal."[38] Other sources confirm that this bell's peal probably sounded an approaching high tide of Buddhism in Annam.

Buddhism may have owed part of its local success to its eclecticism. The Suixi *she*'s 243 named member-donors came from disparate backgrounds and origins. They included not only a Buddhist abbot, presumably of the temple to which the *she* was affiliated, but also a Daoist master (*dongxuan*) and his wife and daughter. The majority of the donors consist of two major groups: Chinese officials, especially military officers, and local women from Annam.[39]

The names of many officials are incised in the four upper panels of the bell's surface, along with those of the eight-member *she* leadership, including its president, two vice-presidents, elders, secretaries, and clerks. More than sixty serving or former government officials are listed on this top half of the bell, including fourteen civil servants who hailed mainly from neighboring Guangdong and no fewer than fifty military officers from all across China. Four of the *she*'s eight administrators were officials, mostly from the army: the president was a retired "district defender," or police chief; both vice-presidents were former military commanders; and one secretary was also a soldier.[40] The imperial security forces seem to have been very prominent in civilian life, reflecting a militarization of Tang authority in late eighth-century Annam.

But most of the named donors to the Suixi association were women. The majority (126 women) were ordinary *she* members whose names are engraved in the four panels on the lower half of the bell. Of the total of 243 members of this *she*, 135 were female and 108 male. And no fewer than 116 were independent women, all ordinary members who contributed a share of money or goods to the *she*. Only nineteen of the women were listed as the mother, wife, or daughter of an official or other donor. Significant autonomous female participation is also recorded among *she* elsewhere in the empire; some included only females, or only elderly women. Significantly, the Suixi *she* membership includes the first verifiable list of women's names in Annam and thus the earliest information on how indigenous women were named there. One hundred of the women listed in the inscription had three-part names including the middle syllable *shi* (V. thị), which became the most common form of name for Vietnamese women in the second millennium and up to the present time.[41]

While its shape revealed a southern Chinese artistic influence, the bronze Suixi bell also reflected an older Vietnamese culture of metallurgy. The eighth-century bell has been termed "a 'marker' of Buddhism and Chineseness in an environment where the bronze drum culture was still alive."[42] Buddhism's appeal to independent women and its eclectic inclusion of other indigenous traditions, even of local material culture, may account for much of its success in Annam.

CONFUCIANISM

Like several of Jiaozhou's Buddhist dharma masters, a tiny group of Confucian-educated scholars from Annam also made successful careers in imperial circles. In the late 700s Khương Công Phụ and Khương Công Phục, two brothers of Chinese background from Jiuzhen (which the Tang dynasty renamed Ái), rose to become doctors, scholars and high officials in China. For a short time Khương Công Phụ even served as premier at the court. However, the numbers of candidates from Annam permitted to take the classical examinations and win positions in the imperial system remained limited. Many such posts were effectively hereditary or filled by recommendation.[43] The imperial system did allow for some promotion by merit and could even be strikingly trans-ethnic. A Japanese named Abe-no Nakamaro, who had arrived in China as a young student and then joined the Tang bureaucracy, headed the Protectorate of Annam from 761 to 767.[44]

However, the indigenous scholarly elite represented by the Khương brothers remained small. A Tang official wrote dismissively in 845: "Annam has produced no more than eight imperial officials; senior graduates have not exceeded ten." Very few natives of Jiao achieved doctorate degree status. One was Liêu Hữu Phương, who passed the classical exams in 816 on his second attempt and became a librarian at the imperial court. He wrote sadly of a fellow student who had complained on his deathbed: "I have toiled through many examinations but not yet found favor." Liêu Hữu Phương commented: "How many rules weary the heart; brush, ink, the examination yard."[45]

Confucian scholarship was not the only imperial contribution to Annam's development. The Red River delta was the largest agricultural plain in the empire's south, and Annam's capital of Đại La became a focus of economic activity. With a genius for organization and imperial experience with water control on the Yangzi and Yellow Rivers, Tang administrators of Annam began construction of dikes to protect the city from flooding and, in some cases, for military purposes.[46] To maintain these earthworks required massive mobilization of workers and skilled managers of labor. The small responsible bureaucratic elite probably increased in importance.

An international economy developed too. Annam produced gold, silver, and silk, and shipbuilding became an important industry. The empire built roads leading up the Red River valley far into the interior, south to Champa, and inland to an emerging Khmer kingdom that Chinese called "Chenla." Sea routes from Annam also led to Champa as well as north to Guangdong. Annam competed strongly for the southern ocean trade. A Cham trader even appealed in 792 to imperial officials for help by closing ports in

Annam: "Lately, the precious and strange [goods] brought by ocean-junks have mostly been taken to An-nan [Annam] to be traded there."[47]

FROM FUNAN AND LINYI TO CHENLA AND CHAMPA

Annam's neighbors were facing a commercial transformation. As the volume of international commerce increased in the sixth century, trading ships became larger, and southern Chinese merchants and shipbuilders benefited. When the new Sui dynasty from the north unified the empire in 590, southern revolts broke out that year both at Guangzhou and at Long Biên, in Jiao. Before reconquering Jiao from the Lý family in 602, the Sui emperor Sun Wendi moved first to break the power and wealth of what is now southern China by limiting its maritime trade. In 598, he banned the construction of large ships. Vessels more than thirty feet long built in the south were to be confiscated.[48] These strictures deterred many foreign merchants. Others who continued to trade with the empire also had larger ships than before and no longer needed to follow the mainland coastal route north from Indonesian islands to China; many began sailing directly across the South China Sea.[49] The coastal trading kingdoms of Funan and Linyi suffered.

The Mekong delta entrepôt kingdom of Funan, ruled by King Rudravarman, sent six trade missions to China between 514 and his death in 540, but in the next eight decades the number dropped to just three as coastal trade seems to have fallen away.[50] Rudravarman was probably succeeded by his grandson Bhavavarman, then by another grandson, Mahendravarman. These brothers appear to have begun to move their kingdom inland and up the Mekong River into what is now Cambodia, where the first Khmer-language inscriptions soon appeared, dating from 611. Mahendravarman's son, King Isanavarman (r. 616–37), is recorded in Sanskrit and Khmer inscriptions as establishing a new capital at Sambor Prei Kuk in northern Cambodia. The Chinese considered this a new polity, Chenla, which they first mentioned in a report of the arrival of a mission from there in 616–17. However, like "Funan," the name "Chenla" appears only in Chinese sources. No indigenous names of these polities survive. The Chinese suggest that Chenla invaded Funan from the north, conquered it, and forced its king to flee southward. China apparently recognized both kingdoms until the 630s, when it received the last envoys from Funan, which then disappears from the historical record. Modern scholars, however, see more continuity from Funan to Chenla.[51] In their view, the Khmer power center had simply moved upriver, inland and northward, away from the delta and coast that now comprise southern Việt Nam. Funan's once-flourishing port of Óc Eo lay abandoned, but Chenla and subsequent Cambodian kingdoms continued to claim authority over the Khmer-speaking rural populations who still inhabited the former Funanese heartland in the Mekong delta.

Compared with Funan's slow decline, the fate of Linyi was dramatic. China's court ministers told the new emperor Sui Yangdi at his accession in 604 that Linyi was "full of the strange and the precious," but that it had paid no tribute for a decade. The emperor dispatched an invasion force of "more than ten thousand soldiers and several thousand criminals." The army sailed south from Jiao in 605, landed on the central coast near modern Đà Nẵng, and sacked the Linyi capital. Imperial forces plundered the city, carting away "eighteen gold statues and 1,350 volumes of Buddhist sutras," along with books written in the local Kunlun language and script. On the march home from Jiao, however, an epidemic wiped out the Sui army, including its commander.[52] For its part, Linyi again recovered, and in 623 it resumed sending tribute missions to China. Imperial annals record the arrival of twenty-six such missions by 749, when Linyi sent "a hundred strings of pearls," thirty catties of gharu wood, fresh cotton, and "twenty tame elephants." However, like Funan, Linyi eventually succumbed to neighboring competition. Chinese sources mention it for the last time in 793.[53] A successor polity known to the Chinese as "Huanwang" (probably the southern Cham port kingdom, Pāṇḍuraṅga) replaced Linyi in imperial histories, and then it in turn disappeared from the record in 877.[54]

The beneficiary to the south was the new realm of Champa. This was probably not a single kingdom but a string of Cham-speaking port states on the central coast, some of which expanded north to occupy Linyi's former territory. Half a century after the sacking of Linyi, Chinese historians record the arrival in 657 of the first mission from "Zhan-po" (Champa). A local Sanskrit inscription dated the next year tells of a Cham prince who had traveled to Cambodia and married a daughter of King Isanavarman, and a Khmer inscription from 667 mentions an envoy sent from Cambodia to a Champa ruler.[55]

The modern central Vietnamese province of Quảng Nam, where a fourth-century Cham inscription was uncovered in 1935, became the initial center of the new kingdom. A score of Sanskrit inscriptions dating from the fifth to the eighth centuries have also been found in Quảng Nam, mostly in the valley of the Thu Bồn River. This was a key region, the location of both Trà Kiệu from the first century CE and the flourishing sixth-century Cham center at Mỹ Sơn.[56] Emerging from a long cultural heritage, this northern Cham area was politically coming into its own and eclipsing both Linyi and Huanwang.

ANTI-TANG REBELLIONS

Despite the flowering of local Confucianism and Buddhist influences from China, there were more anti-imperial rebellions in Annam from the sixth to tenth centuries than there had been in the first to fifth. What was perhaps Annam's first "peasant revolt" wracked the territory in 687.[57] In 722, rebel leader Mai Thúc Loan formed an alliance with Champa and Chenla, occupied the Nghệ An area, and proclaimed himself "the Swarthy Emperor" (*Hắc Đế*).[58] That attempt failed to drive out the empire, but others followed, with increasing frequency. New revolts erupted in 770 and 791. Rebel leader Phùng Hưng mounted a serious challenge to Tang rule from 782 into the 790s. From 803 to 863 alone, rebels killed or expelled no fewer than six protectors-general of Annam.[59]

Troops working on Jiaozhou city's fortifications revolted in 803 and drove out the protector-general. In 819–20, Dương Thanh, a soldier from Hoan (formerly Rinan), took over Jiao's citadel of Đại La. He put to death the governor and his family, as well as more than a thousand other Chinese. Eight years later, another uprising briefly expelled a third governor.[60] Meanwhile, in 824, according to thirteenth-century Vietnamese annals, the Chinese governor Lý Nguyên Hỷ had noticed an indigenous aquatic omen at the old city of Luy Lâu, the regional market town. The Dâu River in front of Luy Lâu's citadel "was suddenly flowing the wrong way." Concerned that this presaged another local revolt, the governor moved the regional market center from Luy Lâu to Annam's capital, Đại La.[61] Then in 843, a modern historian tells us, "When the military commissioner of Annam put his troops to work restoring the walls, they mutinied again, burnt the city, plundered its treasury, and drove the commissioner back to Guangzhou."[62] Two years later a Chinese official underlined the serious security situation in Annam: "At every stream, cave, marketplace, everywhere there is stubbornness. Repression is necessary. Once every three years soldiers have to be taken out to patrol and repress, then to report the situation."[63]

Nevertheless, for most of the Tang era, agrarian lowland Annam was relatively tranquil.[64] The gravest threat to imperial authority there was probably a series of increasingly serious revolts by hill peoples of various ethnolinguistic groups living in the north and west of the protectorate. These uplanders from Annam's mountains and ravines, and beyond, attacked down into the heart of the Red River plain. The threat escalated after they had formed an external alliance with Nanzhao, a formidable new independent upland kingdom across the border in neighboring regions of what is now southwest China. An early omen was an internal rebellion in 791 against the Tang protector of Annam, launched by "a local chief" named Du Yinghan, described in a Chinese source as "chief of the *Man*," or southern barbarians.[65] From the 850s, Nanzhao's successful recruitment of *Man* upland groups inside Annam posed a dire threat to local Tang rule, from which it would recover only briefly before the dynasty itself collapsed in 905.

REVOLT OF THE HILL PEOPLES

After crushing the Trưng sisters' rebellion in 43–44 CE, Ma Yuan erected bronze pillars at the frontiers he had pacified. Some demarcated the far southern region that soon became part of Linyi, and later of Champa. But to mark both Jiaozhi's northwest frontier and the extreme southwestern limits of Han control, Ma Yuan also reportedly placed bronze border posts at the distant hill town of Anning, in the high watershed above the Red River in what is now China's Yunnan province. Anning was a forty-eight-day journey upriver from the capital of Jiaozhi. A little farther, only four days from that border, was the site of the hill town of Chü-mieh.[66] Chinese power rarely extended that far west. However, by the mid-eighth century, the imperial writ had disappeared even from Anning. Frontier patrols had withdrawn far down the valleys to the southeast. The northwest border of the Tang Protectorate of Annam was now near Pu-t'ou, less than thirty-five days' travel from the capital Đại La, or Jiaozhou city.[67] And Chü-mieh, a three-week journey farther north, had fallen way out of Chinese reach to become "the seat of the *Man* king," the capital of Nanzhao.[68] In the ninth century, this mountain realm launched traumatic invasions of both Annam and southwest China.

The peoples whom the Chinese called *Man*, southern "barbarians," were diverse uplanders. Groups of Pai *Man* ("White *Man*") inhabited the hills north of Anning. To its south were the Wu *Man* ("Black *Man*"). Many Wu *Man* lived within the borders Ma Yuan had once demarcated, in the highlands overlooking the Red River plain from the west and northwest. Others lived still farther south, even south of the Tang border at Pu-t'ou, within the northern frontier of Annam (and of modern Việt Nam). Fan Chuo, a Chinese official who served as secretary of Annam in the mid-ninth century, recorded in his work *Man Shu* (*Book of the Southern Barbarians*) the great extent of the territory that the hill peoples of Annam occupied. To depart from the region of the "Southern *Man*," he wrote, "From Pu-t'ou one proceeds by boat" southward, downstream along the Red River "for 35 days."[69]

Founded by a Wu *Man* prince in the seventh century, Nanzhao (Southern Kingdom) soon combined six southern *Man* principalities in the upper reaches of the Red and Mekong Rivers, inhabited by Wu *Man*. They spoke Tibeto-Burman languages related to those of the modern Lolo people who still straddle the Vietnam-China border.[70] Small Lolo groups living in the hills of northern Việt Nam today call themselves Man Di, Man Chi, or Mun Di (*Man* here meaning "people").[71] Fan Chuo's ninth-century depiction of the southern *Man* recalls the ancient Lạc and Yuè: "The traditional custom, at the beginning of the 1st month, at night, is to sound drums suspended from the waist, with singing." In the mid-fifth month, they "order the horse-riding stalwarts to paint paddles and ten boats with horns. A thousand persons all sing in unison and (beat) drums. They knock the sides of the boat and float down the river, riding the waves."[72]

During the eighth century, Nanzhao had expanded south into the lowlands and incorporated diverse groups such as the Mang *Man*, who lived on the west bank of the Mekong and spoke a Tai language.[73] Meanwhile Tang China expanded into the same region, northwest from Annam. According to Fan Chuo, Tang officials "opened the Pu-t'ou road." They seized control of rich salt wells at the former border town of Anning and completed the route linking it to Jiaozhou. They built a walled city at Anning, levying taxes and conscripting labor.[74] This provoked a local revolt, Fan Chuo tells us: "The tribal *Man* were worried and excited. They trapped and killed the officers building the city." The Tang emperor ordered Nanzhao's king Mêng Kuei-i, his then *Man* ally, to punish the rebels. Soon various *Man* groups "were violently at odds." Mêng Kuei-i occupied the Ho *Man* town of Chü-mieh, four days' journey from Anning. He made it his capital and "drove out the Ho *Man*."[75] That was their first deportation.

Nanzhao expanded further under its king Ko-lo-fêng (r. 748–69), who turned to an alliance with Tibet, conquered the Pai *Man*, and fought a war with China. The Tang court sent an army up from Annam to punish Nanzhao. Imperial forces "recovered An-ning city, including the bronze pillars of Ma Yüan." But pursuing the assault against Nanzhao, they "lost 200,000 men."[76]

Ko-lo-fêng's grandson I-mou-hsün used Annam as a conduit to repair relations with Tang China. His mother and wife hailed from a group of Wu *Man* who lived near the former Jiaozhi border at Anning.[77] I-mou-hsün sent an envoy downriver to the imperial protector-general of Annam, Chao Ch'ang, who informed the emperor from Jiaozhou that the *Man* wished "to become subjects of China." A Tang delegation to Nanzhao passed through Jiaozhou city in 794. City officials went all out to display the mission's importance. They "sent out a company of 200 infantry and a company of 100 cavalry to line both sides of the road, and stand in rows. (Also) a company of 60 armoured cavalry to lead the van, and 500 infantry men with spears."[78]

When the envoys reached Nanzhao's capital of Chü-mieh, they found a well-defended multistorey palace, streetscape, and concentric fortifications with rows of high gate towers and a curtain wall. Nanzhao mustered its four armies annually. "Spears, swords, armour, helmets, cutlasses worn at the waist—must all be tempered and sharp." Each company on the march comprised frontline infantry, archers, and thirty cavalry.[79]

Nanzhao forces "plundered the cities and villages of the Tibetans," and in 794 I-mou-hsün conquered the principality of Lang-chao, driving its Ho *Man* residents east, almost to the borders of Annam. There they settled, thirty-nine days' march from Jiaozhou city.[80] With Nanzhao's armies, descendants of these now twice-deported Ho *Man* played a significant role when war broke out again.

A SIEGE

In 854, trouble erupted on both sides of Annam's hill borders. Conflict within the protectorate proved as serious as *Man* attacks from without. Its Tang garrisons would soon find themselves under military assault by forces drawn from eight or more different upland groups, at least three of them from within the borders of Annam. In the northwest, the Tang controlled the Red River valley from Đại La (Jiaozhou city) as far as Gu-yong-bu, a twenty-five-day journey upstream. This area, Fan Chuo recorded, was "all dependent on and attached to the administration of Annam." But a protectorate official (*ci shi*) could also "depute the native chiefs to take a hand in the management." Some of these local chiefs were called "lords of the Ravines" (*wan*). Their regions were known as *jimi zhou*, or tribal frontier prefectures held by "bridle and halter," or "loose reins"—that is, dependent on the empire but governed indirectly, by their own chiefs. Tang Annam included as many as forty-one such prefectures.[81] One *jimi zhou* was the home of the "Peach-Flower" (Tao Hua) people, who lived, according to Fan Chuo, "on each side of the Seven *Wan* and Ravines of Lin-hsi-yüan [Lin-xi-yuan] of Annam. The people wear sheep-skins. Some wear felt. They comb their hair into a knot in front.... The great chieftain, lord of the Seven *Wan* and Ravines, Li Yu-tu [Li Yu Du, *V.* Lý Đô Đốc] administered and controlled them. They also served as frontier-guards on the border. Every year, too, they paid land tax and other duties."[82] These Peach-Flower tribal people would also play a major role in the coming conflict.

First, dissension broke out among the top Tang officials in Annam. The protector-general (*duhu*) developed an "attitude of opposition" to the imperial general (*jing lue shi*). The latter, Li Zhuo, had taken up his post in 854.

Fan Chuo called him "oppressive and cruel." Li Zhuo ordered the men taking salt to barter with the Chong Mo *Man* of the Seven *Wan* and Ravines, to pay them only "1 peck of salt" for each horse or head of cattle. That fixed low price ended the trade: "Relations were blocked and severed." The hill people brought in "no more cattle or horses" for sale.[83]

Also in 854, Li Zhuo refused to deploy the regular garrison of Tang troops to help guard the northwest border during the winter months. According to Fan Chuo, Li Zhuo chose to implement an official request from a local department magistrate "for the dismissal of the winter garrison—6,000 officers and able-bodied men. They did not want a restraining guard on the frontiers."[84] Then the protector-general of Annam, "without authority," compounded the error by dismissing the chief of the Peach-Flower people, Lý Đô Đốc, "and others, seven chieftains of the *Wan*, lords of the Ravines, of the winter-defence forces." Đô Đốc's brothers "could not endure this." They decided to throw in their lot with Nanzhao. Crossing the border, the brothers made the ten-day journey to Chê-tung, where a *Man* official seized the chance to seal an alliance. He appointed Đô Đốc's son to a Nanzhao military command. With that transfer of local allegiance, Tang Annam lost control of its upland border region. "From this time onwards the Seven *Wan* and Ravines were all taken over and administered by the *Man*."[85]

The rebel task was made easier by the cruelty of Imperial General Li Zhuo, who, Fan Chuo wrote, "carried on the work of flaying and massacring. He caused living beings to suffer pain."[86] Before leaving Annam for good in 855, Li Zhuo killed both the governor of the Mã River plain province of Ái (formerly Jiuzhen), and the leader of the upland Ch'i-tung *Man*. Within two years the latter were attacking Tang administrative posts.[87] Fan Chuo reported: "The native areas [literally, 'valleys and ravines'] were divided in heart. The native chiefs within the frontiers were subsequently seduced by the *Man* rebels." Having aligned with the *Man*, the tribal peoples "again became close friends with them. As days passed and months came, we gradually had to encounter raids and sudden attacks.... This caused a number of places to fall into rebel hands."[88] In 858, the Tang court sent a new protector-general to Annam. He upgraded its military and fortified Đại La by planting a thick palisade of reeds around the city, "surrounded by a deep moat and then another thicket of sharpened bamboo." However, his successor provoked a local tribal group by executing its leader. Once again an upland people appealed for help to Nanzhao. Its forces attacked deep into Annam in 860–61 and briefly captured Đại La itself.[89] A Tang army quickly drove the rebels from the capital, but they remained camped a few days away, a continuing threat.

Over the next several years, Fan Chuo penned a vivid portrait of these upland communities on the march against imperial rule of Annam. He had a unique opportunity to observe the interaction of the *Man* invaders from afar with the local hill people, who were led by chiefs like "the petty rebel," Zhu Daogu, apparently a *wan* lord. Jiaozhi's governor (*shang shu*), Tsai Xi, secretly instructed Chuo "to ride alone, with not more than 20 sturdy foot-soldiers, and deeply penetrate the enemy camp and stockade of the rebel commander," Zhu Daogu. He set out in early April 862. After a four-day journey, Chuo later reported to the emperor, "We entered the double enclosure of the rebels."[90] He met with Zhu and visited the Man *panguan* (judge) who had come to the camp from their stronghold of Chê-tung. The judge "had at his command eight *Man* holding bows and spears" guarding his back. Chuo asked Zhu where they came from. "He explained that they were T'ao Hua," that is, local Peach-Flower people of Annam, from "each side of the Seven *Wan* and Ravines." But they had come to consider themselves as *Man*. "Now also they are called T'ao Hua *Man*." Fan Chuo wrote that they yet retained sympathy for the empire despite switching their loyalty to the *Man*, and he speculated that "their hearts are all inclined towards Tang civilization."[91]

Fan Chuo was a resourceful spy. He managed to meet four Wu *Man* (Black *Man*) commanders. "All day long I talked with the *Man* rebel generals.... I got their clan-names and personal names, and (learnt) their reasons for having set up a frontier city and made themselves into a kingdom of their own." But he was not impressed. "Their words were cunning and deceitful. Your humble servant broke off (negotiations) and returned." Back in Đại La, he delivered his report to the protector-general of Annam, Wang K'uan. "Point by point I explained everything." However, "K'uan was conceited and stupid, quite incapable of making farsighted plans. He received your humble servant's written report, but entirely failed to issue any directions." That was costly. Within a week, "five or six thousand" Peach-Flower rebels were "encamped below the west corner of Annam city." It was April 23, 862; another siege had begun. And the attacking commander was a former local magistrate, Ma Kuang-kao, who had defected to the rebels. The *Man* leader, Yang Ssu-chin, had "deputed" him to command the assault.[92] Disaster loomed. It stemmed not merely from external attack but also from a breakdown of the domestic channels of Tang authority and governance, especially in upland Annam.

Fan Chuo stressed the local causes of this threat. "For several years past, because the senior commissioners of the two regions [Jiao and Yung to its north] have been harsh and cruel, licentious, putting to death innocent men, this has resulted in the *Man* masses laying complaints about their wrongs; and so now they are continually coming to attack and raid." He concluded: "The cause of all this cannot but be that the senior administrators were the wrong men." Besides Li Zhuo, he blamed both the protector-general for "failure in his official duty to summon and punish" and the new imperial general, Li Xianggu, who was "reckless, avaricious and injurious, and consequently had to levy troops." Corruption was a serious problem too. Fan Chuo noted the case of the *Zhaotao fushi* ("Assistant Commissioner for summoning and punishing"). "When he entered the court to give judgment on cases, every month the allowance for provender that had to be provided for him amounted to 70 strings of cash." Only Fan Chuo's capable superior officer, the governor of Tonkin, Tsai Xi, was able to mount an effective defense of Đại La. Tsai Xi took command of the troops in place of Wang K'uan.[93]

That winter, the fighting season, a Nanzhao army of fifty thousand invaded Annam.[94] The siege of Đại La began in mid-January 863. Fan Chuo detailed the enemy's order of battle. Apart from the five to six thousand local Peach-Flower forces, leading rebel regiments included two to three thousand Mang *Man*, Tai-speaking auxiliaries from beyond the Mekong who "mustered on the Su-li river bank" near the city on January 14. Fan Chuo recorded that the Mang *Man* "wear trousers of blue cloth and tangle their waists with canes and strips of bamboo. With red silken cloth they bind their headdress, leaving the spill of it to hang behind as an ornament." Another rebel regiment consisted of Lo-hsing *Man*, also "called the *Yeh-Man*" (Wild *Man*), who "wear no clothes, but only take the bark of trees to conceal their bodies." These troops assembled "in the front line of the battle array. If any of them did not advance or charge, the *Man* directing the battle-front would at once cut them down from behind."[95]

By January 20, the *Man* army "closely besieged the moated city." They included Ho *Man* forces from Annam's borderlands, thirty-nine days' march away, who "set up their camp in the old city of Su-li. When stations were assigned to the rebel hosts on the wooden rafts and bamboo rafts, there were ... more than 2000 men." The besieging force also included Hsün-chüan *Man*, who "go barefoot, and can tread on brambles and thorns. Holding bows in their hands and arrows under their arms, they shoot." They adorned their headdress with dog's teeth, wore pig-skin belts, and when in battle "encage[d] their heads with wicker cages, like metal-caps or helmets." On January 20, defenders led by Tsai Xi, using "small spears and pointed weapons," killed more than a hundred of the Hsün-chüan Man attackers. Afterward Tsai Xi asked who they were. A city official named Liang K'o recognized the dead by their distinctive helmets and belts. Chuo recorded what happened to the enemy corpses: "The troops of the Chiang-hsi General took the flesh of these *Man* and broiled it."[96]

Liang K'o himself soon exemplified the breakdown of Tang local authority. He was a P'u-tzu *Man* with a "guest" appointment in the Jiaozhou administration. The attackers included some of his fellow P'u-tzu *Man*, whom Chuo described as "brave, fierce, nimble and active" fighters, dressed in blue silk-cotton trousers. On January 25, Tsai Xi captured some of them alive on the battlefront. His troops then tortured and killed the prisoners. Chuo reported: "When examined under flogging, none of them said a word. When their wrists were severed, they also made no sound." Liang K'o, possibly shocked by these arbitrary executions of his fellow tribesmen, later defected to the invaders. The next year Fan Chuo reported that Liang K'o was "now to be seen among the rebels, arrogating to himself the title of magistrate of Chu-yüan-hsien."[97]

The enemy forces tightened their noose around Đại La. Before dawn on the morning of January 28, "a *Hu* Buddhist monk" appeared outside the city's southern walls, "naked, holding a staff bound with white silk." The Chinese term *Hu* meant "western barbarians," usually Indians, Tibetans, or Central Asians. Fan Chuo described how this monk "strutted forwards and backwards making passes." Then, from the battlements, commanding officer Tsai Xi drew a bow and took aim. His arrow "hit in the breast of this scheming *Hu* monk. Lots of the *Man* helped in carrying him back to the camp." Jiaozhou's defenders were jubilant. "Within the city there were none among the officers or men who did not make a din with the drums."[98]

The vanguard of the Nanzhao armies comprised Wang-chü-tzu *Man* from west of the Mekong. Fan Chuo described these troops as "warlike, nimble, and good at using the lance and the *ch'an* on horseback. When they ride a horse, they do not use a saddle. They go barefoot. They wear a short jerkin barely protecting the breast and stomach—that is all. Their legs and knees are all bare. On their caps and helmets they stick yak-hair. They gallop and charge as if they are flying. Their womenfolk also can do the like." From the city wall on February 14, using a mechanical crossbow or ballista, Governor Tsai Xi "shot down 200 men of the Wang-chü-tzu" and felled "over 30 horses."[99]

Still the besiegers pressed the attack. In a gesture of desperation, Tsai Xi ordered Fan Chuo to have a scribe write out copies of the oath of loyalty to the empire once sworn by the *Man* king I-mou-hsün. "All these documents were fastened on to a mechanical crossbow and shot flying into the rebels' camp." There was no response. Chuo observed bitterly that "the descendants of the Southern *Man* have disregarded and turned their backs on their former oath." Now, he added, "the Way of Heaven is bound to punish them."[100]

But all hope was lost, with "twelve camps of rebel hosts" outside Đại La. Fan Chuo recounted the capital's final agony. By February 28, 863, Governor Tsai Xi had lost all his "principal followers . . . over 70 men, they all perished."

Finally, already "wounded by arrows and stones," the governor was again "hit by an arrow in the left shoulder." A force led by the *Man* commander Yang Ssu-chin now fought its way into the inner city. Fan Chuo's eldest son, T'ao, "and servants and maidservants, 14 persons, all were trapped."[101] Chuo himself was wounded by an arrow in the right wrist. To escape the city and make for the river bank, he had to abandon the mortally wounded Tsai Xi but found and saved the governor's seal of office. "I took off the seal, swam, and crossed the river," he recalled in his memoir. For his part, Tsai Xi made it as far as the bank and pushed off in a boat. However, it capsized in midstream, drowning him.[102] The city's surviving defenders also attempted to escape across the river. Four hundred or more "officers and able-bodied men" armed with cutlasses, "riding on horseback, rushed out to the water-edge east of the city." But all the boats were gone. Three commanders addressed the officers and men: "Now, my lads, we've all reached the river, but there are no boats. If we enter the river, we are sure to die. But if we form a band of brothers, and each of us manages to kill two *Man* rebels, we too shall gain something."[103]

So together they turned their backs to the river and rode once more into the fray. "They entered the eastern perimeter of the city, and crowded inside the gate. On one side they drew up the 'Long Cutlasses,'" on the other their cavalry. Later that morning the rebel horsemen who had unsuccessfully pursued them from the city walls to the river rode back to the city gate, unaware that the defenders had regrouped there. The rebels rode into an ambush, "taking no precautions whatsoever." The defenders charged from the gate in formation, cutting through the surprised *Man* ranks. A Buddhist monk later told Fan Chuo that by noon the desperate defenders had killed "nearly two or three thousand rebels, and over 300 horses." Already inside the inner city, *Man* commander Yang Ssu-chin learned of the debacle only that evening, when he went out to rescue his troops.[104] Jiaozhou finally fell. Surviving Tang forces evacuated Annam for the north, crossing the border to the garrison town of Hepu ("Sea Gate"), which became the new provisional capital of Annam, "temporary Jiaozhou."[105]

Within Annam, the *Man* armies moved to consolidate their victory. On June 25, 863, more than four thousand *Man* troops, with two thousand local rebels under Zhu Daogu, "together rowing several hundred small boats," invested the riverbank prefectural center of Chün-zhou, capturing an Annamese general and officers. But a commander from the headquarters of the governor-general counterattacked. He "took ten large sailing junks and war boats, and rammed and damaged the boats of the Man rebels: over thirty were sunk." Fan Chuo learned that "the Man rebels were unable to swim, so every one of them were drowned." However, the continuing

Annamese resistance received little northern help, Chuo complained. "The native chieftains (*shou-ling*), and military and civil officers (*chiang-li*), . . . both in spring and summer, unceasingly appealed for troops to rescue them. From that time Sea Gate refused to dispatch (troops). At the same time it failed to supply spears, armour, bows, crossbows, thus causing the *Man* rebels to invade and plunder the troops of the divisions (*chou*)." Yet these defenders were still holding out a year later, Chuo reported: "Chiang-yüan and likewise the various *chou* (divisions) each guards itself firmly." He submitted his report in late 864, "at the river-mouth of the divisional headquarters of the commander of Annam."[106]

In two successful attacks on Annam and its capital, in 861 and 863, Nanzhao forces killed or captured more than 150,000 Chinese and their Annamese subjects.[107] A fourteenth-century Vietnamese author, writing in exile in China, assigned a large role to tropical disease: "Of the Chinese sent to defend the country, seven out of ten perished because of the climate, and the brigands were only stronger."[108] In his report at the time, Fan Chuo called the southern *Man* "violent and bad persons, and difficult to reform." He urged the Tang court to "invade and attack them from all four sides," in the "hope to wipe out their host of ant-swarms, and purge for ever" these "barbarian rebels."[109]

Two years later, after a hard-fought reconquest of Đại La, the victorious Tang general Gao Pian captured and beheaded the *Man* chief Duan Qiuqian "along with thirty thousand of his men."[110] The Chinese also captured and executed Zhu Daogu and other local rebel leaders.[111]

Gao Pian (*V.* Cao Biền) then ruled Annam as a military commissioner. In 866 he renamed the protectorate "The Peaceful Sea Army" (Jinghaijun).[112] As well as building roads, bridges, dikes, and canals, he dredged approaches to the harbors to facilitate transportation to and from the north. His grandson, who succeeded him in 868 and ruled for a decade, erected a tablet in Gao Pian's name, proclaiming: "Prosperity comes riding in boats . . . Causing the sea to form a channel, Where boats can pass in safety, With the deep sea stretching out peacefully, A highway of supply for our city."[113]

Gao Pian also built a new citadel at Đại La. By the late ninth century, an eighteen-foot dike encircling four and a half miles of thirty-foot walls protected as many as five thousand new buildings. This unprecedentedly large capital project must have employed a huge labor force and significantly expanded local administrative power. Except for brief interludes, Đại La would remain the regional center for the foreseeable future, eventually becoming Hanoi. Yet, as a classically educated official (who also espoused Daoism), Gao Pian was just as concerned about the past. He wrote, "The land of Jiaozhou is beautiful; So it has been from eternity. The worthy men of old extend their welcome." But he added, in deference to local tradition, "Then one is not ungrateful to the spirits." Gao Pian commemorated the spirit of Zhào Tuó, ancient founder of Nán Yuè. A decade later his former aide-de-camp, Zeng Gun, even called Jiaozhou "the Southern Kingdom":

> The mountains and rivers of the Southern Kingdom are beautiful;
> The place where the Dragon Spirit dwells is blessed.
> Jiaozhou has ceased to be pressed down.[114]

Gao Pian and his successors deftly maintained the unexceptionable long-standing combination of classical scholarship and spirit worship, as well as the delicate balance between imperial and local interests. They also served as a transitional regime. After their departure in 880, power would pass to local figures, beginning with the Sinicized class governing from Đại La in the name of the empire, speaking a local dialect of what linguists call Middle Chinese. Only late in the tenth century would leaders from a more indigenous cultural background displace this Sino-Việt elite.[115] Then, to establish their authority beyond Đại La, throughout the former Tang province of Annam, the new authorities would again require the cooperation of the various regional spirits.

Meanwhile, local unrest continued. A Chinese general campaigned against ethnic minority groups ("aboriginals") in Annam from 874 to 879.[116] Troops from Annam whom the Tang had deployed north to what is now Guangxi province mutinied there in 877, forcing their surveillance commissioner to flee. In the Jiaozhou capital three years later, the army again rose up and drove out military commissioner Zeng Gun, Gao Pian's aide-de-camp during the Nanzhao war. Chinese records state that in the spring of 880 "there was a mutiny of the army in Annam." Zeng Gun, the commissioner for the Peaceful Sea Army, "left the city [Đại La?] and fled." Late that summer a report reached the Tang court: "Now the garrison city in Annam is held by rebellious troops, and the Commissioner is attacking it without success, while many of the remaining [loyal] troops have already gone off home on their own initiative."[117] Zeng Gun withdrew from Annam that year. The Tang dynasty was in decline and, with it, imperial control in Annam. For the next twenty-five years (880–905), no Chinese governor ruled there.[118]

However, two centuries of imperial repression of successive indigenous rebel forces from both the coast and the uplands of Annam ensured that even when the Tang court collapsed in 905, the local Sinicized elite remained in power. They were a group descended in part from generations of Chinese settlers who had arrived in Jiao at different points during the first millennium. They had come from various provinces of China, most bringing their own dialects of Chinese. Settling in Annam, they had developed a new local dialect, dubbed "Annamese Middle Chinese." During the three centuries of the Tang era, most speakers of this Chinese dialect became bilingual, as they or their children or grandchildren also learned the Vietic language or languages of their indigenous neighbors, mostly members of the Viet-Mường linguistic subgroup. Meanwhile, over the centuries of imperial rule several Vietic languages of Annam had adopted some elements of Chinese vocabulary, as well as tones. It was from this successive two-way language shift and the combination of Annamese Middle Chinese with Viet-Mường that the Vietnamese language first emerged in Annam in the late first millennium CE.[119]

SUGGESTIONS OF AN INDIGENOUS WRITING SYSTEM

Possibly even a thousand years earlier, in the late first millennium BCE, Yuè elites in what is now southern China may have already adopted a form of writing based on Chinese characters to record terms from their own languages. If so, such words or scripts could be intelligible only to those who knew both classical Chinese and the indigenous language(s) whose sounds they represented. During imperial rule of Jiaozhi during the early first millennium CE, local texts written in Chinese probably also included some characters adapted to represent Proto-Viet-Mường sounds, usually personal names or Vietic toponyms that had no Chinese equivalent. The fifth-century text *Tá Âm*, for instance, apparently detailed "the method of using sounds to describe Vietnamese objects that do not exist in China."[120] Some scholars date the use in Jiaozhi of demotic characters for this purpose to the Late Han era under Shi Xie (187–226 CE), but many disagree. The first extant specific usage may have been in 791, nine years after Phùng Hưng overthrew the Tang governor and briefly took control of the Protectorate of Annam. Two years after Phùng Hưng's death in 789, his son and successor accorded him the posthumous title *Bố Cái Đại Vương* ("Great *Bố Cái* King"), sometimes translated as "father and mother of the people."[121] A fourteenth-century interpretation of the title's first two terms, then written in characters with an unclear contextual meaning in Chinese, asserted that they were Vietnamese words, eighth-century "local usage" for "father" and "mother." However, the original eighth-century title does not survive in any inscription or other contemporary written form, and it remains possible that its actual words were not *bố cái* but *vua cái* ("great king").[122] The first extant use of any characters of the Vietnamese script that came to be known as "southern letters" (*chữ nôm*) may be the contemporary Chinese inscription dated just seven years later adorning the bronze bell cast in Annam in 798, which includes the earliest record of the recognizably Vietnamese female middle name Thị.[123]

It is just possible that other first-millennium texts might once have existed to link ancient character-based demotic writings of Nán Yuè or other southern kingdoms of the last centuries BCE with the later full emergence of *chữ nôm* in the mid-second millennium CE. Unsurprisingly, no first-millennium documents of this kind survive. Such texts were targets for deliberate destruction at each end of the long historical process of the emergence of a Vietnamese language and demotic script: first in the "burning of the books" by the Qin dynasty of the third century BCE and second during the twenty-year Ming reconquest of Việt Nam in the early fifteenth century CE.

INDEPENDENCE

The Tang dynasty's collapse in 905 led to decades of division in the north. Conflict raged between the Later Liang dynasty, founded in north-central China in 907, and the Southern Han dynasty, established in Guangdong in 917. In the south, an ancient political geography also reasserted itself. Short-lived states with long-familiar names cropped up to rival the Southern Han: the Yangxi river kingdoms of Wu and Ch'u and, on the east coast, Wu-Yuè and Min.[124] The latter two bore the classical names of Yuè kingdoms that the Qin had conquered in the first millennium BCE.

In Annam, a leader named Khúc Thừa Dụ, "from a powerful local family in Jiaozhou," took over in 905 as commissioner for the Peaceful Sea Army, proclaiming allegiance to the Later Liang and keeping Annam out of the war to its north. Six years later his grandson Khúc Thừa Mỹ sent gold, camphor, and vessels made of gold and silver in Southeast Asian kingdoms as tribute to the Liang court. The Liang recognized Thừa Mỹ as "acting governor of Annam" and sent him a ceremonial banner and ax. However the Liang dynasty collapsed in 923, and Thừa Mỹ could expect only hostility from the Southern Han, whose ruler told him: "You, sir, always reckoned me to be a mere pretender." A Southern Han invading force captured Thừa Mỹ and ended Khúc family rule in October 930.[125] But imperial power was limited and temporary. When a former vassal of the Khúc family, Dương Đình Nghệ, launched a rebellion, the Southern Han parlayed, awarded him a title, and sent him back to his home district of Ái, south of the Red River delta. To Jiao, the court dispatched its own officials with instructions to rule in the indirect manner appropriate for non-Chinese "aboriginals" governed by hereditary native chiefs: "The people of Jiaozhi are fond of rebellion; you can simply 'lead them with halter and bridle' and that is all." In Ái, within a year Dương Đình Nghệ had raised a three-thousand-strong army of retainers whom he called his "adopted sons." He seized power throughout Annam in 931 and proclaimed himself "Commissioner of the Peaceful South" (Annam).[126] Like the Khúc family, the Dương clan would hold power for decades.

A usurper murdered Dương Đình Nghệ in 937. His son-in-law Ngô Quyền led an army from Ái against the usurper, who then appealed to the Southern Han for help.[127] An imperial fleet and marines commanded by Emperor Liu Yen's son, Prince Hoằng Thao, sailed to the coast of Annam and headed inland up the Bạch Đằng River, a northern arm of the Red River delta, to confront Ngô Quyền. Liu Yen himself set out from Guangdong, following his son's fleet with additional forces.[128]

Two fourteenth-century Vietnamese accounts tell the story of what happened next. The first history, written by Lê Tắc in exile in China, relates that Ngô Quyền had set up "many lines of stakes" at the mouth of the Red River and "had the piles sharpened and tipped with iron."[129] Quyền determined to bring Hoằng Thao's navy to battle before Liu Yen's reinforcements could reach the seaport of Hải Môn. He ordered his troops at the river mouth, the anonymous author of the mid fourteenth-century *Việt sử lược* says, "to plant iron-tipped sharp spikes under the water, on the river bed."[130] When the tide rose, Quyền ordered fleets of small boats to first head upriver, harass the imperial navy, and then lure it downriver by "feigning a retreat."[131] The Annamese craft, according to the *Việt sử lược*, soon "pretended to be scared" and headed off downstream. "Hoằng Thao chased after them. When the tide dropped, Quyền turned to the attack and pushed [the fleet] back towards the sea. Now the spikes were above the water level. Hoằng Thao's ships were caught on the spikes and broken up. Half of the Southern Han troops were killed. Most drowned. Hoằng Thao was killed."[132] Lê Tắc adds: "At that moment, [Liu] Yen entered Hải Môn, but learning that his troops had not been fortunate, he turned back."[133] Annam was independent. Ngô Quyền proclaimed himself a monarch and set up his court at the ancient Lạc fortress of Cổ-loa.[134]

During a millennium of imperial rule and colonization, the indigenous peoples had learned much from their rulers, especially in the fields of literature and administration. Perhaps it was only coincidence that local knowledge of the rivers and tides, which the ancient Lạc had once mastered, now secured the victory that opened the way to a new kingdom. But it would reclaim the ancient name Nán Yuè, as Lý Bí had done in the sixth century.

PART THREE

Kingdoms

CHAPTER 4

"Rice from the Sky"

Assembling the Spirits of Đại Việt, 940–1340

From the tenth century, Vietnamese history comes into its own. After millennia of undocumented prehistory and a thousand years of imperial rule documented only in Chinese, new indigenous historical sources throw increasing light on political, economic, and cultural developments in the territory that had comprised the Protectorate of Annam. How new were these developments? A tenth-century ruler revived for a second time the ancient name of the kingdom of Nán Yuè in its Vietnamese form, Nam Việt.[1] But this new kingdom would then adopt a new name, Đại Việt (Great Việt), and unlike its classical Yuè predecessors and short-lived tenth-century counterparts in south China, it successfully resisted reintegration into the empire.

The new autonomous Việt realm inherited both the Sino-Vietnamese hereditary aristocracy and the provincial geography of Tang Annam. From north to south, it was a diverse region of five provinces and border marches. Restive ethnic Tai and other upland groups, formerly allied to the defunct Nanzhao kingdom, straddled the mountainous northern frontier.[2] Lowland Jiao province in the central plain of the Red and Bạch Đằng rivers was the most Sinicized region, home to most of the northern settlers and traders and an influential Sino-Vietnamese Buddhist community, as well as Vietic-speaking rice farmers.[3] Here the Vietnamese language was emerging as settlers adopted the Proto-Việt-Mường tongue of their indigenous neighbors, infusing it with much of their Annamese Middle Chinese vocabulary. Indigenous Vietic speakers also lived in Phong province, the western delta, and adjacent highlands and ravines, along with those the Chinese called "aboriginal" ethnic minorities and hill peoples, including Tai speakers.

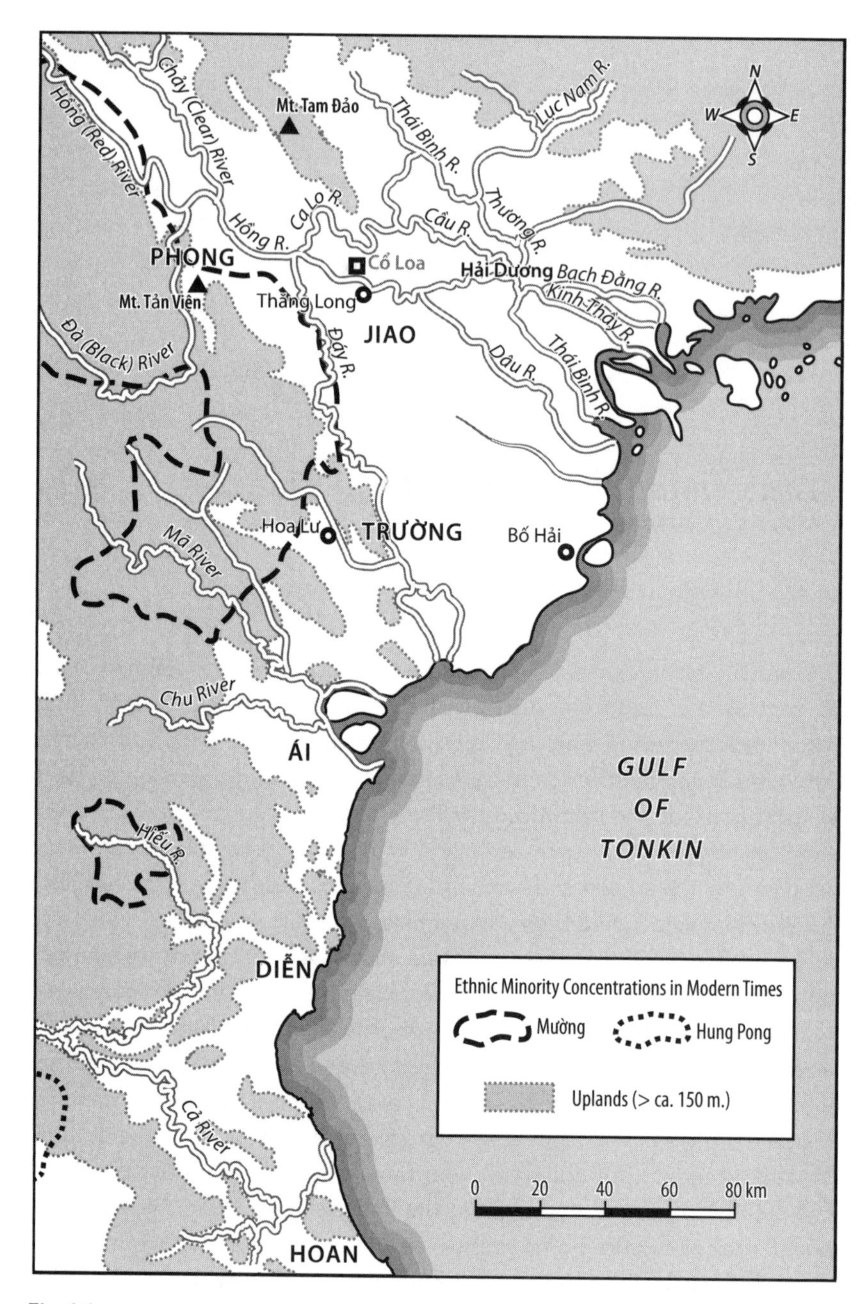

Fig. 4.1

Đại Việt late in the first millennium CE.

Farther south, imperial culture and governance had barely penetrated the other three provinces: Trường, in the rugged southern region of the lower delta; Ái (formerly Jiuzhen) in the Mã River delta; and distant Hoan (formerly Rinan) on the Champa border. All three southern provinces were inhabited by Vietic groups whose languages were slowly diverging into Vietnamese dialects on the narrow coastal lowlands, and dialects of Mường, Nguồn, and other Vietic languages in the nearby uplands.[4]

Over the next four centuries all these communities experienced major transformations. These included the construction of a monarchy, the expansion of literacy in both Chinese and Vietnamese, climate change, significantly enhanced economic prosperity, major wars with China and Champa, and militarization of the Đại Việt royal court along with the first signs of a rising Confucian scholarly and administrative bureaucracy.

Yet there were also continuities. While inheriting the political and cultural legacy of a millennium of Chinese rule, the new tenth-century Vietnamese kingdom also demonstrated a few of the distinct features of ancient Nán Yuè. It was only very loosely unified, at first no more so than the short-lived regionally disparate polity of the Trưng sisters in the mid-first century. Women again played a role in the new royal court. And like the defeated Lạc realm, its much more Sinicized and successful tenth-century reincarnation would slowly become more and more Confucianized. Even after secession from China, not only did the powerful influences of Buddhism and spirit worship persist in Đại Việt, but so did Daoism and other forms of northern culture.

CULTURAL LIFE IN EARLY ĐẠI VIỆT

Vietnamese literature now flourished—in Chinese. One dramatic departure in this story of a newfound autonomy is the proliferation and preservation of texts written by Vietnamese authors. While no such first-millennium texts survive, from c. 990 to 1350 Vietnamese authors are known to have composed at least twenty-five lengthy histories, religious studies, and historical mythologies (shown in the table on the next page). Their inspirations ranged from Buddhism, to spirit veneration, to Daoism and Confucianism. All were written in Chinese; six are extant. Thirty passages of a seventh, Lê Văn Hưu's *Đại Việt sử ký* (Record of the history of Đại Việt, dated 1272), are preserved in a fifteenth-century history. Lê Văn Hưu and other authors drew upon the earliest histories, now lost.[5]

The most substantial of the surviving sources date from the early fourteenth century, an era of prodigious literary production. The first fully extant, extended Vietnamese work of history is the *An Nam chí lược* (Brief annals of

Annam), which the former Đại Việt official Lê Tắc wrote in China after he had crossed the border in 1285 and taken up a new life there.[6] In 1329, Lý Tế Xuyên finished compiling *Việt Điện u linh tập* (*Departed Spirits of the Việt Realm*), twenty-seven legendary tales of kings, subjects, gods, spirits, and heroes. Meanwhile a Vietnamese Buddhist author was composing the *Thiền Uyển Tập Anh* (A collection of outstanding figures of the Zen community), with biographies of dozens of local monks.[7] And around the mid-fourteenth century, an anonymous Vietnamese compiled a lengthy, more secular chronicle entitled *Việt sử lược* (Brief history of Việt). This drew raw material from earlier works composed privately and kept in family libraries but since lost.[8]

More new information about Đại Việt in the tenth to fourteenth centuries exists in voluminous retrospective historical accounts composed in the

Table 4.1 TWENTY-FIVE TEXTS WRITTEN BY VIETNAMESE AUTHORS, C. 950–1350[9]

Author	Date	Title of text	English translation of title	Extant
Pháp Thuận	pre-991	*Bồ-tát-hiệu sám hối văn*	A Bodhisattva's words on repentance	No
Anon.	1069–1090	*Báo cực truyện*	Records declaring the unfathomable	No
Anon.	Trans. into nôm by Viên Chiếu	*Cổ-châu Pháp-vân Phật bản Hành ngữ lục*	Recorded Buddhist proverbs of Pháp-vân Temple at Cổ-châu	No
Viên Chiếu (998–1090)	pre-1090	*Dược sư thập-nhị nguyện văn;*	The twelve vows of Master Healer Buddha;	No
		Tánh Viên Giác Kinh	Elegy on the *Perfect Enlightenment Sutra;*	No
		Thập-nhị bồ-tát hành tu chứng đạo tràng;	Practicing and witnessing enlightenment by the Twelve Bodhisattvas;	No
		Tham đồ hiển khuyết	Hidden and Revealed Truths for Disciples	Yes
Đỗ Thiện	c. 1127	*Sử Ký*	Historical records	No
Thông Biện (d. 1134)	pre-1134	*Chiếu Đối Lục*	Collated biographies	No
Viên Thông (d. 1151)	pre-1151	*Chư phật tích duyên sự;*	Stories and legends of the Buddha's lives;	No
		Hồng chung văn bi kí;	Great bell inscriptions;	No
		Tăng gia tạp lục	Miscellaneous records of the Sangha	No
Thường Chiếu (d. 1203)	pre-1203	*Nam Tông Tự Pháp Đồ*	Diagram of the succession of the dharma of the Southern School	No

Anon.	12th century or earlier (?)	*Phật thuyết đại báo phụ mẫu ân trọng kinh*	Sutra of the Buddha's teaching on the pious duty to the parents' great sacrifice	Yes
Trần Chu Phổ	mid-13th cent.	*Việt chí*	Annals of Việt	No
Lê Văn Hưu	1272	*Đại Việt sử ký (DVSK)*	Record of the history of Đại Việt	Partial
Lê Tắc	1307	*An Nam chí lược (ANCL)*	Brief records of An Nam	Yes
Anon.	1310–13	*Lược Dẫn Thiền Phái Đồ*	Summarized diagram of the Zen schools	Yes
Lý Tế Xuyên	1329	*Việt điện u linh tập*	Departed spirits of the Việt realm	Yes
Huệ Sinh	pre-1337	*Pháp Sự Trai Nghi*	Ritual forms for dharma services and vegetarian feasts;	No
		Chư Đạo Trường Khánh Tán Văn	Celebrations and eulogy of the site of enlightenment	No
Khánh Hỷ	pre-1337	*Ngộ Đạo Ca Thi Tập*	Collected songs and poems on enlightenment	No
Huệ Nhật	pre-1337	*Liệt Tổ Yếu Ngữ*	Essential sayings of the patriarchs	No
Kim Sơn (?)	1337	*Thiền Uyển Tập Anh*	A collection of outstanding figures of the Zen community	Yes
Anon. (Hồ Tôn Thốc?)	1340–77	*Việt sử lược (VSL)*	Brief history of Việt	Yes

fifteenth century, especially Ngô Sĩ Liên's *Đại Việt sử ký toàn thư* (Complete historical annals of Đại Việt, 1479) but also the anonymous Chinese text *An Nam chí nguyên* (Sourcebook on Annam, 1419).[10]

Meanwhile, as in the first millennium, the imperial court kept extensive official records of its dealings with Vietnamese. Especially in the thirteenth century, Chinese visitors and observers continued to pen unofficial accounts of Đại Việt as seen from the north.

Poems and stone inscriptions from this era are also numerous and still being discovered. In 1984–89 alone, twenty-one previously unknown inscriptions of the tenth to fourteenth centuries came to light in rural north Việt Nam. Three are more than two thousand characters in length. Poems of more than thirty Vietnamese writers active during the period 950–1400 are also extant.[11]

The first extant texts written in the Vietnamese language emerged in this period. Chinese characters had been used in Annam to represent

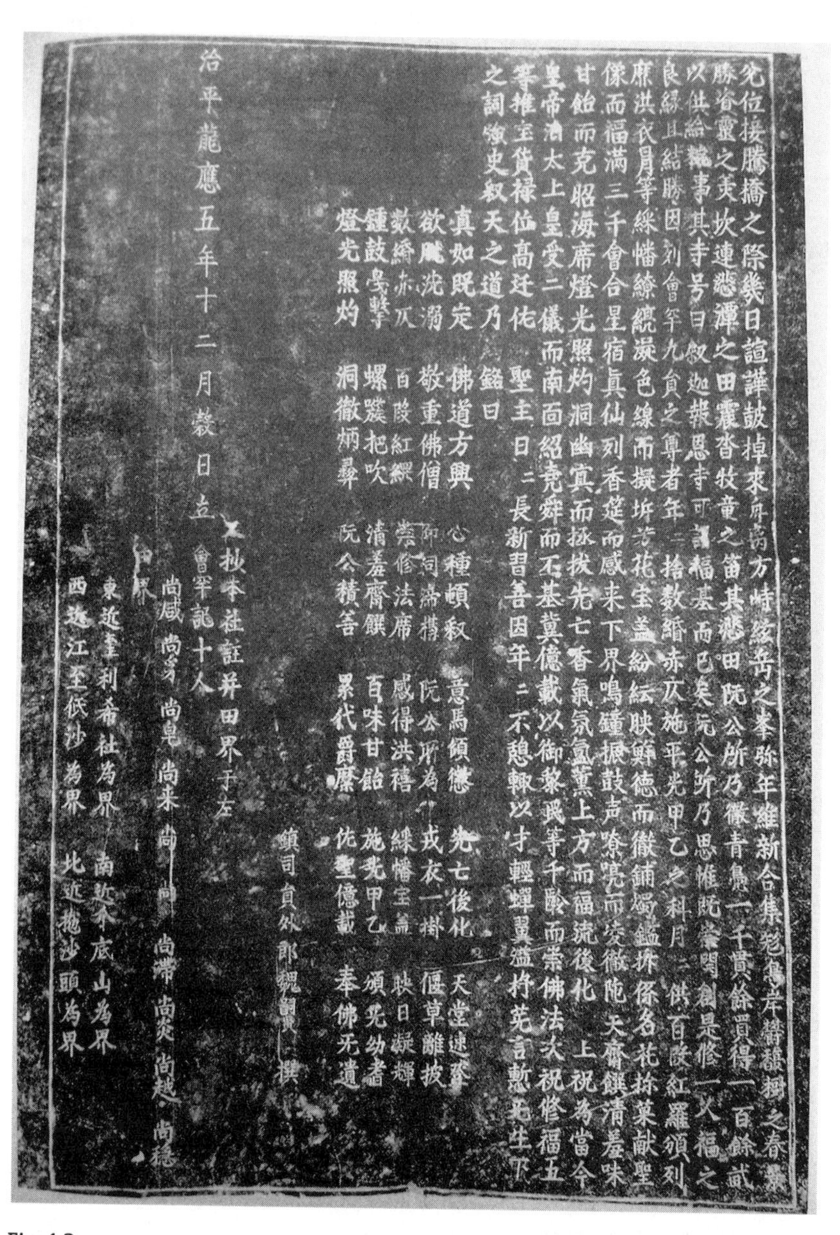

Fig. 4.2
The Tháp Miếu inscription (1210). Courtesy of Prof. Nguyễn Quang Hồng. The photograph originally appeared in *Văn khắc Hán Nôm Việt Nam, Tập 1, Từ Bắc thuộc đến thời Lý* (Hanoi: Institute of Sino-Nom Studies, 1998), 20b, and in Nguyễn Quang Hồng, *Khái luận Văn tự học chữ Nôm* (Hanoi: Education Press, 2008).

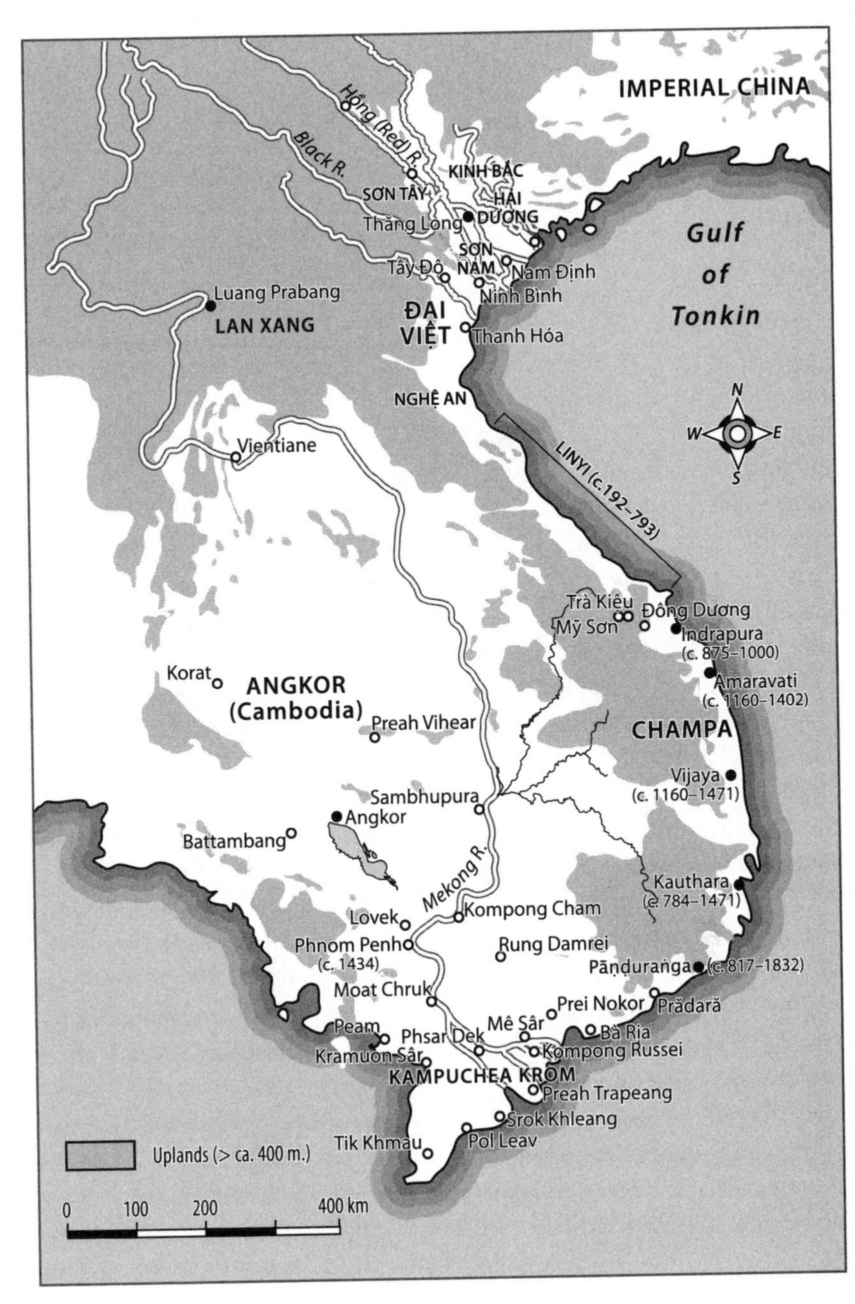

Fig. 4.3
Đại Việt, Champa, and Cambodia in the second millennium CE.

individual Việt-Mường words or sounds, a practice that increased after the tenth century. An inscription dated 1210, found at a pagoda in Tháp Miếu village, listed twenty-one names of people, villages, and hamlets, all written in *chữ nôm* ("southern language").[12] The first extant work in *nôm* is a poem dating from 1282, but there is evidence of possibly earlier *nôm* texts.[13]

Spoken Vietnamese, too, evolved in distinct ways. Classical Chinese remained an important cultural, political, and diplomatic medium, and it continued to be used at the Đại Việt court, but with the separation of the territory from imperial supervision, it was no longer the sole or dominant language of its administration. As Việt-Mường for the first time became the major language at court, it continued to borrow longstanding political vocabulary from Middle Chinese, and also acquired elements of Chinese phonology. As the reach and range of what became the Vietnamese language expanded and evolved, it diverged from its closest indigenous relatives, the upland Vietic languages of the Mường and Nguồn peoples.[14] Vietnamese pronunciation adopted three additional tones, making a total of six.[15] As speakers gradually dropped the first syllable from the many disyllabic Việt-Mường words, Vietnamese emerged as a monosyllabic, tonal language.[16] A new kingdom fostered a new culture.

Meanwhile new climatic conditions nourished a new economy. The period from about 900 to 1340 was the era of a global climate anomaly known as the Medieval Warm Period. In Southeast Asia this produced stronger monsoons. The warmer, wetter climate favored bigger agricultural harvests in mainland Southeast Asia, which also led to substantial population growth. *Việt sử lược* (*VSL*) called one downpour "rice from the sky." The Đại Việt kingdom arose and prospered in the same era that saw strong economic growth in Song dynasty China (960–1279), a period of prolonged vitality of Champa, and the zeniths of the Khmer empire of Angkor and the Burmese kingdom of Pagan.[17] Tree-ring data from the southern Vietnamese highlands, now available to scientists for a period commencing c. 1030, indicate "wetter than average conditions throughout key portions of the Medieval Warm Period." Of the entire second millennium there, the twelfth century was the wettest era recorded.[18] The favorable climatic conditions explain much of the medieval economic trajectory of Đại Việt and its two neighboring kingdoms, Champa and Angkor.

"MEN OF PROWESS" AND ADMINISTRATIVE DEVELOPMENT

The kingdom that Ngô Quyền established in 939 got off to a very shaky start. In its first seven decades it had three different names and was ruled by four dynasties from three capitals. The two kings who reigned from 965 to 1005 alone established ten queens.[19] Even with greater dynastic stability in the eleventh century, royal authority still required multiple marriage alliances to offset regional and political divisions, against a background of continuing invasions from the north, conflict with Champa to the south, and rebellion among Tai hill peoples on the northern frontier.[20]

From the start, Quyền appealed to ancient loyalties, including the propitiation of powerful Việt spirits. He slaughtered a sacrificial ox to thank the spirit of Phùng Hưng, the eighth-century *Bố Cái đại vương* (great *bố cái* king), for his help in defeating the Chinese. Reaching yet further back in time, Quyền established his court at Cổ Loa, the bronze-age walled fortress dating from the first millennium BCE. He "strengthened old rituals, and also provided feathered accessories, yellow banners, brass gongs, and deerskin drums for all the ancient dances with sword and battle axe," reminiscent of scenes depicted on Đông Sơn drums.[21]

Quyền also imposed a new administrative hierarchy. He "assigned a hundred mandarins, decided on the designs and colors of royal robes and hats for everyone," and appointed mandarins to different levels and functions.[22] But his new realm quickly succumbed to prolonged civil conflict, beginning with internecine struggles between members of the Dương and Ngô families, who continued to alternate in power until the mid-960s. After his defeat of the Chinese in 939, Quyền married Dương Đình Nghệ's daughter but failed to unite their families.

After Quyền died in 944, his wife's brother Dương Tam Kha usurped the throne from the four young sons of the dead king. But Tam Kha won control only of Jiao province, the heart of the Red River plain and the region of greatest Chinese cultural influence. To the east, in the vicinity of Trường province, Quyền's eldest son, Ngô Xương Ngập, held out in the delta, escaping Tam Kha's army by hiding in a mountain cave. In upland Phong province to the west, villagers revolted in about 950. Tam Kha dispatched two commanders with Quyền's second son, Ngô Xương Văn. On the march, Xương Văn reportedly told his companions that Tam Kha had "unethical ambitions" and "has ordered me to suppress innocent people." Regional disunity was a perennial problem: "Even if I were lucky to win, they would never completely submit anyway. What can I do now?" The two officers agreed to "obey [his] command." They all marched their army back and overthrew Tam Kha. Yet the monarchy remained weak. Ngô Xương Văn shared the throne with his older brother Xương Ngập and appeased Tam Kha and his followers by assigning him a regional governorship.[23] The resort to a dyarchy suggests the Ngô court had trouble institutionalizing its authority. More resistance erupted in the south of the delta, around Hoa Lư, on the upland frontier between Trường and Ái. In a month of fighting there, the sibling kings failed to suppress a recalcitrant thirty-year-old local leader, Đinh Bộ Lĩnh. Soon after, Xương Ngập "took all power in his hands," banning his brother from "royal meetings."[24]

The first accounts of Đinh Bộ Lĩnh's early career offer a glimpse of village life and hint at the rise, in various localities by the mid-tenth century, of a non-Confucian cohort of indigenous strongmen and village-level elites. Bộ Lĩnh came from a military family that gained prominence in the chaos of the 930s. His father had served as a "commander of the guard" of Dương Đình Nghệ, who made him interim governor of the southern border province, Hoan.[25] But according to *VSL*, Bộ Lĩnh's father "died when he was a child. He lived with his mother and other family members in a holy temple by a mountain" in Hoa Lư. In the 940s the boy emerged as a leader of local youth, who played "royal games in which Bộ Lĩnh was the king." He had them collect wood for his mother, who slaughtered a pig and put on a feast. Villagers sensed a grim future leader: "We'd better follow him now before it is too late." They delivered their youths to Bộ Lĩnh, and he "set up a base" on land of his uncle, who "refused to submit to him." Bộ Lĩnh "sent his friends to attack the uncle," who pursued him, found him trapped under a collapsed bridge, and "almost intended to kill him, but then saw two yellow dragons flying above." The uncle "withdrew and later submitted to him."[26] The story has the ring of the rise of a local strongman, one the historian O. W. Wolters termed a "man of prowess" possessing the "soul stuff" befitting a chief.[27] Traditional accounts of these qualities stressed strength and leadership ability, and often, the backing of both female authority and local spirits, tinged only marginally with Buddhist, Daoist, or Confucian allusion. *VSL*, where Bộ Lĩnh's father is unidentified, tells instead of "a cluster of lotus flowers" in front of his mother's home: "On the leaves, snails crawled and left marks that read, 'Heaven's son.' "[28]

By the early 950s, "arrogant" in his Hoa Lư hill stronghold, Đinh Bộ Lĩnh commanded a force that could resist the Ngô kings. Undeterred when they captured his son Đinh Liễn, he replied in anger, "An honored warrior never gives up just because of his son," and coolly ordered his archers "to shoot arrows at Liễn. The two kings were horrified and withdrew their troops."[29] These stories about Bộ Lĩnh stress the swashbuckling bravado of a military strongman, not a hereditary aristocrat or Confucian official.

Ngô dynasty rule ended in 963. Xương Ngập had died in 954, and during an attack on the still rebellious upland villages in Phong, King Xương Văn, standing in his boat to watch his troops in action, was "struck down by an enemy sniper's arrow."[30] The kingdom dissolved into civil wars. For two years, a twelfth-century Chinese author wrote, Jiaozhi was "in great disorder."[31] *VSL* records that "the country was in anarchy" as "twelve armies" commanded by contending "lords" ranged over the land. Phong fell under the control of a hereditary regional family. Jiao became a battleground for five dukes and two march lords, including sons of a Chinese mandarin and a Vietnamese woman "river merchant." But farther south, near Trường, Đinh Bộ Lĩnh now commanded military units for his adopted father, Trần Lãm, a Cantonese trader and warlord who controlled a seaport near the mouth of the Red River.[32] In Hoan, Chinese sources record, Bộ Lĩnh's son Đinh Liễn (having escaped Ngô custody) raised an army of thirty thousand and marched north.[33] That again suggests a local groundswell. These men vanquished all their rivals, sending "the leaders of the Sino-Vietnamese aristocracy fleeing in all directions."[34] Regional families lost power in a widespread serious of indigenous revolts led by village elites and strongmen recruiting upland and peasant armies.

The *Đại Việt sử ký toàn thư* (*DVSKTT*) describes the last throes of the Ngô and the roles of local leaders and "aboriginal tribes" in the hill country. When Trần Lãm died in 965, Ngô Quyền's son and brother made a last effort. They "assembled at Đỗ-động River" with five hundred warriors and "led the multitude to attack" Đinh Bộ Lĩnh. But a contingent of Ô *Man* people ("Ô barbarians") held off the Ngô loyalists, who were defeated by "a local man." Then Bộ Lĩnh "mobilized his soldiers, and attacked Đỗ-động River." All the "aboriginal tribes in the ravines" submitted to Bộ Lĩnh, and "all the officials and people in the capital gave their loyalty to him."[35]

Taking possession of Cổ Loa fortress in 965, Đinh Bộ Lĩnh rejected the imperial names Annam and Jiaozhi, renamed the kingdom Đại Cồ Việt (Great Việt), and moved its capital south to his home district, Hoa Lư.[36] At first he styled himself "Great Vanquishing King," and his son Đinh Liễn took the old Tang title "Peaceful Sea Military Governor."[37] Then, over the next two years, Bộ Lĩnh promoted himself to emperor (*hoàng đế*) with Liễn as king (*vương*) of "Nam Việt" (Nán Yuè). The new name of Bộ Lĩnh's more august kingdom, Đại Cồ Việt, was written with both the Chinese character for "great" (*đại*) and the *nôm* character reproducing the sound of its Vietnamese synonym *cồ*.[38] A more indigenous monarchy began to take shape. Lê Văn Hưu wrote in *Đại Việt Sử Ký* (*DVSK*) that Bộ Lĩnh "appointed 100 mandarins, built six regiments, and almost all public administrative functions."[39] *VSL* adds that he "built palaces, assigned mandarins, set up rules and law." Bộ Lĩnh also governed by fear. "He placed a giant pot of boiling oil in the middle of the courtyard, and kept tigers in cages, saying 'whoever rebels or commits crimes will be cooked in oil or taken to feed the tigers.' All captives and subjects were scared, submitting to him."[40]

Đinh Bộ Lĩnh enjoyed less success in his effort to win domestic legitimacy and continuity by appeasing the last Ngô claimant to the throne, Ngô Nhật Khánh, who had "formerly styled himself An Vương" (Pacifying King). In an attempt to pacify *him*, Bộ Lĩnh "took his mother as an empress and made his younger sister a wife of Liễn," Bộ Lĩnh's son. Yet Bộ Lĩnh still feared that Nhật Khánh would "foment rebellion." So he gave him his own daughter as "a princess in marriage, wanting to smother his resentment and gain his loyalty." It didn't work. Nhật Khánh's bitterness gave way to brutal desperation. "He subsequently took his wife and children and hastened to Champa. Arriving at a seaport on the southern border, he drew a dagger from his waist and slashed his wife's face, scolding her by saying: 'Your father coerced and ravished my mother and younger sister; how can I, just because of you, forget your father's cruelty? You go back; I will go a different way to look for those who can help me.' "[41] He crossed into Champa.

CONFLICT WITH CHINA AND CHAMPA

Đại Việt faced war on two fronts. From 963 and until as late as 1164, China's Song dynasty recognized kings of Đại Việt only as "internal vassals" (*quận vương*).[42] In 970, the Song even assigned the kingdom its former Tang status, acknowledging Đại Việt's emperor Đinh Bộ Lĩnh as a mere "king of Annam province."[43] The next year, the Song emperor ordered the subjugation of Lingnan (the lands "south of the passes"), implicitly including Đại Việt. This provoked its anxious self-proclaimed king, Đinh Liễn, to request his own recognition as a vassal. The Song emperor duly named him "imperial commissioner and prefect-general of Annam."[44]

Đinh Bộ Lĩnh saw the imperial threat and moved to strengthen his court. He promoted other indigenous "men of prowess," but also Buddhist and Daoist officials. To a new military post, "commander in chief of all armies" (*thập-đạo tướng quân*), he appointed Lê Hoàn, a thirty-five-year-old officer from Ái and former lieutenant of Đinh Liễn. Filling other posts with titles that suggest a continuing transition from subject territory to independent kingdom, Bộ Lĩnh also named both a "chancellor of the protectorate" (*thái sư đô-hộ phủ*) and an "officer of national unification" (*định quốc công*).[45] He awarded additional titles such as "Buddhist Priest Overseer" to Đại Việt's ranking monks, and in 971 assigned Buddhism's top position, that of great preceptor (*đại sư*) for reforming the Việt (*khuông Việt*), to the patriarch of the Vô Ngôn Thông sect, Ngô Chân Lưu, who occupied the post until his death forty years later. Eventually the title itself became the patriarch's own most widely used personal name, Khuông Việt, suggesting that this post remained individual and uninstitutionalized. A Daoist priest became the "Noble and Upright Majesty," with responsibilities that probably included propitiation of local spirits. Bộ Lĩnh's five wives all became empresses, two with the Daoist titles "Cinnabar Wedding" and "Pure and Bright," and two with more political ones, "National Reformation" and "National Vigilance."[46] The fifth empress, entitled Ca-ông, may have been a Cham princess. Writing three centuries later, Lê Văn Hưu was caustic: "So far, there had been only one queen to supervise domestic matters, never before have I heard of five empresses. The emperor had not been fully educated by his predecessors and none of his royal subjects could correct him. Therefore the emperor so much indulged in women that he appointed five empresses with equal privileges."[47]

Hoa Lư's court now comprised, Taylor writes, "an emperor, five empresses, a king, a duke, a judge, a general, two Buddhist priests, a Taoist priest, and a son-in-law"—with the title "Commandant of the Spare Horses."[48] The records describing this small nucleus of central authority add little about Đại Việt regional civil administration. It is unlikely the court exerted much power beyond Jiao. In the provinces of Phong, Trường, and especially Ái and Hoan, some remnants of the hereditary Sino-Vietnamese families may have retained control, but most were probably replaced by indigenous strongmen from the villages who had risen to regional level, as the Đinh family had done in Jiao.

The Hoa Lư court had similarly upgraded itself from village elite to a regional nobility, albeit the paramount one in the kingdom. Events recorded from the Đinh era do not suggest that Hoa Lư's concern was the institution of a transregional bureaucratic or even monarchical administration of Đại Việt, but rather governance of the court itself and the titles and privileges of its members.[49] At first, then, Hoa Lư's interests dovetailed with those of imperial China, which was happy enough to recognize it as a mere regional authority. The *An Nam chí lược* (*ANCL*) says that in 972, the new Song emperor, having received gifts of "cloth, rhinoceros horns, elephant tusks and perfumed tea" as tribute from Hoa Lư, conferred on Đinh Bộ Lĩnh the new title "prince of Jiaozhi, with an apanage of one thousand families."[50] This notional imperial grant may have represented only part of Bộ Lĩnh's new landholdings. By comparison, in 979 his son Liễn erected a large stone column in Hoa Lư, inscribed with Buddhist texts in Chinese characters and asserting that Liễn had been "allotted land of 10,000 households." It is unlikely his father would have done with less. The inscription does not reveal whether Liễn's allotment came from Bộ Lĩnh or from the Song emperor. Two similar stone columns from this era were discovered in Hoa Lư in the 1960s, and fourteen more in 1987. All include Buddhist *Uṣṇīṣa Vijaya*

Dhāraṇī texts. One adds that in 973, Liễn set out to erect a hundred *ratanadhvaja* columns of this kind.[51] The concerns of the court are clear: its landed estates, religious legitimization, and freedom from imperial invasion. Hoa Lư showed less interest in direct governance of the more distant provinces of Đại Việt.

The royal succession wracked the court. In 978, after Đinh Bộ Lĩnh's youngest son, Hạng Lang, was born, the emperor named him crown prince. A middle son, Toàn, aged four, was already a duke. But in 979, the eldest, Đinh Liễn, had his baby brother murdered. Liễn then erected a column inscribed with a long Buddhist text explaining that his "deceased younger brother" had "strayed from the path of loyalty and filial piety toward his King-Father and his elder brother and thereby created grave consequences, and so I had to bring doom to his life for the sake of national security and family ethics." The inscription continues: "As the old saying puts it, 'There is no willingness to withdraw from the struggle for power, but the better way is to eliminate first one's opponents.' The affair has happened as it should. Now I have made one hundred *ratanadhvaja* columns as offerings before the altar and pray for the immediate release of the souls of my brother and others who died before and after him, so that they can escape trials and judgments [in hell]." Liễn's statement in stone concluded with the wish that his father "reign forever over this southern land," while another inscription added the hope that Liễn himself would "be secure in his posts and privileges."[52]

That was not to be. One evening late in that year, as Đinh Bộ Lĩnh, aged fifty-five, "was eating his late luxurious supper, a traitor named Đỗ Thích killed him and his son Liễn." The kingdom had lost its emperor, king, and crown prince. The general Lê Hoàn took power as regent while five-year-old Toàn occupied the throne. Rebellions erupted. Even the "officer of national unification" took up arms. Lê Hoàn captured him in Ái and had him executed at court.[53]

Internal dissension encouraged external intervention. Learning of Đinh Bộ Lĩnh's assassination, the exiled Ngô Nhật Khánh and his host in Champa, King Parameçvaravarman, sailed north with an invading fleet. According to *DVSKTT*, Nhật Khánh "guided the boatmasters of over one thousand Cham vessels, invading for plunder with the intention of attacking Hoa Lư city, through the two estuaries of Đại-ác and Tiểu-khang. After one night's halt, a fierce wind arose and the boats were all sunk. Nhật Khánh and the Chams were drowned and only the Cham king's boat was barely able to return to its home port."[54]

Meanwhile the Song emperor sent Hoa Lư a warning: "The empire's orders extend everywhere, its power is known in every country. Why then has the country of Yuenn-zhi not yet sent in the map of its territory?" (as China required of its vassal states). Since Đại Việt had "ceased to be loyal," the emperor must inflict "on its chief the punishment that Heaven demands." Lê Hoàn complained that Champa had sent "tens of thousands of cavalry and elephants" to raid his kingdom.[55] The emperor dispatched another edict: "China and the *Man* barbarians are like the body of a man and his four limbs.... It is said that the heart is the body's emperor." And "bitter" medicines were "small pain for a great good" that "only he who governs the universe can provide." His imperial predecessor had successfully "practiced acupuncture" on the Yuè and other breakaway regions, and now the Song suzerain was turning his attention to "your Jiaozhou," which is "far away on the horizon.... One might compare it to a finger." He ordered the Việt territories to "conform" as in the past, "forming part of the empire." Refusal would "force us to punish you," he declared, and cause "the ruin of your little kingdom." Imperial power, loftily concerned with neither "the pearls of your waters" nor "the gold of your mountains," offered superior civilization. "Your people wear your hair short, while we wear hats and clothes. Your language resembles the calls of shrikes, while we have a literature in which we will instruct you.... So leave your barbarous islands and come to visit our temples of Confucius." But "if you refuse, our soldiers will set out."[56]

Song armies marched south in the winter of 980–81. Once again an imperial navy entered the Bạch Đằng River.[57] The invaders routed a ten-thousand-strong Đại Việt force, and the following summer, near the Bạch Đằng River, they captured and beheaded a thousand defenders and seized two hundred junks. The imperial army camped at Huabu while the vanguard sailed on upriver with the transports.[58] Đại Việt's generals gathered at Hoa Lư "nicely dressed in decorated military costumes," according to *DVSKTT*. They "marched straight into the court." *VSL* quotes one commander holding to ransom a weak court reliant on reciprocity: "Our king is still an infant who cannot understand our hard work and devotion. Who will then reward us with favors in the future? We'd better promote the commander-in-chief of the armies [*tôn quan thập-đạo*] to be king first, then deploy troops later." The army would fight only for its own candidate and "rewards." It fell to the queen mother to displace her grandson. She "brought out the king's robe to put on Lê Hoàn," offering him the throne."[59]

Lê Hoàn led Đại Việt's armies to battle. Once again a Vietnamese leader "ordered troops to plant stakes in the river."[60] The Song transports and vanguard had advanced too far upriver, into the interior. They now suffered successive defeats before retreating downstream to Huabu. There Lê Hoàn's forces vanquished them again, ambushing and killing the fleet commander while blocking any reinforcements from the army downriver.[61] The imperial forces withdrew from Đại Việt in defeat. The next year, after Champa arrested his envoy there, Lê Hoàn led an invading force south, stormed the Cham capital, killed King Parameçvaravarman, "captured thousands and thousands of civilians," and ordered the destruction of "many" of Champa's "citadels and temples."[62]

Lê Hoàn consolidated his triumphs with diplomacy. Writing in the early fourteenth century, Lê Tắc described him as "energetic and clever," a man who "knew how to win the hearts of the educated." In 983, Lê Hoàn sent the Song emperor tribute of gold, silver, rhinoceros horns, and ivory, and followed this with more two years later, plus tortoiseshell, incense, and "ten thousand pieces of white silk." The emperor granted Lê Hoàn an apanage of three thousand families, adding a thousand more in 988.[63] While maintaining the Buddhist patriarch Khuông Việt in the court post of *đại sư*, Lê Hoàn appointed to the similar position of *thái sư* ("grand preceptor," or chancellor) a Chinese named Hồng Hiến whom he "loved and trusted," who was "well versed in the classics and histories," served as an advisor on Lê Hoàn's military campaigns, and "had great merit in advancing plans and discussing state affairs."[64] Confucian advisors would eventually monopolize this new post of *thái sư*, but in the tenth century Buddhists and Daoists seemed more influential, and Hồng Hiến remained an exception.

EVOLUTION OF A MONARCHY

A Song official depicted a close-up view of the Đại Việt monarchy. In 990, Lê Hoàn dispatched three hundred men in nine junks to the border to escort an arriving imperial delegation. The Chinese envoy, Sung Hao, later reported that after a dangerous two-week sea voyage, travel in the Đại Việt interior was safe. "We arrived at the Bạch Đằng River where we took advantage of the rising tide. In the places where we stopped overnight, there was always a way-station house." Lê Hoàn sent marines out to meet them. Then, as the party neared Hoa Lư, "suddenly, Lê Hoàn and his escort arrived to receive us outside the city, according to the rites. Pulling up his horse, he stopped to ask us for news of the emperor." He offered them betel nut to chew. Hao was unimpressed. "The capital was just a camp, nobody lived there. The palace was small and miserable." Hoàn had even accepted the emperor's written edict without prostrating himself before it as imperial protocol required. "He explained that several years ago while fighting brigands, he had fallen from his horse and injured his leg." After a couple of nights, mats were laid out for a feast. Hao saw "three thousand soldiers and officers, all with the words 'Army of the Son of Heaven' tattooed on their foreheads." Their weapons were "mere bows, crossbows, wooden shields and lances, all very flimsy and barely serviceable." Hao's condescension broke through as he described Lê Hoàn seated on his litter, "a wooden bed, very crudely made. One day he invited me to sit beside him, and turning to me, asked if there was such a thing at the imperial court."[65] Hao considered the Vietnamese "beyond civilization" (*hua-oai*).[66]

Lê Hoàn established five empresses and apparently maintained relations with the queen mother who had appointed him. Of his palace, the fifteenth-century writer Ngô Sĩ Liên lamented that "concerning the customary laws of husband and wife, there were many affairs worthy of shame."[67] At the time, Sung Hao noted a different feature of the inner life of Lê Hoàn's court: "If someone in his entourage commits the least infraction, he is beaten and dismissed. Then, when the prince's anger passes, he recalls him." Lê Hoàn gave higher priority to the court than to developing a provincial administration: "The functionaries who carry out their duties well are chosen to reside with the sovereign."[68] Conversely, to run the provinces, the monarch trusted only members of the royal family, which led to a proliferation of regional "kings." In 991, Lê Hoàn named his brother "king of the Ngự *Man*, governing Phong province." Ten of his eleven sons, including one aged nine, became "kings" of other regions. This did not prevent rebellion erupting in Ái in 997, and again two years later in nineteen of its districts. There was a new revolt in Phong in 1000, and in Aí the next year, Mường rebels trapped the royal army on a river, killing ex-king Toàn in his boat.[69]

The kingdom remained unstable. After Lê Hoàn's death in 1005, his twenty-year-old fifth son, Lê Ngọa Triều, murdered an older brother and ruled for four years. *VSL* asserts matter-of-factly: "The king liked killing." He had criminals burned alive, and enemy soldiers drowned in cages placed in the river at low tide. "When the tide rose, the king enjoyed seeing the captives drown, trying to raise their heads or open their mouths to breathe." He had others tied to boats and rowed back and forth as "big snakes" bit and killed them. Three of his brothers revolted and were suppressed.[70] A fourth defected to China. The Song emperor considered invading Đại Việt again but desisted, saying: "Jiao is a land of deadly climate; if soldiers are sent to take it, many will be killed and injured."[71] Back in Hoa Lư, Lê Ngọa Triều developed hemorrhoids and had to "lie down while listening to mandarins' reports." He died in 1009, aged twenty-five.[72]

The thirty-five-year-old commander of the palace guard, Lý Công Uẩn, quickly seized power. Under the reign name Lý Thái Tổ, he established the Lý dynasty (1009–1225). He granted "amnesty to all people, destroying all the instruments used for torture." The next year he moved the capital back to Jiao, returning it to Đại La, which had been the center of power in Tang Annam from the seventh century until 939.[73] This site was on the right bank of the Red River, where it joined the Tô Lịch and Đuống rivers. There "a golden dragon" appeared to Lý Công Uẩn at the prow of his boat, and he renamed his new capital Thăng Long (Rising Dragon), which eight centuries later became Hà Nội, "between the rivers."[74]

Lý Công Uẩn's twenty-year reign (1009–28) launched a new, more durable monarchy based on economic prosperity and the melding of various regional and ideological influences into an eclectic political culture. The Lý era was "the first long and relatively stable period in independent Vietnam."[75] Đại Việt's territory expanded into both Champa and China. An imperial official later termed "Jiaozhi" the most powerful of the kingdoms "under the Empire."[76]

The Lý dynasty slowly moved to assemble the regions of Đại Việt into a more centralized kingdom. But it did so only by taking advantage of improving agricultural conditions and by acknowledging and incorporating a variety of local and religious traditions. It forged a new Việt political culture that mingled indigenous spirit worship with Buddhism, Daoism, Confucianism, other northern cultural influences, and elements of Hinduism from Champa.

CLIMATE CHANGE AND ECONOMIC GROWTH IN THE ELEVENTH AND TWELFTH CENTURIES

From the late tenth century, *VSL*'s author begins occasionally reporting climatic and agricultural conditions in Đại Việt. The scattered records, consistent with the tree-ring data, suggest that rainfall and rice harvests were increasing over the eleventh and twelfth centuries. A "big flood" came in 997 and "bumper crops" in 1016. In 1029 "it rained hard with rice from the sky, heaping on the courtyard" of Vạn Tuế pagoda. Farmers brought in a "big crop" in 1044. In 1071 there was "no rain from the spring to the summer," but the next year was too wet: "The king sent people to bring a Buddha statue from Pháp Vân pagoda to the capital [in order] to pray for dry weather." In 1078 "the citadel was flooded." A hailstorm struck the following year, and that May "we harvested a great crop." The year 1092 saw another excellent harvest. The spring of 1102 brought "virtuous clouds descending," followed by a flood, and the next spring "the king ordered people from all over the citadel to participate in the building of dikes to block flood waters." Considered a good omen, "sweet water rainfall" was recorded in 1080, 1112, and 1118, and once again "good clouds descended" in 1114. Consistent with wetter conditions, better harvests, and population growth came the first records of "huge epidemics," which occurred in 1100 and 1105. *VSL* reports six "droughts" between 1124 and 1148, but in five of those cases, royally sponsored "prayer sessions" succeeded in bringing rains.[77] Prudent monarchs could usefully take the credit for the now more reliable rainfall by holding more frequent "prayer sessions."

Sponsoring agriculture became a royal duty. *VSL* records that five years after the "great famine" of 982, Lê Hoàn had ceremonially plowed two rice fields and found a pot of gold in each. And in 1030, Lý Công Uẩn's son and successor Lý Phật Mã (reign name Lý Thái Tông, r. 1028–54) "had royal servants carry him to the fields in Ô-lô to watch farmers harvesting." Again, as rainfall increased, a more regular royal ritual developed. In 1032, Phật Mã "joined the plowing work"; farmers presented him with a plant "with nine branches of rice grains." The king again "joined the plowing work" in 1038 and 1042, at coastal locations where farmers were apparently reclaiming land from the sea. In 1056 his successor Lý Nhật Tôn (Lý Thánh Tông, r. 1054–72) "issued a decree that promoted agriculture," and nine years later visited the seaport where his father had plowed the land three decades before and again took part in "plowing and farm work." Lý Nhân Tông (r. 1072–1127) conducted the ritual at Phù Nhân in 1076 and 1080. In early 1101, he returned "to see people plowing" and went to another site "to watch people planting seeds." The next year he revisited Phù Nhân to "watch people plowing" again.[78]

The Lý dynasty's challenge was to build a kingdom from disparate regional fiefdoms, military commands, cultural constituencies, and segmented economies. The Lý family, from the Bắc Ninh region north of Thăng Long, depended on regional support from the western and southern frontier districts—Phong, Trường, Ái, and Diễn.[79] Clan marriage alliances remained crucial. From the outset, Lý Công Uẩn followed Hoa Lư practice by naming six queens; Lý Phật Mã had as many as thirteen, and Lý Nhật Tôn eight.[80] In 1009 the Buddhist abbot Vạn Hạnh had appealed to Công Uẩn to take the throne by remarking that "of all the clans in the realm, the Lý clan is the largest, without equal. You are magnanimous and compassionate, . . . able to gain the affections of the officers and to control the soldiers. Who beside you is able to be sovereign of the people?" Two decades later Phật Mã revealed the continuing combination of clan loyalty and Buddhist merit-making as he pardoned princely rivals: "I want to hide the wicked crimes of my brothers and allow them to withdraw and yield of their own volition for, of all things, my own flesh and blood is most precious."[81]

Conversely, in other lowland Việt agricultural regions, leading local clans flourished, sometimes beyond the court's economic reach. During the Lý era, farmers and merchants paid no taxes on their grain. Even in Jiao, the Lý court left Buddhist monastic estates unsupervised. Taxation in 1013, for instance, applied mostly to goods produced on royal estates (rice, fish, pearls, silk) and in the highlands (salt, rhinoceros horns, ivory, aromatic woods, timber, flowers, fruits). After the bountiful 1016 harvest, Công Uẩn exempted his subjects from all taxation for three years, a feasible gesture from a king who lacked a subordinate administrative class that could consume or even collect such revenue.[82] Yet this unprecedented royal benevolence also suggests new wealth and a more general prosperity, perhaps derived from the improved climatic conditions. Plundering Champa helped too, but as Phật Mã remarked after looting its capital in 1044: "Expeditions to distant lands interfere with and take away from agricultural work. Yet this winter we have an abundant harvest. If the people already have enough, then what do I lack? Therefore, half of this year's taxes are excused so the people can rest from their labours."[83]

By the mid-eleventh century, advancing farmers had cleared much of the forested eastern Red River delta for intensive agriculture, destroying the habitat of the large coastal elephant herds. As rainfall conditions continued to improve, the clearing of new farmland in the coastal western delta would lead to the disappearance of elephants there by the mid-twelfth century.[84] After the Red River's silt deposits had turned salt marshes into dry land, Vietnamese settlers converted its forests into farms.

A BUDDHIST MONARCHY ASSEMBLES THE SPIRITS

Buddhist devotion added authority to the new dynasty. The words of the abbot Vạn Hạnh, a patriarch of the Vinītaruci sect of Thiền (Zen) Buddhism established in Annam in 580 CE, carried weight with Lý Công Uẩn. The Lý family name was that of his adopted father, Lý Khánh Văn, abbot of Cổ Pháp temple near Mount Tiên, whose order of forest monks had raised the young orphan as a boy. Vạn Hạnh had been responsible for Công Uẩn's education and placement at the Hoa Lư court. During the turmoil of the tenth century, Jiao's Buddhist monasteries had provided refuge, protected their estates, and developed political influence.[85] On his accession in 1009, Công Uẩn reflected that influence when he criticized the defunct Hoa Lư court for "ten thousand evil deeds."[86] In the second year of his reign, he built eight Buddhist temples near Mount Tiên and three in Thăng Long, followed by two more in the capital in 1016, and he had a sixth constructed there in 1024.[87] His successor Lý Phật Mã, a patriarch of the Vô Ngôn Thông sect (established in 820 CE), who also wrote a poem in praise of Vinītaruci, had 150 temples and pagodas built in 1031 alone.[88] Phật Mã's reign provides the first evidence in Đại Việt of royal fasts, of the self-immolation of monks to leave body relics that would work miracles, and of the fashioning of images of the emergent Buddha (Bodhisattva) Avalokiteśvara and of the future Buddha Maitreya. In 1049, having dreamed of Avalokiteśvara seated on a lotus, Phật Mã ordered the construction in Thăng Long of the "one pillar pagoda," which survived in twentieth-century Hanoi.[89]

But it was not Buddhism alone that brought the royal capital back to Jiao. Lý Công Uẩn further distinguished himself from his predecessors in presenting a vision of rule over the entire kingdom, from its ninth-century "old capital of Cao Biền [Tang general Gao Pian]." He saw Thăng Long as an appropriate center, "where the four directions meet," as he put it, "between south and north and east and west, with a favorable view of the mountains behind and the river in front, where the earth is spacious and flat and high and clear, where the inhabitants are not oppressed by flooding, where the earth is fertile and prosperous, a location overlooking the entire land of Việt."[90] Though difficult to implement, this was clearly an administrator's view of his kingdom.

History and location did not alone recommend Thăng Long. The site was also the home of the spirit of the Dragon's Belly, the realm's leading genie. Công Uẩn saw Thăng Long as more than Đại Việt's geographic center. It was "the region between heaven and earth, where the dragon-coiled tiger is able to sit."[91] Returning the capital to this site and renaming it "Rising Dragon" assuaged that genie. But it also placed its cult under royal supervision. Công Uẩn's devout Buddhism had led him to mistrust spirit worship for its "obscene" practices that had to be either suppressed or brought under control.[92] He acknowledged the power of the spirits and also deployed them as court ritual assets, alongside Buddhism. When an earthquake struck in 1016, Công Uẩn "prayed to the gods that were in charge of the mountains surrounding the citadel," while also sending "more than 1,000 people to teach in Buddhist schools."[93] Consistent with his geo-administrative vision and his actions to appease and tame the spirit world, during the eleventh century the Lý court "brought back" to Thăng Long a firmament of local spirits that had long dominated more distant regions of the kingdom. The spirits of the Trưng sisters from the western delta, the earth genie of Phù Đổng north of the capital, and the Trống Đồng Mountain god from Thanh

Hóa in Ái to the south were all relocated to the capital and housed there in temples specially dedicated to them.[94] If these spirits were "symbols of regional powers," their pacification involved the extension of monarchical authority to the regions of Đại Việt.[95]

The eclecticism that had long marked Việt religious life also helped Lý Công Uẩn co-opt local spirits into the ruling Buddhist pantheon. In the ninth century, in order to take advantage of the power of the Phù Đổng earth genie, the Kiến Sơ temple that occupied the site of the 820 founding of the Vô Ngôn Thông Buddhist sect had been constructed just beside this genie's shrine, which was still located to the right of the monastery gate. Yet tension divided these neighboring institutions. The late eleventh-century text *Báo cực truyện* relates that in the tenth century Kiến Sơ temple "fell into ruin; the local people consulted witches and wizards on miscellaneous matters and, going to excess, became licentious in their sacrificial observances." Finally the Vô Ngôn Thông patriarch Đa Bảo, "assisting" Lý Công Uẩn before his rise to power, "wanted to put an end" to that. Before the shrine, the monk threatened the spirit with exorcism:

> Be content to dwell in the monastery;
> If you will not defend the Buddha Law,
> Then quickly depart for another place.

A few nights later the genie replied:

> The Buddha Law is extremely compassionate;
> The spirits are covered by Heaven and supported by earth.
> I desire to follow steadfastly the monastic life.[96]

In return, on achieving power Công Uẩn officially made the Phù Đổng genie the guardian spirit of Kiến Sơ temple, bestowing on it the title "Soaring-to-Heaven Spirit King" (*Xung Thiên Thần Vương*). He had an image made of the spirit, to which sacrifices were made.[97] Reflecting the genie's new Buddhist life, the *Báo cực truyện* termed it "the reincarnated local earth spirit of Kiến Sơ temple." Taylor writes that Buddhism was "pulling itself up by grasping sturdy rungs in the spirit world." The same might be said of the monarchy: the *Báo cực truyện* described the period of Công Uẩn's life before he took power as his "concealed dragon time," that is, before he revealed himself as a dragon.[98]

Domesticating and even joining the spirits to ensure harmony across the realm became a major task of Lý monarchs. After the 1016 earthquake, Công Uẩn journeyed around his kingdom both to propitiate its disparate genies and co-opt them by having them "declare" themselves to him. Reaching an "auspicious" riverbank ferry crossing, he remarked: "I see that here the mountains are wonderfully strange and the rivers are beautiful; if there is any hero or earth spirit dwelling here, may it receive this sacrifice." That night a former general of the sixth-century Việt hero Lý Bí visited the king in a dream. Pleased at the long-delayed royal recognition of his protection of the lowlands from upland attackers, the spirit said: "When the realm lies in darkness, the names of loyal ministers are hidden, but at noon, when all is illuminated, who cannot see their forms?" Lý kings ruled by having powerful spirits "declare" themselves to royal power. After Công Uẩn's death, his successor Phật Mã claimed that the Spirit of Mount Trống Đồng, or the Mountain of the Bronze Drum (*Thần Núi Đồng Cổ*), which also inhabited a shrine at Thăng Long, had given him timely warning that his brother was plotting against him at Hoa Lư.[99]

While fighting several new wars against Champa, Lý monarchs enlisted the aid of southern spirits and were even receptive to Cham culture. In 1020, as crown prince Phật Mã was marching his army south through Thanh Hóa, he encountered the spirit of Mount Trống Đồng, which promised to help his campaign. Phật Mã successfully invaded Champa, killed the Cham commander, and destroyed half his army. On his triumphant return to Thăng Long, Phật Mã built the Đồng Cổ temple in the west of the city as a shrine for the spirit of Mount Trống Đồng, which became the protector of the Lý dynasty and guardian spirit of the Buddhist religion.[100] Its assistance to Phật Mã's army foreshadowed the aid a female earth spirit on the south coast provided to his successor Lý Nhật Tôn. During his 1069 march on Champa, she appeared to Nhật Tôn in a dream, saying: "I have been dwelling namelessly in a tree for a long time, . . . and now I have come forth; if you are able to sacrifice to me, . . . your attack on Champa [will] be successful." Nhật Tôn convinced the spirit to "declare" herself; he identified her tree and erected it on his warship. She protected his fleet from storms, and the king promised her a shrine at Thăng Long. The Lý monarch "domesticated" this southern spirit as the "Imperial Earth Lady" (*Hậu-thổ Phu-nhân*), a northern title that had belonged to a goddess of the Tang era.[101]

The official Vietnamese pantheon proved more inclusive still. During Phật Mã's second invasion of Champa in 1044, his army killed its king and captured most of the Cham court. The thousands of prisoners he marched back to Đại Việt included Champa's royal musicians and dance corps, whose legacy was to exert lasting influence on Vietnamese culture. Just before landing in Đại Việt the captured Cham queen Mỵ Ê jumped from Phật Mã's ship in order to escape dishonor. Her suicide not only elicited Phật Mã's admiration but won her, too, a respected place in the Việt spirit world.[102]

This conversion of conquered queen into local deity recalls the Roman conquest in 396 BCE of the Etruscan city of Veii and the victors' removal to Rome of the cult of Veii's leading deity, Iuni. There she assumed her place as Juno, queen of the Roman pantheon.[103] But Vietnamese expropriation of Cham culture was possibly more extensive. Five thousand Cham prisoners were resettled in Hoan province, which Phật Mã renamed Nghệ An. Court ladies in Thăng Long traveled in gilded carriages drawn by elephants captured from the Chams.[104] In 1060, *VSL* says, "The king himself translated the lyrics and rhythm of a Cham dancing song, and ordered entertainers to perform it."[105] The Lý court assigned major Buddhist temples a labor force of Cham prisoners, who worked as artisans and played a key role in the flourishing art and architecture of Đại Việt's proliferating monasteries. Cham slaves also lived and worked in the temple of the Phù Đổng earth spirit.[106]

In 1069, Nhật Tôn's victorious army brought back thousands more Cham prisoners and resettled them near Thăng Long. These captives included Thảo Đường, a Chinese monk who had been living at the Cham court. Under the guidance of his new royal patron Nhật Tôn, he established Đại Việt's third Thiền Buddhist sect. Alongside the popular Vinītaruci sect that Lý Công Uẩn had favored and the more ascetic and scholarly Vô Ngôn Thông sect of Lý Phật Mã, the kingdom acquired a princely order that was patronized by later Lý monarchs and catered to court interests, but also incorporated more cosmopolitan influences, including elements of Chinese Buddhism.[107] And in the same era, reflecting a different religious influence from Champa, the Hindu deities Phạn Vương (Brahma) and Đế Thích (Indra) made their first appearances in the Vietnamese pantheon.[108] In 1057, the court had statues of each cast in gold and placed in a newly built royal pagoda.[109] Both deities remained objects of royal veneration at least until the thirteenth century. Indra, who also served as the Buddhist King of Heaven, passed into Vietnamese folk tradition as the god of chess.[110]

The persistent Lý wars against Champa were also closely connected to the consolidation of court authority over the regions within Đại Việt itself. When Champa's conquerors "brought back" cults of its queen and Hindu deities to Thăng Long and relocated their powers to the Đại Việt court, the Lý simply replicated what they did with regional Việt spirits said to have participated in their victories over the Chams.

The court's appropriation of the regional Việt spirits was perhaps even more important to central power than were its lucrative raids on Champa, which also helped serve the purpose of suppressing regional disunity. When in 1043 Phật Mã noted Champa's failure to send tribute, his advisers replied, "Your majesty has not yet spread far." They counseled that the king had merely "displayed virtue and bestowed favor in order to soothe" the Chams, instead of demonstrating his "military power by attacking them." The advisers concluded that Champa's insubordination could even infect regions within Đại Việt. "This is not the way to show majesty to distant peoples. We fear that the different clans and nobles in the realm will all become like Champa. Why make an exception for Champa?"[111] From 1037 to 1055 the Lý also forcefully suppressed four ethnic Tai efforts to establish a separate kingdom in the northern hills.[112]

EARLY RISE OF CONFUCIANISM

As northern Cham deities accompanied regional Việt spirits in their relocation to the center of the Vietnamese politico-religious world, and Buddhist influence also escalated, the court became ever more eclectic with increasing signs of Confucianism as well. When he visited Bố Hải seaport to "join the plowing" in 1038, Lý Phật Mã ordered a plot of land specially cleared and a shrine erected on it to the Confucian god of agriculture, before which he plowed three furrows. As he put his hand to the plow, "mandarins" tried to dissuade him, arguing that plowing was "the task of farmers, please do not do it." But the king replied, "If I don't plow the land myself, how can I make offerings to God and set an example for the people?"[113] Taylor considers this exchange the first indication in Đại Việt of royal "advisors with Confucian ideas." He speculates that it may have pitted indigenous adepts of an ancient Austroasiatic rite (like the annual royal plowing of a furrow still practiced in modern Cambodia) against Confucian officials and a more Sinic cult of the god of agriculture. Referring to events of the following year, the thirteenth-century historian Lê Văn Hưu praised the king for having accepted advice from Confucian scholars. In 1041 Phật Mã had statues cast of the Buddha Maitreya and two irrigation gods; the latter may again imply the emergence of Confucian associations between the monarchy and agricultural organization.[114]

Confucian scholar-officials were eventually to become central to the effective reach of a political administration. Công Uẩn's construction in 1020 of an administrative palace, separate from the ceremonial palace, may have launched this long process at the court level.[115] A key point in the expansion of bureaucratic administration beyond the capital was the introduction in 1042–43 of a new legal code, which also had some Confucian overtones, such as mourning regulations, harsher punishments for dissidents, and collective responsibility for officials, as well as measures to strengthen central authority such as the minting of new coins, reorganization of the army and navy, enforcement of conscription, and public works programs involving forced labor for vagrants.[116] Along with the command structure and logistical requirements of a standing army, the enforcement of the new civil and penal laws required a significantly expanded official class. Law officers now made their first appearance in the record, followed in 1067 by more junior royal servants, "scribes" (*thư gia*), ten of whom were promoted to law officers that year. In 1122, the court appointed another twenty law officers. In the 1070s, *thư gia* were recruited among monks with the requisite literary qualifications, who must have come from families able to provide an education in Chinese.[117]

Buddhism and Confucianism were both part of an eclectic elite culture, but the latter was gaining some prominence. From 1059 Lý Nhật Tôn ordered all palace officers who would approach him to wear Chinese-style headgear and footwear. This was followed in 1070 by the reconstruction of the Temple of Literature (Văn Miếu), a scholarly shrine and archive in Thăng Long that was stocked with clay statues of the Duke of Zhou and of Confucius and his followers and paintings of seventy-two other disciples of Confucius.[118] It was also in this era, in 1054, that Nhật Tôn dropped the *nôm* term *cồ* from the written form of the kingdom's official name, Đại Cồ Việt, substituting the Sino-Vietnamese term Đại Việt. Yet other Vietnamese-language variants remained in use, including Cự Việt, which also means "Great Việt."[119]

Indeed, the syncretism of Lý institutions remains striking. The records for the year 1043 first use the term *nho thần*, referring to court officials whom the king ordered to "compose a rhyming narrative" in order to publicize his achievement of an "extraordinary supernatural event."[120] Only much later did *nho thần* come to mean "Confucian officials," who took just as long to monopolize the position of *thái sư* (chancellor). The transition to a Confucian monarchy had barely begun. Lý Nhật Tôn erected a "Great Buddha" statue in Thăng Long as the reincarnation of a pantheon of spirits, including the ancient Lạc earth genie Dóng and the Chinese god of war, Chên Wu, while several years later the *thái sư* Lý Đạo Thành erected a Buddha statue and established a garden dedicated to a Bodhisattva in the grounds of the provincial Temple of Literature in Nghệ An.[121] A modern Vietnamese historian described this process as "the seeping of Confucianism into the writing about local gods and spirits."[122]

Those local spirits included the "yellow dragons" that in the mid-tenth century had auspiciously saved Đinh Bộ Lĩnh's life, "dragon shapes" that appeared on Lê Hoàn's back as a boy, and the "golden dragon" that appeared to Lý Công Uẩn in the river at Thăng Long. After Lý Phật Mã's coronation there two decades later, a "dragon" visited a nearby ruined palace that Phật Mã deduced "must be the dragon's ascending land," again suggesting a crocodile emerging from the water. Each of these single "dragon" appearances serves in *VSL* as an early omen of a monarch's rise or reigning glory.[123] *DVSKTT* adds a second incident in Công Uẩn's reign, during his last days in 1028. A Daoist priest entrusted with the old king's robes placed them in the "Southern Emperor Daoist Temple," where a "shimmering yellow dragon" appeared in the night.[124] Then in the late eleventh century, the Đại Việt court developed a full-blown royal cult of Công Uẩn's "golden dragon." In *VSL*, its single recorded appearance for each monarch gives way to no fewer than twenty-three sightings of a "golden dragon" during Nhật Tôn's reign (1054–72), including ten at the height of his triumph over Champa in 1068–69 and another eighteen appearances from 1072 to 1125. Was this a revival of an ancient Lạc crocodile cult, now merged with Daoist mysticism but perhaps also with the imperial image of the Chinese dragon? Yet another indigenous aquatic rite, royal sponsorship of boat races in the river, is reminiscent of Yuè Dragon Boat Festivals and scenes depicted on ancient Đông Sơn drums. *VSL* records Đại Việt kings attending canoe races every couple of decades from 985 to 1055, but then with much greater frequency from the height of Nhật Tôn's reign: nine boat festivals occurred between 1067 and 1104. That reign, and perhaps Nhật Tôn's conquest of Champa, was clearly a key moment in the cultural history of the Đại Việt monarchy. The proliferation of dragons and boat races seems to have accompanied the advent of the warmer, wetter climate, which enhanced the aquatic elements of Đại Việt's environment and culture.

In foreign policy, the Lý monarchs opened diplomatic relations with Champa's southern and western neighbor, the Khmer kingdom that Vietnamese called Chân-lạp (after its Chinese name, Chenla). A Khmer inscription dated 987 records the arrival of Vietnamese traders from across the Annamite Cordillera.[125] *VSL* states that Chân-lạp first sent "tribute" to Đại Việt—in fact probably further peaceful trading overtures—in 1012 and 1014, and then at intervals of eleven to seventeen years.[126] After 1056, the next Khmer mission is recorded in 1069, perhaps precipitated by Nhật Tôn's devastating invasion of Champa in that year. The Vietnamese general Lý Thường Kiệt pushed far to the south in pursuit of the fugitive Cham king, Rudravarman III, capturing him "on the border of Chân-lạp." Nhật Tôn took the prisoner back to Đại Việt for display in a victory parade, "dressed in rough white cotton clothes and hat, silk belt, together with his many close servants . . . all tied up and escorted by five guards." The Khmer king dispatched "tribute" to Đại Việt in 1069 and 1072.[127]

NORTHERN INVASION

Đại Việt fought off another Song invasion in 1076. According to a Chinese account, the Vietnamese kingdom had conducted incursions into Guangxi during Nhật Tôn's reign. It occupied Quảng Yên and "62 townships."[128] But an imperial official warned the emperor not to attack Đại Việt: "The roads through the mountains are remote and arduous, there is much rain with pestilential vapors; the climate is poisonous. It is difficult to take this territory, and I am afraid that it cannot be held."[129] Lê Tắc's *An Nam chí lược* states that the conflict began after Nhật Tôn's death, when the prime minister at the imperial court planned to reconquer "Jiaozhi" and forbade border prefectures from trading with it: "Then the king of Jiaozhi resolved to make war."[130] But that king was Nhật Tôn's nine-year-old son, Lý Nhân Tông. After at least seven years of war, real power at court lay in the hands of his mother, Queen Ỷ Lan, the *thái sư* Lý Đạo Thành, and the *thái úy*, or commander in chief of all military forces, Lý Thường Kiệt.[131] The combination of queen mother and military commander was to prove most potent.

A large Đại Việt army seized three Song border prefectures in 1075. In response, proclaiming that "the king has revolted and attacked my fortresses and towns," the Song emperor dispatched nine armies to "end this tyrannical mode of government." For the first time in a century, imperial forces had to fight on Southeast Asian terrain. First they confronted a corps of war elephants, which the "barbarians" deployed to effect, in their own "method of warfare." But by swinging scythes fixed on lances, the invaders managed to sever some of the elephants' trunks, which drove back the terrified beasts and sent them rampaging through the ranks of the defenders. The Song forces then marched on southward to the Red River, where they faced "three hundred war junks of Jiaozhi... drawn up on the bank." The Vietnamese attacked but, according to Chinese documents, "suffered a great defeat." Then the magnanimous emperor exonerated the "young" monarch Lý Nhân Tông, and invited him to serve as "the true king of Annam" by providing "a protective shield for China"; supposedly, when he accepted, the imperial forces withdrew. However, their commanders gained very mixed evaluations at home.[132] Diseases had ravaged the imperial army, taking the lives of most of its 870,000 troops.[133]

By contrast, *VSL* claims a great military victory over the northerners: "The king sent Lý Thường Kiệt to deploy marines to resist them... The two opposing armies blocked each other in the Như Nguyệt River for over a month. Thường Kiệt knew that the Song troops were about to become tired, so he plotted to cross the river at night and stage a sudden attack, winning a great battle." This Vietnamese source corroborates the Chinese only in contending that the Song "had to retreat," with "losses of 50–60 percent."[134] Before the battle, Lý Thường Kiệt had told his troops: "The Southern emperor rules the Southern land."[135]

But the empire held on to part of Quảng Yên province, and the Vietnamese victory took longer to complete. Reporting to the emperor in 1077, imperial censor Thsai Fong-hi invoked "the rules to observe in relation to distant countries: one should not get involved in their government." Now, despite a continuing occupation, "the brigandage of the people of Jiaozhi has not ceased; the soldiers who die on the roads of that backward country form an uninterrupted line; finally, we have nothing left to send to support the troops, the wealth of the state is exhausted and the losses are counted in the tens and hundreds of thousands. . . . It is a calamity." The censor added that "these Man barbarians have their peculiar customs," and were "beyond the category of frontier countries comprising part of the empire." He minced no words: "Today the court is making the war with these Man barbarians a matter of revenge. We have taken their country and their troops, their chiefs have been put to death, but these people are so stupid that they are again recommencing their disorders." Thsai's advice to the emperor was to "rethink this war," granting the border populations some peace. "Then our current misery will have disappeared, and we will be able to reconsider Annam."[136] Now the empire withdrew its armies. And in unprecedented succession three Khmer missions arrived in Thăng Long—in 1086, 1088, and 1095.[137] These years after Đại Việt's defeat of the Song were the most intense period of its developing diplomatic relations with Cambodia.

THE COURT BUREAUCRACY

Within Đại Việt, too, the Lý court slowly concentrated its power and that of its military commander. The expansion of central authority had first begun with the new posts Đinh Bộ Lĩnh had created at his court in the 960s and 970s: a "commander in chief of all armies" (*thập-đạo tướng quân*), a chancellor (*thái sư*, a post also filled by Lê Hoàn in the 980s), an "officer of national unification" (*định quốc công*), and a "Great Preceptor for Reforming the Việt" (*đại sư khuông Việt*).[138] Only under the Lý from the mid- to late eleventh century did these posts gradually become more distinct, permanent, and powerful, especially that of the military commander in chief, retitled the *thái úy* by 1048. The civilian office of *thái sư* initially involved tutoring the crown prince in the classics and histories. Filled permanently from 1028, it became more significant after 1072. In addition, the new office of *quốc sư* (state preceptor, or master of the realm), a post named and permanently occupied only from around 1069, involved the crown prince's Buddhist education. The rise of the *thái sư* might have undermined Buddhist primacy and necessitated the creation of the post of *quốc sư* for leading monks. But both posts had religious as well as secular functions.[139] It is easy to imagine the power of either position when a minor occupied the throne (as became increasingly common) and, in cases of conflict between them, how the military post of commander in chief, *thái úy*, could later become the most powerful of all. In 1048 the Duke of Quách was the first *thái úy*; his son, the accomplished professional general Lý Thường Kiệt (1019–1105), became the second.[140] Meanwhile, the monarch entrusted the liaison between the throne and the executive branch only to illiterate eunuchs, officials called *hành khiển*.[141]

The court promoted a new bureaucracy. In 1075, soon after the refurbishing of the Temple of Literature, the *thái sư* Lý Đạo Thành began to organize three levels of examinations "to select senior graduates familiar with the classics and broader learning." From the next year, even as Đại Việt fought its war against China, the rudiments of a civil service took shape: "worthy men with civil and military ability" were chosen to "govern the army people," while "civilian officials acquainted with letters" were selected for the Imperial Academy. An examination in 1077 tested officials on "letters and laws." Lý Đạo Thành's protégé Lê Văn Thịnh won highest honors in the 1075 examinations, was appointed the young king's tutor, took charge of the war ministry in 1076, and helped negotiate the border with Song officials in 1084. Lý Đạo Thành died in 1081 after serving twenty-seven years as *thái sư*. Lê Văn Thịnh occupied that post from 1085 to 1096. He set up and staffed the Hàn Lâm Academy in 1086 and a "privy council" the next year. In 1088 the court even sent officials to oversee the "fields, servants, storehouses and valuables" of Buddhist temples, which it ranked in three categories by size. The next year the court underwent reorganization, and in 1092, the "field tax" was revised.[142]

In some ways the institutional extension of Lý power in the development of all these court positions also marked the beginning of the end of the personal authority of Lý monarchs. Their success in building central institutions, especially those of the *thái sư* (chancellor) and *thái úy* (commander in chief) gave occupants of those positions a large staff of their own and made them more powerful. No longer simply reporting to the monarch, they commanded their own bureaucracies. This proved most significant under young or ineffective kings, who were frequent after Lý Nhật Tôn's death in 1072 and especially after 1127.[143] None of the last five Lý rulers (1072–1225) were adults at the time of their accession.[144]

However, the civilian *thái sư*, the key post in the eleventh century and briefly the dominant one after 1072, lost prominence in 1096 when Lê Văn Thịnh was exiled after being found guilty of a plot to murder the king. The Lý court held no further examinations on the classical texts. No subsequent *thái sư* regained the influence that post had previously wielded.[145] Instead, successive *thái úy* dominated the Lý court for six decades (1127–88).[146]

The new predominance of the commander in chief was not simply a result of the importance the army had gained during a long era of warfare and the opportunities it offered for career advancement. During the twelfth century, Taylor writes, it was powerful maternal clans headed by queens who often represented rival regional constituencies that took control of the court through the military authority of the *thái úy*.[147] The court tried in 1136 to limit the problem with a decree warning all families, including those outside the capital, to report court officials who had placed their sons in other households "in order to depend on powerful families." The Lý dynasty's project of assembling Đại Việt's regional family clans into a kingdom run by a central bureaucracy began to unravel. The monarchy's multiple marriage alliances had proved a double-edged strategy. Relocated regional spirits were easier to domesticate in the capital than military strongmen, contending queens from regional clans, and their numerous offspring with claims to the throne. Of the eight Lý monarchs who succeeded the dynasty's founder in the two centuries from 1028 to 1224, the only one to enjoy an uneventful succession was Lý Nhật Tôn in 1054.[148] In the twelfth century, "the Lý family ceased to rule." The court became "the scene of bitter factional feuds."[149] Đại Việt's regional disunity had come to the capital.

The most powerful *thái úy* was Đỗ Anh Vũ (1114–1159), whose assets were economic as well as military. An inscription his mother placed in the Diên Phúc Buddhist temple in 1157 records that Đỗ Anh Vũ possessed a fiefdom of four thousand households and additional land farmed by another ten thousand households—an estate larger than Đinh Liễn had claimed in 979.[150] In the interim, the improved agricultural conditions and increased prosperity of the twelfth century, along with the weakening of the Lý monarchy, had probably led to greater concentration of landholdings and a resurgence of regional landowning families and Buddhist monastic estates. *VSL* reveals a royal attempt to regulate what appears to have been a highly contested land market in 1140, when "the king issued an edict ruling that all the farming fields that had been mortgaged for 20 years could be returned with some payment, but the farms whose ownership was in dispute for over 5 or 10 years could no longer be brought to court. Those farms that had been sold with written documents could no longer be bought back."[151] The large landowners included Buddhist monasteries. The 1157 inscription describes the Diên Phúc temple "in a spectacular manner," giving details of its architecture and statuary, and noting the placement at the center of the altar of the Bodhisattva Avalokiteśvara (representing compassion), flanked on her right and left by the Bodhisattvas Mañjuśrī (embodying the wisdom of all Buddhas) and Samantabhadra (the leading Bodhisattva of conduct), along with statues of the Kim Cương Bodhisattva Vajrapāṇi (representative of the Buddha's power), Hộ Pháp (Guardians of the Dharma), and Tứ Thiên Vương (the Four God Kings, or guardians of the quarters).[152]

Đỗ Anh Vũ's career illustrates the trajectory of leading families and their domination of the Lý court. He was a great-grandson of the first *thái úy*, the Duke of Quách, and grand-nephew of the latter's son and successor Lý Thường Kiệt. His father was a son of Kiệt's sister. The continuing importance of the maternal clan is evident in another long inscription carved at Đỗ Anh Vũ's tomb, where he was buried in 1159 on his mother's family land. That theme is prominent even though this later inscription makes no mention of Buddhism and instead narrates the life of Đỗ Anh Vũ with numerous allusions to Confucian classics propounding models of civilized and correct behavior. It records that his father, Đỗ Tướng, had journeyed as a youth to the capital "and saw the daughter of an honorable family; her thoughts were pure and dignified, her nature was gentle and chaste, her smile surpassed the blossoms of spring, and her behavior was like beautiful jade." After Đỗ Tướng died, the 1159 inscription goes on, their young son Đỗ Anh Vũ attracted the attention of the future Duke of Trương, a court official named Lê Bá Ngọc, who "brought him up as his own son." Anh Vũ himself came to be called "duke." According to the inscription, the young duke was "slender and graceful with a snowy pure complexion and a radiant countenance." When he reached ten years of age, Emperor Lý Nhân Tông, seeing his intelligence and "godlike demeanor," chose him "to dwell in the imperial compound." In his adolescence there, Anh Vũ gained a reputation for "dancing upon embroidered cushions with shield and battleaxe" and for singing "The Return of the Phoenix." He studied geomancy and military tactics, and excelled in "writing, numerical calculation, archery, chariot driving, medicine, acupuncture, and diagnosing illness by taking the pulse."[153] His family was placed to acquire real influence at court. Having risen through the military ranks, Anh Vũ's adoptive father, Lê Bá Ngọc, became *thái úy* after ensuring the accession to the throne in 1127 of his and Nhân Tông's twelve-year-old nephew, Lý Thần Tông. The adolescent king soon took two wives, one of whom, a daughter of Lê Bá Ngọc's nephew, was Anh Vũ's cousin. He and Anh Vũ "had the run of the place."[154] One of the king's first duties was to preside over his predecessor's funeral pyre and "watch royal maids stepping into fires to take their lives following the late Nhân Tông."[155] The two new empresses quickly departed to visit their families. Wolters comments: "Here, surely, is a political marriage which could hardly have been consummated." Thirteenth-century historian Lê Văn Hưu raged that "there were no men at court."[156]

Meanwhile, Đại Việt's diplomatic security in Southeast Asia was deteriorating. After 1095, *VSL* records the arrival of no Cambodian mission for more than two decades. Indeed, even some of the later references to "Chân-lạp" may refer not to Cambodia (known to China as "Water Chenla," the Lower Mekong plain and delta) but to the upriver, inland Lao realm of Vientiane (Văn Đan), which the Chinese called "Land Chenla."[157] But in 1113, after a period of disunity in Cambodia, Suryavarman II, the builder of Angkor Wat, seized the throne and reigned until 1150. *VSL* mentions three missions from "Chân-lạp" in 1118–23. Then in 1128, Suryavarman demanded that Đại Việt in turn send envoys and tribute. It refused.[158] Twenty years of wars followed, which can only have enhanced the position of the *thái úy* in Thăng Long. Twice in 1128, according to *VSL*, Chân-lạp "sent rebels" and "bandits" to plunder Nghệ An province.[159] *DVSKTT* says they numbered twenty thousand Khmer troops.[160] It was at this point that Lê Bá Ngọc assumed the title *thái sư*. By now the post of *thái úy*, which he already occupied, had become the more powerful position. Until he died in 1135, Lê Bá Ngọc dominated the court while his adopted son Đỗ Anh Vũ grew to fill his shoes, with the crucial patronage of Empress Lê Cảm Thánh.[161]

The warfare escalated in 1132 when Chân-lạp and Champa jointly invaded Đại Việt, briefly seizing Nghệ An.[162] Three years later, forces from Vientiane again "invaded the southern bordertowns."[163] Twenty-one-year-old Đỗ Anh Vũ marched against them with the *thái phó* (a military official under the *thái sư*) and thirty thousand troops. He then subdued Sơn Liêu uplanders who had "held the passes." After his adoptive father's death, "All affairs both within and without the inner palace were accordingly entrusted to him."[164]

As the twenty-two-year-old emperor lay on his deathbed in 1137, Lê Cảm Thánh, with the aid of two other queens, bribed a privy councilor and prevailed upon the emperor to revoke his will and name her son as his successor.[165] Đỗ Anh Vũ, who led the two-year-old heir "up the imperial stairs," now saw to "all the numerous affairs of the kingdom." Empress Mother Lê Cảm Thánh immediately appointed him *thái phó*. The next year she again "promoted" him, to *phụ quốc thái úy* (prime minister).[166] Anh Vũ had thus leapfrogged over the post of *thái sư* to become *thái úy*. "Military affairs were completely in his hands." After Anh Vũ defeated the first of a succession of northern hill rebellions, the boy emperor awarded him fiefs of all the kingdom's territories outside the Red River plain: Nghệ An and Thanh Hoá to the south and Phú Lương in the north. Queen, clan, and commander had taken over court and country. Two daughters of Anh Vũ's paternal cousin eventually became royal wives. His tomb inscription tells us: "Both sisters were without jealousy and were zealous to increase in virtue. They worked together with vegetables and were very industrious. They served at bathing and washing without weariness." The elder sister later gave birth to the infant prince who assumed the throne in 1175—yet another royal minor, whose reign would be supervised by Anh Vũ's former leading lieutenant.[167]

Anh Vũ's dominance did provoke a reaction. The 1159 inscription on his tomb did not specify his relationship with Empress Mother Lê Cảm Thánh, but *VSL*, written two centuries afterward and apparently based on private records, says that in 1143 a special palace had been built for the empress mother, where Anh Vũ "pursued a romantic relationship" with her.[168] *DVSKTT* explains how: "Anh Vũ sent his wife, a woman of the Tô clan, into the forbidden palace to serve the Đỗ Empress Mother [his kinswoman]; using this as a pretext, Anh Vũ established secret illicit intercourse with the Lê Empress Mother."[169] *VSL* asserts that he soon "became more and more arrogant, unrestrained." At court "he yelled at people, making mandarins dare to signal only by facial expressions; everyone was scared not daring to say a word." Finally a prince and the chief of the front palace guards "led their army to the Việt-thành gate," shouting: "Anh Vũ has been coming in and out of the forbidden palace, [and has] committed many sins, his notoriety has spread outside. We would like to punish him." The king then "chaired the prosecution" of Đỗ Anh Vũ, found him guilty, and sentenced him to exile. However, the empress mother again prevailed. Anh Vũ was recalled, pardoned, reappointed *thái úy*, "and the king trusted him even more." Anh Vũ had thirty-three of his enemies killed and thirty exiled.[170]

The legacy of the powerful military commander endured after Đỗ Anh Vũ died in 1159. His former leading lieutenant, Tô Hiến Thành, played a similar dominant role at court for the next two decades.[171] In 1175, the dying emperor appointed him *thái sư*. He then became regent to Lý Cao Tông, who assumed the throne at age two.[172] When Tô Hiến Thành died in 1179, Đỗ Anh Di, a first cousin once removed of Đỗ Anh Vũ, became the kingdom's de facto ruler until his own death in 1188.[173]

Meanwhile, from the late twelfth century, economic growth in both Đại Việt and southeastern China strengthened links between them, producing increased circulation of goods, ideas, and people.[174] Chinese immigrants to Đại Việt included "a very large number of literati, Buddhist monks, Daoist priests, merchants and refugees of all kinds," and "hundreds of thousands" of enslaved men and women whom "infamous traffickers" from the empire's southern provinces kidnapped and sold across the border.[175] The two states' increasing integration may have been evident in warmer official relations as early as 1164, when the Song dynasty finally abandoned its claim over Đại Việt as an "internal vassal" (*quận vương*) and recognized its monarch as an "external vassal" ruling the "kingdom" of Annam (*An nam quốc vương*).[176] Equally diplomatic, the Vietnamese court referred to itself in Chinese as "the Protectorate of An-nan" (An Nan Duhufu; *V.* An Nam Đô Hộ Phủ) and even changed its official seal, which had read *Nam Việt Quốc Âm* (Seal of the State of Nán Yuè), to *Chung Shu Men Hsia Chih Yin* (Seal of the [Imperial] Secretariat and Chancellery).[177] Material exchanges also had a ring of reciprocity. In 1172, Đại Việt offered tribute to the Song emperor, who insisted on paying for ten elephants for a sacrifice to heaven. Đại Việt in turn rejected the offer of payment, stating that its elephants were not for sale. When its tribute reached China the next year, it included fifteen elephants. Each animal came bearing a gilded palanquin furnished with embroidered cushions, its tusks encased in golden sheaths and its body festooned with ornaments "such that one could hardly see anything of the animal."[178]

Key aspects of northern culture remained important to Vietnamese. A Chinese visitor wrote that Lý official appointments could be inherited, bought, or won on merit through examination in the classics, but that the last route was "the most respected."[179] Writing in 1225, in the Lý dynasty's last days, another Chinese official noted that the king of "Jiaozhi" had "a Chinese surname" and that "the clothing and food of the people are practically the same as in the Middle Kingdom." But he also noted two exceptions: in Đại Việt "both sexes go barefooted," and "on New Year's day they pray to the Buddha, but they do not make presents to their ancestors (as we do in China)."[180] He might also have noted the absence of Confucian civil service recruitment examinations in late Lý Đại Việt. A temple inscription from 1226, found on the outskirts of Hanoi, describes the new temple's eclectic altar: the Buddha statue was flanked by an Apsara, one of the Hindu water and cloud nymphs, and a Bodhisattva with a clenched fist. Before the altar stood statues of a Guardian of the Dharma flanked by Mỹ Âm, king of the Gandharvas, mythical musician husbands of the Apsaras, and (possibly) Kauṇḍinya, the Buddha's leading early disciple. A modern historian discerns here "a trace of Indian or Cham influence."[181] Another concludes that by the time of its fall, "Lý Vietnam had acquired an armature of Chinese government forms without developing habits of mind which could see these forms as part of a sacrosanct system." Confucianism was far from becoming the organizing principle of the Lý polity. Indigenous "Vietnamese social practices and religious loyalties survived as a source of weakness of the dynasty."[182]

Even the substantial trade with China failed to strengthen the Lý court. The profits probably enriched competing families more. After rule by successive strongmen for the six decades to 1188, the Lý system of government began a "thirty-year slide into ruin."[183] Even as he grew to adulthood, Lý Cao Tông's reign became "increasingly disorderly."[184] Revolts broke out. Cao Tông imprisoned and then killed his own general, whose deputy then briefly seized the capital.[185] The dynasty was in disarray. *VSL* records that in 1209, the emperor "sent Pham Du to Hồng Lộ to train troops." But "when the Hồng Lộ men came to take him at the appointed time, Du was making love to Princess Thiên Cực and had forgotten all about the appointment and missed it."[186]

Meanwhile in Champa, periodic regional conflicts escalated with the emergence around the year 1200 of an independent southern Cham kingdom at Pāṇḍuraṅga (*V.* Phan Rang), a formerly subordinate court that now rivaled the previously predominant northern Cham kingdoms based at Amaravati and then Vijaya (Bình Định).[187] The China trade at the prosperous peak of the Medieval Warm Period probably fueled Pāṇḍuraṅga's ascent, and may also have facilitated the rise of a new dynasty in Đại Việt.

DYNASTIC CHANGE

The Lý dynasty's end came at the hands of a regional family whose marriage alliances had enabled it to "infiltrate and control" the court. The Trần family hailed from the eastern end of the Red River delta, near the coast and the maritime border with China.[188] Its patriarch, Trần Lý, "a rich fisherman who enjoyed great popularity," commanded a "band of pirates" in the region. There the Lý crown prince met and married Trần Lý's daughter Trần Thị.[189] After the prince's accession in 1210 as Emperor Lý Huệ Tông, more revolts wracked the countryside for five years.[190] The new queen, her brothers, and her cousin Trần Thủ Độ became the real rulers. Huệ Tông finally abdicated in 1224 in favor of his seven-year-old daughter. She in turn was prevailed upon to abdicate in favor of her new husband, Trần Thủ Độ's eight-year-old nephew, who became the first ruler of the new Trần dynasty, Emperor Trần Thái Tông (r. 1225–1258).[191] However, his uncle Trần Thủ Độ maintained the late Lý precedent of court strongman and regent. Already the lover of the former queen Trần Thị, Thủ Độ arranged the deaths of the last members of the Lý family and wielded influence until he died in 1264.[192]

The last decades of the Lý also saw the disappearance of all three Thiền (Zen) Buddhist sects in Đại Việt. The Thảo Đường palace sect came to an end with the death of Emperor Lý Cao Tông in 1210, and the last masters of the popular Vinītaruci and the scholarly Vô Ngôn Thông sects all died in 1213–28.[193] The relative decline of Buddhist influence at court is also implied in the Vietnamese annals for the entire thirteenth century, which only once mention the post of *quốc sư*, held by leading monks (in 1237).[194]

Conversely, the Trần dynasty revived public service examinations on the Chinese classics for the first time since 1096.[195] From 1232 to 1400, the Trần held perhaps seventeen competitive examination sessions (compared with seven under the Lý, 1009–1225). These served to recruit not only civil officials but also Buddhist monks and Daoist priests, who were subjected to examinations in all the "three doctrines." The initial impact of the recruitments was limited. The first two examinations, in 1232 and 1239, produced only nine graduates, and from 1247 to 1275 the number averaged thirty-eight per decade.[196] The new graduates did not yet represent a wave of Confucian scholars that could take over the existing administration of Đại Việt. The court continued to patronize Buddhism, and new Zen sects appeared (and disappeared), but slow changes were setting the stage for the later dominance of Confucianism.[197]

The early Trần rulers also moved to strengthen the monarchy, by limiting interfamily rivalries within the court. They each appointed only one empress and further minimized possible succession conflicts by naming an adult son emperor and then stepping back into a role of "senior emperor," while retaining the right to depose the emperor.[198] Trần Thái Tông, for instance, followed his inaugural thirty-three-year reign with another nineteen years as senior emperor, dominating the court until his death at age sixty in 1277.[199] The next two Trần rulers avoided the influence of other families by marrying their cousins. Family members from the senior emperor's generation held the court's highest positions and excluded their in-laws. Throughout the thirteenth century, the Trần family retained firm control of all senior posts.[200]

WARMER WEATHER INCUBATES SOCIAL CHANGE

This was an era of prosperity. The Trần dynasty came to power near the peak of the Medieval Warm Period with its patterns of very high rainfall. The agriculturally productive twelfth century was followed by another

125 years of warm, wet climate. The interval 1250–1325 alone included nine of the twenty-four wettest years of the entire period 1250–2008.[201] In the severe flood of 1270, only boats could navigate Thăng Long's streets. These conditions prompted the construction of dikes to control the flow of water.[202] Hydraulic works also facilitated agriculture, improving both drainage and irrigation. The Red River valley became "a rich granary" and military stronghold.[203] The delta's population doubled, from an estimated 1.2 million around 1200 to about 2.4 million by 1340. Yet this in turn led to increased landlessness.[204] In 1266 Emperor Trần Thánh Tông permitted members of the royal family to round up landless farmers and open up vacant land. "The empire is our ancestors'," he declared at a family feast two years later, and he who inherits it "should share the enjoyment of riches and status with his brothers in the family."[205] Wealthy royal, aristocratic, and Buddhist monastic landowners all employed large numbers of serfs on their expanding agricultural estates.

Widespread rural productivity and cheap labor also fostered a new agrarian class of modestly wealthy "lower landlords," who farmed private holdings with hired laborers and tenants. Among educated sons of these rising smaller landowners, a new school of Confucian literati emerged, particularly in coastal provinces east and south of Thăng Long, such as Hải Dương and Ninh Bình, areas formed by the delta's slow southeastward expansion and reclamation of land from the sea. These new classically educated literati complemented those in the Buddhist-dominated court and competed effectively in the reinstituted civil service examinations for the rising number of midlevel bureaucratic posts.[206] And when tensions heightened with China, the importance of scholar bureaucrats rose with the court's need to draft professional diplomatic communications.[207]

Good relations with the empire continued at first. In 1206, the Song emperor had endorsed the embattled Lý monarch as "king of Annam" and leader of "your maritime country."[208] As the Trần took power, the imperial superintendent of maritime trade in Fujian province explained that military occupation of "Jiaozhi" would be "extremely expensive" and added that "the Government of our present [Song] dynasty, out of affection for the army... deemed it advisable that our troops should no longer be kept in this pestilential climate for the purpose of guarding such an unprofitable territory." Yet he went on to list Đại Việt's valuable products that came in annual tribute: gharu wood, gold, silver, iron, cinnabar, cowries, rhinoceros horn, elephants, kingfishers, shells, salt, lacquer, and cottons.[209] Another sign of the kingdom's closer economic and cultural relations with the north was an order from the Thăng Long court in 1237 that the Trần emperor be offered both "betel and tea" as he embarked from the Eastern Pier.[210]

MONGOL INVASIONS

By the 1250s, the Mongol invasions from the north sent a number of Song officials fleeing south into Đại Việt for refuge.[211] The armies of Kubilai Khan, soon to become founding emperor of the new Yuan dynasty (1271–1368), reached the empire's southern border in 1257. The Mongols demanded that the Trần court grant them passage through Đại Việt territory in order to encircle Song forces. When Emperor Trần Thái Tông refused, the Mongols marched in. Like previous northern invaders, they had to deal with the unfamiliar Southeast Asian environment and methods of warfare. The Vietnamese emperor sent war elephants and infantry to repel them. Mongol archers fired on the elephants, which turned in terror and fled, crushing many Đại Việt soldiers. The invaders pushed on through the riverine landscape, again using their archers to locate fords for their cavalry, testing the depth by loosing "arrows into the air all along the river" and noting where shafts protruded above the water. The Mongol cavalry bounded across the shallows. In a second battle, the northerners killed ten thousand defenders. In 1258 they sacked Thăng Long. But the environment took its toll on them; local resistance, disease, and bad weather soon forced the Mongols to withdraw from Đại Việt.[212]

They returned a quarter century later. First, the Yuan dynasty sent troops against Champa in 1282 and demanded assistance from the Trần court, which again refused.[213] Two years later Kubilai Khan's son Togan and a Yuan fleet landed an army on the south coast between Champa and Đại Việt. Then another Mongol force marched across Đại Việt's northern border in early 1285. Deploying captured Vietnamese junks, it twice defeated a large defending army, crossed the Red River, seized Thăng Long, and sacked the city again. Togan gave a victory banquet in the Đại Việt royal palace. Presented with prisoners of war, he ordered them executed.[214]

Emperor Trần Nhân Tông escaped south toward Thanh Hóa with his army general, Prince Trần Hưng Đạo. Now the second Mongol force marched north from the Champa border to trap the Vietnamese in a pincer operation. First the invaders captured Nghệ An, and a large number of its defenders defected to the Yuan. These included not only the king's nephew Trần Kiện, governor of Nghệ An, but another prince, a marquis, and as many as thirty thousand of their followers. With their help the Yuan took control of Thanh Hóa and beheaded a thousand prisoners.[215]

But other Vietnamese forces escaped west into the mountains, while farther north Trần Hưng Đạo went on the attack with fifty thousand men, including some former Song officers. These armies staged a remarkable comeback, retaking Thăng Long "by surprise" and winning a series of victories over the Mongol army of half a million men. In a final battle, the Vietnamese killed both Togan and Trần Kiện and captured fifty thousand invading troops. By mid-1285, they had driven the retreating Mongol forces from Đại Việt. Furious, Kubilai Khan canceled his planned seaborne invasion of Japan and instead sent his fleet to stage a third assault on Đại Việt. But in the spring of 1288, Trần Hưng Đạo's forces, as Vietnamese defenders had done twice before, placed iron-tipped wooden stakes below the high-water level on the Bạch Đằng River. They sank the Mongol fleet and killed the Yuan commander.[216] Wolters felt that these three victories made the Trần "the most renowned of all Vietnamese dynasties."[217]

LÊ VĂN HƯU, HISTORIAN

Another outcome of the Mongol wars was the emergence of an indigenous Vietnamese historiography. Lê Văn Hưu (1230–1322) is considered the first great Vietnamese historian. Born in Đông Sơn county of Thanh Hóa, at the age of seventeen Lê Văn Hưu took the Trần court's civil service examinations, successfully achieved second rank among the candidates, and was assigned to help draft a new penal code. He rose to become minister of war, and by the 1270s served concurrently in the Hàn Lâm Academy and as director of the Office of Historiographers (*Chưởng sử quan*).[218]

After the first Mongol invasion of 1257, Emperor Trần Thái Tông commissioned Lê Văn Hưu to edit the records of Đại Việt and write its history. This project sprung in part from the emperor's interest in the ancient past, which had led him to launch in 1253 a new court-sponsored program, "learning of antiquity," under the direction of "classicists" (*nho*) teaching from the Four Books and the Six Classics. That year Trần Thái Tông also founded the National Academy next to the *Văn Miếu*, which housed statues for the worship of Confucius and the Duke of Chou and portraits of the Seventy-Two Worthies.[219] In 1258 he passed the throne to his son and became "senior emperor," with a new title, "the emperor who is manifesting Yao's sage (-like) old age," an allusion to Mencius's stipulation that rulers must ensure their succession. Yet the focus of this royal interest in antiquity was also decidedly local. During the 1260s the Trần court incurred Kubilai Khan's wrath for treating his envoys as if they were approaching an independent kingdom, and in 1271 it defended that protocol as befitting the "ancient customs" of Đại Việt. Trần Thái Tông seems to have dated those customs back as far as Zhào Tuó (*V.* Triệu Đà), founder of the classical Nán Yuè kingdom. In him, Đại Việt now saw its own ancient sage ruler. Thái Tông ordered Lê Văn Hưu to begin his historical account with Triệu Đà's foundation of Nán Yuè (207 BCE) and to end at the fall of the Lý in 1225 CE.[220]

Lê Văn Hưu set to work, drawing in large measure on a recent (mid-thirteenth century) history by Trần Chu Phổ entitled *Việt Chí* (Annals of Việt).[221] However, Lê Văn Hưu replicated the structure of the great work of the eleventh-century Song historian Sima Guang, who had chronicled imperial dynasties from the fifth century BCE to the tenth century. And Lê Văn Hưu delved into Chinese sources on the imperial tributary relationship with Đại Việt. In early 1272, he submitted his well-received thirty-chapter work, *Đại Việt Sử Ký*, to Trần Thánh Tông's court.[222] Like *Việt Chí* and works from the early Lý era, this history has not survived. But later excerpts show that Lê Văn Hưu had made a new departure in Vietnamese historiography. His themes included the country's ancient beginnings, sage rulers, imperial status, dynastic succession, officials' loyalty to its ruler, and defense of its polity and territory.

First, following the wishes of his royal patron, Lê Văn Hưu enshrined Triệu Đà as the founding sage who "inaugurated the imperial institution in our country." Since then it had constituted an empire, a peer of China. Lê Văn Hưu compared Triệu Đà to China's legendary sage rulers Shun and Wen Wang, and praised him for "sealing off the frontier, establishing the country's army, following the correct way in . . . relations with neighbouring countries, and safeguarding [the] throne." Lê Văn Hưu bolstered Triệu Đà's sage status by frequently citing the authority of Mencius on the ruler's succession (advice Trần Thái Tông had followed in 1258).[223]

The first-century Trưng sisters, in Lê Văn Hưu's patriarchal estimation, did not qualify as imperial successors to Triệu Đà. Rather, they provided examples of women whose actions simply pointed up the failings of Vietnamese male leaders for "over 1,000 years" of Chinese rule:

> Trưng Trắc and Trưng Nhị were women, but they had only to make one single appeal then the whole provinces of [Jiuzhen, Rinan, Hepu], together with 65 counties in Ngũ-lĩnh, all responded! Setting up the country and conducting a monarchy [*làm vua*] were so easy for them! . . . [But] men were merely kowtowing and resigning to submit to the Chinese! They would not even know that they should be embarrassed by the two Trưng ladies! How shameful![224]

Lê Văn Hưu then praised Ngô Quyền for winning independence in the tenth century and for restoring "the royal lineage for our country." But, he added, Quyền "only proclaimed himself king [*vương*], not yet . . . emperor [*hoàng-đế*]." Lê Văn Hưu refrained from honoring Quyền as a successor to Triệu Đà.[225] Only when Đinh Bộ Lĩnh claimed the title *Hoàng-đế* does Lê

Văn Hưu comment: "Was it not, indeed, Heaven's will that our country should again produce the sage's wisdom so that Triệu vương should have a successor?"[226]

Unlike imperial historians, Lê Văn Hưu relentlessly criticized founders of other dynasties for failing to live up to the model of the ancients. In Đại Việt's case this now meant Triệu Đà's example. Thus the titles that the first Lý monarch conferred on his parents failed to meet Lê Văn Hưu's imperial parity standard.[227] And in his first two years, before establishing "villages and administration," Lý Thái Tổ had new pagodas constructed, "hundreds" upgraded, "and thousands of people at the Buddhist schools" ordained as monks. "So much energy from the people had been wasted just to pray for the harmony of the land," Lê Văn Hưu concluded. "Wasn't that like draining people's blood and flesh?"[228] He praised Lý Thái Tổ's two successors for strengthening the polity militarily, for instance by avenging Cham attacks, but they also received disdain for leniency toward rebellious Nùng hill people. What Lê Văn Hưu called Buddhism's "lesser benevolence" had inappropriately overshadowed the emperor's "major duty" to the kingdom.[229]

Yet this critique of Buddhist failings was still less "Confucian" than meets the eye. The issue at stake was a stronger independent kingdom. Since the first recorded *nho*, whom the king ordered in 1043 to write about a "supernatural event," court scribes had evolved into specialists on classical texts, but they were not necessarily Confucian scholar-mandarins. The court held regular recruitment examinations requiring candidates for public office to demonstrate their knowledge of the classics, and from 1267, *nho* graduates occupied some of the *hành khiển* posts previously reserved for illiterate eunuchs. Yet their familiarity with Đại Việt's Chinese-language archives served them best in drafting diplomatic memorials to defend it from imperial assertions of suzerainty. Several *nho* delivered these to China themselves.[230] But they did not make a Confucian court.

Lê Văn Hưu possibly saw himself as playing a similar role: scrutinizing classical sources to defend the Đại Việt polity. Without a written tradition in their own language, most Vietnamese had access only to Chinese documentary sources. No other archives existed that could reveal precedents and practices for such a defense of their kingdom. Conducting a Confucian domestic administration was another matter, made even more difficult by the suspension of all civil service recruitment examinations from 1275 to 1304 as a result of the Mongol invasions.[231] As one historian has put it, Buddhism remained "the governing ideology of the Trần dynasty," with Confucianism a mere "tool in the selection of government officials."[232]

WATER AND CULTURE

Water motifs retained their cultural power as distinguishing features of the Vietnamese landscape. An early thirteenth-century folktale, *Truyện Trê Cóc* (Chronicle of the catfish and the frog), satirizes a Confucian bureaucrat's unfamiliarity with the Vietnamese environment. In a lawsuit over the paternity of a brood of tadpoles, the mandarin and his corrupt inspectors award custody to a catfish, only to be confounded by a famous legal scholar who advises the frogs to wait until their tadpoles mature. The catfish had to confess to its theft, pay the frogs' costs, and submit to exile. As historian Alexander Woodside points out, the 398-line poem mocks "the Chinese-style mandarin's attempt to thwart the concrete realities of his environment."[233]

If this represented a popular view from the villages, it is unclear that Vietnamese monarchs had any more success than mandarins in imposing their order on amphibian nature. The first extant text written in Vietnamese was composed in 1282, in the *nôm* script.[234] Its author, Nguyễn Thuyên, addressed this poem to crocodiles that had appeared in the Lô branch of the Red River, and Emperor Trần Nhân Tông ordered the text thrown in the river in the hope of driving the reptiles away.

> O crocodiles, do you know?
> The vast Eastern Ocean is your domain,
> While the Phú-Lương [Red] River is part of the sacred territory
> Where you are forbidden to venture?
> Do you not know that the inhabitants of the Việt country [*nước Việt*]
> Are formidable fishermen?
> Since the Hùng [kings], they have tattooed their bodies;
> Even dragons fear them.
> The celestial emperors have ruled down to the present dynasty
> Which from Hải ấp [the Trần home village] has acceded to the throne.
> Its military exploits are famed in all four directions
> And under its power the sea has calmed and the river become clear.
> The tigers have fled the men who farm the land
> Allowing all to live in peace.
> In the name of the Emperor, I order you
> To return to frolic in the Eastern Ocean.[235]

This poem makes the first allusion in any Vietnamese text to ancient "Hùng kings." Pride in recent "military exploits" against the Mongols was apparently pushing the antiquity of "the Việt country" even further back, well before Triệu Đà's kingdom of Nán Yuè. Soon, not only worthy successors to Triệu Đà but also legendary antecedents would become increasingly important.[236]

This was also the first attested use of the Vietnamese term for their land, *nước Việt* (literally, the "Việt waters"). Wolters notes numerous allusions to water in the records of the Trần era: "Every source is coloured by reference to rivers. Rivers are the scene of naval manoeuvres, warfare, floods, dykes, canals, commercial transport, rafting, markets and entertainment held on bridges, princely escapes and escapades, legends, and landscape poetry." Trần emperors meditated, and poets extolled their "land of rivers." "The river coils," wrote Nguyễn Sướng in the early fourteenth century, recalling a serpent.[237]

BUDDHISM PERSISTS

Lê Văn Hưu's initial patron, Emperor Trần Thái Tông, was a devout, eclectic Zen Buddhist. In his preface to a contemporary Zen work, *A Guide to the Dhyana*, he quoted a Chinese Zen patriarch as saying that there was "no difference between the sages and the great Buddhist teachers." Citing Laozi as well as Confucius and the Buddha, Thái Tông wrote: "Those who transmitted rules through the generations and laid guidelines were greatly honoured by the former sages.... I can draw on the example of the former sages when I transmit the teachings of Buddhism."[238] Emperor Trần Nhân Tông, who succeeded Thái Tông's son in 1278, abdicated in 1293, became a Buddhist monk, and founded the Trúc Lâm (Bamboo Grove) sect of Vietnamese Zen Buddhism.[239] He died in 1308, having composed one of the earliest extant texts written solely in *chữ nôm*, his *Cư trần lạc đạo phú* (Rhapsody of Living on earth, enjoying the way).[240] He wrote: "My true nature being veiled, I have sought Buddha; Now it is clear that Buddha is my nature."[241] Up to the mid-fourteenth century, succeeding Trần rulers left a large corpus of Buddhist literature. In a poem on "the Buddha nature," Trần Thánh Tông wrote: "There is no past or future, loss or gain."[242] The new cultural focus on antiquity was eclectic, as ever.

So was the integration of scholarship and politics. Lê Văn Hưu exemplified this in his former role as tutor to the prince, military commander, and poet Trần Quang Khải, who faced the Mongol armies in Nghệ An in 1285.[243] In turn, a member of Trần Quang Khải's entourage, Lê Tắc, was to become the next major Vietnamese historian. As secretary to Nghệ An's governor, Trần Kiện, he defected to the Mongols with Kiện and his army. As they marched north, a Chinese source tells us, "All his compatriots assembled to punish" Kiện. Lê Tắc recalled: "The combat was sharp and the fighting on horseback was fierce." Kiện fell; Lê Tắc fled the field, "making his way across the corpses," carrying his master's body for burial. In 1287, Lê Tắc returned south with the third Mongol invasion force, and after its rout, he escaped north again with the retreating cavalry.[244]

Vietnamese scholarly historiography would thus take root on both sides of the Việt Nam–China border. During retirement in exile, using his new access to Chinese official records, Lê Tắc compiled and wrote a twenty-chapter, four-hundred-page Chinese-language history, entitled *An nan zhi lue* (*V. An Nam chí lược*, "Brief records of An Nam"). In 1307 he showed his manuscript to the editor of the imperial academy, compiler of the bureau of historiographers. For another two decades he added documents and laudatory prefaces by Chinese officials. *An Nam chí lược* finally saw publication sometime after 1339.[245] The first extant extensive work of history by a Vietnamese author, it incorporates at least some authentic early material, whose original Chinese sources are now lost. For instance, *An Nam chí lược* quotes a Han prince saying in 135 BCE: "Yuè is a land beyond this world, with a people who shear their hair and tattoo their bodies. It cannot be regulated by the laws of civilized countries."[246] The quotation resembles statements in extant classical Chinese sources, and it may have been long preserved in others accessible to Lê Tắc but later lost.

In the book, Lê Tắc described his intention to "seize upon and embellish some old hearsay to create an account of An Nam's native land."[247] Despite his reliance on Chinese sources and perspectives, perhaps even betraying the nostalgia of an exile, *An Nam chí lược* abounds with detailed, sometimes almost sentimental descriptions of the country and its inhabitants. But Lê Tắc's history also follows the structure of Lê Văn Hưu, whom he must have read. Lê Tắc mentioned not only Triệu Đà but his predecessor An Dương and the ancient Lạc Việt (*Ch.* Luo Yuè). He gave a straightforward account of "rebels" like the Trưng sisters and Lý Bí, and was the first historian to mention the role of Triệu Ẩu (Lady Triệu) in the rebellion of 248 CE.[248] Vietnamese history had come to life.

And the dead were assuming key roles. While Lê Tắc in China was still assembling documents for his history, the Trần court's keeper of the Tripitaka (the oldest Buddhist scriptures), Lý Tế Xuyên, compiled a collection of twenty-seven legendary tales with thirty biographies of Vietnamese kings, subjects, heroes, gods, and spirits. He completed *Việt điện u linh tập* (Departed spirits of the Việt realm) in 1329. Alongside its eight "sovereigns," including the Trưng sisters, Shi Xie, Phùng Hưng, and the eleventh-century Cham queen Mỵ Ê, were twelve male "ministers," such as the eleventh-century military commander Lý Thường Kiệt. The ten spirits included the Fire Dragon Spirit Lord, the Mountain Spirit and the Water

Spirit, the Lady God of the Earth (or Imperial Earth Lady), the earth genie of Phù Đổng, and the Đồng Cổ mountain spirit.[249] Around 1337, another Buddhist author complemented this growing Vietnamese corpus with a new work, the *Thiền Uyển Tập Anh* (A collection of outstanding figures of the Zen community), which contains more than sixty-five biographical accounts of Zen monks active in Annam and Đại Việt from the sixth to thirteenth centuries.[250]

In four hundred years of independence, the kingdom of Đại Việt had assembled its spirits. An eclectic culture's several traditions of specialist scribes had committed them to writing. The kingdom now possessed a textual pantheon that included both spirits of the land and its distinct geography and ever-present spirits of its people from their long history.

However, that same intellectual eclecticism contained tensions. This was most evident in a text written by Trương Hán Siêu, a onetime protégé of the warrior prince Trần Hưng Đạo who had launched his own career in 1308.[251] In 1339, rejecting a request from two villages for a text to mark the restoration of their pagoda, Siêu instead left his own inscription, in which he sharpened some of Lê Văn Hưu's critiques of Buddhists. Siêu wrote: "Scoundrels who lost all notion of Buddhist asceticism only thought of taking possession of beautiful monasteries and gardens, building for themselves luxurious residences, and surrounding themselves with a host of servants."[252] He added: "That is why, half of the quiet and picturesque places of the country are occupied by pagodas. Bands of black costumes and yellow costumes (bonzes) converge there. They eat without having to cultivate the soil, dress without having to weave. Many have abandoned their wives or their husbands to follow this path."[253] Thus, "monks dupe the people, undermine morality, and waste people's resources. But they are everywhere and wherever they go, they are followed by huge crowds of the faithful, although most of them are little better than bandits." This "prevailing custom," Siêu concluded, was breaking up communities. Spouses "are always leaving their families and villages." To solve this problem Siêu advocated the inculcation of filial piety and quoted the classic *Book of Mencius*: "In the provinces, villages, and hamlets there are 'no schools that discipline the people by teaching them the duties proper to parents and younger brothers.' How can the people be other than disorderly?"[254]

It was an increasingly influential view. Trương Hán Siêu and a dozen other serving officials were later named as the cohort of "perfect men" of 1323, the year following Lê Văn Hưu's death. Yet before his own death in 1354, Siêu turned to Buddhism.[255] It was still unclear in which directions Đại Việt society and governance were heading.

CHAPTER 5

Smooth-Flowing Waters of Government

The Triumph of Confucianism, 1340–1570

The fourteenth century was a watershed in Vietnamese history.[1] Dramatic changes took place, especially from about 1340. Historians describe a "maelstrom," "upheaval," and "breakdown."[2]

One key factor was climate change. The warm weather and higher rainfall patterns of the twelfth and thirteenth centuries ended in the late 1330s. A transitional decade (1326–36) of fluctuating climate extremes prefigured the end of the Medieval Warm Period and the onset of a new era, the "Little Ice Age," which brought to the eastern mainland of Southeast Asia a sharp deterioration in conditions. The period from 1340 to the 1360s saw the most sustained drought of the 759-year Vietnamese climate record. Whereas the nine decades before 1340 had included eleven of the wettest forty years ever recorded and only three of the driest, the pattern completely reversed in the comparable period 1340–1430, with ten of the driest forty years and only two of the wettest.[3] It may have been this post-1340 sudden reversal from frequent flooding to frequent drought that caused the Red River, whose silt over many centuries had built up the eastern delta, to change its direction by the fifteenth century, cutting a new channel southward that began to deposit silt in the salt marshes that became the western delta.[4]

The fourteenth-century social crisis is revealed in the rich contemporary primary sources, which survive in greater numbers than those of previous eras. These sources also disclose the emergence of other important new historical themes that contributed to the crisis, including a demographic downturn, the development of regional differences and divergent patterns

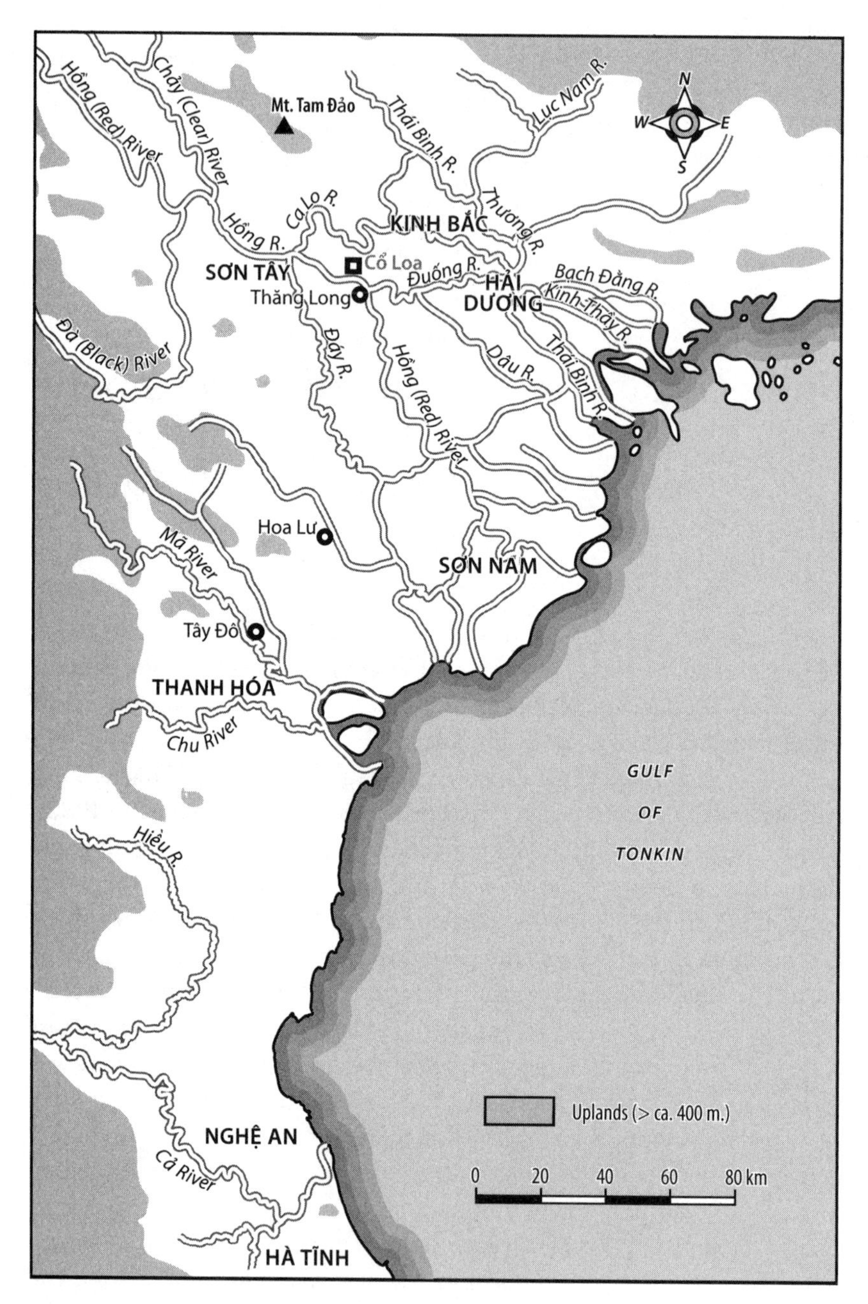

Fig. 5.1
Đại Việt in the mid-second millennium CE.

of landholding (both possibly related to the Red River's change of course), grave threats from Champa and China, the advent of new military technology, and the ascendancy of the new cohort of classically educated scholar officials critical of Buddhism and promoting a new conception of Vietnamese antiquity. Then, after two decades of Ming occupation, the sources for the mid- to late fifteenth century reveal Đại Việt entering a period of stabilization, prosperity, and territorial expansion, with the progressive promulgation of an extensive new legal code, standardization of administrative offices and recruitment, and the rise of a Neo-Confucian ideology of service to the emperor and a sharp distinction between the "civilized" and the "barbarian." Finally, the sixteenth century brought an implosion of the Vietnamese court, leading to both dynastic and territorial division.

The unprecedented wealth of primary sources for the fourteenth to sixteenth centuries also includes more Vietnamese-language texts than before. Most of the extant early works written in *chữ nôm*, or "southern characters," first appear in the historical record from 1300 to 1400. A stele (now lost) was inscribed in *nôm* in 1343.[5] A decade later a Vietnamese Buddhist monk began composing a treatise on medicine written primarily in *nôm*.[6] By the 1380s, nobility and literati alike were composing *nôm* verse, including love poems. At the turn of the century the court even set about replacing Chinese with Vietnamese written in *nôm* as the official writing system, and it indigenized Chinese texts by having them translated into *nôm*.[7]

Translation was feasible because even composition in *nôm* required knowledge of both languages. Written words combined two Chinese characters, one of which presented the meaning in Chinese and the other the word's Vietnamese pronunciation.[8] The proliferation of Vietnamese-language texts, then, was ironically a function of greater familiarity with Chinese and of the rise of the new "classical literati" in Đại Việt.[9] Surviving examples of fourteenth-century Vietnamese verse also include 450 Chinese-language poems composed by fifty authors, just as the indigenous script was "taking to wing in poetry that would go its own way."[10] Yet even in the fifteenth century, the language of *nôm* poetry was "still under the hold of Chinese," including its syntax as well as literary allusions and expressions derived from northern literature.[11]

In addition, the Chinese-language prose works of the 1320s and 1330s were now followed by two other substantial historical texts. The official Trần chronicle *Việt sử lược* (Brief History of Việt) is dated variously from 1340 to 1388, and *Lĩnh Nam Chích Quái* (Wondrous tales of Lĩnh Nam—"south of the passes") was compiled in the period 1370–1400.[12] These and fifteenth-century works on the post-1300 era enable us to draw for the first time upon verifiable, contemporary, or near-contemporary local sources

Table 5.1 *SELECTED TEXTS COMPOSED BY VIETNAMESE AUTHORS, C. 1350–1550*[13]

Author	Date	Title	English title	extant
Hồ Tôn Thốc	late 1300s	*Việt Nam thế chí*	Memoir of the generations of Việt Nam	preface only
Hồ Tôn Thốc	late 1300s	*Việt sử cương mục*	Text and commentary on the history of Việt	No
(?)	1362	*Tam tổ thực lục* (preface only)	True record of the three patriarchs	Yes
Trần Thế Pháp	c. 1370–1400	*Lĩnh Nam chích quái*	Wondrous tales of Lĩnh Nam [*Ch. Lingnan*]	Yes
Tuệ Tĩnh 1330–c. 1400	post-1353	*Hồng Nghĩa Giác Tư Y Thư*	Medical books by Hồng Nghĩa	Yes
Tuệ Tĩnh 1330–c. 1400	post-1389	*Nam Dược Thần Hiệu*	Miraculous drugs of the South	Yes
Anon. (Chinese)	1419	*An Nam Chí Nguyên*	Sourcebook of Annam	Yes
Nguyễn Trãi (1380–1442)	1424–37	*Junzhong ciming* (*Quân Trung Từ Mệnh Tập*)	Collection of writings to the army	Yes
	1428	*Bình Ngô Đại Cáo*	Great proclamation upon defeating the Ngô [China]	Yes
	1430	*Lam Sơn Thực Lục*	True record of Lam Sơn	Yes
	1435	*Dư địa chí*	Geography	Yes
	pre-1442	*Quốc Âm Thi Tập*	Anthology of verse in the national language	Yes
Nguyên Trừng	1438	*Nam Ông Mộng Lục*	Record of the dreams of an old man of the South	Yes
Anon.	1428–68 (?)	*Quốc Triều Hình Luật*	Penal code of the Lê Dynasty	Yes
Phan Phu Tiên	1455	(?)	[commissioned narrative of Trần history; incorporated in next item]	Yes
Ngô Sĩ Liên	1479	*Đại Việt sử ký toàn thư, ngoại kỷ*	Complete historical annals of Đại Việt, outer records	Yes
Anon.	1491	*Hồng Đức Bản Đồ*	Atlas of the Hồng Đức Period	Yes

Author	Date	Title	English title	extant
Lê Thánh Tông & Tao Đàn (Altar of Poesy) club	1495–97 (?)	*Hồng Đức Quốc Âm Thi Tập*	The Hồng Đức Anthology of Verse in the National Language	Yes
Nguyễn Dữ	early 1500s	*Truyền Kỳ Mạn Lục*	Vast collection of marvelous legends	Yes
Dương Văn An	1553	*Ô Châu Cận Lục*	Recent record of Ô Châu	Yes

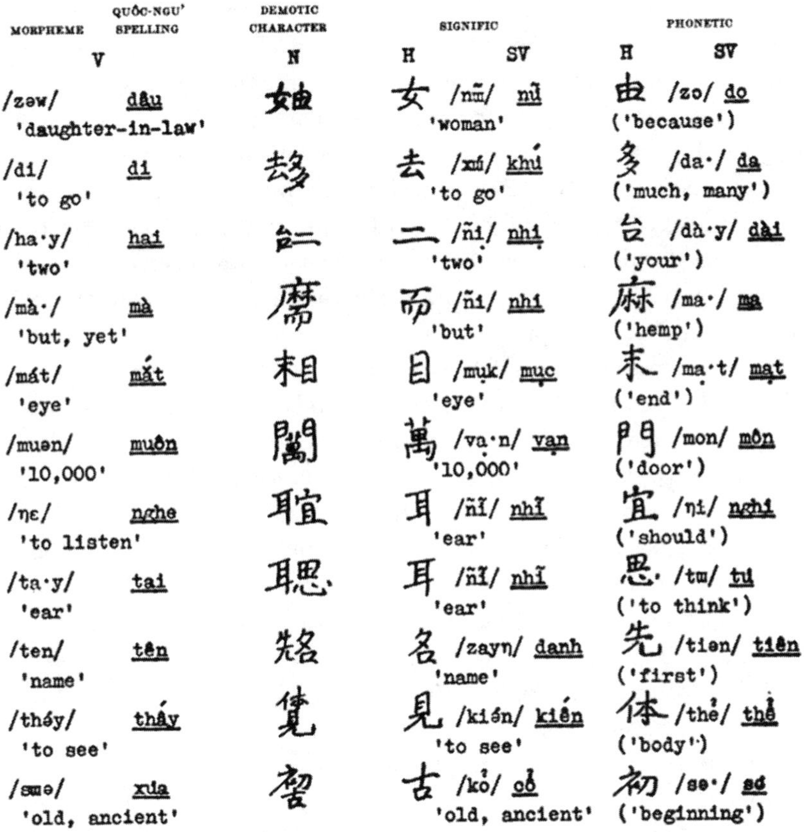

MORPHEME V	QUỐC-NGỮ SPELLING	DEMOTIC CHARACTER N	SIGNIFIC H	SIGNIFIC SV	PHONETIC H	PHONETIC SV
/zəw/ 'daughter-in-law'	dâu	妯	女 /nɯ̃/ 'woman'	nữ	由 /zo/ ('because')	do
/di/ 'to go'	đi	𠫾	去 /xɯ́/ 'to go'	khứ	多 /da·/ ('much, many')	đa
/ha·y/ 'two'	hai	𠄩	二 /ñi/ 'two'	nhị	台 /dà·y/ ('your')	đài
/mà·/ 'but, yet'	mà	𫜵	而 /ñi/ 'but'	nhi	麻 /ma·/ ('hemp')	ma
/mát/ 'eye'	mắt	眜	目 /mụk/ 'eye'	mục	末 /mạ·t/ ('end')	mạt
/muən/ '10,000'	muôn	𨷈	萬 /vạ·n/ '10,000'	vạn	門 /mon/ ('door')	môn
/ŋɛ/ 'to listen'	nghe	𦖑	耳 /ñĩ/ 'ear'	nhĩ	宜 /ŋi/ ('should')	nghi
/ta·y/ 'ear'	tai	𦖻	耳 /ñĩ/ 'ear'	nhĩ	思 /tɯ/ ('to think')	tư
/ten/ 'name'	tên	𠸛	名 /zayŋ/ 'name'	danh	先 /tiən/ ('first')	tiên
/thə́y/ 'to see'	thấy	𧡊	見 /kiə́n/ 'to see'	kiến	体 /thẻ/ ('body')	thể
/sɯə/ 'old, ancient'	xưa	𠸗	古 /kỏ/ 'old, ancient'	cổ	初 /sə·/ ('beginning')	sơ

Fig. 5.2
Examples of the *chữ nôm* demotic writing system. Courtesy of the American Oriental Society. From Nguyễn Đình Hoà, "Chữ Nôm, the Demotic System of Writing in Vietnam," *Journal of the American Oriental Society* 79, no. 4 (Oct.–Dec. 1959): 273.

that include Vietnamese-language texts. These new sources reveal a series of major economic, social, and political transformations.

After 1340, rural productivity fell and famine spread. The fifteenth-century Vietnamese annals, *Đại Việt sử ký toàn thư* (*DVSKTT*) record a dry summer in 1343: "Drought prevailed in the fifth and sixth months. The king, by decree, remitted to the people half of the personal tax. In the second month, the harvest being lost, starving inhabitants formed bands in order to pillage."[14] From that year the price of rice rose as high as one *quan* (a string of hundreds of cash coins) per *thăng* (2 liters, or 2.67 kg of grain).[15] In the contemporary literature, Wolters writes, "As the century moves on, poems describe suffering in the countryside.... And, much more ominous, the annals from 1343 onwards repeatedly refer to uprisings in the countryside, sometimes prolonged ones." Bands of famished rural vagrants taking up arms as robbers, known in official parlance as unregistered "vagabonds," even included "particularly numerous...dependants of princely families." In 1344, many monks joined these bands. Emperor Trần Minh Tông (r. 1320–57) reinforced his provincial administrative staff and established twenty military garrisons in the provinces. The next year he launched repressive operations. But the court was losing revenue and power. Minh Tông's voice, often quoted in the annals chronicling the 1320s and 1330s, almost disappears for the 1340s and 1350s. The annals record: "Officials presented memorials in which they stated that there were many vagabonds. Even in their old age [the vagabonds] had never been registered. They did not pay taxes or contribute services."[16]

In all, at least four serious internal revolts rocked Trần rule in the mid-fourteenth century. After conflicts in the 1320s and 1330s with Tai and Lao hill peoples in the west and southwest, uplanders rebelled in 1351 at two locations, Thái Nguyên in the northwest and Lạng Sơn in the north. Other uprisings wracked the central and south-central provinces from 1343 to the very end of the century. Northeast of the capital, a revolt of peasants and serfs lasted from 1343 to 1360. Its leader, Ngô Bệ, won supporters by erecting wherever he went banners reading "Help for the Poor." After Minh Tông's death, Bệ used this slogan to attempt to proclaim himself ruler in 1358.[17]

Under Minh Tông's son, Trần Dụ Tông (r. 1358–69), the instability became "chronic." In a 1362 poem, the scholar-prince Trần Nguyên Đán recorded:

> For some years the summers have been dry, and moreover,
> the autumns have been very wet.
> The crops have withered and the sprouts have been damaged.
> The harm has been widespread and serious.

Thirty thousand scrolls of writing are of no use.
The white head vainly carries a mind that loves the people.[18]

Several decades later, his son-in-law Nguyễn Phi Khanh (who had wooed Đán's daughter with *nôm* love poems) could still write: "A thousand miles of paddy are red as if they were all burnt. The countryside is groaning and sighing.... The mountains and rivers of the God of the Soil are now parched and dry. The rain and dew of Great Heaven are still far off. The network of local officials is completely exhausted. The people's allotted rations are already half-spent." Khanh may have written these lines during the serious 1392 drought. In another poem, he added, "The people are wailing. They wait to be fed and clothed," and in a tone of resignation recalling that of his father-in-law, Khanh compared himself to a hapless craft tossed upon the water: "In the winds and billows of life I, indeed, am a boat."[19] The result of these "disastrous decades," Wolters concludes, was "the collapse of government in the villages." Even in the capital, Thăng Long, turmoil broke out in 1369–70, provoking a princely coup and a short, bloody civil war.[20]

Worse, Đại Việt now faced a resurgent Champa. After decades of bitter warfare with Cambodia, from the mid-thirteenth century Champa had gained a respite as a result of Siamese (Thai) attacks on Cambodia from the west. The Thai, who expanded southward at the expense first of the Mon kingdoms and then the Khmer, had become a force to be reckoned with in mainland Southeast Asia. By 1371, the Thai kingdom of Ayudhya was threatening the Khmer capital of Angkor. This freed Champa of the threat from its east and enabled it to concentrate its disparate forces against Đại Việt, which had taken over its two northern districts in 1306 but was now engaged in conflicts with Tai peoples to the west.[21] Largely coastal and maritime, Champa was also less of a rice-growing monoculture and therefore less vulnerable than either Cambodia or Đại Việt to the deleterious agricultural impact of the weakened monsoons.

From 1360, under their warrior monarch Po Binasuor, known to Vietnamese as Chế Bồng Nga (r. 1360–90), Cham forces went on the attack.[22] Their fast ships pillaged far up the Vietnamese coast, and mobile infantry struck deep into the Red River delta. In 1371 they sacked Thăng Long, setting fire to the palaces and seizing "women, jewels, and silks." All books held in the royal palace were lost.[23] In attempted retaliation six years later, Emperor Trần Duệ Tông marched south with an army of 120,000 but fell into a trap while occupying Champa's capital. The Chams killed him and decimated his army. They then marched north, again pillaged Đại Việt's capital, repeated their sack of the city in 1378, and did so a fourth time in

1383. All these major defeats dealt severe shocks to the Vietnamese kingdom, which was forced to impose heavier taxes to pay for the war. The introduction in 1378 of a head tax, at three *quan* per person, affected even the landless. More peasant uprisings followed. The largest, in 1389, was led by a Buddhist monk, Phạm Sư Ôn, whose armies of "vagabonds" occupied Thăng Long for three days, forcing Emperor Trần Nghệ Tông and his heir to flee across the river. Thus, in less than two decades from 1370 to 1389, the Trần court lost control of its capital six times.[24]

The demographic impact of these multiple crises was devastating. Drought, falling land productivity and farm sizes, insurgencies, invasions, and disease all combined to reduce the population of Đại Việt by as much as one-third, from 2.4 million in 1340 to around 1.6 million by 1400.[25]

A cultural and political outcome of these disasters was increased regional division in Đại Việt, leading to a fierce contest for influence. The Buddhist elites of the older regions of the upper Red River delta, especially Kinh Bắc and Sơn Tây to the north and west of Thăng Long, confronted challenges from a new group of classically educated scholars hailing from the more recently reclaimed coastal agricultural regions of the eastern and southern delta, such as Hải Dương and Sơn Nam, and from the Thanh Hóa area south of the delta. Historian John Whitmore has noted this "thriving regionalism that would weaken and seriously damage the Vietnamese state."[26] The repeated Cham invasions and prolonged occupation of the border region and southern provinces during the 1370s and 1380s not only disrupted central authority there but also accentuated the different experience of the south from that of the Red River region.[27]

A CULT OF ANTIQUITY

The younger literati forged a new school of intellectual thought, carefully deploying allusions from classical texts to address the new levels of social distress. What Whitmore calls "the rise of 'antiquity'" in Đại Việt began among the generation of scholars who had benefited from the Trần policy launched in the 1290s of employing educated "counselors" (*hành khiển*).[28] In 1343 one of these, Trương Hán Siêu (d. 1354), lamented the decline of Buddhism since the golden age of Asoka: "The present and Antiquity fit together like two tallies."[29] In this view, Đại Việt now needed a new antiquity. Another influential figure was Nguyễn Trung Ngạn (1289–1370), who earned his doctoral degree (*thái học sinh*) at age sixteen and in 1314 served on a diplomatic mission to China, for which he was lauded for "composing poetry on horseback."[30] But the key thinker was probably Chu Văn An

(1292–1370), who also gained a doctoral degree, wrote poems in both Chinese and *nôm*, and ran a private school in his village south of the capital. There he trained a second cohort of scholar-officials who would become prominent in the latter half of the fourteenth century.[31]

Around 1340, Emperor Trần Minh Tông summoned Chu Văn An to court and recalled Nguyễn Trung Ngạn from fifteen years' service in the southern provinces. The emperor appointed An as royal tutor to his sons and heirs and, by 1341, as director of the National Academy (*viện quốc học*), a post An occupied for the next two decades. For a quarter century he was Đại Việt's preeminent scholar and political thinker, reinforcing the role of Trương Hán Siêu, Nguyễn Trung Ngạn, and other like-minded officials at Minh Tông's court who became key ministers in the 1350s. In 1341 the emperor had Siêu and Ngạn assemble a collection of documents on Đại Việt's laws and governance.[32] The next year Siêu was playing a quasi-military role in the troubled, mostly Tai-speaking northern upland region of Lạng Giang, which included Lạng Sơn. There he held the title *kinh lược*, a special commissioner dispatched to an area of unrest. But more dissidence erupted at Lạng Sơn in 1351 and elsewhere in Lạng Giang three years later. In 1355 it was the turn of Nguyễn Trung Ngạn to take up the same sensitive northern post.[33]

Of course these officials did not get all they wanted, and Buddhism remained a major intellectual and political influence in Đại Việt. Responding to a scholar's report that unregistered vagrants were avoiding taxes and corvée labor, Trần Minh Tông "replied that without such vagrants, how could the time be called a period of peace? And he asked what good would be obtained by punishing them?" Before he died in 1357, some of Minh Tông's last poems expressed his devotion to meditative Buddhism.[34] Trương Hán Siêu's late conversion to Buddhism also reflected its continuing appeal.

Nguyễn Bá Tĩnh, a twenty-two-year-old orphan who had been raised in leading Đại Việt monasteries, successfully passed the Confucian examinations in 1352. But he declined an official position and became a Buddhist monk, adopting the name Tuệ Tĩnh (Tranquil Wisdom). He resided in several monasteries, established medical gardens, and became a respected doctor, pharmacist, and expert on plants, wild and cultivated, and their extracts, decoctions, and powders. After 1353 he began compiling his *Hồng Nghĩa Giác Tư Y Thư* (Medical books by "Hồng Nghĩa" [a pseudonym]), which he composed in verse for ease of memorization by illiterates. He also wrote it mostly in *nôm*, probably necessary given both the native language of his target home audience and the number of plants unique to their environment that lacked Chinese names. Tuệ Tĩnh stressed the importance for health of physical exercise, a diet of local fruits and vegetables, and avoidance of imported foodstuffs. His work expressed this philosophy of "a physical and spiritual relationship between human beings and the land where they live."[35]

Meanwhile, Chu Văn An urged a very different approach to healing "the ills of existing society," including a reduction in Buddhist influence. He sought to link his times to the era of "the sage rulers" of ancient China—Yao, Shun, and the Duke of Chou—by "returning to antiquity" (*phục-cổ*) and recreating "the ideals of that past in the present." An fostered what he called "ancient writing" (*cổ-văn*) and a new school of "socially conscious poetry among the Vietnamese elite." An's core teachings were, in Whitmore's words: "Use the Chinese texts, concentrate on Antiquity and how it applies to the present day, be aware of the problems of the Buddhist present... and know the need for such local institutions of textual study as his own." He advocated the founding of more schools to propagate classical learning. One of his former students, Lê Quát, wrote: "I have studied the texts. I focused on (the questions of) Antiquity and today, as well as the *đạo* of the sages by which they transformed their people."[36]

Another of Chu Văn An's former students, Phạm Sư Mạnh, provided Đại Việt with an indigenous antiquity, taken from Chinese records of the Tang era. Mạnh served the Trần court in a military capacity from 1346 to 1362 and as a diplomat in the late 1360s. He undertook at least twenty missions to the northern and northwestern borders to "pacify" upland rebels. During the 1350s or early 1360s, Mạnh succeeded to the title of *kinh lược* in Lạng Giang, where ten thousand Đại Việt cavalry and one thousand infantry patrolled the northern border districts. He considered himself "a fearsome suppressor" of the unrest in that region.[37] It was in the northwest that Tang texts had located the legendary prehistoric Hùng kingdom of Văn Lang, and there, probably in the 1350s, Mạnh wrote a poem entitled "Patrolling the Province," the first Vietnamese document ever to mention Văn Lang. This poem described the Red River's western courses, then known as the Lô and Thao rivers, and it also named Thục Phán, legendary conqueror of Văn Lang, who had taken the regnal name An Dương and supposedly founded the ancient Việt kingdom of Âu Lạc in 258 BCE.[38] Mạnh's poem depicted the landscape:

> I moor my boat by a rock in the river, facing the clear waves.
> The river guards race to hail the official's pennant as it passes by.
> There are tribal stockades along the Lô river and the Thao river's settlements.
> Here Văn Lang's sun and moon once shone upon Thục [Phán]'s mountains and rivers.

Then, when over ten thousand miles there was writing and chariots,
the frontier soil was peaceful.
But for a thousand years there have been disorders in the world.
I am favored with the imperial order to control the border lands.
I shall expel and subdue robbers and bring warfare to an end.[39]

Here Mạnh linked a mythic Việt past to new military conquests—"writing and chariots." As he later put it poetically, he was "trying with a court official's hand / To draft the first chapter of the *Pacification of the Western Barbarians*." Suppression of the rebels contributed to fulfilling an apparently new imperial ambition. In the north Mạnh wrote: "For the control of the world, the flags must be unfurled." In another Lạng Sơn poem, he explained: "On this expedition I am not just seizing the tribes' possessions / I shall take and hold Lộc Châu with all its mountain lands."[40] In Văn Lang, this expansive territorial project had found a local antiquity to serve as its justification. But in a sense the real precedent was the imperial expansion of China, in whose records (albeit late, during the Tang era) "Văn Lang" had first appeared.[41]

Meanwhile, back in the lowlands, Mạnh's colleague Lê Quát, who also served at the court of Trần Dụ Tông in the 1360s, was most critical of the Buddhist practices that prevailed in Đại Việt society, with its more than two hundred temples.[42] Quát wrote scathingly:

> Why have the fear of Buddha's maledictions and the need to implore his mercy become so deeply embedded in people's minds? Royal princes and common folk worship Buddha and squander their wealth on the pagodas. They are as happy as if they had received a written guarantee for the next world. People have faith in Buddhism and drift along with the tide without being ordered to do so, whether they live in the capital or in the most remote village. Wherever you see a house, you can be sure a pagoda is not far away. As soon as one pagoda collapses, another is built. Bells, drums, pagodas and towers are the center of the activities of half the population.[43]

Indeed, Buddhism was so influential that Quát found himself powerless to contest it: "I have not yet been believed in a single village." He complained of the lack of the *học* and *văn miếu* schools that Chinese texts stipulated. "I have always travelled through the country, leaving my footprints over half the empire. But I have never once seen the so-called *học* or *văn miếu*."[44]

Cultural tensions rose. Lê Quát and Phạm Sư Mạnh pushed for changes in the legal system. Trần Minh Tông dismissed them for advocating a Chinese model: "From the time when the state had its system of laws, the South and North have been different. If one were to listen to inexperienced scholars, seeking to obtain their objectives, disorder would break out." Around this time the top Buddhist-held post of *quốc sư* (master of the realm) reappears in the record after more than a century in which it receives only a single mention. Minh Tông's filling of this post may indicate that the court had lost control over the monkhood and was now attempting to reimpose it.[45] Even after Minh Tông's death, in the 1360s the royalist Trúc Lâm Buddhist sect enjoyed a brief resurgence from two decades of weakened influence. On the other hand, at least one prince, Trần Nguyên Đán, preferred to join a new, third generation of literati who composed poetry about current problems, pursued the cause of emulating antiquity, and celebrated Chu Văn An and the first generation of his students like Lê Quát and Phạm Sư Mạnh.[46] In the early 1360s, Chu Văn An himself demanded the execution of seven "treacherous" courtiers, the new emperor's "powerful favourites." Trần Dụ Tông rejected this advice, and so An "resigned from public life."[47] From a hilltop east of Thăng Long, he pronounced caustically: "Fish splash the pond—but where have dragons gone?"[48] During his "exemplary retirement," An's influence persisted; he returned to court in 1370 for the coronation of Trần Nghệ Tông. When An died later that year, he became the first Vietnamese scholar enshrined in the Temple of Literature in Thăng Long. The next was Trương Hán Siêu, who had died in 1354.

During the 1370s and 1380s, at the height of the Cham wars, An's former students and admirers completed the reconstruction of a mythic Vietnamese prehistory and an aggressive new ideology based on the metaphor "writing and chariots." They indigenized the model of China's sage rulers by Vietnamizing the putative primordial Việt realm of Văn Lang. A new ancient ethnic model took shape. Trần Nguyên Đán wrote a poetic eulogy for Chu Văn An, crediting him with key achievements: "The waves of the tide of the ocean of learning were renewed, and customs were again simple and pure." These were the "pure, simple customs" of Văn Lang, introduced by An's student Phạm Sư Mạnh.[49] This prehistory soon extended even further back into the past. By the 1390s, Hồ Tôn Thốc completed his *Việt Nam thế chí* (Memoir of the generations of Việt Nam), a purported history of "eighteen" successive rulers of an ancient "Hồng Bàng" dynasty.[50] These were the "Hùng kings," monarchs undocumented until first mentioned more than six hundred years later in Chinese records of the fourth and fifth centuries CE.[51] The anonymous author of *Việt sử lược* (perhaps Hồ Tôn Thốc himself) explained that the Hùng kings "were all called Lạc" and had ruled the kingdom of Văn Lang, whose "customs were of a simple and pure substance." Just as in ancient China, "for purposes of government, knotted cords were used" to keep records.[52] On thin evidence, "Hùng kings" and Văn Lang attained parity with China's sage rulers.

This new prehistory of Đại Việt began to affect its views of its neighbors. An official edict warned Vietnamese in 1374 not to "dress in the fashion of northerners [Chinese] or copy the speech of the Chams and Lao countries."[53] Historian Nguyễn Thế Anh considers this "the first sign" of Đại Việt unease at Cham cultural influence.[54] Still, Whitmore finds a continuing equilibrium between the Cham and Vietnamese courts, neither yet "viewing the other as culturally inferior." Dissidents from each kingdom gained refuge in the other. Cham exiles in Đại Việt took Vietnamese names; "There was no Confucian condemnation of the Chams as barbarians."[55]

Đại Việt's relations with China's new Ming dynasty (1368–1644), too, initially betrayed possibly fewer stresses between these neighbors than within Đại Việt itself. As a sign of favor, in 1370 the founding Ming emperor invited Đại Việt, Champa, and Korea to send their most accomplished graduates to Nanjing as "tribute" to compete in the Chinese examinations.[56] Then in 1385 China requested twenty Vietnamese Buddhist monks (and the next year southern tropical fruits).[57] While preparing to send a diplomatic mission north in 1385, the Trần court ordered the arrest of Đại Việt's leading Buddhist monk and medical author, Tuệ Tĩnh. It dispatched him to exile in China as a "living gift" of tribute to the Ming royal family. He was never allowed to return home, but he enjoyed fame in China, where he was credited with saving an empress's life. At the Ming court, Tuệ Tĩnh wrote his second work, this one in Chinese. It was an eleven-volume treatise, *Nam Dược Thần Hiệu* (Miraculous drugs of the South). As Thompson explains, this work was "designed to systematize the use of Vietnamese medicaments within the parameters of Chinese drug theory and to present and explain Vietnamese medicine to Chinese physicians at the Ming court." The first volume covers pharmaceutical ingredients; the other ten describe "184 different medical situations from epidemic disease, to chronic complaints such as arthritis, to conditions such as pregnancy." Before he died, Tuệ Tĩnh managed to send copies of this work back to his homeland with a visiting Đại Việt diplomatic mission. At his wish, the epitaph on his Nanjing tomb asked any visitor to his gravesite from Đại Việt to take his remains home.[58]

Meanwhile, in terms of military technology, the Ming dynasty had set off a "gunpowder revolution." From 1368, as historian Sun Laichen has shown, Chinese troops possessed "the most advanced firearms in the early modern world." Some of the new weaponry spread to mainland Southeast Asia. Đại Việt armies had long deployed catapults, scaling ladders, and other siege technologies, and they now quickly acquired and mastered the technology of "war rockets," cannon (using bamboo tubes rather than iron), and other gunpowder weaponry. During a naval battle in 1390, a Cham defector pointed out Chế Bồng Nga's flagship, and Vietnamese marines cut down the veteran enemy king in a volley of fire from handheld muskets. The new weapon sparked chaos among the Cham troops. Severing Chế Bồng Nga's head, the victorious Vietnamese then routed his navy, finally shifting the balance of power against Champa.[59] Chế Bồng Nga has been called "the last great king of classical Southeast Asia."[60] A new era was at hand—but not entirely new. Old political and cultural rivalries and affinities persisted. After the Cham general La Ngai marched his infantry and elephants back to Vijaya and seized the throne of Champa, two of Chế Bồng Nga's sons fled north for refuge in Đại Việt.[61] After the dramatic Vietnamese victory, China stipulated in the 1390s that Đại Việt send tribute only once every three years, and that it must include no elephants or rhinoceros.[62]

Responding in part to the shock of the Cham invasions of the 1370s and 1380s, the Vietnamese intellectual current that had already begun to merge indigenous and classical thought grew ever more vigorous, ambitious, and critical. "The country in former times was an empire with scholars," wrote Nguyễn Phi Khanh, whose father-in-law, Trần Nguyên Đán, had been driven from the government service: "Ordinary men today are those who are officials in the Secretariat." The annals say that in 1385 "worthies and cultivated men grieved over the times and mourned their generation. They had to express their grief in poems." Yet the scholars cherished their common experience and vision. In a later poem addressed to a fellow of his cohort, Nguyễn Phi Khanh recalled "the State College in the spring wind (after) the village examination in the autumn. The examination hall stands out distinctly (as though we were there). I remember our comradeship."[63]

RISE OF HỒ QUÝ LY

In a strong position to harness this new intellectual critique to his own political chariot was Hồ Quý Ly, a cousin of the Trần prince who had staged the 1370 coup. Quý Ly first appears in the annals soon after the 1371 Cham invasion, when he occupied "the key post of *đại sứ* in the secret Council," with a rank just beneath that of the counselors from the Trần royal clan. Within a decade he was able to control the leading Buddhist figure, the *quốc sư*, whose post had been mentioned in the record only once during the thirteenth century but was again occupied by the mid-fourteenth. In 1381, Quý Ly employed the *quốc sư* to lead the monks out of the monasteries, and "wild" monks from the mountains and forests, to join in resistance to the

Chams.[64] By 1387 he was chief minister (*đồng-bình-chương sự*) and preeminent at court, and in the 1390s held the top posts of *thái sư* and imperial regent.[65] It was Quý Ly who drove Trần Nguyên Đán into internal exile, and he executed the father of Nguyên Đán's son-in-law, Nguyễn Phi Khanh. In 1395 Quý Ly presented himself in the role of the ancient Duke of Chou, and later even claimed descent from the mythical Chinese emperor Shun, whom Confucius had praised for governing "efficiently without exertion." While he favored the Five Classics of Confucianism over the more recent Four Books of the Neo-Confucians, Quý Ly also downgraded Confucius, ranking him below the Duke of Chou, and criticized "four dubious places" in Confucius's *Analects*.[66] And he took up the cult of antiquity, melding Văn Lang mythology with Chinese history. He wrote in a poem to a Ming envoy that his country's people were ancient and authentic: "You inquire about the state of affairs in Annam. / Annam's customs are simple and pure." Consistent with this new cult of its antiquity, Quý Ly added that his kingdom was also a genuine Sinic empire: "Official clothing is according to the Tang system. / The rites and music [that control intercourse] between the ruler and officials are those of the Han." In 1395–96, Quý Ly imposed new clothing regulations, first limiting official garb to narrow-sleeved garments only, then enforcing various colored clothing for nine ranks of civilian and military officers and those with no rank, with different types of cloth for the royal clan, the aristocracy, and the censorate.[67]

Hồ Quý Ly was attempting to strengthen the state against both the Cham threat and domestic disintegration. In 1397–98, in the hills of Thanh Hóa to the southwest of the Red River delta, he constructed massive stone fortifications for a new "Western Capital" (Tây Đô), a move that established the Đại Việt court in its southernmost location ever. This undermined the power of Thăng Long, the traditional base of the Trần aristocracy and the Buddhist hierarchy in the Red River delta, now merely the "Eastern Capital" (Đông Đô). In favoring his western capital, Quý Ly faced opposition from his chief counselor and from a member of his Secret Council, who illustrated the regional rivalries when he argued that "the land of Long-đỗ [the 'dragon's belly,' Thăng Long]," with its "Lô and Nhị rivers running deep, lies flat and spacious," in contrast to the "borderlands" of upland Thanh Hóa, which "are closed in and miserable, at the end of the rivers and the beginning of the mountains. It is a rebellious area, unable to be ruled, whose men may be trusted to be dangerous." But Quý Ly overruled the objection and sidelined its author.[68] The southward shift went ahead.

With the support of leading graduates of the classical examinations of the 1380s and 1390s, Quý Ly also began to attack the northern economic base of the Trần aristocracy, with favored exceptions.[69] He moved first against hoarded wealth by introducing paper money in 1395 and banning (on pain of death) the use of coinage. Two years later, he took on large landholders with a new law that allowed only "princes and princesses of the blood" to own more than ten *mẫu* (acres) of riceland. Excess fields had to be surrendered to the state, which loaned them at moderate rents to landless peasants, who became state tenants. In 1398, another edict obliged private landowners to declare their holdings or have them transferred to public ownership (*công điền*).[70] Four years later Quý Ly also raised taxes on riceland, from three to five *thăng* per *mẫu*, while reducing taxes for the poor with exemptions for landless peasants, orphans, and widows.[71]

From 1400, Hồ Quý Ly extended state control to much of the labor force. A census conducted in that year registered the entire population for conscription purposes. In 1401, he limited private slaveholding; as with landed property, the permitted number of slaves depended on their owner's social rank. The state took over excess slaves, paying their owners five *quan* only for third-generation domestic slaves, with no compensation for more recent purchases. In 1404, the Hồ court ordered all landless people throughout the country to enroll in settlements (*đội*) for the poor.[72] It also built up a new army and navy (equipped with troop transports) and established the country's first arms factories. Vietnamese forces developed a new "fire lance," superior to those of the Ming, which Quý Ly's son was an expert at manufacturing.[73]

Through a series of cultural reforms, Quý Ly extended his controls from "chariots" to "writing." They included adoption of *nôm* for administrative texts, reinstitution of the classical examinations on a more regular schedule and with a rigorous new curriculum (abolishing memorized transcription and requiring a policy essay), and the introduction of free courses of study for the examinations. For the first time, such education was available outside the capital.[74] Quý Ly also took steps to control the Buddhist community. The most educated monks were incorporated into a new religious hierarchy; those aged under fifty had to resume a lay life; and the rest became temple servants. The spread of classical expertise accelerated. Whereas the graduates of the examinations held in 1304 had been dominated by scholars from the early bases of the emerging literati in the east and south of the delta (Hải Dương, Sơn Nam, and Thanh Hóa), the successful candidates of 1384, 1393, and especially 1400–1405 also included many from the former Buddhist heartland of the northern and western delta (Kinh Bắc and Sơn Tây).[75] Meanwhile, in 1401, Quý Ly brought the previously excluded scholar Nguyễn Phi Khanh and others into the government; Khanh's son Nguyễn Trãi soon joined the censorate. Khanh wrote in verse to a colleague: "Old am I, an official, fettered to my drafts of edicts.... We have been long separated. Being concerned about the State must indeed be our business."[76]

As Whitmore writes, classical Chinese learning "had grown in influence to the point where the head of state made use of it in a rather eccentric way for his own purposes." Those included Quý Ly's own political dominance and the imposition of central authority throughout the country and even into Champa. In 1400 he had the Trần monarch murdered and formally usurped the throne, provoking a coup attempt that Quý Ly repressed by executing 370 dissidents, seizing their possessions, enslaving their female relatives, and burying alive or drowning males of all ages. He changed the kingdom's name to Đại Ngu after the empire of the mythical northern ruler Shun and adopted a new reign title, "the first year of the sage." The reign of terror continued as "the search for the guilty dragged on for years," with new purges. Having already attacked Champa in 1396, Quý Ly launched four new invasions in 1400–1403, conquering the northern half of the Cham region despite Ming warships helping to defend it. The entire Amaravati region, including the early Cham sites of Mỹ Sơn and Đông Dương, fell into Vietnamese hands. "For the first time," Whitmore writes, "the Vietnamese made a specific attempt to carve out new territory and fill it with their own people." Quý Ly dispatched brigades of landless peasants south to cultivate and patrol the new frontier. He urged a border official in 1405 not to relent but to give priority to military and agricultural tasks: "Instruct the soldiers and the farmers diligently.... Pulling out the border soldiers, what kind of harvest is that?"[77]

The kingdom had adopted an expansionist drive, a preoccupation with cultivation, advanced military technology, and a cult of antiquity. Ethnic divisions, however, remained blurred. Hồ Quý Ly still tried to assimilate captured Cham leaders and woo defectors by giving them Vietnamese names and appointments. He placed Chế Bồng Nga's son Chế Ma Nô Đà Nan in charge of the newly conquered two southernmost prefectures, with the aim of "appealing to the mass of those belonging to Champa" in order to "keep" them pacified. In most cases Đại Việt continued to treat Chams as "legitimate competitors and potential allies."[78] As late as 1406–7, the defector Bố Đông (Kim Tung Liệt) served as a general in the Vietnamese army, and the prince Chế Ma Nô Đà Nan died in battle commanding its forces in the south. But the long conflict had also fostered racialist thinking. In his late fourteenth-century "Wondrous Tales of Lĩnh Nam," the author Trần Thế Pháp drew upon the Ramayana epic for a story entitled "Dạ-xoa-vương" (King of the demons) that he said "explained" the "simian" nature of Chams.[79]

Also ominous was the disastrous weather that struck the eastern mainland of Southeast Asia in the early fifteenth century. The drought years

1401–4, 1416–17, and 1424 were even more severe than those of the mid-fourteenth century.[80] In Đại Việt, the 1401–4 drought was followed in 1405 by a famine.[81] The country faced not only a cultural transformation but also an ecological crisis.

MING OCCUPATION, 1407–28

Then came the Ming invasion of 1406–7, on the pretext of restoring the Trần dynasty. The imperial armies not only overthrew and captured Hồ Quý Ly, but they also put down staunch resistance from organized Trần loyalists and temporarily eclipsed the independence of Đại Việt.[82] The two-decade Ming annexation of the country had major long-term effects. First, it ensured a comprehensive transfer to Đại Việt of the new military technology.[83] But it also strengthened ethnic distinctions all round and implanted the model of bureaucratic government favored under the Ming. For the first time, Đại Việt experienced the sustained influence of Neo-Confucian ideology, which not only included the traditional doctrines of filial piety but also demanded an "activist, state-oriented service" based on officials' absolute loyalty to the dynasty and on the moral superiority of the "civilized" over the "barbarian."[84]

The Ming named their new province Jiaozhi (restoring its classical Han name) and also changed the names of nearly forty of its prefectures, subprefectures, and districts. They set about the destruction of all records of Đại Việt governance, which they saw as signs of independence. They deported leading Đại Ngu officials like Nguyễn Phi Khanh to China.[85] Those remaining in Jiaozhi had to wear Chinese-style clothes. In 1407–10, the new administration upgraded the local state civil service schools to the standards of the Ming Board of Rites and made plans to build, in 1416 alone, forty-six new civil service schools.[86] A "flood of Neo-Confucianism" washed over the country. In 1419 a new Ming edition of the Five Classics and the Four Books, totaling 149 chapters and entitled *The Great Compilation of Neo-Confucianism*, reached Jiaozhi. By the 1420s the Ming were running 126 Confucian schools there.[87]

Ming goals in Jiaozhi also included labor control and economic exploitation. In 1407 Chang Fu, the leading general who commanded the invasion forces, rounded up 7,700 Vietnamese artisans of various trades and dispatched them to Nanjing. The next year, the empire was operating as many as ninety-two merchant tax offices in Jiaozhi. The imperial eunuch Ma Qi scoured the country for "precious gems" and established a large trading interest in gold, silver, pearls, and incense. In 1408 the emperor ordered a minimal taxation regime for Jiaozhi; from 1411 to 1414 the administration lifted the ban on private trade within the province in gold, silver, and copper cash and waived taxes on gold, silver, salt, iron, and fish. However, from 1416 to 23 Ma Qi supervised the imposition of a special tax for the benefit of the Ming imperial household, an annual collection of bulk items including silk, lacquer, sappanwood, kingfisher feathers, fans, and tea.[88]

By 1414 the last member of the Trần family fell into the occupiers' hands. Other revolts were suppressed in 1411 and 1420.[89] Although this early Ming era (1368–1436) was the time of that dynasty's greatest bureaucratic efficiency, the occupation administration confronted serious problems, even in 1415–18 when there were no major revolts in Jiaozhi. A leading imperial official, Hsieh Chin, had predicted to the emperor at the outset that China could not forge a new province from a country that had "from of old" been a separate, tributary state. For his pains, Hsieh Chin was dispatched to a post in Jiaozhi, along with other political exiles, unpromising officials, and even army officers' sons who had failed their military examinations.[90] The top general Chang Fu was recalled to Nanjing in 1408 for service on the northern frontier, but several times over the next eight years he had to return south to combat revolts in Jiaozhi. In 1414 the leading Ming civil official there, Huang Fu, informed him that eight thousand of the ten thousand Guangxi militia forces stationed in Lạng Sơn had deserted and that the army eventually would have to withdraw from parts of Jiaozhi. By 1422, the provisioning and payment of Ming officials and soldiers in Jiaozhi was costing the empire seven hundred thousand piculs of rice annually, yet a Chinese commander in the province reported that insufficient supplies were arriving. In the same year Huang Fu reported that the occupation forces were stagnating, their finances and morale suffering from the war of attrition against a new insurgency that had erupted in the south. The leader of this powerful armed revolt was a landowner from Thanh Hóa named Lê Lợi, who had fought the initial Ming invasion but surrendered with the last Trần loyalists in 1414, gaining appointment to a local post in charge of tracking down smugglers and deserters. In early 1418, Lê Lợi again raised the flag of resistance at the village of Lam Sơn, declaring himself the "Prince of Pacification."[91]

From the start, the Ming had tried to ensure that local opposition forces would not obtain the new weapons technology, including the Chinese musket known as the "magic handgun." The emperor had ordered all firearms counted; "not a single piece is allowed to be missing." In 1407 two Ming "Magic Gun Generals" had commanded possibly as many as 21,000 riflemen in the invading force of 215,000. Breaking into the Vietnamese citadel of Đa Bang, their troops had fired muskets, cannon, and rockets at defenders mounted on elephants. But Vietnamese quickly learned to operate artillery and within a year had killed a Ming general with cannon fire. From 1418, Lê Lợi's growing guerrilla army captured quantities of weaponry and began to challenge the occupiers, using cannon again from 1425. The Ming brought in reinforcements of ten thousand sharpshooters, from whom Vietnamese captured "countless" weapons. Assault charges by troops mounted on elephants regained their effectiveness against imperial units deprived of their superiority in firearms. By 1427, captured northern prisoners also furnished the rebels with siege techniques, "primitive tanks," "flying horse carts," Muslim trebuchets, and possibly another artillery piece that the Chinese called a "thousand-ball thunder cannon."[92]

Lê Lợi and his scholar-counselor Nguyễn Trãi, son of the exiled Nguyễn Phi Khanh and grandson of scholar-prince Trần Nguyên Đán, proclaimed that it was "better to conquer hearts than citadels." They had begun by deploying ambushes and guerrilla warfare to attack the invaders piecemeal. In letters to Wang Tung, the Ming general who then commanded the occupying forces, Nguyễn Trãi used a common Việt water metaphor to assert that "scooping up a dipper of water will not empty the sea; pouring in a dipper of water will not overflow the ocean. Therefore, [those] who [know how to] use armies well are not pleased over a minor victory nor terrified of a major defeat." Trãi claimed that Lê Lợi's movement would prove stronger than the defeated Hồ Quý Ly, because Lê Lợi now possessed the Confucian "Mandate of Heaven." Trãi wrote: "Hồ had a million soldiers, but they were torn by a million different opinions; my men are only a few hundred thousand, but they all fight with one mind." And in a later letter to the occupiers, Trãi added: "Our people have been mobilized to fight for a just cause; they have a common purpose and show great heroism, while your troops are demoralized and exhausted."[93]

In 1424, Lê Lợi deployed his forces along the western frontier into the upland region between Nghệ An province and the Lao border, defeating an army of ethnic minority troops who had joined the Ming cause. Then they headed east down into the coastal lowlands of Nghệ An. They sought to win over the densely settled Việt population by demonstrating discipline and refraining from exactions. Their forces followed a slogan apparently popularized by Nguyễn Trãi, drawing upon another Việt aquatic metaphor: "Like the ocean which supports a ship but can also overturn it, so the people can support the throne or sink it." In Nghệ An, the rebels observed: "Overturn the boat and then you will believe that the people are like water."[94] Lê Lợi gradually raised an army of a quarter of a million.

In two monumental battles in 1426 and 1427, those whom the Chinese had once called southern "serpent-like" barbarians (*Nan Man*) drove them out of Đại Việt.[95] Lê Lợi's successful attack on the Ming-held fortress of Xương Giang ended the war. After a six-month siege, Vietnamese troops "built earth-hills from which they shot into the city," tunneled under it, and carried out assaults with captured weapons such as fire lances, rocket arrows, cannon, and "Duke Lü's overlook and assault carts." After this final victory, the Vietnamese repatriated eighty thousand Ming prisoners to China and confiscated all their weapons.[96] The defeat was perhaps "the greatest policy disaster suffered by the early Ming empire." China would not again invade its southern neighbor for 360 years—after the eventual collapse of the dynasty that Lê Lợi founded. He offered friendship, telling the Ming: "I will be content with my rank of vassal and pay tribute, as has been the custom."[97]

For domestic dissemination, Nguyễn Trãi composed for Lê Lợi the triumphant *Bình Ngô Đại Cáo* (Great proclamation on defeating the northerners):

> From now on our land is safe.
> Rivers and mountains will see a new era.
> Calm comes after the storm,
> Light has driven away darkness.
> For ever we have cleansed ourselves of shame,
> For ever we shall have peace.[98]

This text, written in Chinese, expresses a confident patriotism linked to the Vietnamese landscape, its "rivers and mountains." In a *nôm* poem composed in the period 1429–33, Nguyễn Trãi wrote: "A bond attaches you to hills and streams. Make use of leisure—nourish your true self." The phrase he used there for "hills and streams" was *non nước* (mountains and waters), the Vietnamese term for one's "country."[99]

LÊ LỢI'S REFORMS

The victorious Lê forces reestablished Đại Việt as the name of the country. They also resumed Hồ Quý Ly's renaming of Thăng Long as the Eastern Capital (Đông Kinh, the origin of the European term "Tonkin" for the Red River region), and his use of a second capital, the Western Capital (Tây Đô) in northwest Thanh Hóa.[100] The Lê triumph completed a long regional transition to the predominance of Thanh Hóa and other more southerly provinces over the traditional heartland of the northern and western Red River delta.[101] This process had begun with the influence of Chu Văn An and his followers from the eastern delta in the mid-fourteenth century, accelerated southward under Hồ Quý Ly, and culminated in the rise of Lê Lợi's southern movement, conquering national power from its Thanh Hóa base. This would not be the last southerly shift of the country's center of political gravity.[102]

Within a year Lê Lợi began building up the Đại Việt navy. Each main general commanded ten large warships and a unit headed by an "associate administrator of strong crossbows and flame-throwers," including one "supersized" weapon and one hundred large, medium, and small "flame-throwers." To stockpile ammunition, the new Lê dynasty quickly redoubled the collection of saltpeter and banned its sale in 1428. Records of the smuggling of copper from the imperial province of Yunnan for firearms manufacture in Đại Việt date from 1429. Lê Lợi's new dynasty had launched a military buildup that made Đại Việt "the first gunpowder empire in Southeast Asia."[103]

Đại Việt immediately began to benefit from an amelioration of the severe droughts of the previous quarter century. The period 1400–1424 alone, with its seven drought years, made the fifteenth century the driest in the entire eight-century climate record. But the period 1425–1500 was marked by a milder, moderate climate that allowed the new Lê dynasty to oversee a strong economic and political recovery in Đại Việt. By the second half of the fifteenth century, as elsewhere in Southeast Asia, an era of prosperity reigned.[104]

However, the war against the Ming occupation had polarized ethnic distinctions that were already linked to historical myth. A Đại Việt writer rejoiced: "The soil is again the soil of the Southern kingdom. The people are again the people of the Việt race. Coats and skirts and customs are in agreement with those of the past. The moral and political order is re-established as of old."[105] An indigenous sense of ethnic identity was intensifying. Nguyễn Trãi wrote in his *Dư địa chí* (Geography) in 1435: "The people of our land should not adopt the languages or the clothing of the lands of the Wu [Ming], Champa, the Lao, Siam, or Chenla [Cambodia], since doing so will bring chaos to the customs of our land."[106] Ethnicity and antiquity were now securely intertwined. Trãi was a product of the classical examinations held under Hồ Quý Ly in 1400, and his cohort was a legacy of Chu Văn An. It represented "the culmination of the intellectual development of the 1380s and of Quý Ly's own peculiar brand of classical thought." Trãi himself had reputedly memorized all the Confucian Classics and the Histories.[107]

The kingdom's recovery from the Ming occupation and war was based on reforms in three main areas: the civil service, law, and the landholding system. From the 1430s a Confucian bureaucratic administration slowly began to emerge from the shadow of the Thanh Hóa military clans that predominated at court. Lê Lợi and his successors reestablished the civil service examinations, but despite the proclamation in 1434 of a triennial system of regional and metropolitan competitions, their schedule remained irregular and dependent on official recruitment needs. A thousand graduates passed the first round of lower-level examinations (*học sinh*) in 1434. The first round of the higher, metropolitan-level examinations (*thái học sinh*) was delayed until 1442, and only three others followed in the next two decades.[108] However, talented poor people were encouraged to attend local Confucian schools; some got as far as the National College for Mandarins. In 1429, Lê Lợi ordered all Buddhist and Daoist monks to face examination on their knowledge of scriptures and morality. If they failed, they could not remain monks.[109] As the sole alternative locus of authority, the Buddhist hierarchy continued to feel the pressure of a newly powerful state apparatus.

Drawing on the Tang dynasty's legal code, Lê Lợi set out five degrees of punishment for crimes, from flogging to execution; for example, drinking bouts were punished by one hundred strokes with a cane. Those with money could buy their way out of the three lowest levels of punishment. But political violence continued. Lê Lợi severely repressed upland revolts and even executed several of his previously trusted lieutenants. Then in 1442, on the mysterious death of his successor Lê Thái Tông, Nguyễn Trãi and his entire family were massacred. New penal laws reflected some of this propensity for violence. Article 429, enacted before 1435, prescribed harsher criminal punishments than the Tang and Ming codes: "penal servitude" for those who committed "petty larceny in the daytime," exile "to a distant region" for first-time thieves, and decapitation for recidivists. Also in contrast to the Tang and Ming codes, the same article specified that "female offenders shall be granted a reduction of penalty."[110] As in China, however, polygamy was legal and fairly common.

Agrarian reform was initially limited by Lê Lợi's wartime promise of leniency to those mandarins who collaborated with the Ming, if they were "to repent, to renounce [their] treason, to return to the straight path."[111] However, many did not side with him. After victory, Lê Lợi confiscated their land and handed some over to landlords who had lost estates under Hồ Quý Ly or the Ming.

Then Lê Lợi went much further, launching an attempt to institute a regular "equitable distribution of riceland" (*quân điền*), conducted "by prefectural, district and village officials."[112] This too was based on a Tang dynasty precedent, the "equal fields" allocation and taxation system of the seventh and eighth centuries. In doing so he established an institution that was to form part of Vietnamese agrarian relations for five centuries. In 1428 the Lê regime launched a census and land survey conducted in every village, a massive effort for a new monarchy ruling a population of about 1.9 million in the aftermath of a war.[113] Within a year the administration possessed comprehensive land and population registers, which it revised twice by 1433. A new law established two categories of land: public or state land (*công điền thổ*, *quan điền thổ*) and private land (*tư điền*). The "equitable distribution" affected only the first category. This public land could now be cultivated in state farms run by soldiers or allocated to officials, commoners, or soldiers to enable them to support themselves and pay the state grain tax.[114]

The Lê agrarian vision showed some influence of Hồ Quý Ly's regulations controlling both property and labor, with their sharp distinctions of rank. To implement it, the Lê enacted special laws that comprised further inaugural sections of an expanding legal structure, later known as the Lê Code, based partly on the Tang model but significantly deviating from it (and from the contemporary Ming Code). Lê Lợi promulgated the Lê Code's first thirty-two articles on real property (of which only five bore any resemblance to sections of the Tang Code).[115] Article 347 stipulated: "If in the equitable distribution of riceland there is some surplus, the regulations on public land shall apply; if there is a shortage, the public land of the village in question or nearby... shall be taken for equitable distribution. The land registers shall be amended and submitted to the Throne for approval. Every four years, they shall be revised." Youths turning fourteen would receive a distribution of riceland in the year following their birthday.

The state retained ultimate control of all public land. Articles 342–46 prohibited concealment of "public lands and ponds," their occupation "beyond the amount authorized," the sale of "officially granted land or soldiers' allotment land," and the failure of cultivators of public land to meet the state's requirement for "grain payments" on time. These payments were high. It was permissible to clear virgin land for farming, but article 350 stipulated that after three years, once it became productive, "half of the product" must be "assessed for the state treasury," or the officials responsible "shall be demoted three grades and the farmers shall have to pay the amount due."

The legal protections for private property extended to smallholders. Other proprietors could not make improper claims on farm owners or encroach on their land. Articles 354–55 prohibited forcible contestation of "the ownership of land and dwellings" and the purchase of land by coercion. Law limited the power of large landowners. Article 370 imposed fines or demotion on members of "high-ranking and powerful families who take by force ricelands, dwellings and ponds belonging to commoners." Article 348 sought to control the accumulation of private landholdings, as well as make commoners fulfill state demands for corvée labor, by prohibiting landlords from establishing "estates where they harbor commoners in flight." Article 372 added: "Whoever owns serfs beyond the number he is allowed to have shall be demoted or condemned to penal servitude."

Significantly for the development of a property regime, the new laws also recognized contracts and "tenants of land and dwellings," while offering the latter minimal protection (articles 356 and 361). Tenants faced "sixty strokes of the heavy stick" for contesting terms of their leases; a landowner with a tenancy contract could also obtain "punitive damages." The absence of a contract, however, limited a tenant's liability to "the rent initially fixed." The state as well as private landowners could contract tenants, who were prohibited from harvesting their rice crop "without notifying the responsible supervisory official or the landlord." Only if the latter failed to "come in time" to inspect the harvest, threatening loss of the crop (and the state's grain tax), then "the tenant shall be permitted to harvest after informing the village officials." If he "fail[ed] to notify these officials," he would receive "eighty strokes of the heavy stick" and be made to "pay the grain due without any reduction even if the harvest is poor." Protections for tenants existed only where their interests coincided with those of the state.

Finally, the new system legalized and discriminated between distinct classes of laborers. Articles 363–65 prohibited the sale of "a commoner as a serf" and the purchase of a serf without official authorization. The law punished serfs who "act as if they are commoners" and prescribed "penal servitude" for anyone tattooing "other people's sons, daughters, wives or serfs" to brand them as their own serfs or tattooing "indentured laborers to change them into serfs."[116] In different ways, then, the new Lê landholding system gave legal form to agrarian class differences and imposed strict rural labor controls, but it also limited development of large estates. It fostered the ongoing slow transition from the pre-1400 aristocratic social order with its large-scale employment of serfs to a form of peasant agriculture that included not only tattooed serfs but also tax-paying private smallholders, commoners farming public land, indentured laborers, and, potentially, commercial tenants.[117]

From 1428 Lê Lợi allowed four-fifths of his army to return to farming.[118] This also meant allocating land to peasant soldiers in the form of military colonies (*đồn điền*), based on a system that the Ming had tried but failed to implement during the occupation.[119] The Lê settled many veterans on virgin land or dismantled estates in the Đại Việt heartland. Other peasants gained employment in expanding sectors such as the army, public works, and mining. As a result, apart from several tribal rebellions in the 1430s, the fifteenth century was apparently free of peasant unrest. Nguyễn Trãi expressed a mixture of Confucianism and humanism when he wrote: "The people love those who are inspired by the virtues of humanity" (*nhân*).[120]

CHAMPA IN THE EARLY FIFTEENTH CENTURY

On taking power, Lê Lợi briefly established good relations with Champa's king, Vira Bhadravarman (r. 1400–1441).[121] The Cham lands maintained their important place in an increasingly flourishing Southeast Asian trading network. Vira Bhadravarman's court at Vijaya, in modern Bình Định province, also claimed suzerainty over the southernmost Cham principality of Panduranga, modern Phan Rang.[122] The visiting Ming admiral Ma Huan reported in 1433 that a stone tower on the coast guided ships "from all places" into the harbor of Vijaya's port, modern Qui Nhơn, which the Chinese called "New Department Haven." On the shore, fifty to sixty warriors and their families garrisoned a fort. Ma Huan recorded that Champa offered traders a "very glossy black, and decidedly superior" ebony, a unique black bamboo, aromatic woods, incense, and "very abundant" rhinoceros horn and ivory. In return, using their currency of silver or a "pale gold which is seventy percent [pure]," Chams would purchase blue porcelain Ming ware, which they liked "very much." They kept records in the Cham alphabet, written in white chalk on "goat-skin beaten thin or tree-bark smoked black," which they would fold "into the form of a classical book."[123]

Most of Champa's inhabitants were fisherfolk. They also tended fruits and vegetables, but "rice and cereals [were] not abundant." They lived in squat thatched-roof houses; the kingdom's laws restricted the height of the eaves to three feet. It was also a "capital offence" to wear white clothing, reserved for the monarch. Criminal punishments ranged from flogging with a rattan stick for minor offenses, to branding on the face for adulterers, to transfixing on a stake for heinous crimes. Officials resolved protracted legal disputes in a large brackish lagoon called "the crocodile pool," into which they made "the two litigants ride on water-buffaloes." Crocodiles would supposedly "devour the man whose cause is unrighteous."[124] Inheritance among the Cham was based on matrilineal lines. Centuries later a divorced Cham woman retained the right to her dowry and most of the couple's joint property, and female dignitaries known as *radjas* led annual festivals.[125] Yet at the court level the Hindu practice of sati (widow sacrifice) also persisted for many years.[126]

Ma Huan wrote that the king of Champa went about barefoot like his subjects but wore "a three-tiered elegantly-decorated crown of gold filigree." He traveled by elephant or "in a small carriage with two yellow oxen pulling in front." The palace was "tall and large," its walls "ornately constructed of bricks and mortar," and hardwood doors "decorated with engraved figures of wild beasts and domestic animals." After a Cham king had reigned thirty years, as Vira Bhadravarman had by 1430, "he abdicates and becomes a priest," leaving affairs of state to close male relatives. The king then went alone into "the depths of the mountains" for a year's fasting and penance. Should he survive, he would regain the throne, acclaimed by the Sanskrit title *sri maharaja* (noblest sovereign). It was probably to mark his return from the ordeal that Vira Bhadravarman changed his name to Indravarman in 1432.[127] The next year Lê Lợi died, and Indravarman launched an unsuccessful attack north into Đại Việt territory.[128]

Conflict with Champa escalated as the Đại Việt state strengthened under Lê Lợi's successors Lê Thái Tông (r. 1434–42) and Lê Nhân Tông (r. 1443–59). Vietnamese forces took Vijaya in 1446, then looted and abandoned it.[129] They captured the Cham king and took him to Thăng Long, then invaded Champa again in 1450 and carried off 33,500 captives. Lagging behind Đại Việt in military technology, Champa apparently still possessed no firearms.[130]

GENDER INEQUALITIES

Although maternal clans continued periodically to dominate the medieval Đại Việt court, by the late thirteenth century rising Confucian influence had undermined female status sufficiently for Lê Văn Hưu to express his shame that ancient Việt manhood had failed to rival the Trưng sisters. By the fifteenth century women were far from equal to men in dynastic law, possibly even in village custom. A feature of village life was "ancestor worship," including the dedication of land to the tombs of deceased ancestors and to meeting the expenses of these tombs' maintenance. The produce of specific tracts of land was set aside to keep "incense and fire" (*hương hỏa*) burning on the ancestor's altar and for sacrifices on anniversaries of their death. Although these honored ancestors included women, the task and the management of the land known as *hương hỏa* property was usually entrusted to male heirs, a Buddhist temple, or the village itself.[131]

Vestiges of the customary more bilateral gender relations did persist. The Lê Code set a precedent when it legalized limited consideration for women's inheritance rights in fourteen unique articles promulgated in 1449 under Lê Nhân Tông. Their beneficiaries included childless widows. Some legal scholars argue that article 375, for instance, "gave the wife property rights equal to those of the husband"—aside from acknowledging the customary practice that "the usufruct of the widow ceased upon her remarriage while the same right of the widower only expired at his death."[132] The widow's entitlement was called "nourishment for one generation" (*cấp dưỡng nhất thế*). It presumably also derived from indigenous Vietnamese custom; the degree of equality was unprecedented elsewhere in the Confucian world, where gender discrimination was greater.[133] In the case of property accumulated during the marriage of a childless couple, article 375 of the Lê Code specified that a widow whose husband died intestate could inherit "one" of the "two parts" (perhaps not necessarily half) "with full ownership rights." The remainder was divided into three, with one part "devoted to worshipping the husband" and two parts "entrusted to the wife for her support during her lifetime" and then, "upon her death or remarriage, [were] added to the portion devoted to the maintenance of the husband's tomb." Additionally, property "originating from the husband's clan" was divided in two, with one part "entrusted to a representative of the deceased's paternal relatives for worship," and the other "given to the wife to be used for her support during her lifetime" and then "returned to the husband's clan upon her death or remarriage."[134] Lê laws had yet to address the inheritance rights of daughters, a more difficult issue.[135] However, the incorporation of Vietnamese customary practice in a Confucian system modeled on the Tang had already made the Lê Code a unique, eclectic legal document.

The accumulation of a new legal corpus was not the only large-scale textual project of this early Lê era. In the 1450s, Lê Nhân Tông ordered the scholar Phan Phu Tiên to compile the historical annals of the defunct Trần dynasty (1226–1400), which became known as *Đại Việt sử ký tục biên* (Continued Compilation of the Historical Records of Đại Việt).[136] The first known maps of all the kingdom's provinces and districts were drawn up in 1469 and 1491, indicating that it included approximately 8,000 villages.[137]

LÊ THÁNH TÔNG (r. 1460–97)

The rising generation of Vietnamese literati educated in the Ming era and after finally came to power with the coronation in 1460 of Lê Lợi's grandson, Lê Thánh Tông. Neo-Confucian administrative rationality soon replaced aristocratic and military clan rule. Thánh Tông's court pursued the Tang "grand model of government" with its Six Ministries and "brought the Vietnamese government for the first time into the villages." From 1461, for instance, it forbade the unauthorized construction of new Buddhist and Daoist temples, and later prohibited private casting of "bells and statues" and limited the monkhood of both religions to "persons over fifty years of age having obtained an ordainment certificate." Thánh Tông also disdained trade and discouraged visits by foreign merchants.[138]

In 1462–63 Thánh Tông inaugurated regular triennial examinations on the classical texts. These competitions functioned not only to fill official appointments but also to train and deploy "a country-wide, Neo-Confucian indoctrinated, educated elite."[139] The admissions process accepted only those candidates approved by village or military officials, and it excluded singers, actors, rebels, men of ill-repute, and their descendants. The training was rigorous. The top post-1460 graduates earned doctoral degrees (*tiến sĩ*) that were of a higher level than those awarded over the previous four centuries even to the most qualified "upper-level" graduates (*thái học sinh*). As many as 4,400 candidates presented for the first metropolitan examination in 1463, and forty-four achieved the *tiến sĩ* degree. In each of the twelve triennial metropolitan competitions held under Lê Thánh Tông, the number of candidates never fell below 3,200. By 1497, twelve triennial competitions had produced a total of 501 *tiến sĩ*.[140] These graduates of Lê Thánh Tông's reign alone comprised no less than one-fifth of all the 2,300 leading graduates over eight centuries of Vietnamese classical examinations (from 1075 to 1919). Nine of the very top thirty (*trạng nguyên*) also graduated in the period 1460–97.[141] In the following three decades, ten more triennial contests produced another 381 *tiến sĩ*.[142] Confucian scholarship in Đại Việt had reached its height.

From the 1470s the Lê kingdom was humming. Government was an expanding business. The Six Ministries—interior, finance, war, justice, public works, and rites—each had its own large staff. (There was no foreign ministry; in theory a vassal kingdom left that to the imperial suzerain.) There were also six lower-level departments and six courts. As under Hồ Quý Ly, the government service comprised nine ranks, each with a military and civil branch; each had set salaries and entitlements such as land. Officials regularly inspected the twelve provinces to "check on administrators and express the silences of the people." Whether they could or would express them is unknown, but the formulation suggests a government awareness that many peasants feared criticizing local officials and landlords openly, without support from the state. By 1471 the kingdom employed more than 5,300 officials (0.1 percent of the population), equally divided between the court and the provinces, with at least one official supervising every three villages. Their task was to ensure, in Lê Lợi's aquatic metaphor, "the smooth flowing waters" of government control.[143]

In another innovation, in 1462 Thánh Tông added a unique article to the Lê Code, stipulating that daughters could legally inherit land: "When a father and mother have died intestate and left land, the brothers and sisters who divide the property among themselves shall reserve one-twentieth of this property to constitute the *hương hỏa* [incense and fire] property which shall be entrusted to the eldest brother. The remainder of the property shall be divided among them." That division was not always explicitly required to be equal between brothers and sisters, but in some cases it was.[144] In the absence of male heirs, daughters could also inherit the responsibility for the *hương hỏa* land—before adopted sons, and after 1471 before second sons. Like the earlier provision for property rights for wives as well as husbands, these articles departed from Chinese legal codes.[145] Another unique article of the Lê Code protected a principal wife whose husband "does not personally visit her for five months" (a year if the couple had children) by depriving the husband "of his rights over his wife." It also allowed the woman "to report the case to competent officials of her locale as well as to village officials in order to have the facts publicly recognized."[146] This and other elements of the Lê Code probably expressed some continuing features of "relatively balanced" customary gender roles that accorded women a level of autonomy common throughout Southeast Asia.[147]

Yet other articles incorporated Tang law, in new form and with different penalties that were severe for women. For instance, under the Lê Code, a principal or secondary wife who "leaves her husband's home without authorization shall be condemned to penal servitude as a serf assigned to kitchens." Should she also remarry, the penalty was "penal servitude as a paddy-husking serf." The Lê Code even reduced the Tang Code's penalties for men who injured or killed their wives.[148]

Other unique articles of the Lê Code attempted to suppress such long-standing Việt traditions as levirate marriage: "Whoever marries the widow of his deceased brother or teacher shall be exiled. The female partner shall receive a penalty one degree lower. The marriage shall be dissolved." A 1470 imperial edict prescribed punishment for such marriages even among ethnic minorities.[149] Some ancient practices obviously continued. Others inspired this undated folk song:

> Respecting the rule of fidelity, I have married nine husbands
> Rolling them into balls, I put them in a jar which I then carried on a shoulder pole when I went out.
> Accidentally the supporting basket suspended from the pole broke, and the jar fell to the ground.
> The nine husbands crawled out scattering in different directions.[150]

To the penal laws introduced by Lê Lợi fifty years earlier, the Lê Code added "ten heinous crimes" (such as rebellion) punishable by exile or death. This group of crimes came from the Tang Code, and the Lê Code described and punished six of the ten similarly.[151]

But it also developed Lê Lợi's *quân điền* system by specifying how many rice fields or fish ponds each rank of official could own. This broadly meant that no official could legally own more than a fellow official of equal rank; no able-bodied peasant male could own more than his neighbor (among women, only widows and a few others could own land at this stage); no bonded serf could own more than another, and so on. These "personal shares" (*khẩu phần điền*) made it possible for many Vietnamese to own some land, while the law limited the size of most large estates. (The court could still grant extra land to favored persons.) Later, taxes and rents were reduced as well.[152]

And it was now law that an official's property should return to the king for redistribution to others when he died. This too reduced the power of leading families and increased that of the state, making it more centralized and Confucian than ever before. In the villages, when a person died or turned sixty, his share returned to the village council for distribution to others. Public land was regularly divided up every four or six years. If most of the poor remained poor, many did obtain a secure future to work for, while the rich were discouraged from investing in land. Some probably turned their attention to trade or mining.[153]

The Lê Code reveals a hierarchy of different classes of people. For instance, the severity of penalties for tax collectors who retained state property for two to four months increased with the value of the specific items. The order showed clear social rankings. After the more lenient punishments for withholding less valuable items (demotions of from one to three grades), the law listed progressively harsher forms of penal servitude: as "heavy work menials," or for a more serious case, "as soldiers assigned to elephant stables," or (a yet worse fate) "as paddy-farming soldiers." The most severe punishment tax collectors could receive for that offense was "exile to a nearby region." Exile to "an outlying region" was a punishment for a relative of one or more murder victims who "privately settles the matter with the murderer."[154] A different article applied these same graded punishments to commoners, if they were of insufficient age to become "elders" but posed as "retired scholars" in order to gather "a group of people to commit unlawful acts." In such cases the severity of the penalty depended on the number of people assembled. In the case of a serf, however, exile to a nearby, outlying, or distant region, respectively, was the punishment prescribed for reviling, unintentionally injuring, or unintentionally killing a master. A deliberate injury attracted capital punishment. "A serf who strikes his master shall be put to death by strangulation. If fractures result, he shall be decapitated."[155] By contrast, the penalty for "a master who kills an innocent serf" was penal servitude. The Lê Code even specified that "negligent homicide" of a serf was not a chargeable offense, and the penalty for inflicting serious injuries on one's former serf was "four degrees lower" than for "simple injuring by striking."[156]

Lê Thánh Tông's long reign transformed the social order of Đại Việt. Neo-Confucianism went almost unquestioned, but it could also be adapted to Vietnamese customs and made more or less severe. Officials were, in Whitmore's words, "to comb through libraries for answers and to tour their territories for data."[157] Confucian education flourished throughout the Red River plain, not just in eastern delta provinces like Hải Dương but also in Kinh Bắc and other parts of the former Buddhist heartland of the western and central delta. Doctoral graduates from these regions now far outnumbered those from the southern provinces of Thanh Hóa, Nghệ An, and Thuận Hóa.[158] A well-established, confident regime had achieved a transformation. Cultural life flourished: new writings appeared on history, military science, botany, and mathematics. New prestige was given to the classical examinations. The names of the graduates of 1484 were carved on an inscription that expressed both confidence in the future and a Confucian faith in the ancients: "This stone is like a faithful mirror of the past where already is reflected the most distant future."[159] Đại Việt's leading historian, Ngô Sĩ Liên, wrote: "From the dawn of humanity to the present, no-one has been more important than Confucius."[160]

Equally in conformity with Confucian precepts, agriculture came to the forefront of official preoccupations. Thánh Tông's court aimed to make "full use of agricultural potential." Attention was given to public irrigation works. The Lê Code set out how the irrigation and flood control system should be maintained and repaired and on what days of the year this work should be started and finished. In 1474 the court created new posts for the inspection of dikes and encouragement of agricultural production.[161] Laws banned the killing of farm cattle. Attending to his ritual responsibilities, the monarch "frequently prayed for rain" and issued edicts on cultivation, land reclamation, and farm labor. Historian Sun Laichen notes that in 1498, "an edict was issued to the effect that officials should inspect irrigation works, select officials to be in charge of agriculture, and officials both outside and inside the capital should report on the situation of agriculture." Ngô Sĩ Liên even asserted that "our founding father sprang from the posterity of the Divine Farmer Ruler," Shen-nung, the legendary northern emperor said to have invented the plow.[162]

Ngô Sĩ Liên's backdating of the Lê rulers' ancestors to "the dawn of humanity" polished the prehistory of Đại Việt that had first emerged in the late fourteenth century. Before he presented his fifteen-volume *Đại Việt Sử Ký Toàn Thư* to the Lê court in 1479, Ngô Sĩ Liên added to the work of previous historians a new initial section covering the period from the purported rise of mythical Hùng kings (the "Hồng Bàng dynasty") in the early third millennium BCE to the accession of Zhao Túo in 207 BCE.[163] Đại Việt had produced its own pedigree, as old as China's, and it made no mention of the Lạc Việt era's signature bronze drums, which were now assigned to barbaric hill tribes.[164] This competitive Confucian historiography rather echoed sixth-century Chinese debates between Daoists and Buddhists, who in efforts to prove the precedence of their own religion over the other had backdated the births of the Daoist deity Lord Lao and the Buddha.[165]

GENOCIDE IN CHAMPA

Along with its enhanced administrative reach, Đại Việt's claim to be the inheritor not only of a classical antiquity rivaling China's but also of the empire's alleged agricultural superiority implied a heightened threat to its neighbor Champa. In its foreign relations, the court of Lê Thánh Tông emphasized "the moral question" and the difference, important to Neo-Confucians, between the "civilized" and the "barbarian." As Whitmore puts it, "In both his own villages and other countries, the ruler of Đại Việt now theoretically held the responsibility to tell the occupants how they ought to live."[166]

In 1460, the year Lê Thánh Tông assumed the throne, another new monarch, Bàn-la Trà-toàn (r. 1460–71), became king of Champa. Cham envoys visiting the Ming court protested that "Annam had aggressed against them," and four years later Champa "again complained that Annam had attacked them, and extorted a white elephant." Its envoys asked the Ming to send officials "to pacify" the Vietnamese "and to erect border stelae, in order to end their aggression."[167]

However, Đại Việt was building up to a major campaign. In 1465 Thánh Tông held maneuvers of his land and sea forces, one hundred thousand troops in all. He set down detailed operational rules for the navy, elephant corps, cavalry, and infantry. The next year he organized the armed forces along Ming lines. Each of the five divisions deployed ten warships, one major "fire tube," and ten large and eighty small "fire tubes." Đại Việt was now importing large quantities of copper to make guns and cannon. In 1467 Thánh Tông ordered the manufacture of new types of weapons and prohibited the use of saltpeter for fireworks.[168] He oversaw six naval maneuvers along the Red River and had maps made of the kingdom's twelve provinces, with military needs in mind. In 1469 Champa again protested that "Annam was extorting from Champa rhinoceroses and elephants." Đại Việt demanded that Champa accept tributary status and "serve Annam" as it did the Ming.[169]

Rejecting that status, a Cham army marched north in 1470. Thánh Tông declared war on Champa, stating confidently that Đại Việt possessed more troops and superior weapons.[170] "Your last hour has come," he proclaimed to Bàn-la Trà-toàn. Thánh Tông was ready to "annihilate" his Cham enemies. Champa and its threat were to be destroyed "for good." A 1470 edict stated: "How slow-witted is Champa, unsure whether or not to emerge from its rabbit hole! Like a venomous bee, it has been able to nourish itself and sting again; like animals, they eat their fill and forget their moral debt." Whitmore comments that for the first time, Đại Việt forces "were activated for a moral purpose—the destruction of evil and the establishment of civilization in a foreign land."[171]

The war was short and brutal. Thánh Tông mobilized a large force of reserves, taking personal command of an army now mustering two to three hundred thousand troops, at a reputed daily cost to the Đại Việt treasury of one thousand gold *liang*. They swept south and defeated Cham forces of fewer than a hundred thousand, including a large elephant corps that had marched to meet them. The northern Cham governors of Quảng Nam surrendered, and the Vietnamese overran the coastal strongpoint of Sa-Kỳ. King Trà-toàn immediately requested terms, but Thánh Tông "refused negotiations and pressed on with the offensive." Vietnamese forces next took Thị Nại, port of the Cham capital, and three days later their cannons, firearms, and scaling ladders began to besiege Vijaya itself. Concentrating their firepower against its east gate, the attacking troops broke into the walled city.[172] A massacre ensued. *Đại Việt Sử Ký Toàn Thư* records that the victors put forty to sixty thousand Chams to the sword.[173] China's *Ming shi* annals add that the Vietnamese forces "smashed" Champa: "Annam sacked their country [with] massive burning and looting, and subsequently occupied their territory." Cham officials later told the Ming court: "Annam destroyed our country."[174]

The Vietnamese captured fifty members of the Cham royal family. Troops brought King Trà-toàn kneeling before his conqueror. *Đại Việt Sử Ký Toàn Thư* reports his interrogation by Thánh Tông: "Are you the lord of Champa? I am. Who do you think I am? Just from your face I know you are the Emperor. How many children do you have? More than ten." Thánh Tông spared Trà-toàn and let him keep two of his wives. As Đại Việt soldiers bundled him away, Thánh Tông ordered them to observe the decorum befitting a former "lord of the country." But the Vietnamese deported the royal family and between twenty and thirty thousand Cham prisoners to the north.[175] Trà-toàn died of illness aboard a Vietnamese junk; his head was severed and fixed to the prow.[176] His family was assigned quarters beside the palace in Thăng Long, where they lived for thirty years. Some of the Cham prisoners were enslaved on the estates of Vietnamese dignitaries, and others were ordered to adopt Vietnamese names, marry Vietnamese, and start "correcting themselves."[177] But eventually local prejudice and opposition to their assimilation grew.

The annexed northern and central regions of Champa became Đại Việt's thirteenth province. It settled soldiers on these conquered lands in forty-two military colonies (*đồn điền*).[178] Resistance continued in the upland valleys of the south. Ming annals recorded in 1485 that "Champa is a distant and dangerous place, and Annam is still employing troops there." Cham envoys told the imperial court four years later, "Annam remains unbridled in its encroachments and violence."[179]

Thánh Tông's expansionism also looked west. In 1448, Đại Việt had annexed land from Muong Phuan, in what is today the Plain of Jars in northeastern Laos. Thánh Tông made that territory a prefecture of Đại Việt in 1471, and in 1479 he launched a new western campaign against both the Phuan realm and the Lao kingdom of Lan Xang. Whitmore writes: "Citing the Chinese classics (the *Books of Changes* and *of Poetry* and the *Rituals of Zhou*), he called on his forces to spread righteousness and virtue through the mountains." Vietnamese and Tai chronicles concur that more than 180,000 Đại Việt troops marched west in the fall of 1479.[180] Advancing on several fronts and "seizing the enemy by the throat," they burned the capital of Muong Phuan and took the Lao capital, Luang Prabang, the next year. Vietnamese records assert that in Muong Phuan, "70,000 out of 90,000 households were starved to death," probably a major exaggeration.[181] By September 1480, according to Ming spies, Đại Việt forces took twenty of Lan Xang's strongpoints and killed "over 20,000" Lao. They pushed on, defeating Tai resistance all the way to the upper Irrawaddy River, even briefly invading the Burmese kingdom of Ava. The Vietnamese forces retreated back to Đại Việt only after being driven out of Lan Xang in late 1484. Complementing this offensive across the northern mainland of Southeast Asia came a naval campaign in what is now the South China Sea. Đại Việt fleets clashed with shipping from as far afield as Malacca and the Ryukyu Islands.[182]

DVSKTT summarized Lê Thánh Tông's extraordinary thirty-eight-year reign. He "fixed official ranks, promoted rites and music, chose clean and able officials, sent expeditions to the four directions, expanded the territories;

Trà Toàn was captured, Laos collapsed, Ryukyu was defeated.... The barbarians in the four directions surrendered,... the country was peaceful and well governed. How spectacular was this!"[183] The population of Đại Việt had grown from roughly 1.9 million in 1417 to as many as 4.4 million in 1490.[184] The Red River delta was the most densely inhabited region of Southeast Asia.[185]

Thánh Tông's son Lê Hiến Tông, succeeding him on his death in 1497, saw no reason to alter policy. One of the court's literati quoted Hiến Tông as often saying: "Our Sainted Ancestors originated the civilized world; Our Father [Thánh Tông] reformed inside [the country] and rejected [the barbarians] outside. The model has been set, we have nothing at all to change!"[186] However, official ethnic discrimination escalated. In 1499, a new ruling forbade Vietnamese men of all ranks from marrying Cham women.[187] The rationale given was "so that customs should favor future [generations]"—probably to prevent Cham matrilineal inheritance claims from undermining those of Vietnamese male heirs.[188] The ruling may also have been a response to an internal crisis in Đại Việt, as events now threatened to spin out of control. King Trà-toàn's son escaped back to Champa, taking his father's remains. The Vietnamese "devil king," Lê Uy Mục, seized the throne of Đại Việt in 1505, murdering his grandmother and two ministers and ushering in an era of instability.[189] According to his successor, "Court members interfered in the government, the maternal side seized power, laws and restrictions annoyed and embittered the people, rules led to trouble and revolt, agriculture went into decline."[190] Cham slaves on Vietnamese estates staged a mass escape to the south, and those who remained were distrusted. Finally, the annals of Đại Việt record that in 1509, apparently after uncovering a plot, "the king gave the order to massacre all the Cham" who had remained in the neighborhood of the capital. That autumn, "on the king's order, all the Cham prisoners in custody were executed."[191]

While intermittently pursuing genocidal policies against Chams from 1471 to 1509, Đại Việt had vastly expanded its territory. It annexed twenty-two of Champa's twenty-seven regions and partitioned its southern rump into three small principalities. Only the five southern districts of Pāṇḍuraṅga (modern Phan Rang) retained the name Champa (*V.* Chiêm-Thành), under the Cham general Bố Trì Trì, who had fled there and sent tribute to Đại Việt, which then appointed him its prince. The victors renamed Kauthara on the central-south coast (modern Nha Trang) and Champa's western upland areas (today's Central Highlands), which respectively became the vassal principalities of Hóa Anh and Nam Bàn.[192]

THE CRISIS OF THE SIXTEENTH CENTURY

Đại Việt had taken over this extended new southern region during a period of seventy-five years of milder weather, which now gave way to two hundred years of alternating climate extremes. Severe fluctuations began early in the sixteenth century. The year 1500 was among the fifteen highest-rainfall years of the entire period 1250–2008, but 1503 and 1504 were both among the twelve driest.[193] Đại Việt also suffered from longer-term environmental problems, possibly aggravated by the territorial, demographic, and economic expansion of the late fifteenth century. By 1505–9, according to *DVSKTT*, the cutting of timber for housing construction had denuded the upland regions of Thái Nguyên and Tuyên Quang, leaving "no wood to control the springs," apparently leading to flooding and erosion, while salt production was insufficient to preserve the fish catch of the maritime province of Nghệ An and An Bằng.[194] Almost every year from 1512 to 1517 brought either drought or Red River flooding. The floods of 1517 affected the whole lower delta east of Thăng Long: "The bodies of peasants dead from starvation were piled one on top of the other."[195] Intriguingly, the early sixteenth century proved a period of political instability as well. The same period from 1512 to 1517 also saw eight peasant revolts, and the quarter century from 1502 to 1527 experienced a quick succession of eight rulers, six of whom were assassinated.[196]

The ruling Lê family, originally from Thanh Hóa in the south of Đại Việt, was increasingly dependent at court on two other leading Thanh Hóa military clans, the Trịnh and the Nguyễn. The Lê dynasty increasingly fell victim to intrigue between these competing clans. Bloodshed erupted in 1505–9, briefly forcing the Nguyễn clan back to Thanh Hóa.[197] Two years after the death of the "devil king," his successor Lê Tương Dực was challenged in 1511 by a rebellion whose charismatic leader dressed in red and was possibly a Daoist "sorcerer."[198] Tương Dực attempted a restoration of Neo-Confucian orthodoxy, repairing the National Academy and erecting steles to commemorate graduates of the classical examinations. In 1511, the official stele proclaimed: "Heaven brought the Restoration. (This is) the year for the examinations.... His Majesty, complying with the meeting of Heaven and Man, soothes the people of the land. In the classroom, [he] expounds on the Way [and] honors Neo-Confucian refinement." The inscription, composed by the official Lê Tung, added that "talented men form the basic element of the state," while the examinations "are the rules of the dynasty." He predicted that should chaos return, the inscribed stone would serve to warn the wicked to correct themselves.[199] Several years later Tung lauded

Tương Dực for having "restored the great heritage of Lê Lợi," while "our learning has become even more excellent, [our] territory even more extensive." Thus, Tung concluded, "By bringing prosperity and stability to the state and by giving the people a place to sleep, the great accomplishments of the [prior] kings will last as long as Heaven and Earth."[200]

But chaos did return, within a year. "The decline of the throne started" in the period 1516–22, a sixteenth-century contribution to *DVSKTT* states. During those years, "external bandits were not pacified [and] powerful ministers battled and killed each other."[201] Looking back from the 1550s, the author of a Vietnamese geography added that the Lê dynasty was "beset with weakness and disaster, so that skilled and talented men slowly began to leave, as stars in the morning and leaves in the autumn." Indeed, the climate and environment were in disorder. "Heaven did not continue the [proper] seasons, Earth did not continue the generations, [and] the people no longer prospered.... Heaven's will had gone, the soil went bad, the fields cracked, [and] war appeared."[202]

In 1516, the Buddhist monk Trần Cảo launched a major rebellion against Emperor Lê Tương Dực, claiming to be a descendant of the former Trần dynasty and a reincarnation of the Hindu deity Indra (Đế Thích), who was also the Buddhist King of Heaven and the Vietnamese god of chess.[203] Meanwhile in Thăng Long, the Trịnh clan moved independently against the emperor, who was murdered by one of his generals. The sixteenth-century chronicle records: "Trần Cảo entered the capital and the ancestral temple was destroyed." Then "Sơn-tây revolted and the capital emptied.... The Lê dynasty would not rouse [itself]!"[204] An eighteenth-century Vietnamese historian added that rebels and commoners entered the imperial palaces and plundered "gold, silk, documents, books, maps, and registers and scattered them all over the roads."[205] Trịnh and Nguyễn leaders joined forces again to oppose Trần Cảo and elevated to the throne the teenage prince Lê Y (r. 1516–22). But then the two clans fell out again. After losing a battle against the Trịnh in mid-1517, Nguyễn Hoằng Dụ took his family's forces south to Thanh Hóa once more. The next year, when Lê Y turned on the Trịnh, they drove him north out of Thăng Long.[206]

A new dynasty was in the wings. Mạc Đăng Dung (1483–1541), son of a Confucian family from coastal Hải Dương in the eastern delta, had grown up as a fisherman, then excelled in a military examination and in 1508 gained command of a unit in the capital. Promoted to the nobility three years later, he then served the throne in civil matters. At court he wrote long memorials to condemn advocates of heterodoxy and to punish a leading "traitor," while back in Hải Dương he recruited local troops and led a naval force. Emperor Lê Y now called for his aid. From 1518 to 1521,

Mạc Đăng Dung gradually put down the rebellions and took command of all military and naval garrisons throughout Đại Việt's thirteen provinces. However, as Dung's authority "grew day by day," Lê Y felt threatened. The emperor turned back to the Trịnh, who backed him in a renewed civil war, but in vain. It was their turn to retreat to Thanh Hóa, taking Lê Y with them. In his absence his younger brother Lê An (r. 1522–27) took the throne, but Mạc Đăng Dung dominated the court. Dung captured Lê Y, had both brothers executed, and proclaimed himself emperor. Two years later Mạc Đăng Dung presided over the classical examinations, for which the commemorative stele proclaimed: "This marks the beginning of the civilization of the empire." Đại Việt's Confucian schools and "renewed" examinations would now be held in correct sequence, every three years, and were "fully the equal of those of old." In 1536 another inscription, erected properly to commemorate the 1518 competition held by the Lê, claimed that based on "what (earlier) kings had achieved," the new Mạc dynasty "esteemed Neo-Confucianism and re-established the Way." The Mạc kings "put together again the system of learning and renewed the institutions for gaining talent, extending the (established) model."[207]

However, the Mạc had difficulty explaining their usurpation to the Ming. Lê Y's son Lê Ninh claimed the throne and sent a mission to China in 1536–37. The Ming court sent 110,000 Chinese troops to the border in mid-1540. A Ming text proclaimed: "If the Mạc, regretting their crime, abandon their imperial title, reform their hierarchy, and come to the frontier (with long cords around their necks), leading their officers and their people, to await with submission the decision of China," then the emperor would forgive them. This required a reenactment of the ancient submission to the Qin dynasty of "the princes of the Hundred Yuè, their heads bowed and ropes around their necks," and that of the Lạc lords who surrendered their census records to the Han.[208]

Fearing a Lê revival, Mạc Đăng Dung was ready to kowtow. He wrote the emperor: "Should your gaze illuminate my sincerity and forgive my transgression, I will be able to start anew. The land and the people all belong to the Heavenly Court. In the past I already gave you a true accounting, presented maps and awaited your verdict. I only long for heavenly generosity day and night, the way grain longs for spring rains, how could there be anything else to say!"[209] A few months later, Mạc Đăng Dung "led a number of ministers to the border on foot and with lengths of cord around their necks. On reaching the Ming camp, they crawled in barefoot and, kneeling towards the north, presented their statement of acquiescence, together with records of their land, population, and administrative and military organization to the Ming general." The empire reclassified their country as "An

Nan Dutong Shisi," no longer an independent vassal state, but gave the Mạc dynasty permission to administer it.[210] A Chinese author recorded that with the imperial army at the border, "Mạc Đăng Dung, bound and barefoot, lay prostrate and surrendered."[211] The empire had no need to invade its vassal state.

Mạc Đăng Dung died in 1541, leaving prudent but probably sincere instructions to his successors: "Don't do anything heterodox." The Mạc geographer Dương Văn An, writing in 1553, waxed optimistic: "Heaven's will comes [back], hillocks become solid ramparts, rubble becomes resplendent palaces, barbarian land becomes civilized.... [With] the Mạc dynasty, the wise are established; Heaven and Earth are cared for; truly it is a time of prosperity. Heaven's will has returned."[212] The visiting Portuguese missionary Gaspar da Cruz agreed, commenting in the 1550s that Đại Việt was "a very plentiful country," whose people "feed and dress themselves very well, as they likewise furnish their houses." He added significantly: "The people of this kingdom in their apparel, policy and government, do use themselves like the people of China."[213] The Confucian triumph of the fifteenth century must have seemed irreversible.

Yet a syncretic religious pluralism was widespread in both China and Đại Việt alike. The scholar mandarin Nguyễn Bỉnh Khiêm, who served at the Mạc court from 1535 to 1542, then withdrew from public life to become the leading figure of sixteenth-century Vietnamese literature, wrote in 1578: "I am a Confucian. Although I am not well versed in Buddhism and the Daoism of Laozi, I have read broadly and dispelled my doubts and learned something of their theories. Generally speaking, the Buddhist teaching is rooted in illuminating physical forms and the mind, and analyzing cause and effect. Daoism is based on concentrating the vital energy to make it supple, preserving oneness and keeping to genuineness. The sage Confucius rooted his teachings in morality, benevolence and righteousness, literature, life's realities, loyalty, and good faith. Aren't all of them the teachings that follow human nature in order to cultivate the Way?"[214]

Đại Việt was socially and politically divided. Unless emperors vigorously supervised their officials, they would not hear "the silences of the people," which rang much louder if officials had a free hand to extort their subjects.[215] Some of these "silences" and the social divisions of the time were expressed in the poem "Hatred for Rats," a critique of "predatory men entrenched in positions of power." Nguyễn Bỉnh Khiêm penned these lines on Confucian responsibility:

> Heaven creates all men on earth—
> shelter and nurture they all need.

The sages of long, long ago
taught them the way to grow five grains.
Old parents' wants must be supplied.
Children and wives must be sustained.
O rats, why don't you pity men?
From them you filch and steal their food.
In fields you only spare dried stalks.
In garners, you miss not one grain.
The toiling farmers groan and moan.
The suffering plowmen cry and weep.
The people's livelihood is all—
such harm and havoc you have wrought!
You've burrowed into walls and roofs,
and there you hatch your evil schemes.
Men's bosoms burst with hate for you;
you have incurred the people's wrath,
and someday they will slaughter you.
Displayed at court and in all towns,
your bodies will feed crows and hawks.
The plundered folk will then, at last,
enjoy the blessings of true peace.[216]

The mandate of Heaven had passed.

From 1533 the Lê forces regrouped around the prince Lê Ninh, with the reunited support of both the Trịnh and Nguyễn clans. The latter's leader, Nguyễn Kim (1467–1545), gave his daughter in marriage to Trịnh Kiểm, and with Kim's son, Nguyễn Hoàng, they all launched a military campaign against the Mạc to restore the Lê. By 1542 they had seized the southern provinces of Nghệ An and Thanh Hóa, where they reestablished the Lê court at Hồ Quý Ly's former "Western Capital," Tây Đô, and from there pursued their attacks on the Mạc in the northern delta.[217] The Mạc forces retained the capacity to strike at the south, and had Nguyễn Kim poisoned in 1545, but their court at Thăng Long split. A Mạc faction joined forces with the Lê.[218] By 1554 the Lê were secure enough in Thanh Hóa to hold a special competition of classical examinations at the *tiến sĩ* (doctoral) level.[219] The next year the Mạc staged an unsuccessful attack on Thanh Hóa. The annals describe the debacle: "The bodies of the soldiers of the Mạc stuffed the Đại Lài River, so the water turned red. The Mạc sent several tens of thousands of soldiers to this battle and almost all of them died."[220] Đại Việt was now almost evenly divided between warring dynasties, and it would remain so for another four decades.

Just three years later, in 1558, the Lê camp divided again. Factional lines began to assume geographic form. With the Lê headquarters in Thanh Hóa now dominated by *thái sư* Trịnh Kiểm and the Trịnh clan, rival clan leader Nguyễn Hoàng obtained advice from the scholar Nguyễn Bỉnh Khiêm that the southern frontier territory seized from Champa had "room to stand for thousands of years." He successfully requested a transfer from Thanh Hóa to a new post as garrison commander of the far southern region of Thuận Hóa. In 1569, extending his power yet farther south, Nguyễn Hoàng obtained an additional appointment as governor of the frontier province of Quảng Nam.[221]

In the sixteenth century these southern provinces, Thuận Hóa and Quảng Nam, remained ethnically mixed, with a probable majority of lowland Chams and various Vietic-speaking and other Mon-Khmer hill-peoples. The two provinces had produced only three of Đại Việt's 1,149 classical examination graduates of the entire period from 1463 to 1559. Thus when Nguyễn Hoàng took control there, Thuận Hóa and Quảng Nam lay beyond the kingdom's "Confucian frontier." The nineteenth-century Nguyễn annal says that in Thuận Hóa at that point, "the loyalties of the people were not one." There, Trịnh Kiểm told the Lê emperor, "The people still cherish rebellion in their hearts." That the south formed a natural region of its own was implicit in Trịnh Kiểm's advice that on arrival in Thuận Hóa, Nguyễn Hoàng should "give mutual aid" to his southern colleague, the duke who ruled Quảng Nam, whose post he would also assume a decade later.[222]

The restoration of the Lê dynasty had begun, but their eventual defeat of the Mạc was soon to be followed by a new north-south division, between the Trịnh and the Nguyễn. The Đại Việt kingdom's triumphant expansion over the Cham territories along with the Neo-Confucian intensification of its domestic governance had made the newly extended Vietnamese kingdom more prone to geographic diversification and internal dissension.

PART FOUR

Regions

Ethnic Khmer children on the grounds of a Theravada Buddhist pagoda. Wat Somron, Vĩnh Long province, central delta, January 1975. Photo by Ben Kiernan.

Ethnic Khmer children on the grounds of a Theravada Buddhist pagoda. Wat Somron, Vĩnh Long province, central delta, January 1975. Photo by Ben Kiernan.

Cham Hindu temples at Tháp Chàm, near Phan Rang, built in the reign of Champa's King Jaya Sinhavarman III (r. 1288–1307), January 1975. Photo by Ben Kiernan.

Saigon canal, with Cambodian Theravada Buddhist pagoda Wat Chantaraingsey on the skyline, February 1975. Photo by Ben Kiernan.

Chùa Xá Lợi, a Mahayana Buddhist pagoda in Saigon, February 1975. Photo by Ben Kiernan.

French colonial forestry official at Phú Hộ, northern Việt Nam, 1939. Archives nationales d'outre-mer (ANOM), Aix-en-Provence, France: FR ANOM 3502 COL 4923 (FM INDO NF 4923)—"Tournée d'inspection forestière de M. Consigny," 1939.

Vietnamese Catholic nuns in the Central Highlands town of Đà Lạt, January 1975, after the fall of the border province of Phước Long. The GVN banner reads: *Tấn Chiếm Phước Long Cộng Sản Đã Chà Đạp Trắng Trợn Hiệp Định Ba-Lê 27-1-73* (The communist attack and occupation of Phước Long has blatantly violated the Paris Agreement of January 27, 1973). Photo by Ben Kiernan.

Classical scholar in a Saigon street, February 1975. Photo by Ben Kiernan.

Leaders of the Hòa Hảo Buddhist sect at its headquarters, Hòa Hảo village, Long Xuyên province, late January 1975. Photo by Ben Kiernan.

Regional bus station in south Việt Nam, January 1975. Photo by Ben Kiernan.

Women soldiers in Hanoi, October 1980. Photo by Ben Kiernan.

The fifteenth-century Turtle Tower (Tháp Rùa), on the Lake of the Returned Sword in central Hanoi, 1980. Photo by Ben Kiernan.

Vietnamese soldier with Cambodians in Phnom Penh, 1981. Photo by Ben Kiernan.

CHAPTER 6

Inner and Outer Regions

Contending Shogunates, 1570–1770

The forty major battles fought between Mạc and Lê armies in 1539–1600 comprised only the first in a three-century succession of breakdowns of Đại Việt's political order and territorial unity.[1] With Trịnh and Nguyễn support the resurgent Lê eventually drove Mạc remnants to the far north, but could not regain real power themselves. The seventeenth century saw a long, inconclusive second civil war between the northern Trịnh-controlled and southern Nguyễn-controlled regions of the putative Lê realm. After the country's effective separation into these two kingdoms, known as Đàng Ngoài (Outer Region) and Đàng Trong (Inner Region), both then collapsed from the 1770s in a third round of civil wars and nationwide upheaval under the short-lived Tây Sơn dynasty (1789–1802), whose founders defeated first the Nguyễn and then the Trịnh and Lê.[2] Yet for the greater part of the two centuries of division after 1600, the contending northern and southern rulers had still recognized the powerless Lê emperors as the legitimate symbolic authority for all of Đại Việt.[3] The concept of a united Việt kingdom persisted and reemerged in the late eighteenth century.

Why did these repeated breakdowns of central authority occur in the period 1500–1800?[4] First, the new and extreme climate fluctuations of the sixteenth century, with alternating droughts and floods, escalated in the seventeenth. While the severe weather reduced the resources available to both the Lê and Mạc courts, its fluctuations inflicted more serious long-term damage on the agricultural landscape. Droughts dried out, cracked, and weakened earthen dikes and critical embankments, and then in flood years, fast-flowing waters broke through and swept them away.

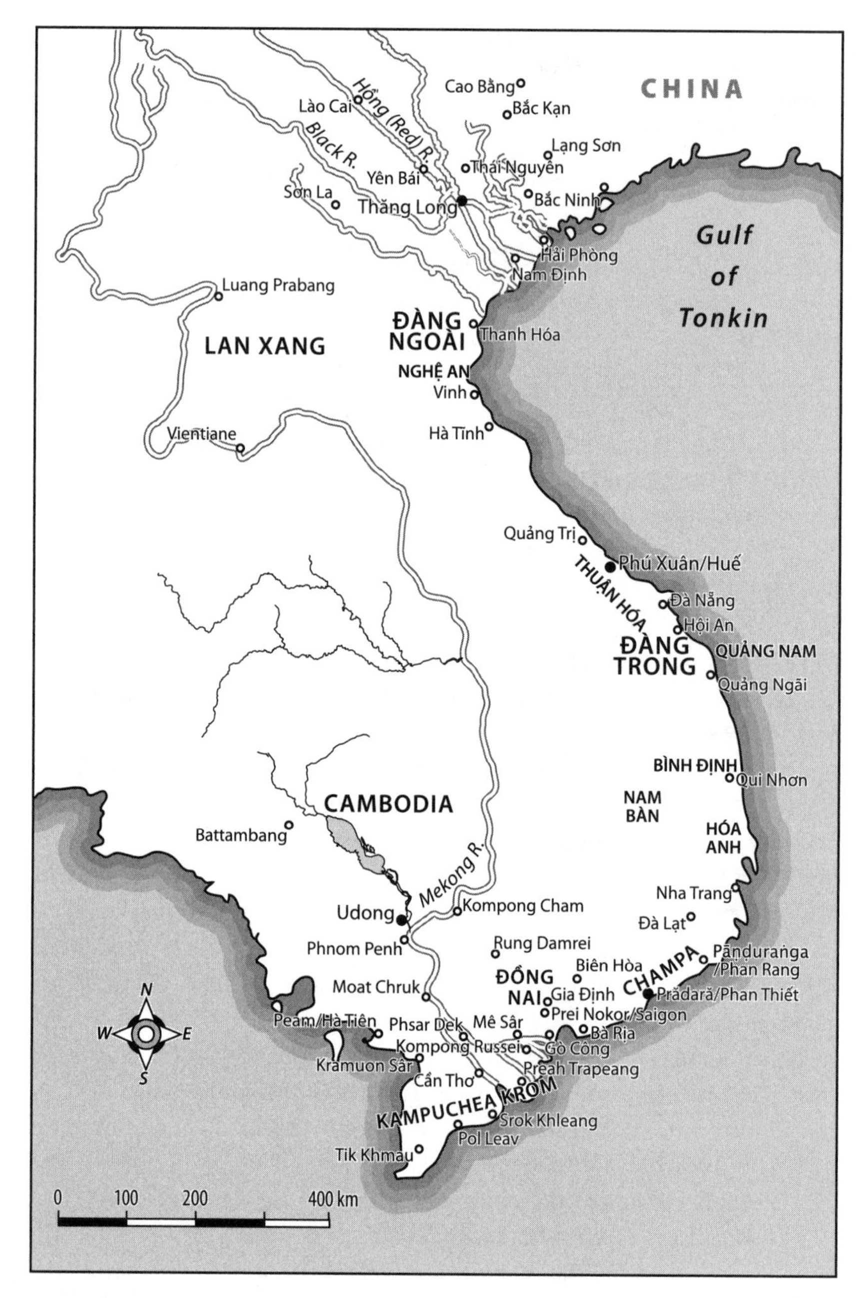

Fig. 6.1
Đàng Ngoài, Đàng Trong, Champa, and Cambodia, c. 1600–1800.

Preventing frequent disasters required the careful design of massive labor projects. Traveling through the Red River delta in 1688, the English buccaneer William Dampier noticed that its villages were "surrounded with great banks and deep ditches." The banks were "to keep the water from overflowing their gardens" in the wet season, and the ditches were "to preserve the water in the dry time, with which they water their gardens when need requires." Dampier pointed out that "the natural floods do very often make great changes in the river, breaking down one point of land, and making another point in the opposite side." Not far upriver from Thăng Long, to protect the capital from flash floods, Vietnamese had erected what Dampier described as

> a massy frame of timber, ingeniously put together, and very skillfully placed on great piles that are set upright in the river, just by its banks. The piles are driven firmly into the ground close by one another, and all the space between them is filled up with stones, and on them great trees laid across, and pinned fast at each end to the piles. . . . This piece of work is raised about sixteen or seventeen foot above the water in the dry time, but in the wet season the floods come within two or three foot of the top. It was made to resist the violence of the water in the rainy season; for the stream then pressed so hard against this place, that before this pile was built it broke down the bank, and threatened to carry all before it, even to the ruin of the city.[5]

Successive extreme fluctuations of drought and flooding not only ruined rice crops in the fields but could also destroy these water control works crucial to people's livelihoods and the economy.

The war-torn period 1570–1670 proved the most drought-stricken century ever. It saw nine of the forty driest years recorded between 1250 and 2008.[6] The second half of the sixteenth century alone included fourteen years of poor crops. For instance, *Đại Việt sử ký toàn thư* (*DVSKTT*) says that in 1572, "Nghệ An harvested nothing this year, what is more, pestilence broke out. Half of the people died. People fled either to the south, or to the northeast." In the eastern delta in 1594, it recorded, "The harvest in several counties around Hải Dương area is very poor, people are so hungry that they eat others. A third of the population has died of starvation." Scholars estimate that during the late sixteenth century Đại Việt's population fell by more than 440,000 (10–15 percent, including "several hundred thousand young men" killed in battles).[7] Yet climate conditions fluctuated even more severely during the seventeenth century, which alone included not only seven of the forty driest years but seven of the forty wettest of the eight-century weather record.[8] That dangerous combination must have seriously eroded and swept away earthen embankments of the delta's critical water control and drainage systems.

A second reason for the long-term instability in Đại Việt was that, despite the stabilization of landholdings under the early Lê, the severe agrarian problems so vividly portrayed by the dissident mandarin poet Nguyễn Bỉnh Khiêm before his death in 1585 remained unresolved. Many landless or land-poor peasants were available for recruitment or conscription into rebel, usurper, or restorationist armies, in those of the rival Trịnh and Nguyễn clans or in a vast uprising like that of the Tây Sơn. Hunger and agrarian turmoil were never far away if regimes or their opponents began to live off the fat of the land or neglect the maintenance of public works such as dikes and irrigation canals, as they often did after 1505.[9]

Third, the wars and natural disasters of the second half of the sixteenth century sent "thousands of desperate colonists" southward. *DVSKTT* increasingly records refugee movements from 1559, and particularly after 1570.[10] Not all displaced people went south, but the settlement opportunities there following the destruction of the main Champa state were such that Vietnamese peasants began heading for former Cham lands at a rate no kingdom could control. As they moved down hundreds of miles of coastline, many of these people escaped the grip of the Vietnamese state, which once again had overreached itself. In the three centuries after 1471, Đại Việt's territory doubled in size, mainly in its coastal length. Vietnamese courts found it much more difficult to retain control of far-flung domains, newly mobile subjects, and even their own officials.

Fourth, in this context the strengthening of the Vietnamese state apparatus by the early Lê may have proved counterproductive. The fifteenth-century reforms had brought benefits to some Vietnamese, for instance, by ensuring that public land was regularly and somewhat equitably distributed. But the state now depended on its officials to supervise regional and village affairs, for instance, to ensure that landlords and notables surrendered their excess fields. This put weight on the relationship between the monarchy and its bureaucracy. The state needed strong local authority. For example, *thái sư* Trịnh Kiểm advised the Lê emperor in 1558 to give Nguyễn Hoàng command of Thuận Hóa not only to "stand guard against the eastern pirates" but also to take control of "all local matters whether great or small and including all tax assessments, everything." Hoàng would have the power to "receive each year the taxes that are due."[11] But the court needed to restrain that power, too. Otherwise, one result could be the emergence of new regional magnates in place of the old landholding families, merging with them by striking deals at the local level, or even forming a new breakaway court. At least in the event of a weak monarchy, the delegated authority of regional officials could strengthen local autonomy rather than restrain influential families.

Fifth, a new era of international commerce brought opportunities that favored inhabitants of the extended southern coastline, which protruded into the South China Sea and provided many havens for the increased numbers of ships sailing to and from China. Just as ports in Champa had for centuries attracted and exploited the passing Asian trade, another "age of commerce" had begun, fueled in part by the Portuguese capture of Malacca in 1511 and their establishment of Macao in the 1550s. The Spanish, too, occupied Manila from 1571. But most important for the independent rise of Nguyễn Hoàng's southern region was the Ming court's decision in 1567 to rescind China's ban on trade across the South China Sea, while maintaining its prohibition on direct trade with Japan. The two new southern Vietnamese provinces—Thuận Hóa and Quảng Nam—soon became an entrepôt region for China's indirect commerce with Japan.[12] Ships commanded by Chinese, Japanese, and Europeans (known in Đại Việt as "Western Sea Kingdom bandit chieftains") plied Vietnamese coasts in the sixteenth century.[13] Japanese vessels visited both Manila and the port of Hội An in Quảng Nam, which became "the meeting place of Chinese and Japanese merchants."[14] Portuguese vessels brought Catholic missionaries who made the first Vietnamese converts. Trading ships from the Muslim world brought Islamic preachers to the rump kingdom of Champa. From 1600, Dutch and English ships also frequented the shores of the eastern Southeast Asian mainland. While the new international trade benefited both northern and southern regions of Đại Việt, it also accentuated the geographic advantages of the more commercially oriented south.

For all these reasons, then, the aftermath of the fifteenth-century Lê conquest and dismemberment of Champa proved ironic. Indeed, just a century later, from 1570 to 1677, the contending Vietnamese political forces split Đại Việt itself into no fewer than three regions.[15] At first the Mạc court at Thăng Long controlled the Red River delta, the northern region by then known as Đông Kinh ("Tonkin" to Europeans). Under the revived Lê banner, Trịnh forces held the central region of Nghệ An and Thanh Hóa, and the Nguyễn clan separately administered the southern provinces of Thuận Hóa and Quảng Nam.

Then around 1586 the Lê and Trịnh escalated their war against the Mạc, inflicting increasingly heavy casualties and generating a decade-long dispersal of refugees. In one battle in 1589, the annals assert, "The heads of more than one thousand Mạc soldiers were chopped off."[16] That proved only a start. In 1592, armies under the command of Trịnh Kiểm's son Trịnh Tùng overran Thăng Long. The Mạc retreated northward. Occupying the capital, the Lê emperor proclaimed triumphantly in 1593 that Lê Lợi's

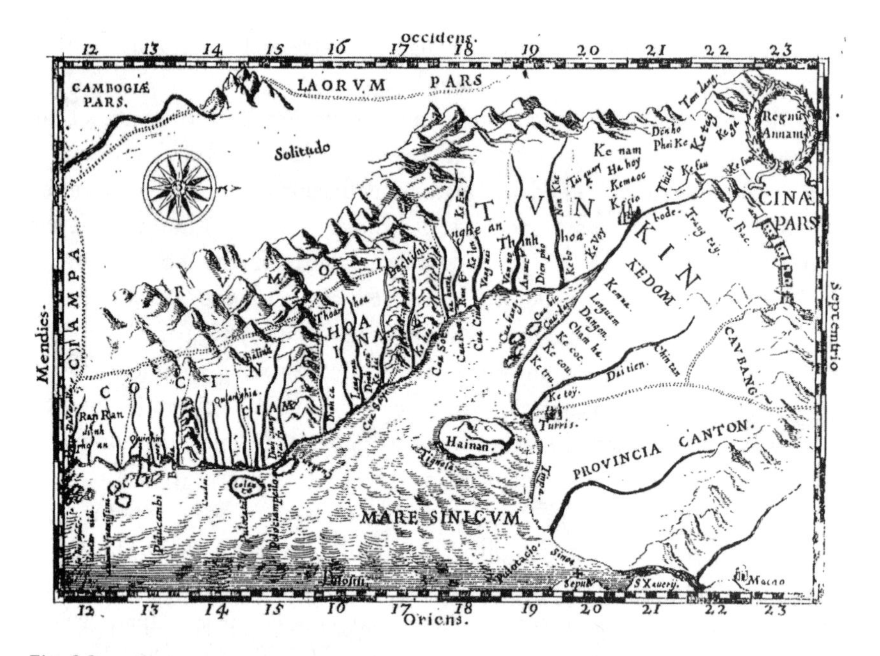

Fig. 6.2
Alexandre de Rhodes's 1651 map of Việt Nam, showing the succession of rivers along its central coast from Thanh Hóa to Phan Rang, flowing west to east down from the Annamite mountain chain. In the "Tunkin" plain, the town of "Kecio" (Kẻ Chợ), depicted by the church de Rhodes had founded, is modern Hanoi. From Alexandre de Rhodes, *Histoire du royaume de Tunquin* [History of the kingdom of Tonkin], published in Lyon in 1651.

fifteenth-century "model" had established "the state, widely and for a long time."[17] Yet the Mạc fought on. Even Nguyễn Hoàng, after three decades in the south, returned north and spent seven years campaigning alongside Trịnh Tùng and the Lê armies, deploying "large cannon of all types" in a bloody campaign to clear the Mạc from most of Đông Kinh. *DVSKTT* catalogues the decapitations of up to thirty thousand enemy Mạc soldiers between 1591 and 1596. The years 1592–97 also saw the greatest intensity of refugee flight. Only in 1600, after confining the Mạc to Cao Bằng province on the Chinese border, did Nguyễn Hoàng finally abandon northern political life and set off south to pursue an increasingly independent path in command of the maritime coastal area that stretched southward from Huế.[18] Many northern refugees preceded and followed him there.

ASSEMBLING SOUTHERN SPIRITS

Just as Lê Lợi's 1428 triumph had shifted power southward from the Red River delta to Thanh Hóa, Đại Việt's center of gravity again moved south as it incorporated the new cultural and economic zone that had long been part of Champa. In establishing its own political authority in this largely unfamiliar landscape, the Nguyễn clan participated in the formation of a new southern Việt identity, part of which involved taking up the worship of local earth and water spirits, especially female ones. In the mid-sixteenth century a Vietnamese fisherman near Huế reported the discovery of a rock goddess, Thai Dương Phu Nhân. Before long Nguyễn officials sponsored a cult in her name.[19] Then in 1572, in the face of seaborne attacks on the southern provinces conducted by Mạc forces from Đông Kinh, the regional commander Nguyễn Hoàng called upon the assistance of a local female water spirit. Close by his armed camp at Ái Tử (near modern Quảng Trị) was a riverbank from which he heard the sound "trao trao" emanating from the water. Suspecting the presence of a spirit, he prayed for its aid. In a dream during the night, a "woman dressed in green holding a white silk fan" appeared to Nguyễn Hoàng, promising him her help if he sent a beautiful woman to lure his enemy into a trap. Following the spirit's advice, his forces were able to ambush and kill the Mạc commander who had followed the woman to the water's edge. A grateful Nguyễn Hoàng bestowed a title on the spirit of Ái Tử River and had a shrine erected in her honor.[20] The Việt gathering of the spirits had recommenced, in the new southern region.

That coincided with the start of a new political era in the south. Soon afterward, according to a Lê annal compiled in the north a century later, a Trịnh envoy arrived to "inspect" and "speak kindly" to the southern troops who had just fought off the Mạc. As Nguyễn Hoàng feasted his northern guest, the two men "exhausted reminiscences and emotions from the old days." For those days were coming to an end. The later Nguyễn annal reports that when a northern "inspector general" came south in 1586 "to investigate the cultivated fields and to collect the tax due," Hoàng treated his guest with such "esteem" that the Trịnh inspector was supposedly moved to end the practice of calculating southerners' taxes, henceforth allowing "each district and village to prepare their own registers."[21] This administrative demarcation may be said to have launched the new southern polity that became known as Đàng Trong (the "Inner Region," in fact most of old Champa), henceforth ruled separately from the northern Đàng Ngoài ("Outer Region"), which was now limited to Đại Việt's pre-1400 territories—Đông Kinh, Thanh Hóa, and Nghệ An.

During the 1570s and 1580s, the Lê annals say, Nguyễn Hoàng "soothed" the southern provinces, Thuận Hóa and Quảng Nam. He governed them "with geniality," "applied law with impartiality, kept the local strongmen in check, and put an end to the cruel and crafty." Hard work and military discipline prevailed, "public morality was improved," banditry decreased, and people left their doors unlocked. Mạc forces "dared not" return, and "the borderlands were at peace."[22] In 1585, when five large Japanese pirate ships "plundered the coast" of Thuận Hóa, Hoàng's son sailed ten galleys out to attack them, sank two ships, and drove off the rest.[23]

The Lê annals add, however, that other "seaborne merchants from foreign kingdoms all came to buy and sell, [and] a trading center was established." In the 1570s fourteen Chinese junks brought copper, iron, and porcelain ware from Fujian.[24] Portuguese visited from Macao, and by 1584 some were seasonally resident in Đàng Trong.[25] A decade later, the governor of Fujian reported that three Japanese "Red Seal" ships, of only ten that Kyoto officially authorized to engage in international trade, were visiting Thuận Hóa to buy lead and saltpeter that Portuguese ships had brought there from Cambodia and Siam. By 1600 the highlands of Thuận Hóa were producing commercial quantities of pepper, which local merchants sold to Portuguese traders.[26]

The Nguyễn annals, for their part, state that Nguyễn Hoàng was strict and "kept close guard," but add that he "was cunning and seized opportunities," and enforced a fixed price for goods, with the result that "a large city" grew up in the south. This was Hội An, a bustling entrepôt port known to Europeans as Faifo. In 1602, on his only journey into the south of his realm, Hoàng chose a site about ten miles upriver from Hội An for the establishment of a garrison, a storehouse, and a temple.[27] The last of these was one of five temples he built in his territory between 1600 and his death in 1613. The annals record Hoàng visiting these places for "fasting and penance," to "give alms," and for "enjoyment of the scenery."[28] In 1601 he ordered the construction of the Thiên Mụ pagoda on the left bank of the Perfume River near Huế, at the site of the shrine of yet another powerful female spirit, the Cham earth goddess Po Nagar (the Lady of the Realm).[29]

Much of Nguyễn Hoàng's ritual activity recalls the eclectic style of the eleventh-century Lý monarchs. To some extent he was fostering a new Việt identity in a new land, but his emerging southern kingdom also retained important features of indigenous Việt tradition, including its receptivity to Cham culture, the spirit world, and seaborne trade. These specific continuities contrasted with the dramatic post-1460 Neo-Confucian transformation of the northern delta, which the Mạc had maintained and the Trịnh inherited. That, too, was a relatively new way of being Vietnamese, but not one that the Nguyễn pursued. They used classical examination competitions for lower-level recruitment only. Unlike the previous triennial system, the seventeenth-century Đàng Trong examinations were held only every six or nine years, and they tested candidates only on poetic composition and political analysis, not on the Confucian classics or history. There were no "metropolitan" palace-level examinations until as late as 1695. Confucianism in Đàng Trong, in the words of historian Nola Cooke, "became a matter of private choice and practice to an extent unknown in the north since the thirteenth century." Significantly, the Nguyễn "built no schools and created no prestigious central organ of learning akin to the Lê National College."[30]

It was Buddhism that thrived in Đàng Trong. In 1665 a Chinese monk from Guangzhou established the new Lâm Tế sect of Vietnamese Zen there. He built temples in Bình Định and in the capital, Phú Xuân (modern Huế). In the 1680s the Nguyễn sent him on a mission to Guangzhou to bring back Buddha statues, cult items, and many more monks. For nearly two centuries, Cooke writes, Buddhism was "effectively the state religion" of Đàng Trong.[31]

Nor was the Confucianization of the north irreversible. Under the early Trịnh the number of graduates of palace examinations plummeted, from 481 in the sixty-five years of Mạc rule of Đông Kinh (1527–92) to only 184 in the period of similar length up to 1657.[32] Indeed, in the early seventeenth century, following a long absence from the royal chronicles reflecting the withdrawal of court patronage for Buddhist sects after 1460, Đàng Ngoài too saw a revival of Zen Buddhism, with the foundation of the Tào Động Vietnamese sect.[33] Several of the figurehead Lê emperors (*vua*) patronized Buddhism, and leading monks returned to the palaces especially under Lê Thần Tông (r. 1616–43 and 1649–62), whom the annals described as "a deep thinker, a fine writer, a good and praiseworthy king. But his weak points were that his palace was disorganized and he believed in Buddhism."[34]

This double-edged critique suggests the rise of a new political configuration. Historians have compared the Lê monarch's ritual role to that of the Japanese emperor, "enjoying the trappings and not the substance of sovereignty," while the Trịnh lord (*chúa*) "occupied a position similar to that of the Shogun." The Japanese title *shogun* originally meant "the great general who subdues the barbarians."[35] From 1599 Trịnh rulers assumed the Vietnamese title "generalissimo" (*nguyên soái*). They took a close interest in military affairs and restricted most civil officials to less important posts. They established a military college and even instituted a triennial system of provincial and central military examinations, paralleling the civil competitions. Its graduates earned equal status to civil graduates, and often gained better posts. The annals record only two pre-1625 civil graduates of the Trịnh classical examinations who won promotion to high posts. Critiquing the "inferior state of learning" in the early seventeenth century, a later scholar wrote that during the 1631 competition, even the examiners failed to grasp one candidate's literary allusions, and they had to seek help from an elderly, well-read former Mạc concubine.[36]

INTERNATIONAL COMMERCE

Lacking the north's rich agricultural base, Đàng Trong needed to accumulate economic as well as spiritual resources. Nguyễn Hoàng and his successors adopted a policy of openness to trade, and in the early seventeenth century the south became a commercial center. On his return from the war in the north in 1600, Hoàng found that his officers had captured a Japanese pirate commander. Seizing this opportunity, Hoàng wrote to Japan offering "to continue relations." From Edo, the Tokugawa shogunate responded positively, and for five years Hoàng corresponded annually with its ruler, Tokugawa Ieyasu. A Japanese source recorded the arrival in Nagasaki in 1602 of a very large ship from Đàng Trong supposedly carrying 1,200 passengers and crew and gifts that included a tiger, an elephant, and peacocks. Hoàng adopted a Tokugawa emissary as his son in 1604. From then until 1620, Japan sent fifty Red Seal trading ships to Đàng Trong, which became its top trading partner.[37] The Japanese brought silver, still scarce in Southeast Asia, and purchased large quantities of Đàng Trong silk.[38] When a storm blew ashore a Japanese vessel bound for Siam in 1611, Hoàng immediately wrote to Japan: "Siam was in chaos and I could not bear to let the ship get into trouble, so I invited them to stay here to trade and treated them with sincerity." When the vessel sailed again, it carried more gifts from Hoàng and a letter asking the Japanese to "send the ship back to our country next year."[39]

In the early 1600s Nguyễn Hoàng also became a familiar figure to other foreign traders, who described him as "the king" of "Cochinchina" (Đàng Trong). In 1602 a Dutchman who came to Đà Nẵng to buy local pepper reported that Hoàng not only took a close interest in that trade but also treated the visitor to "a lengthy discourse on what the Portuguese had said about us, our country and our religion," and then listened to the Dutch Protestant defense, which "seemed to give him great pleasure." Hoàng then asked if the Dutch "had seen those crucifixes on the roads" erected by Portuguese Dominican missionaries. Perhaps keen to play the Westerners against each another, he authorized the Dutch to "pull down the crucifixes as they liked."[40]

As international commerce expanded, Chinese interest in Đàng Trong also remained high, partly because it offered opportunities to trade with Japan. By the beginning of the seventeenth century Chinese ships were already not only frequenting Hội An and Thuận Hóa to its north but also regularly trading as far south as the port of Qui Nhơn, near the former Cham capital Vijaya, in modern Bình Định province. Both Chinese and Japanese residents of Hội An established their own local community

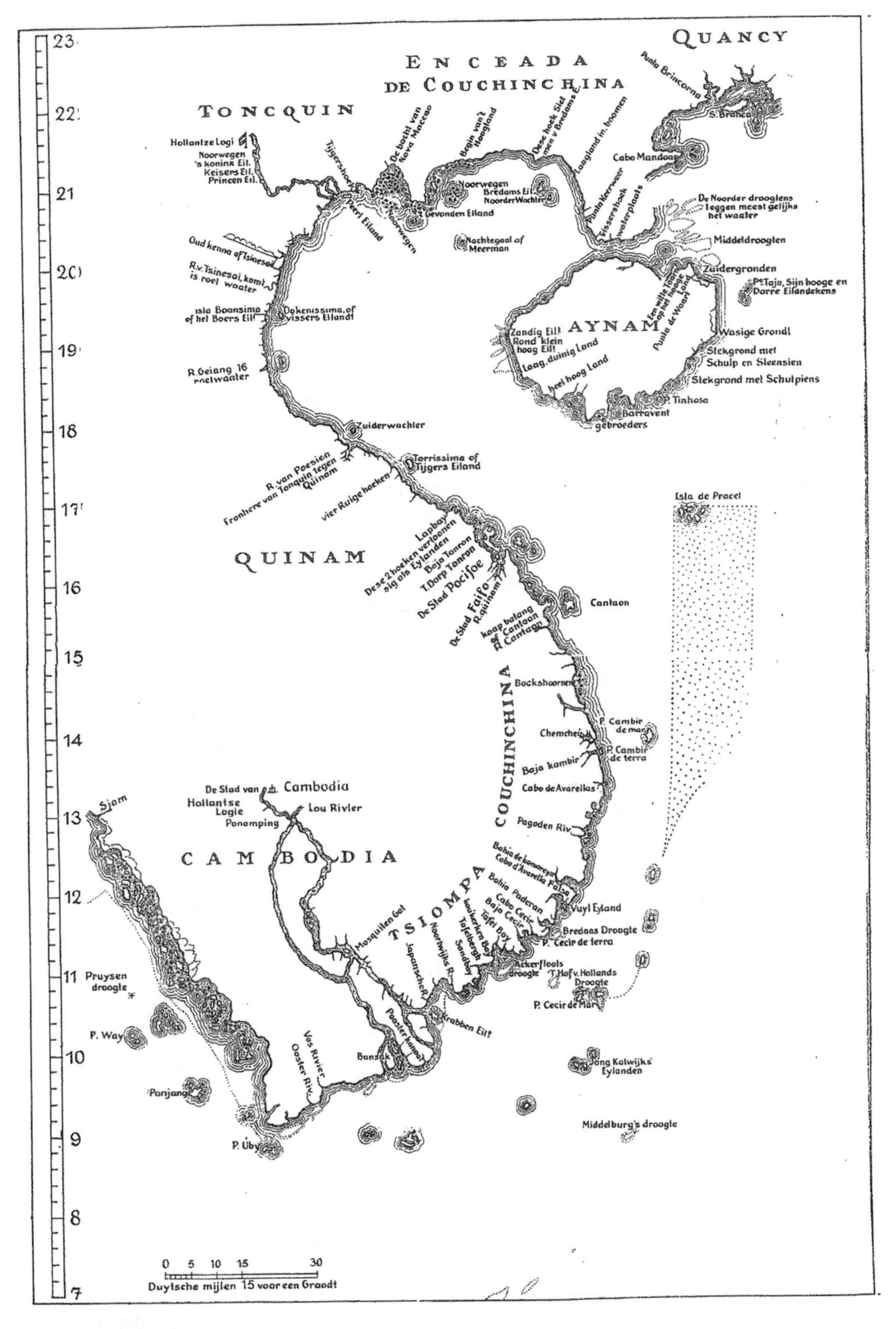

Fig. 6.3
Dutch map of the coasts and navigable rivers of Tonkin, Annam, Cochinchina, Champa ("Tsiompa"), and Cambodia, 1658–59. On the central coast, "Faifo" is the port of Hội An; "Tonron" appears to represent Tourane (Đà Nẵng). Upriver in Cambodia, Phnom Penh is spelled "Ponomping." An eighteenth-century copy of a map held in the State Archives in The Hague, reproduced in *BEFEO*.

organizations there in the 1610s.[41] Of the twenty junks that sailed south from Chinese ports in 1631, five went to Đàng Trong and five each to Cambodia and Batavia (modern Jakarta), the new headquarters of the Dutch East India Company (VOC). From 1621 to 1635, twenty more Japanese Red Seal ships sailed to Đàng Trong, where many farmers turned their riceland over to the cultivation of mulberry bushes and sugar cane for the Japanese market. Đàng Trong increasingly met its food needs by importing Cambodian rice. From 1635, when Japan forbade its own subjects to travel abroad, the port of Nagasaki continued to admit Chinese junks that had sailed from Southeast Asia, and Hội An remained the most important Southeast Asian port of origin for merchants trading into Japan, bringing Đàng Trong silks, sugar, and rare woods.[42] In 1642 a Japanese Christian who had spent the previous decade in Đàng Trong told the Dutch that forty to fifty Japanese still resided in Hội An, along with ten to twelve Portuguese visitors annually and more than four thousand Chinese. In the period 1647–1720, a total of 203 Chinese junks set sail for Japan from Quảng Nam in Đàng Trong, compared with 138 from Siam, 109 from Cambodia, and 90 from Batavia.[43]

In Đàng Ngoài, too, commerce thrived, though there it was mostly domestic exchange based on peasant agriculture supplying local markets. In the seventeenth century Thăng Long became known as Kẻ Chợ ("marketplace"). Samuel Baron, probably the first Westerner born and raised in Đại Việt, was the son of a Vietnamese woman and a Dutch official whom the VOC described in 1651 as "a longtime resident of Tonkin and fluent in the language." Baron was probably born in Thăng Long in the 1640s.[44] In a manuscript completed in 1686, *A Description of the Kingdom of Tonqueen*, he wrote of an "infinite number of boats trading up and down the country," mostly to and from the capital, which each month hosted two market days when crowds from the nearby villages thronged the streets.[45]

But the northern agrarian heartland could not compete commercially with Đàng Trong. Đàng Ngoài engaged in a "mutual and constant" overland trade with China, but the Trịnh rulers were less open to seaborne commerce, which they subjected to taxes and impediments.[46] From 1604 to 1635, only thirty-six Japanese Red Seal ships sailed for Đàng Ngoài, compared with seventy for Đàng Trong. When Trịnh Tráng (r. 1624–1657) assumed the throne in Thăng Long, he immediately wrote to solicit relations with Japan, but his letter stressed official political ties: "We are interested in getting on good terms with your government rather than those small traders." Three years later Trịnh Tráng's second letter, accompanied by gifts, may have offended the Japanese with its brusque hauteur: "Ten bolts of silk granted to the Japanese king." In 1628, Japan banned trade with Đàng Ngoài. Partly for this reason, the Trịnh had more success with the Dutch, who began trading in Đàng Ngoài in 1637 after finding that the Japanese living in Hội An had cornered the Đàng Trong silk market. The VOC reported Đàng Ngoài's annual production at more than 1,500 piculs of raw silk and five thousand bolts of silk fabric. From then until 1668, Đàng Ngoài was the source of the VOC's most profitable cargoes of silk bound for Japan.[47]

However, the Trịnh carefully controlled the silk exports, especially through a monopoly run by high-ranking eunuchs.[48] From 1647 to 1720, only sixty-three Chinese junks sailed to Japan from Đàng Ngoài (against 203 from Đàng Trong). Few northern Vietnamese profited, in contrast with the flourishing mercantile culture of Đàng Trong society. Comparison of mid-seventeenth-century donations to two Buddhist pagodas, one in the south near Hội An and one in the main northern port of Phố Hiến, reveals that the southern pagoda received mostly cash contributions, which were eight times more valuable than gifts made to the northern one, which received its donations mostly in rice.[49]

MISSIONARY SUCCESSES

The cosmopolitan mercantile world of the South China Sea attracted a spiritual counterpart in the multiethnic missionary orders who landed on Vietnamese shores. During the sixteenth century, Portuguese and Spanish members of the Franciscan, Dominican, and Augustinian Catholic orders proselytized in Mạc, Trịnh, and Nguyễn regions.[50] Then in 1615, a group of five Italian, Portuguese, and Japanese Jesuit priests and lay brothers established the first Catholic mission in Đàng Trong. Two years later a second Portuguese, Fr. Francisco de Pina, joined them and became the first Westerner to master the Vietnamese language.[51] Meanwhile, however, a major drought struck in 1614 and 1615, and "a universal barrenness" prevailed in 1617. Leading Buddhists blamed the missionaries, and a crowd burned down their new church at Đà Nẵng. But the drought broke immediately after the arrival of a third Portuguese Jesuit accompanied by another Italian, Christoforo Borri.[52] As Borri landed and said mass by the shore, he later wrote, "It rain'd so abundantly day and night, without ever ceasing, that every man apply'd himself to tilling of the ground" and "never gave us any farther trouble." Jesuits could now "live freely throughout the kingdom."[53] They attracted hundreds of converts in missions at Hội An and farther south at Qui Nhơn, where Borri lived until 1622. Two years later the French Jesuit Alexandre de Rhodes arrived, studied Vietnamese under de Pina, and then moved with a Portuguese confrere to Đàng Ngoài, where he spent most of the years 1627–33.[54]

While de Rhodes was away in the north, the Nguyễn court in Đàng Trong became more suspicious of missionaries. In 1631 the southern ruler, Nguyễn Hoàng's son Nguyễn Phúc Nguyên (r. 1613–35), outlawed Christianity.[55] But by 1639, the Catholic orders claimed to have attracted 82,500 converts throughout Đại Việt. When de Rhodes returned to Đàng Trong in 1640, he was unable to stay for long periods and left finally in 1645, a year after the first execution of a foreign missionary, Fr. André, killed by the Nguyễn in Đà Nẵng.[56] By then there were nearly fifty thousand Catholics in Đàng Trong alone.[57] De Rhodes estimated in 1650 that the total number in north and south had risen to three hundred thousand and was increasing by fifteen thousand per year. But within thirteen years the Trịnh court, too, prohibited Christianity as "a false doctrine capable of troubling the people's minds."[58] Yet by the 1680s northern Catholics numbered as many as two hundred thousand.[59] And after a relaxation in Đàng Trong, southern numbers reached sixty thousand before the Nguyễn ruler again banned Christianity in 1690.[60] In 1696, the Trịnh ruler burned Christian texts, but four years later a missionary wrote: "The people of Tonkin possess wit, politeness, and docility. It is not difficult to win them to Jesus Christ for they have little attachment to their pagodas." In 1712 King Trịnh Cương had Vietnamese Christians arrested and their foreheads marked with the words "student of Dutch religion."[61] Yet neither the Trịnh nor Nguyễn regimes succeeded in suppressing their now substantial Catholic minority communities.

The Catholic presence in Vietnamese life and impact on its culture only grew. In 1651, de Rhodes published a three-hundred-page catechism in Latin and Vietnamese. This was the first book to be printed in the new Romanized alphabet that he had helped devise for writing Vietnamese, which would eventually become known as *quốc ngữ* (the national script), a term previously reserved for *nôm* characters. Before he died in 1660, de Rhodes also completed a history of Tonkin and his massive *Từ điển Annam-Lusitan-Latinh*, a trilingual Vietnamese-Portuguese-Latin dictionary, which is now a key source for the history of the Vietnamese language.[62]

GENDER RELATIONS

The autonomy of Vietnamese women and their activities in public space shocked several foreign religious visitors. Early in the 1620s, Borri wrote that Đàng Trong's women wore "the modestest garb of all India for even in the hottest weather, [and] they suffer no part of the body to be uncovered."[63] But increasing contacts with crews of trading ships altered some marital arrangements. In the 1680s a Spanish priest reported that Đàng Trong women "even make it an Article of Marriage with their own Countrymen, that when Ships come in, they shall be left to their own Will, and have the Liberty to do what they please." Thus, "the Women there being too free and immodest, as soon as any Ship arrives, they presently go aboard to invite the Men." In 1667, a ship from Macao had arrived in Đàng Trong, "and during its stay there, the Portugueses had so openly to do with those Infidel Harlots, that when they were ready to sail, the Women complain'd to the King, that they did not pay them what they ow'd them for the use of their Bodys. So the King order'd the Vessel should not stir till that debt was paid."[64]

Vietnamese women dominated the trading sector. Sailing into Đàng Trong in 1694, the Chinese Buddhist monk Da Shan could see from his ship "more women than men, and their clothes were colourful." He later reported: "All the commerce was carried out by women, with no consideration of the differences between *nei* and *wai*," the Chinese distinction between "inside" and "outside" tasks. He found Vietnamese women "very good at trade, so the traders who came here all tended to marry a local woman."[65] Eight decades later the visiting northern scholar-official Lê Quý Đôn remarked that it was "ordinary" for Quảng Nam's female traders to ride horses to market, and that southern girls all wore fine silk tunics embroidered with flowers.[66]

Gender relations in private spaces also tended toward the bilateral. Possibly reflecting preexisting local Cham custom, southern households formed on matrilocal lines. Husbands, Borri recorded, "leave their own houses to go to the wife's; upon whose fortunes they live, the women managing all the household affairs and governing the family." Northern practice, Baron recorded some decades later, was not matrilocal. A bride moved to the groom's home, bringing "all her moveables, household stuff, and whatever else her father and mother gave for her portion," along with the groom's contribution in gold, silver, or cash. Yet although the law allowed only husbands to initiate divorce, in common practice even in the north it seemed more reciprocal: "Among the meaner sort, when a man and his wife disagree, and mutually desire a separation, they are divorced in the presence of some small judge and publick officers, by mutual discharges in writing."[67] The Jesuit priest Fr. Marini asserted that "Tonkinese women, like many other women, often tax their husbands' patience," and a wife's "cunning and malice" could force the "miserable man" to leave her, "as long as she pays him twice the amount he gave when he married her." Marini similarly condemned Đàng Ngoài's women traders, who "busy themselves incessantly in buying and selling," and worse, "become bold and free thinking." He went on: "They navigate the boats and carry by water everything one could want, and they pass from one side of the river to the other," conducting business "with all sorts of people . . . without worrying about their reputation," and "prostitute themselves shamefully and brutally without even being solicited." Đàng Ngoài village life, on the other hand, drew Marini's praise for its rural "simplicity and innocence." Northern women "allow themselves such criminal liberties only in those places where there are a great many people and where the merchant ships dock."[68]

Household relations clearly affected women's roles in commercial life. William Dampier, more interested in trade than Marini was, also proved more sympathetic: "This custom among them of buying wives, easily degenerates into that other of hiring misses, and gives great liberty to the young women, who offer themselves of their own accord to any strangers, who will go to their price." As a result, he wrote, "Most of our men had women aboard all the time of our abode there." Many Dutchmen, he added, "have gotten good estates by their Tonquin ladies, and that chiefly by trusting them with money and goods. For in this poor country 'tis a great advantage to watch the market; and these female merchants having stocks will mightily improve them, taking their opportunity of buying raw silk in the dead time of the year. With this they will employ the poor people, when work is scarce; and get it cheaper and better done than when ships are here."[69]

CHAMPA SURVIVES

The small rump kingdom of Champa, too, prospered from the rise in international trade. In 1594, Chams were able to help the Malay sultan of Johor combat Portuguese attacks, and in 1611 they launched an unsuccessful attempt to recapture territory from Đàng Trong. Throughout the seventeenth century, Cham merchants sailing from ports such as Pāṇḍuraṅga (*V.* Phan Rang) traded actively in Siam, Manila, Macao, Malacca, Johor, Pahang, Patani, and Makassar. Ships from as far away as Japan and Banten (in western Java) visited Cham ports.[70] However, from 1609 the rise of Hội An appears to have diverted most of the Japanese trade from Champa. Five Red Seal ships visited the kingdom after 1603, the last docking in 1623.[71]

Boarding the ships of Islamic merchants sailing from Indian ports, Sufi Muslim preachers also reached the shores of Champa. Like Christianity, Islam spread across the island world of Southeast Asia and registered some successes on the mainland as well. In 1595 a Spanish observer asserted that "many Mahometans" lived in Champa, whose Hindu king wanted Islam "spoken and taught," with the result that "many mosques" existed in the kingdom alongside Hindu temples. In 1607, when a Dutch fleet anchored off Champa, a Muslim *orang kaya* (a Malay word literally meaning "high-ranking person," denoting an official responsible for foreign traders) came aboard to inspect the vessels. The Hindu king's younger brother supposedly "wished to embrace the religion of the Moors, but he dared not do so because of his brother." Cham traditions record that King Po Ramo (r. 1627–51) invited Muslim dignitaries to Hindu ceremonies and had Hindu priests attend mosques during celebrations of Ramaḍān. He chose a Muslim as one of his wives, as did his successor.[72] Champa was experiencing politico-religious transition even as it faced continuing territorial losses.

WARFARE

As the Trịnh and Nguyễn drifted apart, these two regimes descended from former Thanh Hóa military clans each fought wars on other fronts. In the far north the Trịnh continued to combat the last of the Mạc, staging a major attack on its Cao Bằng redoubt in 1644 and finally destroying the rival dynasty in 1677. In the south, from the outset the Nguyễn rulers of Đàng Trong had constituted a military administration of a subjugated frontier. It too resembled a shogunate streamlined for war.[73]

Christoforo Borri wrote in the 1620s that the southern ruler Nguyễn Phúc Nguyên was "generally" waging "war in three parts of his kingdom": a civil war against two of his brothers, a war against Champa in the south, and a conflict with Đàng Ngoài to the north.[74] After Champa's irredentist attack in 1611, Đàng Trong annexed its territory of Phú Yên down the southern coast, provoking many Chams to flee into Cambodia.[75] Then Phúc Nguyên routed and captured his rebel brothers, who had sided with the Trịnh.[76] A forty-five-year Nguyễn-Trịnh civil war broke out. From 1624, the Nguyễn lords refused to hand over their southern tax collections to the northern court of Đàng Ngoài. The Trịnh then attempted to reconquer the south, and the Nguyễn built two defensive walls at coastal passes near Đồng Hới.[77] Over the next half century they not only held their ground against seven major Trịnh assaults from the north but continued to impose conquest, expulsion, and forced assimilation on the Chams in the south. After a major battle with Trịnh forces in 1648, Đàng Trong took thirty thousand northern prisoners and resettled them in Phú Yên on appropriated southern lands whose inhabitants had fled its incursions there. Đàng Trong proclaimed, "Previously, this land was of Cham barbarians. Now the population is small but land is large." The Nguyễn put their northern Vietnamese captives to work clearing new land among the cultivated plots.

They were "divided into villages, fifty to each village, and given half a year's supplies." The ruler Nguyễn Phúc Lan (r. 1635–48) predicted that "in several years they could produce enough for their own needs. After they marry and have children, in twenty years the children can be soldiers of the country."[78]

In 1653, Đàng Trong invaded Champa, captured and decapitated its king, and imprisoned a Cham religious leader and his wife in a structure "like a dogbox." Nguyễn forces seized the coastal district of Kauthara (Nha Trang) and moved the border farther south as far as Cam Ranh Bay. This reduced the territory of Champa to four remaining districts of the kingdom of Pāṇḍuraṅga, including its capital of Phan Rang, Phan Rí and Phan Thiết.[79] Very quickly, Đàng Trong then turned north again and launched an offensive against the Trịnh. From 1653 to 1657, Nguyễn forces occupied seven counties of Nghệ An and deported some of their population to the south.[80]

Đàng Trong enjoyed several advantages over Đàng Ngoài. The half century of the Nguyễn-Trịnh civil war (1627–72) coincided with a period of alternating climate extremes that probably favored the maritime southern power over the more agricultural north—just as the weakened monsoons of the mid- to late fourteenth century had given Champa an advantage over Đại Việt. The severe dry weather of the war's early decades must have particularly punished the rain-dependent northern economy: three successive years of drought in 1633–35 were followed by two very wet years in 1640–41, then another drought in 1646.[81] Yet the regional economies were now partly interdependent. When agricultural Cambodia also suffered a poor rice harvest in 1636, its king prohibited rice exports, bringing famine to northern Đàng Trong the next year.[82]

Though of modest numbers, the Nguyễn forces were well armed and relatively mobile. The Spanish priest Domingo Navarrete considered the Đàng Trong army "the best in all those parts," and "well-disciplined."[83] The Japanese who had lived there in 1632–42 estimated the army at four thousand paid infantry armed with firearms, pikes, bows and arrows, and spears. Unpaid conscripts numbered 30,000 in the 1630s but increased to 160,000 after 1648.[84] By the 1680s, Navarrete wrote, "The King keeps 40,000 Men at Court who most days shoot at a Mark and those that aim best are rewarded with pieces of Silk. I have several times heard Spaniards and Portugueses say, they are all excellent Marks-men."[85] There was no equine cavalry, but the king had "600 elephants suitable for war." The army fielded two hundred cannon of various calibers, fifty of which it had obtained from the Dutch and Portuguese. Vietnamese military craftsmen could cast artillery pieces of brass, but not of iron. Đàng Trong also possessed 230 naval galleys, each equipped with a cannon and two smaller artillery pieces and manned by sixty-four rowers and marines.[86] Most Đàng Trong conscripts served in the navy, which historian Li Tana considers "central" to the Nguyễn order of battle: "Its basic fighting unit was actually called a 'boat' (or galley, *Thuyền*)."[87]

By contrast, Đàng Ngoài's standing army was much larger, though less mobile, and its navy less effective. Navarrete described Đàng Ngoài as surpassing Đàng Trong "in all respects, not only in number of Men, but in Wealth, and the multitude of Elephants." In the 1640s Alexandre de Rhodes wrote that one hundred thousand troops from Thanh Hóa and Nghệ An occupied the Red River plain, of whom no less than half garrisoned Thăng Long itself.[88] In 1688 Dampier reported between seventy and eighty thousand soldiers still "constantly in pay." Baron estimated total infantry forces at 140,000, plus eight thousand cavalry and three hundred elephants. However, Đàng Ngoài's 220 oar-powered galleys, each with a single four-pound gun, were "more fit for the river than the sea, and rather for sport and exercise than war."[89] Navarrete described these as "many light Galleys, with which they do Wonders in the great River that runs up to the Court." Despite its numerical superiority, the Đàng Ngoài infantry could not overrun Đàng Trong's defensive walls blocking the narrow coastal passes, while the smaller northern ships could not land sufficient troops farther south. The war ended in a stalemate in 1672, with Đàng Ngoài maintaining a garrison of forty thousand soldiers near the border.[90]

In far-southern Pāṇḍuraṅga, the last principality of Champa, by 1675 most of the population were said to have become Muslims.[91] The next year saw the accession to the throne of the first Cham monarch to convert to Islam. His full name is now unknown, but he used the Malay title "Paduka Seri Sultan" and ruled until 1685. Cham Muslims were Sunnis and followed the Shāfiʿī school but retained many of their traditional beliefs and practices. A French missionary wrote of the Chams in 1678 that "more than half are Moors with the King, without however understanding their religion; the other part worship the sky, and in their sicknesses, or in accidents which overtake them, offer sacrifices to devils to be cured."[92] The Cham earth goddess Po Ino Nagar, who had previously metamorphosed into Uma, consort of the Hindu god Siva, reemerged now as Po Havah, or Eve, wife of the Muslim prophet Adam.[93] In 1680–82, the Cham sultan sent ambassadors to Batavia and merchant ships to Malacca. He or his successor shifted Pāṇḍuraṅga's capital southward to Phan Rí while continuing efforts to retake lost territory from Đàng Trong.[94]

The Nguyễn turned south again to crush Pāṇḍuraṅga. They seized its last remaining port, the former capital Phan Rang, in 1692. A Cham rebellion the next year successfully secured Pāṇḍuraṅga's continued recognition as a tributary kingdom, renamed as the march (*trấn*) of Thuận Thành. However, in 1697, the Nguyễn created, within the Cham kingdom, a new Vietnamese prefecture (*phủ*), Bình Thuận. In this way their magistrates took charge of the increasing numbers of new Vietnamese settlers in Pāṇḍuraṅga. The Nguyễn instructed Cham leaders to "change their clothes and to follow the customs" of the Vietnamese and "to govern their people" in Confucian manner. Đàng Trong recruited only Vietnamese for its armies.[95] About five thousand Chams fled to Cambodia, and fifty thousand remained in the small, now almost powerless principality of Pāṇḍuraṅga.[96] In 1712, the Cham ruler Po śaktiraydaputiḥ obtained the agreement of the Nguyễn court that he maintained the authority to judge disputes between his subjects, but that those among ethnic Vietnamese in Bình Thuận would be resolved by Đàng Trong prefectural authorities, and disputes between Chams and Vietnamese by a council including the ruler himself and two Vietnamese officials of Bình Thuận. By 1720, Đàng Trong's monarch Nguyễn Phước Chu had appointed a mandarin and a garrison in the Pāṇḍuraṅga court, and the death of its ruler in 1728 led to an abortive Cham revolt against the Vietnamese.[97]

CAMBODIA

Cham refugees and Vietnamese troops had already become involved in an additional series of conflicts in neighboring Cambodia. From the west, invading Siamese forces had razed its capital, Longvek, in 1594, attacked Cambodia again in 1601, and occupied lands in its north. The Khmer king, Barom Reachea VII, reputedly told his court in 1617 that they "will certainly raise troops to come and attack our country again. It is fruitful for us to contract an alliance with the Vietnamese kingdom.... If the Siamese raise troops to come [to attack us], we will take the troops of the Vietnamese kingdom to help us make war."[98]

Hoping to settle matters on the eastern front, Cambodia's crown prince married a Nguyễn princess.[99] Two years later he ascended the throne as Chey Chetta II, and when Siamese invasions recommenced in 1621, Đàng Trong provided help to Cambodia. In 1623 the Nguyễn ruler successfully persuaded Chey Chetta to cede the coastal Khmer border villages of Prei Nokor ("forest of the realm") and Kompong Krabei ("buffalo port") to Đàng Trong. However, with commercial opportunities expanding, Buddhist Cambodia soon became a battleground for a new confrontation between rising Islamic influences and the VOC. With help from local Malay Muslims, a young Khmer prince named Ponhea Chan seized the Cambodian throne in 1642, took the regnal name Ibrahim, and ordered his court to "enter the religion of Allah."[100] He launched a war on the Dutch East India Company, fighting naval engagements and seizing its ships.[101]

The Buddhist Khmer chronicle of the era later denounced Ibrahim for having given Islamic Cham and Malay mandarins "more power than the Khmer." His half-brothers accused him of "discarding his faith." Fearing that "the Khmer nation will disappear," they requested help from Đàng Trong to overthrow Ibrahim.[102] In 1658, Nguyễn forces marched through Champa and into Cambodia. Storming its capital of Udong, they captured and deported Ibrahim, who later died in exile. Cambodia regained its status as a Buddhist kingdom as a result of this first Vietnamese military intervention there.[103] However, in 1667 pirates from Taiwan descended on Cambodia by ship and massacred possibly a thousand Vietnamese living in the country. The Nguyễn monarch held Cambodia responsible, and hostilities persisted until 1672. From then until 1700, Đàng Trong armies intervened four more times in Cambodia, mostly at the invitation of claimants to its throne who faced Siamese-backed rivals.[104]

POLITICAL AND CULTURAL CHANGE IN ĐÀNG TRONG

The farther south and west Nguyễn power extended, the more Đàng Trong's center of gravity moved away from the old northern heartland. From the late seventeenth century, the Nguyễn took steps to distance their polity not only from the Trịnh but from the figurehead Lê emperors as well. They began by ritually defining their territory, then applying to it the term *quốc* (nation), and finally instituting a separate monarchy. First, from 1687 successive Nguyễn rulers conferred royal honors on selected spirits of the south. In the 1690s, rulers assumed for themselves the title "national lord" (*quốc chúa*). Then in 1702, the Nguyễn requested Chinese recognition of Đàng Trong as a separate independent vassal state. The Qing court rejected this request, but Đàng Trong soon began to employ "national" seals, including one in 1729 that proclaimed its ruler "king" (*vương*) of Đại Việt. This may have maintained a ritual link to the entire Vietnamese territory and left open a possible southern claim to rule both Đàng Ngoài and Đàng Trong. Finally in 1744, at the southern capital, Phú Xuân (Huế), the ruler Nguyễn Phúc Khoát (r. 1738–65) ascended "the kingly throne," which, as Li Tana writes, "completed the transformation from warlord to monarch."[105] By 1750, he claimed the title *vua trời* (celestial emperor) with status previously reserved for the Lê emperor (*vua*), ending any southern pretense of ritual loyalty.[106] The break was incomplete as the Nguyễn continued to use

Lê reign titles and eras in their documentation and calendars, an implicit acknowledgement of Lê sovereignty.[107]

Thus even in more distant Đàng Trong, despite or perhaps because of the break with Đàng Ngoài, the importance of Chinese imperial and even cultural models was clear. On first taking the title *vương*, Nguyễn Phúc Khoát not only had his civil and military officials wear imperial uniforms copied from a Ming illustrated encyclopedia, but he even ordered all his subjects in Thuận Hóa and Quảng Nam to dress in "Chinese" clothing styles.[108] A sense of belonging to the empire and belief in its tributary system of world order was not a monopoly of the imperial court, nor of Vietnamese envoys visiting China from Đàng Ngoài, who commonly expressed it in heartfelt verse.[109] At a more prosaic level, it was during the political separation of north and south in the seventeenth and eighteenth centuries that in both regions the Vietnamese language even borrowed the Chinese term for "empty," pronounced *không* in Vietnamese and employed not just as an adjective but more frequently as a negative particle meaning "not."[110]

The Nguyễn move from warfare shogunate to imperial monarchy also marked the high end of a slow demilitarization of the Đàng Trong regime. In 1695 it finally introduced palace-level examinations, if only to judge the poetic skills of serving officials rather than their knowledge of the Confucian classics or history. A separate special competition now tested candidates' familiarity with taxation and government finances. That was about as far as it went in Đàng Trong. In 1740, Nguyễn Phúc Khoát finally introduced a test on the Confucian classics, but after that no further examinations of any kind were held until 1765.[111]

Buddhism remained more influential, but in a local form. In the 1690s the Chinese monk Da Shan found "Buddhists everywhere but very little knowledge of the principles of Buddhism," with "immoral conduct" more common "in the temples than in secular society."[112] A Nguyễn ruler left an inscription in 1714 stating that he, "the king of Đại Việt," lived "in the Kun Ye garden inside the temple." By 1750 the Huế area alone boasted about four hundred Buddhist temples, as well as large numbers of shrines dedicated to the female deity Thiên-Y-A-Na, the Vietnamized reincarnation of the Cham goddess Po Nagar.[113]

A continued expansion in foreign trade and the peace with Đàng Ngoài after 1672 encouraged the trend away from military rule, yet probably also reinforced suspicion of Confucian orthodoxy with its disdain for commerce. Da Shan called Hội An "an international port," with a large Chinese quarter, a Japanese quarter and "Japanese Bridge," and "endless streams" of local products, including fish, shrimp, vegetables, fruits, and medicines—"a crowded town bustling with activities."[114] A British merchant estimated in 1695 that each year ten or twelve Chinese junks came to trade in Hội An, bringing cargoes from Japan, Canton, Siam, Cambodia, Manila, and Batavia. Then from 1715, Japan admitted only thirty Chinese junks annually; many others transferred their business to Hội An. By the 1750s Hội An's ethnic Chinese population may have reached ten thousand. Eighty Chinese junks traded there each year in addition to the mostly European ships coming from Macao, Batavia, and France. An eighteenth-century Cantonese trader visiting Hội An considered it "superior to all other ports of Southeast Asia," with "ships, boats and horses" arriving from six regions of Đàng Trong. They brought goods of all kinds "so abundant that even a hundred big ships cannot carry them out of here."[115] The Nguyễn lords committed substantial human resources to servicing and taxing this trade: 175 superintendents and managers of ships and of ship registers, defense superintendents, clerks, soldiers, sailors, and interpreters.

The northern official Lê Quý Đôn, visiting in 1776, remarked on Đàng Trong's prosperity that southerners "regard gold and silver as if it were sand, and rice paddy as if it were mud."[116]

ESCALATING CRISES IN ĐÀNG NGOÀI

Meanwhile in the north, the Trịnh rulers of the mid-seventeenth century had also launched a new program of civilian administrative reform. This eventually brought Confucian literati from the Red River plain into high positions that rivaled the entrenched warrior clans from Thanh Hóa and Nghệ An. Since the 1620s the palace examinations had already begun to produce more top-level graduates from the Đông Kinh heartland. Of the eighteen successful candidates in 1628, for instance, sixteen came from the Red River plain. By 1649 some had gained positions of authority and were promoting prohibitions of "bad habits" such as cockfighting, gambling, chess, sorcery, and promiscuity.[117] The civil bureaucracy expanded in numbers and influence. It set about updating population registers and taxation records and attempted to revive its role in the construction and repair of roads and dikes. By 1660 Thăng Long was "overrun with young, freshly-polished scholars and clerks." This new literati reached their greatest numbers and influence in the period 1663–72, with a proliferation of edicts, starting with one entitled "Forty-seven rules for teaching and changing the people," stressing submission to the ruler and filial piety. Other innovations ranged from regular lectures on the classics for leading officials to the sponsorship of Confucian rituals of marriage and ancestor worship; restrictions on Buddhism, Daoism, and Catholicism; and the imposition of central power down to the local level by taking taxation decisions away from village officials, condemned for their "swindling, knavish tricks." The state now assigned each village a fixed taxation and manpower quota.[118] In a break from customary practice, inhabitants could no longer appoint their village chiefs, who for the first time required state approval as being "educated and of good conduct."[119] The Trịnh court also tightened controls on international trade. It decreed in 1662 that European merchants "residing in the kingdom and long living side by side with the inhabitants, having come to despise the laws and to infringe upon them, it has become necessary to separate them from the rest of the population."[120]

Nevertheless, Đàng Ngoài experienced a brief commercial resurgence.[121] Edicts banning gambling and cockfighting were repeated three times in 1662–64, suggesting they were a response to an atmosphere of relative prosperity and leisure. From 1671 to 1690, the number of Chinese junks sailing to Japan from Đàng Ngoài doubled, though it barely exceeded one per year.[122] Domestic commerce remained more pervasive. Dampier, who spent several months in Đàng Ngoài in 1688, twice traveled inland to the capital, by water and on land. He reported "markets duly kept all over Tonquin once a week," one serving each group of four or five villages. They sold rice, pork, poultry, eggs, fish, and "all sorts of roots, herbs, and fruits, even in these country markets." In Thăng Long Dampier found daily bazaars offering these products along with beef and cuts of buffalo, goat, horse, cat, and dog meat. He also noted "the multitude of fine silks that are made here, and the curious lacquerwork" that merchants bought each year. Vietnamese craftsmen were skilled, Dampier wrote, but they lacked capital and needed advances from foreign traders, so that "though the country is full of silk, and other materials to work on, yet little is done, but when strange ships arrive." The Trịnh court closely regulated commerce in the capital, assigning entire villages to specialized crafts. Samuel Baron wrote in 1685–86: "Every different commodity sold in this city is appointed to a particular street, and these streets again allotted to one, two or more villages," whose inhabitants monopolized the shops in the assigned streets.[123]

However, in rural areas the new Trịnh officialdom had to confront ever more serious problems. Vietnamese annals record floods or droughts and consequent famines in Sơn Nam and Thanh Hóa in 1663 and 1667, a three-year drought in 1668–70, and more famines in Thanh Hóa in 1679 and 1684, the latter extending to Sơn Nam and Sơn Tây as well. Japanese sources record a major famine in 1681. Popular revolts broke out that year in Hải Dương and in 1683 in Sơn Tây.[124] Then in 1685 the region experienced one of the forty wettest years in its climate history.[125] Floods devastated Đàng Ngoài's rice crop. The next year Baron lamented, "If this grain would have grown only by the rains of the months of June and July, we should not have experienced the sad effects of a most dreadful and calamitous famine that swept away so many millions of souls, in these two preceding years." Inequitable distribution of land and food probably accentuated the death toll. Dampier reported in 1688, "'Tis through the poverty of the meaner people, that so many perish or sell their children, for they might else have rice enough, had they money to buy with it." He added, "The villages and land about them do most belong to great men, and the inhabitants are tenants that manure and cultivate the ground."[126]

With its newly qualified bureaucracy that may have numbered 3,500 civil and military officials by the early eighteenth-century, the Trịnh regime was in its best position ever to resolve these issues administratively.[127] But it eventually proved unequal to the task. Seven decades of palace examinations from 1657 to 1729 produced 346 top-level graduates, almost twice as many as in the early Trịnh years. In the last month of 1674 alone, 1,239 lower-level officials received posts in the capital and provinces. A "new generation of literati" from the delta was filling ever more positions in the bureaucracy, where they held their own against the previously dominant Thanh Hóa military officers.[128] But some sided with the latter, and factional rivalries within the administration provoked a debilitating and violent mutiny in the capital in 1674. They probably also contributed to the countryside gradually slipping out of control. For two decades the inhabitants of a village in Ninh Bình that offered a rest house for passersby would routinely storm it at night, kill all the guests, and steal their property. The villagers' criminal enterprise remained undiscovered until 1694.[129]

Neither faction at the Trịnh court was able to address Đàng Ngoài's serious agrarian problems, even though the extremes of climate eased from 1686 to 1740, the longest such respite to that date. In 1698 the regime again had to ban cockfighting, chess, and gambling.[130] Vietnamese annals even describe the period from the 1680s to 1719 as "prosperous" with domestic conditions "almost calm."[131] But that was a relative statement. International trade gradually withered. The English and Dutch closed their counting houses in Thăng Long in 1697 and 1700.[132] In the eighteenth century a Cantonese trader even reported that Đàng Ngoài offered "nothing but rice."[133] Soon even rice was in short supply.

Bad weather, though less severe, overwhelmed the northern agricultural and administrative systems. In 1694–95, famine struck Sơn Nam, Hải Dương, and Thanh Hóa.[134] In Thanh Hóa in 1702, floodwaters broke through the dikes of the Mã and Chu rivers, contributing to three poor harvests there in the years 1700–1705, which were followed by several years of drought. Then in 1712 and 1713 floods swept away tens of thousands of homes and much livestock, causing successive famines in both Thanh Hóa and Đông Kinh.[135] After another famine in 1721, a government attempt to register taxpayers in a canton of Nghệ An caused the flight of much of its able-bodied population. That led to registration of the old and weak and an increased burden, so more people left. In 1726–28, suffering in Nghệ An and Thanh Hóa was so extensive that the Trịnh allocated two hundred thousand strings of cash (*quan*) from the treasury to relieve it. Flooding struck the Red River delta in 1729, and the next year the populations of 527 northern villages fled their homes. Pestilence spread in 1736. Two years later the Qing annals reported that Chinese had bought a number of fleeing Vietnamese refugees, most likely as slaves. A nineteenth-century chronicle records that in the delta during the late 1730s, "the whole area was in chaos, especially in Hải Dương, where people planted nothing and all the stored rice had been eaten." The roads were "congested with starving people" heading for Sơn Nam, where conditions were "slightly better." A hundred *quan* could not buy a single meal. "The land was strewn with bodies of those who had starved to death. Only one out of ten people survived this famine." Of some Hải Dương villages "only three to five families were left."[136]

Apart from offering relief aid, the Trịnh responded to these serial crises in several ways. A first measure was restatement of the Lê Code's provision for "equitable redistribution" of public riceland. Trịnh Cương (r. 1709–29) decreed in 1711 that this should occur every six years under the control of qualified officials. Redistributed fields were to go only to the poor and to soldiers, and not to officeholders and farmers with sufficient landholdings.[137] Another decree of that year attempted to curb the abuses of landlords and to dismantle large private estates: "From now on, officials and rich people are forbidden from taking advantage of the poverty and dispersion of the villagers to usurp their land through purchase and to create farming estates where registered people in flight could take refuge and are used as farm labor." The landowners were given three months "to abolish themselves" or face prosecution, after which the provincial military chief would "abolish the farms."[138] Tillers of the land were to receive full title to the area they cultivated. But this legislation was never implemented, nor was the 1740 proposal of a Trịnh prince to collectivize all landholdings, which the court rejected "for fear of stirring anxiety and resistance on the part of the rich."[139]

In 1718 the Trịnh began to reorganize taxation. They adopted the former Tang tripartite system of taxes, on land, individuals, and sectors like commerce.[140] The administration conducted a cadastral survey in 1719 and four years later introduced a tax on private landed property. But privately owned riceland was taxed at a lower rate than public land. Officials, Buddhist pagodas, the capital, and the population of the Trịnh heartland, the Thanh Hóa-Nghệ An region, also gained preferential rates or exemptions, from both the land tax and the head tax. The poor peasantry of the Red River plain continued to bear the heaviest tax burden. In 1728 Trịnh Cương conceded that "the lands are falling into the hands of the rich, while the poor have nothing to subsist on." The tax on the produce of the soil led to iniquities and was abolished in 1732 for most products, leaving state monopolies on salt, copper, and cinnamon.[141]

Part of the problem was a failure of administration. When Trịnh Giang assumed power in 1730, he asked his officials whether the government's books balanced. They reported: "Recently, it has not mattered if the amounts collected and paid out came out even, and at the end of the year [they] were not even checked." The officials now requested and obtained permission to investigate the previous year's accounts, "to see whether the revenues are sufficient or fall short."[142]

One reason financial prudence had previously "not mattered" was that from 1658, just at the point when the Confucian revival was taking wing, the Trịnh had begun formally to offer for sale government posts (not merely honorific titles as under previous regimes) in order to cover the costs of the war with the Nguyễn. Twenty years later a decree revealed that examination candidates were paying others to sit the tests for them. After the regional examinations of 1696, investigation showed that many successful candidates were in fact underqualified. By 1700 the price of offices had risen to three thousand strings of cash for a district magistracy. By then, however, only 64,000 of the country's 206,000 fiscal units were actually paying taxes; the other households were exempt nobility and civil and military officials whose property was untaxed.[143] Worse, in Đàng Ngoài's population of around six million, probably an additional eight hundred thousand households remained simply unregistered.[144] From 1732 the administration lost the power to nominate village chiefs, whose appointments by default returned to the hands of the local inhabitants, especially the more influential notables.[145] Despite all its new recruiting and training since the 1660s, the Trịnh regime could neither govern most of its subjects nor afford to staff a central and regional administration even at one-tenth the size of the Lê bureaucracy at its height (during the Hồng Đức period, 1470–97).[146]

The intellectual level of its recruits was also inferior. The court acknowledged in 1732, "Recently, those who study the classics are researching the commentary annexes and neglecting the essential chapters; those who study history give attention to distant events and not to those of importance; their knowledge is superficial." Six years later a new set of promotions went on sale, at six hundred strings of cash for a step up the administrative ladder, and new posts became open for purchase even by nonofficials, for 1,800 and 2,800 strings of cash.[147] The problems plaguing the countryside of Đàng Ngoài went far beyond Confucian moral definitions of "bad habits," and they could not be resolved by edicts.

As if in acknowledgement that training more Confucian officials could not resolve these problems, the years following 1730 saw a precipitous decline in top-level graduation rates. This was unsurprising, given that from 1750 anyone could take the provincial examinations by paying three strings of cash. The result was chaos, as "everyone, merchants, butchers, and shopkeepers," presented themselves. The day the new competition opened, so many candidates stampeded into the examination field that some died of asphyxiation in the crush. Cheating was transparent. Some candidates were visibly consulting books, others selling their knowledge. Mandarins took bribes to look the other way. "From that time on, the competition tests were completely discredited."[148] The number of successful candidates in the palace-level examinations fell back to the level of the early Trịnh years: the nearly six decades to 1787 produced only 183 graduates, half the number for the period 1657–1729.[149] The historian Nguyễn Thế Anh comments that the attempts to employ Confucian thought "to advance a more rational system of administration" already seemed "to have come to naught."[150]

Nor had the Confucian revival proved very successful in reversing the renaissance of Zen Buddhism that had begun in Đàng Ngoài in the early seventeenth century. The late 1600s saw another wave of Buddhist innovation with the formation in Thăng Long of a third new Vietnamese Zen sect, Liên Tông, under the influence of a contemporary Chinese monk who practiced the "ritual of ceremonies to honour the souls wandering in water and on land." In this form even new, foreign practices were easily compatible with indigenous Vietnamese spirit worship. Confucians, too, often found "refuge and consolation" in Buddhism, and many literati entered the monkhood. Theories arose positing the common origins and interrelatedness of the Three Doctrines of Confucianism, Buddhism, and Daoism. Historian Lê Thành Khôi dates the "specific syncretism" of modern Vietnamese folk religion to this period. In the face of resurgent Buddhism in a new Chinese form and the successes that Catholicism also enjoyed, Trịnh officials sought to standardize and control indigenous tradition and manage local cults by authorizing "exemplary" spirits but prohibiting the worship of "unworthy" ones.[151] No fewer than 2,500 deities populated the royal register by 1722.[152] Their numbers were increasing, and even their titles became inflated. From 1729, the Neo-Confucian scholar Lê Quý Đôn wrote later that century, "civil and military officials possessing the title of Duke and their relatives, royal teachers, royal deputies, and those with military merit when they passed away were appointed to become beneficent deities, and all were given the title of Đại Vương [great prince or great king]."[153]

At court, Buddhism gained spectacular influence. Trịnh rulers had many temples repaired and new ones built. Trịnh Cương made frequent pleasure trips to pilgrimage sites and composed poetry about them. From 1713 he forced inhabitants of three districts of Bắc Ninh to work for six years on the restoration of a single temple. But in 1719 he feared unrest, abandoned the project, and exempted the districts from a year's taxation. Several years later he resumed the conscription of labor for temple construction. A year after his death, his son Trịnh Giang (r. 1729–40) began a similar project, obliging the people of three districts of Hải Dương to work day and night on two pagodas there, digging canals, building roads, and transporting timber and stone. In 1731 he had the Lê emperor strangled and a number of courtiers executed. While Trịnh Giang was having other officials investigate the budget, he expended much of it on Buddhist construction, left trusted eunuchs in charge of the court, and allowed local officials to impose exactions on villagers. A series of major rural revolts broke out in the 1730s, one lasting until 1769.[154]

Rural conditions in Đàng Ngoài deteriorated further in the 1740s, when very severe weather fluctuations returned. The years 1741 and 1742 were extremely wet, while 1746 and 1747 were extremely dry. Rebellions intensified across Đàng Ngoài, led by "disaffected scholars, Lê princes, Buddhist monks, local peasants, and minority peoples."[155] One major revolt lasted from 1738 to 1769, another from 1740 to 1767. For thirteen consecutive years from 1742, the Trịnh regime had to waive all taxation. It eventually conceded local power to leaders chosen within the cantons and communes. In 1742 and 1743 more refugees fled north into China, where purchasers continued to buy Vietnamese youths.[156] Other refugees headed south. A French visitor reported that around 1745, "four thousand Tongkingese, dying of hunger, came and surrendered to the Cochinchinese mandarin who is in command of the fortress situated on the banks of the river separating Tongking from Cochinchina."[157] A prominent scholar informed the Trịnh court around 1750 that 1,070 of the 9,668 villages in the Red River Delta were simply "gone," along with 297 of Thanh Hóa's 1,392 villages and 115 of the 706 in Nghệ An. Thirteen percent of Đàng Ngoài's 11,766 villages were empty.[158]

Worse was to come. In the second half of the eighteenth century, Đại Việt experienced its first multidecadal drought since the 1420s, in fact the longest period of dry weather since 1250.[159] Data from the northern highlands, not far to the west of the Red River delta, identify a "mega-drought" beginning over Đàng Ngoài around 1745 and lasting "nearly thirty years."[160] Vietnamese annals record famine in Cao Bằng in 1754, drought in the delta in 1756, and the next year a famine and epidemic in Sơn Tây, where in eleven counties "the people who survived numbered only one or two out of ten." The year 1764 was one of the forty driest years in the eight-century climate record.[161] Institutional, agrarian, and climate crises had all set the stage for a vast conflagration.

KHMER-VIETNAMESE CONFLICT IN THE EIGHTEENTH CENTURY

While the Trịnh battled agrarian disaster in the north, Nguyễn armies confronted Cambodian resistance to the south. In the Mekong delta, colonization and competition for resources increasingly plagued relations between local Khmers and Vietnamese. In the sixteenth century the first few Vietnamese settlers had reached the Gia Định region adjacent to the eastern delta. In 1679 the Nguyễn regime granted land there, on Đàng Trong's southern frontier but still within what a later Nguyễn history termed "the territory of Cambodia," to three thousand Ming refugees who had fled the collapse of their dynasty in China. By 1698, five years after Đàng Trong had completed its conquest of the central coast and seized the former Cham capital of Phan Rang, forty thousand Vietnamese households had independently moved farther south, settling near the delta. In that year Đàng Trong officially established its new prefecture of Gia Định, adjoining the eastern delta.[162] From 1700 to 1772, Đàng Trong armies intervened eight times in Cambodia.[163]

Upriver at Udong, the Cambodian court claimed the delta region, still inhabited mostly by Khmers, who contested Vietnamese encroachment. French missionaries there reported witnessing a genocidal Cambodian attack, led by a self-proclaimed Buddhist monk, on the Cochinchinese-controlled port of Hà Tiên in 1731: "People say that the war originated because of a certain woman who claimed to be the daughter of their god sent to punish the excesses of the Cochinchinese against the Cambodians, magic is mixed up in it and a great deal of prestige. She raised a considerable army of Cambodians.... Thus armed and protected by several mandarins [they] marched against the Cochinchinese and made an enormous carnage of them[;] they counted more than ten thousand of them lost as they were not at all ready to oppose her." From there the genocidal massacres spread. "Thus they ravaged all the provinces of the south of Cochinchina, putting all to fire and blood, killed the great mandarin of the place called Say Gon

[Saigon], and burned down the fine church of a Franciscan father." Yet "they were not content with this. They killed all those [Cochinchinese] that they found in Cambodia, men, women and children."[164] Đàng Trong armies responded with two unsuccessful attacks on Cambodia in 1731–32.[165] The Khmer court at Udong retained control of most of the Mekong delta.[166]

However, internecine strife plagued the Cambodian court. In 1737, a royal chronicle records, "Armies fought against each other."[167] A former Khmer ruler tried to regain the throne with the help of a Vietnamese invading force, but it was defeated after Siamese intervention in 1750, and once again a Khmer ex-monarch died in Đàng Trong. His successor Ang Snguon (r. 1749–55) escalated the violence. A French missionary in Cambodia reported in 1751 that war "raged" inside the country "every day," and that the previous year, conflict with Đàng Trong had led to more genocidal massacres. "It is also war outside, against the Cochinchinese who are not far away.... There have been great cruelties on both sides. The Cambodians have massacred all the Cochinchinese that they could find in the country, including three mandarins; several Christians were caught up in this murder.... At first they took no prisoners, but killed all those they could find. Now they are sent as slaves to the king of Siam."[168]

A few months later another missionary, M. d'Azema, identified the author of this massacre. King Ang Snguon's Cambodia was "in a very sad state," d'Azema wrote. "Last year the king had his son, who had been at the court of Cochinchina, killed on some suspicion of rebelling." Then, in July 1750, the Khmer king launched the attacks on every Vietnamese residing in Cambodian territory, including the Mekong delta; "He gave orders or permission to massacre all the Cochinchinese who could be found, and this order was executed very precisely and very cruelly; this massacre lasted a month and a half; only about twenty women and children were spared; no one knows the number of deaths, and it would be very difficult to find out, for the massacre was general from Cahon to Ha-tien, with the exception of a few who were able to escape through the forest or fled by sea to Ha-tien." Of Cambodia's "numerous" Vietnamese residents, d'Azema reported finding no survivors, "pagan or Christian."[169]

Other Cambodian authorities condoned these royally sponsored anti-Vietnamese massacres. In Phnom Penh, d'Azema informed "the great mandarin of this place, who is the first after the king, and who governs everything," that the Christian missionaries had been expelled from Cochinchina "on almost the same day" that the mass killing had begun in Cambodia. D'Azema reported that the delighted Cambodian mandarin "even told us that God was punishing the Cochinchinese for their iniquities, and especially for the impieties committed against our holy religion." The king and "princes, great and small," saw Đàng Trong's mistreatment of missionaries and burning of churches as a justification for massacring local Vietnamese.[170]

THE LAST DECADES OF ĐÀNG TRONG AND ĐÀNG NGOÀI

Nguyễn involvement in conflict in Cambodia symbolized Đàng Trong's vulnerability to the same centrifugal forces that had fostered its creation two centuries earlier. Like its fifteenth-century predecessor, the Lê dynasty, after its own major military successes and southern expansion, the southern kingdom had overreached and began to fall apart.[171] Đàng Trong's fragmentation was both economic and territorial.

The monetization of the southern economy, with taxes increasingly levied in cash and even some wages eventually paid in cash, led to a deepening shortage of the traditional copper coinage, which mostly came from Japan. But in the early eighteenth century, the price of copper rose in China, and Japan began to limit its copper exports. The Nguyễn decided to mint their own cheap, thin, light, low-quality zinc coins. Private minters could then follow suit, and they did so on a large scale. The results were massive inflation and the "disintegration of overseas trade."[172]

Another problem was environmental. Hội An harbor began to silt up. As mud from the Thu Bồn River slowly formed sandbanks in the channel of its estuary, they blocked the entrance to the port. From the high point in the 1750s, when eighty Chinese junks had visited Hội An each year, the number of ships arriving there decreased to sixteen in 1771, twelve the next year, and only six in 1773. The kingdom's tax revenues from shipping fell from 38,000 *quan* in 1771 to just 3,200 two years later.[173] In 1776 Hội An was still exporting gold, silk, pearls, aloeswood, cinnamon, black pepper, areca, nutmeg, sappanwood, ebony, cypress wood, cardamom seeds, elephant tusks, rhinoceros horn, tortoise shells, birds' nests, deer tendons, fish fins, dried shrimps, "fragrance snails," sugar, iron, zinc, sea slugs, and hundreds of traditional Vietnamese pharmaceutical products. Yet the port of Hội An gradually became a quiet backwater, a historic riverbank town.[174]

As southern expansion proceeded, the Mekong delta rice basket took Hội An's place. Chinese settlement started there in 1679, when the Nguyễn granted land at Gia Định to the Ming refugees. During the eighteenth century, more ethnic Chinese moved south from Hội An. The delta region of Mỹ Tho and Biên Hòa became commercial centers where "Chinese, Westerners, Japanese, and Malay traders were bustling."[175] Chinese merchants moved upriver and established themselves near the former Khmer village of Prey Nokor, now the Vietnamese town of Saigon (Sài Gòn). Its

Chinese quarter grew into the distinct township of Chợ Lớn. Other Chinese settlers in the western delta port of Hà Tiên transformed that previously Khmer region into an autonomous trading power. In 1708, under threat from an expanding Siamese kingdom farther west, Hà Tiên's ruler, Mạc Cửu, sought Nguyễn protection, giving Đàng Trong control of much of the trade from the Mekong basin and delta. With denser settlement and new markets, the far south began to produce vast quantities of paddy (unmilled rice grain) for export, as well as for the rice-poor regions of the central coast.[176] Once again the country's center of gravity had shifted southward. Saigon became a major port with "a forest of masts everywhere." A northern merchant who had made more than ten visits to Saigon reported: "Nowhere else can people buy rice as cheaply as here."[177]

Yet the deteriorating climatic conditions of the mid-eighteenth century, while less severe than in Đàng Ngoài, had an impact even in Đàng Trong. The Nguyễn chronicle records a famine in 1752 in which "many people died of starvation," and adds that in 1774 "a major famine struck Thuận Hóa." Of course, neither the Nguyễn nor the Trịnh regime was undergoing "irreversible" decline. At their centers, both ruling houses were capable of confronting political threats and in the mid-eighteenth century stronger rulers temporarily reestablished political stability for several decades.[178] But their deaths, in 1765 in Đàng Trong and fifteen years later in Đàng Ngoài, brought crises of succession and legitimacy. In the southern kingdom, the deceased ruler's maternal uncle imprisoned the royal heir and seized the throne himself; then in the north the crown prince plotted against his ailing father, who named another son as his successor, but on his death the disinherited prince staged a coup. In both cases military commanders played a major role in the outcome.[179] Both polities were ill-equipped to deal with the deepening challenge of a deteriorating climate.

Nor could either regime fully subjugate the varied ethnic and religious minority populations of the large areas each claimed to administer, especially the still-expanding Nguyễn regime. Its claim from 1757 to control of the entire multiethnic Mekong delta was an ambition that not only drew it into deeper conflict with Cambodia but also, even as the new frontier offered economic advantages, stretched thin Đàng Trong's administrative capacity. Its attempted absorption of the distant Mekong delta generated centrifugal pressures on the Nguyễn state similar to those that had brought about the breakup of the kingdom of Đại Việt after the Lê conquest and incorporation of Champa in 1471.

Moreover, from the late 1740s, after two centuries of peace, the Đá Vách (Hrê) people in upland Quảng Ngãi began to raid lowland settlements. In the 1750s Bahnar hill peoples, a Mon-Khmer group, some of whom lived in

Quảng Ngãi and others farther south in Quảng Nam, took up arms. The unrest spread south, and by 1761 "open warfare" raged in the highlands of both Quảng Ngãi and Quảng Nam. This was the point at which Đàng Trong's fiscal crisis propelled its tax collectors into the hills, imposing an "unendurable tax burden on uplander peoples." The Nguyễn ruler attempted in 1769 to further specify "detailed and clear" tax demands, and the following year, military forces drove the upland rebels back into the hills.[180] But victory was temporary. The later Nguyễn chronicle reported a series of "earthquakes and landslides, and shooting stars, and disturbed waters."[181] The era of Đàng Trong and Đàng Ngoài was coming to an end.

Over the course of the sixteenth to eighteenth centuries, Đại Việt's political center of gravity continued to shifted southward. As its territory expanded, the country divided into two kingdoms, whose geographic variety fostered further diversification into three distinct economic regions.

The populous rice-growing northern plains, Đại Việt's traditional heartland region, known as Đàng Ngoài, still supported the largest Vietnamese city, Thăng Long (now called Kẻ Chợ, later Hanoi), as well as the country's greatest concentration of artisanry and artistic development. Dutch, English, and French merchants visited Thăng Long and its seaport, Phố Hiến. Inland, Chinese ran mining enterprises near the northern border. However, from the mid-eighteenth century serious agrarian, climatic, and cultural crises threw Đàng Ngoài into turmoil.

On the less fertile, more sparsely populated central coast, the newer kingdom of Đàng Trong enjoyed closer access to the hills and a more tropical climate. Like Champa before it, Đàng Trong exported valuable forest and animal products such as aloeswood and birds' nests, as well as rice, fruits, sugar, fish, and Vietnamese fish sauce (*nước mắm*). Đàng Trong's capital region of Thuận Hóa and its court at Phú Xuân (later renamed Huế) were now populous and well established. The long coastline to their south was dotted with seaports, especially around Qui Nhơn and Phú Yên, which conducted extensive trade with Portuguese, Chinese, and Japanese merchants. Farther south, Đàng Trong officials dominated the small remaining Cham principality of Pāṇḍuraṅga, which they now called Thuận Thành.[182] Yet after the mid-eighteenth century, Đàng Trong too fell victim to a serious economic and fiscal crisis.

In the far south was the luxuriant alluvial Mekong delta and its environs, a pluri-ethnic frontier region that Vietnamese called Đồng Nai. Known to Cambodians as Kampuchea Krom (Lower Cambodia), much of the delta was still formally part of the Khmer kingdom and was inhabited mostly by Khmer farmers, though increasingly settled by Vietnamese speakers. The names of several Cambodian ports on the delta's coast and rivers suggest that Khmer traders were also active there: Kompong Russei (Bamboo Port), Srok Khleang (Warehouse District), and Phsar Dek (Iron Market). The region was low-lying and its population thinly dispersed, but it was "very rich in rice and agricultural products of all kinds," which ethnic Chinese merchants exported from the eastern port of Gia Định or Sài Gòn (Saigon), and from the far west on the Cambodian coast, the until recently autonomous ethnic Chinese entrepôt port of Peam, known in Vietnamese as Hà Tiên.[183] The Mekong delta had become the granary of Đàng Trong. In some months of the year, as many as a thousand boatloads of rice would set sail from there to the central coast.[184]

Đồng Nai escaped the serious agrarian, cultural, environmental, and economic crises that plagued the central and northern parts of the country. Prolonged political and military upheaval would soon bring down the Nguyễn and Trịnh regimes and end the Lê era.

CHAPTER 7

Alternative Unifications

Rebellion and Restoration, 1771–1859

The environmental and other crises that debilitated Đại Việt in the second half of the eighteenth century had their counterparts in the other major regions of mainland Southeast Asia. In 1752 and 1767–82, respectively, the powerful neighboring kingdoms of Burma and Siam both collapsed, giving way to energetic new dynasties there.[1] What happened in Đại Việt was similar but more complex and prolonged.

During the 1770s and 1780s, a three-way civil war raged up and down the full length of Đại Việt, ravaging both the southern and northern kingdoms and all three geographic regions of the country. The war began in the center of the country as a revolt in Đàng Trong, spread both south and north, and drew in massive military invasions from Siam and China in support of the southern and northern regimes. The rebels, known as the Tây Sơn, defeated them all, conquered most of Đại Việt, and briefly instituted several reforms. But fighting continued throughout the 1790s, and finally, in 1802, the Tây Sơn fell to a new nationwide dynasty. Three Vietnamese regimes—the Nguyễn, the Trịnh, and their Tây Sơn successors—had all collapsed in turn. The eventual victor emerged not in Đại Việt's northern or central heartlands but on its far southern frontier, in the newest and economically most dynamic region, Đồng Nai and its Mekong delta hinterland, and with aid from new foreign sources—especially Siamese and eventually, French. Đồng Nai's economic vitality and new importance also had significant cultural implications for the future unity of Đại Việt. As historian Alexander Woodside has written: "If mainland Southeast Asia was a crossroad of civilizations, . . . traditional Vietnam was a crossroad within this crossroad, especially after it had seized the Mekong delta."[2]

The three geographic regions of Đại Việt were culturally diverse, and they proved difficult to combine into a single polity for the first time. The tumultuous military history of the three-decade conflict known as the Tây Sơn rebellion reflected this extraordinary cultural variety and the chaotically rapid changes that convulsed early modern Đại Việt society in a period of ecological crisis.

THE TÂY SƠN REBELLION, 1771–1802

The upheaval that began by bringing down Đàng Trong started in the hills of Quảng Nam in 1771. The rebellion's leaders hailed from the hamlet of Tây Sơn (Western Mountains), where the mid-central coastal plain meets the highlands, sixty miles inland from the walled port city of Qui Nhơn.[3] The three "Tây Sơn brothers" grew up in this region, where the Nguyễn regime had resettled their northern ethnic Vietnamese forefathers captured during the wars of the previous century. Descendants of those northerners lived alongside local Chams and traded with upland peoples. The eldest Tây Sơn brother, Nguyễn Nhạc, a betel-nut merchant, took as his second wife a Bahnar woman who tamed elephants.[4] A public clerk and minor tax collector for the Nguyễn lords, Nhạc apparently kept his hands on some of the takings. In 1771, fearing arrest, he took to the hills and assembled a following of "malcontents, peasants, malefactors and soldiers." They started to seize property from the rich and give some of it to the poor.[5] They recruited strongly among the Bahnar hill people. Within two years, Nhạc's men sallied out of the forest to slaughter a Nguyễn tax official and his family.[6]

Nhạc then led his small force of minority uplanders and Vietnamese farmers down from the hills and across the coastal plain. In September 1773 they approached the walls of Qui Nhơn, the former Cham capital Vijaya.[7] Nhạc had his followers pretend to turn on him and arrest him. They put him in a cage and handed their "prisoner" over to the town's Nguyễn garrison. After dark, Nhạc freed himself from the cage as planned and opened the city gates to his army outside. The rebels stormed in and butchered the garrison. They routed reinforcements sent from Đàng Trong's capital, Phú Xuân. By late 1773, the Tây Sơn controlled the entire central region from Quảng Ngãi in the north to as far south as Bình Thuận (the former Cham district of Phan Thiết, adjacent to the rump Champa principality, Thuận Thành). In a few months, the rebels had killed in battle as many as

1,600 Nguyễn troops. They burned tax registers and canceled tribute requisitions.[8]

As Đàng Trong dissolved in civil war, a Trịnh army of thirty thousand invaded from the north and stormed Phú Xuân. The Nguyễn capital fell in early 1775. The young ruler Nguyễn Phúc Thuần (Định Vương) fled south along with his nephew, Nguyễn Phúc Ánh. Repulsed by the Tây Sơn, who dominated the central coast, the Nguyễn royal family sailed on and reached safety in the citadel of Saigon, capital of the far southern Nguyễn prefecture of Gia Định.[9]

In Đàng Trong's central region, the Tây Sơn had drawn upon a significant cross section of local support. They recruited their troops not only from the Bahnar and other hill peoples but also from lowland Cham, local members of the ethnic Chinese Heaven and Earth Society, Chinese pirates, and Vietnamese merchants.[10] In the early 1770s, the Cham princess Thị Hỏa and her followers in the Thuận Thành principality joined forces with the Tây Sơn, who appointed two successive Cham monarchs, and from the mid-1780s, one of them, the Cham prince Chưởng Cơ Tá also fought as their ally.[11] His title *chưởng cơ* means "regimental commander" or "captain," but a later Nguyễn account indicates that he also held the royal title "King of Thuận Thành."[12] Two ethnic Chinese generals commanded most of the Tây Sơn troops until 1775, when Nhạc dismissed one of them and the other, Lý Tài, defected to the Nguyễn in the far south.[13] Local Vietnamese merchants from Qui Nhơn and other south-central ports were among the other early supporters of the rebellion. They may have resented competition from the ethnic Chinese merchants who were by now well established in the southern ports of Gia Định and Hà Tiên and whose trading houses penetrated the Mekong delta and prospered on its burgeoning rice exports. After 1775 the Tây Sơn began to persecute ethnic Chinese, and from 1780 Nhạc (but not his youngest brother, Nguyễn Huệ) also attempted to crack down on Đàng Trong's Vietnamese Catholic minority.[14]

For more than a decade the dramatic three-way civil war turned the length of Đàng Trong into a battleground. In 1775, as the Trịnh force pursued their advance from the north against the Tây Sơn rebels, a Nguyễn army pushed back from the south, retaking Bình Thuận from them. This former Cham district was to prove pivotal in the long Vietnamese civil conflict. Caught between the northern and southern regimes, Nhạc made a tactical decision: he offered to join forces with the Trịnh. The northerners accepted Nhạc's offer and enlisted his army to pursue their longstanding campaign against the Nguyễn. Nhạc's brother Huệ marched south and again took Bình Thuận. For its part, the Trịnh army turned back and marched north to Phú Xuân, where an epidemic almost wiped it out. That allowed the Tây Sơn to reoccupy Quảng Nam as well, while the Trịnh held on to Phú Xuân and the northern prefecture, Thuận Hóa. Nhạc then sent his middle brother, Lữ, back to attack the Nguyễn holdouts in the south. Saigon fell in early 1776, but a Nguyễn counterattack quickly recaptured it.[15] Meanwhile Nhạc had himself crowned "Heavenly King" (*thiên vương*) in a ceremony held in the citadel of the former Cham capital, Chà Bàn, near Qui Nhơn town. The Trịnh recognized Nhạc the next year but accorded him only the rank of "grand duke" of Quảng Nam.[16]

Nhạc sent his two brothers south on another expedition against the Nguyễn. Again Saigon and Gia Định fell. The Tây Sơn victors pursued the southern monarch Định Vương across the Mekong delta, killed him, and massacred almost his entire family. In Qui Nhơn, Nhạc triumphantly assumed the new more ambitious title of the Thái Đức "Emperor" (*hoàng đế*) in 1778, thus not merely displacing the Nguyễn but also forswearing any allegiance to the Lê emperor in Thăng Long and, by implication, claiming suzerainty over the Trịnh. But he continued to stress his southern character by maintaining his court at the former Cham citadel of Chà Bàn. The surrounding region of Qui Nhơn was dotted with "Việt-Cham" temples like that of Nhạn-sơn, whose monks hung Vietnamese clothing over two Cham statues in the temple grounds, assimilating these forgotten deities into local Vietnamese ritual.[17] In similar fashion, Nhạc metaphorically draped his imperial robes over the silent stone monument of Chà Bàn.

But Nhạc still faced an enemy in the far south. Định Vương's nephew, Nguyễn Ánh had escaped the slaughter. This last surviving Nguyễn prince rebuilt an army in the Mekong delta. In 1779, he hit back. Saigon changed hands for the fourth time in four years. Pushing north once more, Nguyễn forces returned to Bình Thuận. They also marched west and imposed Nguyễn rule over the kingdom of Cambodia. In 1780, Nguyễn Ánh in turn proclaimed himself king (*vương*) and consolidated his control over the delta by incorporating the previously autonomous port kingdom of Hà Tiên. A major Siamese invasion of Cambodia threatened to end Nguyễn rule there, but in 1781 the Siamese commander received news of trouble in the court at home. He offered a truce, marched his army back to Siam, and seized power. He took the Siamese throne as King Rama I, founding the Chakri dynasty in Bangkok in 1782.[18]

In the same year the Tây Sơn returned south to attack the Nguyễn. Nhạc and Huệ sailed a hundred war junks into the Saigon River and took the citadel by storm. The victorious Tây Sơn troops massacred more than ten thousand local Chinese merchants and their families, burning and pillaging their shops and warehouses in the city and neighboring Chợ Lớn. The battle lines seesawed as control of Saigon changed hands three more times in as many years. Nguyễn Ánh fled to Siam. His new ally Rama I mustered twenty thousand Siamese troops and three hundred junks in Nguyễn Ánh's support. In early 1785 their combined forces marched east across Cambodia to the Mekong delta, where Nguyễn Huệ ambushed and routed them. The defeated Nguyễn Ánh sailed back to Bangkok.[19] But the delta remained a chaos of contending claimants. The next year Nhạc acknowledged that his Tây Sơn regime was merely one of "six forces competing with each other" in the Mekong delta. He named the other five as "the Khmer, Siam, Hà Tiên, the female leader [Cham princess Thị Hỏa], and the Chinese Li [Lý Tài]."[20]

Nguyễn Ánh could not be written off either. From Bangkok, he sent his young son Prince Cảnh to France in the company of the French bishop Pigneau de Béhaine, who had been proselytizing in Hà Tiên since 1767. Nguyễn Ánh entrusted the bishop with the Nguyễn seal and the authority to negotiate a treaty with France.[21]

Meanwhile the Tây Sơn turned north. Nhạc dispatched his young brother Nguyễn Huệ with an army to conquer Thuận Hóa, including the Đàng Trong capital, Phú Xuân, which he seized from the Trịnh in June 1786. Huệ then paused at the northern border, contemplating the rebellion and famine that for two years had plagued Đàng Ngoài after the death of Trịnh Sâm in 1782. A defecting Trịnh general, Nguyễn Hữu Chỉnh, assured Huệ that the north now possessed no leadership, "only incapable generals, undisciplined troops, a government in total confusion." The Tây Sơn invaded Đàng Ngoài by land and sea, with four hundred ships. Terrifying the northern literati, Huệ's assault from the south earned him the nickname "Chế Bồng Nga," identifying him with Champa's last great warrior monarch (r. 1360–90), who had repeatedly invaded Đại Việt. Both Nghệ An and Thanh Hóa fell quickly. The last Trịnh prince committed suicide, ending more than two centuries of his family's rule of the north. Brandishing banners reading "Long Live the Lê, Down with the Trịnh," Huệ's Tây Sơn army marched into Thăng Long on July 21, 1786. First on the coast and then in the capital, the victorious rebels opened official granaries and distributed food to the people. Huệ received an audience with the elderly Lê emperor, who died a few days later and was succeeded by his nephew, Lê Chiêu Thống. The latter quickly gave an audience to Nguyễn Nhạc, who had hurried north to gain some of the limelight for himself.[22] For the first time in nearly 250 years, Đại Việt was unified.

Yet this was a tentative and barely successful unification. It required no fewer than three more Tây Sơn expeditions into Đàng Ngoài.[23] The north's distinct geography and history seemed to keep generating autonomous commanders. First, the Tây Sơn brothers marched south again and left Đàng Ngoài to the new Lê emperor under the occupation of the forces of their recent ally, the former Trịnh general Chỉnh. But Chỉnh withdrew southward to Nghệ An, allowing a brief Trịnh resurgence in Thăng Long. At the emperor's secret invitation, Chỉnh again marched on Thăng Long, retaking it in December 1786. He then disobeyed Nguyễn Huệ's order to withdraw south again, and even advised Lê Chiêu Thống to demand that the Tây Sơn return the Nghệ An region to northern control. Huệ responded by sending another army to the north, whose commander drove out the Lê emperor's forces and in late 1787 seized Thăng Long for the third time, killing Chỉnh. In turn, the victorious northern Tây Sơn command fell out; its new viceroy of Đàng Ngoài assumed personal power, provoking the enmity of the military commander, who sent word back to Huệ soliciting a fourth invasion. Yet another Tây Sơn army recaptured Thăng Long in early 1788. Two of Đàng Ngoài's leading Confucian scholar-mandarins joined the new Tây Sơn administration, soon to be followed by many others. Meanwhile at the far end of the country, in the Mekong delta, in 1788 two local Khmer officials (*oknya*) also took up the Tây Sơn cause against the returning Nguyễn.[24]

As in the south, Tây Sơn power in the north remained insecure, and a fifth invasion force became necessary. Lê Chiêu Thống, whose deposed dynasty retained the loyalty of some northern literati, had fled to China. There he convinced the Qing emperor to send an army of up to two hundred thousand, which marched in, occupied Thăng Long in October, and briefly restored the Lê dynasty. In retaliation, Nguyễn Huệ had himself crowned in Phú Xuân, also taking the title "emperor" and the regnal name Quang Trung. In recognizably Neo-Confucian tone, his northern literati counselors composed a proclamation in which he even laid claim to the title "Son of Heaven" (*thiên tử*) along with the authority to foster "humanity, fidelity, loyalty, and righteousness," and to "use moral education to rule all under Heaven."[25]

Quang Trung marched north once more, this time to overturn the Lê, leading an army of one hundred thousand men and a hundred elephants. He himself fought mounted on an elephant.[26] Nguyễn Ánh's son the future emperor Minh Mạng would later comment: "The Tây Sơn impostors used elephants lavishly in their battles with the Northern soldiers. The Northern horses are afraid of elephants. When they saw them, they fell prostrate. For that reason they were defeated."[27] Addressing his troops, Quang Trung no longer sounded like a Son of Heaven. He asserted that "on earth, each country has its own government. The Chinese do not belong to our racial stock, therefore their intentions must be completely different from ours.... Today the Qing have returned once again. They are determined to annex our country and to divide it into provinces and districts." He appealed to his men to help "expel them," and sternly warned the audience: "Should you maintain your old vice of having two hearts, I shall immediately exterminate all of you, without exception."[28] In a major victory after a surprise attack on Thăng Long during the lunar New Year of 1789, Quang Trung's Tây Sơn forces routed and drove out the Chinese army. Thousands of fleeing Qing troops drowned after they crowded onto a bridge that collapsed into the Red River.[29] The rest were captured or fled north to the border.

The Tây Sơn rebellion had founded a new dynasty with a nationwide claim. For the first time since the 1530s, a single ruling family controlled all or most of Đại Việt. But this new regime also replicated some of the divisions and warlordism of the intervening centuries. The Tây Sơn brothers had already begun to fall out among themselves and resorted to dividing the country along regional lines. In 1786 they had assigned the far south to the third brother, Nguyễn Lữ, who became the "Eastern Stabilization King," with his capital at Gia Định. From the central coast at Chà Bàn, the oldest brother, Nguyễn Nhạc continued to rule as suzerain "Emperor." The youngest, Nguyễn Huệ, became the "Northern Pacification King," based at Phú Xuân and ruling Thuận Hóa, to which he soon added Nghệ An to its north. As Huệ then pushed farther into Đàng Ngoài and his successes multiplied, Nhạc resented Huệ's burgeoning independence. As fighting broke out between them, Huệ drove the point home by marching south and even besieging Chà Bàn, forcing Nhạc to reinforce it with troops withdrawn from Gia Định. That left Lữ and the south vulnerable. In the center, Huệ defeated Nhạc's forces in mid-1787 and seized some of his territory south of the Hải Vân pass.[30] The next year, Huệ's assumption of the title emperor entrenched this rivalry, while his defeat of the Qing invasion in early 1789 enhanced his prestige and power. Now even the Middle Kingdom acknowledged Huệ as "national king" (*quốc vương*) of "Annam."[31]

Meanwhile the fighting among the Tây Sơn had allowed Nguyễn Ánh, sailing from Bangkok, to land at Hà Tiên in August 1787. Marching east across the Mekong delta, the returning Nguyễn prince gathered his local supporters and recruited Tây Sơn defectors, Chinese pirates, and Cambodian leaders and mercenaries. He drove Lữ northward, seized the citadel of Gia Định in September 1788, and took full control throughout the delta region by early 1789.[32] Nguyễn Ánh attacked and defeated the two Khmer commanders who had sided with the Tây Sơn the previous year.[33] In 1790 he marched north into Phan Rí and even briefly reoccupied Bình Thuận before being repelled.[34] Meanwhile Lữ, who had fled to his brother Nhạc's territory, died in Qui Nhơn. The Tây Sơn would never regain the far south. Once again Đại Việt was divided, this time into three domains with rulers drawn from two contending dynasties. A new phase of the civil war began. It would be a fight to the end.

Nguyễn Ánh's hopes for a treaty with the French government were not realized, but he received unofficial aid from the bishop Pigneau de Béhaine, who joined him in southern Đàng Trong in July 1789, bringing two ships carrying mercenaries and military supplies. Pigneau had adopted the Vietnamese name Bách Đa Lộc, while Nguyễn Ánh diplomatically addressed the French missionaries as "spiritual shepherds" (*linh-mục*). By 1792, about forty Europeans were fighting in the Nguyễn armies, along with military advisers and two warships serving in the Nguyễn navy.[35] They made a notable but not decisive contribution to the war.

In the north, Nguyễn Huệ, ruling as Emperor Quang Trung, consolidated his hold on Đàng Ngoài. He recruited prominent local Confucian scholars, but during his four-year reign he maintained a regime that was led by Tây Sơn military officers, whom he appointed to head each of Đàng Ngoài's thirteen provinces. However, the more southerly provinces maintained priority. Quang Trung returned to the central region, where he ruled his new realm from Phú Xuân, but he gave orders for the construction of a new, mid-northern capital, to be located at Nghệ An. To secure that region's western flank, in 1790 and 1791 Quang Trung dispatched his forces on two massive invasions of the neighboring Lao kingdom of Luang Prabang, which the Tây Sơn plundered before advancing as far west as the Siamese frontier. But the greatest challenge Quang Trung faced was the economy. The repeated fighting in the north had devastated large areas and many displaced peasants became landless refugees. Quang Trung ordered them to return home and offered tax incentives for the cultivation of abandoned riceland. He organized a general population census in 1790, obliged each person to carry an identity card, and began the creation of a national network of schools run by local Confucian scholars. And for the first time he ordered the translation of the classical corpus from Chinese into *nôm*. Quang Trung not only reintroduced Confucian civil service examinations but also presided over a provincial-level competition that included a test on verse and prose composition in *nôm*. Prominent mandarins and scholars wrote works in *nôm*. Military proclamations and public decrees were also issued in the vernacular rather than in Chinese.[36] This was part of a wider cultural phenomenon that included a golden age of *nôm* literature in which the Tây Sơn participated, not a specific result of their policy.[37]

At the time of his unexpected death in September 1792, Quang Trung was only forty years old. His eleven-year-old son Quang Toản ascended the throne under the title of Cảnh Thịnh Emperor. The young monarch reigned under the supervision of a maternal uncle who served as regent but harbored plans for his own son and faced opposition from other Tây Sơn commanders. In the last decade before its collapse in 1802, the regime suffered from internal instability, exacerbated by continual Nguyễn attacks from the south. These included, in 1793, the occupation of the coastal ports from Bình Thuận as far north as Phú Yên and an aggressive siege of Qui Nhơn itself by land and sea. Yet the Tây Sơn forces continued to fight effectively. From Phú Xuân, the Cảnh Thịnh Emperor was able to send Nhạc substantial reinforcements: eighteen thousand troops, eighty elephants, and thirty war junks. They raised the Nguyễn siege but then pillaged Qui Nhơn. The enraged Nhạc died later that year, and the Cảnh Thịnh Emperor simply annexed his central realm.[38]

Meanwhile the Nguyễn reoccupation of Bình Thuận had also led to the defection from the Tây Sơn cause of several Cham leaders there and, in 1794, to their betrayal and assassination of the Tây Sơn's leading Cham ally, the king of Thuận Thành, *Chưởng Cơ* Tá. A later Nguyễn account records: "Tá was killed. The title of King of Thuận Thành was immediately abolished." Instead, the Nguyễn promoted their allied "tribal chief" (*tù trưởng*), a Cham known to them as Nguyễn Văn Hào, but gave him the lower status of "primary leading captain" (*chưởng cơ lĩnh chánh*) of the Thuận Thành principality. The Nguyễn now "ordered" Hào and his Cham assistant, a longtime follower of Nguyễn Ánh, "to gather together the peoples and every year to submit taxes; and they would be attached to the Bình Thuận military camp."[39] Champa had become merely the Thuận Thành "march," or border zone; the prefecture of Bình Thuận now included as many as two hundred villages of Vietnamese inhabitants. Nor did the Tây Sơn abandon their claim to the area. Bình Thuận briefly changed hands again in 1795, and an anti-Nguyễn Cham revolt led by Tuần Phù, broke out ineffectually the next year. The surviving Tây Sơn–appointed Cham king, Po Ci Bri, accompanied by a large number of followers, fled to Cambodia, where they settled permanently. The Nguyễn appointed their trusted Cham partisan Nguyễn Văn Chấn as ruler of Thuận Thành in 1799. But the local Cham population held on to their historical identity, increasingly referring to their principality not as Thuận Thành but as Prădară, a term devolved from its ancient name Pāṇḍuraṅga, in contrast to the Vietnamese derivation Phan Rang.[40]

Even after the Nguyễn had wrested Bình Thuận from the Tây Sơn, fierce fighting raged all the way up the coast into the north. But the political convulsions of 1792–94 proved a turning point in the long war. Once again a contest for former Cham territory, not only the seesawing battles for Bình Thuận but also the siege of Qui Nhơn and its former Cham citadel Chà Bàn proved pivotal. As internecine rivalry wracked the northern Tây Sơn court at Phú Xuân, in 1797 the Nguyễn returned to their assault on Qui Nhơn, again unsuccessfully besieging the southern capital but also penetrating farther north and plundering Quảng Nam, then withdrawing. In mid-1799 a third, four-month siege of Qui Nhơn ended in a Nguyễn victory. Nguyễn Ánh changed the city's name to Bình Định ("Pacification Established"). But early the next year, the Tây Sơn besieged it in turn, and after a seventeen-month campaign even recaptured it in 1801. They held it only briefly, and for the last time. Within a month, the Nguyễn forces had taken Phú Xuân and pushed north into Đàng Ngoài, finally seizing Thăng Long in July 1802.[41]

Though itself short-lived, the Tây Sơn dynasty seems to have envisaged the length of Vietnamese history in distinctive ways, emphasizing not only Cham antecedents but indigenous Vietnamese themes, beyond the resort to *nôm* as the official language of government. In his proclamation to his army in 1789, Quang Trung placed himself in a long line of Vietnamese leaders who had fought successive Chinese dynasties: "Under the Han, there were the Trưng Queens"; Đinh Bộ Lĩnh and Lê Hoàn defeated the Song; "Under the Yuan, there was Trần Hưng Đạo. Under the Ming, [Lê Lợi]. . . . Throughout all these periods, the South [Đại Việt] and the North [China] were clearly separated."[42] Tây Sơn documents from 1792 and 1802 show that Quang Trung and his successors even accorded noble status to two long-dead Việt women generals, Nguyệt Thai and Nguyệt Độ, who had served with the Trưng sisters in their revolt of 39–43 CE. In 1798, the Tây Sơn court established a new historical bureau with the mission to revise the old annals and compile a new national history of Đại Việt.[43]

Yet the partial reforms launched by the Tây Sơn support historian George Dutton's argument that the new dynasty was neither revolutionary nor even ideological in inspiration. Its militarized governance replicated features of both the Trịnh and Nguyễn regimes, and in the north the Tây Sơn also drew upon the aid of Confucian scholars as the Trịnh had done there. Quang Trung's 1789 Edict Seeking Worthy Men, a rather successful appeal to the same northern scholars who had earlier scorned him as "Chế Bồng Nga," and his prudent diplomatic reconciliation with China after his victory over it both suggest a nonideological approach to governance. His successor the Cảnh Thịnh Emperor's holding of a second census in 1801; his attempts in the mid-1790s to centralize control over the influential northern Buddhist hierarchy, including even the dismantling of local pagodas; and his sporadic crackdowns between 1795 and 1800 on northern Catholics suspected of sympathies with the European missionary backers of the Nguyễn also suggest historically tested pragmatic inclinations, though they were unsuccessful in ensuring the Tây Sơn regime's longevity. In neither Đàng Trong nor Đàng Ngoài did the Tây Sơn regime show any sense of religious inspiration, quite unlike the Vietnamese peasantry from whose ranks most of its followers came.[44]

On the other hand, the Tây Sơn political strategy, at least initially and perhaps of necessity for a rebel movement seeking to build an army, was to appeal more directly to the peasantry than its predecessors had done. Dutton suggests that the idea of "promoting economic justice" seems to have been "central to the early movement."[45] After it had gained power and was ruling at least in the north with the help of prestigious local mandarins, it is possible that a residual influence of indigenous and peasant themes explains in part not only the Tây Sơn's formidable military response to the Siamese and Qing invasions but also the dynasty's continued pursuit, even after its charismatic founding leadership passed from the scene in 1792–93, of innovative, vernacular-oriented cultural initiatives that partially distinguish it from its predecessors.

Another Tây Sơn innovation may have been, as one northern mandarin noted of Nguyễn Huệ with apparent surprise, the fact that he "behaves towards scholars without differentiating between those of south or north." None of this was enough, however, for the Tây Sơn either to permanently pacify their new subjects or to impose a new nationwide form on the political stakes of the Vietnamese civil war. The victorious Nguyễn dynasty's chronicle for the year 1791 asserts that even in the central region where the rebellion had begun, the people of Thuận Hóa and Quảng Nam "hated the cruel policies of the Tây Sơn," and that "every time they felt the blowing of the southern wind they all said, 'Our old lord is arriving.'" Even when Nguyễn Ánh's forces finally moved farther north into Đàng Ngoài, he maintained the formality of restoring Lê rule there.[46] This too could be seen as reflecting a separate southern perspective on the north, though it was of course the same tactic that the Tây Sơn had also used to conquer Đàng Ngoài and try to bring all of Đại Việt under a single administration.

In at least one sense the Nguyễn regime was distinctively southern. In 1800 its armies advancing from the south into Quảng Nam included a force of five thousand Cambodians, who apparently proceeded no farther north. When he pushed on to conquer Đàng Ngoài, Nguyễn Ánh took power with the help of a multicultural coalition that in part reflected his base in the far south and its historical connections abroad. During his long war against the Tây Sơn, he had received aid not only from European naval and infantry forces but also from an army raised by a Cambodian former palace slave, two fleets of war junks commanded, respectively, by a Siamese rebel and a Sichuan-born Chinese pirate, and at one point the twenty thousand Siamese troops contributed by Rama I.[47]

The Tây Sơn movement had drawn some strength from traditional indigenous Vietnamese sources, especially rural communities but also including Cham and highlander constituencies and in one case even a female commander. Repression and misrule squandered much of the Tây Sơn's early popular support, but their military showed some of this strength until the end. Their forces besieging Qui Nhơn, for instance, included Bùi Thị Xuân, the wife of a Tây Sơn general. Trained in the martial skills of the Tây Sơn mountain people, she rode into battle on an elephant.[48] In early 1802 she led five thousand troops northward to join forces with the Cảnh Thịnh Emperor, who had retreated into Đàng Ngoài. Together they turned and attacked Nguyễn positions from the north. The emperor then fled, but Bùi Thị Xuân continued to fight aggressively until her capture later in the year. The victorious Nguyễn condemned her to be thrown under an elephant along with her husband and fourteen-year-old daughter.[49] One account has it that Bùi Thị Xuân "died as she had lived: when faced with the elephant which was about to trample her to death, she remained calm and tried to stir it to greater fierceness."[50]

Bùi Thị Xuân's executioners probably considered her to have transgressed, like the Tây Sơn generally, in more ways than one. Trampling by an elephant as a mode of execution was not only for defeated political foes; it was also the form of capital punishment occasionally administered to upper-class women who had become pregnant out of wedlock. The offender was condemned to be crushed lifeless with her unborn child as the elephant trod on her stomach.[51] Bùi Thị Xuân's transgressions as a woman were not unique.

A WOMAN'S LITERARY LIFE: HỒ XUÂN HƯƠNG

A very different unconventional woman of the era was Hồ Xuân Hương, who lived another extraordinary life from the 1780s to the 1820s. She was an intractable literary opponent of the subjugation of Vietnamese women, demonstrating "an audacity not found in any male poet of this epoch." Unlike Bùi Thị Xuân, she was in no way politically associated with the Tây Sơn, though she grew up in Thăng Long under their rule.[52] She probably composed most if not all of her dozens of poetic works (estimates range from 25 to 148 poems) in the two decades after 1802. She usually wrote in *nôm*, but several of her poems are in Chinese.[53] Hồ Xuân Hương is famous for her disrespect for convention, especially patriarchal authority and what she saw as the fraudulent patronage and practice of Confucianism and Buddhism. Her sexual allusions are explicit, almost uniquely in Vietnamese literary culture.

Thus, Hồ Xuân Hương scandalized various Vietnamese constituencies. The historian Alexander Woodside describes her as "an improbable figure" whose poetry, "for all its playfulness, may have been the darkest assault upon Confucian ethics ever delivered by a literate scholar of a classical East Asian society." Often her attack exploded from within, targeting the false pretensions of scholars rather than the content of their studies. In "Young Scholars," she wrote:

> Jostling about by the temple door,
> they'd like to be scholars but they can't even talk.
> Someone should teach these illiterate fools
> to take their brushes and paint the pagoda wall.[54]

But her most iconoclastic assaults targeted the patriarchal relations fostered by the Confucian family model. "The Condition of Women" is a rallying cry:

> Sisters, do you know how it is? On the one hand,
> The bawling baby, on the other your husband
> sliding onto your stomach,
> his little son still howling at your side.
> Yet, everything must be put in order.
> Rushing around all helter-skelter.
> Husband and child, what obligations!
> Sisters, do you know how it is?[55]

Hồ Xuân Hương was the daughter of a mandarin's second wife or concubine (*vợ lẽ*) and became one herself, before being twice widowed.[56] Her poem "On Being a Concubine," has been called "the most succinct and eloquent attack on the institution by one of its victims." It begins: "One gal lies under quilts, the other chills. / To share a husband—damn it, what a fate!" And it ends:

> I labor as a maid,
> a wageless maid.
> Had I but known I should end up like this
> I would have sooner stayed the way I was.[57]

Hồ Xuân Hương made different enemies with other poems like "The Lustful Monk" and "Buddhist Nun."[58] Taking aim at a monk's gluttony and violations of the vow of sexual abstinence, she portrays "a head without one hair, a hemless frock:" "Under his nose lie three or five rice cakes. / Behind his back lurk six or seven nuns." She openly scorns Buddhist music and chanting:

> Now he claps cymbals, now he pounds the gong.
> He hees, he haws, he heehaws all the time.

Keeping at it, he'll rise to be top bonze:
he'll mount the lotus throne and sit in state.[59]

She did share with Quang Trung and others a sense of Vietnamese antiquity, which she felt had been lost by the time she wrote under the victorious Nguyễn dynasty. In "Trấn Quốc Temple," an ode to Thăng Long's oldest temple dating from the first millennium, she wrote:

Weeds sprout outside the royal chapel.
I ache thinking of this country's past.
...Old heroes, old deeds, where are they?

She immediately closes with another barb at the monkhood: "One sees only this flock of shaved heads."[60]

However, Hồ Xuân Hương is probably best known for the nimble, thinly veiled sexual imagery and relentlessly bawdy puns that carried her work and reputation way beyond the constraints of both Tây Sơn and Nguyễn society. Her poems "Weaving at Night" and "Swinging" are very explicit.[61] Some contemporaries considered Hồ Xuân Hương a "monster."[62] Her poetry spiced traditional Vietnamese themes, including rural imagery, with sexual allusion:

My body's like a jackfruit on the tree
The skin is rough—the pulp is nice and thick.
If you love me, drive into it your plug.
Don't fondle it or sap will stain your hand.[63]

Another indigenous theme appears in her water-laden metaphors. One example ends with yet another swipe at official Buddhism:

Three times the bell tolls echoes like a wave.
We see heaven upside-down in sad puddles.
Love's vast sea cannot be emptied.
And springs of grace flow easily everywhere.
Where is nirvana?
Nirvana is here, nine times out of ten.

Water also dominates her poem "Country Scene":

The waterfall plunges in mist.
...the long white river sliding through
...fishnets stretched to dry on sandy flats.

In "Confession," she compared a woman (herself?) to a

> lonely boat fated to float aimlessly
> midstream, weary with sadness, drifting.
> Her hold overflowing with duty and feeling,
> bow rocked by storms, adrift and wandering.[64]

Indeed, Hồ Xuân Hương traveled extensively in the countryside. Her modern translator retraced some of her journeys and was "struck by the distances and rugged terrain she would have encountered journeying by horse, boat, and foot."[65] She was a sad, lost soul of the society she lived in. Bitterness about her fate probably kept her writing: "Father and mother joined to breed a snail. / I grovel night and day among foul weeds."[66] But so did her imagination. She was "obsessed by sexual desire as by a real illness."[67] Her "Snail" continues: "Sir, if you love me, take my breastpiece off. / Don't wiggle, please, your finger in my hole!"[68]

Her major innovation, a literary scholar writes, is that she brought to her writing "a total liberation from all traditions, from all rules, from all habits which bound the national literature in imitation of Chinese literary works." It was with unprecedented originality that Hồ Xuân Hương expressed "her feelings, thoughts, ideas, in short her universe." Her poetry was restricted to her intimate life, but it transmits "echoes of the society of her time."[69]

GIA LONG (r. 1802–19)

In 1802 the victorious Nguyễn Ánh adopted the reign title Gia Long.[70] He built his new Nguyễn dynasty on the Chinese bureaucratic model and the traditional Neo-Confucian base. Gia Long's court replicated the imperial Six Boards—of appointments, finance, rites, war, justice, and public works. Beyond the court, official propriety and rules had to be reestablished and autonomous folk culture brought under control. Some of Gia Long's first acts as ruler were to promulgate regulations for controlling village communities, prohibiting their consumption of wine and meat during communal deliberations, to ban the construction or repair of local Buddhist temples, and to "deeply commend" a new local education program, designed in 1802 by a Nguyễn military man, which stipulated punishment for villagers "addicted to songs and ballads" and obligated children to read the Confucian Five Classics.[71] As Gia Long explained in 1814, "Filial piety can be transferred to matters of state, so the prince who is searching for loyal ministers must visit households with filial sons." A quarter century later his own son and successor Minh Mạng would note one disadvantage of this: "Cliques inevitably issue primarily from the father-son and elder brother–younger brother relationship and later spread to other men."[72] The status of women was low on the Nguyễn agenda.

Affinity with China was significant from the beginning, though not predominant. As early as the 1790s, the Nguyễn construction of the new fortified citadel of Gia Định followed the imperial design of an "eight-diagrams city," in the shape of a lotus with eight sides and eight entrances. In 1802, however, Gia Long established his capital at Huế, affirming his Đàng Trong heritage. The attention he gave to his ancestors also revealed his identification with Đàng Trong over and above the Sinic rituals of his predecessors, even those of the Tây Sơn.[73] Yet Gia Long also departed from his southern heritage by petitioning the Qing for permission to rename his new kingdom. From Huế he wrote in Chinese requesting imperial acknowledgement of the name Nán Yuè (*V.* Nam Việt). But Qing officials on the border insisted instead on reversing these Chinese words, creating the entirely new term "Yuè Nán."[74] Thus it was that in 1804, for the first time, but only briefly and at Qing stipulation, the Chinese equivalent of the Vietnamese "Việt Nam" (Southern Việt) entered political vocabulary.[75] While Chinese continued to refer to the country as An-Nam (Pacified South), the Qing court amended its monarch's official seal to read "King of the Southern Việt Country."[76]

Although Gia Long acceded to this Qing behest, and also restored Chinese to its status as Việt Nam's official language of state, he departed in other ways from orthodox Qing ideology and ritual. In 1805 he even referred to his own country as the "middle kingdom," an intimate imitation that would have scandalized any northern court. The next year he assumed the title of emperor.[77] In recruiting his own imperial bureaucracy Gia Long relied on his longtime partisans, usually appointing southerners whom Woodside calls "militarists with homespun learning," like his local education enforcer, who had read no Chinese texts before age fifty. Until 1815, just as many Nguyễn court memorials were written in *nôm* as in classical Chinese. As late as 1814, Gia Long promulgated a law stipulating that the new official secretariat for the northern region must recruit its fifty staff among those "skilled at writing Southern and Northern character styles." Here *nôm* still had precedence over Chinese.[78]

To take another example, China's official holidays included celebrations of the New Year, its emperor's birthday, and the winter solstice. But in fixing Việt Nam's "three great holidays," the Nguyễn dynasty replaced the winter festival with a summertime Dragonboat Day, based on the ancient aquatic festival that southern China had shared with the neighboring Lạc culture—not to mention with ancient Nán Yuè. Each year on the fifth day of the fifth lunar month, both Gia Long and Minh Mạng (r. 1820–41) would suspend official business and corvée labor. In Huế, yellow banners flew, cannon were fired, and the Nguyễn emperors gave "formal Dragonboat Day banquets" at the Hall of Supreme Harmony. When his own board of rites objected to this irregularity, Minh Mạng maintained that environmental differences explained the departure. A winter solstice holiday suited Beijing's colder northern climate, he replied, whereas Việt Nam's tropical location and traditions favored the summer festival. In a more obvious departure from Chinese ritual, the Nguyễn court instituted and funded a cult of the spirits of its army's corps of elephants, worshipping these symbols of indigenous "anti-Chinese military tradition" in ceremonies held every three months at a special temple near Huế.[79]

Thus to some extent the early Nguyễn resembled both their Đàng Trong forefathers and their defeated Tây Sơn enemies in their eclectic choices of indigenous and Confucian cultural models. That was also the spirit of the time. The most famous and beloved of all Vietnamese literary works, *Truyện Kiều* (*The Tale of Kiều*), a romantic epic in *nôm* verse composed in the early nineteenth century by the northern classical scholar Nguyễn Du (1765–1820), was based on a seventeenth-century Chinese prose novel. According to his translator, Huỳnh Sanh Thông, Nguyễn Du achieved for the Vietnamese vernacular language "what Dante had once done for Italian, liberating it from its position of subservience to Latin."[80] Nguyễn Du was a loyalist of the ousted Lê dynasty, was unaffiliated with the Tây Sơn, and then served as a reticent collaborator with Gia Long and as the new monarch's envoy to China, where he probably obtained a copy of the novel. His poem, unlike Hồ Xuân Hương's works, ends with its long-separated lovers Kim and Kiều finally reunited in a platonic marriage:

> Of love and friendship they fulfilled both claims—
> They shared no bed but joys of lute and verse.
> Now they sipped wine, now played a game of chess,
> Admiring flowers, waiting for the moon.
> Their wishes all came true since fate so willed,
> And of two lovers marriage made two friends.[81]

The epic also brims with classical allusions, including fifty quotations from the Confucian *Book of Odes*. Yet in Kiều it portrays a strong, gifted female protagonist. Nguyễn Du also included a sympathetic portrait of the Tây Sơn leader Quang Trung (as the pseudonymous character Từ Hải), and even recorded in veiled fashion the 1789 defeat of the Qing invasion: "He beat the world / in wit and grit, shook heaven by sheer might. / Leading a hundred thousand seasoned troops."[82] Equally eclectic, the early nineteenth-century northern Vietnamese poetess Bà Huyện Thanh Quan, who also wrote in *nôm*, mingled Vietnamese water symbolism with a Confucian respect for past models: "And the waters still ripple with frowns at the rapid changes. / This thousand year old mirror reflects the present and the past."[83]

Compared with its predecessors, the Nguyễn dynasty's heightened attraction to the "Chinese model" was intense. In 1812 Gia Long decreed the wholesale adoption of the Qing legal code as Vietnamese law, making few if any changes or additions. This contrasted with the now discarded Lê Code's departures from northern legal discriminations against women. Under articles 143 and 144 of the new Nguyễn Code, an official who allowed his wife or daughter to visit a Buddhist or Daoist temple received forty strokes of the cane, and "men and women expounding pernicious doctrines" were to be exiled.[84] Hồ Xuân Hương must have bristled, as Woodside remarks, at the clause that held "that the wife was noble and the concubine was vile and that elevating the latter to the status of the former upset morality." A Chinese model prevailed even in official salary levels: in 1813, after his court had discussed the establishment of salaries for its bureaucrats, Gia Long curtly decreed: "My intention is to consult and institute the stipends for officials of the imperial Qing."[85]

Yet Gia Long also maintained some of the other international connections that had helped him to power. From the 1780s to his death in 1819, more than three hundred Frenchmen served in his entourage and court, mainly as his personal servants with adopted Vietnamese names. However, they were not members of the court bureaucracy, and their role was limited to offering military advice and shielding the emperor from other foreigners. Gia Long also accorded French Catholic missionaries in Việt Nam favorable treatment. In 1815, France and England even appeared on Gia Long's list of Việt Nam's thirteen supposed "vassal" countries, along with Burma, Cambodia, the Lao kingdoms of Luang Prabang and Vientiane, and the Trấn Ninh plateau of eastern Laos, as well as two Jarai chiefdoms of the Central Vietnamese highlands, known as "Water Haven" and "Fire Haven." Whether inclusion of France as a vassal reflected Gia Long's assessment of its power or simply a sentimental relationship, his assignment of the French military engineer Victor Olivier to supervise the building of Vauban-style fortified walls at Huế and elsewhere, unlike the Chinese-style citadel at Gia Định, and the later spread of French "citadel art" into northern Việt Nam suggest Gia Long took advantage of broader cultural options than the northern model alone, even when he formally replicated it.[86]

Geography did restrict his political options. The newly unified country had now reached its greatest extent. To govern this vast territory from north to south, Gia Long's board of war in Huế set up a series of postal stations and inns. By 1805 thirty-six of these were strung along the road north to Hanoi, for the five-day journey. Seven more way stations served couriers taking official documents from Hanoi to the Chinese border. The south, however, remained remote. Messengers from Saigon were flogged if they failed to reach Huế within fifteen days of departure. By 1820, transportation improvements sped up this journey, but even "most urgent" communications between Saigon and Huế still took at least nine days. The Cambodian border and the Gulf of Siam were even farther away. Power was still dispersed between the country's three regions. The central coast and hinterland was under the direct control of the Huế court, while appointed viceroys or military governors ruled the two distant deltas from their citadels, Gia Định (Saigon) in the south and Bắc Thành (Hanoi) in the north.[87]

Gia Long also ordered the construction of a new fleet. In his *Voyage to Cochinchina*, the American John White wrote: "The king has a fleet of gallies at Huè, and was building, in 1819, two hundred more, some of which were pierced for fourteen guns." Their design demonstrated traditional features of creative syncretism and nautical prowess. Fifty of these new ships were "schooner-rigged, and constructed partly in the European style; their sterns are completely European, while their bows are a mixture of that and the Onamese [Annamese] model." White added that the Vietnamese "have, under the instruction of the French, made considerable advances in naval architecture." He concluded that Việt Nam "is perhaps, of all the powers in Asia, the best adapted to maritime adventure," in part because of its excellent harbors and in part due to "the aquatic nature of her population on the sea-board, the Onamese rivalling even the Chinese as sailors."[88]

However, a postal network and naval capability could not perform the unification work that ritual could. Like the first dynasties of medieval Đại Việt and then the early Nguyễn rulers in sixteenth- and seventeenth-century Đàng Trong, the restored Nguyễn dynasty found it prudent to assemble and appease the regional spirits of the expansive lands it claimed for the new kingdom. In 1802 Gia Long gave homage to his clan's ancestral spirits in Thanh Hóa, located in a district which he said had "poured forth spirit vitality." From the start of his reign he also gave particular attention to the cult of the rain-bringing rock goddess, Thai Dương Phu Nhân, whose shrine was near Huế. He raised her in spiritual rank, funded her pagoda and annual offerings, and in 1813 ordered the construction of a new brick temple for her cult. Elsewhere Gia Long constructed dozens of temples to local and ancestral spirits, including not only "royally recognized southern protective spirits" but also village tutelary deities. In 1804, when the northern citadel of Bắc Thành requested that the Huế court "invest the miraculous spirits (*thần thiêng*) residing in its local jurisdictions," Gia Long ordered the identification of influential northern spirits. In 1810 he decided to award them royal diplomas.[89]

The geographic limits of Huế's cultural reach are nevertheless illustrated by the successful Nguyễn imposition of Chinese-style dress only in the central region, where women adopted trousers, while across the Gianh River in northern Việt Nam they still wore the customary skirts. To the south, Cambodians in the Mekong delta wore sarongs. The south remained "more Cambodian, more Buddhist, less Confucian, less Sino-Vietnamese" than either the center or the north.[90]

RELATIONS WITH CAMBODIA AND SIAM

The Nguyễn restoration and unification of the country opened the way to its further western expansion into Cambodia. Despite sharpening ethnopolitical divisions between Khmers and Vietnamese in Cambodia, including the genocidal massacre of almost all Vietnamese in the country in 1750, Vietnamese settlement in the Mekong delta continued. In 1769 Khmers again slaughtered many of the newcomers.[91] But collaboration remained an alternative to ethnic conflict. At local levels, Vietnamese attempted to reproduce in their own tongue the historic Khmer names of many delta provinces: Phsar Dek (Iron Market) became Sa Đéc; Mê Sâr (White Mother), Mỹ Tho; Srok Khleang (Warehouse District), Sóc Trăng; and Tik Khmau (Black Water), Cà Mau. They translated other Khmer toponyms directly into Vietnamese: Kompong Russei (Bamboo Port) became faithfully rendered as Bến Tre. At a higher level, although Gia Long's victorious army included thousands of Khmers and Siamese, by then, a historian comments, "Ethnic differentiation and stratification were more finely developed in the Vietnamese imperial outlook" than in the Buddhist kingdoms of Cambodia and Siam.[92] Meanwhile in 1794 Siam, pursuing its own eastward expansion, occupied Cambodia's northwest provinces.[93]

Gia Long believed that "the Vietnamese and the barbarians must have clear borders." He combined this policy with Confucian paternalism and regional pragmatism: "Cambodia is a small country.... We will be its mother; its father will be Siam." Cambodia was "an independent country that is the slave of two."[94] Vietnamese paternalism and Siamese suzerainty were both unwelcome in Cambodia, but their contention gave it room to maneuver. Disenchanted with Siamese power, the Khmer king Chan (r. 1806–35) offered to become Gia Long's vassal, and the Khmer court moved closer to Việt Nam, relocating downriver from Udong to Phnom Penh. Gia Long ordered his officials in the delta to "separate people of Chinese descent, Chinese merchants, Cambodians and Malays."[95]

Contention over Cambodia gradually led to closer colonial encroachments. Siam invaded Cambodia in 1811, clashing with Vietnamese forces. Withdrawing in defeat, Siamese troops destroyed both Udong and the Phnom Penh citadel, and then deported thousands of Cambodians to the Siamese-controlled northwest.[96] As Gia Long restored his country's traditional name Đại Việt in 1813, a thirteen-thousand-strong army enforced its protectorate over Cambodia.[97] He withdrew Vietnamese residents from there in 1815 to avoid "trouble with Cambodians in the future," and later ordered his officials to "prevent my people from intervening in their lives." Twice a month the Khmer king had to bow to a tablet inscribed with Gia Long's name, and a thousand Vietnamese soldiers were garrisoned in the capital, but their demands and controls on Cambodia were mainly political and not yet severe. Huế's formal policy was "to strengthen the preservation" of Cambodia. Siamese forces still threatened it and reoccupied its northern provinces in 1814.[98]

Việt Nam tightened its grip on the rest of Cambodia. In 1816 Nguyễn authorities began recruiting five thousand Khmers in both kingdoms to dig a canal along the northern edge of the Mekong delta. More laborers joined the project before construction was completed in 1820.[99] Gia Long's administration demonstrated its organizational reach. A Buddhist poem composed decades later offered a total estimate of "one hundred thousand Khmer and Vietnamese workers." The vast digging project, wrote the Khmer poet, a monk named the Venerable Pich, "killed many people and exhausted many others."[100] The workers were paid and supervised by corrupt Vietnamese officials under harsh conditions. A visiting English diplomat reported a death toll on the project of ten thousand laborers.[101]

Resistance erupted. In eastern Cambodia, a Buddhist monk named Kai raised a rebel force in 1820, joined by a Cambodian general whom the Nguyễn authorities had demoted.[102] Led by Kai, the rebels "annihilated all the Vietnamese soldiers" sent to arrest him. Vietnamese commanders denounced Kai for "daring to exterminate their compatriots." But rebels continued to massacre ethnic Vietnamese in eastern Cambodia. According to Pich's poem: "The number of dead was high. The soil was bathed in blood. Many abandoned bodies lay on the ground. For the Vietnamese it was a general debacle." Launching a fleet of thirty boats on the Mekong, the rebels sailed on Phnom Penh, only to be routed.[103] "Vietnamese, Chams, and Malays attacked them mercilessly from their boats, with axes, rifles, and swords," and many Buddhist monks fell fighting. Vietnamese forces captured and killed Kai, tried and executed the Cambodian general, and beheaded many other rebels.[104] After Gia Long's death in 1819, Minh Mạng declared: "Peace has been restored, but... little has been accomplished."[105]

MINH MẠNG'S DOMESTIC POLICIES AND IDEOLOGY

Minh Mạng was more aggressive and ideologically rigid than his father. Repressive and haughty, but deeply concerned with agricultural welfare and development, Minh Mạng exhibited a Confucian preoccupation with models from antiquity while imposing centralized administration and ethnic assimilation at home and pursuing territorial expansionism in response to conflict abroad.

Minh Mạng's reign was wracked by domestic discord. His succession divided the court.[106] Though he would prove an unusually inflexible ruler, like perhaps many of his predecessors he ascended the throne feeling apprehensive—as he put it, "like sitting on a boat." With a nod over the side at Nguyễn Trãi's fifteenth-century reflection, he added: "The king is the boat and the people are the water beneath. So, water can overturn the boat and the king can lose his position."[107] Minh Mạng's 1820 coronation coincided with a major epidemic of plague that reduced the population by more than two hundred thousand people. Yet one of his first acts was to order the banning of the *nôm* script from all court memorials and all essays written in the examination system. Vietnamese scholars have estimated that 105 individual revolts, mostly scattered and local, had broken out during the two decades of Gia Long's reign, but that nearly two hundred rebellions erupted under Minh Mạng. Several were serious, especially a multifaceted revolt in Tonkin in 1826.[108]

In contrast to his father's acceptance of Western advisers at the Vietnamese court, under Minh Mạng none remained after 1824.[109] The next year he attempted to ban Catholicism, later denouncing it as a "vicious religion" and "false teaching" and stating explicitly, "We burned its books, destroyed its residences, and chased people away so that they no longer could gather together."[110] From 1833 Minh Mạng began to target Western missionaries, and in 1836–41 a total of 130 priests, missionaries, and lay church leaders were executed, along with many Vietnamese Catholics. In 1837 an old woman from a village near Huế who refused to renounce her faith was thrown under elephants.[111]

This was more than a "closed-door" (*bế quan tỏa cảng*) policy toward the West. Also at stake was a rigid social policy that brought state expansion and intrusion down to the local level. From 1828, Minh Mạng ordered northern Vietnamese women to wear trousers instead of skirts, issuing a second edict on the matter nine years later. He also had to repeat in 1832 the ban on *nôm* "rustic books" and "privately-assorted characters." In his last years he tried to prohibit village theatre performances, saying: "I hear that a stupendous number of males and females, old people and young people, watch these plays. This must definitely be an evil custom."[112]

Minh Mạng inherited his father's southern-dominated regime but did not wish to entrench it. In the mid-1830s an official Nguyễn censor noted "discrimination between south and north" in the bureaucracy: "Through good fortune the southerners are flatterers and braggarts, and everything they say and do occupies the position of advantage. Consequently, the northerners are ashamed within themselves."[113] Minh Mạng was attempting to remedy this. His reign brought a northern "influx" into the mandarinate, and 85 percent of the northern graduates of the years 1822–35 won positions at court. But Confucian ideals of meritocracy and uniformity probably faced their greatest obstacles in the far south, where Khmer Theravada Buddhism remained influential. Minh Mạng was distressed to learn from Gia Định in 1838 that local wooden Buddhist idols had even replaced the Confucian-style tablets of Saigon's tutelary deity in the city's temple, and that other southern towns were experiencing a "tense struggle" between the Sinic and Indic cultural worlds.[114]

The impositions Minh Mạng placed on domestic ethnic communities resembled those on divergent Vietnamese beliefs and practices. For the Khmer and highland minorities of southern Việt Nam, he abandoned Gia Long's policy of muted segregation and insisted on assimilation: "We must hope that their barbarian habits will be subconsciously dissipated, and that they will daily become more infected by Han [Sino-Vietnamese] customs." Significantly, the emperor associated this cultural assimilation with both agriculture and state supervision of the population: "The surveying of land and the erecting of settlements, the promulgation and completion of the quotas and the registers, these things are essential" in order "to change barbarians."[115]

Strict Confucian controls provoked multiethnic responses. Immediately upon the death in 1832 of the powerful viceroy of Gia Định, its military governor general Lê Văn Duyệt, Minh Mạng dismantled the southern autonomous Gia Định government, replaced it with six provinces (*tỉnh*), appointed central and northern officials to head them, and totally prohibited Christianity, whose adherents, like Khmer Theravada Buddhists, had lived largely unmolested under Lê Văn Duyệt.[116] The next year a son of the deceased viceroy, Lê Văn Khôi, led rebels in a revolt in the Mekong delta.[117]

They won support from Vietnamese Christians, local Khmers, Chinese merchants in Saigon, the leader of the Cham principality of Thuận Thành, and the king of Siam.[118] After crushing Khôi's rebellion in 1834, Minh Mạng proclaimed: "The number of rebels, like herds of dogs and foxes, grew daily, and the revolt became an extremely serious problem.... I cannot hide my vexation.... How was the disaster able to extend through the six provinces and resist the court for three years?" Not content with dismantling Gia Định, defeating Khôi, and suppressing the Cham revolt, Minh Mạng extinguished Thuận Thành, removing that last Cham principality from the map and turning it into a Vietnamese administrative unit.[119] In 1838 he ordered the forcible assimilation of Cambodians in the delta: "Force the sons of Khmer people [*thổ dân*] to go to officials in charge of education at the level of district and prefecture to learn *hán chữ* [characters], not to stay in humble habits. Forbid them from going to their own monks to learn. Whoever learns *hán chữ* will be appointed head of the village, so let them know what is demanded. Afterwards, let them also learn the Vietnamese language [*hán nhân ngôn ngữ*], clothes, and food."[120]

Yet Minh Mạng also saw himself as a Confucian ruler with Heaven's Mandate to be benevolent. He established a genuine agrarian "relief" system to help the poor cope with drought, flood, and fire. He explained: "The relationship between a king and his people is like that of a good father with a young child who does not wait for the child to be cold to put clothes on him." He ordered the rich to hand over some of their private land to village communes and forbade the sale of commune land at a profit.[121]

Minh Mạng's agricultural vision was powerful. An 1831 ordinance offered free grants of uncultivated land "to any person who asks for it." Minh Mạng revived the Đại Việt institution of royal land grants in the south to groups of military colonists, for payment in rice and performance of military duties. A French historian credited him with pioneering "a new doctrine" on irrigation. An 1833 edict proclaimed:

> When the ricefields are flooded by the rains and the water-courses are still at a rather low level, it is useful to dig drainage canals and to clear the ricefields of water into the water-courses; in this way one can avoid flooding and the rotting of the summer harvests. Inversely, if the rains are lacking and the ricefields are drying off, and if at the same time the water in the river is rather high, then it is useful to bring the water into the fields by means of small channels.... It is thus preferable to entrust the care of all dykes, public and private, to the provincial mandarins, who will maintain them according to the prescribed rule.... During the summer and winter crops, they should introduce water from the water-courses, according to whether the ricefields are dry or flooded.[122]

Minh Mạng left twelve thousand pages of writings, which include "hundreds of poems and pieces of prose about agriculture and the peasant."[123] Much of it was genuine reporting; some gave a monarch's view from Huế's imperial citadel:

> In the citadel, people are happy because of continuous good crops
> I am leisurely and less worried
> In the autumn, rice plants are full across the fields
> In the autumn, rice paddies are across the villages
> People have a positive outlook on the world
> Farmers are tired but smiling.[124]

In 1836 the emperor announced a new program of land measurement throughout southern Việt Nam. "It is very important to clarify the borders of fields," his edict stated. Landed property had to be recognized. Minh Mạng overruled his officials to ensure that public lands were not augmented, and he reduced taxes to encourage the clearing and farming of new land. As he put it, "Private land has been possessed for a long time, and ownership has already been recognized." Rejecting his mandarins' proposal to "cut away and take their private property," Minh Mạng responded, "It is natural to see the rich provide the land and the poor provide the labor." His main goals were land clearing, rice production, and private property. As he put it, "[I] do not worry whether the amount of rice fields is small for each peasant, . . . [I] only worry that people are not diligent." He required cultivation efforts on the part of landlords too. It was a crime to accumulate land beyond the owner's capacity to farm. Minh Mạng ordered his officials: "Any owner who has relatively too much land to be able fully to cultivate it, then take half of 30 percent." At the other end of the social scale, convicts who had cleared public lands were also to become small landowners: "If they want to stay there, . . . give the cleared land to them as the form of private land to live on. If they want to go back home, sell the cleared land to others." The Huế government provided buffalo, tools, and seeds to individuals setting out to clear new land, and it rewarded or punished local officials on the basis of the area of their region that was brought into cultivation.[125] He urged farmers in the Mekong delta to cultivate "every morsel of earth."[126]

But Minh Mạng also saw agrarian policy as a way to strengthen the Nguyễn state. In 1839 in Bình Định province, he rushed through an unprecedented, top-down administrative intervention. In 645 of the province's 678 hamlets, where private landholdings exceeded the area of communally owned land, he forcibly imposed a severe redistribution in which the court seized half the land held in private hands and converted it to communal property. The reasons are unclear. Bình Định's ratio of private to communal land was well above average (10:1), and Minh Mạng and his officials asserted that "rich landlords" owned most of the land there. But a sample of the province cadastral records from 1815 shows that smallholder peasants had seized much of the farmland after the Tây Sơn revolt first broke out in the province. Vietnamese historian Phan Phương Thảo argues that Minh Mạng aimed to dispossess the original beneficiaries of the Tây Sơn and impose closer state control over their province's land area. The measure was not repeated elsewhere, such as the six frontier provinces of the Mekong delta (Nam Kỳ), where the ratio of private to communal land (14:1) was even higher.[127]

Another way to strengthen the newly extended state was horizontally, by means of seaborne transport and communications. Early in Minh Mạng's reign the viceroy of Gia Định, General Lê Văn Duyệt, wrote: "I, yielding to an Imperial edict, ordered my underlings in the Section of Public Works to select wood of good quality to build big ships after the standards established by the Board of Public Works. Now, the ships have been built. In my opinion, they are quite beautiful." In June 1826, Gia Định citadel's engineers completed the construction of "three big ships," which sailed for Huế the next month, bringing a range of construction materials from the south: 160,000 measures of "standard-sized iron," 20,000 of cast iron, and 32,000 of "cast steel."[128] During Minh Mạng's reign rice stores were shipped to Huế by sea from both the northern and southern deltas. In a memorandum probably dating from the 1830s, Minh Mạng wrote, "This year, we have found a new way to transport the paddy.... More than 900 boats came from both extremities. The rice paddy transported and placed into the storehouse was more than 760,000 baskets of rice." A single boat was lost, sunk in strong winds with forty tons of northern rice.[129] At least in terms of its domestic surplus, the economy was now seaborne. Minh Mạng even attempted to have his engineers build steamships.[130]

His administration's strong interest in antiquity, on the other hand, expressed a special Confucian orthodoxy. As Woodside has pointed out, "The Vietnamese elite's sense of Chinese history was strong. Its faith in Chinese allusions, classical and historical, momentous and trivial, was romantic and unlimited." A performing elephant at Minh Mạng's court in the 1820s, the historian adds, provoked an allusion to an eighth-century elephant "that had held a goblet in its mouth" at the Tang court. When soldiers digging a gate for the imperial city excavated a skeleton in 1833, Minh Mạng ordered it solemnly reburied on a precedent set by a classical monarch. He would tell stories at any pretext about the first Ming emperor, "complete with dialogue." Minh Mạng's historical curiosity extended to Cambodia.

In a slightly condescending tone, he remarked that the Khmer "have been a nation for over 1,200 years, but we do not know precisely what year they began, in terms of the Vietnamese and Chinese dynasties that were then reigning."[131]

Yet the strong southern and Mahayana Buddhist heritage of the early Nguyễn dynasty persisted despite Minh Mạng's assertion of Confucian ideology and policy. Minh Mạng himself resolved tensions between his Đàng Trong background and his imperial obligations, historian Nola Cooke writes, by "relocating Buddhist gestures to the personal or family domain." He held Buddhist ceremonies for the souls of his deceased officers, converted temples to pagodas, and built several new pagodas, including one at his birthplace in Gia Định. He rebuilt another pagoda on the site of a Cham temple that his "royal ancestor," the seventeenth-century ruler Nguyễn Phúc Tần, had replaced with a Buddhist pagoda.[132]

Also seeking ritual continuity between past and future, Minh Mạng would survey the heavens for omens, following the tradition of early northern emperors and the *Book of Songs*. One day in late 1834, he predicted with optimism: "On every winter solstice day the ancients ascended the Spirit Tower to examine the clouds.... Today in the early dawn I saw that the color of the sun was radiant and the cloud ornaments were luxuriant, and I reflected that the peace and happiness of men next spring could be foretold."[133] War over Cambodia would prove him wrong. Minh Mạng's involvement in conflict abroad was yet more serious than the continuing discord at home.

ANNEXATION OF CAMBODIA IN THE 1830S

After a brutal Siamese intervention in Laos, Minh Mạng annexed parts of that country in 1827–31. Under similar circumstances, he soon added Cambodia.[134] In 1833, a Siamese army marched through Cambodia to invade Đại Việt in support of Lê Văn Khôi's revolt in the Mekong delta. Siam's King Rama III (r. 1824–51) aimed to rule Cambodia through two pro-Siamese Khmer princes or, failing that, to depopulate it. Rama III ordered his military commander, Chaophraya Bodin, to restore Siamese control of Cambodia. "If this is not possible, you should turn Cambodia into forest... carry off Khmer families to be resettled in Thai territory, do not leave any behind."[135] Bodin's army marched into Cambodia, headed by shock troops with "a multitude of enormous elephants."[136] When they approached Phnom Penh, its Vietnamese garrison retreated, massacring four hundred ethnic Chinese who had settled there from Việt Nam.[137]

Pursuing the offensive, the Siamese invaded Việt Nam, but met defeat and had to fall back in early 1834. In Cambodia, Khmer rebels had begun massacring Siamese forces, and much of its population sought refuge in the forest.[138] The retreating Siamese carried off Khmer and Chinese residents of Phnom Penh but, on learning that their protégé Khmer princes had taken many Vietnamese captives, ordered them, ominously, not to "hold a single Vietnamese."[139]

On retaking Phnom Penh, the Vietnamese hardened their policy too. At the end of 1834, Minh Mạng formally declared Cambodia a province, Trấn Tây thành, "the citadel of the western protectorate." He also renamed central and southern Laos as Cam Lộ and signaled his expansion policy by changing the kingdom's name from Đại Việt to Đại Nam, "Great South." Minh Mạng now laid claim to much more than the old Việt realm.[140] The 1838 edict announcing the change reflected his ambitions: "This dynasty owns the whole southern part.... All creatures that move belong to our territory," which "our court... is constantly expanding."[141]

A Vietnamese general in northern Cambodia, according to the poet Pich, press-ganged the entire population of Kompong Thom, "some to build fortresses, to dig the earth; the others cultivated rice and transported it into granaries." In the five northern provinces, even top Khmer officials had to perform this labor. "No one dared revolt for fear of the Vietnamese and everyone collaborated."[142]

However, Minh Mạng's viceroy in Cambodia, Trương Minh Giảng, quickly encountered problems establishing Vietnamese authority there. He reported to the emperor in 1834: "We have tried to punish and reward the Cambodian officials according to their merits and demerits.... Offices are sold; nobody carries out orders;... for the last four months, nothing has been accomplished."[143] Assessing Cambodia's resources six years later, Đại Nam officials still complained that "posts were acquired by paying money" and that Khmer family ties were closer on the maternal than the paternal side. But "the worst aspect" of Cambodian society was that people "do not know the ethical codes. Although they accept the supreme power of our country, they still keep their own customs."[144]

One of Huế's major problems was feeding its occupying forces. An 1834 memorial complained that Cambodia did not practice basic rice and grain storage.[145] In their 1840 assessment of Cambodia's resources, Đại Nam officials wrote: "Land is abundant here and the population is scarce. Only 30–40% of the land is under cultivation, mainly for cotton and betel nut and a little rice." The document added: "It is customary here that the king has no granary, and the country has no [standing] army."[146]

So, while enjoining Vietnamese officials there to "teach them our customs," Minh Mạng also meant to impose his agrarian vision on the land. He told his viceroy:

> I have heard, for example, that the land is plentiful and fertile, and that there are plenty of oxen... but the people have no knowledge of agriculture, using picks and hoes, rather than oxen. They grow enough rice for two meals a day, but they don't store any surplus.... Now all these shortcomings stem from the laziness of the Cambodians... and my instructions to you are these; teach them to use oxen, teach them to grow more rice, teach them to raise mulberry trees, pigs, and ducks.... As for language, they should be taught to speak Vietnamese. [Our habits of] dress and table manners must also be followed. If there is any out-dated or barbarous custom that can be simplified, or repressed, then do so.[147]

At first Minh Mạng's approach was paternalistic and gradualist. "The barbarians have become my children now, and you should help them," he advised his viceroy, Giảng. "Let the good ideas seep in, turning the barbarians into civilized people.... As for winning the hearts of the people, and teaching them, we plan to do this rather slowly." Minh Mạng requested reports from Cambodia on its "customs, people, and agricultural produce. I want to know whether the people are prosperous, and whether or not the Cambodian militia have been trained... if the barbarian people have learned Vietnamese ways, and if they are happy."[148]

The new requirements of intensive cultivation involved official Vietnamese monitoring of previously mobile populations. Huế's 1834 memorial complained, "The Cambodian territory is broad... but up until now its soldiers and adult males have wandered about and have not been registered and controlled." In 1835 alone, Minh Mạng dispatched more than a hundred Vietnamese officials to staff the new administration.[149] He also arranged for the deportation of new Chinese immigrants, landless Chinese, and Chams from Việt Nam into Cambodia: "Give them some land, and divide up parcels of land for them to cultivate unused soil. The government will provide those lacking means with seed grain and farming tools."[150] Minh Mạng ordered progress reports: "After three years, surmise the number of people, of farming plots; organize the data in record books, and report them."[151] By the late 1830s, Minh Mạng's officials also brought Vietnamese crops to Cambodia and supervised their systematic cultivation. Viceroy Giảng reported: "We have often advised them to till the land diligently and cultivate crops accordingly, to plant beans and rice." However, food shortages now threatened an "emergency" in the area west of Phnom Penh, which was "in very bad shape."[152] Minh Mạng finally complained in 1840 that for six years he had insisted in vain on the measurement of Cambodian cropland and compilation of records on its rainfall, granaries, and irrigation works, and once again he ordered these tasks to be performed.[153]

In part, Minh Mạng's policy reflected Confucian preoccupations with benevolence, border security, and cultural superiority. When Giảng reported in the late 1830s on the distribution of "10,000 measures of rice" to Khmer delta communities, the king replied: "It is right to do that. You should allow your compassion to keep the outside [Cambodia] peaceful so that the inside [Đại Nam] can be comfortable."[154] In establishing Huế's control over Cambodian communities, Minh Mạng also followed China's traditional Sinicization policy of regularizing court appointments in minority regions by replacing hereditary chiefs, thus changing from "aboriginal" rulers to "circulating" bureaucratic appointees. He planned to replace Cambodian province chiefs with Vietnamese who possessed a combination of agricultural and military skills, starting in the provinces near Phnom Penh. But few if any of these new positions were ever filled.[155]

Đại Nam officials who appear to have shared Minh Mạng's historical perspective wrote around 1840: "Ah! The expansion of the earth goes from north to south." Just as in ancient times south China was "deserted and beyond the reach of civilization," so southern Đại Việt, too, had once been "the land of Chams and Khmers." However, they reported, "Since our ancestral sages [the early Nguyễn lords] began to open it up, it has now become a superior civilised country." In Cambodia itself, the officials wrote, it was also necessary to "open the land up, then to civilize uncouth people with writing, cover fish scales with clothing, turn unhealthy air into good, and transform barbarians into *Hoa* [Vietnamese]... Heaven cannot let it be a barbarian wilderness. Now that our country is changing things in a significant way and registering [Khmer] households, the day of transforming old customs into *Hoa* has come!"[156]

The optimism was unmerited. At this height of Đại Việt's historical expansion, the kingdom had again overreached. Cambodians welcomed neither Vietnamization nor repression, nor the colonial condescension in Minh Mạng's description of King Chan: a "fresh wind or the cry of a bird could make him flee." In 1834, Khmer court brahmans apparently counseled Chan to accept bribes and "let criminals out of jail." Giảng had these advisors executed as "magicians," and when Chan died the next year, the viceroy crowned the king's daughter, Mei, as queen.[157] Cambodia's history had precedents for female rulers, but Giảng probably saw Mei as a pliable puppet.[158]

Đại Nam's repression of Cambodians intensified. Giảng "gave the order to arrest, in the citadel, all the Khmer dignitaries and to put them to death."

Kompong Thom province's "entire Khmer population... fled into the forest." A Vietnamese force marched north to arrest the leading Khmer officials there, but they "rapidly mustered troops to massacre the Vietnamese." The massacres "began in Kandal province and extended to all the fortresses... and all the populations rose up."[159]

Scattered Khmer uprisings recurred from 1837 to 1839.[160] Rebels "were murdering the Vietnamese in the whole country." The occupying forces, unable to locate the rebels, "arrested only frightened individuals," incarcerating a thousand prisoners in cages. Giảng cruelly "eliminated the rebels as if he were uprooting trees."[161]

Minh Mạng took a piqued, personal interest in Cambodia's pacification. Addressing Khmers in an 1838 decree, he complained that they had ignored his "generosity." For instance, "Imperial troops were dispatched to Cambodia, costing millions of coins, and brought you security by destroying the Thai. Troops were stationed to bring peace. This action was like bringing the Cambodian people out of the mud onto a warm feather bed.... Why are there people who hate us and believe the rebels?" A year later Minh Mạng again complained that Cambodian officials who had all been "given titles from my court" continued inexplicably to use their Khmer titles. "The Cambodians should be told that it is an honor to have titles bestowed on them by this court. In conversation, therefore, they should use our titles." Another Vietnamese asserted that Cambodian officials "collect the taxes that are owed to us, and still rule over one another." Vietnamese personnel took over direct administration of Cambodia's provinces in 1840. That June, Minh Mạng demoted Queen Mei and imposed a Vietnamese taxation regime, including new taxes on food products. The arrest of six prominent Khmer officials was followed in August by that of Mei and two princesses. All went off to exile in Saigon.[162] Đại Nam officials explained: "[Our king] thus ordered the army to... manage the land and set up administrations."[163]

Meanwhile, challenges to Huế's authority proliferated at home. The 1830s had seen three more major rebellions; a fourth broke out in 1841. As Minh Mạng's ambitious land measurement program got under way in southern Vietnam in 1836, he asked a mandarin about popular attitudes in the south. The response was ominous: "All people are shaking and sighing." Minh Mạng's agrarian program was needed to raise more tax revenue to feed the troops in Cambodia, defending five to six thousand military posts there. Each year, this cost Đại Nam seventy to eighty thousand *hộc* of unhusked rice, at a monthly salary of one *hộc* per soldier.[164] Besides tripling tax revenues in rice, land registration facilitated conscription for the Cambodian front. Vietnamese soldiers there were all landowners (tenants were exempt).

The proportion of southern Vietnamese men conscripted also tripled, from 7 to 20 percent. After 1836, Huế drafted twenty-one thousand southerners for military service until age fifty or fifty-five. From 1839, wealthy Vietnamese received government rank for donating and delivering over 2,500 *hộc* of unhusked rice to Cambodia or the border. The war increasingly militarized Minh Mạng's regime. By 1839 he was advising his administrators: "All civil officials ideally should be forced to learn the military arts and all military officials should be forced to learn civil business. . . . Civil officials must not consider guns and cannon to be the sphere of responsibility of military bureaucrats."[165]

Đại Nam's problems escalated when a serious rebellion erupted in southern and eastern Cambodia in September 1840. The imprisonment of the Khmer princesses and courtiers had provoked Cambodia's officials and population to revolt. "The rebellion spread to the whole country."[166] Minh Mạng exploded in a letter to Giảng in Phnom Penh: "Sometimes the Cambodians are loyal; at other times they betray us. We helped them when they were suffering, and lifted them out of the mud. . . . Now they are rebellious: I am so angry that my hair stands upright. . . . Hundreds of knives should be used against them, to chop them up, to dismember them." He added in another edict that rebels must be "crushed to powder." Cambodian rebel leaders reciprocated the sentiment: "We are happy killing Vietnamese. We no longer fear them; in all our battles, we are mindful of the three jewels [of Theravada Buddhist teaching]—the Buddha, the Law, and the monastic community." Minh Mạng expressed his own view before his death in early 1841: "The Cambodians are so stupid, that we must frighten them. Ordinary moral suasion has no effect." In a sad sign of his dashed hopes for agricultural development of the annexed territory, he ordered the burning of Cambodian orchards and crops.[167]

Siam now returned to the offensive. Bangkok's thirty-five-thousand-strong army overran the Vietnamese fort at Pursat, but then fell back. The war had exhausted all sides. A Khmer rebel reported difficulties from the interior: "We are unable to continue fighting the Vietnamese. We lack the troops to do so, the rifles, the ammunition, and the supplies." Their enemies were also chastened. Bodin estimated that ten thousand Khmer rebels were in the field, but the Vietnamese thought they faced thirty thousand.[168] A captured Vietnamese official from Phnom Penh told the Siamese: "I heard that Thai and Khmer troops were everywhere. I was so afraid that I and another 160 people decided to flee."[169] A Vietnamese report stated in 1841 that Khmer rebels "appear and disappear at will," avoiding contact unless they had the advantage. "They concentrate their forces where the jungle is thick, and in swampy areas where our troops cannot manoeuver."

Culturally the Vietnamese were even more isolated; "We have no intelligence about the enemy, and no guides."[170]

Minh Mạng's death, in a fall from a horse in January 1841, had a pronounced impact.[171] A year later a French missionary stated that Vietnamese "persecution" in Cambodia had "at least greatly slowed."[172] Under Minh Mạng's successor, Emperor Thiệu Trị (r. 1841–47), Vietnamese forces abandoned Cambodia. In late 1841 Viceroy Giảng evacuated Phnom Penh's six thousand inhabitants to Việt Nam. He accepted responsibility for "losing" Cambodia and committed suicide.[173]

Now mostly under Siamese control, Cambodia saw no peace after the Vietnamese withdrawal. Bodin ordered "the general massacre" of the "numerous" Vietnamese still resident there. According to a missionary, the Siamese "fell upon Cambodia, rallied the whole population around them, and massacred the Annamites dispersed in the country."[174] Also, Siam's depopulation campaigns devastated areas near Việt Nam, such as Phnom Penh, and "remarkably diminished the size of Cambodia's population."[175]

Siam now confronted some of the same difficulties in Cambodia that had defeated Đại Nam. The Siamese abandoned Phnom Penh in 1844, and Vietnamese forces again returned to the capital. Vietnamese attacks on Udong in 1845 led to peace talks.[176] Bodin wrote to Rama III: "Cambodia knows famine. During the recent Vietnamese intervention, a good number of Khmers rallied to Annam for the sake of peace."[177] Both sides implemented a mutual withdrawal in 1847. Đại Nam's hold on Cambodia ended.[178]

ĐẠI NAM, 1841–59

Regionalism within Đại Nam reasserted itself after Minh Mạng died. Thiệu Trị presided over the reversal of Minh Mạng's efforts to include northern literati in positions of power. Faithful to his Đàng Trong background as he saw it, Thiệu Trị allowed Huế's dominant southern court faction to retain control through manipulating the examination competitions. He reinstituted ceremonies honoring the Nguyễn soldiers who had died fighting the Trịnh in the seventeenth century and discriminated against northerners by refusing to allow imperial princesses to marry anyone from the Đàng Ngoài region north of the Nguyễn ancestral home of Thanh Hóa.

Unlike his two predecessors, Thiệu Trị also brought the public performance of Buddhist rites into the court. He constructed a seven-story tower at the Thiên Mụ pagoda in Huế, stating: "These works have been undertaken with the aim of propagating the Buddhist doctrine, of bringing beings to the truth who are still plunged in ignorance and error." He left a poem inscribed at Thiên Mụ, expressing his confidence that "as its Buddhist wheel turns, forever in motion, so will the imperial fortune develop without cease." During his short reign he also built a new pagoda in Huế, recording in an inscription there his desire "to be myself enlightened on the way of the Buddha [and] to help initiate all creatures into Buddhism."[179]

Like many previous Vietnamese monarchs, Thiệu Trị saw no contradiction between private Buddhist and public Confucian practice: "How can meditating on goodness harm the royal way?" Yet there is a decidedly Buddhist and eclectic flavor to Thiệu Trị's self-conscious riposte to a court censor who had rebuked him for his love of poetry:

> According to the acting supervising secretary at the office of scrutiny of justice, Giang Văn Hiển, my self-indulgent abandonment of myself to reciting and chanting successive works of poetry... is a distressing expenditure of energy. He requests that in my leisure from my duties I should read widely in the classics and histories.... Diligently from day to day I have obliged myself to seek what ought to be done, sometimes considering and investigating masses of arguments.... Has it ever happened that in the depths of the palace I have written the odd song... [and] indulged irresponsibly...? Merely in the leisure that remains from affairs of state to grasp a brush and record something in order to test myself, surely such diligent labor is more worthy than idly confronting my wives and servants![180]

Thiệu Trị's death in 1847 led to a traumatic succession. The court passed over his eldest son, Hồng Bảo, in favor of a twenty-year-old younger brother, Tự Đức (r. 1847–83). In 1848 Hồng Bảo's sponsors made a final attempt to seize the throne, and he was executed along with eight members of his family. The accession of the "doctrinaire Confucian" Tự Đức brought another about-face in royal policy toward Buddhism. Between 1849 and 1874, Tự Đức made five attempts to reduce the numbers of monks and nuns, and on four occasions he imposed restrictions on pagoda construction.[181] Under this youthful Confucian emperor, Đại Nam would face French invasion.

Before Minh Mạng died he had begun to have doubts about the wisdom of his closed-door policy.[182] He had sent an embassy to France to attempt to negotiate a treaty and discuss the question of the Vietnamese Catholics. He also sent missions to London and to the British colonies of Penang and Calcutta, and to Batavia, the capital of the Dutch East Indies. But the French government refused to negotiate with the Đại Nam court. Thiệu Trị was also conscious of Western power and tried to obtain more information from his officials about a possible British attack on Siam.[183] In 1847, as French vessels offshore prepared to attack Đà Nẵng, Thiệu Trị told his ministers:

"Of old, the use of guns and of projectiles was unknown. But since [Westerners] employed these engines of war, they have never lost a single battle and no fortress, however solid, has been able to withstand their assaults. At present everybody must agree that rifles and cannons are the Gods of Might."[184] The French ships opened fire and destroyed the Vietnamese fleet at anchor in Đà Nẵng harbor. An enraged Thiệu Trị "ordered every article of European provenance in his palace to be smashed, and decreed the immediate execution, without legal trial, of every European caught on Vietnamese territory." The emperor died soon afterward, but over the next twelve years, the regime of his successor Tự Đức killed "27 European missionaries, 300 Vietnamese priests, and 30,000 Vietnamese Christians."[185]

In 1856 French ships again shelled Đà Nẵng's fortifications, then sailed away. Vietnamese officials concluded: "The French bark like dogs but flee like goats."[186] Early the next year, a missionary and lobbyist wrote to Emperor Napoleon III: "The occupation of Cochin-China is the easiest thing in the world.... France has in the China seas ample forces for this task.... The population, gentle, hardworking, very accessible to the preaching of the Christian faith, groans under a frightful tyranny. They would welcome us as liberators and benefactors. In a little time the entire population would become Catholic and devoted to France."[187] There was some truth to the claim that the Vietnamese were suffering, particularly in the north. A plague of locusts devastated Sơn Tây and Bắc Ninh provinces in 1854.[188] A major rebellion then wracked the countryside in 1854–55. Tự Đức was presiding over a succession of natural disasters. Looking back on this era in 1879, the first French consul in Hanoi asserted that the Nguyễn dynasty had not only neglected the key Red River dikes but had also introduced an inferior system of repair:

> The construction of these levies, which line the Red River and its various branches over a considerable distance, dates from several centuries ago. They were once very well maintained, and the former kings of Tongking who had had them constructed and understood their full importance, had placed them under the supervision of a special administration led by responsible high functionaries. The current dynasty has not shown the same solicitude, and the maintenance of the levies in each of the districts through which the river passes is left without control to the *quan huyện*, or local sub-prefect. Should only one of these functionaries fulfill his task badly, the dikes break at the first flood, and half a province is inundated.[189]

A Vietnamese historian has noted that, indeed, "government supervision of hydraulic works was so inefficient that the Red River dike at Văn-giang was broken eighteen years in succession."[190]

A folk poem proclaimed: "Since the accession of Tự Đức to the throne / The crops are often lost." Another verse offered graphic detail:

> There is no rice,
> Not even thin gruel or vegetables.
> The parched fields are covered with salt.
> The rich seal their doors hermetically.
> Like living skeletons,
> People go begging far and near...
> Corpses fill the graveyards
> and rot near the bridges.
> The sky is dark and sad,
> Everywhere is desolation and misery...
> With my brush I write
> These few lines of verse
> So that even a thousand years from now,
> People may still know of the hunger and sufferings
> In the reign of Tự Đức.[191]

A southerner visiting Tonkin in 1876 reported without explanation that the adult male population of Ninh Bình province, which had numbered 9,800 in the early nineteenth century, fell to only 3,192 by the last decade of Tự Đức's reign.[192]

Meanwhile, in late 1858, a combined French and Spanish expeditionary force landed at Đà Nẵng. It ordered the city to surrender. Vietnamese resistance was strong; the invaders' positions were besieged. The Spanish departed, and the French fleet sailed south to Saigon, seizing it on February 18, 1859. The French declared the southern city a free port open "to all friendly nations," halved its customs duties, and overturned Huế's ban on rice exports. In 1860, Saigon exported fifty-seven thousand tons of rice from what became French Cochinchina.[193] Việt Nam's colonization had commenced.

PART FIVE

Colonies

CHAPTER 8

"World Trends" and French Conquest, 1860–1920

The combination of "barbarian" invasion and natural disasters delivered a powerful shock to the Vietnamese polity and economy.[1] Both reflected the arrival of a new global era. The second half of the nineteenth century brought not only the high tide of Western colonialism in Asia and Africa but also, from the 1860s to the mid-1920s, a series of severe worldwide droughts.[2] Vietnamese responded to both with a variety of views and initiatives.

The impact on Việt Nam of the new climate conditions was extreme. After some unusually wet rainy seasons during the period 1847–61, the weather pattern reversed. The second half of the nineteenth century was the driest period the country had experienced since at least the early seventeenth century. The annual rainfall in Việt Nam in 1864 was the lowest for a century. That year and 1865 were both among the country's forty driest years since 1250. Then 1877 and 1878 were two of the *ten* driest. Still lower rainfall in 1888 and 1889 put each of those two years among the *six* driest in Việt Nam's seven-century climate record. The droughts of 1877–78 and 1888–89 were both associated with El Niño "warm episode events."[3] The first brought a "once-in-200-year" global drought. In 1876–79 perhaps sixteen million people died in famines in India, China, and Brazil, and as many again in 1896–1902.[4]

In his poem "Drought," the patriotic satirist Trần Tế Xương (1870–1907) used dry weather as a metaphor for the French colonial conquest of Việt Nam, with the word *nước*, meaning both "water" and "country," representing a double loss:

These days the sun could melt both gold and stone.
The people, wild and frantic, pray for rain.
In happier times, carefree, they ate and slept.
Now, robbed of water, they fear for their land.

The fourth line literally reads, "Now they do nothing but worry about *nước-nôi*," which may be translated as "water," "country," or "water and country."[5]

Domestic changes were underway too. More than a few Vietnamese scholars and peasants were coming to believe that Emperor Tự Đức had lost the Mandate of Heaven and that the Nguyễn dynasty was illegitimate. Some even thought the Lê, deposed in 1788, should be restored. Tạ Văn Phụng, a Catholic raised by French missionaries in Penang, Malaya, who claimed to be a member of the Lê family and had served as an interpreter for French forces besieging Đà Nẵng in 1858, led a revolt that wracked eastern Tonkin from 1861 to 1865.[6] As climatic conditions deteriorated, Tự Đức's court could barely deal with this internal unrest and face French encroachment too.

Major transformations lay ahead, political and economic but also cultural. Beginning in 1859 with the seizure of Saigon, France's progressive territorial conquest of Đại Nam and its partition of the country into three administrative territories accentuated the geographic and historical distinctions between the south, center, and north—regions that the French renamed Cochinchina, Annam, and Tonkin, respectively. The colonial project's southern start further integrated Cochinchina's strong export sector into transnational trade, but it also sparked Vietnamese literary innovations in the south that undermined Confucian political culture and soon spread to the center and north. New international influences had begun to transform the country's social, political, and economic life. A spectrum of Vietnamese addressed these changes and challenges with passion, vigor, creativity, collaboration, and resistance. Even the extended colonial conquest, somewhat chaotically conducted by competing French interest groups, depended in large part on the agency of Vietnamese allies.

FRENCH COCHINCHINA

After settling the Second Opium War with China in 1860, French forces turned to expanding their control around their new outpost in the city of Saigon. They inflicted defeats on the Vietnamese defenders, and in 1862 Tự Đức surrendered the three eastern Cochinchinese provinces. This separated the three remaining western provinces from those of Đại Nam's center

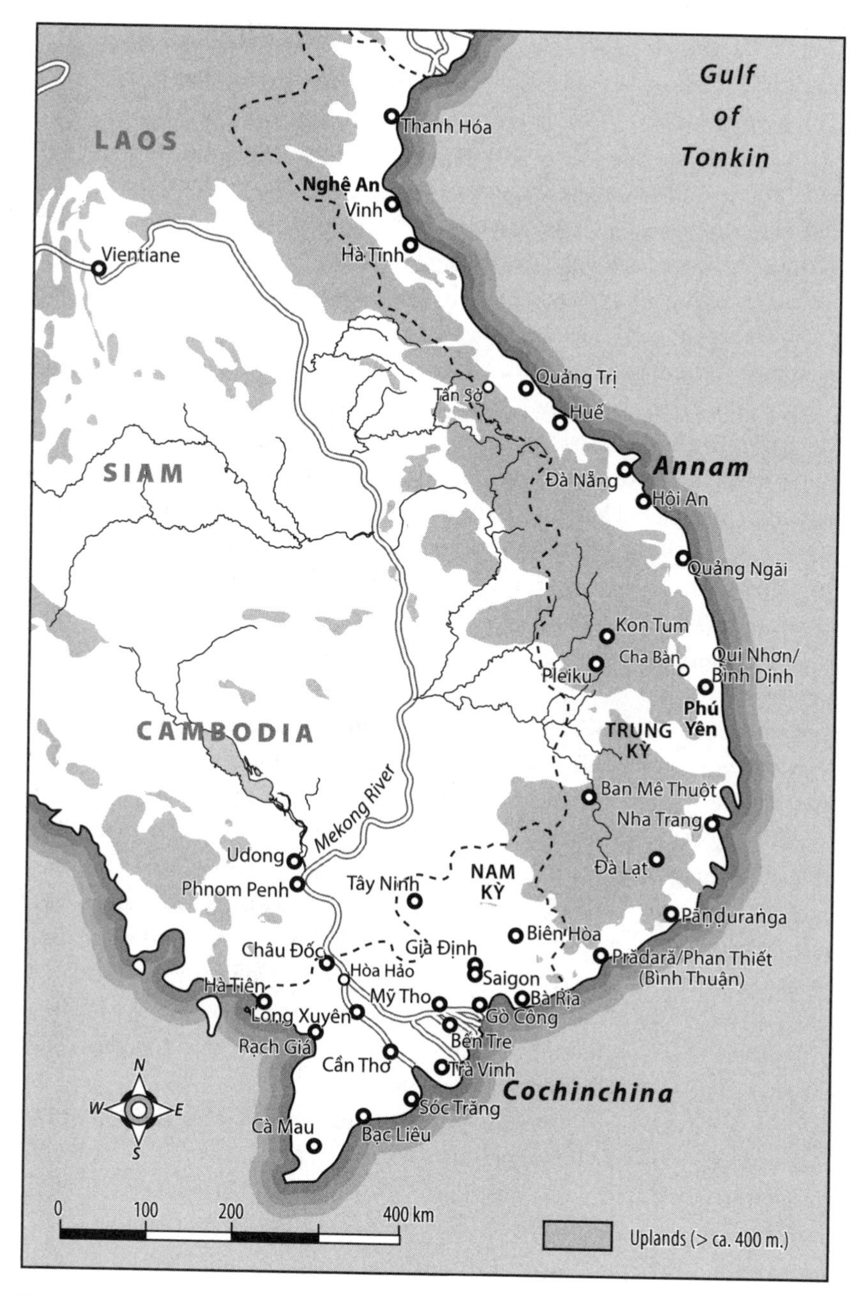

Fig. 8.1
Cochinchina and Annam in the late nineteenth century.

and north. The kingdom was cut in two. Tự Đức withdrew his mandarins from the French-held area of Cochinchina, and the French began setting up their own administration there.

Cochinchina, which retained its large Khmer-speaking Theravada Buddhist population, was the last region to be extensively settled by ethnic Vietnamese, and now, only decades later, it became the first to fall to France. For both reasons Vietnamese village institutions in Cochinchina departed from the model prevailing in the long-established communities of Tonkin and Annam. The more recent settlement of most Vietnamese families living in the south meant that their family tombs were not so long established in southern villages and Vietnamese ancestral cults were less rooted in their localities. Moreover, the flatter expansive terrain of the Mekong basin in Cochinchina, along with its more even rainfall pattern, permitted southern farming on a more individual basis (as Cambodians already practiced it there) without requiring the level of collective organization and regulation of labor for flood control or irrigation that characterized the older Vietnamese communities further north.[7]

In addition, Huế's Confucian model of classical education and literati governance had had only six decades to take root in Cochinchina. The French navy's "admiral governors" quickly made plans to nip it in the bud. They established schools in Saigon that taught the Vietnamese language in the romanized *quốc ngữ* script—hitherto restricted largely to the Catholic community. As early as 1862, Governor Admiral Bonard denounced "this official language *Chinese*" as "*incompatible* with all progress," and two years later his successor La Grandière hoped that "we will have in less than a year at least a thousand young Annamites knowing how to read and write their language in Latin characters; we will thus strike a deadly blow to mandarinism, and we will finally rid ourselves of the scholars who are always inclined to troublemaking."[8] The colonial adventurer Francis Garnier, too, described the literati as a "hostile class *par excellence*."[9]

In stages over the next twenty years, French forces seized the rest of Đại Nam. In 1867 they acquired the three western provinces of Cochinchina, from which Tự Đức then recalled his remaining mandarins. Over 1.5 million Vietnamese now lived under colonial rule.[10] By 1879, the French collected from the population of Cochinchina in annual taxes a total of nineteen million gold francs, ten times the amount they had paid to Đại Nam two decades earlier, when climatic conditions were more favorable. Then in 1882–83, colonial power expanded to conquer the center and north of the country. The French now ruled all eleven million Vietnamese.[11] They divided Đại Nam into three territories—the colony of Cochinchina and the Protectorates of Annam and Tonkin. Meanwhile in 1863 they also imposed protectorate status on the kingdom of Cambodia and finally, in 1893, on Laos, completing their construction of the new colonial state of French Indochina in 1897. The pace of this French advance was twice as rapid as the phased British conquest of Burma, which took three wars from the 1820s to the 1880s.

Vietnamese who worried about their nation's future felt at a loss. Confucianism, based on authority and stability, was no sure guide. It was also based on the past, while French control brought a new future and raised the possibilities of modernization.

Tự Đức, aged forty in 1867, was scholarly, introspective, and sickly. He had contracted smallpox at age eighteen and produced no heirs, unlike his predecessor monarchs, who had each sired at least fifty children.[12] Tự Đức compared his ship of state to a becalmed bark, lacking "solid oars" for officials:

> The wind hardly manifests its presence.
> The bark sits still.
> Stars emerge from the mist.
> Who then shall soothe my distress?
> How do I suffer when I cannot dispel sadness?
> Had I a bark and solid oars,
> In tranquility, I should row across the river.[13]

Historian David Marr describes the royal capital Huế at the time as "a rather modest court, an oversize citadel, and a satellite town" lining the Perfume River—"all surrounded by an ocean of ricefields and hamlets." Huế was a place to which "scholar gentry at various times in their lives came and went," and it exercised a powerful ideological influence on them.[14]

Yet the Vietnamese mandarinate also had deep roots in the country's villages, and it had rarely been a hidebound, ideologically rigid community. The country boasted perhaps twenty thousand "accomplished literati" and at least twice as many others who could read government edicts, treatises on family morality, and anthologies of poetry, folklore, and social satire written in Chinese and *nôm*.[15] Vigorous debates raged about the French challenge. An important catalyst was the findings of the sixty-nine-member Vietnamese embassy that Tự Đức dispatched in 1863 to visit France, Spain, and Italy. The mandarin viceroy of Cochinchina, Phan Thanh Giản, who had just lost the first three of his six provinces, led the embassy, whose main goal was to repurchase them from France.[16] On this unsuccessful mission, Giản saw the power of the West and its industrial development.

He wrote in a poem on his return, "I was startled by what I saw," and complained, "No matter how I insist no one believes me."[17]

Giản's deputy, second ambassador Phạm Phú Thứ, kept the diary of their European journey. Back in Đại Nam, Thứ presented it to Tự Đức and asked that the emperor read it with "a penetrating eye." Thứ pointedly noted that the French state employed both Catholics and Protestants; that Egypt, too, made use of both minority Christian and majority Muslim officials; that European capitals welcomed resident foreign ambassadors; and that Đại Nam's neighbor Siam had established an embassy in Paris. The diary described Europe's railroad networks, industrial capacity, military strength, and commercial wealth. Yet Tự Đức showed no sign of adjusting his policy to address this power, so Phạm Phú Thứ continued to write to the throne, appealing for the creation of a foreign language school, for local translations of books about the West, the opening of diplomatic and trade relations with Western countries and of a Đại Nam consulate in Hong Kong, and the development of mines and industry. Thứ had books printed on international law, administration, science, navigation, and coal mining, all prefaced with his hope that "men of good will could widen their knowledge" for "better results."[18]

Some Vietnamese believed collaboration with France their only choice, partly because the French seemed unbeatable, partly because they seemed modern, with ideas and technology that might benefit Đại Nam. This was the view of an anonymous "Letter from Cochinchina" ("Thơ Nam Kỳ") composed in the 1860s: "Alas, let us moderate our love for the fatherland. The wind of the West has blown lightly over us and made us shiver and tremble."[19] It was not Tự Đức's breeze that "hardly manifests its presence."

Others who had seen the West were more specific and insistent. The Catholic mandarin Nguyễn Trường Tộ, for his part, had studied in seminaries in Hong Kong and Penang before returning to join the new French administration in Saigon. He wrote in an 1863 memorial *Thiên Hạ Đại Thế Luận* (Discussion of the dominant trends of the world): "I have studied world affairs and realized that to try for peace with France is the best thing we can do. In Europe, France is a great military power."[20] Three years later he spoke of the need to "bend ourselves in order to adjust our position," to temporarily "part with some of our territory" and "send young students to foreign countries" to study "technical civilization," allowing the Vietnamese to "accumulate our strength, waiting for the day when we shall go into action" and finally recover "in the evening what we have lost in the morning."[21]

Still others saw France as an enemy to be resisted now whatever the cost. Some of them charged further that Vietnamese who "serve the enemy" also "contribute to the division of the South from the North," and so would "dye half the silk thread blue and the other half gold."[22] But anti-French fighters had their own pragmatic instincts. They would not submit to foreign rule or division of their country, yet they were prepared to accommodate some French interests. Around 1862, a group of Cochinchinese wrote this message in Chinese, on a wooden board that French forces found by a riverbank near Saigon:

> If you wish for peace, give back his territory to our king.... Do you wish a ransom in exchange for our territory? We will pay it on condition that you will stop fighting and withdraw your troops to your possessions. We will even have gratitude for you, and your glory will be like the universe. Do you wish a concession to watch over your commercial interests? We will consent to this. But if you refuse, we will not cease to fight in order to obey the wish of heaven.... We ask you to examine this request with care and to put an end to a state of affairs as disagreeable for your interests as it is for ours.[23]

New thinking was also evident in the still unoccupied north and center of the country. Some saw a model in Siam's moves to reform and therefore strengthen its traditional institutions. Mandarins like Nguyễn Hiệp, who participated in a Vietnamese mission to Siam in 1879, and others who visited Hong Kong in 1868 or traveled elsewhere, "memorialized" (reported to) the court on the need for a new, more open policy of adaptation to the new international environment.[24]

Yet others saw a third way out as the only option. The viceroy of Cochinchina, Phan Thanh Giản, committed suicide after surrendering the last of his territory in 1867. He had written of the French after his 1863 mission to Europe, "Under Heaven, everything is feasible to them, Save only the matter of life and death." His suicide was something that the conquerors of Cochinchina could not deny him. The celebrated general Nguyễn Tri Phương also took his own life after French forces briefly seized Hanoi and other citadels in 1873.[25] So did Hoàng Diệu, viceroy of Tonkin, when the French again successfully attacked Hanoi in April 1882.[26]

CONFUCIANS AND THE COURT

In the 1860s time-honored Confucian precepts remained the guiding discourse of the Vietnamese elite, especially in the center and north, but they proved of limited use in the face of the kingdom's new dilemma in the south. Phan Văn Trị, a scholar who opposed the French in Cochinchina, also mocked the Vietnamese monarchy (symbolized by the dragon) for its passivity in the face of their threat: "I can, while walking, trace a dragon with my urine." Trị himself attracted criticism from a Vietnamese Catholic official, Tôn Thọ Tường, who had participated in Phan Thanh Giản's mission to France and now cooperated with the French.[27] Their exchange was preserved in verse in 1866:

> TÔN THỌ TƯỜNG:
> Three provinces of our territory are left.
> To be at such an extremity is undoubtedly the result of the will of Heaven and Earth.
> Swiftly, telegraphic cables were installed, straight.
> Like black clouds, the smoke of battleships rose to the sky.
> Wavering in their actions, they [who resist the French] are furthermore slow in devising plans; I truly have much pity for them.
> As for me, I too am apprehensive of future days.
> It is indeed not easy to play with the mouth of the tiger or the jaws of the dragon.
> I therefore advise these children not to act recklessly.
>
> PHAN VĂN TRỊ:
> The outcome of the struggle between here and there is not yet definitive. . . .
> We cannot allow our determination to falter because of the many fires in [Saigon]. . . .
> There will be days when the nets we now string will trap the deer.
> Do not rely on the tiger's smell to terrify the monkey.
> My heart is of iron, it shall never waver.

Tường retorted that Trị was "over-confident in your intellectual abilities. And yet you belong to the category of those who sell shadows and move their lips." Taking up Trị's metaphor of the French tiger, Tường was prudently wary of such a powerful enemy: "The wind which carries the tiger's odor sufficiently terrifies the fox." And the moral case was too complex for anyone to say "who is right and who is wrong." Trị then rejected all three points:

> It is indeed the mark of an intelligent person to speak highly of what he does rightly.
> How can the perfidious belong to the same category as the just? . . .
> The tiger, once cornered, is overcome by the fox.

Warned that "the water will soon reach your waist," Trị drew faith from a classical Chinese sage, who was "not perturbed."[28] But the sage had drowned. Where did Đại Nam's interests and future lie? Despite his own criticism of the throne, Trị saw pro-French Vietnamese as disloyal rebels, yet when the court gave up territory, loyal Vietnamese might soon become rebels too.

Within a half century, Confucianism would lose its appeal to many Vietnamese on both sides. But its decline was uneven. Tự Đức conceded French control of Cochinchina and withdrew his mandarins there, but other Vietnamese ignored the "Son of Heaven" and fought on. For a couple of years, a peasant movement led by Trương Công Định harassed the French in Cochinchina. Định wrote to Phan Thanh Giản: "As long as you speak of peace and surrender, we are determined not to obey the court's orders."[29] Định was killed in a French offensive in 1864. But his example inspired others, who, as under Tự Đức's predecessors, rebelled against the court, and their dissent was more determined once they saw Tự Đức as surrendering to France. Revolts, mainly peasant movements, broke out every year from 1860 to 1883, when Tự Đức died.[30]

Stirrings among the literati are well documented. In 1861 the best-known poet in southern Đại Nam, the blind Nguyễn Đình Chiểu, eulogized peasants who had fallen attacking French positions: "You did not wait for an authority to summon you or to draft you." Obedience to the emperor, in Chiểu's eyes, was now apparently a lesser virtue than what he called "patriotism" in the defense of a "united and sumptuous kingdom." Chiểu wrote his eulogy in *nôm*, disdaining the court's preference for Chinese. Just as interesting, he wrote, "Our ancestors and parents still live on the land of Đồng Nai" (now Cochinchina), and he reassured the fallen heroes: "Your debt to your country has been fully honored, and your reputation shall be praised by the whole population of the six provinces"—suggesting his dual attachments, to the south and to a "united" kingdom.[31] Later the French tried to win Chiểu over and offered him back his family's land, which had been confiscated. He replied: "You took my whole country, why do you trouble to give back my land?"[32] Yet Chiểu must have seriously considered the offer because of the importance Vietnamese accorded to family and ancestral tombs.

In Huế in 1864, scholars who had come from many provinces to sit for the classical examinations submitted a petition to Tự Đức, laying blame for the loss of the three Cochinchinese provinces on Vietnamese Catholics, advocating their extermination as a means of "striking at the root of the evil" and accusing Phan Thanh Giản's embassy to France of having betrayed the country. The literati candidates demanded that the court harden its policy toward France before they would agree to take the examinations. At the northern examination center in Nam Định province, candidates rioted and attempted to assassinate a former member of Giản's embassy. Meanwhile Tự Đức's cousin Prince Hồng Tập plotted to seize power, massacre Catholics, reconquer the south, and expel the French. But the court uncovered the plot, executed Hồng Tập and his lieutenants, and forced the candidates to sit for their examinations.[33]

Also in 1864, in the first of two successive years of severe drought, construction began on a mausoleum for Tự Đức, a three-year project with working conditions so harsh that in 1866 the corvée laborers and soldiers employed on it briefly revolted and made common cause with a new group of coup plotters. Workers in the mausoleum's construction yard sang: "The walls are made of the workers' bones, and the moats are filled with the people's blood." The mandarin Thân Văn Nhiếp warned Tự Đức: "In the present situation, when our territory in the South is lost, when revolts in the North are increasing, when reports of typhoons, of flood and of droughts come from all parts of the country, is it right to build the Monument of Ten Thousand Years which costs ten times more than [Thiệu Trị's] Tomb of Heavenly Longevity?" That was not the only example of imperial profligacy, Nhiếp went on: "A pavilion inside the palace walls is no sooner erected than another is being built out on the riverside. Does Your Majesty think that there is no harm in acting in this fashion?" The leading conspirator in the 1866 plot, Đoàn Trưng, described the mausoleum construction site:

> Soldiers can be seen working up and down the hills.
> Their shoulders are worn away by carrying stones,
> Their buttocks are whipped until the skin is flayed...
> Their mouths are parched and their stomachs cry out for food.

Đoàn Trưng planned to displace Tự Đức in favor of his nephew, to end the court's appeasement of the French, and to repress the Catholics. This coup attempt also failed. Trưng was imprisoned and executed.[34]

Catholics too were searching for new Vietnamese paths. The priest Nguyễn Hữu Thơ served the Huế court in several capacities. Tự Đức sent him to France with a French bishop to plan the creation of a school of "Sciences, and Arts and Crafts" in Huế, but the emperor then went cold on the project. Nguyễn Hữu Thơ authored the diaries of both this second Vietnamese embassy to Europe and a separate royal mission to Saigon. Writing in Ninh Bình province in 1868, Đinh Văn Điền suggested not only that Đại Nam's army needed reform and upgrading to face the French threat but also that the court should invite European technicians to help build railroads and expand the mining industry, and that Đại Nam should develop relations with Britain to counterbalance France. Meanwhile the leading Catholic Nguyễn Trường Tộ left the service of the French in Saigon and returned north to his Nghệ An home in 1863. During the next decade, he submitted to Tự Đức no fewer than forty-three memorials in attempts to convince the court to adapt to the modern world. In 1866, Huế sent Tộ on the third Vietnamese mission to Europe, to recruit technicians and teachers for a Western-style school, but that project also foundered when the French annexed western Cochinchina in 1867.[35]

Nguyễn Trường Tộ mounted a campaign against Confucianism. He wrote Tự Đức the next year: "Today, our country is besieged, threatened, and will perhaps be occupied by men of another race. This is a problem we have to face." The past was no guide. "The Classics have been annotated time and again by ancient Confucian scholars; we need add nothing to them. We should on the contrary discard them all and question our students on the present state of the administration of our country." He denounced "the evil that has been brought on China and on our country by the Confucian way of life."[36]

> What we now study, what the professors teach and what the students learn, is all related to things past.... Why do we spend all our time, day and night, ceaselessly invoking Chinese heroes who died several thousand years ago? Do we owe them a debt of gratitude? Are men of the present inferior to those of the past?

"No other country in the world has so irrational a system of education," Nguyễn Trường Tộ concluded.

Instead, he argued for educating Vietnamese officials in what he called "realistic studies" (*những cái học thiết thực*)—agricultural administration, astronomy, geography, mechanics, law, and foreign languages. "The first act should be to issue a book on agriculture." The next step was to select and translate "Occidental books" that "deal with useful matters such as mines or mechanics (I recently bought two big volumes of such books in which one can find everything)." He also drew upon practical Chinese texts, particularly Xu Jiyu's ten-volume 1848 work, *Ying huan Zhi lue* (Short account of the maritime circuit). Based on information from American missionaries, this was a major Chinese attempt to describe the geography and political boundaries of the modern world, including Europe and its expansion. Historian Lorraine Paterson notes that when Nguyễn Trường Tộ incorporated much of this content in his memorials to the Huế court, he "brought the globe to Vietnam."[37]

Nguyễn Trường Tộ conveyed four interesting conceptions of the country he wished to strengthen. First, he combined religious and scientific understandings that made his argument for independence. "Our country has the support of Heaven above it, the support of the Earth under it. These are astronomic and geographical foundations. In this world our country is, after all, an independent country. It is not a Chinese colony. Within our borders, we have problems of organization and of maintenance of order, problems that we ought to think of in the present, for the future." Second, he defined "our territory" as a modern geo-body while using traditional Vietnamese terms in which water (*nước*) remained a motif as predominant as land: "Our mountains and our rivers [*non nước*] our borders and our frontiers, our seas and our lakes, our military posts and our citadels." Third, all these features required study: "We must know them well." And for the language of these studies, Nguyễn Trường Tộ proposed Vietnamese—written in *nôm*: "We shall then use Chinese characters, but we shall read them according to our national spoken language. At that time, when a document is read aloud, all in the country will be able to understand it.... I suggest that all books of history, geography, and arts and crafts be written in this writing and distributed to the population." Fourth, he considered the Vietnamese population in proto-egalitarian terms, as he lashed out at social injustices of the traditional system: "Among our people today, there are persons who do not labor in the ricefields but who wish to eat, people who do not weave but who wish to dress, who have no talent but who wish to occupy high positions, who have no education but who wish to be officials.... These people constitute a real danger to our country."[38]

FROM COCHINCHINA TO TONKIN

In France, a new wave of colonial fervor peaked in the 1870s. Missionary interest in the fate of long-persecuted Vietnamese Catholics combined with new French nationalist ideology and ambitions, a cultural "civilizing mission," the demands of France's naval and military power, and burgeoning commercial imperatives. The latter focused increasingly on China. French exploration in the 1860s had found that the Mekong River provided no navigable inland route there.[39] By 1873, when the explorer Francis Garnier published his account of the search, *Voyage d'exploration en Indochine*, French attention had shifted north to Tonkin, and to the Red River as an alternative waterway to China's Yunnan province.[40]

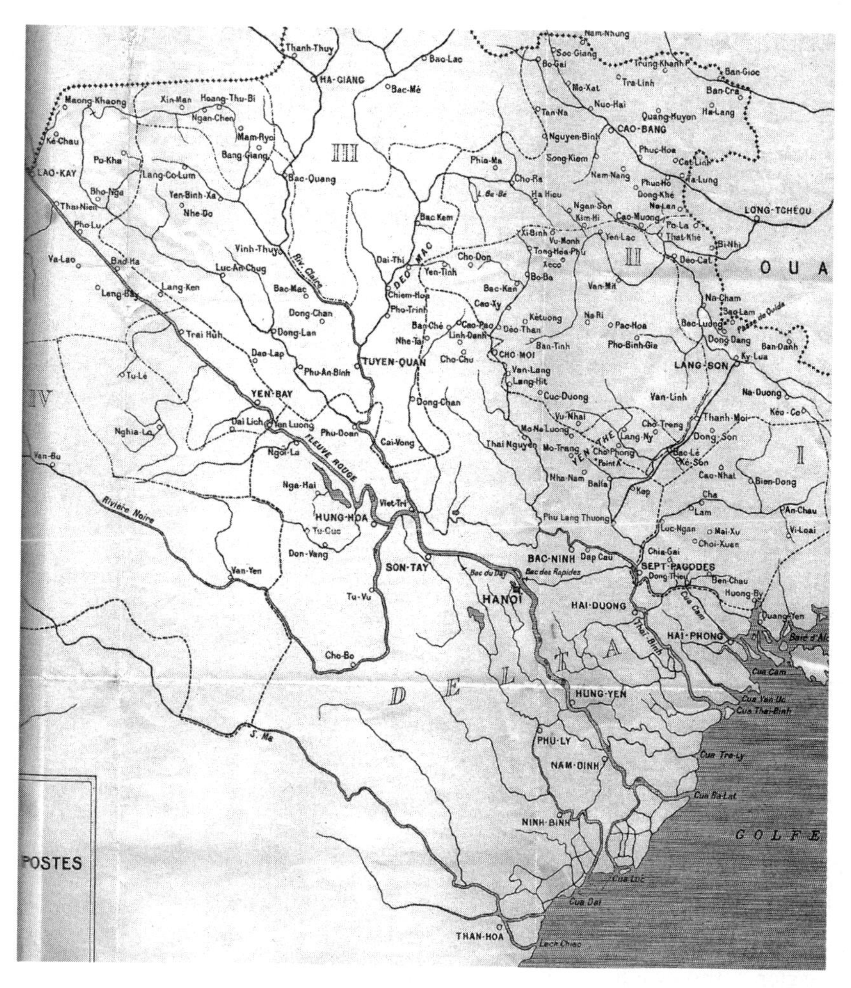

Fig. 8.2
French map of Tonkin, 1895. From Marshal Louis Lyautey, *Intimate Letters from Tonquin* (London: John Lane, 1932).

An 1873–74 incursion into the north of Đại Nam resulted in the imposition on Huế of two new treaties with France. In November 1873, Garnier led a successful French surprise attack on the Hanoi citadel, outmaneuvering the city's seventeen-thousand-strong Vietnamese garrison, and quickly capturing five provincial citadels of the Red River delta. These defeats exposed Tự Đức's ineffectual authority in the north, despite Garnier's death in December at the hands of Black Flags—exiled Chinese Taiping rebels now fighting on Huế's behalf—and even after the withdrawal of the French forces.[41] During the incursion, Vietnamese officials had abandoned some of the delta areas, and a number of local Catholics took their positions there or enrolled in French-sponsored militias. Commanded in some cases by

French missionaries, they stormed and looted "pagan" temples and villages and killed the inhabitants. One priest led his flock "truly to make war."[42] Catholics burned the home village of the governor of Nam Định and killed most of his family. On a visit to Tonkin two years later, the southern Catholic Petrus Trương Vĩnh Ký lamented that "bad Christians" had pursued "religious wars." It is unlikely that these represented most of the eight hundred Catholic communities of Tonkin.[43]

Brutal reprisals began in January 1874. Literati summoned the non-Catholic population to "Expel the Westerners and Exterminate the Christians," citing Catholics' collaboration with France and their supposed influence at court. This violent campaign became known as the "Scholars' Revolt" (*giặc Văn Thân*). In western Tonkin in January, rebels killed three Vietnamese priests and twenty-five catechists, and pillaged and destroyed 107 Catholic communities. By March the revolt had spread south to Nghệ An and Hà Tĩnh provinces. Local literati Trần Tấn and Đặng Như Mai proclaimed: "Although the Court has made peace with the Westerners, the scholars of the country do not accept it. First, we should kill all the Christians, then we should fight and expel the French, in order to preserve our culture which is over a thousand years old." Rebels in southern Tonkin murdered as many as 4,500 local Catholics and ravaged three hundred communities. This was doubly tragic: several leading Vietnamese Catholics had attempted to reform and strengthen the kingdom, and yet had largely failed to impact Tự Đức's policies, for which they then received the blame. Only on March 15, in exchange for French withdrawal, did Huế sign a treaty renewing the legal status of Christianity in Đại Nam. It also ratified French rule of western Cochinchina and the establishment of French consulates and land concessions, and of joint customs houses. In a second treaty in August 1874, Huế permitted free trade along the Red River.[44]

It took the forces deployed by the court four months to put down the 1874 Scholars' Revolt in Nghệ An. Meanwhile another rebellion broke out in eastern Tonkin, a second attempt at a restoration of the Lê dynasty. In July 1874, ten thousand rebels with thirty armed junks attacked the town of Hải Dương. Tự Đức's loyalists required French assistance to lift that siege. By December, Tonkin was experiencing another famine, which severely affected seven hundred Catholic communities there. After visiting Tonkin more than a year later, during the first year of a global drought, Trương Vĩnh Ký asserted in a secret report addressed in April 1876 to the French governor of Cochinchina that famine and "misery" afflicted Tonkin's farmers and workers, an "immense population" that "groans in the deepest poverty and spends long days without rice and without work."[45] And Đại Nam's severe drought of 1877–78 was still to come. Tự Đức's kingdom was in desperate straits. Having gained French recognition in 1874 of Đại Nam's "entire independence" from China, two years later Tự Đức sent an embassy to Beijing in an attempt to secure its help in evicting the French. In 1879, Chinese troops did arrive to help Đại Nam combat more Chinese rebels who had crossed into Tonkin, and two years later Beijing dispatched thirty thousand troops to contest French designs there.[46]

Reporting to the governor on his return to Saigon in 1876, Trương Vĩnh Ký added that "everywhere" in Tonkin "one hears demands for changes and for an administration capable of maintaining order, of giving the people a future." Even Tonkin's mandarins were "disgusted" at having "to slavishly follow outmoded practices" incompatible with ideas of progress and relations with the West. Ký thought that the Huế court, for its part, "would like to adopt these new ideas, but it appears powerless and all its good will is cancelled by the quite preponderant influence of certain obstinate personages who are great enemies of the new political doctrines."[47]

"On the other hand," Ký went on, "there is no shortage of intelligent men, capable administrators who know that salvation lies in a revolution of the policy of the Government, and who struggle with all the force of their conviction and authority to move the policy of the Court their way. Up to now they have been the weaker side." Even former deputy ambassador to France Phạm Phú Thứ (with whom Ký had served as interpreter on that 1863 mission) had been sent off to Tonkin because of "the fear that he inspires among the opposing party for his political ideas." Ký knew that Thứ and others had written to the Court to request changes and reforms, and even ministers insisted on them. "But the King, dominated by the [Privy] Council" (*cơ mật viện*), took no action. "The ministers wanted to resign their portfolios, but the King's pleas convinced them to stay at their posts." In addition, officials received small salaries, which led to "the cupidity of the whole hierarchy of officialdom." Ký therefore proposed deeper French intervention in Đại Nam. He asserted that "the influence of the French Government can without difficulty become quite preponderant"—indeed, "a great weight" in favor of the necessary reforms. The Huế government, "without aid, is powerless to do this great work," and "France alone," given the confidence of the local administration, was "capable of helping up this nation that is wilting."[48]

Trương Vĩnh Ký was possibly unaware that the French did not necessarily share a positive assessment of "the local administration" in Tonkin. Just months earlier the new consul in Hanoi, M. de Kergaradec, had also written to the governor of Cochinchina, stating that it was "precisely the officials chosen by the court from among the most intelligent, to facilitate the establishment of the new state of affairs, like Phạm Phú Thứ and the vice-governor of Hà Nội who create the most difficulties for us." These very reformers, the consul claimed, "raise the most puerile objections" to France's "just requests," while other officials "who unlike them have not only fulfilled no missions to France and China, but also have never even seen Europeans, find everything simple and easy." Kergaradec asserted that local populations, too, "even in the places where Europeans had never been seen," were "far from hostile to us." And, he added, "The mandarins know it as well as we do, which does not however prevent some of them from continually speaking of objections that must be presented to us and of the fright we give the inhabitants."[49] This explicit colonial distrust of Phạm Phú Thứ and other Vietnamese modernizing reformers and the preference for indigenous counterparts unspoiled by any foreign contacts pointed to diverging French and Vietnamese interests.

Back in the south, Trương Vĩnh Ký was already forging another path to Việt Nam's modernization. Having long collaborated with the French, Ký was also playing a key role in the advocacy for and official adoption by French Cochinchina of the romanized Vietnamese script *quốc ngữ*. But neither of these activities reveal the full extent of Ký's international connections and cosmopolitan culture, which helped determine his responses to the challenges the modern world posed to Vietnamese.

Born in 1837 to a Catholic mandarin family in Vĩnh Long province of the Mekong delta, Trương Vĩnh Ký began learning Chinese characters at age five. Then a Vietnamese priest taught him *quốc ngữ*. When Thiệu Trị's court sent his father on a mission to Cambodia, the young family moved to Phnom Penh, where his father died. From 1847 to 1852 Ký attended the small Catholic junior seminary located next to the Phnom Penh home of the French missionary Monseigneur Miche. He then spent six years studying at the seminary of the Société des Missions Étrangères in the British settlement at Penang. To his Vietnamese, Chinese, and Khmer linguistic skills, Ký added French, English, and Malay, along with philosophy, science, and mathematics. He eventually learned to read and speak fifteen languages and write in eleven.[50]

On his mother's death in 1858, Ký returned to southern Việt Nam just as the French were imposing their authority in and around Saigon. He married and settled near Chợ Lớn, the largely Chinese town bordering the city. He worked with the French military as an interpreter, and the bishop of Saigon employed him to teach in the city's seminary. By 1868 he could write, "My heart is always with France, my feeble services belong to her."[51] But his skills were also recognized at the Huế court. After a first visit there in 1862, Tự Đức appointed Ký as the interpreter for Viceroy Phan Thanh Giản's mission to Europe. He thus visited France, Spain, Italy, and the

Vatican, where he met the pope. Back home, he launched his publishing career in 1866–68 with three works, in Vietnamese and French, on Vietnamese culture and language. In 1869, Admiral Ohier appointed Ký editor of the first periodical published in Vietnamese, the official *Gia-định Báo* (Gia Định news), which French officials in Saigon had launched as a monthly in 1865. As one of his three Vietnamese writers, Ký appointed Tôn Thọ Tường, who had argued with Phan Văn Trị on the necessity of an accommodation with France. Another was Paulus Huỳnh Tịnh Của, who had asserted in *Gia-định Báo* in 1865 that "the King of Annam has understood the power of the French and weighted the pros and cons and seen that there is no longer any reason to be distrustful or difficult.... The Huế government knows that the French have no intention of putting aside the authority of Annam."[52]

Along with this pro-French position, the team of Catholic interpreters that Trương Vĩnh Ký assembled was to have a major impact on modern Vietnamese culture. They and *Gia-định Báo* quickly established *quốc ngữ* as "an indispensable instrument for spreading new ideas," ending the hopes of Nguyễn Trường Tộ (who died in 1871, aged forty-four) for a revival of *nôm*. Their work set off a "wave of public written expression in Vietnamese." By 1882 *quốc ngữ* had become French Cochinchina's official Vietnamese script. In it Huỳnh Tịnh Của was to publish the first monolingual Vietnamese dictionary, in 1898.[53] And Ký, before he died in that year, published up to 120 titles, including works on the grammar and vocabulary of Vietnamese, Chinese, Khmer, Malay, Burmese, Cham, Lao, Tamil, and Hindi and, in *quốc ngữ*, essays, translations, and poetry on geography, history, morality, philosophy, and the sciences, as well as "witness accounts, literature, legends, and short stories."[54] Between 1868 and 1907, eight *quốc ngữ* newspapers appeared in Cochinchina, along with the first *quốc ngữ* prose novella, a thirty-two-page melodrama about a Vietnamese Catholic interpreter entangled in love, revenge, and remorse. It found many readers on its publication in 1887.[55] The dissemination of *quốc ngữ* as a script and literary vehicle eventually made it much easier for Vietnamese readers to absorb Western ideas and technology. Ký wrote in 1877:

> Thanks to this writing, our poor disinherited country will be able to enter into the community of peoples and the great issues which the West has brought before the world; the sciences whose unexpected revelations strike the spirit and confound the intelligence will no longer be unfathomable mysteries to us, and these old errors, prejudices, absurd beliefs will disappear, giving way to true knowledge, to the high and serious inspiration of a wise philosophy. But for that one must have books, books, and still more books.[56]

Ký wrote these words less than a year after his three-month tour of Tonkin, undertaken, as he put it, "for the purpose of acquiring knowledge."[57] To the French he had immediately reported the northern delta society's difficult economic and political straits. Yet his later, fuller account also showed Tonkin, on the brink of a severe drought and a major political transformation, to be a region of remarkable cultural diversity that retained many traditional Vietnamese traits.

A SOUTHERN VIEW OF THE NORTH

After disembarking at Hải Phòng port in the northeastern delta, Ký had continued to travel within Tonkin mostly by water, along its network of rivers and canals. He journeyed by boat even when he left the delta, heading southward for Thanh Hóa: "We sailed along the Truy-lộc canal to the stream known as Càn and then from the Ngạt-kéo river junction into the Thần-phù estuary. From there we sailed along the river Trường-giang." Noting the mountain landscape through which his boat was passing, Ký recorded a local saying on the significance of water: "Highest of all is Mount Chóp-chài. / Widest of all is the ocean. / Longest of all is the river." Sleeping aboard, they sailed on along two more rivers to Thanh Hóa.[58]

Ký also observed the still relatively important role of Vietnamese women. Traveling on three more rivers between Hanoi and Hải Dương, Ký watched closely as "the old boatwoman" skippering their sampan navigated a dangerous stretch of rapids. His account conjures up ancient Chinese reports of Yuè female water shamans:

> We saw the fast flowing water looking most threatening and ominous then, as the boat drew near to the rapids, the old woman lit some joss sticks and burned some pieces of gold and silver paper. Next she commenced a series of low and solemn bows while she shrieked out prayers at the top of her voice. After this performance she and her daughter seized the oars with which they guided and steadied the boat, allowing the swift current to sweep it through the rapids. Suddenly we found ourselves in smooth calm water again.

Ký noted the key participation of northern women in agricultural life too. Echoing a 1651 observation made by Alexandre de Rhodes, he remarked that in Hanoi "the men and boys sit about in shops and cafes drinking tea or wine, while the actual working of the land is done by the women and girls."[59]

Ký saw "nothing unusual about the dress of the men up here": knee-length coats and black turbans or palm-leaf conical hats. But he carefully described Tonkinese women in their red bodices and tunics tied against the northern cold with a cloth belt where "they keep their money." Yet "whatever the weather," mothers nursing babies and even the younger girls "always" fail to button their tunics "properly," and they leave "the shoulder fastening undone so that it flaps down." A cord drawn under the chin held their three-tasseled palm-leaf hats, "large as winnowing baskets." "Over their lower portions they wear skirts and are shod in varnished or painted sandals. Their complexions are fair and satiny, and their cheeks are rosy. Their skin is lightish in colour, and they look attractive and a little plump. The teeth are covered with a shiny black lacquer."[60]

Ký also found his attention drawn to an apparent fertility ritual in rural Hà Nội province, again connected with water. In a village "sculpting contest," he wrote, a "seductive singing girl wearing a thin diaphanous silk dress and shiny taffeta trousers sits on a platform erected in a pond." Young men wearing only paper loincloths go out and "pretend" to sculpt the girl. "When a competitor is unable to restrain his passion any longer his penis rises into an erection and bursts through the paper loincloth," eliminating him from the competition. He then "dives head first into the water to hide his shame."[61]

Northerners reciprocated Ký's curiosity about their society. As he reached Ninh Bình, he wrote, onlookers, "hearing that people from Cochinchina were arriving, crowded around us and followed behind just to watch. We were hemmed in on both sides by large noisy crowds of people. Even after we had gone inside the citadel the crowd was still behaving in a rowdy fashion, and some of the people were climbing up to look at us."[62]

On his first arrival in Tonkin, Ký had a fine reunion with Phạm Phú Thứ. Removed from the Huế court, Thứ had become governor of Hải Dương and Quảng Yên provinces and customs chief for Tonkin. He had just convened all the mandarins of Hải Dương: "The feasting, the drinking, and the conversation went on night and day," with daytime theatrical productions. "Whenever we tired of dramatic performances the singing girls entertained us." None too soon, one suspects, Ký left for Hanoi, in a palanquin.[63]

In the northern capital Ký met the new French consul, Kergaradec. Hanoi's Vietnamese governor, implementing the concession in the 1874 treaty, had initially assigned the consulate offices at a large hall inside a vast walled enclosure with nine gates that was traditionally used for the regional classical examination competition. Here in the "Camp des Lettrés" Kergaradec had planned to house the French customs service. But soon six thousand literati candidates would assemble there for the triennial examinations, and the governor had to convince the consul to move offices—in return for a yet larger territorial concession.[64]

Ký's description of the city of Hanoi reveals the syncretism of Vietnamese religious and cultural life, as well as the ritual importance of water. Strolling down Mother of Pearl Street, he found that "the people living in the whole string of houses there were all Roman Catholics." Next he visited a Buddhist pagoda constructed during the reign of Thiệu Trị, which "must once have been very fine." Tall stupas flanked its entrance beside Hồ Hoàn-gươm Lake. Spanned by bridges on four sides, water surrounded the pagoda and passed underneath its floor. Inside were large imposing Buddha statues "covered in gold leaf." However, Ký reported, "the bonzes in charge of the pagoda are tearing off the tiles and prising out the bricks," which they sell "for money on which to live." The government neglected the building's upkeep, and it was "falling into ruins." A few days later Ký visited the eleventh-century Chùa Một Cột (Single-Pillar Pagoda). Atop a wide stone pillar rising from the middle of a pond, this small tiled pagoda resembled "a lotus flower protruding out of the water."[65]

Ký went on to inspect the Confucian temple of literature (Văn Thánh Miếu), another eleventh-century site. In its courtyard stood rows of marble tablets dating from the Trần dynasty (1225–1400) onward, set on the backs of carved turtles and inscribed with "the names of the learned doctors." On the same day, at the edge of West Lake, Ký visited the Daoist temple of Trấn-võ-quan, "the bronze saint," a tall, seated statue with curly hair and facial features that reminded Ký of a Buddha image. The eclecticism did not stop there. To Ký, from the neck down the figure resembled "a statue of St. Paul," his hand "on the hilt of a sword whose tip is supported on the back of a turtle." Ký also went out the citadel's western gate to visit the shrine of the indigenous seventeenth-century goddess Liễu Hạnh.[66]

Spirit cults were more prominent in the countryside, even around Hanoi. In Hải Dương province, two years after the second Lê revolt erupted there, Ký recorded that villagers customarily held sacrifices and festivals for spirits "on a very large scale, offering pigs and buffaloes without any fear of the enormous expense." A popular maxim named one village as an ideal location to spend one's youth, but another, where buffalo were slaughtered for sacrifice, was the best place to "become a spirit" after death.[67]

In contrast to the 1876 French-language report that Ký composed for the governor of Cochinchina, which briefly stressed Tonkin's dire economic straits and the discontent of its mandarins, the long Vietnamese account of his visit saw publication only in 1881 and in the words of its translator was "silent about the endemic poverty and insecurity" of Tonkin. Indeed, Ký described a functioning urban and rural economy yet to be debilitated by the coming drought. In the southeast of Hanoi, for instance, sixteen of the "21 streets of fine houses with tiled roofs" specialized in the sale of different products: Chinese books and medicines, religious paraphernalia, silks, silverware, copper and tin utensils, black and blue cloth, chests, baskets, shoes, cane, salt, and tea. Hanoi also offered fifteen varieties of rice and sticky rice, thirteen different silks, nine potatoes and root vegetables, five varieties of fruit, five of wood, three of bamboo, colored writing paper and "various types of paper produced in the north," fans, conical hats, tiles, bricks, pottery, treacle, sugar, chalk, cakes, popcorn, and rice wine. All around the city "a broad flat plain enriches it," with "very numerous" markets "found throughout the whole of the province," as elsewhere in Tonkin.[68]

Ký did not journey inland west of Hanoi. But the consul Kergaradec, on a visit to Sơn Tây a few months earlier, found its wide level plain "admirably cultivated as far as the eye can see," impressing on him "the richness" of the province. Beyond the citadel of Sơn Tây, and steaming farther upriver, the consul found the same productive agricultural scene. His return land journey took him on a twenty-kilometer march down the Clear River plain. "On the road one finds numerous pagodas," and "curious monuments" including large stone elephants. A companion took the river route back, also describing the country as "peaceful and well populated."[69] Kergaradec took note of Sơn Tây's large stone citadel, its walls "perfectly maintained" (and likely to be "difficult to storm"). Outside the walls were the homes of ten to twelve thousand people, protected by a second fortification eight thousand meters in circumference.[70]

The central delta was yet more impressive. Ký traveled south from Hanoi soon after Kergaradec returned from the west. Ký visited Nam Định, a province crisscrossed by rivers and, like Hanoi, enjoying a climate permitting two annual rice harvests. Ký found Nam Định "the richest province in the whole of Tonkin. It has fine ricefields, wealthy and prosperous people, a considerable trade, and crowded markets." The Catholic population there was large, and the parish priest of Nam Định city, Fr. Nghiêm, was "very well known and highly skilled in dealing with practical matters . . . a brilliant man who is also on very friendly terms with the mandarins in the province"—presumably including the governor, whose family Catholic rebels had murdered two years before.[71]

If the north was still prosperous, international trade was most important in central Đại Nam. The new French consul in Qui Nhơn reported that in the first days of November 1876, fifteen Chinese and Vietnamese sailing barks from various harbors along the coast had docked at Qui Nhơn's port of Thị Nại, and as many more vessels departed with local cargo. That month Thị Nại exported to Saigon alone four hundred piculs of sugar, more than one thousand lengths of silk, 1,365 piculs of raw silk, and 112 piculs of peanut oil. In addition, a steamer from Singapore spent several months each year at Thị Nại, buying silk and peanut oil from a local Chinese merchant and making two journeys back to Singapore, then sailing to Siam for a cargo of rice that it would ship to Hong Kong, and returning to Qui Nhơn loaded with opium and cotton goods. Each year the Chinese trader in Thị Nại also hired a four-hundred-ton sailing vessel to carry to Hong Kong a load of peanut byproducts (used in China as fertilizer) from Qui Nhơn or Phú Yên to its north.[72] The region's economic potential was of course uneven. The consul considered Phú Yên province "very poor," with sterile soil and a rugged landscape that made even coastal communications difficult; few ships sailed there. But, he wrote, "Bình Định, by contrast, is almost rich; its soil is fertile, its products diverse; ships easily find cargo there. Commercial interests are developed." Swatow as well as Hong Kong houses maintained clients and warehouses in Bình Định. Sea traffic was slow, the consul reported, but "customs receipts are increasing and can go even higher."[73]

These various impressions of Tonkin and Annam qualify Trương Vĩnh Ký's initial depiction of a ruined economy, ideological disillusionment, and sectarian strife. Despite its poverty and misrule, and before a major drought, Đại Nam remained to a large extent economically self-sufficient as well as culturally pluralistic.

Tonkin in particular, however, was still subject to both drought and flash floods, which severely challenged the imperial administration and its Confucian commitment to welfare and relief. The years 1877–78 were two of the ten driest since 1250.[74] Extended drought could crack and crumble the earthworks on the Red River, making them more vulnerable to floods. In mid-August 1879, when the Red River rapidly rose to its highest levels in twenty years, it broke through the dikes in many places and flooded all of Bắc Ninh province, half of Sơn Tây, nearly all of Hưng Yên, and parts of Hải Dương, Hà Nội and Nam Định provinces. More than thirty of Tonkin's richest districts lost at least three-quarters of the December harvest. By April 1880, famine ravaged Hanoi. The consul reported that the city authorities organized six public rice distributions per month, for women, children, the old, and the sick. "Every five days, the beggars of the city and its environs, a veritable army," crowded one at a time through the gates of the examination center, each receiving about five hundred grams (1.1 lbs.) of husked rice; the late April distribution fed twenty-two thousand people. Soldiers would then simultaneously open all nine gates to let the crowd quickly depart. These large-scale food distributions did not prevent starvation: "Every morning the police pick up bodies in the streets." But the return of good weather promised an abundant July harvest, which the consul predicted would reach forty to fifty million piculs and include a surplus of several million piculs for restocking the government's rice reserves and for the export trade.[75] Indeed, he reported in September 1880 that Bắc Ninh province had recovered to the extent that rice was "more abundant and cheaper" than in Hà Nội, while prospects for the harvest throughout Tonkin seemed to justify "the finest hopes." The more cautious Vietnamese authorities modulated their policies. The governors of Bắc Ninh, Sơn Tây, Hưng Yên, and Thanh Hóa reported that their provinces still suffered from the flooding. The governor general of Hà Nội and Ninh Bình and the governor of Hà Nội continued to prohibit exports of rice from those provinces, explaining to the consul that if "the people suffer from shortages, the Governors will be held to blame." However, they added that rice was now "cheap" in Hà Nội, Ninh Bình, Nam Định, and Hải Dương, and so for the months of October and November 1880 these four provinces were authorized to export rice "by sea."[76]

THE FRENCH INVADE TONKIN

In 1882 French military units returned to Tonkin in force, this time to stay. The conquest would not be easy. As the first French résident at Sơn Tây would later recall, "The whole territory of the empire was divided into provinces" (*phủ*), each with "a vast stone citadel," and districts (*huyện*) with smaller earthwork forts, all defended by soldiers. These strongpoints were "rather large," sheltering many inhabitants.[77] In mid-April 1882 consul Kergaradec reported from Hanoi: "The arrival of our troops has produced a great effect in the country. The mandarins of Hanoi especially have been very upset.... They immediately began defensive preparations in the citadel and refused us entry." Soldiers' leaves were canceled, additional forces brought in from nearby provinces, and orders issued "everywhere" to call up new recruits. "The Hanoi authorities are mustering all the forces at their disposition." The consul predicted that the commander of the naval division of Cochinchina, Henri Rivière, would soon attack the citadel in Hanoi. Kergaradec urged that France "maintain the administration in the hands of the ordinary magistrates, while really keeping over the affairs of the country the influential role that it would suit us to exercise."[78]

On April 25, French troops led by Rivière stormed the citadel after subjecting it to a seven-hour naval bombardment.[79] The governor of Hà Nội province, "alone among the mandarins, was found alive in the citadel." Kergaradec reported the next day that the governor general of Hà Nội and Ninh Bình "has just been found dead," while "the quan bố or treasurer has fled towards Sơn Tây." The victorious forces quickly carried out what the consul called "an inventory of the valuables that the mandarins have left in the citadel," though he feared "everything has been sent to Huế."[80] Rivière's attack on Hanoi launched what became a fourteen-year conflict against a multiplicity of Vietnamese and Chinese forces. Despite superior French arms, disarray in the Huế court, and lack of regional coordination of a dispersed Vietnamese resistance, the French conquest of the north and center of Đại Nam required prolonged fighting.[81]

Huế resolved on September 6, 1882, to fight the French, but the court remained divided. Tensions brewed in Hanoi as more French troops marched in. On March 19, 1883, Rivière wrote to inform M. Rheinart, the chargé d'affaires in Huế, of a "serious" new situation: "The arrival of 4 companies of reinforcements has produced the same effect as our arrival last April. . . . Death threats against the French are loudly made." Rivière would brook no risk to "all our navigation" in the Red River delta. He told Rheinart he would attack on March 27: "I plan to seize Nam Dinh, the center of the resistance." He intended to "act with extreme vigor and probably with extreme rigor."[82]

The new offensive provoked sharp dissent in the French ranks. The perfect storm of rival colonial interests involved as much confrontation as collusion. In a dispatch from Huế to the governor of Cochinchina, Charles Thomson, chargé Rheinart protested his "extreme embarrassment" at learning of Rivière's intent to attack Nam Định. French forces, Rheinart concluded, were to "make war" on Đại Nam "without prior declaration of any kind, at the same time as we were undertaking a mission charged with attending to the execution of the treaty" and fostering "friendship between the two countries." Rheinart felt, he said, "no more consulted than I was at the time of the taking of Ha Noi."[83] He considered Rivière's new assault contrary to "ministerial instructions" and "very prejudicial to our interests." As for the Vietnamese, he added, "Their *defense* preparations are criticized as threatening our security and serve as a unique pretext for our unexpected attacks." Noting that his mission had become "a fiction, a lie," and having received "indications" of his "coming replacement," Rheinart closed the Huế consulate and, "like the captain of a sinking ship," evacuated it with all personnel on April 3, 1883. He concluded his protest by adding that "the very regrettable taking of Hanoi has brought us a Chinese intervention and Chinese claims."[84]

Indeed, Chinese Black Flags killed Rivière in a battle on May 19. But French reinforcements occupied the Red River delta, and other units captured forts outside Huế. Tự Đức died in his capital on July 19, aged fifty-six. The next month France's new "general civil commissioner," Jules Harmand, forced the court's two regents to surrender Tonkin and northern Annam, to transfer to French Cochinchina Annam's southernmost province of Bình Thuận (the largely Cham district of Phan Thiết), and to accept a French résident in Huế who could demand royal audiences. Otherwise, Harmand threatened the regents, "The name Vietnam will no longer exist in history."[85] The substitution of résidents for consuls made no pretense that the country remained independent, though it preserved in the new "protectorate" regime the figment of French detachment, in contrast to the title of governor for the head of the colony of Cochinchina. Yet that was not the major difference between the French officers involved in the conquest of Đại Nam.

THE CONTEST FOR ANNAM

After Rivière's offensive in the north, the French consul in the south-central port of Qui Nhơn reported in June 1883 that "the Tonkin events have had only a late echo in the population," and that "tranquility reigns" in Qui Nhơn and "all the neighboring provinces; . . . so for the moment, nothing to fear." Yet he thought it "inadmissible" for the French in central Đại Nam "to remain under the Annamite cannons, even inoffensive" as they were—or to abandon to their fate Annam's sixty thousand Catholics.[86]

By contrast, in January 1884 the new French résident in Huế, like his predecessor, opposed military action. He reported a reduction in the Vietnamese "defense preparations that the threats and arbitrary acts of M. Harmand had caused the citadel to make." The "war party" in the divided Huế court, the résident added, was "very timid at present." He urged an end to "the annexation of Tonkin begun by M. Harmand, in violation of his treaty." If not, the résident predicted a "general uprising of Annam and Tonkin" along with "the flight of the court and provincial mandarins into the high country, abandoning to us the ruined plains infested by wild bands." That, the résident feared, would "bring on us the just and severe reprimands of France and the outside world."[87] Then in May 1884, China undertook to withdraw its forces from Tonkin. On June 6, France imposed a new treaty on Đại Nam that took over its foreign policy, ended its tributary relationship with Beijing, returned Bình Thuận from French Cochinchina to Annam, divided Annam from Tonkin, and confirmed the dominance of the French résident in Huế.[88]

The next year, however, the résident's fears materialized. Turmoil had wracked the Huế court in 1883–84 as three young princes in turn succeeded Tự Đức, each being quickly removed or executed. Finally, in August 1884, his fourteen-year-old nephew, Prince Hàm Nghi, ascended the throne. The court planned to fight in his name. The regent who also served as minister of war, Tôn Thất Thuyết, secretly organized the building of a strongly fortified hill camp in the mountains at Tân Sở, in the Mường ethnic minority region of northern Annam. There Thuyết shipped artillery pieces, ammunition, provisions, and a third of the court's treasury. On July 4–5, 1885, one month after the ratification of the 1884 treaty, imperial troops unsuccessfully attacked French positions at Huế. French forces repulsed them and immediately sacked the Forbidden City, seizing possibly 2.6 tons of gold and thirty tons of silver. At the end of July they imposed on the rump kingdom of Annam a protectorate regime similar to that already established over Tonkin and empowered the French résident général in Hanoi to preside over the imperial Secret Council (Cơ Mật Viện). Meanwhile, however, Tôn Thất Thuyết had whisked the teenage monarch Hàm Nghi northward out of Huế and into the hills around the Tân Sở fortified base. In the king's name on July 13, Thuyết issued an edict appealing for opposition to the French, entitled *Cần Vương* (Aid the king).[89] A royalist resistance began. The response from scholars was nationwide. For now (unlike in Cochinchina since 1863), they could be loyal to both king and country.

The revolt included new massacres of Vietnamese Catholics. In July 1885, in the central Annam provinces of Quảng Nam and Quảng Ngãi, rebels slaughtered five thousand Christians. From September in northern Annam, under the slogan "Hunt the Westerners, kill the Catholics!" as many as forty thousand more were killed.[90] These massacres would also have significant repercussions in southern Annam.

In the south-central province of Bình Định, site of the former Cham capital Vijaya, the French consulate at Qui Nhơn was well prepared. Some 125 troops and three officers defended its fortifications. But Đại Nam's forces there were also strong. Just beyond the consulate's walls was the Vietnamese fort at Qui Nhơn, garrisoned by three hundred men with seventy-seven artillery pieces. A few miles away, the mandarin in command of Bình Định had also made "defensive preparations" in the citadel there, a Vauban fort with corner bastions that French engineers had built in the late eighteenth century. The citadel was protected by thick stone walls thirteen feet high, on which were mounted forty-nine artillery pieces overlooking a deep moat and exterior wall. Its eight-hundred-strong garrison was equipped with seventy Minié rifles, 3,500 cartridges, and three war elephants. The French consul had reported in 1883 that the Bình Định citadel "does not worry us"; French forces could comfortably shell it from batteries placed above the Cham ruins just 2,500 meters away. "The walls and bastions are weak and one could easily storm them, or the gates could be smashed in with cannon and the defending artillery cast down."[91]

However, when news of the fall of Huế in July 1885 reached Bình Định, candidates taking their classical examinations there broke out of the enclosed camp and joined the Cần Vương anti-French struggle. And it was these civilian literati, outraged at the French seizure of Huế, who first stormed into the citadel of Bình Định, evicting the mandarin in charge and taking over the fortifications. The advance French intelligence on the citadel no doubt proved valuable to General de Courcy and his several hundred troops, who in turn seized it from the local Cần Vương forces in late August.[92] By 1886 two French companies of three to four hundred soldiers garrisoned the Bình Định citadel.[93] But that force was insufficient to control rural Bình Định and Phú Yên provinces, which were in revolt. In Bình Định, at the former Tây Sơn fort of An Nhơn, the rebel literati (*văn thân*) even appointed a twenty-seven-year-old, Mai Xuân Thưởng, as their new monarch.[94]

The ensuing French campaign to put down the uprising in Bình Định and Phú Yên highlighted both the key role of France's Vietnamese allies and the continuing rivalries among the French actors in this ongoing colonial expansion. In this case it was not a contest between advocates and opponents of further conquest but a competition for control of the new territory between French Cochinchina and French officials of the new "Protectorate of Annam."

Much of the military initiative seems to have come from a leading Cochinchinese Catholic and colonial militia commander, Emmanuel Trần Bá Lộc. In September 1886, Lộc drew up a proposal to subjugate the provinces of Bình Định and Phú Yên.[95] Six years earlier, he had told the director of Cochinchina's department of the interior: "If I have served France to this day, it has been so as to cover the object of my affections with the shadow of my influence." But Lộc was in fact an active agent rather than a servant of the French cause. In July and August 1886 he proved brutally effective in French Cochinchina's repression of the Cần Vương revolt in neighboring Bình Thuận when he worked with the French officer Étienne Aymonier, who defeated the rebels and conquered Bình Thuận by arming Cham militias there and neighboring Khánh Hoà by arming local Catholic militias. For his part, Lộc ordered the burning of many villages in Bình Thuận and reported graphically on the beheading and dismembering of his victims.[96] Now, in November 1886, he wrote to Cochinchina's director of the interior, noting, "Our enemies have lost ground," but they had retreated north to "our coasts in Bình Định" where they now had to be "pursued and exterminated without delay." Among these enemies Lộc mentioned the young Mai Xuân Thưởng, "named as a king" in Bình Định. Lộc recommended a new expedition to impose colonial control there and in Phú Yên.[97] He estimated he would need eight hundred Cochinchinese militia volunteers each armed with a Gras rifle and two hundred cartridges, plus two hundred piston rifles for local recruits.[98]

As Lộc pushed for intervention in Annam from the south, in Hanoi a second expedition was preparing to embark from the north. By early December 1886, Résident Général Paulin Vial was planning to conquer Phú Yên "in eight or ten days with our troops." General Munier, commander of the French occupation division, drew up plans for its deployment there and to Bình Định.[99] Vial prudently wrote Governor Filippini of Cochinchina, requesting support from Lộc's southern militia: "Once the occupation of the country [Phú Yên] is over, this fine partisan chief will help to organize the local militias and will be a great support to the résident whom I shall designate." Vial promised Filippini that "the expenses incurred by this expedition" would be raised from Phú Yên ("the country itself") and so the new Protectorate of Annam would guarantee French Cochinchina's costs.[100] Yet Vial took pains to underline that Lộc's militiamen were "not indispensable." The protectorate would pay their salary and ensure they were "armed and equipped at our expense," but it would "keep them only for a month." Vial also asked Filippini to send "administrators from Cochinchina who would get on perfectly" with Lộc and "create the police of the province," but only after Protectorate of Annam troops had "occupied the citadel where they would remain to serve in support of our domination."[101]

The French protectorate's "domination" was to be exercised not merely over its new Vietnamese subjects. Its use of that term, like the limitations it sought on Trần Bá Lộc's role, also expressed the rivalry of the new Annam administration with the older Cochinchina colony. The rivalry was mutual. Cochinchina, stung by the formal loss to Annam of its brief suzerainty over Bình Thuận, still nourished hopes of its own expansion.[102] General Munier would later complain that in February 1887, after his field commander Lieutenant Colonel Dumas had marched to Phú Yên to confer with his Cochinchinese "inferior," Commandant Chevreux, the latter's first words to him served curt notice that Dumas was now supposedly "on the territory of Cochinchina."[103]

Behind that confrontation in the field lay the two expanding colonial territories' continued squabbling over the role of Trần Bá Lộc, as well as his own demands for influence and benefits. Vial insisted to Filippini that Lộc arrive "only after the military occupation" of Phú Yên had been completed by protectorate troops.[104] Saigon quickly objected: "According to *Phủ* Lộc [Trần Bá Lộc's title], the pursuit of the rebels and pacification would be more difficult, almost impossible, if the militia do not act immediately after the taking of the citadel and strongpoints. Treasure will be carried off by those fleeing and will be lost to us." Demanding that the two territories' operations be "simultaneous," Filippini also revealed Lộc's own power in the colonial structure: "It would otherwise be very difficult for me to obtain support of the Phu Loc." He offered to send one thousand militiamen and suggested the combined expedition against Phú Yên and Bình Định commence on January 20, 1887.[105] Hanoi gave in: "Loc and his 1,000 militia will arrive in a manner to act immediately after the taking of the citadel. . . . The action will be joint." Lộc's militia would occupy "the most propitious points to arrest those fleeing" and seize their "papers and valuables," but Phú Yên citadel "will be in the hands of our troops."[106]

The protectorate's options soon narrowed further. In the northern province of Thanh Hóa in late December 1886, the Cần Vương rebels launched new attacks. That challenge, a frustrated Vial informed Filippini, "no longer permits the general to send troops to Phú Yên." He now asked Cochinchina to deploy "a sufficient detachment to support Phủ Lộc and reoccupy the citadel" of Phú Yên.[107] The governor of Cochinchina then pressed his advantage. He urged joint "pacification" not only of Phú Yên but farther north, of Bình Định "as far" as Qui Nhơn.[108] Vial again responded positively: "I voluntarily accept the occupation of Phú Yên by your troops and the intervention of the Phủ Lộc." He even offered Filippini the possibility, "once the cleaning up of the rebel bands is accomplished," that Munier might require deployment north of the protectorate's two companies holding Bình Định citadel; Cochinchinese forces could replace them at the protectorate's expense, extending "your salutary influence northwards."[109] The next day Vial confirmed that Cochinchina had agreed to "carry out this expedition by your own means" and "at my expense," adding that "Phu Loc and his militia would be more at ease with officers and troops that they have known for a long time."[110] Filippini then asked for the two hundred piston rifles that Lộc had first requested two months earlier.[111] Vial agreed to send them, noting that the revolt in Thanh Hóa now required "all our available forces" and had inspired more unrest "in several provinces of Annam."[112] Cochinchina would contribute an "expeditionary corps" comprising 450 regular troops in addition to Lộc's thousand-strong militia.[113]

Meanwhile, however, in its northern province of Quảng Ngãi, the Annam Protectorate was recruiting its own Vietnamese militia force. And Cochinchina's sensitivity to the new protectorate's expansion boiled over just as its expedition was to embark from Saigon on January 20, 1887. Filippini was shocked to learn via Qui Nhơn that Commander Dumas of the Annam forces had already set out to attack "the chief of the rebels of Phu Yen and Binh Dinh." He protested to Vial: "This news, entirely contrary to all the information contained in your correspondence, surprises me enormously. . . . I should have been informed for it is indispensable that the operations be combined." Within days Filippini heard worse: Dumas had reached Bình Định with three thousand militiamen from Quảng Ngãi, and the protectorate forces were already "raising contributions, naming functionaries, receiving surrenders." The enraged governor of Cochinchina suspected that "all this" had "been organized only to hinder the mission of the Phu Lộc." He asked Hanoi to stop "all these movements" which "make the expedition from Cochinchina useless," and to "bring order to this anarchy which seems to reign in the administration of Bình Định where everyone acts without orders, without understanding, and probably without profit."[114]

Vietnamese resistance aggravated the dissension among the French and accentuated their dependence on Vietnamese militias. Offering Filippini little consolation, Vial's reply from Hanoi conceded that lack of telegraph communications with Bình Định made transmission of orders difficult but protested that the report from Qui Nhơn was "exaggerated, and out of context." Just two days before, General Munier had told Vial that now "Quảng Ngãi is in the hands of the rebels, like Phú Yên."[115] Vial insisted that the deployments from Quảng Ngãi should not hinder the joint assault on Phú Yên, the expedition's first target. Next would come Bình Định, where, he wrote, "we continue to struggle almost without direct control against the insurgents who are still very powerful." Indeed, since July 1885, Vial went on, "the rebels of Quang Nam and Bình Định" had even attempted to invade Quảng Ngãi. Probably, he thought, it was the Vietnamese militiamen from that province who had pursued the attackers back into Bình Định. Vial expressed "full confidence" in his protectorate's Vietnamese commander, "the Sonphung of Ngãi Đinh," whom he credited with keeping order in Quảng Ngãi.[116] It is clear that both of the rival colonial forces relied heavily on Vietnamese militia.

The 1,500-strong Cochinchinese expeditionary corps set sail from Saigon under Commandant Chevreux. It landed at Phú Yên on February 6, 1887, while two hundred troops from Tonkin under Lieutenant Colonel Dumas garrisoned the citadel of Bình Định.[117] In its first three days in Phú Yên the expeditionary corps seized two forts and drove the Cần Vương resistance into the hills. Trần Bá Lộc quickly captured and executed one of its two leaders; the other defected and joined forces with him. Dumas's force set out from Bình Định and reached Phú Yên on February 12, then met its cold reception from Chevreux. The rivalry dividing the two French forces had left Lộc's militia with major effective power.

Lộc used his power forcefully. On February 28, he sailed to Bình Định with 1,200 men and began to attack the Cần Vương there.[118] A month later the Phú Yên résident reported the surrender of rebel "king" Mai Xuân

Thưởng.[119] But this report was false, and a resurgence of the revolt even led Dumas to countermand Chevreux's imminent recall to Cochinchina.[120] Then on April 12 Lộc claimed that some 1,531 of the 1,723 "rebel chiefs" in Bình Định had surrendered. Supposedly only 144 military and 48 civil chiefs remained at large in the province.[121] Cochinchina's governor continued to weigh in on Lộc's side, arguing that he was "probably upset" at being "immobilized" by Dumas's Tonkin contingent.[122] The résident at Bình Định reported later that "the provincial mandarins were very annoyed" at Lộc's presence.[123] But Lộc was soon conducting a prolonged manhunt for Mai Xuân Thưởng. On May 4 he captured the rebel leader, then his family members and twenty-six other "chiefs."[124] Lộc publicly executed all twenty-seven rebel chiefs in early June.[125] By month's end, "no real organized bands" of rebels remained in Bình Định or Phú Yên, and Lộc returned to Saigon with 558 of his Vietnamese volunteers. The governor underlined their importance to French Cochinchina and its rivalry with the Protectorate of Annam, in an angry letter he sent to Hanoi upon learning that Lộc's forces had "not received their pay for May and June." He wrote, "That has produced a very bad effect. I gave the order to have them paid immediately."[126]

The French failed until 1892 to capture the last resistance leader in Bình Định.[127] But a long century of unrest in central Việt Nam that had begun with the Tây Sơn uprising was now ending, as one of Lộc's reports revealed. At seven in the morning on June 7, 1887, in the last hour of his life, "Mai Xuân Thưởng, led to the place indicated for his execution, was again interrogated and declared that he was the grand-nephew of the rebel Nguyễn Nhạt [Nhạc] of Tây Sơn."[128] Thưởng met his death not far from the former Cham citadel of Chà Bàn, where his great-uncle, the senior of the three Tây Sơn brothers, had maintained his own capital from 1776 until his death in 1793.[129]

Trần Bá Lộc won his victories at great human cost, as he had in Bình Thuận in 1886.[130] Reports of his forces' "regrettable" acts came in from "the various posts of the interior" of Bình Định, its French résident informed the governor of Cochinchina. The résident added that Dumas and his successor also "very much wished to pass on this information to me and I immediately did what I could to remedy this situation." But he expected to learn of still more atrocities, for which France "must not assume the responsibility but at which we should not be too astonished." This was because both Vietnamese sides—not only "the Văn Thân rebels" but also "the mandarins still attached to the Court" after the French had crowned a new emperor, Đồng Khánh (r. 1885–89)—allegedly practiced a brutality that the résident conveniently termed "Annamite customs."[131] A racialized notion of authentic indigeneity formed an integral part of the colonial project. But so did indigenous colonial society itself. Its cohesion, in contrast to the rivalry that plagued official French circles, was demonstrated by the marriage in Cochinchina of Trần Bá Lộc's granddaughter to a son of the literary reformer Trương Vĩnh Ký.[132]

VARYING IMPACTS OF FRENCH RULE

In both the north and center of the country, as earlier in the south, Vietnamese fought ferociously for and against the French conquest. And the conquest itself inflicted significant material damage and human losses. After the seizure of Hanoi, the citadel of Sơn Tây became the major bastion of Vietnamese resistance, but it fell to a French siege in December 1883 after a royal officer opened the citadel gates.[133] The first French résident there reported that Sơn Tây and the many other provincial citadels of Đại Nam had each contained a large rice warehouse for the collected stocks of the government's taxation in kind, intended "partly as a reserve in case of famine or shortage." The résident went on: "When we took possession of the country, some of these rice warehouses fell into disuse, the others were destroyed.... The rice reserves were wasted." He concluded: "In Tonkin we found immense warehouses full of rice, and today [October 1886] they are almost gone, and those which remain are empty." The long war of conquest also brought floods and epidemics, causing historians to describe the period 1883–96 as "the terrifying years," in which "a genuine demographic disaster" occurred. Tonkin's population in 1913, at six million, was no higher than it had been in 1880.[134]

It took the forty-two-thousand-strong French expeditionary corps nearly three years of sporadic fighting in most provinces of the north and center to capture Hàm Nghi in October 1888. A group of ethnic Mường handed over the young emperor. The regent Tôn Thất Thuyết had departed for China to appeal for help, without success. The Cần Vương movement was over.[135] Trần Bá Lộc even claimed that in Huế under Emperor Đồng Khánh, the royal family no longer considered Thuyết one of its members and officially altered his family name from Nguyễn to Lê, his mother's name.[136] In 1886 Đồng Khánh also chose to depart from his predecessor Tự Đức's single-minded Confucianism; he revisited the Nguyễn dynasty's local roots by sponsoring a state cult of Thiên-y-a-na, a Vietnamese incarnation of the Cham earth goddess Po Nagar.[137] This ritual turn to the indigenous, with its parallel in colonial ideology, could not compensate for the new monarch's selection by the French, which in the eyes of many Vietnamese discredited the dynasty. Nor did it help the colonialists subjugate the indigenous upland populations; in the north Mường fighters had delivered Hàm Nghi, but most of the Central Highlands remained "unconquered" as late as 1899.[138]

In Nghệ An and Hà Tĩnh provinces north of Huế, anticolonial resistance continued until 1896, led by the mandarin Phan Đình Phùng, former chief censor at the court.[139] Even without royal support many scholars were prepared to fight on. They managed to keep a spirit of resistance alive because of their links to the villages, where most of them had grown up. As Marr has pointed out, scholars had "spent most of their existence far from court and close to the annual harvest cycle, teaching, writing, or serving in district and provincial positions." Thus, "the ricefields" gave scholars and peasants alike "a reason for being and sealed the contract between man, soil, and sky." The examination system, which allowed talented rural people to achieve promotion, had fostered this link. Many other scholars who had not attained mandarinal rank and were teaching in villages also led peasants into the nationwide revolt. Phan Đình Phùng reportedly put it this way:

> I determined to forget questions of family and village.
>
> Now I have but one tomb, a very large one, that must be defended: the land of Vietnam.... Our rivers and our mountains have been annexed by them at a stroke and turned into a foreign territory. These events affected the whole country, the entire population. It is not any particular region or any particular family alone that has suffered this trial.[140]

Moreover, China had renounced its suzerainty over Đại Nam. To throw off French imperialism, the country would have to rely on its own resources, and even Confucian governance would not be one of them. A number of southern Vietnamese on both sides had already come to this conclusion. Đại Nam's Sino-Confucian heritage was under concerted attack. The last round of classical examinations would be held in 1919, ending nine centuries of tradition and intermittent adaptation.

The French slowly put together their new colonial state of Indochina. This was not just a matter of visibly ruling large populations who before the 1870s had "never even seen Europeans."[141] It was also about France guiding the life of the colonized nation. In 1886 the protectorate's résident général in Hanoi, Paulin Vial, shared the view of Governor Filippini of Cochinchina that the three Vietnamese territories belonged to a single state: "Like you, despite the different constitutions of Cochinchina, Annam, and Tonkin, I think that our efforts must tend toward bringing together the institutions of these three countries destined to be reunited later just as they have been in the past."[142] Vial specifically asked Cochinchina to send to Hanoi

"Annamites of distinction, among the most devoted," so that he could "show them to their compatriots of Tonkin."[143]

French Indochina was also about introducing its diverse populations of Vietnamese, Cambodians, Lao, and various ethnic minorities, to one another and to the geography of the new colonial state. The Governor and the résident général further agreed on the desirability of an "exchange of decorations between the sovereigns of Annam and Cambodia."[144] At the same time the French scholar-official Aymonier sparked concern in Hanoi by provoking dissension between Vietnamese and Chams in Bình Thuận. While working with Trần Bá Lộc there, Aymonier had widened social divisions along fault lines that Emperor Minh Mạng had first accentuated in the 1830s when he both suppressed the Cham principality and stepped up persecution of Catholics. Vial complained to Filippini that Aymonier had "decidedly upset the Annamites by showing preference to the Cham and openly favoring them. In Huế they are very irritated." Vial had visited the court and "found the ministers worried and very upset." He urged that Aymonier "manage with care the *amour propre* of the Annamites who are very susceptible." The résident général was concerned to prevent the discontent spreading to "those who are with us in the provinces of the North."[145]

The new colonial state would incorporate uplanders as well. Two months later, for instance, a party of rebels from the Bình Định hills came down to the coast to surrender. The résident in Phú Yên noted pointedly that they were of Chamic origin, from "a small group of 14 villages who called themselves Ya-Pang," and until now they "had never seen the sea."[146] A French official stationed at Saravane in south Laos later brought a group of Lao mandarins eastward down from the hills into central Việt Nam. He made the same point, that these Lao now "saw the sea for the first time," and he mused that they wondered "why the French built roads across mountains instead of around them, following the Laotian method, and also how it could be that an ocean, even if wide, had banks on only one side."[147] Colonialism demanded the proclamation of a new geography.

In Cochinchina in particular, colonial rule had two major internationalizing effects. One was to further weaken the southern village institutions, which were already more tenuous than in the north and central regions of Đại Nam. From early in the conquest the French applied their own law in Saigon. The promulgation from 1880 of the French penal code throughout Cochinchina (and, from 1883, of the French civil code) ended the applicability of the Gia Long code there. Increasing colonial control over Cochinchina's village census and land records permitted the French to abolish the traditional collective taxation obligations of its Vietnamese villages in favor of individual impositions, including a head tax on all adult

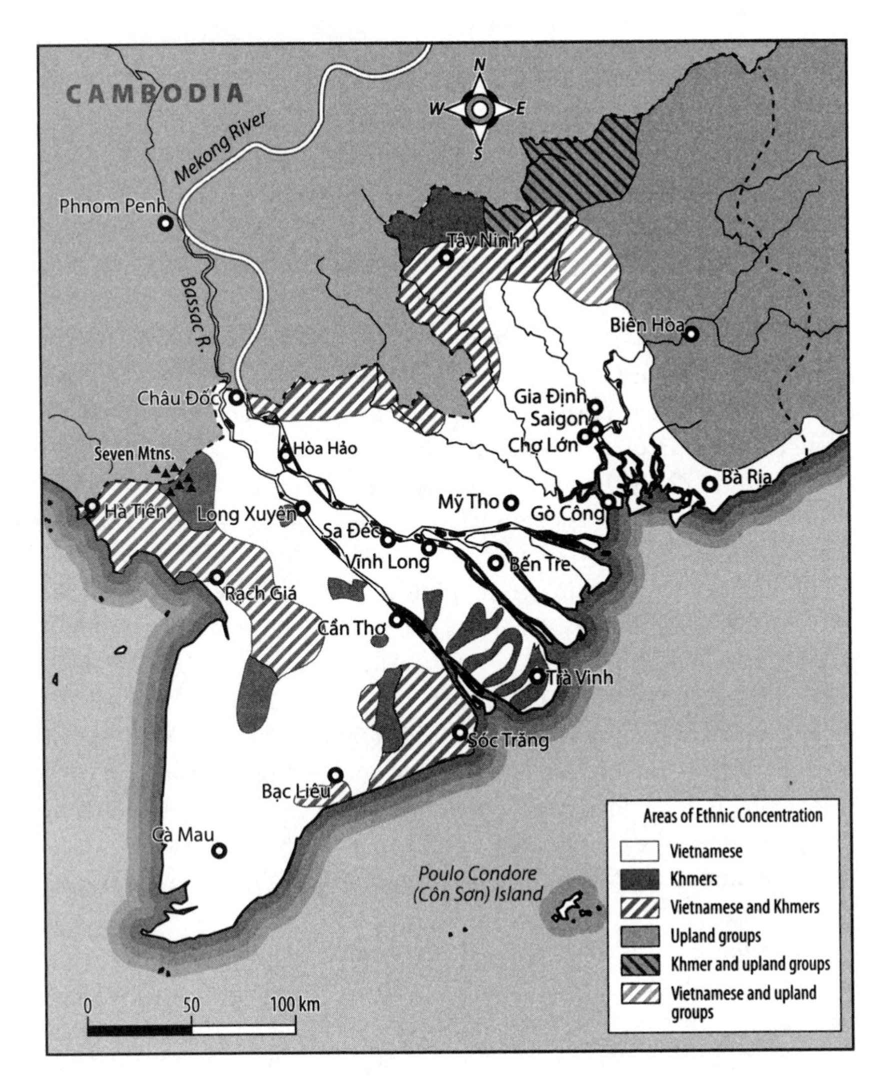

Fig. 8.3
French Cochinchina (Nam Kỳ)

male villagers. Unlike in Annam and Tonkin, direct colonial rule of Cochinchina significantly undermined village autonomy and local leadership.[148]

French rule also brought to Cochinchina a massive expansion of the cultivation and export of rice and, to a lesser extent, of its import of manufactured goods. The colony's economy became increasingly tied to external markets. In the years 1860–77, Cochinchina's annual rice exports rose from 57,000 to 319,000 tons. The number of European ships entering Saigon harbor each year rose from 272 in 1865 to 403 in 1877, while the number of junks and barges fell from 5,500 to 3,500.[149]

Exploitation of the international rice market brought major changes to the geography and ethnic makeup of Cochinchina. In the countryside, French officials and entrepreneurs began to supervise the draining of large swampy areas, especially those long inhabited by Khmers in the western Mekong delta, digging canals and opening up much new land to cultivation. The years between 1886 and 1930 saw the draining of 1,425,000 hectares (ha) of land in western Cochinchina, whose population increased from 391,000 to more than 1.45 million.[150] This increase affected all three major ethnic groups of western Cochinchina.[151] But Khmers lost ground to Vietnamese westward internal migration. From 1886 to 1928, in-migration plus natural increase in the western delta saw the number of Vietnamese there rise to 1.13 million, while the number of ethnic Cambodians grew more slowly to 224,000, and the ethnic Chinese population reached 44,000.[152] Every year small numbers of ethnic Khmer families chose to move upriver into Cambodia.[153]

Throughout Cochinchina from 1873 to 1920, the area of cultivated riceland increased sixfold—from 275,000 to 1,752,000 ha. The population more than doubled to 3.8 million. Cochinchina's rice production increased tenfold from 300,000 tons in 1870 to 3 million in 1930. Its rice exports continued to soar, quintupling from 295,000 tons in 1880 to about 1.5 million tons in 1920.[154] The increases in Cochinchina's cultivated area and labor force more than compensated for the local impact of the successive El Niño droughts during the period 1876–1902, and later when the years 1913 and 1914 fell among the forty driest years in southern Việt Nam's entire climate record.[155]

But in social terms the fruits of the economic expansion were ever more unevenly distributed. A small number of absentee landlords with large estates, both French and Vietnamese, monopolized most of the new riceland in the west, and landlordism also became dominant in central and eastern Cochinchina. Trần Bá Lộc, for instance, became one of the south's leading landowners. By 1930 only one-quarter of the rural families in Cochinchina owned any land. Tenants farmed four-fifths of the cultivated area.[156]

Rural society in Tonkin and Annam remained rather different from Cochinchina. From 1884 each of these Protectorates came under the authority of a French *résident-supérieur*, but unlike in Cochinchina, Vietnamese mandarins remained in place and Vietnamese law in force. At the village level, councils of notables retained much of their influence, and the proportion of communal land (*công điền*), which came under the village council's authority, remained significant: 20 percent of the cultivated area in Tonkin and 26 percent in Annam (more than 50 percent in Quảng Trị and Quảng Bình provinces), compared with only 2.5 percent or less in Cochinchina.[157] While notables on the village councils had privileged access to much of this communal land, some of it was also regularly rented out to landless peasants, who made up only a third of the rural population in Tonkin in the 1930s, compared with three-quarters in Cochinchina. Moreover, again in contrast to Cochinchina, nine-tenths of Tonkin's landowners were smallholders who owned less than 1.8 ha. Yet their holdings totaled only a third of the riceland, and the richest one-tenth owned nearly two-thirds of it. In northern and central Việt Nam, both the hierarchy of village life and its sense of solidarity remained stronger than in the more landlord-dominated, proletarianized, individualized southern rural economy.[158]

For example, offshore of the densely populated southern Tonkin delta province of Ninh Bình, the vast silt deposits of the Red River continued to create many small coastal islands. As these emerged slowly from the sea, the local Vietnamese Catholic community, led from the 1870s by the priest Trần Lục (known as Père Six), who maintained excellent connections with the colonial authorities, built dikes around the mudflats and opened the new lands up for cultivation.[159] Lục also organized the construction in Kim Sơn district of the famous Phát Diệm Cathedral, a triumph of ornate Vietnamese Buddhist-style architecture dedicated to the Queen of the Rosary and completed in the year of the priest's death in 1899.

By 1930, French property-owners had taken over much smaller areas of land in Tonkin (104,000 ha) and Annam (168,000 ha) than in Cochinchina (607,000 ha, more than a quarter of its cultivated area). Unlike even Cochinchina's villages, which direct French rule integrated more closely into the colonial legal structure and the international economy, Tonkin and Annam both imported and exported less than Cochinchina did.[160]

The urban populations of the north and center were also proportionately smaller and less cosmopolitan. Only about 4 percent of the people of Tonkin and Annam lived in urban areas, compared with 14 percent in Cochinchina. Hanoi's population of 80,000 in 1900 included only 1,000 French (4,000 by 1908), and 3,000 Chinese by 1912. Saigon's 70,000 residents in 1910 included 40,000 Vietnamese, but also 20,000 Chinese, Indians, and Khmers, and 10,000 French.[161] By 1921 the southern city was also home to more than 5,000 registered residents who had moved there from Tonkin and Annam.[162]

Colonial conquest also fostered cultural convergence in some spheres. In 1899, after the establishment of French Indochina with its capital in Hanoi, a decree amalgamating the civil services throughout the new colonial state exempted French officials from an obligation to know the Vietnamese language. This distanced them from their subjects but also raised the pressure on Vietnamese to study French and have their children learn it, which in turn earned them access to the romanized *quốc ngữ* alphabet. A network of French-medium schools established in Cochinchina in 1879, known as "Franco-Vietnamese" education, expanded to Hanoi.[163] By 1910, 4,900 Vietnamese students in Tonkin were enrolled in French-medium public primary schools, along with, by 1914, more than 40,000 in Cochinchina—where the first Vietnamese-language novels appeared in 1910–12.[164]

VARYING VIETNAMESE RESPONSES

As the economy and culture of colonial Việt Nam became increasingly internationalized, so did its political life. This occurred in both the intellectual and activist realms, in response not only to the conquest of Việt Nam but also to dramatic developments in China and Japan. In 1895–96, after Japan's victory in the Sino-Japanese War, the Vietnamese scholar Nguyễn Lộ Trạch borrowed the title of Nguyễn Trường Tộ's 1863 memorial for his own pioneering work *Thiên Hạ Đại Thế Luận* (Discussion on the dominant trends of the world), which drew attention to Japan's successful innovations. This was arguably Việt Nam's first indigenous work of "current affairs."[165] Analysis of contemporary "world trends," and global "conditions," including contemporary "trends in East Asia," soon became a key element of Vietnamese thinking which aimed to "suit the time."[166]

Then came the brief "Hundred Days of Reform" in China in 1898, and the repressive reaction there. Chinese-language works of the modernizing scholars Kang Youwei and Liang Qichao, who fled into exile in Japan, soon reached Huế. There, Vietnamese literati gathered to discuss them at the home of the scholar Đào Nguyên Phổ, who purchased copies despite the court's move to suppress these works.[167]

Meanwhile in the hills, the last anti-French rebel to survive was Đề Thám (1846–1913), who fought on with a couple of hundred followers until his capture in 1913. Thám, whose parents had been active rebels against the Nguyễn in the 1840s, carried on a dissident tradition.[168] And he held out just long enough to pass on that torch to Việt Nam's first generation of modern anticolonialists. These were led by two literati from central Việt Nam, Phan Bội Châu (1867–1940) and Phan Châu Trinh (1872–1926). The pair first met in Huế in 1903 but later fell out over different visions of the country's future and how to achieve them. The story of their interactions, disagreements, successes, and failures offers a window on Vietnamese political aspirations and choices under French rule.

Phan Bội Châu was the son of a poor scholar-teacher "whose ink bottle served as his rice paddy and his brush as his hoe." In mid-1885, aged eighteen,

Phan was taking the classical examinations in his native Nghệ An when word came of the Cần Vương revolt. He later recalled how he and sixty fellow students, like those in Bình Định, began organizing themselves into an anticolonial "Army of the Examination Candidates." Suddenly French troops "burst on the scene, burning and ravaging, shooting and killing. Smoke and flames obscured the sky."[169] Phan made himself scarce, and he stayed out of politics for a decade, studying and supporting his widowed father. But his 1885 experience, followed by the patronage of the principal of the Imperial Academy while he was teaching in Huế in the late 1890s, set his mind on "escaping from my cage." By 1900 he was absorbing the "new ideas" in Nguyễn Lộ Trạch's *Thiên Hạ Đại Thế Luận* and in Chinese works like Xu Jiyu's seminal *Ying huan Zhi lue* and Liang Qichao's histories of the Franco-Prussian and Sino-Japanese Wars. He wrote: "I began to have a rough idea of the rivalries in the world, and I was profoundly struck by the tragic prospect of the ruin of nations."[170]

Phan Bội Châu won first place in the 1900 Nghệ An regional examinations, earning the bachelor's degree (*cử nhân*, recommended men), but he eschewed an official career. In 1902, Phan made contact with Đề Thám and spent ten days in his jungle camp, finding there "an island of independence, even after the loss of our country." He also became interested in China's modernist reform movements. He read more of Liang Qichao, who aimed to reform China by modeling it on the West while preserving its monarchy. This led Phan to China, then to imperial Japan. For twenty years, in cooperation with Đề Thám and a dissident Vietnamese prince, Cường Để, Phan led an underground movement against the French occupation of Việt Nam. But he spent much of the period 1905–9 in Japan and another four years in a Chinese jail.[171]

Phan Châu Trinh had also participated as a youth in the Cần Vương movement, alongside his father, a Quảng Nam military official who was apparently murdered by others in the movement.[172] In 1900, at age twenty-eight, Trinh took the imperial examinations in Huế and received the *cử nhân* degree, advancing the next year to the doctoral level of *phó bảng* (supplementary list of "presented scholars").[173] But he was a critical student. He favored Mencius and the Analects of Confucius for their humane emphasis on the responsibilities of rulers to their subjects.[174] But he resisted prevalent trends "to adopt everything Chinese" and ignore "our national history," and he spurned Confucian etiquette and literary conventions such as the "eight-legged essay," a rhythmic format of four sections each comprising two couplets. He soon denounced "weak-kneed scholars who have been trained in eight-legged essays and who care only for their personal life." Trinh had already become "indignant with the world." He wrote later that his teachers considered him "ignorant and idiotic," as did fellow officials in 1903–4 when he worked as a secretary at the ministry of rites in Huế. As early as 1902, after Đào Nguyên Phổ acquired copies of Liang Qichao's "New Books" (*tân thư*), he provided them to Trinh.[175] Delighted, Trinh told himself: "This is the time that the ignorant and the idiotic may be useful!"[176]

Phan Bội Châu was also in Huế in 1903–4, as an intern at the Imperial Academy, and the two men met at the 1903 metropolitan examinations. Later, Trinh recalled, Phan Bội Châu "came to look for me at my boarding house in Huế." They became friends and briefly worked together to urge civil service candidates "to petition for the abolition of the civil-service examinations" and push for "political reform." They launched what Marr terms a "full-scale political assault on the mandarin system." Trinh blamed "the illusion of the examinations" and "the evil of the civil-service scholarship" for obscuring Việt Nam's "time-honored great national traits" and stunting its "shining spiritual qualities." But Phan Bội Châu was the first to come to the notice of the French. Trinh records that "in 1903, they wanted to arrest him twice." Having "arrested, questioned, and released him," the French pursued him again "but could not catch him."[177]

The two literati went their own ways. Phan Bội Châu traveled south to Cochinchina, back to Huế, and into the north. Having made connections with former Cần Vương activists, including upland minority leaders, he sought funds for a new organization. An associate counseled that Cochinchina was "the storehouse of money and provisions . . . the land that the Nguyễn dynasty opened up." Since the "financial resources" of the dynasty's founder Gia Long "all came from there," recruiting a Gia Long descendant had to be "the first move." Phan Bội Châu did win the secret cooperation of Marquis Cường Để, grandson of Gia Long's eldest son. But he also reached "a mutual understanding" with several "senior Catholics." A quarter century later he would proudly recall that the "overhanging clouds and murky fogs that separated Catholics and non-Catholics were swept away in an instant," leading to the "great support rendered to the patriotic cause by the Catholic people."[178]

A more inclusive vision of the country was slowly emerging, symbolized in the organization that Phan Bội Châu and Cường Để secretly founded in May 1904, the Việt-Nam Duy-Tân Hội (Vietnam Modernization Association). Theirs was the first political group to adopt in its title the name "Việt Nam," still rarely used at the time.[179] It was a logical choice for a new national movement that wished to avoid both the imperial tone of the Chinese "Annam" (Pacified South) and the regional limitation of its French usage (for central Việt Nam only). Phan Châu Trinh shared this vision when he wrote in 1910 of "our nation, Việt Nam." But in contrast to Phan Bội Châu, he registered a critique of the monarchy and its history, recording his sorrow that "because our current dynasty came from the South, the South and North have been treated differently. This is an evil." When he insisted that "the Vietnamese people are . . . not a single entity," he meant they were divided by politics, not geography.[180]

After hearing of Japan's first victories over Russia in their war of 1904–5, Trinh concluded that Việt Nam had to modernize. In late 1904 he and two friends who had just graduated with the highest degree (*tiến sĩ*, "presented scholars"), Trần Quý Cáp and Huỳnh Thúc Kháng, all resigned their posts in Huế. Early the next year they too headed to the south of the country on a "fact-finding" mission. Kháng later quoted Trinh as saying, "When the winds of change are blowing in all directions, you have to go and look to see what is happening." Passing through Bình Định, the three masqueraded as provincial examination candidates and submitted a poem and composition denigrating the mandarinal system. Trinh's poem went: "Thousands of people are slaves, underneath the stronger / Eight-legged literature is just a dream."[181] Like Phan Bội Châu, Trinh also targeted the arrogance of "Mandarins," the title of this text he wrote in 1904:

> One of them is said to have told his associates: "If you want to become a mandarin, you'd better be careful and don't read new [modern] books or look at new periodicals." Alas! Not knowing about the existence of new books and periodicals is one thing. But knowing about them and yet sealing off, blocking out, insuring that the story is not heard or seen—that is building and preserving for oneself a fundamentally slave-like character. People of that type should really make us sick![182]

Phan Bội Châu set out on his first visit to Japan. His guide was a native of Bình Định named Tăng Bạt Hổ. A veteran of the Black Flags and Cần Vương who had served in the retinue of the regent Tôn Thất Thuyết, escaped to China, worked on merchant ships, and visited Russia, Formosa, and Siam, Hổ was now "hiding in Hanoi."[183] In Hải Phòng in February 1905, he and Phan boarded a Western merchant vessel for China. They reached Tokyo in June and met with Liang Qichao and several sympathetic Japanese political leaders. Hổ served as interpreter, but Phan frequently engaged his Chinese and Japanese interlocutors in written "brush-conversations." Their common facility with Chinese characters led them to see themselves as members of the "same culture and same race" (*đồng-văn đồng chủng*) of East Asia. Phan told Count Ōkuma Shigenobu: "We have come here across the waves of the boundless ocean only because we are seeking a way to save the people in our country from death." Another Japanese politician told Phan he was "the first Vietnamese who has come to the Land of the Rising Sun to meet with our men in high positions." Before returning home, Phan set out his country's predicament in the rapidly written *Việt-Nam vong-quốc-sử* (History of the loss of Việt Nam), to which Liang added a foreword.[184]

This work betrayed Phan Bội Châu's rather naive understanding of the high colonial era. He excoriated France for having both conquered Việt Nam and "tricked foreign countries." Thus, he wrote, "No one investigates their evil deeds. Now isn't that treacherous cunning on the part of the French?" Yet Phan also wondered if perhaps France had "not necessarily tricked... the powerful nations of the five continents.... There may be another reason that I am just not able to explain yet."[185] He was only very slowly grasping the consonance of interests, the collusion as well as the competition that drove diverse colonial powers to divide up the globe among themselves. A lack of direct personal access to foreign societies hampered Phan's understanding. Of course he had mastered written Chinese as well as *nôm*, but he never learned to speak Chinese or Japanese, let alone French or any Western language, nor did he become proficient at writing in *quốc ngữ*.[186]

When Phan Châu Trinh visited Japan in early 1906, the outcome was different. En route in Guangdong, he met up with Phan Bội Châu. "Our joy was indescribable," the latter recalled. Cường Để secretly joined them, and after hearing Trinh urge abolition of the monarchy, the prince signed a self-admonition as "Enemy of the People Cường Để." All three went on to Japan. Phan Bội Châu showed them around Tokyo. Trinh was most impressed with the schools he saw. He became convinced that Việt Nam's future lay in popular education, without monarchism or anti-French violence. He advised Phan Bội Châu: "That some students now can enter Japanese schools has been your great achievement. Please stay on in Tokyo to take a quiet rest and devote yourself to writing, and not to making appeals for combat against the French."[187] It was unwelcome advice.

In Hong Kong on the return journey, the Phans fell out. It was their last meeting. Trinh, competent in French and *quốc ngữ* as well as literary Chinese, was moving intellectually beyond the East Asian cultural world. He was soon criticizing Phan Bội Châu's "shallow knowledge" and ignorance of "world trends," to which his books paid "no attention," while his writings were "molded by the eight-legged compositions, which are not worth a penny." Trinh asserted that Phan Bội Châu alternately "curses people" and "weeps bitterly," aiming to inculcate "malicious feelings among the people," and pursuing a "commitment to revenge" against France that "goes against world trends and does not follow reason."[188] Phan Bội Châu, as Trinh now described him, "adored" Japan for its "brute force" and sought aid from "this utterly unprincipled" state. Trinh "bade farewell to him on foreign soil. I did not look back and returned to our homeland."[189]

But the bitter break was not over eight-legged essays or faith in Japan. As Phan Bội Châu summed it up, Trinh "wished to overthrow the monarchy in order to create a basis for the promotion of popular rights; I, on the contrary, maintained that first the foreign enemy should be driven out.... My plan was to make use of the monarchy, which he opposed absolutely." Thus on the return home, according to Phan Bội Châu, Trinh "championed the position of 'Up with Democracy, Out with Monarchy,'" and "assailed the monarchy without questioning the French regime." Trinh himself put it differently: "He advocates violence, but I believe in 'holding on to France and looking for independence.'"[190] In Hong Kong he told Phan: "From the nineteenth century onward, the countries in the world have competed against one another more fiercely than ever. The fate of a country must be left in the hands of a large number of people. I have not seen any country survive in which the people's rights were lost. How can you uphold monarchism in this moment?"[191] The dilemmas Vietnamese faced were real enough to deeply divide men of similar background who saw in each other much to like and admire.[192]

Phan Bội Châu stayed mostly in Japan, where by 1908 he, Cường Để, and their Đông Du (Go East) movement managed to attract up to two hundred Vietnamese to pursue their studies. But in 1907, Tokyo made alliances with the colonial powers France, Britain, and Russia. The Franco-Japanese Treaty enabled Paris to demand Japan's support for French "territorial rights" in Asia. So in 1909, Tokyo deported Phan Bội Châu and Cường Để.[193] Their exile continued in Siam, China, Hong Kong, and Singapore. From 1913 to 1917, Phan Bội Châu even served a four-year prison sentence in Guangdong.[194] In 1915, Cường Để was able to return to Japan, where he lived until his death in 1951.[195]

Of course both Phan Bội Châu and Phan Châu Trinh deeply valued education, and their writings made frequent use of Confucian thinking and classical allusions.[196] Yet Trinh urged "getting rid of Chinese characters," while Phan Bội Châu's group favored "invigorating, improving Chinese studies." In both cases, their humanistic literary culture placed emphasis on "new ideas" and had little in common with the traditional Neo-Confucian ideology of imperial service, based on absolute loyalty to the emperor and moral superiority over "barbarians."[197] Much more rethinking was also necessary for most classically educated scholars to envision a future that would be very different from the past. But some eagerly took up the challenge identified in a popular song calling on Vietnamese literati to abandon the traditional practice of wearing their hair long. This song began to circulate in 1907 after Phan Châu Trinh made a rousing speech to students at the short-lived Tonkin Free School (Đông Kinh Nghĩa Thục):

> Comb in the left hand,
> Scissors in the right,
> Snip, snip, clip, clip,
> Watch out, be careful,
> Drop stupid practices,
> Dump childish things
> Speak openly and frankly
> Study Western customs
> Don't cheat or bluff
> Don't lie
> Today we clip
> Tomorrow we shave![198]

Phan Châu Trinh was now devoting his efforts to building schools and commercial and agricultural societies in his native Quảng Nam. In this way, from within Việt Nam, he aimed "to ally with France" and "petition the French government for improvements to the people's conditions," in the hope of "working within the French system for self-rule."[199] His hopes were dashed in 1908 by the forcible closure by the French of the Tonkin Free School and fierce repression of the peasant antitax revolts that erupted in Quảng Nam and eleven other provinces of central Việt Nam. From his base in Japan, Phan Bội Châu was encouraging violent protests, but Trinh was not involved in them.[200] Neither were his two literati friends, Huỳnh Thúc Kháng and Trần Quý Cáp, both of whom were also working to establish new schools in Quảng Nam and Nha Trang.[201] But the colonial authorities seized the excuse to arrest all three. Huỳnh Thúc Kháng and Phan Châu Trinh both received jail sentences on Poulo Condore island, far off the Cochinchina coast, serving terms of thirteen and three years, respectively. Trần Quý Cáp was convicted of treason in Nha Trang, and, at the order of a local mandarin, he was executed by being chopped in half at the waist.[202] The next year a missionary in Nghệ An informed French authorities that he had caught three local Vietnamese priests with papers revealing their involvement since 1906 in Phan Bội Châu's Đông Du movement. All three were sentenced to nine years' hard labor on Poulo Condore, where one of the priests died.[203]

In 1910 Phan Châu Trinh was released from Poulo Condore. Under house arrest at Mỹ Tho in the Mekong delta, he quickly wrote *A New Vietnam Following the Franco-Vietnamese Alliance*. He recorded what he knew of the

1908 repression: "I heard that, after the insurrection, wherever there were schools and agricultural societies, local soldiers came to occupy them and harassed people. . . . Many people have been murdered or sent to prisons." He lamented that "every single suspect was imprisoned," including "many innocent people," while "the number of people who have fled abroad is extremely high." Now, "men of high purpose are about to perish in remote mountains and on a distant island." Trinh later estimated that "the number of the literati and others who were murdered or imprisoned amounted to several thousands."[204]

While Trinh hoped to "promote a Franco-Vietnamese alliance," he had long found the French "highly skeptical" of Vietnamese who "called for such an alliance" from "outside of the country." That was one reason he returned from Japan, only to find that the French in 1908 "even wanted to murder those within the country."[205] He recalled having "presented my position to the Vietnamese officials; they thought that I was ignorant." Trinh now wrote: "I have met the French officials; they shared the Vietnamese officials' view of me. During the past several decades, the French have not adopted an enlightened policy in Vietnam." Yet his release from jail did come through the aid of French supporters, such as Ernest Babut of the Ligue des Droits de l'Homme. Trinh retained the hope that "great France" and its "progressive people of Europe" with their "chivalrous" spirit of "philanthropy and equality" would still "provide our Vietnamese people a lifeline to survive in the twentieth century." Conversely, he urged Vietnamese to "rid ourselves of our disposition to rely on China!"[206]

With Babut's help, Trinh was able to leave house arrest and take his son into exile in France. They arrived in Paris in April 1911, and for several years received funds to support themselves. Trinh spent much of this time translating into Vietnamese Liang Qichao's Chinese version of a Japanese novel exploring popular rights and revolution. The project didn't stop Trinh thinking about home; in a passage of the novel recording a poem sung by an Irish woman patriot, Trinh even replaced her reference to Japan ("At the end of the sea there is Japan, whose customs and manners are elegant") with two lines of his own, portraying instead Việt Nam's mythical origins and aquatic self-image: "The vestiges of Lạc Hồng still remain, after four thousand years of history, / In the mountains and in the sea, in the rivers, in villages, and in cities."[207]

Trinh continued to criticize French policy in Indochina, and when the First World War broke out he refused to serve in the French army. Arrested on a false charge of conspiring with Germany, he spent ten months in France's Santé political prison—while Phan Bội Châu languished in a Chinese jail. Again sympathetic French politicians, including Marius Moutet, secured

Trinh's release from incarceration, in July 1915. His son had been repatriated to Việt Nam and had died of tuberculosis in Huế. It took another decade, once more with the help of Moutet, who took up his case in the French Chamber of Deputies, before Trinh himself was allowed to go home. Within a year of his return, at the age of fifty-six, he too succumbed to tuberculosis. One last moment was an emotional reunion with Huỳnh Thúc Kháng, released from Poulo Condore in 1921.[208]

Phan Bội Châu and Phan Châu Trinh both assessed their careers as failures.[209] Each spent most of the period 1905–25 in prison and/or exile. Japan and China let Phan down; France disappointed Trinh. Yet the two brought new ideas into Vietnamese politics. And their campaign against the Chinese-based civil service examinations system succeeded. Classical examinations ended in Tonkin in 1916 and in Annam in 1919.[210]

The end of the traditional examinations system opened up new avenues of communications and advancement. In Cochinchina alone, the years 1916–18 saw the launch of no fewer than nine *quốc ngữ* periodicals (seven in Saigon and two in the Mekong delta towns of Cần Thơ and Long Xuyên). These included the first Vietnamese journal run by women, *Nữ Giới Chung* (Women's bell). Its editor in chief, Sương Nguyệt Anh, was the fifth daughter of the anticolonial blind poet Nguyễn Đình Chiểu (1822–88). She composed poetry in both Chinese and *nôm*—one of the last generation of Vietnamese to do so. Within five months of its appearance, the French authorities shut down Nguyệt Anh's *quốc ngữ* magazine after it published a "subversive" piece alluding to the patriotism of the first-century Trưng sisters.[211] Her death in 1921 at the age of fifty-seven signaled the close of a literary era. Meanwhile in 1917, two wealthy Saigonese with French citizenship launched the first Vietnamese-owned, Vietnamese-run political newspaper, the French-language *Tribune Indigène* (Native tribune), which appeared biweekly and called itself "the barometer of Vietnamese public opinion." The next year they established an affiliated weekly *quốc ngữ* edition, *Quốc Dân Diễn Đàn* (National forum).[212]

Phan Bội Châu and Phan Châu Trinh led a generation of the country's classical-educated anticolonialists into twentieth-century nationalism and political reform and inspired a cohort of younger activists to take up the cause of Việt Nam's independence. Yet their critique of traditional thinking was not entirely new or imported from abroad. It was in part a legacy of pioneering nineteenth-century Vietnamese thinkers. Thus their critical approach had become apparent early in the careers of both men. So had their own influence. Writing his autobiography at age sixty-two, Phan Bội Châu recalled "a convivial occasion" three decades before, in Nghệ An in 1899, when he was reciting a few lines of Chinese poetry. The verse mentioned

Phan's hope at the time, "To leave a name for future generations; / But what worse way to stand out from the crowd / Than fame for passing the examinations!" A ten-year-old boy in the audience, Phan wrote in 1929, had not forgotten the experience or the lines of verse, "and he is still able to recall them now."[213] The boy was Nguyễn Sinh Cung, who later took the name Hồ Chí Minh.

Nghệ An was the heartland of the 1885–95 Cần Vương anticolonial revolt led by Phan Đình Phùng. Like the latter and Phan Bội Châu, Hồ came from a family of scholars. Hồ's father knew Phan Bội Châu and was also a friend and fellow 1901 *phó bảng* graduate of Phan Châu Trinh's.[214] By 1911 the Sûreté in Annam "strongly suspected" him of "complicity with Phan-Boi-Châu, Phan-Châu-Trinh and others" and considered his daughter, Hồ's sister Thanh, a "good friend" of "bandits."[215] As manager of a barracks, Thanh used her post to smuggle weapons to Đề Thám's guerrillas.[216]

Hồ learned French as well as Vietnamese in secondary school, and then taught *quốc ngữ* and French for a year in Cochinchina. In late 1911, at age twenty-one, he enrolled in a navigation course in Saigon. For two years he worked as a kitchen hand on a ship traveling back and forth between France, Boston, and New York. From Boston and then London, where he spent part of the First World War as a hotel dishwasher and cook, Hồ wrote to Phan Châu Trinh in Paris.[217] Meanwhile one hundred thousand Vietnamese peasants and artisans were dispatched to the defense of France. Hồ denounced this in *The Trial of French Colonialism* (1923): "They perished in the poetic desert of the Balkans," where France had sent them "to be hacked up."[218] The 1916 Easter Rising against British rule in Ireland caught his attention as an anticolonial movement. Late in 1917 he moved to Paris, just before news arrived from Russia of the first communist revolution. Hồ joined the French Socialist Party, because of its "sympathy for the struggle of the oppressed peoples." He also worked closely with Phan Châu Trinh. At the Versailles Peace Conference in 1919, Hồ tried to present a request for equal rights and freedoms for French and Vietnamese. This made him well known in France. When the Socialist Party split and the French Communist Party formed in 1920, Hồ became a founding member as a "Representative of Indochina."[219]

"I, Trinh," began the letter from Paris to Đại Nam's Emperor Khải Định in 1922, "love democracy" and "abhor the tyranny of autocratic monarchy." Phan Châu Trinh was writing in the literary Chinese favored by the Nguyễn dynasty.[220] But he departed from Vietnamese tradition not only in critiquing the monarchy but also in using his personal name. At that time literati used either their family name, full name, or a pseudonym. Phan Bội Châu was known as Phan, and no one would have used the personal name "Trinh" to refer to Phan Châu Trinh. Only he did. Not until the postwar era did Vietnamese leaders come to be formally known by their personal names.[221] Even then, some from the older generation, Hồ Chí Minh for instance, continued to be known by their family name (or pseudonym). For "Trinh" to depart from this practice as early as 1922 was an innovation.

In "Monarchy and Democracy," a lecture delivered just before his death, Trinh even called the former emperor "Mr. Tự Đức." Quoting Tự Đức asking his court, "How could we possibly go to learn from the barbarians?," Trinh added wryly: "Well, I am not going to pass judgment on that king." His audience could "decide on [their] own what kind of king he was." Trinh's wish was "to ensure that everyone is equal"; even husbands and wives merited "equal footing." He aimed at "genuine democracy" through adopting "liberal ideas from Europe." In addition, he wrote, "Although socialism is so popular in Europe and has been widely expanded, people in our country are completely unaware of it, as if sleeping. How pitiful!" Trinh urged that in place of their divisions, "the Vietnamese must have solidarity" as a first step toward their country's "freedom and independence." To foster that, he added, "What can be better than circulating socialist ideas among the Vietnamese?" Trinh neither specifically mentioned communism nor renounced his longstanding objection to violent revolution; when he spoke of "revolutionary ideas," he seemed to mean European social democracy.[222] In a single speech he had urged the introduction to Việt Nam of "liberal," "revolutionary," and "socialist" ideas. A new era had begun. As Trinh saw it, "The world trends are . . . unrelenting. Those who go with them are sailing with the wind." Yet in the 1920s, these "winds of change" were still "blowing in all directions."[223]

CHAPTER 9

Writing and Revolution from Colonialism to Independence, 1920–54

Before his death Phan Châu Trinh lamented that Vietnamese still "know only their family and do not know their country." He wrote this in *quốc ngữ* in 1925, when only a few significant works of Vietnamese literature had been published in the romanized script.[1] Yet change was coming fast among a new generation of Vietnamese learning *quốc ngữ*. People born before 1900 still predominated among Vietnamese members of Cochinchina's colonial elite as late as 1943, but a much younger elite that included far more writers was about to inherit Việt Nam's cultural and political future.[2] As different historians put it, from 1920 to 1945 the French authorities not only "lost control of language strategy" but also lost control of Vietnamese politics.[3]

The romanized script enabled a revolution in print media and literature.[4] The 1920s saw the appearance of sixty Vietnamese daily and weekly newspapers, followed by no fewer than 428 newspapers and journals from 1932 to 1945.[5] The first great works of *quốc ngữ* literature were serialized in some of these new periodicals.[6] The rapid cultural transformation also fostered a new sense of national identity. Việt Nam in the 1920s and 1930s became the stage for a multiplicity of modern political parties amid alternating colonial repression and liberalization, economic depression, anticolonial and revolutionary revolts, a Buddhist revival, Vietnamese Catholic self-assertion, and the emergence in Cochinchina of new popular religious sects.[7]

The 1920s also brought more favorable weather for Vietnamese farmers. That decade, after sixty years of intermittent severe droughts associated with global El Niño events, was the country's wettest ever recorded. The years 1923, 1924, 1928, and 1929 were all among the forty highest-rainfall years since at least 1250—as were 1942 and 1943.[8] However, colonial neglect of the northern dike system, then the global depression, and finally World War II all undercut the economic impact of this sustained improvement in climate conditions.

From 1920 to 1954 two revolutionary processes swept Việt Nam into a new era: a cultural transformation of the educated elite and a distinct grassroots upsurge of local activism and nationwide protest provoked by colonial injustice and material deprivation. The communist movement that rose to dominate the country's political future was not a cause of either phenomenon but to some extent a product of each, as well as both an agent and a beneficiary of their powerful combination. Meanwhile Việt Nam became subject to a greater range of international influences than at any time in its history. The arrival of Japanese occupation forces in 1940 was followed by the outbreak of the Pacific War, catastrophic famine in northern Việt Nam, postwar revolution, an attempted French reconquest, and a long, debilitating, successful struggle for independence.

A VIETNAMESE CULTURAL REVOLUTION, 1920–40

The abolition of the classical examinations in Tonkin and Annam by 1919 meant that an administrative career there no longer required knowledge of Chinese. The future lay with the Vietnamese language and the *quốc ngữ* script. This and other reforms introduced under the governor general of French Indochina Albert Sarraut (1916–19) led to the expansion of Franco-Vietnamese school enrollments in both protectorates. Beginning in 1918 the Indochina government ended school tuition charges for the six primary-level years.[9] From fewer than five thousand in 1910, the number of public primary pupils in Tonkin by 1920 exceeded thirty-nine thousand, in a nationwide total of 123,000.[10] By 1922, Cochinchina alone had ninety thousand. Although French remained the sole official medium of instruction, in practice elementary schools in rural areas could offer classes in Vietnamese. This became official from 1924 with the introduction of a three-year sequence of elementary education in Vietnamese, designed to give "the native children the minimum of instruction indispensable to every man." Two years later, under socialist governor general Alexandre Varenne (1925–27), Vietnamese villages obtained the right to open local schools, at their own expense. In 1926, 229,000 Vietnamese pupils attended primary schools (including sixty-eight thousand in Tonkin).[11] In the next four years, this figure almost doubled to 435,000, including more than forty thousand female pupils, while an equal number of girls likely received *quốc ngữ* lessons at home or in the informal study groups proliferating across the country. Marr estimates that between 1920 and 1938, perhaps 1.2 million Vietnamese children obtained some primary education, usually enough to equip them to read their native language in *quốc ngữ*. By 1939 the government employed more than 6,500 Vietnamese primary teachers, 10 percent of whom were women. The number of Vietnamese able to read a newspaper rose from fewer than 750,000 in the mid-1920s to 1.8 million, or 10 percent of the population, by 1939.[12] In the next five years, school enrolments rose from 450,000 to 700,000. This was still only one in seven school-age children, but a new elite was forming, including one thousand Vietnamese students at the University of Indochina, in Hanoi.[13] Those who could read Chinese and (except among traditional healers) *nôm* characters were fast declining in number.[14] Moving into a new cultural future, Việt Nam was becoming cut off from its literate past.

The colonial administration had long fostered *quốc ngữ* in the Cochinchinese press, through Trương Vĩnh Ký and other former interpreters. Well-established in Saigon, from the 1910s a *quốc ngữ* public culture also spread in Tonkin. First, two new government-financed *quốc ngữ* journals began publication in Hanoi, edited by graduates of the French School of Interpreters there.[15] The founding editor of *Đông Dương tạp chí* (Indochina review), Nguyễn Văn Vĩnh (1882–1936), had participated in Hanoi's short-lived Tonkin Free School; he now aimed to highlight "the good work done by the government." More importantly, Vĩnh believed that the country's future, "good or bad, will depend on *quốc ngữ*," the study of which was "a question of life and death for Vietnam." In 1913–18, *Đông Dương tạp chí* published *quốc ngữ* translations of works in French (including those of Dumas, Hugo, Balzac, and Molière) and Chinese (e.g., *The Romance of the Three Kingdoms*). Vĩnh did some of the translations himself. He also edited an offshoot *quốc ngữ* weekly newspaper called *Trung Bắc Tân Văn* (Central and northern news), which became a daily in 1919 and ran continuously until 1945, "the longest-surviving *quốc ngữ* daily of the colonial period." In 1920, a commercial and landowning group established another Hanoi *quốc ngữ* daily.[16]

Nam Phong (South wind), a second government-funded Vietnamese journal, appeared in Hanoi in 1917. A monthly magazine edited by the established savant Phạm Quỳnh (1892–1945), it published articles in *quốc ngữ*, French, and Chinese.[17] As Quỳnh stated in its inaugural issue, he aimed "to disseminate the sciences of the West, in particular French thought and culture, to preserve the national essence of Vietnam, and to defend the economic interests of the French and the Vietnamese." But *Nam Phong* was "particularly intent on the elaboration of a literature in *quốc ngữ* to form a national literature." It was imperative, Quỳnh added, to build "a new elite culture to replace the old one which is almost lost."[18] In his view, Vietnamese should avoid politics and focus on their culture and education: "As long as our language lasts, our country will last."[19] Culture (*văn hoá*), he wrote in 1930, comprised the nation's "roots" and required cultivation before its "branches" could grow successfully.[20] Quỳnh was confident colonial rule would permit this. French policy was "not deviating from humanity," he asserted, because "to conquer the land of other people and then to endeavour to guide them along the road to progress is not an unjust action."[21] Quỳnh was editor of *Nam Phong* for seventeen years until it ceased publication in 1934.

Also founded in 1917, the French-language biweekly *La Tribune Indigène* was for three years Cochinchina's sole legal Vietnamese political newspaper. Edited by the older Paris-educated agronomist Bùi Quang Chiêu, it billed itself as "the only indigenous newspaper enjoying freedom of expression." But from 1920 to 1924, Chiêu and other Vietnamese participants in "public politics" gradually asserted more independence of the government, and six new Cochinchinese newspapers began publication in *quốc ngữ*. The lively French-language press, too, was published and read not only by Europeans (who in 1921 comprised 6 percent of Saigon's population, rising to 10 percent by 1928).[22] In July–August 1919, the Vietnamese-run *Tribune Indigène* even serialized Hồ Chí Minh's recent declaration in Paris, *Revendications du peuple annamite* (Demands of the Vietnamese people), which caused a stir in colonial Saigon. In 1922 the young Nguyễn An Ninh, who had attended Franco-Vietnamese schools in Mỹ Tho and Saigon, returned home from Paris, where he had earned a law degree and become a confidant of Hồ and Phan Châu Trinh. In Saigon in 1923 he launched a new newspaper, *La Cloche Fêlée* (The cracked bell), in which he campaigned against colonial injustices and corruption.[23] Already in 1922 the British consul general had expressed his surprise that "the Saigon papers" (presumably the French-language ones) enjoyed "apparent immunity" from government repression. "From time to time they contain direct charges of malfeasance of one sort or other directed against some highly placed official or prominent merchant."[24] For two years, Nguyễn An Ninh advocated Vietnamese cooperation with the French and acceptance of their tutelage. But in March 1926, he announced to a large rally: "The French have nothing more to do here. Let them return the land of our ancestors to us. Let them quit the country so that we can govern ourselves." Three days later, as 140,000 Vietnamese converged on Saigon for the funeral of Phan

Châu Trinh, French police arrested Nguyễn An Ninh, jailing him for a year. His newspaper changed its name to *L'Annam* and moved in a Marxist direction until his successor's arrest led to its closure two years later.[25]

Saigon's first independent *quốc ngữ* daily, *Tân Thế Kỷ* (New century), appeared in November 1926 and quickly gained a circulation of six thousand copies per issue. Its staff included reporters from Cochinchina but also some from Annam, who campaigned vigorously against both French authorities and the Huế court and mandarins ("slaves in the hands of the powerful barbarians"). In the Protectorate of Annam, court-imposed censorship delayed the establishment of any independent newspaper. But the Saigon press published articles written by correspondents there. *Tân Thế Kỷ* was banned first in the protectorate (and three of its local contributors arrested), and then finally in 1927 it was also banned in Cochinchina.[26] However, the resourceful Huỳnh Thúc Kháng, longtime friend of Phan Châu Trinh, won election to the new consultative Annam Chamber of Representatives for a three-year term and also managed to launch Annam's first independent newspaper, *Tiếng dân* (Voice of the people), which he edited and published in Huế from 1927 to 1943. *Tiếng dân* became central Việt Nam's "most important and longest-lasting newspaper" of the colonial era.[27]

Modern Vietnamese literature, which had emerged in Cochinchina in the 1910s, grew faster in the 1920s as *quốc ngữ* literacy and printing expanded rapidly north into Tonkin and then Annam. Along with the newspapers, the 1920s to 1940s saw the publication in Việt Nam of nearly fourteen thousand different books and pamphlets, including about ten thousand *quốc ngữ* titles—fifteen million volumes. About 10 percent of these have been called "modernizing essays and translations," mostly inspired by Western thought and technical achievements. But *quốc ngữ* printers also published modern novels and short-story collections (24 percent of the total) and religious works (20 percent).[28]

Việt Nam's fast-growing two major cities provided an audience. The population of Saigon–Chợ Lớn, 232,000 in 1918, increased to 324,000 in 1931, while Hanoi's population doubled between 1921 and 1937, to 154,000.[29] The first Vietnamese prose novels, printed in Saigon in 1910–12, had retained a traditional focus on Confucian morality, but the first to appear in Hanoi, serialized in *Nam Phong* in 1925, did not.[30] A tragic romance written by twenty-nine-year-old Hoàng Ngọc Phách, it was entitled *Tố Tâm*; its eponymous heroine cannot marry her lover because her parents have promised her to another. She dies of sorrow on the final page. Noting the novel's "rupture with the past," Lê Thành Khôi attributes its "immense success" to a sensitivity to the mindset of its time: "the helplessness of youth in the face of colonial violence and the loss of traditional values." Philippe Papin adds that *Tố Tâm* demonstrated the possibilities for Vietnamese to write "desinicized" literature shaped by a Westernized form and content. Between French and Confucian cultures, and old and new generations of Vietnamese, Hanoi became "the distinctive, hybrid capital" of avant-garde literature.[31]

Hanoi was home to the Self-Reliant Literary Group (Tự lực văn đoàn), launched in 1932 by the twenty-six-year-old Montpellier- and Paris-trained Nguyễn Tường Tam (alias Nhất Linh) and his younger brothers. This mostly French-educated circle, which included a novelist, poets, and the fashion designer who pioneered the modern form of Vietnamese women's traditional dress, ran two weekly newspapers and its own publishing house—Tonkin's most influential press in the 1930s. The youthful members of this group are classed as romantics, but they wrote with a terse clarity, eschewed staid classical images and allusions, and vigorously opposed Phạm Quỳnh's attempts to both preserve Việt Nam's "natural essence" and limit Vietnamese political activism.[32] The Self-Reliant Literary Group's ten-point manifesto began:

> 1) Modernize completely, without hesitation, and modernization means Westernization; 2) Have faith in progress, believe that things can get better; 3) Live according to an ideal; 4) Work for the good of society; 5) Train your character; 6) Encourage women to go out into the world; 7) Acquire a scientific mind.[33]

A very different example of the vitality and rapidity of the urban cultural transformation occurring in Hanoi was the realist style of the *quốc ngữ* writings of Vũ Trọng Phụng.[34] Phụng was a member of the first generation of northern Vietnamese students to receive a free primary education only in French and *quốc ngữ*. He left school at fourteen and began working in publishing as a clerk for Tonkin's first professional journalistic daily, *Hà Thành Ngọ Báo*, to which he contributed short stories from 1930. Then, historian Peter Zinoman notes, from 1932 until his death at age twenty-seven in 1939, Phụng wrote for thirteen other journals and newspapers in the lively literary world of Hanoi and Hải Phòng. His work revealed the influence of French and Russian writers, from Zola to Malraux, Dostoevsky, and Gorky.[35] In 1934 he took his approach into the Vietnamese countryside when he interviewed foreign legionnaires and local women in Bắc Ninh for his documentary narrative *The Industry of Marrying Europeans*.[36] But Phụng was above all a close observer of Hanoi's urban scene, publishing reportage on prostitutes, gamblers, con men, domestic workers, and actors. His serialized *Số đỏ* (*Dumb Luck*), a modernist "sidewalk novel," satirized characters from Hanoi street life and pilloried Nhất Linh as "Mr. Civilization," ridiculing his mild legal reformism and the Self-Reliant Literary Group's obsession with "modernization, Europeanization, and progress."[37]

In yet other literary circles, however, age-old themes persisted. The poet Vũ Đình Liên (1913–96) "instinctively reached for a water-related metaphor," guiding readers in a boat up the silent "stream of time" to voice his nostalgia for the precolonial era.[38]

NEW RELIGIOUS MOVEMENTS

Confucianism, Buddhism, and Daoism—the "three religions" (*tam giáo*) of traditional Việt Nam—had long coexisted and intermingled. Colonial displacement of the Confucian cultural worldview now occasioned the rise not only of a new Westernized literary culture but also of Buddhist literature, resulting by the 1930s in an "explosion of cheap or free religious tracts" in *quốc ngữ*. Like the advent of indigenous political newspapers, Việt Nam's "Buddhist Revival" has also been dated to around 1920 in Cochinchina. One of its founders was Lê Khánh Hòa, a monk from Bến Tre in the Mekong delta, who aimed "to launch a movement to revive Buddhism in the six provinces," meaning Cochinchina. This again was a "text-oriented movement," one of whose goals was the publication and dissemination of Buddhist scriptures, including the translation into Vietnamese of important Chinese religious texts. Việt Nam's first Buddhist journals were *Pháp âm* (Sound of the law), which Lê Khánh Hòa launched in 1929, and a periodical that addressed the newly literate younger generation, *Phật hóa tân thanh niên* (New Buddhist youth). Cochinchina was the home of most Buddhist publications, including one newspaper printed in Chợ Lớn and another at a temple in Rạch Giá in the Mekong delta. Saigon had two Buddhist magazines; the delta had two in Trà Vinh and two more in Baria and Sóc Trăng. By contrast, in the north French restrictions prevented the establishment of the Tonkin Buddhist association until 1934, when it quickly registered twenty-one thousand paying members. Its Hanoi publications backed both the French government and the Vietnamese monarchy. A similar association in Huế published a magazine entitled *Viên âm* (Words of the Buddha).[39]

The more autonomous and syncretic Buddhism of Cochinchina was evident in what intelligence agents of the French Sûreté (security police) called "a religious demonstration consisting of a procession of two hundred

Vietnamese and Cambodian monks," presumably from both the Mahayana and Theravada schools, who gathered in November 1922 in the sacred Seven Mountains area of the Vietnamese border province of Châu Đốc. Their ostensible purpose was to mourn victims of a boat accident on the Bassac River. The Sûreté suspected "a political motive," and its investigation concluded that "individuals" had made "requests of the inhabitants in order to raise money in the hope that it would one day be used in the cause of revolution."[40] However, the Seven Mountains region's history of religious syncretism would persist in Cochinchina's millenarian Buddhist circles.[41]

A different example of the Buddhist revival in Cochinchina was newspaper editor Nguyễn An Ninh's interest in the religion after his release from jail in 1927. He returned to his native village outside Saigon, "arranged his house in Buddhist fashion, shaved his head, wore the simple black pajamas characteristic of southern peasants, and began to bicycle around the countryside selling his own brand of medicinal ointment." He recruited a modest following until October 1928, when the authorities imprisoned him once again (this time imposing a three-year sentence for clandestine activities) and arrested hundreds of his peasant supporters. Ninh studied Buddhism seriously, though he was eventually unconvinced and in 1937 published a book entitled *Phê Bình Phật Giáo* (A critique of Buddhism).[42]

In 1936 a monk from Rạch Giá could look back proudly and stress the role of print culture in his religion's rejuvenation: "For the last seven or eight years, the movement to revive Buddhism in our country has developed vigorously.... Whether it is with weekly newspapers or monthly reviews, monks and lay believers cooperate with one another, publish on and study the canonical classics, translate into Vietnamese and publish collections of Buddhist books, speak out on the aims of the Buddha, and proselytize among humanity."[43] This new religious movement could not have occurred without a *quốc ngữ* readership and press. Additionally, the Buddhist revival probably could not have first emerged in either Tonkin or Annam, which despite their long Buddhist heritage offered less fertile ground for innovation than Cochinchina, with its plurality of rural cultures, relatively brief Confucian implantation, longstanding French policies that delegitimized mandarinal authority and classical texts, and less repressive colonial legal system than those of the protectorates.

Vietnamese Catholic communities had been using the *quốc ngữ* script since the seventeenth century. But paralleling the rise of a national consciousness among Vietnamese in general, Catholicism in Việt Nam was undergoing a major transition from a missionary-run pastoral institution to a self-consciously national and nationwide religious community. The first Vietnamese Catholic periodical was a *quốc ngữ* religious bulletin that appeared in 1908. By 1945, Việt Nam boasted more than twenty Catholic periodicals.[44]

One of the most independent was Tonkin's first Catholic *quốc ngữ* periodical, *Trung Hòa Nhật Báo* (Impartial), published in Hanoi from 1923 to 1945, which by 1927 had achieved a circulation of four thousand throughout Việt Nam. Another was *Công Giáo Đồng Thinh* (Catholic voice), a biweekly published in Saigon from 1927 to 1937. Both papers addressed contemporary social and anticolonial issues and ran into trouble with the authorities. Nguyễn Bá Chính, the founding editor of *Trung Hòa Nhật Báo*, considered Catholicism at least compatible with Vietnamese patriotism and hoped his newspaper would dispel "ill-grounded doubts about Catholics," who were unjustly "written off as traitors in this nation." Bishop Gendreau of Hanoi wrote of the paper in 1925: "I barely read the articles at all, having not enough time or enough knowledge of the new modernized language." However, he thought the paper required "surveillance," and by the late 1920s both it and its new Saigon counterpart suffered from Sûreté censorship. The founding editor of *Công Giáo Đồng Thinh* was Đoàn Kim Hương, who described it as "a social organ" that would "struggle for citizens to live in security and good health, struggle for Vietnam's progress, cultural growth and prosperity in the countryside." Another early editor was the youthful Huỳnh Phúc Yên, former correspondent in Laos for the French-language *Echo Annamite*. Yên favored a "social nationalism" wherein "all individuals were equal before God and would cherish their homeland." He urged his readers to "pray to God" that "the three regions of north, center, and south be as one." After he took up anticolonial and labor causes in the late 1920s, Yên found himself removed from the editorial board of *Công Giáo Đồng Thinh*. Similarly, in Hanoi Nguyễn Bá Chính resigned as editor of *Trung Hòa Nhật Báo* in 1932 because, as he complained to the governor general's office, foreign missionaries had "transformed" the paper "into a purely religious journal."[45] Its circulation fell by more than half to around 1,500 in 1937. But by then, Việt Nam's fifteen Catholic newspapers and journals were together printing tens of thousands of copies a month.[46]

The development of a national church gathered pace. The year 1933 saw the establishment of the country's first Catholic secondary school and the ordination in Rome of the first Vietnamese bishop, Jean-Baptiste Nguyễn Bá Tòng. In 1935, the Catholic writer Lê Thiện Bá greeted the ordination of a second Vietnamese bishop as a national achievement: "Now we see Vietnamese—not only one from the south several years ago, but now another from the center—who have risen to the position of bishop, an important position that in the past in our country was a title that only Europeans held, which proves that Vietnamese are not inferior to Westerners."

The first two Vietnamese bishops took over the populous northern dioceses of Phát Diệm and Bùi Chu (the latter alone ministered to a quarter of a million Catholics), based in the Red River delta provinces of Ninh Bình and Nam Định, respectively. The third bishop, Ngô Đình Thục, educated in Rome and ordained in 1938, took over the Mekong delta diocese of Vĩnh Long. When he visited Tonkin in 1940, local Catholic students welcomed Thục with a song, "We see clearly that CENTER SOUTH NORTH three regions are linked," and he responded with a Latin version of Psalm 133, "How good and pleasant for brothers to live in unity." As historian Charles Keith notes, Thục infused Saint Augustine's prescription of monastic brotherhood "with a different meaning," inclusive of a national fraternity.[47]

If the social and cultural transformation of colonial Việt Nam could be considered in part the modernization and internationalization of Vietnamese elite culture, the emergence in Cochinchina in the 1920s of the Cao Đài religious sect was an example of its extension from urban society to the rural population.[48] It also showed that the rapid dissemination of a "national" script had not just privileged the emerging modern nationalism but facilitated regionalism too: with few exceptions the Cao Đài's growing mass appeal was limited to Cochinchina. Even there, in its first decade the sect quickly broke up into six provincially based subsects.[49]

The Cao Đài sect arose in the early 1920s in overlapping circles of educated Vietnamese midlevel colonial civil servants who had held posts in provinces throughout urban and rural Cochinchina. Its beliefs and practices drew on Sino-Vietnamese Daoism, a Buddhist concept of salvation, Chinese immigrant secret society ritual, the institutional structure of Catholicism, and French secular urban spiritism and séances. All of these had taken root in Cochinchina, in Saigon–Chợ Lớn or the Mekong delta, or both.[50]

The Cao Đài's founder, Ngô Văn Chiêu, son of a rice-mill employee, grew up in Chợ Lớn and the delta town of Mỹ Tho, attended French schools, and joined the Cochinchina civil service in 1899. He served in Saigon, Tân An, Hà Tiên, and the island of Phú Quốc in the Gulf of Siam. Around 1918, Chiêu attended séances at a temple near Cần Thơ in the central delta. It was there, and again in 1920 at Hà Tiên, much of whose population is of Chinese and Cambodian extraction, that he made contact with a spirit he named Cao-Đài Tiên Ông (His Excellency the Immortal).[51] Cao-Đài (literally "high tower") is a Daoist term for the Supreme Being. Unlike other Caodaists, Chiêu was also familiar with the practice of European spiritism.[52] In 1919, he befriended a dignitary of one of the Daoist Minh ("light") sects, the Minh Sư, a China-based vegetarian sect that had previously dedicated itself to the overthrow of the Qing dynasty and maintained a temple in Saigon named Ngọc Hoàng Điện (Jade Emperor Palace). The head of the Minh Sư in the delta had also been a key secret leader of Phan Bội Châu's movement there. On Phú Quốc in 1920–24, Chiêu became a vegetarian and an adept of the Cao Đài spirit. He adopted the "great eye" as its symbol.[53]

Back in Saigon in 1925, Chiêu hung out at the Jade Emperor Palace and began to convert friends, including several Saigon and Chợ Lớn officials, to his new Caodaism. Two were fellow graduates of Saigon's Collège Chasseloup-Laubat. Nguyễn Ngọc Tương had also been educated in Chinese. In 1920, Tương also made contact with the Minh Sư sect and began to study its doctrines, and he served as district chief near Hà Tiên in 1920–24 while Chiêu was offshore on Phú Quốc. Of a similar age and education, Lê Văn Trung, son of a small farmer from Chợ Lớn province, had also joined the civil service but left in 1905 to start a successful business career. By 1925 Trung had gained a prestigious colonial appointment to the Conseil Supérieur de l'Indochine.[54]

A slightly younger group, who held more junior posts in the colonial administration and seem to have had Catholic backgrounds, were already practitioners of spiritism, using a Ouija board in the "European manner." Historian R. B. Smith observed that the Ouija board had become "perfectly suitable for the Vietnamese language, once it had begun to be written in the roman script of *quốc-ngữ*." An organizer of these séances, and a spirit medium himself, was the Saigon customs clerk Phạm Công Tắc.

These Saigon circles merged when Lê Văn Trung held a séance at his house in January 1926. The most senior colonial officeholder, he began to organize the religious movement formally, and officially became its leader in May 1926. He then set out to expand it to the countryside. That year Trung gained official permission to establish twenty Cao Đài "oratories" in east and central Cochinchina and organized a petition to the government requesting the religion's formal recognition. It was signed by twenty-eight Cao Đài dignitaries, one of whom would later also head the Daoist Minh-Sư sect. In November, Trung moved Cao Đài headquarters to the provincial town of Tây Ninh, northwest of Saigon. There the sect built its Main Temple, which became its "holy see" and Trung its first "pope."[55] The Cao Đài established a hierarchical structure of priests, bishops, archbishops, and cardinals, whose *quốc ngữ* titles resembled those of Vietnamese Catholicism.[56] In addition, the sect proclaimed its own eclectic pantheon, including the Buddha; "Great Immortals" such as Confucius, the Mother Goddess, and Tang poet Li Po; and numerous "saints," including Laozi, Moses, Jesus, Muhammad, Pericles, Julius Caesar, Joan of Arc, the sixteenth-century Vietnamese literatus Nguyễn Bỉnh Khiêm, Victor Hugo, William Shakespeare, Louis Pasteur, Sun Yat-sen—and later Winston Churchill.

The Cao Đài quickly attracted many Vietnamese peasant followers. By mid-1928 the movement had recruited two hundred thousand adepts.[57] Not all were ethnic Vietnamese. Along with most of the Mekong delta provinces, Tây Ninh was home to a minority Khmer population. Lê Văn Trung proclaimed that the Cao Đài represented "Renovated Indochinese Buddhism," and he advocated mutual aid among Khmers and Vietnamese to improve their welfare. In the sect's possibly most eclectic gesture, its adepts erected a statue near the holy see, of a rider on a white horse quickly recognized as the Khmer folk figure Neak Mian Bon, a "man of merit" who would arrive to end all misery, and who in this case was identified with both the Buddha and a prince whose reincarnation was imminent. In late 1926 and 1927, tens of thousands of Cambodian peasants flocked across the border to Tây Ninh, alarming the French authorities, the Khmer Buddhist hierarchy, and Cambodia's king. In June 1927, five thousand Khmers prostrated themselves before the equestrian statue, and eight thousand attended a November Cao Đài festival. The next month King Monivong prohibited Cambodians from participating in this "heretical" sect. But in June 1928, when the Cao Đài proclaimed that a new Khmer king would appear to them at Tây Ninh, nearly ten thousand Cambodians traveled there.[58]

Cao Đài religious activity remained legal for Vietnamese, including those in Cambodia. Branches flourished among Phnom Penh's twenty-eight-thousand-strong Vietnamese community.[59] In Cochinchina by 1930, according to its French governor, the Cao Đài had converted more than half a million peasants, in a population of four million that included eighty thousand Catholics. By 1932, the sect claimed to have 135 oratories in the colony.[60]

Explanations for this success vary. In 1932, after his Buddhist phase, Nguyễn An Ninh published a skeptical work entitled *Tôn Giáo* (Religions). He dismissed Cao Đài philosophy: "You have to be very ignorant to dare to put Catholicism, Buddhism, Confucianism, the cult of the spirits, and mediumism all together." But Ninh thought the Cao Đài filled a vacuum in Cochinchina where, as a compatriot put it, "Buddhism had degenerated, Confucianism had disappeared, and Christianity was regarded as the religion of the conquerors."[61] Cao Đài themselves claimed to represent not only the "three religions" of Vietnamese tradition but also a combination of the world's faiths, of East and West, so that "Christianity and the wisdom of the Orient could meet under the umbrella of Caodaism." Historians describe the Cao Đài as, in turn, a "surrogate" for Cochinchina's "faltering rural leadership," a sect that formed "a link between town and country in a way that no previous movement was able to do," and a movement "in the van of the Vietnamese search for equivalence with the West."[62]

The Cao Đài movement's eclecticism contributed to its appeal, but also made it more liable to fracture. From 1926 until his death in 1932, even its founder Ngô Văn Chiêu associated himself with a more introspective, less political Cao Đài group in Cần Thơ, while Tây Ninh appears to have repudiated the oratory in Saigon.[63] In 1930 the movement began to suffer serious divisions, and in 1935 Phạm Công Tắc, heading his own inner sect, the Phạm Môn, became pope after the death of Lê Văn Trung. By then the holy see at Tây Ninh was only the largest of four such centers. In 1934 Nguyễn Ngọc Tương established a breakaway group in Bến Tre, which soon claimed thirty thousand members and sixteen temples. Two more "holy sees" affiliated with different Minh sects sprung up in Mỹ Tho (sixteen thousand members and seventeen temples in 1938) and Bạc Liêu (8,500 members, four temples). Along with a "Western Sect," the latter two formed a Caodaist Union in 1936, centered in Saigon and more amenable to French authority than Tây Ninh was. As the movement successfully spread across Cochinchina, it splintered into as many as twelve subsects by 1938. Geographically it also remained mostly confined to the south, though the Caodaist Union was later able to form branches in parts of central Việt Nam.[64]

Despite its institutional fragmentation and geographical constriction, the Cao Đài movement was capable of meeting the cultural and material needs of its faithful. While most of the original Cao Đài founders came from the landowning elite and salaried middle classes of Saigon and Chợ Lớn, most other Cao Đài dignitaries were local religious leaders and rural notables who often brought their peasant followings into the movement. Others were wealthy delta landholders who brought employment and social services to Tây Ninh.[65] The Cao Đài thus filled not just a religious need but a sociopolitical vacuum that was a function of the frontier nature of Cochinchina's rural society, the Huế court's early withdrawal of Confucian mandarins from the region, the colony's direct exposure to French power and culture, the weakening of its village institutions and communal solidarity, and the spread of absentee landlordism and wage labor there.

The Cao Đài thus flourished in a "crossroads" region.[66] Tây Ninh itself was Cochinchina's newest frontier, a historically and ethnically syncretic home for this eclectic faith. In 1860, the province was populated mostly by Khmers, with only four thousand Vietnamese residents, but from 1879 to 1936 settler in-migration multiplied the number of Vietnamese by a factor of twenty-five. Yet in 1930 Tây Ninh remained quite diverse, with its thirty-five Vietnamese villages, fourteen Cambodian villages, and one Cham village, as well as groups of forest-dwelling uplanders (whom the French called Montagnards) and 1,500 Chinese and mixed Chinese-Vietnamese who controlled local commerce from the provincial town.[67] Above the town and the holy see loomed Núi Bà Đen (Black Woman Mountain), named for an ancient Cham earth goddess.[68]

Unlike the Mekong delta provinces, Tây Ninh's soils were infertile, and it remained mostly forested, with few large landlord estates or tenant farmers. Two-thirds of its peasants owned small plots, but they were insufficient to feed a family, and most farmers depended on additional work, for instance in the large French-owned rubber plantations established there in the 1920s. The Cao Đài offered peasants alternative employment in collective farming groups, in handicrafts, and in small-scale manufacturing, and social services such as schools, adult instruction circles, a sports field, and a hospital. Eventually the sect's Tây Ninh education branch served twenty thousand students, and its Office of Social Services employed six thousand workers in three rubber plantations, a hundred public enterprises, and its seventy-five-bed hospital staffed by thirty-six nurses.[69] The Cao Đài's level of social organization was rare in Cochinchina.

ECOLOGICAL AND ECONOMIC CHALLENGES

One reason for the popularity of the Cao Đài and its mutual aid system was the material difficulties Cochinchinese were experiencing. From 1920 to the mid-1930s, the region's population rose from 3.8 to 4.5 million. The area of cultivated riceland in Cochinchina also continued to increase, from 1.75 million ha to 2.4 million.[70] But the major beneficiaries were a small number of large landowners: 244 property owners in Cochinchina each owned at least 500 ha of riceland in 1930–31. One man, Trần Trinh Trạch, owned 15,000 ha, and another controlled 18,000 ha. By the 1930s, tenants farmed four-fifths of the cultivated area of all Cochinchina.[71]

New land was also available for cultivation in Tonkin. In the southern delta province of Ninh Bình the Red River's silt deposits continued to create small offshore islands. Around 1906, a large mudflat appeared off the coast of Kim Sơn district, between two river branches. As alluvium slowly built up and extended the mudflats, some remained above sea level even at high tide. These new islands were named Cồn Thoi. The notables of Phát Diệm and three other densely populated, impoverished Catholic coastal villages applied to the authorities for a concession to establish communes there, build protective dykes, and bring the land under cultivation. But Tonkin's French résident supérieur withheld permission, instructing the communities to wait for natural siltation to complete the buildup of the islands. The villagers' second request and then a third, submitted in 1927, were also denied. Even a 1930 administrative order to regulate the ownership of mudflats and assign "riverine villages the necessary lands to safeguard their needs" failed to elicit a favorable ruling on this case. Five years later, Governor General René Robin also rejected a petition from Vietnamese Buddhist leaders and mandarins to allow peasants from other provinces of Tonkin to exploit the offshore land.[72]

Yet cultivation of new land was the only major form of agricultural growth in French Indochina. Vietnamese rice exports, mainly from Cochinchina to southern China via Chợ Lớn's ethnic Chinese trading houses, reached 1.55 million tons in 1937.[73] Significantly, however, neither the increasing concentration of landholdings nor Việt Nam's improved climatic conditions from the mid-1920s seems to have led to greater productivity. French Indochina's highest level of rice exports was 1.8 million tons in the record year of 1928. Yields per hectare even in the extremely wet years of 1928–29 remained lower in Tonkin, and were barely higher in Cochinchina, than they had been in the severe drought of 1912–13.[74]

Decades of low rainfall since the 1860s had once again left the northern dike system dry, crumbling, and vulnerable. The frequency of disasters increased after 1893; the two-decade "black" period of 1905–26 saw thirty-five serious breaks in the Red River's dikes. In 1915 a quarter of the Tonkin delta flooded, destroying the rice harvest over an area of 200,000 ha. The record wet years 1923–24 (the wettest two-year interval since 1258),[75] were followed in Tonkin in 1926 by breaches in the dikes opposite Hanoi and serious flooding, leading to poor harvests and deadly epidemics. In the face of the unprecedentedly high rainfall, colonial neglect of the dike system contributed to the lack of productivity gains even after the easing of the long years of recurrent drought. Dam reinforcement work in 1909 was apparently ineffective and was not undertaken again until 1918–24, 1926, and 1931; the more catastrophic breaches in the dikes ended only from 1927 on. Another factor in the absence of higher yields in Tonkin and Annam was overpopulation there, especially after 1920, and the limited extent of land reclamation (on the mudflats of Kim Sơn, for instance) before 1930.[76] In parts of the south, Tây Ninh at least, yields per unit of land did rise in the 1920s, but elsewhere in Cochinchina, as in Tonkin, peasant production increases came more from new land reclamation than from better yields. This was rural "growth without modernization."[77]

However, population growth and economic change fostered the rise of a new labor market. Tonkin's traditional skilled craft sector employed (in 1937) 1.3 million rural artisans, 7 percent of the population of the Red River delta, mostly well-integrated into its villages and its economy. But a modern sector had also emerged in some urban areas and colonial industries. In the decade 1919–29, the Vietnamese industrial workforce doubled in size from 100,000 to 221,000, making a fourfold increase since 1900.[78]

Indochina's first mechanized plant and the largest French industrial operation was the Ba Son shipyard in Saigon, which employed one thousand Vietnamese and Chinese workers. They staged strike actions in 1925 and, in concert with other workers, in 1927, prefiguring the nationwide grassroots activism of the next decade. During the 1920s, the number of northern Vietnamese who worked in French-run coal, zinc, and tin mines increased from twelve thousand to more than fifty thousand.[79] Coal exports, mainly to Japan and coastal Chinese cities, quickly expanded from about two hundred thousand tons in 1900 to 1.8 million tons by 1939. Miners' working conditions were poor, hours long (ten- to twelve-hour shifts were common), wages low, disease and death frequent. Workers on new coffee and tea plantations fared little better. Others labored on the new railways, cotton mills, cement factories, and petroleum refineries. More than seventy thousand northerners and central Vietnamese were drafted into laboring on Cochinchina rubber plantations, whose area expanded fast in the late 1920s from 18,000 to 79,000 ha, then to 103,000 ha by 1942. Northern Vietnamese "coolies" were also sent to plantations in Cambodia. As early as 1927 a French official remarked that workers at Cambodia's Mimot rubber plantation were "treated like human cattle, terrorized by the overseers."[80] Another official added: "Already 450 coolies have fled. Most of them have been recaptured and sent back to Mimot, and have undergone punishment that should frighten the rest."[81] From rice to coal, rubber, tea, and coffee, Việt Nam was for the first time producing exports on a large scale. Like its culture, the country's economy was undergoing rapid internationalization.

Việt Nam was also coming closer together. Work on a railway system commenced in the 1890s, and by 1942 it comprised nearly three thousand kilometers of rail lines that could quickly transport Vietnamese from the north of their country to the south. As early as 1920, "natives" comprised 94 percent of railway passengers, and in 1937 the system carried 1.2 million tons of freight. Moreover, "one of the finest road networks in East Asia" included, by 1943, thirty-eight thousand kilometers of paved roads carrying eighteen thousand vehicles. Colonial rule and capital also fostered a new seasonal, mobile wage labor force, up to 2 percent of the population, who escaped the reach of "traditional mechanisms of social control" such as "fathers, family elders, [or] village notables." In the 1920s "at least 600,000 Vietnamese men and women spent several years as non-rural wage laborers," subjected to more modern forms of social control. Thus not only laborers but a significant minority of peasants, in all "a rather large portion of the population" in the words of French economist Charles Robequain in 1939, experienced a "new way of life."[82]

Then in 1929–30, the Great Depression struck Việt Nam as no other world crisis had affected it before. By late 1933, rice prices plunged to one-twelfth of their 1928 level. Ruined peasants in Cochinchina left 400,000 ha of land uncultivated. To pay their taxes, small farmers had to put their land up for sale; in the already landlord-dominated four major provinces of western Cochinchina, 13 percent of the riceland changed hands in 1930–34. In the wake of crop failures, many landlords abandoned their tenants or raised the rent, "in an attempt to maintain their incomes by selling more rice."[83] Nguyễn Thị Định, then a ten-year-old peasant girl in Bến Tre in the Mekong delta, recalled many years later how the village landlord, named Muôn, "came to my house and demanded paddy in a threatening manner"; her parents had to ply him with alcohol, "catch the hen about to lay eggs which I had been raising, and slaughter it for him to eat."[84]

Throughout Việt Nam at least one hundred thousand workers, including a third of the country's industrial labor force, lost their jobs and returned to rural areas during the Depression.[85] In northern Việt Nam alone, a conservative newspaper reported in May 1930: "There are now one million persons who do not have enough clothes to wear or food to eat." In Annam, catastrophic flooding compounded the falling rice prices and caused peasants to abandon large areas of riceland. French reports noted that 30 percent of Annam's population suffered from hunger.[86] However, the government still attempted to collect taxes, even in advance in some cases, which provoked major peasant protests in the south, center, and north alike. Only Cao Đài–dominated Tây Ninh province, with its new, modest but unprecedented welfare system, remained "calm."[87]

THE RISE OF MODERN POLITICAL PARTIES

Việt Nam's "first public political movement" announced its existence in 1919. That April, Bùi Quang Chiêu's newspaper *La Tribune Indigène* added to its banner a new subtitle, "Organ of the Indochinese Constitutionalist Party." This moderate, relatively pro-French group officially registered itself in France in 1926 as the Constitutionalist Party of Cochinchina—it did not register in that colony until 1937. Most of its leadership, like Chiêu, were landed, prosperous, French-educated urban southerners committed to French-Vietnamese collaboration in the interests of what they saw as Việt Nam's modernization.[88] Constitutionalists, along with the newspapers Chiêu edited, *La Tribune Indigène* (1917–25) and its successor *La Tribune*

Indochinoise (1925–42), also promoted colonial recognition of the qualifications of educated Vietnamese professionals and their right to play a role in the political life and development of Cochinchina. In the colony, unlike in the Protectorates of Annam and Tonkin, this was a feasible goal. Cochinchina's economically successful Vietnamese were able to demand greater rights and equality under French law. In 1920, most Constitutionalist Party members were in the thirty-five-to-forty-five age group. The leaders were older, and included prominent names in Chiêu's French-language press and other Saigon-based organizations: the Association Mutuelle des Indochinois (founded in Paris in 1920) and its local branch that functioned as a government employees association, Le Cercle Franco-Annamite, the Cochinchinese Mutual Education Association, and the Association of Alumni of the Collège Chasseloup-Laubat. This was not an anticolonial group but one that comprised senior indigenous colonial figures seeking to maximize the benefits of French rule. Its first political campaign, launched in August 1919, was an anti-Chinese boycott targeting the grip on Cochinchina's commerce of Chinese Saigon–Chợ Lớn businesses.[89]

The party also called for electoral reforms, to raise the number of Vietnamese eligible to vote in elections for the Colonial Council of Cochinchina (which could ratify or reject budgets proposed by the colony's governor) and to raise the number of council seats set aside for Vietnamese members. Of Cochinchina's population of about 3.8 million, for instance, only 1,800 Vietnamese were eligible to vote in the elections of 1920; at stake were seven seats for French citizens and only four for *indigènes* ("natives"). But in 1922, the authorities widened the franchise to twenty thousand voters, including those landowners and businessmen who paid certain levels of taxation, officeholders of various levels, high school graduates, and decorated war veterans.[90] The number of seats reserved for Vietnamese increased to ten (with ten to twelve French seats); in the 1922 elections, Constitutionalists and their allies won five. A successful candidate captured the party's ethos with his campaign slogans, "Vive la France. Vive la Cochinchine," to which he added, in reference to the land reclamations in western Cochinchina that formed the economic base of so many of Saigon's French-educated elite, "Vive l'Ouest Agricole."[91] Along with their Cochinchinese focus, Chiêu and other leading Constitutionalists also welcomed the colonial state of "Indochina." They accepted its *mission civilisatrice* and saw themselves working alongside the French, playing leading roles in Cambodia and Laos as well as representing nonelite Vietnamese.[92] By 1939 Cochinchina's bureaucracy included at least 159 Vietnamese in its *cadre supérieur* of officials, twenty of them at the top administrative grade. Yet before 1945 the French promoted few Vietnamese even to the level of province chief. The colonial army of Indochina had only about fifty Indochinese in its 1,400-strong officer corps.[93]

The Constitutionalists' loyalty to the colonial enterprise did not permit them to accept exclusion within it. In 1923, when some Vietnamese in the Colonial Council voted with its French majority to allow colonists a virtual monopoly on the port of Saigon, it provoked the party's first split. The next year Constitutionalists summed up their demands as educational expansion, judicial reform, increased access to French citizenship, and a representative political body with a wider franchise.[94] Voter turnout was high in the 1926 elections for the Colonial Council, and this time Constitutionalist candidates won all ten of the Vietnamese seats. But the party continued to split over its contradictory policies of loyalty and reform, along with the difficulty of playing the role, in the words of one historian, of "a subject elite."[95] By the end of the decade the Constitutionalists had divided into three factions and begun to lose influence to younger rival political groups. They still won eight of the ten Vietnamese seats in the 1930 Colonial Council elections but garnered many fewer votes than they had in 1926.[96]

As the educational system opened up, these leading Cochinchinese had won the right to offer advice to the French authorities and were approaching equality in the professions and middle ranks of the bureaucracy. However, the Constitutionalist Party itself never recruited more than thirty members. It relied on a restricted, largely urban electoral base and remained disinclined to court the rural population—even their own tenants. Historian Megan Cook writes: "As absentee landowners the Constitutionalists had little opportunity and probably little incentive to observe in detail conditions on their properties."[97] That role would be left to other Vietnamese political groups.

COMMUNISM

Living and working in Paris in 1917–23, Hồ Chí Minh (using his earlier pseudonym Nguyễn Ái Quốc) joined the French Socialist Party in 1919.[98] He worked at pricking the conscience of the French left by reminding them of the hardships France imposed on Vietnamese. In December 1920, Hồ became a member of the French Communist Party. At its founding meeting he announced: "I didn't understand what you said about strategy, proletarian tactics, and other points. But there is one thing that I understood clearly: The Third International is interested in the problem of liberating the colonies." The next month the former reformist governor general of Indochina, Albert Sarraut, became France's minister of colonies. He invited

Hồ to a face-to-face meeting, in which the Vietnamese "spoke frankly about his feelings and his goal—the liberation of his country—showing a quiet audacity." That year Hồ and other foreign nationals in Paris founded the Intercolonial Union and in 1922 launched its newspaper, *Le Paria*, in which Hồ wrote about French colonialism in Algeria and Madagascar. In 1924 elections, *Le Paria* supported the Communists, "the only party to put up a colored candidate in Paris."[99]

But Hồ had moved to Moscow. He spent most of 1924 in the Soviet Union; he took a course in politics and met communists from across the world, including India and China. The Communist International (known as the Comintern) then sent him to China, where he was based for the next twenty years, evading arrest, organizing a Vietnamese communist movement, training its officers, and coordinating its activities with other Asian communists and anticolonialists, and with the policies of the Soviet Union.

Phan Bội Châu had known the young Hồ Chí Minh in Nghệ An in the 1890s but unlike Phan Châu Trinh had not seen Hồ since then. In mid-1924, Phan returned to the Chinese city of Guangzhou, scene of his 1913–17 imprisonment and now the nerve center of the first United Front between the Chinese Nationalist Party (Guomindang) and the Chinese Communist Party (CCP). On this visit, Phan toured the Whampoa Military Academy with its director, Guomindang leader Jiang Jeshi, and met some of its Soviet instructors. Phan proposed to his Vietnamese supporters in Guangzhou the creation of a new political party to be called the Vietnamese Nationalist Party (Việt Nam Quốc Dân Đảng), modeled on the Guomindang, Quốc Dân Đảng in Vietnamese. Three months later, when Hồ, still as Nguyễn Ái Quốc, arrived in Guangzhou from Moscow, Phan had just left for Hangzhou. But Hồ exchanged letters with Phan with a view to revising the proposed Nationalist Party's constitution and program.[100] Hồ was critical of Phan but managed to win him over. Hồ wrote the Comintern in December 1924:

> The sole objective of this man is to avenge his country for the massacres committed by the French. He does not understand politics and above all he does not understand how to organize the masses. In our communications I have explained to him the necessity for organization and the futility of ill-prepared actions. He has agreed with me. . . . The work we have started is as follows: (i) I have drawn up a plan of organization . . . (ii) having agreed to this plan, he has given me a list of fourteen Vietnamese who have been working with him up to now.

From these supporters of Phan Bội Châu, the next year Hồ selected the founding members of a new party, the League of Vietnamese Revolutionary

Youth (Việt-Nam Thanh-niên Cách-mạng Đồng-chí Hội). Thanh Niên became the country's first communist organization.[101]

Within months, in June 1925, French agents in Shanghai tracked down and apprehended Phan. They brought him back to a Hanoi jail and subjected him to a criminal trial. He was sentenced to death, but after large-scale Vietnamese protests the French commuted his sentence. By the time of Phan Châu Trinh's final illness in Saigon in early 1926, Phan Bội Châu was forcibly confined to house arrest in Huế, where the pair had first met in 1903. On the first anniversary of Trinh's death, Phan published a eulogy for his old sparring partner in the Huế newspaper *Tiếng dân*, in which he proclaimed: "If he were still alive, we would ask him to lead us."[102] This high praise reaffirmed the two men's different critiques of the discredited Huế monarchy. Phan may also have implicitly targeted the Constitutionalist Party, and perhaps the other Vietnamese political groups that were proliferating.

From Guangzhou in 1925–27, Hồ Chí Minh and his Thanh Niên organized the secret departure from Việt Nam and reception in China of about three hundred young Vietnamese activists for training, including one hundred at the Whampoa Academy. Most received instruction in communist theory and methods and returned to their country to help found a communist movement there, aiming especially at recruitment of workers and peasants. Some helped set up Tonkin's first ever industrial workers' unions. From 1926 to 1927, Thanh Niên members crisscrossing the upland China-Tonkin border also included local ethnic Tày and Nùng activists who began organizing among the hill peoples there, forming a Thanh Niên section in the Cao Bằng-Lạng Sơn region in 1929. A few Vietnamese graduates of Guangzhou went on to Moscow for training at the Soviet Union's University of the Toilers of the East.[103] As historian Huỳnh Kim Khánh showed, Thanh Niên successfully "grafted" Leninism onto the sapling of Vietnamese patriotism, ensuring that "communism remained an integral part of Vietnamese nationalism."[104] However, in China in 1927, Jiang Jeshi's crackdown following the collapse of the Guomindang-CCP United Front ended any opportunity to safely train Vietnamese communists in Guangzhou. Tipped off in advance, Hồ fled back to Moscow, later returning to the region via Siam.[105]

The communists became almost as susceptible to splits as the Cao Đài and Constitutionalists. In Annam in 1926, some Phan Bội Châu supporters had formed the New Việt Nam Revolutionary Party (known as the Tân Việt). They approached the Thanh Niên for discussions about an alliance but were initially rebuffed. In January 1930 the Tân Việt changed its name to the Indochinese Communist League.[106] By 1929, Thanh Niên had built up its own membership of about a thousand, including about five hundred in Tonkin, plus newer probationary members. It helped form peasant associations, and in 1929 six thousand workers staged twenty-four strikes, but the upsurge in labor action was also a result of jockeying within the revolutionary movement. In Hanoi in mid-1929, a Thanh Niên breakaway group formed an "Indochina Communist Party" and quickly mobilized nearly all Thanh Niên members in Tonkin and Annam, while the rump league's Central Committee, active mostly in Cochinchina, set up the competing party "Annamese Communism," with about four hundred members and eight hundred probationers. In October 1929, the Comintern's executive committee sent orders from Moscow to end the factionalism. It arranged for Hồ Chí Minh to return to southern China and impose unity from there. He convened a secret meeting in Hong Kong on February 3, 1930, which achieved the amalgamation of the Vietnamese factions and formation of the Vietnamese Communist Party (Đảng Cộng Sản Việt Nam), which it also invited Tân Việt members to join.[107]

Still competing with the communists was the Việt Nam Nationalist Party, or Việt Nam Quốc Dân Đảng (VNQDD), founded in 1927 and modeled on the Guomindang. By 1929 the VNQDD had recruited 1,500 members organized into 120 party cells. It was strongest in Tonkin, with more than a thousand members in Red River delta towns, mostly students, small traders, and low-ranking civil servants.[108] However, the party split, and in February 1929 the authorities succeeded in arresting most of the VNQDD Central Committee. In desperation the rump party, led by former chairman Nguyễn Thái Học, moved to win over Vietnamese troops enlisted in colonial forces. The French uncovered its plans for a mutiny centered on Yên Bái barracks in the upper Tonkin delta, and the revolt went off half-cocked on February 10, 1930. Almost all VNQDD leaders were arrested. The French prosecuted one thousand suspects; six hundred were sentenced to forced labor and eighty to death. Many more were exiled. Nguyễn Thái Học and twelve others went to the gallows on June 17, 1930.[109] The VNQDD never recovered.

Vietnamese discontent still seethed. From April 1930 to November 1931, a more widespread and sustained revolt erupted. In more than five hundred rural demonstrations, peasants seized land and rice stores all over Việt Nam. There were also more than one hundred workers' strikes, many in support of the peasants. Peasant violence targeted landlords, Catholics, and Frenchmen, killing up to 130 people in the north-central provinces Nghệ An and Hà Tĩnh alone.[110] Members of the new Vietnamese Communist Party quickly became involved, attempting to lead the movement, often succeeding, and the colonial government responded with brutal and overwhelming force. In one confrontation in September 1930, troops and aircraft killed nearly two hundred peasant demonstrators. Hundreds more were killed before the French regained control, taking nine thousand prisoners.[111]

The newspaper editor and former member of the Annam Chamber of Representatives Huỳnh Thúc Kháng tried to warn the authorities against fueling a cycle of violence. He drew upon a traditional image of the power of water. Kháng wrote to Governor General Pasquier in September 1930: "Man's ideas evolve with the social milieu, and in times of crisis sweep the masses up in the impetuous torrent, drawing them along with the irresistible current. The only opportune policy is to open wide the gates to the tempestuous waters, which if savagely blocked, will overflow and cause irreparable devastation." Nevertheless, in central Việt Nam the colonial repression was heavy, with three thousand peasants killed and as many imprisoned in Nghệ An and Hà-Tĩnh.[112] In the south of Annam, one Vietnamese official involved in suppressing communist dissidence in 1930–31 was the new chief of Ninh Thuận province (seat until 1832 of the Cham principality of Pāṇḍuraṅga/Phan Rang), a thirty-year-old Catholic mandarin from Huế named Ngô Đình Diệm. Telling his subordinates that "fear is the beginning of discipline," Diệm ordered "ruthless, fast arrests," which helped win him promotion to chief of the nearby larger province of Bình Thuận.[113]

Meanwhile the Comintern had again intervened to have the Vietnamese Communist Party change its name in October 1930 to "Indochina Communist Party" (Đông Dương Cộng Sản Đảng), reflecting the goal of a more international anticolonial revolution that would include Cambodia and Laos, though communist recruits in those protectorates remained few. But in Nghệ An and Hà Tĩnh, a French police commissioner reported a year later that six out of ten peasants had joined the Indochina Communist Party (ICP) or its other organizations such as the Peasants' Associations.[114] It was in this region of northern Annam that the revolt was strongest, as in 1885–95. In September-December 1930 the movement there established what became known as the "Nghệ-Tĩnh soviets" (*xô viết*), comprising about thirty armed rural councils inspired by the workers' councils of the Russian Revolution.[115] Some of these soviets already existed when the ICP Central Committee convened its First Plenum, in Saigon in October 1930. The party faced a fait accompli at a time when, the Central Committee warned, the takeover of villages and redistribution of land was "not appropriate," because the ICP and "the masses in our country have not yet reached a sufficient level of preparedness and because we still do not have the means for armed violence."[116] The communist leadership had not started the revolt, nor ever fully controlled the peasant movement. The involvement of communists at the side of the protestors throughout the country helped establish the ICP as the new leading party of Vietnamese anticolonialism. But the 1930–31 unrest expressed genuine peasant and worker grievances and a spirit of local activism, often independent of communist organizing efforts, that persisted in many parts of Việt Nam until 1940.

Of the ICP's two major rivals, the VNQDD, decimated by the 1930 repression, almost disappeared for a decade. Based in northern towns, it failed to recruit many members in rural areas or in the south and center. Most surviving VNQDD leaders took up exile in China. In the south, the Constitutionalist Party of Cochinchina appealed to Saigon's landed and educated elite, offering moderate leadership but little else to the peasantry—or to Vietnamese of the north and center. In Tonkin the French blocked the loyalist savant Phạm Quỳnh from even organizing a similar party.[117] In October 1931, Bùi Quang Chiêu expressed the Constitutionalists' belief in their own elite rule: "All the [Vietnamese] live together, pursue the same ideal; masses and elite interpenetrate, intermingle, and when the latter translates the race's aspirations, it only lends its voice to the intimate and confused desires which trouble the national soul."[118] But of all the peasant protests in the previous eighteen months, the most extensive had occurred in Cochinchina itself, where the ICP led them from start to finish.[119]

In Bến Tre sometime in 1930, ten-year-old Nguyễn Thị Định noticed, she wrote later, "that my brother Ba Chan came and went at odd hours. Sometimes men came to the house, sat and whispered for a while and then disappeared." One day she saw "my brother hand to my father a piece of red cloth embroidered with something yellow inside." Her father "quietly went into the garden, climbed to the top of the coconut tree, and hid the package there." It was a communist hammer-and-sickle flag, which Định later saw flying over a nearby river junction. Village officials arrested Ba Chan, and he spent six months in a prison at the mercy of the local canton chief, Muôn, the very landlord who had demanded rice from the family earlier in the year.[120]

The ICP paid a high price for coming out into the open in 1930–31. After its Central Committee (CC) reassembled in Saigon for its Second Plenum in March 1931, French police apprehended one of its members and soon managed to arrest nearly all the others. Within months the authorities had imprisoned the entire Standing Committee of the ICP CC, all six members of the Nam Kỳ (Cochinchina) Regional Committee, and the entire Bắc Kỳ (Tonkin) Regional Committee. Of the ICP's Trung Kỳ (Annam) Regional Committee, three members had been killed and one arrested.[121] Those jailed in 1930–31 included nearly all the future top leaders of Vietnamese communism: Võ Nguyên Giáp, Phạm Văn Đồng, Lê Đức Thọ, Phạm Hùng, Hoàng Quốc Việt, and the three men who over a fifty-year period would occupy the communist movement's highest post, party secretary-general:

Trường Chinh, Lê Duẩn, and Nguyễn Văn Linh. In 1930 Giáp and Chinh went to Tonkin jails, but the other six spent much of the period 1930–36 together on Poulo Condore prison island off the Cochinchina coast. Then, in Hong Kong in June 1931, British police apprehended and jailed Hồ Chí Minh, leaving his whereabouts and leadership of the ICP in doubt for the next decade.[122] Hồ, then, spent most of the 1930s first under cover in Siam, then under detention in Hong Kong, then under suspicion in the Soviet Union, and finally incognito in Mao Zedong's CCP base at Yanan. Meanwhile a small cohort of Moscow-trained Vietnamese cadres assumed leadership of the ICP.[123]

PEASANTS AND POWER

So far, at least, communist and nationalist efforts had failed to resolve the problems facing the Vietnamese peasantry, which persisted well beyond the Depression. Addressing the Tonkin Chamber of Agriculture in August 1934, Dr. Le Roy des Barres described the "miserable" plight of "numerous Tonkinese farmers." He explained that local authorities often demanded double the amount of the head tax; that peasants had reportedly been forced to sell their children, land, stock, or religious items; and that "the Administration would deny this state of affairs" which he could prove in "a hundred cases." The chamber set up a commission to investigate, gather testimonies, "assemble the grievances of the farmers," and report on their situation, "which is much more serious than is thought."[124] But the résident supérieur instructed Tonkin's French province administrators to "recommend to the mandarins" against any cooperation with this "inopportune" investigation, and to withhold any information it requested.[125]

Colonial power confounded peasant interests. As the Red River continued to deposit quantities of silt offshore, new land became available. The first Vietnamese Catholic bishop, Nguyễn Bá Tòng, wrote from Phát Diệm cathedral to the French résident at Ninh Bình in November 1936 that most of the population of coastal Kim-sơn district was "excessively poor," some of them often eating "only one meal per day, and alas! what a miserable meal." More and more of them frequented the now "immense" alluvial Cồn Thoi islands to gather *cỏ ngạn* grass to feed ducks and saltwater reeds for matting, and to fish with traps they had set up there. But unscrupulous officials were dividing up the new offshore land between them and demanding high payments for its use, as if they owned it. Conflicts and "continuous trouble" had erupted. The bishop asked the résident to temporarily rent the island to him, to establish the authority and supervision necessary to give "the inhabitants, especially the poor, a provisional distribution of land on which they may peacefully earn their living," pending a definitive concession based on the 1930 administrative order.[126] But successive résidents at Ninh Bình proved unable to help.

The next year Bishop Tòng sent his request on to the résident supérieur in Hanoi. He added that the high population density of Phát Diệm and other villages of southern Ninh Bình was "found almost nowhere else, even in this delta." For the previous fifty years, it was only from the mudflats "that these hardworking populations [had] been able to gain a livelihood." Recently, the bishop went on, they had built dikes to block saltwater inflow at high tide and create rice fields from "vast areas" previously suitable only for marsh grass. Beyond these, Catholic villagers had also built a perimeter dike within which they could raise the ground level and plant marsh grass. They made this onerous labor commitment, Tòng concluded, only to house and support their surplus population. He asked the résident supérieur for the same authority that Fr. Trần Lục had wielded in the nineteenth century, to "maintain the peace," with the land settled and farmed pending a "definitive concession" giving its new residents the right to occupy it.[127] Résident Supérieur Yves Chatel replied with a skepticism that suggested a refusal to delegate power to any Vietnamese. He asked only that the bishop "detail to me the direction and the weight of the authority with which you wish to have yourself invested as well as the manner in which you intend to exercise these powers." The file contains no response from Bishop Tòng. This long-running issue seems to have reached a close.[128]

POPULAR FRONT POLITICS

The ICP slowly recovered from the mass arrests of 1930–31, while the influence of the Constitutionalists and Nationalists declined. Even in Saigon the ICP registered gains, alongside other leftist Vietnamese parties, now including Trotskyists.[129] In all of French Indochina up to 1945, the elections closest to a democratic competition were those held for the Saigon Municipal Council from 1933 to 1939. The election of April 30–May 7, 1933, coincided with a five-day mass political trial of 121 leaders and members of the ICP arrested in 1930–31 and a second trial of jailed Trotskyists. The vote gave the Constitutionalist Party four of the six seats reserved for Vietnamese. But an unprecedented combined ICP-Trotskyist opposition campaign, supported by the jointly run leftist *quốc ngữ* daily, *Trung Lập* (Neutral), established in 1932, and a new French-language paper, *La Lutte* (Struggle), both edited by the independent leftist Nguyễn An Ninh, ensured that a Communist and a Trotskyist candidate won the two other seats. The French authorities then canceled their election on technical grounds.[130]

Two years later, Communist-Trotskyist candidates registered their first achievement in Colonial Council elections, which were held in Cochinchina in March 1935; the list supported by *La Lutte* won 17 percent of first-round ballots and significantly reduced the Constitutionalist vote. Then, in May 1935 elections for the Saigon Municipal Council, the ICP and the Trotskyists each won two seats, for a total of four of the six. "For the first time the administration lost control of the electoral game."[131] The Constitutionalists never recovered from this defeat. Meanwhile in the rural areas of Cochinchina, local Communist cadres were guiding six hundred "action committees" that had sprung up by the mid-1930s—peasants' federations, youth and women's leagues, trade unions, and mutual assistance and fraternal associations.[132]

Meanwhile the Comintern reversed its opposition to moderate or socialist political parties. From 1935, Moscow adopted a policy of international unity between communist and other antifascist forces (but not Trotskyists). In France, a Popular Front government, including Socialists and Communists, won election in May 1936. Socialist Marius Moutet, who had helped Phan Châu Trinh, became overseas minister. Some 1,500 political prisoners were freed in Indochina. Future ICP leaders Phạm Văn Đồng, Lê Duẩn, Lê Đức Thọ, Phạm Hùng, Nguyễn Văn Linh, and Hoàng Quốc Việt all returned from Poulo Condore island; Trường Chinh gained release from Sơn La jail in Tonkin. Political repression diminished but did not end.[133] Meanwhile the ICP continued to disregard Moscow's ban on collaboration with Trotskyists. In the April 1937 Saigon municipal elections, the combined leftist list of two ICP members (1928 Comintern Congress delegate Nguyễn Văn Tạo and Moscow-trained Dương Bạch Mai) and the leading Trotskyist Tạ Thu Thâu again won three of the six Vietnamese seats.[134] But the colonial authorities quickly arrested Tạo and Thâu, along with *La Lutte*'s editor Nguyễn An Ninh, imprisoning them. Ninh was sent to Poulo Condore; his five-year sentence was his third lengthy jail term in a decade.[135]

Several important Vietnamese groups opposed the Popular Front strategy of an alliance between communists and moderate nationalists. Vietnamese Catholic leaders in particular tended to reject it as a dangerous flirtation with atheistic communism, and some, especially in Saigon, also emphasized the threat to "property." In Annam, meanwhile, anticolonialism escalated among Catholics in the imperial cabinet. In May 1933, French officials removed its prime minister, the Catholic mandarin Nguyễn Hữu Bài, who had pushed for a restoration of monarchical powers, and promoted his protégé Ngô Đình Diệm to interior minister. But within two months, Diệm resigned from the cabinet. He wrote to the young emperor Bảo Đại protesting in particular the French refusal to concede more power to Annam's advisory Chamber of People's Representatives.[136] Diệm's new anti-French stance, however, did not make him any more inclined to an alliance with communists.

Most Trotskyists, for their part, opposed the Popular Front as a dilution of working-class activism by compromise with other groups. In March 1938, the ICP proposed the creation of an Indochinese Democratic Front, and in June it proclaimed that "all strata of the people—whether they are Frenchmen or natives" should "demand the democratic rights and reforms in the living conditions of the people." But in Cochinchina the Constitutionalists and Trotskyists both refused to work with the ICP, whose Cochinchina branch failed even to establish the Democratic Front there.[137] The Trotskyists then defeated the ICP in the April 1939 Colonial Council elections, winning four of the ten Vietnamese seats. Three Constitutionalist candidates were also elected.[138]

The ICP had more success in elections in Annam and Tonkin, where landowning and commercial interests were less powerful than in Cochinchina. In August 1937, ICP-supported candidates won election to eighteen of the thirty-three seats in the advisory Chamber of People's Representatives of Annam; three of them became the chamber's chairman, deputy chairman, and general secretary.[139] The successful candidates included ICP member Phan Thanh, elected by Quảng Nam voters. In 1938–39, workers staged several strikes in Huế, Quảng Ngãi, and Vinh, though otherwise the local Democratic Front came to little. The ICP's strategy registered its best results in Tonkin, where members of the French Socialist Party established a branch and both parties pursued the Popular Front approach. Phan Thanh traveled north to Hanoi and infiltrated the Socialist branch along with other ICP members. Hanoi's 1938 May Day demonstration drew a crowd of twenty thousand.[140] The July election campaign for the Tonkin Chamber of People's Representatives, another advisory body, one-quarter of whose members were appointed civil servants and notables, saw more protest meetings in Hanoi and large worker demonstrations in Hải Phòng, with many arrests. ICP-supported candidates won fifteen seats, about half of the elected seats in the chamber.[141]

Protests also wracked the Hanoi Municipal Council, which by 1937 included several communists or nationalists who enjoyed ICP support.[142] The Council comprised twelve seats for French representatives but only eight for Vietnamese, including two reserve seats to be filled in case of resignations.[143] Four of the Vietnamese members elected in 1934 had resigned their seats in protest of the higher number reserved for French members.[144] Then, in the lead-up to the December 1938 municipal elections, the *quốc ngữ* press campaigned for voters to protest this democratic imbalance by staying away from the polls.[145] Nearly all 3,800 eligible Vietnamese voters abstained from the first round of voting.[146] The Sûreté reported that "certain circles" noted an emerging alliance between the four members who had vacated their seats and were standing again and the new Socialist electoral "list," which included Dr. Phạm Hữu Chương, Phan Thanh, and a second ICP member, Bùi Ngọc Ai. This alliance competed with the more accommodating "monarchist" Vietnamese list, one of whom had already broken ranks.[147]

The second round of voting delivered, in the words of Tonkin's résident supérieur, a "stinging" defeat to the monarchists. "Complete success" went to the four candidates who had resigned and were reelected with more than twice the monarchist vote. The Socialists also gained a "partial" victory with both Phạm Hữu Chương and Phan Thanh winning seats, and two others the reserve seats. The résident supérieur commented that the election of the ICP's Bùi Ngọc Ai as a reserve councilor seemed to vindicate the party's Democratic Front policy, "this alliance having permitted their candidates to obtain a brilliant result thanks to the support of the socialist votes."[148]

At the meeting of the Hanoi Municipal Council on December 19, the Socialists planned to resign their seats unless the council unanimously passed a motion establishing numerical equality of French and Vietnamese representatives. The four other elected Vietnamese council members supported this Socialist demand but did not plan to emulate their resignations.[149] Back in Annam, a government official immediately summoned Phan Thanh, still an elected member of the Annam Chamber of Representatives, to appear there in person on December 20.[150] Unintimidated, Phan Thanh resigned his Hanoi Council seat, as did two others elected on the Socialist list—Dr. Phạm Hữu Chương and Bùi Ngọc Ai. They aimed to submit the question of democratic representation to the voters, in a virtual referendum on the council's institutionalized French majority.[151] So in April 1939 they stood again in the new elections to fill their vacant seats. Once again the Socialist list, including both ICP members, won all three. Phan Thanh, Phạm Hữu Chương, and Bùi Ngọc Ai all won back their seats with more than two-thirds of the 1,149 votes cast, easily defeating three "moderate" candidates in a low-turnout first round, and again a week later with a higher voter participation.[152] The ICP newspaper *Đời nay* celebrated the Democratic Front's victory over "those who take orders from the government" and an "alliance of the property owners and Catholics."[153]

Later that month, Phan Thanh died suddenly, aged thirty-one. A crowd assembled for a big public funeral "reminiscent of that given for Phan Châu Trinh in 1926." In the July 1939 by-election to fill Thanh's seat in the Annam Chamber of Representatives, the Democratic Front candidate Đặng

Thái Mai, also a covert ICP member, assumed Thanh's mantle; stressed his own syncretic grasp of Western, Chinese, and Vietnamese studies; assailed his opponent for lacking sufficient facility in *quốc ngữ*; and won the election. The ICP's rather successful Popular Front strategy in Annam and Tonkin (though not in Cochinchina) prefigured its creation of the Việt Minh Front two years later.[154]

Meanwhile other Vietnamese anticolonial movements were drifting toward the ICP. When he wrote his autobiography in 1928–29, Phan Bội Châu referred to Hồ Chí Minh as *tiên-sinh* (teacher, scholar), and before he died in 1940, he described Hồ as a "very reliable" custodian of the mission to achieve independence. In Huế during his last years, Phan Bội Châu also became friendly with the young anticolonial mandarin Ngô Đình Diệm, whom he called "a truly great man."[155] During the 1920s and 1930s the independent radical Nguyễn An Ninh moved toward close cooperation with the ICP, especially through their work together with Trotskyists in the newspaper *La Lutte*.[156] In the late 1930s, "several leading members" of the VNQDD collaborated with the ICP too, including the former head of the VNQDD's Southern Section, Trần Huy Liệu, who joined the ICP. One of the three founders of the VNQDD, Phạm Tuấn Tài, wrote his fellow party members a last "Political Testament," urging them also to join the ICP, which Tài now considered "the only party capable of leading the masses in their effort of liberation from the yoke of the imperialists and capitalists." In particular it was communist fellow inmates of French prisons who won over Tài and other VNQDD leaders. He and two others went on to occupy leading posts in the ICP.[157]

By 1937, the ICP was the only Vietnamese party operating nationwide, and it "unquestionably controlled national opinion in Tonkin and Annam." Politics in Cochinchina, also involving the Trotskyists, Constitutionalists, and Cao Đài, was more complex.[158] But the ICP remained strong in the south too. The region was still stirring with unrest. The teenage peasant girl Nguyễn Thị Định later recalled that "the movement was on the rise" from 1936. Her family in the delta province of Bến Tre often hosted meetings with people from "many areas." Frequent visitors included two men "who had shaved their heads and become monks." Revolutionary propagandist Co Trà would arrive at her home "disguised as an itinerant merchant selling the ointment produced by Nguyễn An Ninh"—in his Buddhist phase. Trà, in his disheveled coat and uneven pajama trousers, was a "spellbinding" orator: "Once in a while, I rowed him to the market to sell his ointment. After I finished selling fish I went to where he was and saw many people still surrounding him and listening to him talk." Định's parents were also Buddhists, fasting six days each month, and several of their secret visitors were "living in the pagoda disguised as monks." Định recalls, "I thought that Buddhism and revolution were the same." In 1939, the French police estimated that the ICP had two thousand cadres, organized into 150 cells. Like the Trotskyists, Constitutionalists, and Cao Đài, the ICP's stronghold now was Cochinchina.[159]

AGRARIAN POLARIZATION

Absentee landlords had long been accumulating Cochinchina's arable land, and the Depression had accelerated this trend. "Much land changed hands," wrote R. B. Smith, as "ruthless men with money" could buy up estates "in all parts of the country, not just in the new lands of the West." In the 1930s Trần Trinh Trạch added another 10,000 ha to his landholdings.[160] By 1938, the wealthiest 2.5 percent of Cochinchina's landholders each owned more than 50 ha, totaling 45 percent of all riceland there. The poorest 72 percent of peasants, with less than 5 ha each, accounted for only 15 percent of the riceland.[161] Many were landless tenants, sharecroppers, or rural laborers; by the 1940s those groups made up 80 percent of the Mekong delta population.[162] The combined effect on Cochinchina of the depression, population increase, lack of technological improvements, and the end of the frontier meant that from 1930 to 1945, "the share of land farmed by owners fell, and conversely, the share farmed by tenants rose."[163] The colonial phenomenon of the increasing concentration of landholdings was relentless.

In the north, poverty was more prevalent and the agrarian structure more complex, though also polarized. Tonkin annually produced two million tons of rice and exported forty thousand tons to China, but local consumption required similar rice imports from Cochinchina as well as a corn supplement.[164] In 1939, Tonkin's inspector of political and administrative affairs submitted a report on "the overpopulation of the Tonkin delta" that detailed "the misery of a very prolific population" and the "impoverishment" fast spreading "behind the false decor of our urban centers."[165] That year anthropologist Nguyễn Văn Huyên wrote that in "the poor villages" for two-thirds of the year, "80% of the population has only one meal a day." Feeding a family of six required more than 1.5 ha of riceland. "A million and a half mouths could not be fed," a statistic similar to the number of landless farmers in Tonkin in 1940.[166] 62 percent of its farming families owned less than 0.4 ha, while 20 percent owned less than 0.2 ha. The poorest 90 percent of the landowners owned only 37 percent of the farmland, while the richest 10 percent controlled 43 percent of it.[167] However, most of the rich were villagers, not urban absentee landlords as in Cochinchina, and in Tonkin in the early 1950s they still lived side by side with the 58 percent of villagers who were landless.[168]

In contrast to Constitutionalists and Nationalists, leading members of the ICP set out to study the Vietnamese peasantry. In 1937–38 two emerging ICP leaders published *The Peasant Question* (*Vấn Đề Dân Cày*), "the first detailed study in Vietnamese of rural socio-economic relations."[169] The authors, Võ Nguyên Giáp (who had been released from jail in 1932) and Trường Chinh (released in 1936), wrote:

> [The] misfortunes are so numerous that the peasant cannot catch his breath, but still people think that the peasant is secure and well-off. Aristocratic and bourgeois writers set out in their cars and speed through the countryside; they see the green and fragrant fields, the thick smoke rising from the thatched roofs in the evening and immediately invent a picture full of "poetic flavor," but they don't know....
>
> They don't know that at times the peasants can eat only one meal every two days, and that they must work at night by the light of the moon or in the dark. The children have bloated bellies and their skin is as pale as wilted leaves.[170]

The authors blamed "greedy mandarins and corrupt officials who use any means, from honeyed words to whipping and punishment in stocks, to extract money from the peasants." But changes introduced by French rule were partly responsible too:

> In former times, the life of mandarins and Confucian scholars was relatively simple. They were influenced by Confucianism and were concerned about public opinion to a certain extent. Some people who studied the Confucian classics became very greedy once they became mandarins, but for the most part mandarins in the old days were not as corrupt as they are now. Nowadays, mandarins of the new school compete with one another in making money and living in a European manner.

The lesson the authors drew from all this was as follows: "Peasants comprise a majority of the people, and suffer many layers of oppression and exploitation. Therefore the peasants have a hidden force, worthy of attention and worthy of respect. We must be aware of all the strengths and weaknesses of the peasants, but we absolutely must not underestimate them."[171] Though the colonial grip on the country still seemed unshakeable to many Vietnamese, communist revolution was now on the agenda.

Other social upheavals were possible too. Floods in late 1938 ruined 65,000 ha of riceland in Tonkin, but in the central Mekong delta, the devastation covered 200,000 ha, including 125,000 ha in Châu Đốc province alone. In July 1939, Huỳnh Phú Sổ, a twenty-year-old from Hòa Hảo village in Châu Đốc, declared himself the emissary of the Jade Buddha.[172] Within months he recruited a following of ten thousand for a dynamic new delta sect that came to be known as Hòa Hảo Buddhism. It drew on the sacred syncretic tradition of the multiethnic Seven Mountains region on the Cambodian border, especially local religious movements known as Bửu Sơn Kỳ Hương (Strange Fragrance from the Precious Mountain). The Hòa Hảo rejected the intermediary role of a Buddhist monkhood and focused on the laity, and was influenced by millennial aspects of Khmer Buddhism more than the Cao Đài were. Huỳnh Phú Sổ's leadership was charismatic, even apocalyptic. A 1941 pronouncement began: "Disaster of every sort; Fire, floods, epidemics. / Children will catch the measles, / Old and young will drown." Some Hòa Hảo leaders were far more violent than the Cao Đài, resorting to public immolations, beheadings, and, later, mass killings of both ethnic Khmers and Vietnamese.[173]

The odds against a Vietnamese communist revolution remained high. Japanese expansion recommenced in China in 1937, and war loomed in Europe. After the Munich Conference in September 1938, the ICP began to order its more public activists to "withdraw into deep cover." Then in August 1939, Moscow signed the Nazi-Soviet Pact, and the next month Paris outlawed the French Communist Party. In Indochina on September 28, the colonial government banned all communist organizations, forcing the ICP underground. It smashed the Democratic Front and arrested hundreds of members of nationalist parties and Trotskyists. Two thousand ICP members were arrested, including eight hundred in Cochinchina. Then in November-December 1939, the French jailed the ICP's secretary-general, its former secretary-general, three other CC members, and the Comintern representative to the ICP.[174] Among those arrested in 1939–40 were Nguyễn Thị Định, a future leader of the National Liberation Front of South Vietnam, and her husband, Bích, a young intellectual from Bến Tre who was a member of the ICP's province party committee. Định served three years with other women in a jungle prison camp, before learning that Bích had died in jail on Poulo Condore.[175]

In 1940, the ICP's Cochinchina (Nam Kỳ) branch launched an ill-prepared revolt known as the Nam Kỳ uprising. French forces devastated whole villages, arrested eight thousand people, and killed thousands of peasants. They executed a hundred members of the ICP's Nam Kỳ branch, which did not recover until early 1945. After the ICP's decimation in much of the Mekong delta, the Cao Đài and Hòa Hảo Buddhists continued to expand. Hue-Tam Ho Tai notes that to many peasants, the sects "provided some protection against colonial repression, but also seemed to hold out promise of a future not very different from the one for which the Communist cadres had claimed to be working."[176]

Between 1931 and 1942, the ICP's first four general secretaries perished one after another in French colonial detention. The first three were all graduates of Moscow's University for the Toilers of the East.[177] In 1939, the surviving ICP leaders began a crucial departure from the more internationalist and class-oriented lines the party had followed in the previous decade, while pursuing its recent moves toward a united front policy. The CC directed ICP members on September 29, 1939, that "the situation in Indochina will lead to the issue of national liberation." Its Sixth Plenum in November described "national liberation" as "the foremost task of the Indochinese revolution," and it proclaimed the need "to overthrow the French imperialists and resist all types of aggressors—white or yellow."[178] The ICP was the only Vietnamese party to oppose both the French and the Japanese, staking its claim to lead a national liberation movement.

WAR AND REVOLUTION, 1940–46

Germany invaded France in May-June 1940, occupying Paris and the country's north. From Vichy in the south, Marshal Pétain's new German-allied regime assumed responsibility for French Indochina. Then in September, Japan's South China Army began moving troops into Indochina, provoking some resistance. A Japanese plane bombed Hải Phòng, killing thirty-seven civilians. French officials reluctantly agreed to a Japanese military occupation while retaining control of the colonial administration. The French allowed Japan to garrison 6,000 Japanese troops in northern Tonkin, use four airfields, and deploy another 30,000 troops through the Protectorate. By 1945, Japanese force levels in Indochina reached 55,000, plus 4,000 civilians. The French Indochina colonial army of 60,000 comprised mostly Vietnamese troops, with fewer than 12,000 Europeans and foreign legionnaires. The 40,000 French civilians in Indochina included 18,000 women and children.[179]

This wartime French-Japanese condominium opened a new phase in Vietnamese history. The two colonial powers had reached a compromise that protected their own closest interests but not necessarily those of their respective Vietnamese clients. Both powers also competed uneasily for the loyalty of the native population. In November 1940, the French discovered that some of their disaffected Vietnamese infantrymen had engaged in a plot to join an ICP revolt. Yet the Vichy-appointed governor general of

Indochina, Admiral Jean Decoux, became the first leading French official to use the term "Việt Nam," and colonial propaganda celebrated the country's "peasant thought."[180]

The Japanese, for their part, would discreetly protect some favored Vietnamese politicians from French repression, including Catholic mandarin Ngô Đình Diệm and Hòa Hảo firebrand Huỳnh Phú Sổ. But despite their anticolonial rhetoric, the Japanese failed to offer the Tokyo-based Vietnamese aristocrat Marquis Cường Để the chance he had long awaited in exile. In 1937–38 Cao Đài spokesmen had begun proclaiming Hitler and Mussolini as Cao Đài disciples "sent down to the world to change the situation in Europe," and the sect declared its allegiance to Cường Để. From Japanese-occupied Shanghai in 1939, Cường Để formed the Vietnam National Restoration League (Việt Nam Phục Quốc Đồng Minh Hội), which the South China Army helped build to a force of possibly two thousand Vietnamese auxiliaries. Then the 1940 French-Japanese agreement left them all high and dry. The auxiliaries scattered, and Cường Để had to return to Tokyo. In August 1940 the French raided the Tây Ninh holy see, and the next year they arrested the sect's pope, Phạm Công Tắc, and five other Cao Đài leaders, dispatching them all to exile in the Comoros Islands off Africa for the war's duration. Phạm Công Tắc was not allowed to return to Việt Nam until August 1946.[181] In exiling both the monarchist Cường Để and Cao Đài leader Phạm Công Tắc, the Japanese and the French between them removed from the country's wartime political stage two of the most popular figures of traditional Vietnamese society.

French repression of reformists and radicals continued throughout the war. After the respected reformist scholar Huỳnh Thúc Kháng corresponded from Huế with Cường Để, the French shut down Kháng's newspaper *Tiếng Dân* in 1943.[182] That year the formidable Nguyễn An Ninh died at the age of forty-three on Poulo Condore island, allegedly under torture, and in Hanoi the French captured the ethnic Tày communist Hoàng Văn Thụ, a member of the ICP's Standing Bureau and head of its Tonkin branch. Thụ was executed in 1944. Three thousand ICP members spent the years 1941–44 in French Indochina's prisons.[183]

In February 1941, Hồ Chí Minh crossed the Chinese border and returned to Việt Nam for the first time since 1911. At the ICP's eighth plenum in May, Hồ and other communists resolved to "awaken the traditional nationalism in the people." They set up a new front organization, the League for the Independence of Việt Nam (Việt Nam Độc Lập Đồng Minh Hội), or Việt Minh. Like the ICP, the Việt Minh aimed to fight "a national liberation revolution" against both French and Japanese. Trường Chinh, coauthor of *The Peasant Question*, became ICP secretary-general. By 1943, the Việt Minh had taken over three border districts of Cao Bằng province and in one district tripled its local strength to three thousand.[184]

Hồ also set out to win favor among the Allies. In early August 1942 he headed back to China, seeking to meet the Soviet and U.S. delegations in the Guomindang capital, Chongqing. But the Guomindang sponsored a rival, anticommunist organization, the Vietnamese Revolutionary League (Việt Nam Cách Mệnh Đồng Minh Hội). Chinese officials arrested Hồ on August 19. He spent a year in Chinese jails until his release under guard in September 1943. Guomindang leaders had discovered Hồ's real identity, but now hoped he could be "converted." He won their confidence as a source of information from Indochina, and they included him in the Revolutionary League's leadership. Then, like many other Vietnamese political groups, it split apart. Not until March 1944 did Hồ finally obtain the right to travel.[185] U.S. officials had joined the negotiations for his release, and by mid-1944 Hồ was also "cooperating with the Americans in propaganda activities."[186] A convinced communist, he was funded and supplied by anticommunist China and had begun a relationship with the United States. In a stronger position than before his arrest, Hồ returned to Việt Nam in September 1944 with two hundred other Vietnamese exiles.[187]

One reason Japan had occupied Indochina was to secure supplies for its armies in South China. The Japanese did not challenge French rule, but they requisitioned large amounts of Indochinese rice and forced many Vietnamese peasants to convert their rice fields to industrial or cash crops such as jute and cotton. Cotton cultivation expanded from seven thousand acres in 1939 to fifty-two thousand in 1944, though little cloth reached the Vietnamese; "Poor adult Vietnamese often owned only one tattered pair of shorts and a shirt, while their children went naked." By mid-1944 serious famine loomed, especially in Tonkin. There the Việt Minh began to urge farmers: "Don't turn over a single grain of rice,... don't grow another jute plant for the bandits."[188] In December 1944 the Việt Minh set up the core of its armed forces—thirty-four fighters, mostly from northern Tonkin's Tày, Nùng, and Yao ethnic minority groups, with seventeen rifles. Its commander was Võ Nguyên Giáp. The two coauthors of *The Peasant Question* had become the communists' political and military leaders. The Việt Minh mobilized peasants to "destroy the granaries, solve the problem of hunger." Its propaganda proclaimed:

> Hunger! Hunger! Keep your paddy and rice! Destroy the granaries of the bandits. Chase out the French and the Japanese! Our land we till, we don't pay taxes. Our paddy we eat, don't let it be robbed of us! To accomplish this, compatriots ought to quickly join the Việt Minh.[189]

In November 1944, Việt Minh fighters rescued the U.S. pilot Lieutenant Rudolph Shaw after his plane, flying south of the Chinese border, experienced engine trouble over Cao Bằng. Hồ Chí Minh personally escorted Shaw back to his U.S. base in China. There Hồ met with American officials, this time including Office of Strategic Services (OSS) personnel and General Claire Chennault. He returned to Việt Nam in May 1945 with a team of forty OSS advisers and military instructors, including two Asian Americans, dispatched to help the Việt Minh rescue more downed Allied airmen and step up attacks on the Japanese.[190]

With the liberation of Paris in August 1944, General de Gaulle had taken power in France. As Japan suffered more defeats in the Pacific, its leaders began to suspect the French administration of Indochina of loyalty to de Gaulle. On March 9, 1945, employing effective surprise, the Japanese military rounded up nearly all the French forces and top officials in Indochina. The coup led to the formation of a Japanese-sponsored Vietnamese royal government. To lead it, Emperor Bảo Đại tried to recruit Ngô Đình Diệm, who had eluded French arrest in Huế the previous year when Japan's consul there smuggled him out dressed as a Japanese officer; he then lived in Saigon under Japanese military protection. Diệm declined the appointment, to his immediate regret. The new premier was the Confucian scholar and historian Trần Trọng Kim, whom the Japanese had also saved from the Sûreté.[191]

Few Vietnamese believed their country could be independent while still occupied by Japanese troops. When the new government appealed for support, the newspaper *Tin mới* reported that after seven days there had been "not one voice of support."[192] Another pro-Japanese newspaper reported:

> Thanks to the power of the Imperial Army of the Japanese Empire, our enemy has been destroyed.... Yet, strangely enough, among the patriotic personages who have for a long time sacrificed and devoted themselves for the Fatherland, representing the nation, there is now suddenly a non-committal, observing attitude. They watch from afar, guarding their silence.[193]

An exception again was the south, where the Cao Đài and Hòa Hảo had also cooperated discreetly with the Japanese and received weapons, training, or supplies from them.[194] In 1942 the Kempeitai rescued Huỳnh Phú Sổ from French detention, then protected him in Saigon. By 1944 his Hòa Hảo adepts numbered as many as a million. The Cao Đài following was larger. Both sects benefited from their ability to operate openly, as religious rather than political groups. Yet local communists, despite the 1939–40 French repression and the disastrous Nam Kỳ uprising, retained a strong underground network in Cochinchina and were expanding it. The Japanese organized the Vanguard Youth movement with more than forty thousand, unaware that its founding leader, Dr. Phạm Ngọc Thạch, had secretly joined the ICP. Bảo Đại also appointed Thạch the royal government's youth representative in the south. Vanguard Youth took on administrative tasks vacated by the French, such as disaster relief and sending rice north.[195]

Meanwhile famine raged in Tonkin and northern Annam. By mid-1945, a million people had died from hunger, one in ten of the inhabitants of Tonkin. Half the deaths occurred in four of its overpopulated coastal provinces, and another third in Nam Định alone. A poem penned by an eyewitness recounted: "At dawn you'd gingerly push your door ajar / To check if there was someone dead outside."[196] Then, after the two very high rainfall years of 1942–43, the Red River dike system suffered major breaches in August 1945. Tonkin suffered its most catastrophic floods of the twentieth century, which inundated 230,000 ha, about one-third of the summer rice crop.[197]

As soon as they had learned of the March 9 Japanese coup, the ICP and Việt Minh went on the offensive in the countryside. The ICP declared Japan "the principal, concrete, immediate and unique enemy." The Việt Minh armed forces, led by Giáp and Chu Văn Tấn, a member of the Nùng minority, organized attacks on rice stores, distribution of food to the peasants, and assaults on selected Japanese outposts. In June 1945, Japanese forces withdrew from military positions along the Chinese border, leaving six provinces of northern Tonkin to expanding Việt Minh control. In Cochinchina in late March, Communist leaders formed an alliance with the Hòa Hảo sect. Huỳnh Phú Sổ requested and was assigned a communist cadre to help train his followers. But the Japanese also tried to employ Sổ, to encourage peasants to hand over their rice crop. Instead, he urged them to stop farming, in turn threatening his new alliance with the ICP, which saw southern rice as crucial to ending the northern famine. Local communists managed to persuade peasants to partially restore production levels, and the ICP held to its tenuous united front with the Hòa Hảo in the common cause of independence.[198]

The Việt Minh concentrated on probing for Japanese weak spots, rather than mounting frontal attacks. Their biggest battle, on July 16, 1945, was for a position km outside Hanoi. After Vietnamese enrolled in Japanese units had defected to the Việt Minh, the latter attacked the post, killing seven Japanese and capturing a major. The next day the U.S. military "Deer Team" parachuted in to train Việt Minh forces to use the latest weapons.[199] Also in July Việt Minh groups north of Hải Phòng took over coal mines there, but kept in place their French overseers and technical staff. The communists put most of their efforts into secret political organizing. Estimates suggest that by late July the Việt Minh had enlisted or recruited possibly 150,000 people in Tonkin, 20,000 in Annam, and 10,000 in Cochinchina.[200] Throughout the country, the ICP itself had 5,000 members. But there were only sixty in Hanoi. Another six hundred or more in Hanoi were members of the Việt Minh; but they had only eighty rifles between them.[201]

On August 13 word arrived that Tokyo had agreed to surrender to the United States. The Việt Minh moved fast. Its local committees, patiently set up over the previous few years, took the initiative. They rode to power on a tide of revolution that swept the country from north to south, as yet with little widespread violence.[202] This was possible because the French and then the Japanese had each in turn suffered defeat, while Hồ had secured the backing of the victorious Americans. But the communists and their Việt Minh movement would never have been able to fill the power vacuum if the population had not seen them as the leading champions of Vietnamese independence against both the French and Japanese. And no other Vietnamese group was seriously attempting to tackle the famine.

After large demonstrations in Hanoi on August 16 and 17, the Việt Minh took power there on the nineteenth. Armed Japanese troops stood by watching. The Việt Minh were careful not to further antagonize them, in most cases negotiating a transfer of power with local commanders. To forestall Japanese retaliation they even handed over a supporter who had killed two Japanese soldiers; he was released later. After demonstrators in Hanoi killed about ten French personnel, the Việt Minh forbade further attacks. This convinced the Japanese commander that they could maintain order, and it showed Americans that the Việt Minh were loyal to the Allied cause. The situation demanded a balancing act; popular feeling ran high. Peasants in a northern province drew up a banner saying "Down with the French colonialists" and hung it upside down for emphasis.[203]

The situation also demanded speed, for the French were keen to resume their position of power. Võ Nguyên Giáp, his U.S. advisers, and his small army of two hundred mostly upland minority troops were still in the hills north of Hanoi when local Việt Minh committees took over Huế on August 23. In Saigon the previous day, the Vanguard Youth announced it had joined the Việt Minh. Cochinchina's Japanese-sponsored United National Front, which included the Cao Đài and Hòa Hảo, did the same on August 24.[204] It was under these conditions of coalition with better-armed allies that Việt Minh forces, led by ICP member Trần Văn Giàu, took power in Saigon on the twenty-fifth, and in Hà Tiên on the far west coast three days later. A Việt Minh–led Southern Provisional Administrative Committee occupied the former governor general's palace in Saigon.[205]

Formally the whole country was now under Việt Minh rule. On August 30, Emperor Bảo Đại abdicated. On September 2, Hồ Chí Minh declared independence in front of half a million people in Hanoi's Ba Đình square. He proclaimed the establishment of the Democratic Republic of Việt Nam (DRV). The Nguyễn dynasty, and a millennium of Vietnamese monarchies, had come to an end. The crowd watched as two U.S. P-38 Lightning aircraft approached Hanoi and, in an unplanned manoeuver, flew in low over the square.[206]

The fast pace of events was nowhere more pressing than for the three thousand Vietnamese inmates on the French prison island of Poulo Condore, sixty miles off the Mekong delta coastline. The island's Japanese garrison left on August 25, but it took three more weeks for Việt Minh forces in the south to send boats to ferry the impatient prisoners back to the Vietnamese mainland. A storm scattered seven of the rescue sampans, but the rest of the flotilla, twenty-five sampans and the ship *Phú Quốc*, reached the island on September 16. Some 1,800 of the Vietnamese political prisoners crowded aboard the vessels and sailed for the mainland, bringing many Cambodian political prisoners with them.[207] The thirty-year-old Vietnamese prisoner Nguyễn Văn Linh piloted the sampan that carried to safety his fellow inmates and future communist leaders Lê Duẩn, Phạm Hùng, and Mai Chí Thọ, younger brother of their comrade Lê Đức Thọ. The escapee fleet reached the delta mainland on September 23 to a rousing welcome, "with national flags and platforms and food," as Cambodian prisoners told the story after heading on to Phnom Penh.[208]

In a few weeks Việt Nam had been transformed, but it sat in the eye of the storm. Giáp's Việt Minh army numbered only 1,200 trained troops.[209] The Allies had divided Asia between their military commands, bisecting Việt Nam at the sixteenth parallel. In September two Allied armies arrived to take the Japanese surrender and restore order. Guomindang forces entered northern Việt Nam, and British forces the south.

The Allied occupying armies both had plans for different Vietnamese postwar governments than the one they found in power. The Guomindang wanted a regime friendly to them, not to their communist opponents. The British, fearful that the idea of independence would spread to their own Asian colonies, aimed to both extract the surrendered Japanese forces and pave the way for a French return. Two British battalions flew into Saigon on September 13, bringing a company of French soldiers.[210] The DRV hoped to cooperate with the Allies, but the British commander, General Douglas Gracey, dismissed local ICP leader Trần Văn Giàu and the city's embryonic Việt Minh administration: "They came to see me, and said 'welcome' and all that sort of thing. It was an unpleasant situation and I promptly kicked them out."[211] Gracey's First Gurkha Battalion evicted the Vietnamese Southern Provisional Administrative Committee from the governor general's palace and handed over to the French forces the Saigon docks, military storehouses, and ammunition depots.[212] Tensions rose in the city. Gracey instructed Lt. Col. E. D. Murray: "You're taking over Saigon. Clear the area. I want the whole of Saigon cleared." "What of?," Murray asked. Gracey replied, "'You'll find out.' Which I did," Murray later recalled. "I found out that there were inside Saigon, let's call them Annamites, who were being a bloody nuisance.... It was a question of clearing the area of these Annamite types and making it peaceful."[213]

Saigon's Vietnamese factions were divided. The DRV in Hanoi had counseled cooperation, while Trotskyist, Cao Đài, and Hòa Hảo leaders urged armed resistance to the British. Instead, after a fraught internal debate, Trần Văn Giàu's DRV Southern Committee called a general strike in Saigon for September 17. Two days later Gracey banned all newspapers and declared martial law. He released and rearmed 1,400 French prisoners of the Japanese, and deployed two battalions of surrendered Japanese troops. On September 23, French ex-prisoners conducted a violent anti-Vietnamese pogrom across the city. The next night uncontrolled armed groups of Vietnamese murdered a hundred French civilians. The DRV Southern Committee overruled Hanoi's representative Hoàng Quốc Việt and voted to launch an appeal drafted by Trần Văn Giàu calling on Vietnamese to "grab weapons and rise up to drive out the invading forces."[214] However, profiting from the disunity among Việt Minh, Cao Đài, and Hòa Hảo, over the next few weeks the British and French drove the independence forces out of Saigon.[215] Murray recalled several "*really* organized battles." Japanese, French, and British units all inflicted heavy casualties on the Vietnamese.[216] Việt Minh forces began to retreat to base areas in the Mekong delta and Central Highlands, where they recruited Cambodians and uplanders.[217]

Meanwhile on August 19, the day the Việt Minh took Hanoi, the ICP set up the "Vietnamese People's Police" (Công An Nhân Dân Việt Nam)—two weeks before the foundation of the DRV itself.[218] It was possibly under Công An control and that of ICP secretary-general Trường Chinh that ICP and Việt Minh units in central and northern Việt Nam quickly began targeting Vietnamese "collaborators" and others who opposed the new DRV regime or its strategy for achieving independence. The Trotskyist leader Tạ Thu Thâu was making his way north to Hanoi; in late August, Việt Minh forces in Quảng Ngãi intercepted and assassinated him. From Hanoi, Trường Chinh began calling for the elimination of Trotskyists. In Huế in early September, the ICP city committee sent squads to assassinate the intellectual and former royalist premier Phạm Quỳnh and the Catholic former minister Ngô Đình

Khôi. At the time, two of Khôi's younger brothers, Bishop Ngô Đình Thục and the anti-French mandarin Ngô Đình Diệm, were both visiting Hanoi. Thục held a meeting with members of the new government, but the DRV kept Diệm under detention for months in the hills outside Hanoi. In Cochinchina, ICP units murdered the former Constitutionalist Party leader Bùi Quang Chiêu in Saigon and others elsewhere. Also in September, superior Việt Minh forces put down a Hòa Hảo revolt and coup attempt in Cần Thơ city. On October 7, they executed two Hòa Hảo leaders, including Huỳnh Phú Sổ's brother, and one of his Trotskyist advisers. Then, retreating from British-controlled Saigon in mid-October, ICP squads began pursuing and killing two dozen more Trotskyists.[219]

The one-hundred-thousand-strong Chinese forces in the north were undisciplined and spent much of their time looting. Unlike the British in the south, they did not declare martial law.[220] Given his past relations with the Guomindang, Hồ Chí Minh's position was delicate, but the Việt Minh held on to power in Hanoi. They were careful to discourage violence against both the French and Vietnamese "class enemies," as occurred in 1930–31. Hồ wanted a phased Guomindang withdrawal as well as continued U.S. support, even though he calculated that Allied pressure would soon become too strong for the DRV to resist some form of negotiated French return. He hoped U.S. influence on France would favor Vietnamese independence. So his new regime also met opposition from Vietnamese nationalists, who preferred the Guomindang occupation to a French return, or neither.

In November 1945, Hồ acceded to Chinese pressure by announcing the "disbanding" of the ICP, which simply went underground and continued to be led by Trường Chinh. With nationwide DRV National Assembly elections to be held in January, Hồ agreed in December to assign in advance seventy of the four hundred assembly seats for non–Việt Minh opposition parties, giving the VNQDD fifty seats and the Revolutionary League twenty.[221] In January, Hồ brought Ngô Đình Diệm out of detention and offered him a cabinet post. Diệm refused and was allowed to leave for China.[222] The cabinet appointed in early March 1946 remained dominated by Việt Minh and ICP leaders, including Phạm Văn Đồng as finance minister and Võ Nguyên Giáp as chairman of the Military Commission. Three VNQDD leaders joined the cabinet. Nguyễn Tường Tam (Nhất Linh), former leader of Hanoi's Self-Reliant Literary Group, became foreign minister, with Vũ Hồng Khánh as deputy resistance commissioner and Chu Bá Phượng as economics minister. Nguyễn Hải Thần of the Revolutionary League briefly became the DRV's vice president. A significant new appointment was that of the veteran anticolonialist Huỳnh Thúc Kháng, onetime close friend of Phan Châu Trinh. Previously unaffiliated with the Việt Minh, Kháng became interior minister in March 1946 and later served as acting DRV president from June to October while Hồ traveled to France for negotiations. Also during 1946, the Việt Minh and Hòa Hảo made several attempts at mutual reconciliation, after their first united front collapsed in September 1945.[223]

In March 1946 Hồ secured the withdrawal of the Chinese armies from the north, at the high price of allowing the return of fifteen thousand French troops. France in turn had to recognize the DRV "as a free state with its own government, parliament, army, finances, forming part of the Indochinese Federation."[224] With British help the French had already reoccupied Cochinchina, refused to consider it part of the DRV, and continued to augment their forces there. But they agreed to withdraw from the DRV by 1952, with further negotiations stipulated to finally resolve the relationship between France and Việt Nam. By October 1946, French forces in Tonkin, Annam, and Cochinchina had increased to seventy-five thousand troops, mostly in the south. The VNQDD strongly opposed the DRV's agreement to this; the Việt Minh threatened that party's leaders and arrested many of them. Two of the three VNQDD cabinet members fled, as did DRV vice president Nguyễn Hải Thần of the Revolutionary League. When the National Assembly met in October, only thirty-eight of its seventy opposition party members attended, including at most twelve of the fifty VNQDD members, whose party newspapers in Hanoi had by then closed or fallen victim to DRV censorship. The DRV had gained most of the year to build up its own forces, which increased from twenty-eight thousand in late 1945 to more than fifty thousand troops and regional guerrillas in December 1946 and a growing ICP political apparatus of similar size.[225]

Meanwhile Hồ's hopes for U.S. backing for Vietnamese independence were dashed. After his unsuccessful visit to France, negotiations broke down. On November 23, 1946, four French warships bombarded Hải Phòng, massacring thousands of civilians. Two days later French forces attacked the Chinese border town of Lạng Sơn. In December Việt Minh units attacked French forces in Hanoi.[226] The First Indochina War had begun. Vietnamese would fight it with a functioning state and a national army, both established in 1945–46 for the first time since the nineteenth century.[227] The war itself would bring full-fledged development of the communist DRV state.[228]

WAR FOR INDEPENDENCE, 1946–54

The French moved into Hanoi in force in December 1946. Some Việt Minh units defended parts of the city until February to protect the withdrawal of their main forces into the hills to the west and north. The French took Huế after a six-week siege, and most of the towns in Tonkin and north Annam. Their military power was far superior, but the Việt Minh had political resources and continuing control of much of Tonkin's rice-rich delta. As in 1945, their nationalist appeal to many Vietnamese was an underlying factor in their eventual victory in 1954. The DRV assigned its interior minister, Huỳnh Thúc Kháng, to his home region of central Việt Nam, where he died in 1947.[229] By contrast, Emperor Bảo Đại's return to the French fold in 1948–49, and his participation in the creation in Cochinchina of a dependent "State of Vietnam," made little difference to the widespread Vietnamese demand for an end to French colonialism.

But Cochinchina remained a theater of brutal civil war as well as anticolonial conflict. As the French initially expanded their control of the Mekong delta countryside in 1945–47, members of the large ethnic Khmer populations of the central delta attacked and killed many ethnic Vietnamese, targeting them as "Việt Minh."[230] In February 1947, the Việt Minh and Hòa Hảo joined forces in a fourth attempt at an anti-French united front, but that too broke down after a Hòa Hảo commander, Trần Văn Soái, accepted French overtures for an anticommunist alliance. The Việt Minh leader in Cochinchina, Nguyễn Bình, ordered assaults on Hòa Hảo positions and the assassination of Huỳnh Phú Sổ, who was killed in April 1947, aged twenty-eight. Later Nguyễn Bình himself was recalled north, ambushed, and executed, presumably by a Việt Minh unit.[231] Meanwhile the ethnic Khmer in the central delta were caught in heavy fighting between Việt Minh, Hòa Hảo, and French forces, with each now also targeting them directly. The Khmers suffered numerous casualties, causing many to flee their homes and lose possession of much of their land along the Mekong waterways.[232] All sides continued to perpetrate atrocities throughout the war, including in the north, such as the Việt Minh mass killing of more than a hundred VNQDD prisoners, murdered by an escaping DRV security unit as the French attacked Phú Thọ in October 1947.[233] There were other similarly bloody incidents.

The French assault on Phú Thọ was part of a two-stage offensive against DRV base areas in northern Tonkin that inflicted ten thousand Việt Minh casualties and almost succeeded in capturing Hồ Chí Minh. But as the Việt Minh began to recover from their extended withdrawal from the cities, they recruited heavily among the large rural populations still under their control. By early 1948, French forces started to suffer battalion-sized assaults, and by 1949 the Việt Minh army (known as the People's Army of Việt Nam, PAVN) had grown to as many as 250,000 men. From 1947 to 1948 the ICP's political apparatus tripled in size to 150,000 cadres, and in 1949 it administered more than half of Việt Nam's villages and population, about twelve million people.[234]

Along with the appeal of the independence cause, two other factors gave the Việt Minh a long-term advantage over the French. One was the December 1949 communist victory in China. Mao Zedong's new CCP government recognized the DRV as the legal government of Việt Nam, as did Stalin's Soviet Union. Võ Nguyên Giáp visited China in January 1950 and obtained its agreement to send military aid, establish training camps, and build roads in border areas. Beijing shipped weaponry across the frontier to the Việt Minh, eventually supplying eight hundred recoilless cannon and machine guns, among other assistance. During 1950 alone, for instance, twenty-four thousand Việt Minh regulars received training in three Chinese camps. That year an unprecedented Việt Minh offensive along the border, mobilizing thirty well-armed battalions and a full-strength division, wiped out two French columns, captured eleven thousand tons of ammunition, and seized almost all northern Tonkin. PAVN could now launch regular assaults into the Red River delta. By early 1951 it had eighty well-armed battalions within twenty-five miles of Hanoi. Material aid from China, still below twenty tons per month, rose to 1,500 tons per month by March 1954.[235]

Also from 1950, especially in response to the "loss of China," the United States began to fully back the two-hundred-thousand-strong French forces in Indochina. In 1950 and 1951, Washington delivered five thousand tons of military equipment per month to Indochina, including Bearcat fighter aircraft, B-26 bombers, and Dakota transport planes. French forces extended their air superiority; they faced increasing antiaircraft fire, but PAVN possessed no air force. In four days in January 1951, French airstrikes killed up to six thousand of the Việt Minh soldiers attacking Vĩnh Yên. Two more PAVN attacks into the delta also failed, but in February 1952 the French had to abandon the provincial town of Hòa Bình in the hills southwest of Hanoi. By the end of 1952, the U.S. military had provided the French forces with 228 aircraft, 253 naval craft, thirteen thousand transport vehicles, and 777 armored fighting vehicles. U.S. aid eventually totaled 1,400 tanks among 160,000 tons of durable items.[236]

Meanwhile Ngô Đình Diệm found his way to the United States. In August 1950, having abandoned his efforts to influence the Bảo Đại regime in an anti-French direction, Diệm left Việt Nam for what became four years in exile. He took up residence in the United States in December 1950 and over the next thirty months attempted to build support there.[237] It was in 1950, too, that the U.S. Central Intelligence Agency first opened its Saigon station. The next year a CIA officer met Diệm's younger brother, Ngô Đình Nhu, whom the station made "the Agency's main political action contact in Saigon."[238] Nhu provided the CIA with valued intelligence on Vietnamese anticommunist circles. The internal Agency history, *CIA and the House of Ngo*, concluded: "The Ngo family's relationship with CIA had its beginning long before Diem's accession to office."[239]

Neither of the Ngôs was a liberal anticommunist. While studying in France in the 1930s, Nhu had imbibed the political philosophy of the Catholic thinker Emmanuel Mounier, who offered his concept of "the person" in answer to the materialism of liberals and communists alike. While Diệm was in the United States, Nhu drew on this personalist philosophy as he worked with support from Bảo Đại's State of Vietnam officials to build Ngô family connections to Vietnamese anticommunists. In a 1952 speech Nhu informed a group of non-Catholics, "The anxieties of Catholics are like an echo answering the worries that are roiling your own hearts and souls," and he urged Vietnamese to join together to "preserve the person" against the "false liberation" of both liberalism and communism. This struggle required a full "politico-economic revolution" in Việt Nam. It was necessary not merely to "patch over the fissures in a creaky house," but rather to "transform the entire internal structure of the house."[240] In Saigon during 1953, Nhu brought together a small, secretive, anticommunist political group, known from the next year as the Revolutionary Personalist Workers Party (Cần Lao Nhân Vị Cách Mạng Đảng), or the Cần Lao. His key recruits included nationalistic junior officers in the French-controlled Vietnam National Army, Catholic labor organizer Trần Quốc Bửu, and a Saigon group of Catholic intellectuals involved in the journal *Tinh Thần* (Spirit). The latter were led by Trần Văn Đỗ, scion of a delta landowning family and uncle of Nhu's wife, Trần Lệ Xuân.[241]

According to *CIA and the House of Ngo*, Nhu remained the Agency's top political contact in Saigon until April 1953, when its Saigon station temporarily ceased covert action programs. A CIA contract employee, Virginia Spence, stepped in late in 1953 and "maintained the relationship on a social basis." She noticed "the importance to Nhu of her CIA affiliation, and how material support helped save the relationship." Nhu responded fast to Spence's requests to meet his brother, Bishop Ngô Đình Thục, and others. She concluded that Nhu "needed us far more than we needed him."[242]

An anticolonial war of independence and sporadic civil war had also become a confrontation between capitalism and communism. In February 1951 the ICP returned to the public arena at its Second National Congress, held in Tuyên Quang province of Tonkin. The two hundred delegates claimed to represent five hundred thousand members, but they were now organized into a separate party for Việt Nam, and others for Cambodia and Laos. Vietnamese ICP members became members of the Vietnamese Workers' Party (Đảng Lao Động Việt Nam), or VWP. Its ruling Politburo was largely unchanged: Hồ Chí Minh (VWP chairman), Trường Chinh (secretary general), Lê Duẩn, Phạm Văn Đồng, Võ Nguyên Giáp, Nguyễn Chí Thanh, and Hoàng Quốc Việt.[243]

From 1952, the Việt Minh drew on its second major political resource, the appeal of land reform to many peasants. First, in their areas of control the Việt Minh imposed widespread reductions in land rents. Then in January 1953, the VWP CC decided to enforce the seizure of the estates of those landlords not supporting the resistance. In May the Politburo, chaired by Hồ Chí Minh, authorized the execution of landlords by a ratio of one for every thousand people. In Việt Minh–controlled areas of the north, including about half the villages in the Red River delta, 15 percent of the land was handed over to one-fifth of the peasantry; the proportion of landless laborers fell from 20 to 14 percent of the northern population. In Cochinchina, Việt Minh cadres seized 410,000 *mẫu* (c. 160,000 ha) and assigned 307,000 peasants farm plots of their own. Under guidance from CCP cadres, this program accelerated in December 1953 to include almost all landlord estates.[244] Though it is hard to quantify, the VWP promise to redistribute land to the tiller probably stiffened peasant resolve to fight to the end.[245]

Việt Minh forces in 1953 numbered 350,000 troops, in eight mobile infantry divisions and one artillery division. Parts of six PAVN divisions were poised within easy striking range of Hanoi. The Việt Minh successfully tied down in static defense positions 350,000 of the 500,000-strong French Expeditionary Force, leaving only three mobile divisions, seven regimental combat units, and eight paratroop battalions. Việt Minh numbers had also grown steadily in central Việt Nam, and in the Central Highlands in early 1954 Việt Minh assaults forced the French to abandon the provincial town of Kontum, isolating nearby Pleiku from the coast. Twenty percent of Việt Minh forces were located in Cochinchina. By 1954 PAVN mustered 450,000 regular troops, almost matching the forces they opposed.[246]

Victory came on May 7, 1954, after nearly one hundred thousand Vietnamese laborers lugged supplies from the Chinese border, including heavy artillery pieces from the Soviet Union, over two hundred miles through northern Tonkin's mountains and forests, to a PAVN force of 105,000 combat and support troops, plus a CCP contingent, surrounding the large French entrenched camp at Điện Biên Phủ near the Lao border. In a two-month siege, the French garrison of sixteen thousand was slowly strangled.[247] The Việt Minh captured eight thousand prisoners of war and marched them to camps in the Red River delta. A French commander, Lieutenant Colonel Bigeard, later called Giáp's army "the greatest infantry in the world." Peace talks began at Geneva the day after Điện Biên Phủ fell. Within days Bảo Đại

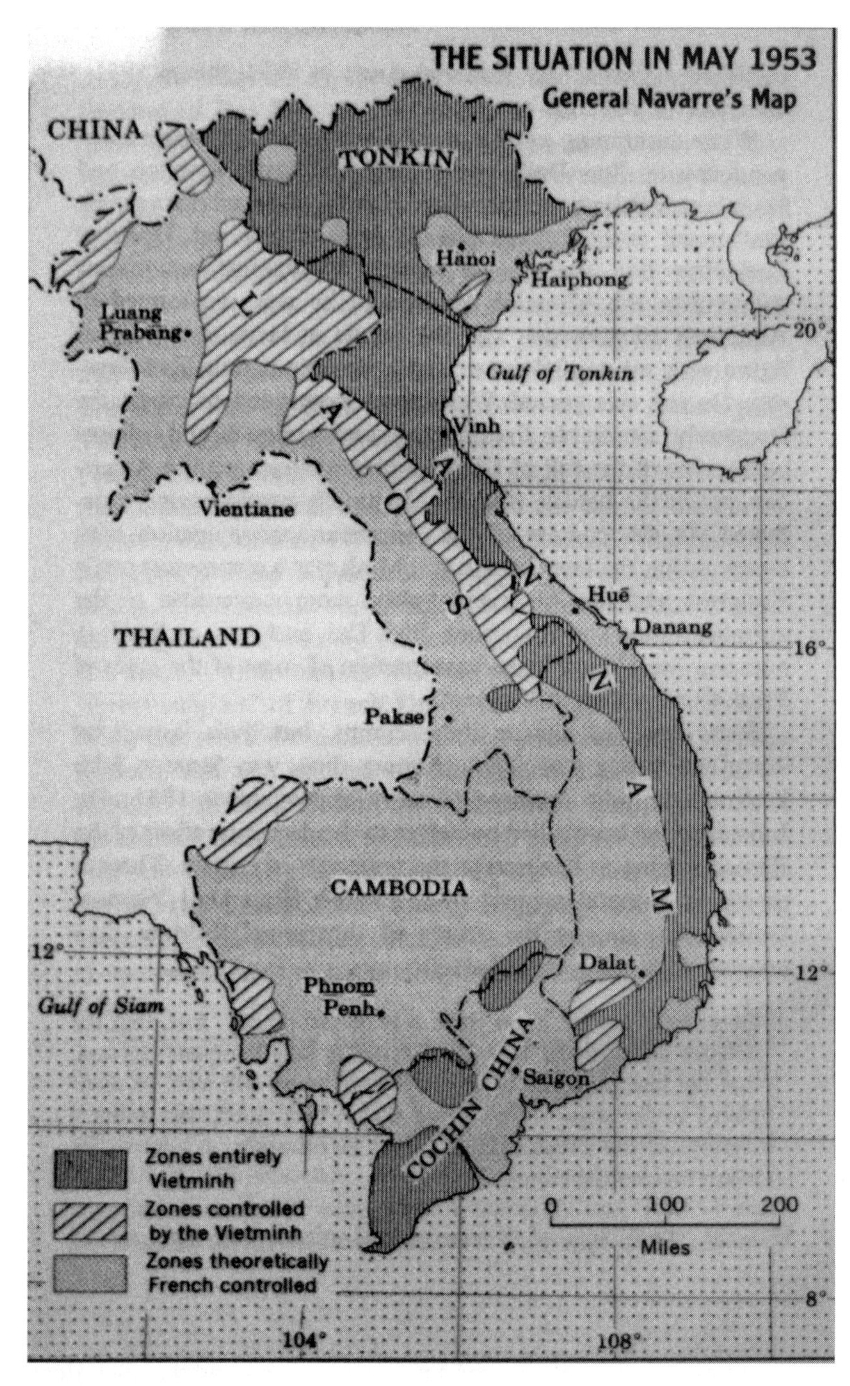

Fig. 9.1
The First Indochina War: General Henri Navarre's map, 1953. From George McTurnan Kahin, and John W. Lewis, *The United States in Vietnam* (New York: Dial, 1967), 34. Courtesy of Audrey Kahin.

contacted Ngô Đình Diệm in exile and offered him the premiership of the State of Việt Nam.[248]

After two months of bargaining among the great powers at the Geneva Conference, it was agreed that the French forces and the hundred-thousand-strong State of Việt Nam army they had trained would regroup south of the seventeenth parallel and PAVN forces to the north.[249] Saigon and Hanoi fell into separate zones. Within two years, internationally supervised nationwide elections were to be held to decide on a government for all of Việt Nam. The temporary dividing line, the parties agreed, would represent a military demarcation, not a political border between states.

Việt Minh troops at Điện Biên Phủ learned the slogan "Gain independence for the fatherland, return the fields to the peasants, advance to socialism." One historian has commented that "this had been the call of the radical intellectuals since the 1920s." Yet much had changed since Phan Châu Trinh's lament that Vietnamese did not "know their country."[250] They did now. *Quốc ngữ* had become the national script, giving birth to a modern print culture in a country with a new name. The Vietnamese had endured repression, depression, World War, and revolution. They were at last free of colonial rule. Trinh might have celebrated the country's new independence, but the violent means of its achievement would have appalled him even though his own peaceful approach had failed. About to be divided between two homegrown dictatorships, Việt Nam also remained at the mercy of great powers.

PART SIX

Republics

CHAPTER 10

The American-Vietnamese War, 1954–75

Việt Nam had won independence, only to be divided on regional and political lines. In the north, the communist DRV state sprang fully grown from its long anticolonial struggle. But the State of Việt Nam (SVN) that inherited the south from the French was hardly a state at all.

Its head of state, Bảo Đại, lived in France. His family had moved to Cannes in 1947. He joined them on April 10, 1954, a "broken playboy," never to return.[1] Before departing, Bảo Đại replaced the SVN premier Nguyễn Văn Tâm, a French citizen, with his cousin, "caretaker" Prince Bửu Lộc, who in turn appointed an acting premier, Dr. Phan Huy Quát of the nationalistic, formerly pro-Japanese Đại Việt Party.[2] The SVN was still occupied by about 150,000 troops of the French Expeditionary Corps, which fully withdrew only in April 1956. French officers also controlled the SVN's two-hundred-thousand-strong Vietnam National Army (VNA), which in June 1954 included only three Vietnamese generals, seven colonels, and eleven lieutenant-colonels. The VNA commander Nguyễn Văn Hinh, a thirty-eight-year-old dual citizen with a commission in the French air force, was the son of ex-premier Tâm. He saw France as "the far-off motherland."[3]

The SVN's colonial status was not the only limit on its authority as a state. Its internal administration included regional governors who, like its French overseers, held more power than did the central government in Saigon. Even in the capital, in return for information on Việt Minh operatives there, the French had allowed the Bình Xuyên criminal syndicate to run Saigon's vice rackets and a Chợ Lớn "nationalist zone." In addition, Bảo

Đại and Bửu Lộc sold off to the Bình Xuyên the Saigon–Chợ Lớn municipal police force and even the Cochinchinese Public Security Service, inherited from the French and still known as the Sûreté.[4] Among authentic political groups, the Việt Nam Nationalist Party (VNQDD) had dissolved into four factions. The Đại Việt Party filled its role, with possibly ten thousand members and sympathizers in the Saigon administration and in central Việt Nam, though it was divided over support for Bảo Đại.[5]

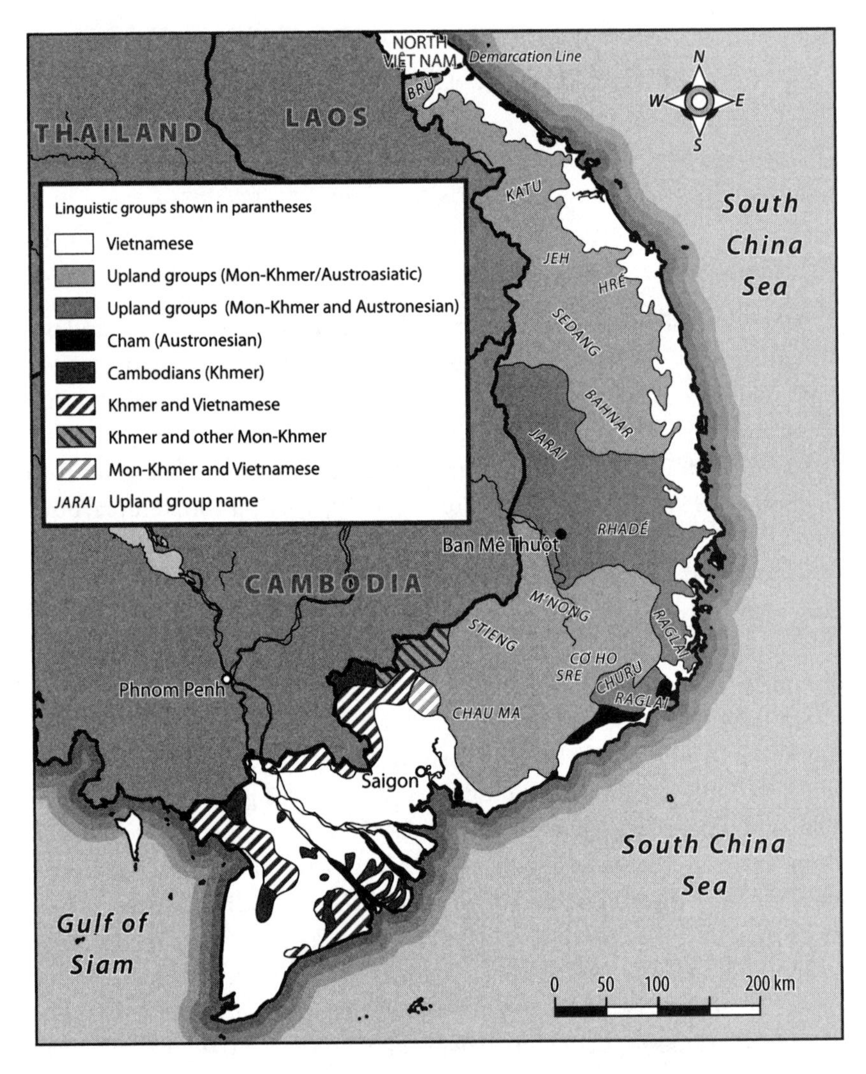

Fig. 10.1
Ethnic groups of South Việt Nam. Source: Thomas L. Ahern, Jr., *CIA and Rural Pacification in South Vietnam* (Washington, DC: CIA, Center for the Study of Intelligence, 2001), declassified 2009, 39, available online at https://www.cia.gov/library/readingroom/collection/vietnam-histories.

The southern countryside, too, was a collage of mini states in 1954. This was a result not only of the region's historic cultural heterogeneity but also of French attempts since 1946 to deny territories to the DRV by sponsoring secessionist areas like the "Republic of Cochinchina" and by funding the armed religious sects there. The French made most of the Central Highlands into a separate crown domain, the "Pays Montagnards du Sud," legally reserved for its five hundred thousand indigenous uplanders.[6]

The rural political patchwork also reflected southern communist-led resistance to the French. By 1953–54, the hundred-thousand-strong Việt Minh forces in the south dominated large populous areas, including most of southern Việt Nam's central coast (especially Quảng Ngãi, Bình Định, Phú Yên, and Bà Rịa provinces), key Mekong delta provinces such as Mỹ Tho, and most of the western delta.[7] By the time of the Geneva ceasefire, the Việt Nam Workers Party (VWP) had recruited about sixty thousand members in Cochinchina, including a thousand in two districts of Saigon. Across the south the VWP "controlled over half of the rural villages outside the sect areas," administering a population of 2.1 to 3.6 million.[8]

American journalist Joseph Alsop toured Việt Minh areas of the rural south in December 1954. He described a "palm-hut state" with "a loyal population of nearly two million." He wrote: "At first, it was difficult for me, as it is for any Westerner, to conceive of a Communist government's genuinely 'serving the people.' I could hardly imagine a Communist government that was also a popular government and almost a democratic government. But this is just the sort of government the palm-hut state actually was while the struggle with the French continued."[9]

FOUNDATIONS OF U.S. POLICY

The United States had emerged from World War Two "at the summit of the world," as Winston Churchill put it in 1945. America controlled half the globe's manufacturing capacity, electrical power, and monetary reserves, owned two-thirds of its gold stocks, and produced two-thirds of its oil. By 1948 the United States controlled 48 percent of world trade.[10] In that year George F. Kennan, the State Department's director of policy planning and author of the doctrine of "containment" of the Soviet Union, warned that with "about 50% of the world's wealth, but only about 6.3% of its population," the United States must "maintain this position of disparity" without "detriment to our national security." He added:

> To do so, we will have to dispense with all sentimentality.... We need not deceive ourselves that we can afford today the luxury of altruism and world-benefaction.
>
> For these reasons, we must observe great restraint in our attitude toward the Far Eastern areas.... We should cease to talk about vague and—for the Far East—unreal objectives, such as human rights, the raising of the living standards, and democratization.... We are going to have to deal in straight power concepts.
>
> ... Our influence in the Far Eastern area in the coming period is going to be primarily military and economic.

But when it came to Asian threats to U.S. security, Kennan was less bleak. As a foreign policy "realist," he opposed U.S. involvement in a land war on the Asian continent. He considered "absolutely vital to our security" only the archipelagoes, Japan and the Philippines. Given "effective control over these areas there can be no serious threat to our security from the East within our time."[11]

The next year the "loss of China" convinced many U.S. officials of a threat from continental Asia.[12] In 1950 the United States intervened in the Korean War and launched large-scale military support for the French war in Indochina. George Kennan, however, considered the French cause "hopeless." He warned, "We are getting ourselves into the position of guaranteeing the French in an undertaking that neither they nor we, nor both of us together, can win." Washington should allow Việt Nam's "turbulent political currents" to "find their own level," even if the Việt Minh won. America, he thought, need not include Việt Nam in the key strategic contest with the Soviet Union.[13] In 1952, Kennan became the only U.S. ambassador ever to be expelled by the Soviet Union, but the next year he was fired from the State Department by the incoming secretary of state, John Foster Dulles.[14]

Then and later, many of the actions of U.S. policymakers in Việt Nam may be explained by their view of a continental Asian threat to American security. To meet it, U.S. control of Japan and the Philippines would not suffice. In early 1954, the U.S. National Security Council asserted that a "loss of Southeast Asia" would adversely affect "many nations of the free world" and "add significant resources" to the Soviet Bloc. "Southeast Asia, especially Malaya and Indonesia, is the principal world source of natural rubber and tin, and a producer of petroleum and other strategically important commodities. The rice exports of Burma, Indochina and Thailand are... important to Malaya... and... Japan."[15] Two months later the Joint Chiefs of Staff reaffirmed that Japan was "the keystone of United States policy in the Far East" but added that "the loss of Southeast Asia to Communism" would "drive Japan into an accommodation with the Communist Bloc."[16]

That Southeast Asia must not be "lost" formed part of the strategic thinking dominant in the United States at the time of the 1954 Geneva Agreements on Indochina. Reflecting this thinking, the confidential 1969 U.S. Department of Defense historical compilation on the Vietnam War, known as the "Pentagon Papers," asserted that the agreements specifying nationwide free elections in Việt Nam in July 1956 had amounted to "a major disaster for US interests."[17] This was partly because, as the CIA predicted in August 1954, should those elections take place, barring any missteps "the Viet Minh will almost certainly win." President Eisenhower later wrote in his memoirs that in 1954 "possibly 80 percent of the population would have voted for the Communist Ho Chi Minh as their leader."[18] Washington faced a dilemma. It consented to the Geneva Agreements, undertook "to refrain from the threat or use of force to disturb them," and pledged "to seek to achieve unity" in Việt Nam "through free elections." But it declined to vote for the July 21, 1954, conference resolution, declared that the United States was not bound by its decisions, and did not agree to participate in consultations to "ensure that the agreements... are respected."[19] To stem or reverse the tide of communism in Asia, Washington soon began an effort to establish, without free elections, a separate state in southern Việt Nam and to support "operations against North Vietnam."[20]

U.S. technological superiority and political will precluded any thought of failure. In Washington, Vietnamese democracy and national or social aspirations were not the key issues. Rather, Eisenhower and Dulles saw their task in more global and mechanical terms. They described Việt Nam in April 1954 as one of a "row of dominoes," whose fall might provoke a "chain reaction" but could be prevented by a "cork in the bottle, the bottle being... all the surrounding areas of Asia." In these high-level mixed metaphors of world power projection, one scholar has remarked, Southeast Asian countries became "undifferentiated," without "histories, cultures and social structures." Since the United States possessed the most advanced weaponry, "defeat by a nationalist social revolution in a peasant society" was "unthinkable."[21]

The American-Vietnamese war pitted a global military superpower against a South Vietnamese communist-led peasant insurgency. But South Vietnamese fought on both sides, and the war involved other players—and two more theaters. Along with U.S. policy, Việt Nam's varied political and ecological landscapes played their parts in shaping the coming conflict.

THE RISE OF NGÔ ĐÌNH DIỆM

The Pentagon Papers described "South Vietnam" in 1954 as "essentially the creation of the United States." The U.S. analysts considered that its founding president, Ngô Đình Diệm, owed his survival to Washington:

> Without U.S. support Diem almost certainly could not have consolidated his hold on the South during 1955 and 1956. Without the threat of U.S. intervention, South Vietnam could not have refused to even discuss the elections called for in 1956 under the Geneva settlement without immediately being overrun by the Viet Minh armies.[22]

Though no puppet, Diệm depended on U.S. support to implement his vision for his country. In turn, U.S. anticommunist imperatives made Washington itself dependent on the small circle of Vietnamese who fit its required political mold.[23] The last French commander in chief, General Paul Ely, described Diệm as "the only Vietnamese politician" whose anti-communism was total.[24] The CIA's Saigon station had been working with his younger brother Ngô Đình Nhu since 1951, but Washington still sought additional options.

The CIA's internal history, *CIA and the House of Ngo*, says that early in 1954, as the French military position deteriorated, "the Agency started trying to identify Vietnamese leaders with whom it might work directly to resist further Viet Minh expansion." At a January meeting of the U.S. National Security Council (NSC), "someone suggested that Colonel Edward Lansdale, USAF, renowned for his work as 'kingmaker' in the Philippines, be commissioned to find a Vietnamese" to play a role similar to Ramon Magsaysay, the Filipino president, whom Lansdale had served as key adviser. For its part, the CIA decided that its Saigon station would "resume the direct assessment of nationalist politicians there."[25] In April 1954 a new covert action chief, Paul Harwood, arrived at the station to assume the task. Separately, the NSC approved the Lansdale mission; Secretary of State John Foster Dulles and his brother, Allen Dulles, director of Central Intelligence, "directly participated in creating the assignment." In June, Lansdale followed Harwood to Saigon and set up a second CIA station there, reporting personally to Allen Dulles.

For several weeks after his arrival, Harwood left the station's contact with Nhu to the "capable" contract employee Virginia Spence, who told CIA headquarters in April that Nhu believed the French premier favored Diệm. As Harwood sounded out other noncommunist nationalist politicians in

Saigon, "Nhu quickly emerged as the most promising of an unimpressive lot." By early May 1954, "before Diệm emerged as a candidate to head the government, Nhu's talent and willingness to work with the Agency had helped make him the focus of CIA covert action planning."[26]

Within "a few days" of Điện Biên Phủ's fall on May 7, Bảo Đại, in France, first offered Diệm, now in Belgium, the premiership of the SVN. Diệm held out for "full powers"—not only over the SVN government but also over its armed forces and economy. And he wanted U.S. backing. In Saigon in mid-May, the CIA history informs us, Nhu approached Harwood "about the terms under which the US would support Diem's bid to become prime minister."[27] The two parties were thinking alike. Dulles and the State Department were separately "discussing with the French a new government for non-Communist Vietnam," and in Washington, also around mid-May, the CIA decided to involve Nhu. "At Headquarters' request, Harwood told Nhu at a meeting in May that there were 'plans which might involve Diem.'" He asked "if Diem would accept a position other than that of prime minister." By May 21, Nhu had replied with "a categorical 'no.'" At some point in May, CIA headquarters also asked the Saigon station to ascertain Diệm's intentions and Nhu's own ambitions. Nhu wanted no cabinet post; Spence thought he had "worked so long covertly he couldn't bear to do otherwise." The Agency history reports the views of three subsequent Saigon station officers that Washington, without need of CIA urging, either supported or insisted on Diệm's appointment. It adds: "In fact, John Foster Dulles and the French seem to have concluded, more or less simultaneously, that there was no alternative to Diem. On 24 May, the US Embassy in Paris moved to 'reestablish contact' with Diem to discuss his negotiations with Bao Dai."[28]

In Saigon in mid-May, seeking to answer Nhu's question about U.S. support, Harwood had asked his station chief and CIA headquarters to specify "the terms on which he could commit covert assistance through Nhu." Harwood received no reply for two weeks, and so, at the end of May, he drew up what he thought the U.S. mission in Saigon wanted from "any new government": direct U.S. training of the SVN army "even over French objections"; "uncompromising resistance by the government to any Viet Minh encroachment on southern territory"; "prosecuting the war against the Viet Minh," and opposition to "coalition and partition." Significantly, the terms also required "CIA access to Bao Dai" and "the continued secrecy of the liaison with CIA." Spence took these terms to Nhu, who agreed to them. By June 2, Harwood had transmitted them to CIA Headquarters. The ramifications were clear: "Once Nhu accepted the terms, Harwood was committed to support the effort to install Diem as prime minister." Headquarters in turn accepted this commitment "and proceeded directly into a discussion of operational programs." While Harwood "explored the operational possibilities with Nhu," he also wanted to use their relationship for "covert action." The Station "pressed Nhu to describe his influence over Diem." Nhu replied, "probably with tongue in cheek," that he could "direct" his brother. Precisely when the CIA obtained its desired access to Bảo Đại and whether it encouraged him to meet Diệm's terms remain unclear.[29] But the CIA's historian of the Diệm era concluded in 2001 that since "the southern rump state had to have a leader," the United States "chose" Diệm for that role.[30]

Diệm was ready for the challenge. On June 16, 1954, he officially accepted Bảo Đại's offer of the SVN premiership. He flew to Saigon on June 25 to assume the office. Lansdale, who had just arrived to establish the city's second CIA mission, had still "never heard of Diem."[31] But Saigon's other CIA station certainly had.

CONTENDING FORCES

The U.S. State Department's Division of Research reported in February 1955: "Almost any type of election that could conceivably be held in Vietnam in 1956 would, on the basis of present trends, give the Communists a very significant if not decisive advantage." And in the South, "maximum conditions of freedom and the maximum degree of international supervision might well operate to Communist advantage."[32] Sharing this view, most southern communists had accepted the DRV's commitment to the Geneva Agreement, disarmed, and stood down at least for the period 1954–56.

Some did so more begrudgingly than others. Two of the South's three leading communists were southerners: Lê Duẩn, born in Quảng Trị province, was its top communist; its third-ranking VWP leader, Phạm Hùng, came from Vĩnh Long in the Mekong delta; and Duẩn's deputy, northerner Lê Đức Thọ, had come south in 1948. In that year Thọ and Hùng played roles in Duẩn's marriage to a young southern resistance fighter, Nguyễn Thụy Nga.[33] The VWP's fourth-ranking leader in the South, Nguyễn Văn Linh, born in Tonkin in 1915, had grown up in the South and had piloted the getaway boat on which Lê Duẩn, Phạm Hùng, and Lê Đức Thọ's younger brother all escaped from Poulo Condore prison island in September 1945. They cannot have been happy to hand over the South to their SVN opponents.[34]

Yet in 1954–55 about 130,000 mostly southern VWP members and Việt Minh regrouped to North Việt Nam, including 87,000 of the 100,000 communist-led troops in the south, and 43,000 civilians. Up to 10,000 of these regroupees were members of southern ethnic minorities from the Central Highlands—about 5,000 Rhadé (also called Edé) and 4,000 Jarai, Bahnar, and Sédang, along with smaller numbers from a dozen other upland groups. A few regroupees were Chams, and about 1,000 were Khmers from the Mekong delta and Cambodia.[35] After arrival in the DRV, some of the southern regroupees remained in recognizably southern military units, including PAVN's 325th Division, which "at least until 1959," according to the U.S. State Department, was "reportedly composed entirely of South Vietnamese."[36]

Lê Duẩn's deputies Lê Đức Thọ and Phạm Hùng, and most other officials of the VWP Central Committee's Directorate for Southern Việt Nam, headed north in 1955. They first conducted a reorganization and purge that significantly reduced party numbers in the South. Of the region's sixty thousand VWP members in 1954, about fifteen thousand remained active there the next year.[37] Their leader Lê Duẩn worked undercover in Saigon in 1955 and 1956, alongside his former Poulo Condore fellow inmate Nguyễn Văn Linh, now secretary of the VWP City Committee for Saigon–Chợ Lớn.[38] Most other Việt Minh members and VWP cadres who stayed in the South laid down their weapons or returned to their villages and restricted their activities either to unarmed "political struggle" or "lying low for a long time." The political struggle was to be waged by "legal, semi-legal, and secret" groups of communists and their allies. Some would be armed, but no more than two thousand, dispersed in a few secret base areas.[39] Of the graduated Vietnamese communist strategies, "political struggle" was the lowest level of armed activity. It could be escalated progressively through later stages, from "political struggle supported by arms," to "combined armed and political struggle," to the highest level of armed struggle, "all-out people's war."[40]

The different armed groups who dominated other areas of southern Việt Nam were not parties to the Geneva Agreement and did not demobilize in 1954. The Bình Xuyên syndicate continued to run parts of Saigon and rural pockets to its south and east. The Cao Đài controlled larger areas, mostly north of the capital but also interspersed throughout the Mekong delta. The Hòa Hảo ruled most of the upper central delta.[41] Areas of French control in the South became strongholds of the Diệm regime. These included coastal Catholic communities of the lower central delta; the south-central provinces of Khánh Hòa, Ninh Thuận (Phan Rang), and Bình Thuận (Phan Thiết), with their Catholic and Cham minorities; and north-central areas around Huế and Đà Nẵng.[42]

Like the leaders of the Bình Xuyên, Cao Đài, and Hòa Hảo, as well as Bảo Đại himself, Ngô Đình Diệm was not a party to the Geneva Agreement. He denounced it and dissociated his new government from implementing it.

Yet his refusal to treat with the DRV did not make him a southern secessionist. Diệm considered southerners to be "more thinly spread geographically and more naive politically" than northerners, and he hoped his SVN regime could hold on to parts of the north. Diệm flew to Hanoi in its last days of colonial rule in an unsuccessful attempt to prevent French withdrawal from the northern Catholic dioceses Phát Diệm and Bùi Chu and to retain the Hanoi–Hải Phòng corridor for the SVN. Diệm did not fully abandon his frustrated northern ambitions. But on returning to Saigon, before turning on the disarmed southern communists and Việt Minh, he first set about defeating the noncommunist southern groups.[43]

Diệm conducted these campaigns with massive U.S. aid to his regime, totaling 60 percent of its revenues. In October 1954, President Eisenhower ordered a "crash program" of military assistance, and in February 1955, the U.S. Military Assistance Advisory Group (MAAG) took charge of advising, training, and equipping the VNA. From 1954 to 1960, Washington provided Diệm's government with $444 million in military aid and $1.4 billion in economic aid. Diệm's dependence on U.S. aid was such that in 1957–61, even while (as he later asserted), he "advocated for four years" a twenty-thousand-man increase in the size of his army, he did not pursue that expansion in the absence of U.S. provision for its funding.[44]

Diệm appointed his first cabinet on July 7, 1954. Catholic intellectuals of the *Tinh Thần* group gained four cabinet posts. But other close allies had already broken with the new leader. Twelve days after Diệm's June 25 return to Việt Nam, Catholic labor leader Trần Quốc Bửu regretted siding with the Ngô brothers and was "so disillusioned" with them that he "briefly considered an accommodation with the Việt Minh." Trần Văn Đỗ of *Tinh Thần* and Phan Huy Quát of the Đại Việt Party soon complained of Diệm's refusal to share power with fellow anticommunists.[45]

Yet a new constituency for Diệm was emerging. During the three-hundred-day period of free movement between the northern and southern zones, about 860,000 anticommunist northerners migrated to the south, with the assistance of the U.S. Navy. Most were Catholic civilians from Tonkin (including five of the north's ten bishops), but they included about twenty thousand members of northern Catholic militia units and two hundred thousand VNA soldiers, officials, and their families. Of the total, 209,000 were Buddhists.[46] In 1955–56, the Diệm regime resettled about a hundred thousand of the northern Catholics on a single 77,000 ha tract of land formerly controlled by the Hòa Hảo, in An Giang province in the upper Mekong delta. Another twenty-five thousand refugees were soon resettled in two areas in the lower delta and the Plain of Reeds.[47]

These local concentrations of mostly Catholic refugees added another distinct regional religious community to the "leopard spot" political pattern of rural southern Việt Nam. Diệm also maintained the SVN's supraprovincial regional administrative divisions, while quickly replacing the regional governors and other officials who had run them.[48] A third brother, Ngô Đình Cẩn, took over central Việt Nam, which he ruled for nine years as its "uncrowned king" with his own ruthless security force and continued autonomy from Saigon.[49] The CIA's internal history later termed Diệm's government a "proliferation of quasi-feudal fiefdoms."[50]

As the massive refugee migration from the north proceeded during 1954–55, Diệm suppressed his southern noncommunist rivals one by one. He first moved to temporarily neutralize the Cao Đài and Hòa Hảo armies, meeting with their commanders in July 1954. In September Diệm brought eight of their leaders into a reshuffled cabinet alongside the *Tinh Thần* ministers, and he bought off several sect commanders with CIA-supplied cash. Diệm also arrested two junior officers of the VNA commander General Hinh, provoking a confrontation that led to Hinh's permanent departure for France in November.[51]

But in March 1955 the eight Hòa Hảo and Cao Đài ministers quit the cabinet. Diệm then deployed the VNA against his armed noncommunist rivals. First, in the "Battle of Saigon" in April-May, the army drove the Bình Xuyên crime syndicate from the capital at a cost of hundreds of civilians killed or missing, and pursued its remnant forces into the swamps south of the city. Then in June the VNA attacked and overran the Hòa Hảo stronghold near Cần Thơ, capturing (and later beheading) Ba Cụt, one of the sect's two leading commanders; the other fled over the Cambodian border. Only four Hòa Hảo battalions held out. In October, VNA units surrounded the Cao Đài holy see at Tây Ninh, placed its pope Phạm Công Tắc and his family under house arrest, and attacked a Cao Đài center in the western delta.[52] Tắc soon fled to Cambodia, which accepted him as a political refugee. Meanwhile, in northern South Việt Nam, Đại Việt members led a revolt of one thousand national guard deserters who set up a base near the Lao border. By August 1955 Diệm and the VNA crushed them too.[53]

THE REPUBLIC OF VIỆT NAM (RVN)

In October 1955 Diệm staged a one-sided "referendum" on his regime. He campaigned strongly against Bảo Đại, who remained in France while his supporters were barred from campaigning. The vote was heavily rigged. Diệm himself then replaced Bảo Đại as chief of state, and proclaimed the new Republic of Việt Nam (RVN), to be run by the "Government of Việt Nam," or GVN.[54] Diệm had eclipsed his noncommunist rivals. He could now deploy the newly renamed Army of the Republic of Việt Nam (ARVN) against his last opponents, the southern communists.

The communists in the south were no military threat but were politically potent. In April 1955 the U.S. International Security Agency had predicted the communists would still "easily" win a free election in the south as well as the north: "Nationalist appeal in Vietnam is so closely identified with Ho Chi Minh and the Viet-Minh movement that, even in areas outside communist control, candidates and issues connected with 'nationalism' and supported by the Viet-Minh would probably be supported by the majority of the people."[55] Maintaining his opposition to the Geneva Agreement, and with support from Lansdale, Dulles, and the U.S. Government, Diệm continued to reject DRV attempts to engage him in talks about holding the stipulated July 1956 nationwide elections.[56] He also refused to allow free elections within South Việt Nam.[57] Vietnamese of both North and South were denied any choice of their rulers.

Diệm believed, Nhu informed his CIA contact Harwood, that "to rule, it was enough to have an army and an administrative apparatus." In June 1956 Diệm abolished villagers' traditional right to vote in local elections for their village chiefs and councils.[58] Thenceforth the GVN's province chiefs would name an unelected committee to run each village; Diệm himself, it was announced in October, would directly appoint the province chiefs. This alienated a large cohort of previously elected village chiefs who had the respect of their fellow villagers and had mostly collaborated with the former Việt Minh administration. The GVN province chiefs now ran the entire administration of each province. The next year they also assumed military command of all its armed forces; from then on, most of those who gained appointment as province chiefs were field-grade ARVN military officers.[59] The top-down approach to local government also impacted the newly resettled communities of northern refugees in An Giang. After first enlisting their priests in the local administration, Diệm supplanted them in August 1956 with a government-appointed village council. The priests objected. The GVN had them investigated and accused of corruption.[60] That August Diệm issued Ordinance 47, prescribing a death sentence for "any deed performed in or for any organization designated as Communist."[61]

In other 1955–56 ordinances, Diệm overturned the 1953–54 Việt Minh land reform in the South, instead legally recognizing the titles of the expropriated landlords. Peasant beneficiaries of the Việt Minh reform had to abandon their claims and even pay back rent for their plots. Diệm instituted his own land redistribution that exempted the property of absentee landlords, French citizens, and the Catholic Church, while other landlords could retain as much as 145 ha of farmland. Though the average family plot size was 1.5 ha, and 80 percent of Mekong delta farmers were landless tenants, only 10 percent of southern tenants benefited from Diệm's reform, which required them to rent or purchase their new holdings from the government.[62] In 1961 more than 44 percent of Cochinchina's peasants remained landless, and another 29 percent were partial tenants; only 22 percent of farmers were owner-occupiers. When some northern Catholic refugees resettled in An Giang objected to the government's imposition of tenancy contracts, the GVN withheld their subsistence payments "to bring them around."[63]

DIỆM'S PROJECT

What kind of a regime and society did Diệm wish to build? Some have described him as an adherent of traditional Vietnamese ideology, the "last Confucian" or "last of the mandarins," who had gained "the Mandate of Heaven."[64] He was well-schooled in the classical texts and demonstrated a scholarly elitism when he officially changed the name of the province of Bến Tre (colloquial Vietnamese for "bamboo port") to Kiến Hòa, a more literary synonym. To address Diệm, his officials employed a term of deference used under the mandarinate, Ngài ("Excellency" or "Majesty," also used for deities).[65] Diệm's rigid but authentic rejection of ideological compromise recalls the mindset of the nineteenth-century emperor Minh Mạng; even so his abolition of local elections distinguished Diệm's project from the traditional Vietnamese adage that "the emperor's writ stops at the village gate."

Diệm and his secretive brother Nhu were twentieth-century politicians. Despite their anticolonialism, European political ideology influenced them as much as Vietnamese and Confucian thought. Strong Catholic beliefs were central to both men, as were Nhu's creed of personalism and his borrowings from French colonial counterinsurgency doctrine, including its pioneering of "strategic hamlets." The brothers exhibited a "long-standing interest in synthesizing Eastern and Western cultural elements in a modern political philosophy."[66] One observer saw Diệm as an aristocratic amalgam of "a Confucian scholar-statesman, a Platonic philosopher-king and a devout Christian."[67]

Like some European and Asian Catholic leaders, the Ngôs' instincts were as autocratic as they were nationalistic. They had little interest in democratic electoral competition or even the compromises that political coalitions require.[68] After launching his anticolonial career in 1933, Diệm saw himself as a natural leader of his country, yet never built a political party or movement. He tried to gain the leadership of existing groups and coalitions, proposing that they accept his claim for "full powers." The strategy failed for two decades. Then, taking power in 1954, Diệm shunned or destroyed most noncommunist potential allies, requiring loyalty of his constituents and deploying force to impose it. His brothers worked out of public view. Nhu's Cần Lao Party "operated mostly in the shadows," and Cẩn ran central Việt Nam "from behind the scenes." By 1955 the CIA worried over the "enormous gap between the Government and the people."[69]

The Ngôs were Vietnamese nationalists who saw few others as such. Several CIA and U.S. observers, including Lansdale, concluded that Diệm's regime was an emerging "fascist state," one "more messianic than Confucian."[70] Nhu told his main CIA contact in 1958 that their regime "could never get the support of the people because they had to tax and discipline the population which in turn would not respond to them with affection."[71] He later added:

> People say that our cadres should go out, work with the peasants, and establish a relationship of affection and confidence with them to learn their needs. But if the cadres do this, they are overwhelmed by the people's claims and demands. The only thing for the government to do is issue orders and back them up with force.[72]

Autocratic impulses undermined even the Ngôs' attachment to French Catholic personalism. While opposing communist materialism, most personalists rejected capitalism and imperialism too; they advocated "social pluralism," along with people's rights to employ "direct pressures" such as strikes and uprisings. These tenets were anathema to the Ngôs, who opposed independent popular actions to achieve social change. Nhu "blamed virtually all political unrest" on communists and asserted that "the people never march against their government unless they are instigated to do so by Communist terrorism."[73] Diệm and Nhu used personalist ideology, rather, to justify their demands that citizens take full responsibility to implement GVN projects and to develop themselves in "self-sufficiency" without expecting government aid. That often meant compulsory unpaid labor—especially building rural "agrovilles" and "strategic hamlets" to relocate peasants and forcibly separate them from the reach of communist cadres.[74] The government saw its own task mostly in terms of defeating its political rivals. Around 1956 Diệm told the CIA station chief that, given limited resources, GVN officials should "rely on speed and force rather than thoroughness." Nhu told a French journalist in 1960: "Although what transpires in Saigon may not conform to the ideal of Mounier, in political action one is sometimes obliged to dirty his hands." Under the Ngôs, an analyst wrote, almost all "Personalist scholars in Vietnam" professed "disillusionment at what Personalism has become in its official guise."[75]

Diệm launched the Anti-Communist Denunciation Campaign (ACDC) in July 1955. It began in Saigon with a GVN-sponsored "demonstration against the International Control Commission, representing the Geneva signatories."[76] From October the ACDC applied "real pressure" on the communists' rural political organizations. But it caught many others in its net. A CIA contact in the Cao Đài sect told Lansdale that in early 1956 Saigon's Chí Hòa prison housed seven thousand political detainees.[77] In May 1956, the GVN reported that since 1954 it had imprisoned fifteen to twenty thousand suspected communists and procommunists in "political reeducation" centers. The GVN then launched "period II" of the ACDC, aiming "to destroy the whole network secretly woven by the adversary which covers the whole of free Vietnam." By the end of 1956 a French scholar estimated the number of political prisoners in the RVN at fifty thousand.[78] A lull from March 1957 was followed by the ACDC's most intense phase from November 1957 to February 1959, "directed indiscriminately at opponents of the Diem regime." One was the former Trotskyist and well-known writer Hồ Hữu Tường, who spent the years 1957–63 in jail on Poulo Condore island. Police records in Long An province alone showed that in each month of 1959, an average of twenty-six people were arrested there for communist activities. The GVN estimated the total number it arrested from 1954 to 1960 at 48,200. The numbers of detainees held from year to year ranged from 15,000 to 30,000.[79]

The GVN's transfer into the Central Highlands in 1957–58 of 128,000 settlers, including many northern Catholics, provoked racial tensions with upland groups, some of whom the army forcibly removed from their homes. In 1958 highlanders from the Bahnar, Rhadé, Jarai, and Cơ Ho ethnic groups formed the Bajaraka Movement to air their grievances and claims for political autonomy. When they appealed for a general strike, Diệm was outraged at this "highland gang" and ordered all its leaders arrested.[80] The top Rhadé leader, the Protestant Y Bham Enuol, spent the next four years in jail. Another, Y Bih Aleo, escaped and joined the communist underground.[81]

The historian Trương Bửu Lâm returned to Việt Nam in May 1957, after a decade in Europe. He became director of the RVN's Institute of Historical Research, with appointments at the Universities of Saigon, Huế, and Đà Lạt. In 1957 and 1958 Lâm and his staff were constantly on the road. They drove their institute van "all over South Vietnam, region by region, to inspect its historical monuments," including long trips "from the southernmost point of the country to the demarcation line at the 17th parallel," and enjoying "very extensive" contacts with local people where they worked. Lâm recalls: "I found that a great deal of cynicism toward the regime had spread among the common people." Those "born and raised in the South complained about discrimination" and about the regime's "favoritism" to the mostly Catholic northern refugees. Pursuing "a sinister path with more and more restrictions on the basic human rights," South Việt Nam was gliding toward "dictatorship, totalitarianism, one-party and one-family rule." In the government, "the Ngô family and their in-laws occupied almost all the key positions."[82]

Much of this barely perturbed some of the leading American officers on the spot. The head of the U.S. MAAG from 1955 to 1960, General Samuel "Hangin' Sam" Williams, like his successors, saw the main problem as the threat of North Vietnamese invasion. Williams seemed to disregard the political ramifications of GVN domestic repression when he asserted in 1959 that "the population of South Vietnam . . . is more responsive to fear and force than to an improved standard of living." He concluded: "The paramount consideration is to gain and maintain a superiority of force in all parts of the country."[83]

In April 1960, eighteen of Saigon's prominent political figures, mostly former RVN high officials, disagreed. They published a "manifesto" appealing for democratic reforms. They accused Diệm of having, among other things, "crammed the jails and prisons to the rafters." A number of the manifesto's signatories were themselves jailed, some in Côn Sơn prison on Poulo Condore. Within months Diệm further tightened his grip on the RVN. He replaced his information minister and other leading officials and centralized government power in the hands of three trusted personal associates. The Cần Lao Party extended its reach within ARVN, provoking the resignation of the deputy defense minister in October 1960.[84] The next month, three U.S.-trained ARVN paratroop battalions staged an abortive coup in Saigon. The fighting took four hundred lives before Diệm regained control.[85] It was in this context of repression and of growing unrest in Saigon that a southern communist insurgency emerged in the countryside.

INSURGENCY

Southern communists had begun to amend their "political struggle" strategy as early as mid-1956, close to the July deadline for holding the nationwide elections. That June, before gaining approval from Hanoi, the southern communist leadership responded to appeals from its cadres whom the GVN was hunting down, by authorizing them in special cases to use "self-defense." Then on July 22, the "Vietnamese People's Liberation Movement" announced its formation in Long An province. It urged people to help "smash" and "defeat" the "rebel" GVN authorities, but apparently it did not yet advocate the use of armed force. In the last months of 1956 Lê Duẩn, the VWP secretary for Nam Bộ (Cochinchina), circulated among southern party cadres a document entitled "The Path of the Revolution in the South." It urged them to "strongly push the revolutionary movement in the South," but to do so in accord with the party's line of "peaceful political struggle." At the same time higher councils of the party in the South were openly discussing future plans for an armed uprising after this period of political rebuilding of its forces.[86] The VWP's Nam Bộ Regional Committee, meeting in December 1956, approved the use of "self-defense and armed propaganda forces in order to support the political struggle and eventually use those armed forces to overthrow U.S.-Diệm" in a "violent general uprising." A secret directive that accompanied Lê Duẩn's text ordered cadres to prepare for a campaign of "executing tyrants" (*trừ gian*), which the party launched in mid-1957. In Long An that year, a unit calling itself "Company 12" announced the formation of the "Liberation Army" of the Vietnamese People's Liberation Movement. The statement also denounced "the American-Diệm regime" for having "sabotaged the Geneva Accords" and for moving to "massacre, imprison or exile patriots who demand peace." It appealed for funds "in order to suppress the stubborn tyrants" and overthrow the regime.[87]

Thus, particularly after October 1957, "the Communist underground struck back." In 1957 alone it killed at least seventy-five GVN military personnel, village chiefs, officials, and private citizens, and about two hundred more officials each year in 1958 and 1959. Highlander unrest in central Việt Nam, including a Rhadé revolt in 1957, also led "the Party's most senior official in Trung Bo" (Annam) to order, in March-April 1958, preparations for "the first armed uprising." That year southern communist fighting units inflicted casualties on GVN paramilitary forces "at the rate of 40 men per week."[88] GVN repression continued, reducing VWP membership in the south from fifteen thousand in 1957 to a low point of possibly as few as five thousand in 1959.[89] Yet Diệm's ruling party newspaper lamented in February 1959 that "the situation in the rural areas is rotten."[90]

As in Saigon in September 1945, when the DRV's Southern Committee had overruled Hanoi's preference for diplomacy and urged Vietnamese to "grab weapons and rise up to drive out the invading forces," a new southern insurgency had commenced despite Hanoi's refusal to formally support an armed struggle. Southern representatives making the case in Hanoi found the DRV focused on internal issues and its response limited.[91] A few hundred of the southern regroupees had started to return from the north from as early as 1955, and in April 1956, the DRV's Voice of Việt Nam began broadcasting radio programs in three of the main languages unique to the Central Highlands: Rhadé, Bahnar, and Jarai.[92] That June the Hanoi Politburo followed the initiative of the southern communist leaders by authorizing "self-defense." Otherwise Hanoi held to its policy of "political struggle" for the South, unprovoked by what the CIA termed "a modest program of harassing attacks on coastal facilities in the North," conducted by the RVN and financed by the Agency from 1955 to 1956.[93] But southern communists who had initially stayed in the south made visits to the north. In 1957 Lê Duẩn was recalled north and even promoted to VWP acting secretary-general.[94] Nguyễn Văn Linh succeeded him as VWP leader in the South.[95] In late 1958 Duẩn briefly returned south for "a secret inspection trip."[96]

In January 1959, after Duẩn's return to Hanoi, the VWP Central Committee (CC) met there for its Fifteenth Plenum. Four southern party leaders also traveled north to attend. Another southerner present, PAVN deputy chief of staff General Trần Văn Trà, later recalled that Hồ Chí Minh presided over the meeting, which reached a resolution only in May: "There was heated discussion between those who advocated the use of arms and those who didn't. Hồ Chí Minh always tried to avoid war, to favor political struggle and avoid bloodshed. But those who came from the South said that without armed struggle the revolutionary forces would be destroyed." Of the three thousand cadres in 1954 in Mỹ Tho province, for instance, only three hundred remained in 1959. "So we asked that armed struggle be allowed... to support political struggle."[97] The plenum finally authorized an "insurrection" in the South, involving the use of both "armed force" and "political force." Yet this was not the conventional main force warfare that the Việt Minh had marshalled against the French; "political struggle" remained the "primary" strategy.[98] The operational guidelines for implementing this VWP resolution, transmitted to southern communist leaders on May 7, 1959, permitted the use only of "armed propaganda units" and "armed self-defense forces" to support "political struggle."[99] This was precisely the southern communist policy that the Nam Bộ Regional Committee had adopted two years earlier, in December 1956. Still, Hanoi ruled out launching a "people's war."[100] It approved armed force only under restrictions, and provided "limited" DRV support to the southern insurrection.[101] In late May 1959, Hanoi established "Group 559" to open up what later became the Hồ Chí Minh Trail. PAVN engineering units set up marine and jungle infiltration routes into the South. In 1959 and 1960 about 4,600 former southern regroupees returned there, including political cadres, technicians, military advisers, armed propaganda units, and medics.[102]

But the southern insurrection was already in progress. By April 1959, "before infiltration from the North had even begun, the CIA reported that the Viet Cong had already achieved virtual control over whole villages and districts in the Cà Mau peninsula," in the western delta. After two years of traveling the southern countryside "without any incident," one day in 1959, as Trương Bửu Lâm and his staff from the RVN Institute of Historical Research were driving through the delta, "five armed men all dressed in pajamas of different colors and qualities" intercepted them. "They stopped and boarded our van without a word. Since they looked well equipped with weapons, we chose not to object." After fifteen minutes driving along in silence, one of the men signaled the driver to stop. The group "got off the van without a word of thanks, and disappeared into nowhere." Two months later, Lâm's team went deeper into the delta by car and boat, visiting the village of Hoà Hảo "without a hitch." But the next day "insurgents armed with machine guns" ambushed and killed the RVN deputy province chief and his entire entourage, who were "following exactly the same itinerary."[103]

News of Hanoi's Fifteenth Plenum reached Bến Tre province in the eastern delta before the end of 1959. Nguyễn Thị Định attended the local meeting at which the new policy of "political struggle in conjunction with military action" was announced. She recalled: "The moment they heard military action mentioned the conference burst out in stormy applause. The higher levels had followed exactly the aspirations of the lower."[104] However, local communists in other delta provinces such as Kiến Phong, Kiến Tường, and Mỹ Tho had already launched "unauthorized military actions," which Hanoi considered "adventurous" and was as yet unwilling to back.[105] Nevertheless, the September 1960 VWP Third Congress in Hanoi confirmed Lê Duẩn as party secretary general and promoted "almost a dozen southern or central Vietnamese" to CC membership. Nguyễn Văn Linh, still in the South, became a secret CC member. As U.S. intelligence later reported, these southerners were soon chosen to form a "Central Office for South Vietnam" as an "extension" of the VWP.[106]

The civil war in the south escalated. Both sides took heavy casualties. By the end of 1960 the communist rebels had killed or kidnapped 1,400 GVN officials.[107] This figure reached 13,000 by late 1963. According to GVN statistics, communist losses in the south between January 1957 and June 1962 totaled 79,000 people—compared with 35,000 on the government side, and fewer than twenty Americans.[108]

In December 1960, the communists established the National Front for the Liberation of South Việt Nam—usually known as the National Liberation Front (NLF) or Việt Cộng (VC). Its membership at that time has been estimated at about 37,500.[109] A month later the "Liberation Army of South Việt Nam," first unveiled in Long An province in 1957, was declared to be a branch of PAVN.[110] Also in January 1961, the VWP CC established its "Central Office" for South Việt Nam (COSVN).[111] Led by COSVN and its VWP cadres, the NLF also included ten of the eleven Cao Đài subsects, a former Bình Xuyên officer and the remnants of two Bình Xuyên companies, and several ethnic Cambodian religious leaders.[112] The founding president of the NLF was Nguyễn Hữu Thọ, a Paris-educated Saigon lawyer who in 1950–54 had campaigned against the French and worked with Nguyễn Thị Bình, a granddaughter of the early twentieth-century nationalist reformer Phan Châu Trinh. Jailed by the French, Thọ pursued his activism against Diệm and spent six more years in prison until his escape in 1961. Mme. Bình also joined the NLF and became its "foreign minister." The Christian ethnic Rhadé leader Y Bih Aleo served as NLF vice president.[113]

But until 1965 the leading role in the NLF was probably that of Lê Duẩn's successor, the senior VWP representative in the South, Nguyễn Văn Linh. He became "secretary of the COSVN" on its foundation in January 1961.[114] Linh's key role and his membership in the party CC remained undisclosed, possibly in case he were to be captured. A CIA history described Linh as "quiet, scholarly, and heavy-browed," working from an office in his jungle headquarters "lined with books, both Marxist tomes and recent novels. When he reads, which is often," the report noted, "he uses glasses." He read Vietnamese, French, and Chinese.[115] Born in Tonkin but raised from childhood in the South, Linh had worked as a communist there for a quarter century—apparently unknown to U.S. intelligence. He was not listed among the thirty-three "major figures of the NLF" (only two of them northerners) that U.S. government analysts had identified by 1965.[116]

The GVN's continuing repression in the South had backfired. It provoked a local communist-led southern insurgency that grew rapidly from 1960, taking over many rural provinces of South Việt Nam.[117] By 1961 the Diệm government estimated it had lost control of more than half the population. In his study *War Comes to Long An*, Jeffrey Race suggested why: "The government terrorized far more than did the revolutionary movement—for example, by liquidations of former Vietminh, by artillery and ground attacks on 'communist villages,' and by roundups of 'communist sympathizers.' Yet it was just these tactics that led to the constantly increasing strength of the revolutionary movement in Long An from 1960 to 1965."

Although it had won northern approval and support, the local movement was largely indigenous to Long An. The number of personnel "infiltrated" there from the DRV was "extremely low," increasing "from about ten a year in 1960 to less than one hundred a year in 1965."[118] Until 1964, nearly all infiltrators arriving in the South were returning southern regroupees.[119] The insurgency remained local, but this was far from unique to Long An; military historian Eric Bergerud found a similar story in neighboring Hậu Nghĩa province, west of Saigon. In the northeastern delta province of Mỹ Tho, too, the NLF amassed "overwhelming popular support" during 1961–63.[120] By 1962, in the five provinces of the northern delta alone, the NLF was fielding two thousand regular troops, three thousand provincial forces, and ten thousand guerrillas.[121]

The impact of GVN repression on ethnic minorities was also severe, with a similar political blowback. Some 429 Khmer peasants, including 284 women and children, from thirty Khmer-majority villages in An Giang province in the northern delta, fled across the border into Cambodia in early 1962. They brought accounts of the Diệm regime's forced resettlements, closure of Khmer schools, and, in the words of a Khmer monk, "the slaughter of our people, the destruction of our villages, the repression of our culture and language."[122] This helps explain a CIA report that in the Seven Mountains border area of An Giang until at least October 1962, "the ethnic Cambodian majority . . . supported or tolerated the VC." The local GVN authorities harbored views of the Cambodians that ranged from "apathetic at best to hostile at worst." And fifty miles east of Saigon, Long Khánh province, with its mixed population of Vietnamese and uplanders, was "largely under enemy control" by 1963. CIA teams, for instance, "could circulate no farther than into the hamlets adjacent to the district towns."[123]

Washington had meanwhile escalated its commitment to the GVN and against the DRV. In 1961 the CIA and ARVN began launching a new series of joint "black entry" military operations into North Việt Nam.[124] That year Washington also increased the corps of 685 U.S. military advisers in the South (the Geneva Agreement allowed up to 888) to more than 3,000. In February 1962 it transferred these personnel to a new U.S. Military Assistance Command, Vietnam (MACV). By December 1963, some sixteen thousand American military personnel were deployed in South Việt Nam. U.S. aircraft began strafing and bombing in the southern countryside in 1962, flying 2,048 attack sorties that year and more than 6,000 in 1963.[125] Also in 1962, they began spraying herbicides to kill vegetation that might hide enemy troops.[126] Americans were playing a direct role in what was still a South Vietnamese civil war.

COUNTERINSURGENCY IN THE HIGHLANDS

The CIA launched its first counterinsurgency program in 1961, in the Central Highlands. Local tensions were rising; the GVN had by now resettled 180,000 ethnic Vietnamese there, antagonizing many of the indigenous uplanders, whom the French and Americans called Montagnards. A CIA officer would soon warn that twenty-one highland districts were considered "ripe for complete VC control." The Agency's covert Military Operations Section (MOS) elected to start off its counterinsurgency efforts by setting up "intelligence nets directed at Viet Cong military forces thought to be based in that area." For its first project, MOS selected one of the villages of the hundred-thousand-strong Rhadé minority, most of whom lived in Đắc Lắc province in the southern Central Highlands. MOS proposed to start by building a medical dispensary and a perimeter fence around the village of Buon Enao, four miles from the province capital, Ban Mê Thuột.[127] The fence would bar entry to "Communist personnel" and would be posted with RVN flags and anticommunist notices.[128]

The Rhadé village of Buon Enao comprised between fifteen and twenty thatched longhouses, built on stilts for protection against animals and floods.[129] It had as yet suffered no "VC attacks" and was "not immediately threatened with Communist attack or infiltration." But a mid-1961 GVN bombardment had destroyed several local villages. "Most of the survivors had joined the Viet Cong," according to a CIA account of the counterinsurgency program. Some twenty-six Rhadé refugees who had instead moved to Buon Enao were to become the nucleus of MOS's proposed "village defense leadership." First, however, MOS had to secure the cooperation of the elders of Buon Enao. A U.S. Special Forces medic and a Rhadé-speaking American civilian made an initial visit to the village in October 1961.[130] On arrival they found "no younger men present." Women, children, a shaman, and the village chief Y-Ju "watched the Americans," who offered to treat the sick. Y-Ju presented his daughter, "a frail girl in black pajamas," ill with a fever. The medic successfully treated her with an injection of antibiotics.[131]

For three weeks the MOS team visited Buon Enao daily. The medic recorded its negotiations there. Villagers appreciated the medical attention, but the elders registered a list of objections to participating in the counterinsurgency program. One gains the impression that these Rhadé much preferred to be left alone without voicing any confrontational opposition to the American proposal or antagonizing either side in the Vietnamese civil war. First came objections on carefully even-handed political grounds: construction of a fence around their village "would provoke tension with the Army"—that is, ARVN. The MOS team responded by promising "a letter of authorization from the province chief." Next the elders argued that the fence would also "provoke VC attack." The Americans replied, "We'll arm you." But the elders worried, "We don't know how to shoot." The reply: "We'll teach you." The Rhadé remained skeptical. Perhaps prudently unwilling to reject the U.S. approach outright, they next raised environmental and cost problems: "We have no bamboo for the fence." The Americans promised to "go into the jungle and cut it"—if any Rhadé needed such help. But, the elders continued, "the fence will displace crops and fruit trees." The American answer was, "We'll replace them." That might have been harder. But the CIA history reveals what came next. The Americans "pointed out to the elders: eventually they would have to choose sides, because 'any bug between the foot and the rug is going to get squashed.' "[132]

The Rhadé acceded at the end of October 1961. Village chief Y-Ju "committed himself to help build both the dispensary and the fence." MOS employed fifty Buon Enao villagers on the project, and another 125 from adjacent villages, including the 26 whose fellow villagers had joined the NLF. But during the construction the Rhadé raised more obstacles. According to the CIA, their "religious beliefs and superstitions" continually threatened progress on the project. At one point, a Western-educated Rhadé had to be called in to explain to the Americans that the villagers considered fence building "foolish" and believed that "a monkey follows a man who does something foolish." This required a temporary halt to the fence construction and the formation of a "monkey patrol" to scour the surrounding jungle and clear it of simians. Finally, the Rhadé argued, a crow alighting on an unfinished building would require its construction to be abandoned, so a "crow patrol" also had to be formed to keep the birds away from project housing.[133] The CIA commended its personnel for negotiating a thicket of exotic surroundings. Yet it is hard to see the Rhadé behavior as anything but understandable foot-dragging, a resort to the arsenal of what political scientist James Scott calls the "weapons of the weak."[134] The elders would have felt they had little choice. But they negotiated hard.

Buon Enao's elders also insisted on an end to "all attacks by government forces" on Rhadé and Jarai villages—"even if such villages were perceived to be co-operating with the Communists." GVN and ARVN officials agreed to this. But they rejected the elders' further stipulation that any Rhadé "who had been forced to train with or support with the VC" but now declared "allegiance" to the GVN should receive an immediate amnesty. The Đắc Lắc province chief and local ARVN commanders demanded that these Rhadé be "re-educated to the government cause" and "carefully observed." The Americans, too, asked chief Y-Ju "to certify the loyalty of each villager." He identified three men from Buon Enao "as having attended training camps run by the Communists." The three, subjected to effective "re-education," in turn "identified other Rhadé who had been involved with the Communists."[135]

Buon Enao's perimeter fencing and dispensary were completed in early December 1961. Within a week U.S. Special Forces arrived to commence training a village militia of fifty armed Rhadé as well as members of a mobile "Strike Force" for deployment over a wide area of Dắc Lắc province. In mid-December Ngô Đình Nhu visited Buon Enao, seemed "greatly impressed," and authorized the project's expansion to other Rhadé villages. Then "VC attacks began, in 1962." CIA sources credit "Buon Enao forces" with killing two hundred and capturing four hundred "VC" by the end of that year.[136] The program, to become known as the Civilian Irregular Defense Groups (CIDG), spread out from Buon Enao like an "oil slick." By July 1962, "the Strike Force at Buon Enao had about 650 armed and trained men deployed in support of 3,600 unpaid village defenders." Some eighty-eight villages in the area had resident medics. By late 1962, the CIA estimated that the CIDG "had drawn under its protection" up to a third of the 100,000–140,000 total Rhadé population. And beyond Đắc Lắc, MOS also recruited members of the Jarai, Bahnar, and Sédang in the more northerly upland provinces, Kontum and Pleiku. Looking back on this period, a British military analyst describes "the Buon Enao experiment" as "one of the most sophisticated counterinsurgency efforts that Americans have ever conceived and mounted."[137]

Yet the CIA's Montagnard pacification program collapsed. One reason was MACV's tendency "to ignore the guerrilla problem" in favor of large-scale operations.[138] From February 1963, the U.S. military took command of the Montagnard program from the CIA and increasingly directed it to more conventional warfare, rather than village defense. The GVN, which opposed uplander empowerment or autonomy, also stepped in and in many cases disbanded Montagnard units. ARVN disarmed eight hundred Strike Force troops and cut the pay of the others and of the hamlet militias. Rhadé Strike Force leaders were displaced by "haughty, cocky Vietnamese," who aimed "to ride hard on the Rhadé."[139] When the CIA received a report in late 1962 that the NLF vice president, Rhadé leader Y Bih Aleo, would consider surrendering to the GVN in return for the release of Bajaraka Rhadé leader Y Bham Enuol, who had languished in a GVN jail since 1958, negotiations were arranged. But in March 1963, on the order of the GVN's Đắc Lắc province chief, the South Vietnamese Air Force bombed the site of the talks, a medieval Cham tower in the province. Unhurt, Y Bih Aleo stayed with the NLF.[140]

All this played into the hands of the growing communist forces. The Việt Minh had dominated the Central Highlands up to their withdrawal in 1954.

Some six thousand Rhadé warriors had regrouped north with them, and many had undergone leadership training at the Southern Ethnic Minority Cadre School in Hanoi. The NLF inherited a substantial Việt Minh political following in the Central Highlands and could match U.S. and GVN military expansion there. In 1961 the VWP Politburo established a special military region for the highlands, separate from the Mekong delta.[141] By 1963, the "Communist tribal regular units which had slowly strangled the French" in the Central Highlands were "back in business" there. These included the 126th regiment, composed of Rhadé fighters, but also the 108th (Jarai) and 803rd (Bahnar) regiments, and the 120th, an ethnic Hre regiment commanded by Colonel Y Bloc. A July 1963 communist offensive in central Đắc Lắc met little resistance, "villagers apparently surrendering quite readily the inadequate armament the government had left them."[142] In the fall of 1963, an Australian officer visited Buon Enao and found the village "half-empty."[143] By year's end the security situation in Đắc Lắc province was "extremely serious." From 1964 the NLF successfully staged three attacks on highlands Special Forces camps, with the aid of Montagnard agents inside.[144]

IN THE DELTA

In 1962 the CIA's MOS also turned its attention to An Giang province on the Cambodian border. It set out to "make" GVN officials there "realize their responsibilities" to the ethnic Khmer majority of the Seven Mountains area and bring "the latter into active support of their government." An MOS officer hoped to make An Giang "the first province fully under GVN control." In April 1963, however, the officer found "little to encourage him" after visiting the four camps that U.S. Special Forces set up among Khmer communities there. A declassified CIA history records his view at the time that "the US Army failed to grasp the causes of the insurgency and therefore lacked any prescription for a cure."[145]

The insurgency continued to spread. Throughout the South, U.S. experts estimated that from December 1960 NLF membership quadrupled to 150,000 by late 1961, and reached in 1962. Within the Front, the VWP in the South, which had 10,000–15,000 members in 1955–57 and many fewer in 1959, rebounded to number 30,000–35,000 by January 1962, when the VWP's southern branch renamed itself the People's Revolutionary Party (PRP). In December 1962 its membership reached 69,580, organized into 4,400 party chapters, half civilian and half military. Some PRP members served in the army and another 33,000 were stationed in South

Vietnamese villages and hamlets. The party had more than 5,000 female members and 8,000 from ethnic minorities.[146] By 1963 U.S. officials in Saigon agreed that "about one half of the South Vietnamese support the National Liberation Front."[147] It was also true that, in the words of a CIA officer who served in six provinces of South Việt Nam from 1963 to 1965, "many peasants hated them [the communists]."[148] But the NLF enjoyed far greater political support than the GVN, which, if it had wished, could not afford to negotiate a coalition with the NLF for fear that "the whale would swallow the minnow."[149]

The NLF showed its fighting capacity at the battle of Ấp Bắc in the Plain of Reeds in January 1963. A three-hundred-strong delta battalion defeated 2,500 ARVN troops, who were supported by thirteen U.S. warplanes and fifteen helicopters. The communists shot down five helicopters, damaged nine others, and killed eighty-three ARVN soldiers and three Americans, while losing of eighteen of their own. The hope that improved weaponry and air mobility would give ARVN military superiority foundered.[150] Later in 1963, the NLF introduced conscription and taxation, which dented its popularity but bolstered its military and economic power.[151] Its main force and local force units, organized at province and district level, were backed by equal numbers enlisted in village and hamlet guerrilla and militia units.[152] Meanwhile the top communist party leader in the South, Nguyễn Văn Linh, was joined by southern regroupee Trần Văn Trà, who left his DRV post as PAVN deputy chief of staff in 1963 and took command of the People's Liberation Armed Forces (PLAF) of South Việt Nam, a post he occupied until 1975.[153]

The rapid growth of the southern revolution was probably not surprising. As Jeffrey Race noted, what had initially enabled the GVN to both survive and "grind down" the communists in the late 1950s was the VWP CC's pre-1959 "policy of nonviolence, and not any intrinsic superiority of the government apparatus."[154] Diệm's early successes against the religious sects, other noncommunist oppositionists, and the communists pursuing an unarmed "political struggle" proved to be no guarantee of GVN prospects in the face of a communist-led armed insurrection that now drew members from all three groups.

THE BOWL OVERFLOWS: BUDDHIST PROTESTS

In 1959 Diệm formally dedicated South Việt Nam to the Virgin Mary. In political appointments, especially at the middle and lower levels, his regime favored Catholics over the far more numerous Buddhists. The church ran the government's academy for senior civil servants, led by Diệm's brother, Bishop Ngô Đình Thục.[155] Meanwhile Diệm declined to rescind the 1950 French colonial Ordinance no. 10, which permitted Catholics to publicly display religious banners yet denied the same right to adherents of Buddhism, defined in the ordinance as an "association" rather than a religion.[156] In 1960, Thục became archbishop of Huế, strengthening his brother Ngô Đình Cẩn's grip on central Việt Nam, the home region of the Ngô family but also a traditional stronghold of Vietnamese Buddhism. It was in Huế that the Buddhist revival had culminated in 1951 with the founding of the General Buddhist Association of Việt Nam (GBA), which advocated "national Buddhism" (*Phật Giáo dân tộc*). Three years later a northern GBA activist, Thích Trí Quang, fled south and took up residence in Huế. Trí Quang and other Buddhists encountered few problems with Cẩn before 1960. But after Thục's arrival in Huế, the archbishop's moves to convert locals to Catholicism and build a "National Marian Center" near the northern border sparked Buddhist concerns. In 1962, GBA president Thích Tịnh Kiết complained to Diệm, whose interior minister reported that Catholic officials had provoked the Buddhists. Diệm failed to resolve the issue.[157]

On May 4, 1963, the historian Trương Bửu Lâm traveled by train from Saigon to Huế. "Along the whole way, at every train station, at every railroad crossing, Vatican flags were flying high and low, sometimes alongside the national flag, sometimes all alone. I learned, afterwards, that some high officials of the government or of the Catholic Church had taken the train one or two days before me." The occasion was the May 4 celebration in Huế of the twenty-fifth anniversary of Thục's 1938 consecration as Việt Nam's third bishop. This was just days before the Wesak festival celebrating the Buddha's birthday and enlightenment, when Vietnamese believers bathe a Buddha image in sacred water. Trí Quang appealed to ARVN to admit Buddhist chaplains into the armed forces alongside Catholic ones. Diệm and Thục did not respond, but on May 6, the president's office sent an order to all GVN province chiefs and mayors prohibiting the public flying of any religious flags or banners. After the display of Vatican flags over the previous days, this enraged Buddhists assembling for Wesak. The next day, at Thục's insistence, police all over Huế pulled down Buddhist flags, banners, and lanterns. The following morning monks and faithful gathered at Huế radio station in anticipation of a special Wesak program, but the broadcast did not go ahead. As the crowd protested, troops opened fire, killing nine people. Trí Quang later described the government's tactics as "the drop that makes the bowl of water overflow."[158]

This was more than a religious crisis. It soon involved Diệm's secular noncommunist opposition. The public self-immolation in a Saigon street on June 11, 1963, of the monk Thích Quảng Đức, who left a statement inspired by the Buddhist revival asserting that "when Buddhism declines, the nation declines," was followed on July 7 by the suicide at home of leading intellectual Nguyễn Tường Tam (Nhất Linh), who had been a founder in 1932 of the Self-Reliant Literary Group and later briefly a member of both the VNQDD and of the early Democratic Republic of Việt Nam (DRV) government in 1946.[159] Nhất Linh's final note explained: "The arrest and detention of nationalist opposition elements is a serious crime, and it will cause the country to be lost into the hands of the Communists. . . . I kill myself as Thích Quảng Đức burned himself to send a warning to those who are trampling on our freedoms."[160]

The televised image of Quảng Đức calmly dying in the street for his views brought South Việt Nam to world attention. Four more Buddhist self-immolations followed in August. On August 20, ARVN troops invaded twelve Saigon pagodas and arrested more than seven hundred people. All this convinced many Americans and Vietnamese army officers that Diệm had to go. The CIA, which had assisted the rise of the Ngô brothers a decade earlier, now played a role in their downfall through the Saigon station. With the support of U.S. officials, a military coup overthrew the regime on November 2, 1963.[161] General Dương Văn Minh ("Big Minh") took power; unidentified ARVN soldiers murdered Diệm and Nhu. Their brother Cẩn was arrested, and he was executed the following year. Archbishop Thục, who was in Rome attending the Second Vatican Council, never returned to Việt Nam. The GVN was in crisis.

COMMUNISM IN THE NORTH

The DRV's victory over the French had barely interrupted its land reform campaign in the North. While Diệm reversed it in the South, the campaign intensified in the northern countryside until its completion in July 1956. Led by then–VWP secretary general Trường Chinh and backed by Hồ Chí Minh from the start, it involved two major processes. The first comprised successive phases, a "mass mobilization for rent reduction," followed by land reform proper, the redistribution to poor peasants of lands held by landlords, "rich peasants," and even many middle peasants. The second process was the reorganization and purge of local VWP branches, to expel landlords and members of "other exploiting classes" from the party.[162] A 1953 VWP investigation found that landlords comprised as much as 14 percent of party village committee members, rich peasants 15 percent, and middle peasants 61 percent. The VWP targeted many of these people for replacement by poor peasants, who in 1953 represented 44 percent of the rural population but fewer than 4 percent of VWP members.[163] In February 1956, the DRV vice minister of the interior, Lê Văn Lương, who also headed the VWP's Organization Commission and was the Politburo member responsible for party "rectification," publicly favored (in what became known as Maoist parlance) the promotion of people with the correct "spirit" even if they were not fully qualified for the post.[164]

As in the south before 1954, the land redistribution was relatively successful according to official figures. By 1957, northerners whom the VWP had classified as poor and landless peasants now held on average three to five times as much land as they had in 1953, while middle peasants had slightly increased their average ownership, but rich peasants had lost more than half of their holdings. On average, members of all four groups now owned roughly similar amounts, around 1,500 square meters of land (0.15 ha). Former landlords, for their part, retained 12 percent of their previous holdings, an average of only 738 square meters, or about half as much as the four peasant groups. On its own terms the party reorganization, again according to official figures, also succeeded. In VWP village committees, the proportion of former poor peasants and landless laborers rose from 4 percent to 53 percent, and that of middle peasants fell from 61 percent to 44 percent.[165]

Yet the results had come with a high level of violence. Landlords and rich peasants had not merely lost their lands. Thousands were killed, including some of those who formerly comprised 29 percent of the membership of village party committees. In the first six hundred villages affected by the preliminary phase, the mass mobilization for rent reduction, VWP Politburo member Hoàng Quốc Việt announced in August 1954 that villagers there had identified 10,147 landlords, of whom 1.3 percent had been executed, a death toll of over 130. This rent reduction phase eventually covered 1,875 North Vietnamese villages; if executions continued at the same rate, its toll may have exceeded four hundred. Then came the land reform proper. In its first, experimental wave, affecting only six villages of Thái Nguyên province, Việt also reported that ninety-eight of the households had been denounced as landlord families: thirty-eight in the rent reduction campaign and sixty families (ten per village) newly classified as landlords during the land reform campaign. Việt added that each of these ninety-eight landlords had been made to confess their crimes to the villagers and that 8 percent of them (an average of 1.3 per village) had been executed.[166] Others were imprisoned, including some inaccurately classified as landlords. The number of people killed during the entire 1954–56 land reform campaign, which covered a total of 3,314 villages in northern Việt Nam, remains unknown.

But it most probably exceeded three thousand and was possibly higher than fifteen thousand.[167]

The "absolute power" wielded by DRV land reform teams, writes political scientist Kim Ninh, had led to both "violence and opportunism." The writer and journalist Tô Hoài, while he was reporting for the North Vietnamese press on sessions in which peasants recounted their exploitation at the hands of landlords, observed the fanaticism of one team leader "bent on prevailing at all costs, fierce in every aspect," who not only called a village meeting to preside over the execution of a landlord but also insisted on marrying a poor peasant woman "to enhance his political credentials." Tô Hoài recalled: "I could not open my mouth. He could imprison me in a buffalo pen any time!"[168]

The DRV in this period was subject to a variety of international influences. Members of the International Control Commission (ICC), established at Geneva and comprising representatives from Canada, India, and Poland, were still able to move relatively freely throughout northern Việt Nam and report on violations of the 1954 agreement.[169] And in 1956, as members of the world communist bloc, leaders of the DRV and the VWP experienced the varied repercussions of Nikita Khrushchev's denunciation of Stalin's crimes at the Communist Party of the Soviet Union's Twentieth Congress in Moscow in February, Lu Dingyi's May speech in Beijing on the "Hundred Flowers" dissent, and also the June Poznań workers' protests in Poland and the October Hungarian uprising, both of which the communist governments severely repressed.[170]

From June to September 1956, the VWP newspaper *Nhân Dân* (The People) began to report "mistakes" in the DRV's land reform campaign that needed to be corrected. On August 17, Hồ Chí Minh addressed a letter "To the Compatriots in the Country," in which he asserted: "Errors have been committed in the implementation of unity in the countryside.... The Party and the Government have taken up seriously the subject of those lacks and errors and have determined a plan for their correction: Those who have been wrongly classified as landlords and rich peasants will be correctly reclassified. Those members of the Party, the cadres, and the population who have been the subject of an erroneous judgment will be re-established in their rights and prerogatives and their honorable character will be recognized."[171] Finally, on October 29, addressing a public meeting in Hanoi, General Võ Nguyên Giáp launched a more general critique: "We committed deviations in not emphasizing the necessity for caution and for avoiding the unjust disciplining [*xử trí*] of innocent people. We attacked on too wide a front, and used excessive repressive measures on a wide scale.... Even coercion was used in order to carry out party reorganization." Giáp then urged: "Correct the classification of people who have been wrongly called landlords, rich peasants, and small renters. Abolish the category 'other exploiting classes'; everyone so classified must be reclassified.... Do not treat the rich peasants like landlords. Carry out correctly the policy of allying with the rich peasants."[172]

Giáp's criticisms of the campaign that VWP secretary general Trường Chinh had led represented a sharp break between these two coauthors of *The Peasant Question*. In *Nhân Dân* the next day, Trường Chinh announced his resignation as secretary general, a post he had held for fifteen years. In addition, three of his allies on the VWP Politburo, also northerners, lost their positions in that body: Hoàng Quốc Việt; Lê Văn Lương, who additionally resigned from his DRV posts; and Hồ Viết Thắng, who also stepped down as vice minister of agriculture. *Nhân Dân* added in an editorial: "The mistakes were due to shortcomings in leadership" and in the leaders' "guidance of the application of policies," as well as "insufficient understanding" of many CC policies, which meant that the land reform administration had "formed a separate system with excessively broad power."[173] Its "serious mistakes" required "rectification" of the "general errors of our Party" that had "harmed the whole people," as *Nhân Dân* acknowledged on November 2, 1956.[174] This was equally true of the bloody repression on that very day of a revolt by Catholic peasants in Quỳnh Lưu district of Nghệ An province. As they protested at being prevented from emigrating to the South, troops of PAVN's southern 325th Division opened fire on the crowd.[175]

Hồ Chí Minh briefly took over from Trường Chinh as VWP Secretary General. On November 8, the land reform tribunals were abolished.[176] Chinh was not purged; he remained a Politburo member and announced in December the release of twelve thousand prisoners detained during the land reform. His three Politburo allies remained VWP members, but were not readmitted to the Politburo or to government posts.[177] Chinh's demotion had created the opening that Lê Duẩn filled the next year when he moved north and became VWP acting secretary general. His absence in the South and noninvolvement in the DRV domestic crisis probably helped him.

Duẩn benefitted not only from the fall of the four northerners but also from the rise of his former VWP comrades in the South, Lê Đức Thọ and Phạm Hùng, who had regrouped north to the DRV in 1955. Thọ joined the VWP Politburo and became head of its Reunification Commission. Now he also resumed the position he had occupied in 1945–48, head of the CC's Organization Commission, with responsibilities that included making future appointments to top party posts. And in the wake of the demotions of Trường Chinh and his northern associates, Hùng gained promotion to the Politburo in 1957. He became the DRV's deputy premier the next year.

By 1960 all three—Lê Duẩn, Lê Đức Thọ, and Phạm Hùng—were members of the VWP Reunification Commission.[178] The party's former southern leaders had all assumed top posts in Hanoi and were now in a strong position to guide the DRV's policy toward the South.

Therefore, when Lê Duẩn was confirmed as party secretary general in 1960, his closest allies in the Politburo were fellow southerners or, in the case of Lê Đức Thọ, had worked in the south from 1948 to 1955. They had shared the experience of lengthy terms in French colonial prisons in the South.[179] Two more future allies of Lê Duẩn were, like him, southerners from central Việt Nam and had also served time in colonial prisons. Both came from Thừa Thiên province, near Huế. General Nguyễn Chí Thanh had risen through ICP ranks there, serving jail terms in Huế, Ban Mê Thuột, and elsewhere from 1938 to 1945. He then became head of PAVN's General Political Directorate in 1950, joining the VWP Politburo the next year. The VWP's literary czar Tố Hữu, another southern former inmate of a French prison, did time in Tonkin until his release in 1942. In the VWP's central apparatus, he assumed responsibility for intellectual and cultural activities in 1947 and joined the CC as a full member in 1955, the year after his appointment as DRV vice minister of information.[180] Tố Hữu was not a member of the Politburo but served with Thọ, Hùng, and Thanh on Lê Duẩn's VWP Secretariat and on the Central Executive Commission.[181] In these posts Hữu played a major role in the repression of writers during the literary controversy known as the *Nhân Văn Giai Phẩm* affair of 1955–58.

In January 1955, Tố Hữu urged writers to glorify "positive" revolutionary heroes and to "bring about the unification of politics and art."[182] But the following month Trần Dần, a twenty-nine-year-old poet and veteran who had written a book on Điện Biên Phủ entitled *Người Người lớp lớp* ("Men upon men, waves upon waves"), joined a group of twenty army intellectuals in a meeting with General Nguyễn Chí Thanh. As their spokesman, Trần Dần called for their creative work to be freed from military regulation and to be moved under the auspices of the professional Association of Art and Literature, rather than Thanh's General Political Directorate of the army. Dần presented a statement that asserted: "Revolution needs no apostle to burn incense and praise programs and has even less use for shamans who celebrate its cult as they clap cymbals and intone litanies. . . . A writer must be allowed a quasi-absolute freedom in the choice of his subject, of his characters, of his style to express attitudes and feelings." Dần added, anticipating by a year China's "Hundred Flowers" campaign: "Realism encourages a hundred schools to thrive."[183] The often jovial, blunt General Thanh shocked the assembled intellectuals when he retorted, "Capitalist ideology has begun to attack all of you comrades!" But this didn't stop Trần Dần. He dismissed Tố Hữu's volume of poetry *Việt Bắc*, which had appeared at the end of 1954, as a work that was "small and bland in the face of the grandness of life." Dần fell in love with a Catholic Hanoi woman, and he requested discharge from both the army and the VWP in May 1955. In June, he was put under house arrest for three months. Then in March 1956 the official Association of Art and Literature awarded Tố Hữu its poetry prize. Dissent swirled. A new critical magazine, *Giai Phẩm* (Masterworks), appeared in February 1956, featuring a poem by Trần Dần (who was arrested again, then rereleased). A weekly newspaper, *Nhân Văn* (Humanity), started up in September, as did five new independent journals, all fueling a raging cultural debate in Hanoi.[184]

Contributors to *Giai Phẩm* and *Nhân Văn* included many of Việt Nam's best-known intellectuals, such as Phan Khôi, founder of the New Poetry movement in the 1930s, and the historian and lexicographer Đào Duy Anh.[185] Many of the dissident writers saw themselves as reformist communists, moved by Khrushchev's denunciation of Stalin.[186] In the inaugural issue of *Giai Phẩm*, Phan Khôi urged, "Politics must tap art and literature on the shoulder and say: I am attached to you because I want to use your art. Once that is out in the open, art and literature agree." Yet the creativity required, he added, "is a separate component of art and literature. Politics cannot be in charge of that, too, and art and literature must demand freedom in that arena." Six months later Phan Khôi scolded the DRV's cultural commissars: "They make me recall the old dynastic Vietnam of the Emperors Thiệu Trị and Tự Đức when the source of all authority lay in the Chinese classics. Vietnam today is still a dynasty with the main difference being that the source of authority is Marxism. But the fidelity to authority is unchanged." In the first issue of *Nhân Văn*, Đào Duy Anh asserted: "No one denies another the freedom to conduct research and create, but if you do not have the means to conduct research and create then in reality you do not have any rights. . . . Since in reality the bulk of the means of publishing, distribution, and all the means of research and creation have been consolidated in government units, the issue is not so much the struggle to demand what kind of freedom but the struggle to win the genuine support of the government so as to generate conditions favorable to achieving those freedoms."[187] In the third issue of *Nhân Văn*, another author wrote: "We mean to adopt the following method in our criticism: say it openly, say it truthfully, and say it all."[188]

Instead, the VWP opted for cultural repression. In December 1956 it forcibly closed down the two critical journals and their publishing house.[189] The official press attacked some of the dissident authors but most remained active, publishing even in government journals, for another year or more.[190]

Then in June 1958, Tố Hữu presented a report of the Association of Art and Literature on "three years of struggle against the *Nhân Văn Giai Phẩm* clique." He described the critics as "subversives" who were "dangerously operating in the cultural and art and literary arena, intending to oppose the nation. . . . Leading the clique are professional 'intellectual agitators,' long time Trotskyists, [and] sophisticated antirevolutionary characters . . . They rely on a number of intellectuals from the resistance, who since their return to the cities have been transformed by the depraved urban style of living and reactionary thought." In 1960 the authorities put five of the leading dissidents on trial, and jailed them for terms of five to fifteen years. Phan Khôi died aged seventy-two, just as he was to face trial. Đào Duy Anh joined the Institute of History, retired in 1965, and kept writing until his death at age eighty-four. Most of the other dissident writers suffered "expulsion from professional associations and brief terms of political rectification through hard labor," followed by decades of "bureaucratic harassment, low-level surveillance, and institutional discrimination."[191] Now dissenters had to resort to oblique literary analogies and to "talk with shadows and winds."[192]

Harsher repression struck those dissidents who lacked VWP connections. In December 1960, a twenty-two-year-old Hanoi-born man named Nguyễn Chí Thiện volunteered to take the high school class of a friend, a Hải Phòng history teacher who had fallen ill. Teaching the class, Thiện noticed an assertion in the textbook that the Soviet Union had defeated Japan in Manchuria, thus ending World War II. "Oh no, he told his students, the United States defeated Japan when they dropped the atomic bomb on Hiroshima and Nagasaki." Police arrested him soon afterward, and Thiện was sentenced, without a trial, to hard labor for three and a half years.[193] During his incarceration, he composed dissident poems, committed them to memory, and after his release recited them to friends. He likened his heart to a rice paddy awaiting the flood rains, "so that it can overflow into a thousand waves, / White-crested ones that will sweep everything away!"[194] Meanwhile in 1961 the first CIA-sponsored ARVN commando teams sent into the North were captured there. The DRV heightened its search for "counterrevolutionaries" and set up concentration camps for "educational reform" of suspects.[195]

In economic terms, the DRV made a more impressive postwar start. From 1954 to 1959, rice production in North Việt Nam doubled, from 2.55 to 5.19 million tons of unmilled rice per year. That reflected a substantial increase in the cultivated area, but especially higher yields, which rose from 13.7 quintals per hectare in 1954 to 22.9 quintals in 1959. This productivity far exceeded that of the colonial era, when average annual yields in Tonkin in 1913–43 had ranged from 13 to 15.8 quintals per hectare and, in Annam, from 10 to 13 quintals per hectare.[196] The creation of a middle-peasant majority through more equitable division of landholdings significantly raised peasant incentives and capacity to produce, despite rising taxation.

The DRV's next step was the collectivization of landholdings. It conducted this transformation in stages, gradually at first, and with much less violence than the 1954–56 redistribution of land.[197] From late 1958 the VWP accelerated the collectivization, and by 1960, 85 percent of the North Vietnamese peasantry belonged to one of forty thousand "low-level" farming cooperatives. Most of those, as political scientist Benedict Kerkvliet puts it, rested "uneasily on wobbly foundations," being largely the result of the government's "resolute determination" to collectivize agriculture. He concludes: "Villagers by and large went along with what party and government leaders wanted. Few did so enthusiastically. Coercion was one reason people complied. Another was considerable trust in the Communist Party government, which had already done more for the majority of peasants than any regime they had seen before. Third, people could keep some land and thus not be entirely dependent on collective farming. Finally, people joined expecting, primarily because of what officials had promised, that the cooperatives would mean better living conditions. The combination amounted to a tacit agreement between them and the authorities."[198] The results were mixed. In economic terms, collectivization proved slightly less productive than the immediate post–land reform period had been. During the decade 1958–67, average annual rice yields in the DRV routinely exceeded 17.3 quintals per hectare, and production always exceeded 4.1 million tons, but the cooperative system still took fifteen years to match the 1959 bumper harvest.[199]

In 1961 a southern member of the Đại Việt Party, the literary scholar Huỳnh Sanh Thông, commented on both Vietnamese regimes from his exile in the United States. In the South, he noted the "paradox" that Ngô Đình Diệm, though "starting out as an enemy of communism," had "ended up by copying its worst features: rigged elections, a puppet National Assembly, a muzzled press, a monolithic party with secret cells and underground members, mutual spying elevated into a patriotic duty, arbitrary arrests, concentration camps, 'Agrovilles' reminiscent of Mao Tse-tung's communes, etc." However, Thông saw "one difference" between the regimes of North and South: "Because they have lived ostensibly austere lives, the Communist leaders in Hanoi have succeeded in palming off their totalitarian methods on the people as short-term means necessary to the achievement of long-term goals. They are not loved, but they still command respect. On the other hand, Diem has allowed complete license to members of his own family while he has denied freedom to the people."[200] Escalating warfare was about to test these two regimes, north and south.

ESCALATIONS: NEW THEATERS OF WAR

In December 1963, the month after Diệm's overthrow in Saigon, the VWP CC's Ninth Plenum met in Hanoi. After heated debate it resolved that now "armed struggle plays the directly decisive role" in the southern insurrection. "Political struggle" supposedly remained decisive too, but, the resolution insisted, "We have to go all out to strengthen our forces in every respect, especially the military forces." Hanoi had endorsed a "people's war" in the South. But it was to be carefully managed in two distinct environmental theaters. The conflict would involve not only continuing guerrilla warfare in the delta and the rice-growing coastal lowlands but soon also the use of regular PAVN large units in the thinly populated mountain and forest (*rừng núi*) regions, especially the Central Highlands and northern uplands, "where we have the necessary conditions for big battles in which we can annihilate a large part of the enemy's forces." As a CIA officer later put it, "The foothills and plateaus of the Annamite Chain provided safe areas for larger combat formations than could be maintained in the flat, sometimes flooded, terrain of the Mekong Delta."[201] Soon PAVN main force units prepared to march south to fight in the hilly northern region of South Việt Nam, northwest of Huế, and in the Central Highlands. With them, in late 1964 Lê Duẩn sent his fellow southern-born military ally, General Nguyễn Chí Thanh, to take command of COSVN. The VWP leader in the South since 1957 and COSVN chief since 1961, Nguyễn Văn Linh, became Thanh's principal deputy.[202]

The Ninth Plenum was a victory for Lê Duẩn and his mostly southern colleagues on the VWP Politburo and Secretariat: Lê Đức Thọ, Phạm Hùng, and Nguyễn Chí Thanh. With the support of another southerner, Võ Chí Công, who had remained active in the South but joined the Politburo in 1961,[203] and of the now rehabilitated Trường Chinh, the group led by Lê Duẩn had overruled supporters of a DRV "North-first" approach, as well as moderates and other northerners who shared Khrushchev's "peaceful coexistence" policy. The plenum's resolution criticized a "small number of cadres" influenced by "modern revisionism." It went on:

> When the Nhân Văn-Giai Phẩm clique took advantage of the fact that our party criticized its own shortcomings and errors during the application of the land reforms... [and] of the opposition to the cult of Stalin's personality to engage in sabotaging activities, a number of our cadres and party members sided with it.

The next month Lê Đức Thọ even accused such "modern revisionists" of endangering the northern and southern revolutions. They included pro-Soviet Vietnamese, one of whom soon defected to the Soviet Union, while others were purged.[204] The sudden death in April 1964 of the sixty-year-old veteran communist Dương Bạch Mai—who had studied in the Soviet Union, twice won election to the Saigon Municipal Council, and served as DRV finance minister—dealt another blow to the dissident "revisionist" camp. Mai was posthumously expelled from the party.[205]

For a brief period the VWP had returned to its closer alliance with China of the early to mid-1950s. But that was unlikely to last, given the party's contemporaneous and equally assertive denunciation of those who lacked a "spirit of independence" and the desire to "wash away the mentality of servitude to foreign countries produced by the residue of influences of having been ruled for a thousand years"—a clear allusion to China's millennium-long domination of Việt Nam.[206] The VWP's divisions were mostly internal. During the plenum, Lê Duẩn reportedly criticized Hồ Chí Minh for having compromised with the French in 1945 and 1954. This prefigured a 1966–67 "war of words" over military strategy between Duẩn and Nguyễn Chí Thanh, on the one hand and, on the other, Võ Nguyên Giáp, whom Hồ continued to support. But Hồ was ailing, and he died two years later. Meanwhile, twelve thousand northerners were sent to reeducation camps in 1964 alone. Arrests continued. In 1966, after reciting his earlier prison poetry to friends while working as a bricklayer, Nguyễn Chí Thiện was jailed without trial for eleven more years.[207]

According to the U.S. State Department, PAVN personnel moving into the South in the first eight months of 1964 included several thousand northern regulars, though still mostly dispersed in small groups or company-level reinforcements rather than large combat units. Others date the first departures of PAVN regulars to September 1964.[208] General Nguyễn Chí Thanh probably traveled with them. The DRV later announced that "in 1965 he took the post of leading the army."[209] PAVN was preparing to open up a new theater, of conventional "main force" warfare in the "mountains and forests" of South Việt Nam, especially its Central Highlands and northern borderlands.

Diệm's demise had brought some initial gains for the GVN. Until his overthrow the NLF recruited heavily among those he alienated, but now NLF membership reportedly fell by "perhaps 50,000 or 100,000," stabilizing at around 250,000. The four rebel Hòa Hảo battalions returned to the GVN fold.[210] The Hòa Hảo home province, An Giang, became a government stronghold until the last months of the war.[211] Cao Đài pope Phạm Công Tắc had died in Phnom Penh in 1959, but another exiled Cao Đài official now returned from Cambodia and became GVN province chief of Tây Ninh.[212]

In general, however, the GVN's position continued to deteriorate in 1964. NLF forces seized most of the countryside, and ARVN suffered several dramatic military defeats. It also won victories, but its U.S. support became more crucial. A hundred U.S. pilots were now flying combat missions over the South; the first was shot down in May 1964.[213] Yet the political base for U.S. involvement had narrowed. As early as January 6, U.S. ambassador to Saigon Henry Cabot Lodge remarked that "the Vietnamese generals . . . are all we have got" and that Việt Nam needed "to be dragged into the twentieth century."[214] Worse, the generals in power started to make noises about peace talks and a coalition government that might include elements of the NLF. Washington, already drawing up plans for expanding the war by bombing North Việt Nam, resisted this and sponsored another coup.[215] The next RVN president, General Nguyễn Khánh, "a longtime Agency contact," later recalled that in January 1964 his U.S. advisor "told me a coup d'état was planned in Saigon and I was to become President. . . . On 8 February 1964 I took over as Premier."[216]

That second coup also failed to settle the issue of power in Saigon. Instead, it opened the way to further revolving-door changes among the GVN's military rulers. A new MACV commander, General William Westmoreland, arrived in August, and four months later the U.S. ambassador, Lodge's successor General Maxwell Taylor, told a meeting of Vietnamese generals:

> Do all of you understand English? (Vietnamese officers indicated they did, although the understanding of General Thi was known to be weak.) I told you all clearly at General Westmoreland's dinner we Americans were tired of coups. Apparently I wasted my words. Maybe this is because something is wrong with my French because you evidently didn't understand. I made it clear that all the military plans which I know you would like to carry out are dependent on governmental stability. Now you have made a real mess. We cannot carry you forever if you do things like this.[217]

After a reported naval incident in the Tonkin Gulf in early August 1964, the U.S. Air Force began bombing North Việt Nam as well as the South. The U.S. Congress quickly gave President Lyndon Johnson open authorization to escalate the war.[218] Washington opened up a second theater of the war, waged from the skies over the DRV and what had become PAVN's "Hồ Chí Minh Trail" through Laos into the South. George F. Kennan, who had returned to the State Department and served as ambassador to Yugoslavia, wrote in his diary in February 1965 that "this bombing of points in Vietnam is a sort of petulant escapism" that would "lead to no good results." By May, Kennan was "absolutely appalled at what [was] going on" and worried that Johnson had "lost his head completely."[219] During Operation Rolling Thunder, from 1965 to 1968, a daily average of eight hundred tons of U.S. bombs fell on North Việt Nam alone. During the years 1964–72, a total of one million tons of bombs fell, many of the major northern cities were destroyed or damaged, and more than five hundred U.S. pilots were shot down and captured.[220] The DRV evacuated sizeable urban populations and industrial facilities and relocated them in the countryside.[221]

In the countryside of the South in 1964, the political situation was turning against the GVN. A CIA officer recalled the Saigon station's "desperate need to do something, anything, to stem the Communist tide." The U.S. RAND Corporation chose Đức Lập village in Hậu Nghĩa province for a two-month study in 1964. Near the province capital, it was "one of the very few villages in Hau Nghia secure enough to be examined over any extended period." Đức Lập's GVN village chief estimated that 70 percent of his villagers were pro-NLF, 30 percent were neutral, and that "only 1 percent openly supported the government."[222] In mid-1964 the majority of the eight "most seriously threatened" provinces in South Việt Nam were those around Saigon itself. That fall U.S. intelligence predicted victory within six months for the NLF's army, the PLAF, unless the United States responded dramatically.[223]

The VWP CC, meeting in Hanoi September 25–29, 1964, resolved to "take advantage of this opportune time to try and defeat completely the puppet army before American forces intervened."[224] More southern regroupees returned from the DRV; elements of the 325th Division reached the South between December 1964 and March 1965. These were the first PAVN combat units that the U.S. detected there.[225] In December 1964 the PLAF's Ninth Division occupied the village of Bình Giã in forested Phước Tuy province (formerly Bà Rịa) of eastern Cochinchina. In the ensuing battle it "virtually destroyed two ARVN battalions" and mauled an armored relieving force—"the first time a VC unit engaged in sustained combat against large ARVN forces." This was a "turning point in the war."[226] PLAF and now PAVN main forces were operating in a third military theater: mobile conventional warfare in the forests and highlands of south-central Việt Nam.

A U.S. general toured the GVN's four military zones in February 1965 and concluded that "unless the situation was reversed soon, South Vietnam would not survive."[227] GVN survival required either peace talks with the NLF or a massive intervention of U.S. ground forces far beyond the twenty-three thousand military advisers by then active in the South. Even General Khánh had made contact with the NLF, and in February 1965 he too was ousted and exiled.[228] In March the first American combat troops landed at

Đà Nẵng, while U.S. aerial bombardments and the ground war in the South escalated. By 1973 American forces would drop four million tons of bombs, four hundred thousand tons of napalm, and nineteen million gallons of herbicides on South Việt Nam's rural areas.[229]

In Saigon, GVN instability persisted. Phan Huy Quát, who had been premier briefly in 1954, returned to office. During his five-month administration in 1965, Quát held elections for provincial advisory councils and announced legislative elections for August 1965.[230] But in June, Air Marshall Nguyễn Cao Kỳ took over as premier, with General Nguyễn Văn Thiệu, head of the Armed Forces Council, as chief of state. The legislative elections were again canceled, as Diệm had canceled them after Quát's first ouster.

The U.S. ground troops disembarking in early 1965 found much of the South Vietnamese countryside in NLF hands. General Thiệu estimated that the communists "controlled seventy-five percent of the countryside. We controlled only the chief towns."[231] On the central coast, Bình Định province had "fallen under the nearly complete control of the NLF," and in Phú Yên, the CIA reported "little of the province" under GVN control "except for district and province towns and some of the main lines of communication." Farther south, "the NLF had effectively won the war" in Phước Tuy, fielding a "dangerous" mobile battalion "raised, reinforced, and succoured by local inhabitants," as an Australian army history later put it.[232] West of Saigon, the CIA representative in Hậu Nghĩa province estimated in 1966 that "98 percent of the insurgents in the province were local and that they neither got nor needed substantial aid from Hanoi." The NLF's four thousand cadres and guerrillas in the province, historian Eric Bergerud writes, had "won the war" in Hậu Nghĩa also. Its GVN province chief remarked that of the 220,000 people in Hậu Nghĩa, "two hundred thousand of them are ruled by the VC.... I am not a province chief; I am a hamlet chief." In Bến Tre, south of Saigon, in 1964 and 1965, GVN officials confronted a "tradition of Viet Minh sympathies," against which they fought "what amounted to a province-level civil war, in which the combatants were often known to each other by name."[233]

But along with this village-level guerrilla war in the rice-growing lowlands and the escalating U.S. air war over the North, a third, "big-unit" war was fought out mostly in South Việt Nam's sparsely populated highlands and remote border regions. The escalation of fighting in this theater was ideologically and logistically a product of DRV decisions, though PAVN's military role in the South did not match the expanding U.S. commitment. After PAVN units joined the war in late 1964–early 1965, regular northern combat forces in the south numbered 5,800 troops by March 1965 and, a year later, 13,000. By then U.S. forces in the South had reached 216,000,

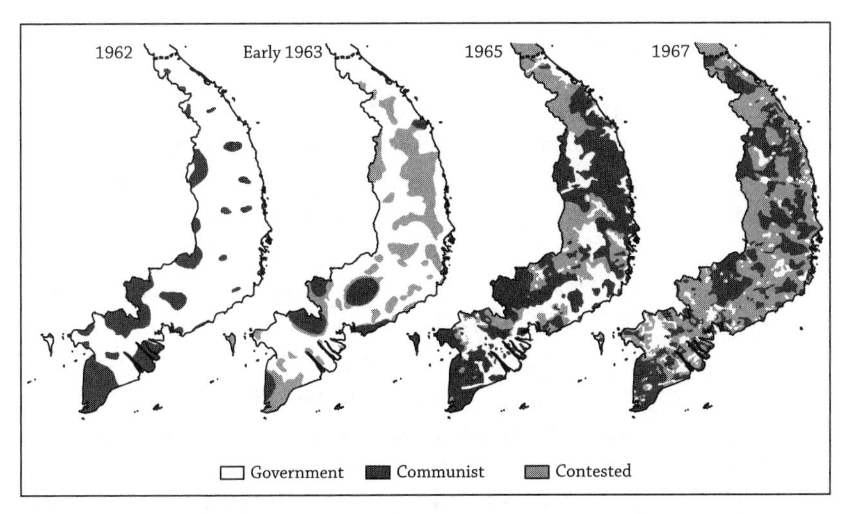

Fig. 10.2
Areas of government and communist control, South Việt Nam, 1962–1967. Sources: Thomas L. Ahern, Jr., *CIA and the Generals: Covert Support to Military Government in South Vietnam* (Washington, DC: CIA, Center for the Study of Intelligence, 1999), 14, 37, 66, and Ahern, *CIA and Rural Pacification in South Vietnam* (Washington, DC: CIA, Center for the Study of Intelligence, 2001), 100, 173, 243, both declassified 2009, available online at https://www.cia.gov/library/readingroom/collection/vietnam-histories.

a fifth of them combat forces, the rest being service troops. The PAVN forces were far fewer and were deployed mostly in the hills and forests of central Việt Nam.[234]

The U.S. challenge of confronting PAVN in the Central Highlands was accentuated by the earlier failure of the pacification program there. In September 1964, Rhadé and other uplanders serving in the Special Forces, who were secretly organized in a new highland autonomy movement entitled Front Unifié de la Lutte des Races Opprimés (FULRO) that was spreading among Montagnard troops, turned their guns on the GVN. The FULRO rebels killed seventy ARVN soldiers in five CIDG camps around Ban Mê Thuột, took the surviving Vietnamese and Americans as prisoners, marched on the provincial capital, and briefly took over its radio station. U.S. Special Forces stationed at their original Buon Enao site had "received no hint of Montagnard planning there for the revolt." Negotiations ended the crisis, and the main FULRO leader, the Protestant Rhadé elder Y Bham Enuol, withdrew to Cambodia with some of his armed units. Then in December 1965, a second revolt erupted in Special Forces camps throughout the highlands, which ARVN violently repressed. Rather than foster local guerrilla warfare, the GVN continued to fight a big-unit conventional war in the highlands. In Pleiku in April 1967, the GVN forcibly relocated eight thousand Jarai villagers from their highland homes in order to clear "a free-fire zone along the Cambodian border" and to interdict PAVN infiltrations.[235]

On the communist side, at least, the two theaters of the war in the South were complementary but distinct. From 1965 PAVN "controlled the northern battles," including much of the heavy fighting in the highlands, while the southern-led COSVN commanded the war against the GVN and U.S. forces in the delta and most central coastal regions. COSVN also contributed some of its PLAF main forces to the conventional unit war in the hills and the north, while it maintained more of a holding action in the populous lowland provinces that mostly took the form of intense guerrilla warfare. In the delta as much as half of what the U.S. called the Viet Cong infrastructure and local force leadership were "transferred into main force units."[236] Conversely, PAVN units did not appear in Long An province of the delta before December 1967, nor in Hậu Nghĩa until 1968.[237] They began operating in the central delta only in 1969.[238] COSVN remained responsible for most military operations south of Huế until at least 1968.[239]

U.S. forces in the South built up at a much faster rate than PAVN and were deployed in both theaters. By January 1968 they numbered 498,000 (PAVN troops in the South then numbered 80,000). American troop levels would peak in April 1969, at 543,000.[240] U.S. and ARVN troops were also supported by allied contingents: 50,000 South Korean combat troops, 7,500 Australian, 500 New Zealand, 11,000 Thai, and 2,000 Filipino soldiers.[241]

From 1965 on, the United States and its allies faced a challenge similar to that which had confronted the French in 1946: how to reverse a near-complete communist takeover of the populated rural areas. The NLF were entrenched in the vast majority of South Việt Nam's 2,500 villages, comprising twelve thousand hamlets.[242] Washington faced a major task in helping the GVN reconquer most of them. Instead, however, from 1965 to 1968, "the U.S. military favored large-unit engagements designed to inflict ultimately intolerable attrition on North Vietnamese and Viet Cong military forces."[243] This strategy took less account of the guerrilla war in the villages and tended to overlook the dual impact of large-unit conventional war there, first on villagers: frequent devastation of homes and lives—and then on the guerrilla insurgency: increased recruitment.

THE U.S. WAR IN THE LOWLANDS

The American impact on southern Việt Nam from 1965 was twofold: military destruction and political backlash. First, levels of violence and war damage rose.[244] The quantity of U.S. heavy weaponry was one reason. The

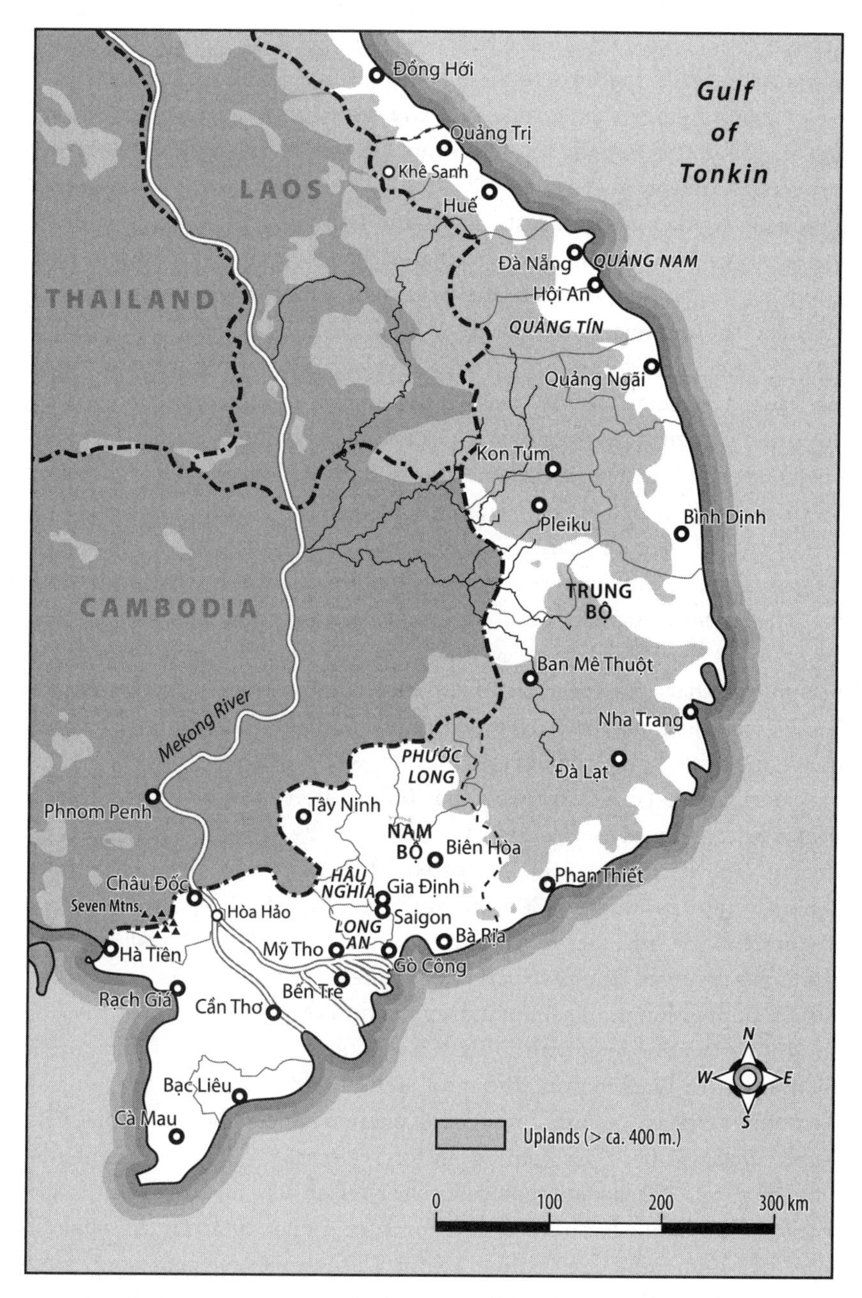

Fig. 10.3
The Republic of Việt Nam, 1955–1975.

veteran French observer Bernard Fall worried in 1966, "Viet-Nam to all accounts is really taking a terrible beating for a small country.... We've never really fought that intensive a war over that small a piece of real estate.... So, in a way for the first time I'm just wondering what's going to be left of 'my old Viet-Nam.' "[245]

In Hậu Nghĩa province, historian Bergerud writes, "The attitude of the American soldiers on the spot was that if the villagers did not warn them of enemy infiltration, the villagers were responsible for their own safety." He links "the innate destructiveness of US combat operations" to the "structure of American ground forces," with "the vast majority of civilian casualties caused by American fire" resulting from officers' practice of preferring any other casualties to their own. U.S. commanders deploying massive firepower to shield their men was half the story.[246] In addition, enough South Vietnamese civilians opposed the American war for U.S. troops to frequently see them as legitimate targets. A historian retroactively made this case: "If guerrillas live and operate among the people like fish in the water, then, legally, the entire school of fish may become a legitimate military target." By contrast, in 1966 George Kennan told the Senate Foreign Relations Committee that "the spectacle of Americans" attacking "a poor and helpless people, and particularly a people of different race and color," was damaging America's global image.[247]

America's image in Cambodia certainly suffered from the war. Many ethnic Khmers from the Mekong delta escaped the escalation in fighting by fleeing Việt Nam. From 1965 to March 1968, more than seventeen thousand Khmers, including 2,300 Buddhist monks, left the RVN to resettle in Cambodia.[248] A Khmer refugee who defected from U.S. Special Forces in the South reported "the destruction of Khmer villages and massacres of the Khmer population in our mopping-up operations."[249] In May 1965, as U.S. combat troops landed in South Việt Nam, Phnom Penh broke off diplomatic relations with Washington. Though Cambodia was still formally neutral, part of its territory became a refuge for Vietnamese communist troops, who established fortified "sanctuaries" in forests across the border. Cambodia was safer for VWP leaders too: each year Nguyễn Văn Linh drove from the frontier to Phnom Penh airport, bound for Hanoi to attend annual CC meetings. Cambodia's half million ethnic Vietnamese residents were "more and more sympathetic to the Communist cause."[250]

A similar political backlash on the ground in South Việt Nam was the U.S. war's second major impact. To many Vietnamese, Bergerud writes, American intervention justified NLF claims about "the dangers facing the fatherland." Expelling United States forces was the Front's "most widely heralded and supported goal." Thus in a way, he concludes, "American intervention made the situation worse: After 1966, followers of the Front could claim very plausibly that they were defending national sovereignty." Two years later a U.S. after-action report on large-scale military operations in Bình Định province asserted: "It becomes relatively easy for the VC to replace losses from a population resentful and disgruntled at the destruction of their lives and property and therefore hostile to the GVN and its allies."[251]

From 1964 to 1966, matching the new U.S. and ARVN forces and their firepower, the NLF stepped up its conscription in the South.[252] Recruitments quadrupled; the 1964 tally of 45,000 new Front recruits shot up to 160,000 for 1965.[253] Membership of the southern communist PRP also rose, to a high of nearly 100,000 in 1966.[254] The size of the NLF armed forces became the subject of prolonged dispute between MACV and the CIA. But the evidence for 1966–67 suggests a total of about 500,000, including PLAF main force units, local forces, and guerrilla-militia. In the villages and hamlets of Bình Định, captured NLF documents recorded totals of 50,000 guerrillas and militia, in Phú Yên 20,000, in Phước Long 300, and in Long An 7,000. PLAF main forces suffered huge losses in their battles with American units, but they could make them up, even if at declining levels, by "upgrading" members of local guerrilla and militia units into main forces.[255] In mid-1967 the Front was reported to be recruiting 3,500 new troops per month.[256]

The COSVN commander, General Nguyễn Chí Thanh, appears to have spent much of this period in Hanoi, first sparring with General Võ Nguyên Giáp and then, after an apparent limited reconciliation, conducting a series of meetings with Giáp and the PAVN general staff in the second quarter of 1967 to draw up a plan for attempting a "decisive victory" during the 1968 U.S. presidential election campaign. Thanh returned south, but in June the Politburo quickly recalled him to Hanoi. There he died of a heart attack on July 6, 1967.[257] His predecessor and deputy since 1965, Nguyễn Văn Linh, had been running COSVN in Thanh's absence and initially replaced him. But in August Lê Duẩn sent a more trusted member of his close southern circle in Hanoi, Phạm Hùng, back to the South to take charge of COSVN.[258] This was the second time Duẩn had downgraded Linh, but Linh also gained a secret promotion to the Politburo in 1967. Led by Hùng, Linh, and General Trần Văn Trà, COSVN remained "dominated by southerners."[259] But Hùng alone had the full confidence of Duẩn, who would attempt to sideline the other two after victory.[260]

After their June 1965 takeover in Saigon, Kỳ and Thiệu revived Ngô Đình Nhu's shadowy Cần Lao party, which General Khánh had banned the previous year. The Cần Lao remained influential in the South Vietnamese capital for another decade, an exclusive organization known for securing draft deferments on behalf of its members. In 1965–66 Buddhist unrest again erupted, this time centered in Huế and Đà Nẵng as well as Saigon. Monks and student protesters demanded democratic elections. Successive ARVN commanders of I Corps (the five northern provinces), disregarded GVN orders to suppress the protests. With U.S. support Kỳ cracked down hard in May-June 1966, sending in ARVN forces from Saigon to put down the I Corps mutiny, raid the pagodas in Đà Nẵng and Huế, and arrest hundreds of monks and students.[261] In protests from May 29 to June 4 alone, four Buddhist nuns, two lay women, and several monks immolated themselves in Huế, Đà Lạt, Saigon, Nha Trang, and Quảng Trị. One author asserts that the GVN arrested 5,000 Buddhists, and another that 1,665 Buddhists remained in Chí Hòa prison two years later. Of the top Buddhist leaders, Thích Thiện Minh was seriously wounded in a grenade attack, and Thích Trí Quang was placed under house arrest in Saigon.[262]

In mid-1966, General Westmoreland's MACV insisted that "the US will must be asserted" without the GVN leaders being "identified as US puppets."[263] But that October, U.S. Secretary of Defense Robert McNamara reported to President Johnson: "Pacification has, if anything, gone backward. As compared with two, or four, years ago, enemy full-time regional forces and part-time guerrilla forces are larger. . . . Full security exists nowhere (not even behind the U.S. Marines' lines and in Saigon)." In December General Phạm Xuân Chiểu, chief political adviser to Kỳ and Thiệu, remarked, "We are very weak politically and without the strong political support of the population which the NLF have."[264]

In Hậu Nghĩa by early 1966, villagers' attitude to the GVN already seemed "worse than it was before pacification began."[265] NLF forces there, "although controlled from the outside," remained "locally recruited and self-sustaining." During 1966, "the Front was expanding" in Hậu Nghĩa, "very likely sending out much more in terms of taxes, food, and recruits than it was receiving in the way of weapons." Like other delta provinces, it was probably contributing troops to the buildup of communist main force units in the other theater, the Central Highlands and the foothills of eastern Cochinchina. Despite these transfers and heavy combat losses after 1966, the NLF in Hậu Nghĩa was still "able to keep its forces up to strength through local recruitment."[266] The "frequent reports of mistreatment of villagers detained by American units" and "nearly daily incidents" in which U.S. vehicles caused injuries and damaged crops probably helped NLF recruiters. Even "cruelty on the part of American soldiers toward civilians" was "common enough" in Hậu Nghĩa. In a 1970 study of displaced Vietnamese refugees, a U.S. rural technical team reported: "American tanks pushed down their houses, they often shot into their hamlets—people were killed and crops were damaged. They lived in anxiety night and day." Most villagers, the team found, had been "effectively propagandized by the Communists" and "show[ed] hatred toward the American troops because of the many casualties and damage they have caused." Serious tensions, even "mutual hatred and loathing," divided American forces from the people of Hậu Nghĩa; "no hamlet" in the province was "genuinely safe" for Americans. The U.S. province senior adviser there, observing a link between greater American activity and increased enemy terrorism, concluded that "the civilians are often caught in the middle; therefore their security has been reduced," but added, "This present situation is unavoidable" if the war was to be won. Historian Bergerud agreed: it was "impossible for the US Army to fight the necessary military campaign without causing great destruction and much loss of innocent life."[267] Those outcomes certainly occurred in the three northern RVN provinces of Quảng Nam, Quảng Tín, and Quảng Ngãi in 1965–68.[268] As for Hậu Nghĩa, the U.S. Twenty-Fifth Infantry's "three years of bloody operations" made "a shambles of much of the province," which apparently "lost a large number of its people," mainly to refugee flight but also to lethal U.S. firepower. A political consequence was that in many ways the NLF did "very well during the three years beginning with 1966" in Hậu Nghĩa and throughout the South.[269]

Across South Việt Nam the number of refugees displaced from their homes ran to many hundreds of thousands. In the five northern provinces, they numbered 539,000 by October 1967 and 690,000 two years later. Neighboring Bình Định had another 180,000 refugees by May 1968. In Quảng Nam in the north and in two delta provinces, 60–80 percent of refugees surveyed in 1965–70 blamed U.S. and/or ARVN forces for their displacement.[270]

By early 1968, the 80,000 PAVN troops in the South were fighting alongside 160,000 NLF infantry and service troops.[271] NLF village- and hamlet-level forces mustered an additional 250,000–300,000 guerrillas, who were responsible for inflicting as much as 20 percent of the casualties that Americans suffered in the South.[272] The communist forces confronted 492,000 U.S. troops and 342,000 ARVN regulars. The U.S. expeditionary force deployed 2,600 airplanes, 3,000 helicopters, and 3,500 armored vehicles. PAVN units also began using tanks for the first time in 1968.[273] But in the Mekong delta, where some of the fiercest fighting was occurring, the NLF still carried the brunt of the effort without northern troops. General Thiệu, who took over from Kỳ as RVN president in 1967, commented in early 1968: "The main reason the Viet Cong remain so strongly entrenched in the Mekong Delta is that people there still believe there is little difference between the French, whom they called colonialists, and the Americans whom they call imperialists."[274] Another French legacy the Thiệu regime still faced in Cochinchina was the fact that 70 percent of its peasants did not own the land they worked.[275]

CONVENTIONAL WAR IN THE HILLS

An NLF raid on the Central Highlands town of Pleiku had provoked the dispatch of the first U.S. ground troops in early 1965, and the buildup of PAVN conventional forces in this northerly theater continued to draw large U.S. units there. In January 1966, fourteen miles south of the demilitarized zone (DMZ) between North and South, PAVN and NLF forces attacked Khe Sanh, a former CIDG outpost established among the Bru upland minority in 1962 and expanded into a U.S. Special Forces base in 1964. In mid-1966, while PAVN began to deploy substantial forces in the south of North Việt Nam, within the DMZ, and across the border in Laos, U.S. Navy Seabees constructed a 1,500-foot airstrip at Khe Sanh, and in January 1967 a marine regiment took over command of the base from the Special Forces.[276] From 1966 on, big-unit operations and set-piece battles there and in other forested, thinly populated areas of northern South Việt Nam caused some of the highest U.S. casualties of the entire war. PAVN forces themselves suffered much greater losses, made up only by continued reinforcements from the DRV.

This was high-stakes, grinding conventional warfare. From July 1966 to March 1967, some 542 U.S. marines were killed and 2,732 wounded in fierce fighting near the DMZ. Then in April-May at Khe Sanh another 155 marines were killed and 424 wounded (and 920 Vietnamese communists killed). In the southern foothills and forests of the Central Highlands and eastern Cochinchina, 444 Americans were killed and 2,400 wounded in large-unit operations dubbed "Attleboro" and "Junction City" that lasted from November 1966 to May 1967. From July to November 1967 a series of four more "border battles" broke out along South Việt Nam's western frontier from the northern to the southern highlands. In an extended contest in September and October, elements of a PAVN division attacked a marine base and shelled it with 130 artillery pieces. They were repelled with the aid of offshore U.S. naval bombardments and "massive airstrikes," including as many as 790 B-52 bomber sorties. In November fighting erupted in the Cambodian border area of the Central Highlands near Kontum. The United States lost another 289 men killed and more than 900 wounded; PAVN lost 1,400 killed. PAVN initiated most of these battles in the northern theater, without extensive southern COSVN or PLAF participation. But also in November 1967, two PLAF regiments attacked the southern foothills rubber plantation town of Lộc Ninh, followed in support by elements of two PAVN regiments. It was the first time that COSVN had "staged coordinated attacks by large units from different divisions." U.S. intelligence discovered later that this was a "rehearsal" for both PLAF and PAVN forces in "street fighting techniques."[277] The communists now had the cities in their sights.

Although their casualties in each battle ranged from a third to half of their number, the communist forces, including smaller units, nevertheless retained the fighting initiative. U.S. defense analysts who studied 289 engagements fought by platoon- and company-level units of all U.S. Army divisions throughout South Việt Nam between October 1966 and May 1968 found that the communists had initiated between 68 and 79 percent of the actions.[278]

In the hills around the U.S. Marine base at Khe Sanh, fighting raged on for most of 1967. By January 1968, twenty thousand communist troops surrounded the base; over twelve thousand more were within "easy reinforcing distance." To support the six thousand marines in Khe Sanh, General Westmoreland deployed more than two thousand warplanes, including U.S. B-52 bombers and South Vietnamese Air Force Skyraiders. The MACV commander was convinced this would be a key battle of the war. He believed General Giáp "hoped to annihilate a major U.S. force at Khe Sanh just as the Viet Minh had destroyed the French garrison at Dien Bien Phu." Communist assaults on Khe Sanh began on the night of January 21, 1968. The battle lasted seventy-seven days. By March 31, U.S. Air Force and Marine fighter-bombers had flown twenty-four thousand tactical air strikes over the Khe Sanh battlefield, supported by 2,700 B-52 bombing missions.[279] But most of the communist forces attacked elsewhere.

THE TẾT OFFENSIVE AND ITS AFTERMATH

In the night and early morning of January 30–31, 1968, during the Vietnamese lunar new year holiday (Tết), about eighty thousand communist troops, three quarters of them NLF and PLAF southerners, suddenly stormed more than a hundred of South Việt Nam's cities and towns; others attacked almost all major air bases, military garrisons and supply installations, and hundreds of village centers and hamlets.[280] What became known as the Tết Offensive achieved "nearly complete tactical surprise." Communists had "infiltrated not only the major cities but 110 province and district capitals, in most cases reaching their targets before GVN defenders knew they were there." A squad of nineteen PLAF sappers briefly seized the grounds of the U.S. embassy in Saigon. The subsequent fierce fighting destroyed parts of the cities and some suburbs of Saigon, Chợ Lớn, and Huế.[281] Communist forces occupied Huế for four weeks before U.S. and ARVN troops could evict them. Throughout the South some forty thousand NLF soldiers were killed in the Tết battles, which ended in a communist tactical military defeat. But in the words of a U.S. Army historian, "The sheer fact that the enemy had pulled off such an offensive and caught the allies by surprise ultimately contributed to the strategic Communist victory and the turning point of the war."[282] On February 6, George Kennan wrote in his diary that the "disturbing news" of "further expansion of the fighting in Saigon" marked "the beginning of the end."[283]

The impact on civilians was horrendous. During and after the Tết Offensive, a million more South Vietnamese civilians lost their homes. As the communist forces retreated from Huế, they assassinated thousands of RVN officials and supporters, possibly the largest atrocity of the war.[284] In Hậu Nghĩa province, the Tết violence "created a dangerous and very ugly chemistry between U.S. soldiers and the local inhabitants," Bergerud reports; "many villagers fled to hamlets controlled by the Front."[285] In the northern coastlands of South Việt Nam, an American massacre of about five hundred villagers at Mỹ Lai in March 1968 was probably the most extreme case of U.S. anticivilian violence, but there were many others before and after the offensive.[286]

MACV maintained that the U.S. and ARVN had won a decisive victory, but that the best means of securing it required more American troops. In late February Westmoreland asked President Johnson to send 206,000 reinforcements.[287] For his part, Kennan publicly denounced the Vietnam War as a "grievously unsound" enterprise. America, he said, had committed extensive resources in a "single secondary theater of world events," while forgetting that it owed "a decent respect to the opinions of mankind." Kennan now endorsed Johnson's primary challenger, antiwar Democratic presidential candidate Eugene McCarthy.[288] In late March, Johnson rejected the additional troop request, suspended the bombing of North Việt Nam, and called for talks with Hanoi. He also announced that he had decided not to run again in the November U.S. elections. But in their August convention, the Democrats denied McCarthy the nomination, helping to ensure, Kennan predicted, that "the whole bloody business will continue indefinitely" with "further loss of life."[289]

The post-Tết remainder of 1968 proved "the bloodiest year" of U.S. involvement in Việt Nam.[290] Heavy fighting continued in the highlands of the north. In April-May 1968, 142 Americans were killed and 731 wounded in an operation against PAVN forces garrisoning an infiltration route through the A Shan valley near the Lao border. In the same valley a year later, in just ten days of May 1969, the 101st Airborne Division killed 505 PAVN troops while driving an entrenched force from "Hamburger Hill," at a cost of fifty-six Americans killed and 420 wounded. The 101st Airborne then destroyed the complex of PAVN bunkers and abandoned the hill.[291] This battle epitomized the mobile (and, some observers added, futile) nature of the conventional warfare in the sparsely populated highlands.

In the densely populated upper Mekong delta, by contrast, the U.S. military's Operation Speedy Express stormed three provinces from December 1968 to May 1969, claiming more than ten thousand "enemy" killed (but only 748 weapons captured) for the loss of 267 American dead. Both ratios were unusually high. The Ninth Infantry Division commander explained, "Viet Cong units dispersed and blended very effectively with people in the numerous villages and hamlets, greatly complicating reconnaissance difficulties and problems of fire control." U.S. official observers raised "the suspicion that many VC supporters, willing or unwilling, and innocent bystanders were also eliminated," and noted "particularly incidents in which civilians had been killed by 9th Division fire [which] had a significant negative impact on the population." In two of the three provinces, all the hamlets rated "secure" still contained only 45 percent and 37 percent of the population apiece. Later investigations by both *Newsweek* and the MACV inspector general concurred that Operation Speedy Express had killed at least five thousand Vietnamese civilians.[292]

Throughout the South, in NLF-controlled regions that U.S. forces labeled "free fire zones," a U.S. Senate study concluded that American troops killed three hundred thousand Vietnamese during 1965–68.[293] A later estimate by U.S. political scientists for the period 1965–72 suggested a toll of 475,000 civilians dead at U.S./GVN hands (from starvation, exposure, execution, massacre, bombing, shelling, or murder).[294] Other U.S. studies found that from 1957 to 1972, Vietnamese communists killed 27,000–36,000 noncombatants and abducted 40,000–60,000.[295] Like U.S. and South Korean forces, both contending Vietnamese armies committed war crimes.[296] During and after the Tết Offensive, ARVN troops often fought well, as did the communists. ARVN continued to suffer numerous desertions; communist morale tended to be higher.[297]

Thiệu's "Second Republic" (1967–75) attempted to repair some of the political damage previous RVN regimes had done, but its reforms came too late or too haltingly to make enough of a difference. In April 1967 Kỳ and Thiệu introduced elections for village chiefs based on a limited franchise, but in the aftermath of Tết, on March 1, 1968, Thiệu reimposed the top-down appointment of unelected hamlet and village officials.[298]

From 1967 to 1973 the GVN held state-level elections on a wider though still limited franchise. In the September 1967 presidential election, with U.S. "aid, collusion, and tacit support," Thiệu prevented "his two or three leading opponents" from standing against him.[299] Even so, his presidential slate won just 34.8 percent of the vote; the noncommunist opposition labeled Thiệu a "minority president." The election law also barred candidates with alleged "pro-communist" links, but a Buddhist-supported slate won first place among the six successful lists in the 1967 Senate election.[300] In the 1970 election for half the Senate, the Unified Buddhist Association's list, sponsored by Ấn Quang pagoda and led by former judge Vũ Văn Mẫu (1914–98), again topped the polling and gained ten seats, for a total of eighteen of the sixty Senate seats. The new upper house also included five Cao Đài senators, three from the Hòa Hảo, three Confucianists, two Montagnards, a Cham, and an ethnic Cambodian. In 1971 the Buddhist opposition also won twenty-five seats in the lower house elections, doubling its representation. Thiệu officials engineered the defeat of other opposition leaders such as the delta Catholic Ngô Công Đức; pro-government deputies, including twelve Hòa Hảo, retained a majority of the 159 seats.[301] But unlike in the North, a nascent civil society emerged in urban areas of the South.[302]

In 1970 the GVN enacted a significant land reform, legally redistributing one million hectares. This finally erased the French legacy of agrarian polarization in Cochinchina, though it "seems not to have generated any visible surge in peasant allegiance to the government."[303] Many farmers had first obtained their land from the Việt Minh or the NLF. The predominance of a middle peasantry in South Việt Nam was now entrenched and uncontested.

Thiệu's regime never won democratic legitimacy.[304] Dương Văn Minh ("Big Minh"), whom Thiệu had kept in exile during the 1967 elections, withdrew from the 1971 presidential contest, as did the third candidate, Nguyễn Cao Kỳ. Both charged that the regime would not conduct the vote fairly. The Ấn Quang Buddhists urged a boycott. Thiệu ran alone, in "the embarrassment of a totally uncontested election."[305] In May 1973 the GVN ordered the dissolution of twenty-six political parties. It authorized three approved parties to contest that year's "noncompetitive and thus nonrepresentative" Senate election.[306] Along with communists, "pro-communist neutralists" were explicitly barred. The GVN remained a military-dominated regime.[307]

Meanwhile the Johnson administration had opened peace talks with Vietnamese communist representatives in Paris. These dragged on for four years, after the new U.S. president, Republican Richard M. Nixon, took office in 1969 and attempted to "Vietnamize" the war. This required building up ARVN to about one million men as American troops were slowly withdrawn. To buy time for their departure, Nixon expanded the war with a U.S. conventional ground invasion of Cambodia in 1970, while ARVN staged an unsuccessful foray into Laos the next year. In the meantime the U.S.-sponsored "Phoenix Program" killed another thirty thousand NLF members and others in an attempt to root out communist officials and supporters in the South. The program was not fully successful, but to a large extent the 1968–72 period saw the communist side of the war "northernized," as so many southern communists were killed during and after Tết. U.S. agencies argued over how to count the civilian "Viet Cong infrastructure" in the South, but intelligence estimates of the size of its membership declined from 84,000 at Tết to 82,000 in late 1968, to 74,000 in 1970, to 56,000 in 1972. North Vietnamese "fillers" replaced NLF losses. By 1970 some 70 percent of all main force Communist troops in the South were northerners, and even predominantly southern PLAF units no longer existed.[308]

In the political arena, however, the NLF was able to partially withstand this U.S. assault and eventually begin to recover from its military defeats by superior arms. Viewing the possibility of future elections resulting from the ongoing Paris peace talks, the Front began to create political "liberation committees" in the countryside, even in GVN-controlled areas. By mid-1968, a U.S. estimate calculated that "about one-third of the hamlets classified by the GVN as either contested or relatively secure harbored such a committee." A later count found a rapid increase from 397 NLF liberation committees in September 1968, to 3,367 in mid-January 1969.[309] By a different measure of the size of the southern communist political movement, after four years of fierce fighting against U.S. forces, NLF civilian membership in early 1969 was estimated at three hundred thousand, including forty thousand full-time cadres, still higher than 1965–66 levels. Including its PLAF soldiers, the Front retained "about 750,000 hardcore supporters" in South Việt Nam. In October 1969 Hậu Nghĩa's U.S. province senior adviser (PSA) saw the population there "slipping through our fingers." By the end of the year, though the NLF in Hậu Nghĩa had become "weaker than at any previous time since American intervention," and was finally "growing dependent on all types of aid from the North," yet "the GVN was never able to convert Front weakness into government strength." The GVN remained the weaker party in Hậu Nghĩa, "totally dependent upon forces from outside" the province.[310] As of early 1970, communists still controlled four hundred of the South's 2,500 villages.[311]

During 1970, the United States and ARVN conducted a major pacification campaign in Hậu Nghĩa. Bergerud calls it "one of the strongest allied efforts directed anywhere against the Front during the entire war." Again the political outcome failed to justify this military effort. The GVN chief of Đức Lập village in 1964 had counted 70 percent of his villagers as pro-NLF.[312] By late 1970, after six years of "very heavy allied pressure," assessments by an NLF official *and* the American PSA concurred: the Front now had "100 percent support" in Đức Lập. Even by 1971, the attrition that continued to weaken the NLF militarily was still "not accompanied by any important change in allegiance on the part of the rural population in favor of the GVN."[313]

In 1968–69 the NLF suffered higher casualties in Long An than in other provinces. By late 1969 the communists had evacuated all Long An's main force units to the Cambodian border, leaving "only a few dozen village guerrillas" in the province. But in 1970 five battalions from Long An returned there to rebuild its district and village guerrilla units. After October 1970 northern reinforcements arrived. Communist forces partially recovered in Long An, with seven battalions active there.[314]

PAVN's spring 1972 offensive in South Việt Nam proved "a great and decisive victory," according to Bergerud, in which the communists "seized a third of the country." The year 1972 then saw "a marked revival of the Front" in Hậu Nghĩa.[315] A CIA study of the war found that the 1972 offensive weakened "Saigon's hold on a substantial part of the countryside it had reclaimed after Tet 1968," in Hậu Nghĩa and four more provinces abutting Saigon. Communist military recovery occurred to the south in Mỹ Tho and elsewhere in the delta.[316] East of Saigon, in Phước Tuy province, an Australian officer who had served there six years earlier remarked in 1972 that the security situation remained "as it had been in 1966 . . . as if we had never really been there." That September, Thiệu again abolished the election of hamlet officials.[317]

THE END OF THE WAR

In response to PAVN's 1972 offensive, Nixon recommenced and progressively escalated the bombing of North Việt Nam. On May 8, he ordered extended aerial bombardments throughout the DRV, with the exception of a buffer zone along the Chinese border, and the mining of North Vietnamese harbors and a coastal blockade. Two days later, Nixon had a White House aide call George Kennan to ask for "a quick reaction" to these announcements. Kennan's diary records his response:

> I could give the President small comfort here. There were important points on which I simply could not go along with him. One was the bombings. I had never seen evidence that strategic bombing was very effective when it came to interdicting the flow of supplies to the battlefield, and to the extent it *was* effective, I thought it was inordinately costly in terms both of extraneous destruction and of our international reputation.... I thought that as far as the future was concerned, we ought to go ahead and get the troops out of there as fast as possible.[318]

From April to October 1972, in Operation Linebacker, U.S. fighter-bombers and B-52s flew forty-two thousand sorties over the DRV, dropping 155,000 tons of bombs. The North Vietnamese shot down some seventy-five U.S. aircraft. Then in October, the Paris talks produced breakthroughs on both sides. The United States, having in May 1971 effectively dropped its demand for a PAVN withdrawal from the South, now agreed on a limit to arms replacements after a ceasefire, while Hanoi withdrew its insistence that Thiệu leave office. Nixon suspended U.S. bombing north of the twentieth parallel, and on October 26, National Security Adviser Henry Kissinger announced, "Peace is at hand." But Thiệu opposed the agreement vigorously. On December 19, Nixon ordered additional bombing of the DRV, Operation Linebacker II. In twelve days, more than 1,700 U.S. sorties dropped twenty thousand tons of bombs on Hanoi and Hải Phòng. Antiaircraft crews shot down twenty-six U.S. planes, including fifteen B-52s. Thirty-three pilots were killed and as many captured.[319]

Talks resumed on New Year's Day. On January 23, 1973, Washington and Hanoi again agreed on a ceasefire, the return of Hanoi's 566 American prisoners of war, and a U.S. withdrawal from the South.[320] The Paris Agreement thus ended the American combat role in the war. More than fifty-seven thousand Americans had been killed in Việt Nam, more than half of them since 1968.

There was no ceasefire. President Thiệu held on as the Vietnamese civil war raged for another two years. In Tây Ninh in 1974, a visiting scholar found the Cao Đài holy see in a surrealistic "eerie calm, like the eye of a storm." Fighting continued elsewhere, but Thiệu also faced new domestic opposition from both conservative Catholics and a range of Buddhist organizations.[321] Tensions rose in Saigon as the anticommunist priest Fr. Trần Hữu Thanh accused the Thiệu family of corruption and organized street protests. In May 1974 Thiệu began to crack down even on the anticommunist Hòa Hảo sect's militia.[322] That December the communists fired the opening shots of what would become a massive offensive. On January 6, 1975, they seized Phước Bình, capital of Phước Long province on the Cambodian border north of Saigon. It was the first provincial town the communists had occupied since 1972.

But the GVN was also collapsing from within. In late January 1975 it assaulted the Hòa Hảo for the first time since 1963. Thiệu's government arrested Lê Trung Tuấn, director of the Hòa Hảo Central Institute, and Trần Hữu Bẩy, commander of its Bảo An military wing, which the GVN then banned. The men were sent to a military court in Cần Thơ, which later sentenced them to six years' hard labor. In Saigon the Hòa Hảo senator and chancellor of the Hòa Hảo University, Lê Phước Sang, reported in February that as many as six hundred Hòa Hảo had "been arrested by government forces." Fighting erupted in the delta. ARVN troops killed seven Hòa Hảo militiamen and wounded sixteen, after surrounding ten thousand Hòa Hảo, including Bảo An forces dug in around a pagoda. Those besieged there included the head of the Hòa Hảo, Lương Trọng Tường, and members of the sect's high council.[323] Meanwhile in early February the GVN shut down five Saigon newspapers and arrested thirteen journalists from nine papers that had published Fr. Thanh's charges that Thiệu had "betrayed the people."[324]

ARVN's military collapse began in March, in the southern Central Highlands town of Ban Mê Thuột. When PAVN's 316th Division quietly crossed the border from Laos, local FULRO Montagnard units decided not to warn ARVN; the "non-cooperation of the Montagnards" with the GVN permitted a communist surprise attack.[325] PAVN succeeded in taking Ban Mê Thuột, as FULRO had almost done in 1964. Concerned that a PAVN strike from there to the coast would cut the South in two, Thiệu ordered a hasty ARVN pullout from the northern Highlands. The retreat became a rout. Huế fell, and, on March 30, Đà Nẵng. The GVN's end was near. Washington's $150 billion investment since 1965 was lost.[326] An internal CIA history of the American war concluded: "The North Vietnamese tanks rolling into Saigon on 30 April 1975 sealed a victory that the Southern insurgents had won more than a decade before."[327]

Politically, the Agency history argues, "The issue in South Vietnam was decided" two decades before, in the mid-1950s. The turning point was the doomed CIA attempt to help Diệm and Nhu "mobilize the countryside using urban-bred cadres in an organization developed from the top down." The die was cast when Diệm decided to "take peasant loyalty for granted while he tried to extirpate former Viet Minh adherents" and set about the "evisceration of village government." In a foreword to this CIA study, the Agency's chief historian agreed. At the end in April 1975, he wrote, "The CIA and the US government were no closer to 'pacifying' the countryside than they had been when the effort began almost two decades earlier."[328]

The destruction wreaked on Việt Nam extended over three decades. Four months after Saigon was renamed Hồ Chí Minh City, a reunified country commemorated the thirtieth anniversary of the August 1945 revolution. Two massive foreign interventions, aimed at returning the country to its pre-1945 condition, had failed. Just as a million Vietnamese had lost their lives in the wartime famine of 1944–45, three million more, mostly civilians, had died on both sides in the thirty years of war that followed.[329]

CHAPTER 11

The Making of Contemporary Việt Nam, 1975–2016

President Nguyễn Văn Thiệu flew out of Saigon for Taiwan on April 21, 1975. General Dương Văn Minh, who had recently assembled Catholic and Buddhist opposition leaders to call for the "despotic" Thiệu to step down, became the last president of the Republic of Việt Nam.[1] As his new prime minister Minh appointed the leading Buddhist in the RVN Senate, Vũ Văn Mẫu, head of the National Reconciliation Force. Mẫu had called for Thiệu's resignation as "the first necessary step" toward national reconciliation and peace. Only then, he predicted, could Vietnamese "direct our attention to the reunification of North and South."[2]

National reunification proved to be the single major outcome of the war's end. Reconciliation and peace were much more difficult. Over the next few years three huge waves of refugees fled Việt Nam, and two neighboring states attacked across its borders. The Vietnamese economy suffered a disastrous postwar decade. Before it finally took off in the late 1980s and 1990s, recovery required a long struggle within the ruling Communist Party for domestic reform (*đổi mới*, "renovation"). Important economic successes were then accompanied by a modest cultural renaissance.[3] But Việt Nam remained a one-party state. The free nationwide elections that Diệm canceled with U.S. backing in 1956 were not held under communist rule either. In 2016, political democracy remained distant, and territorial tensions with China simmered.

REEDUCATION AND NEW ECONOMIC ZONES

A camouflaged PAVN tank "crashed into the cast-iron gates" of Saigon's Presidential Palace on April 30, 1975. With the aid of offshore U.S. naval craft, some 135,000 Vietnamese followed Thiệu into exile, mostly in the United States.[4] General Dương Văn Minh surrendered to PAVN's Colonel Bùi Tín, who had also fought at Điện Biên Phủ in 1954.[5] COSVN's southern commander, General Trần Văn Trà, set up a Military Management Committee to run Saigon, renamed Hồ Chí Minh City.

The Republic of Việt Nam came to an end with the Vietnamese civil war. Up to two hundred thousand political prisoners, including students and Buddhists held since 1966, now gained release.[6] But the new government quickly set up twenty-one new "reeducation" camps and detained up to three hundred thousand GVN officials, ARVN officers, and soldiers. Some were released after a few weeks or months, but many thousands were held for several years.[7] At least twenty-six thousand remained in detention in 1979, and possibly twenty to forty thousand people served terms of ten years or more.[8]

The postwar repression was not limited to former RVN personnel. In the Mekong delta, the Hanoi government incarcerated Hòa Hảo Buddhist leaders, including those whom ARVN had assaulted in January 1975, and outlawed their anticommunist organization. Activities of the Hòa Hảo membership were restricted to the spiritual realm. Most of the Cao Đài subsects remained legal, but only as religious organizations. In Tây Ninh the Communist Party took over the holy see, imprisoned more than one thousand Cao Đài officials and members, and executed thirty-nine Caodaists between 1975 and 1983.[9]

The communist victors also severely curtailed freedom of speech. Saigon's remaining RVN-era newspapers were closed. The five that Thiệu had shut down in February 1975 were not allowed to reopen. The only exception was a paper whose publisher the Thiệu regime had targeted and driven into exile. Ngô Công Đức returned home and reopened his noncommunist *Tin Sáng* (Morning news) after six years of GVN prohibition. Đức and his staff had to tread a careful line between self-censorship and some independent reporting.[10] Also in Saigon, the onetime Trotskyist and veteran writer Hồ Hữu Tường, who had been jailed twice on Poulo Condore, by the French from 1938 to 1943 and by Diệm from 1957 to 1963, mailed a printed protest statement to the new government in 1977. Police arrested him the next year. Released due to ill health in 1980, Tường died that same day, aged seventy.[11] In the North, freed in 1977 from his second jail term, the former history teacher and construction worker Nguyễn Chí Thiện carefully wrote down about four hundred of his prison poems. Two years later he smuggled a copy into the British embassy in Hanoi. As he was leaving the premises, Vietnamese police arrested him yet again, and he spent six more years in jail. While he was incarcerated, Thiện's book of verse appeared in English as *Flowers from Hell*.[12]

North and South were reunified in 1976, becoming the Socialist Republic of Việt Nam (SRV). As in 1945, Hanoi became the national capital. At its Fourth Congress in December 1976, the ruling Việt Nam Workers Party also changed its name, to the Vietnamese Communist Party (VCP). National reconciliation would take longer than reunification, but armed antigovernment opposition was limited to a few hundred FULRO guerrillas in the Central Highlands and CIA-trained ethnic Khmer "Mike Force" paramilitaries in the Mekong delta.[13]

War damage to the environment was a more serious problem. Unexploded ordinance littered the southern countryside, killing possibly a thousand people each year for decades.[14] U.S. aircraft had defoliated two and a half million acres with chemical agents. Twelve million of the nineteen million gallons of herbicides sprayed consisted of Agent Orange, with its dangerous levels of dioxin, one of the deadliest toxins known.[15]

Another serious postwar issue was urban and rural unemployment, with different levels of urbanization in the North and South. Although the North was more heavily populated, its cities contained three million people (12 percent of the northern population), while the figure for South Việt Nam was seven million (31 percent of southerners).[16] In an attempt to reclaim large areas of land uncultivated during the war and to relieve both rural overpopulation in the Red River delta and urban overcrowding and unemployment in Hanoi and the South, the unified Vietnamese government opened up "New Economic Zones" (NEZs), often in remote regions inhabited by ethnic minorities.

This NEZ policy brought Vietnamese from various regions into new contact with one other. For instance, from 1976 to 1979 some 8,500 people from urban Hanoi moved to the southern Central Highlands. They went to Lâm Đồng, a province whose four hundred thousand people included one hundred thousand members of upland ethnic minority groups. The SRV government set aside a 47,000 ha NEZ for a planned influx of a hundred thousand settlers. Newcomers from Hanoi began clearing a forested district south of Đà Lạt. Along its main road, eleven thousand existing residents lived on an 11,000 ha strip of land: three villages of ethnic Vietnamese and two villages of several thousand Cơ Ho, Chin, and Mạ uplanders whom the United States and RVN had relocated there. Like the RVN, the SRV continued to discourage hill peoples from practicing their traditional shifting agriculture, and it attempted to house them on sedentary sites using the slogan "Stable cultivation, stable dwelling." In the first postwar years the movement of ethnic Vietnamese to this NEZ and others appears to have been largely voluntary. By 1980 fewer than ten thousand settlers had arrived there from Hanoi, a tenth of the projected number.[17]

VCP general secretary Lê Duẩn upped the ante in 1978. He visited the Central Highlands and urged, "All Đắc Lắc must become one huge construction project." Over the next decade, the government organized the movement south of more than one hundred thousand more northerners to Lâm Đồng alone.[18] The influx alienated many local uplanders. But the newcomers' living conditions in NEZs were often harsh, wages on the state farms and cooperatives were low, and compulsion became more common. A former South Vietnamese religious figure who fled the country in 1979 stated: "The people were transported to the NEZs and told to produce crops with no equipment guidance. The people received no food and were reduced to eating the leaves off the trees and bushes. There were well known cases of people on the NEZs dying from eating manioc leaves that they had cooked.... The people fled back to Saigon from most of the NEZs."[19] In Saigon in 1978, the last independent newspaper *Tin Sáng* published articles on suicides among "deportees" to NEZs. By 1985 two million people, mostly from the north but also large numbers from southern cities, had been moved to these zones, bringing more than 600,000 ha into production.[20] Despite the hardships, the economic impact was low. National-level yields fell as Việt Nam's population increased to sixty million by 1985, and the rural economy remained locked in its historic pattern of "growth without modernization."[21]

CONFLICT WITH CHINA AND CAMBODIA

On Việt Nam's borders, the postwar peace was brief. Even in the last stages of the civil war, Beijing military forces had already expanded their control across the Paracel Islands, forcibly seizing Pattle Island and the Crescent Group from the South Vietnamese navy in January 1974.[22] Beijing proclaimed the Paracels to be part of China along with the entire South China Sea (which China had first claimed in 1948), including the far southerly Spratley Islands and shoals occupied or claimed by South Việt Nam and the Philippines, as well as distant territorial waters claimed by Indonesia.[23] In 1974, still at war with the GVN, Hanoi was unable to restrain its Chinese ally's ambitions. But that June the editor of the VCP daily *Nhân Dân*, Hoàng Tùng, told a Thai journalist: "Southeast Asia belongs to the Southeast Asian people... so China should not have such big territorial waters as it claims." In April-May 1975, the DRV navy quickly occupied most of the Spratleys. "I tasted ash in my mouth," recalled a Chinese journalist visiting the south. Another war had silently begun.[24]

Hanoi moved to strengthen its control along the land border with China. In 1976 it abolished the DRV's former northern ethnic minority autonomous zones, the Việt Bắc and Tây Bắc regions. The VCP also abruptly retired two PAVN generals from the Nùng and Tài northern upland minorities, Chu Văn Tấn and Lê Quảng Ba, both full CC members who now lost their posts. The party also dropped from its Politburo the most pro-Chinese member, Hoàng Văn Hoan (1905–91).[25] In 1977, Hanoi sought closer control of those members of Việt Nam's ethnic Chinese minority, known as Hoa, inhabiting the frontier region near China. The government "tried to get the Hoa living on the border to adopt Vietnamese citizenship," and also, in "an obvious security move," it "began to clear out ethnic Chinese" from the frontier zone.[26] And on the Spratley Islands in the South China Sea, Hanoi stationed 350 troops armed with coastal artillery and antiaircraft guns.[27]

Hanoi had long attempted to balance its relations with Moscow and Beijing.[28] After the 1975 victory it declined to antagonize China by siding openly with the Soviet-led Eastern Bloc and did not provide the Soviet Union with military facilities in Việt Nam. Hanoi also hoped to establish diplomatic relations with Washington, as well as attract its economic aid. In 1977 Việt Nam joined the U.S.-dominated International Monetary Fund, becoming the only communist state to do so.[29] It took another year, after Hanoi's relations with Beijing had publicly soured over Cambodia and Washington had moved to establish relations with China but not Việt Nam, for Hanoi to also join the Soviet-led Council for Mutual Economic Assistance, in November 1978. Only in 1979, after China's overland invasion of northern Việt Nam, did Hanoi for the first time allow Soviet ships to dock at the former U.S. base at Cam Ranh Bay.

There in the South, a long fuse had been lit by a serious conflict that ignited on the Cambodian border. In April 1975 the Khmer Rouge forces led by Saloth Sar (Pol Pot) took power in Phnom Penh. Also communist but far more extreme, violent, and closely allied to China, the Pol Pot regime immediately launched armed attacks across the Vietnamese border in May and June 1975. It also expelled about 150,000 Vietnamese residents of Cambodia.[30] Disagreement in Việt Nam over how to respond to the Cambodian attacks resulted in the demotion and recall to Hanoi of the Seventh Military Region commander, Trần Văn Trà.[31] At first, China discouraged military action by either side, and inconclusive peace talks were held in Phnom Penh in May 1976. But the Pol Pot regime, now known as Democratic Kampuchea (DK), was viscerally anti-Vietnamese. In April 1976 it secretly slaughtered sixty-nine ethnic Khmer "Mike Force" guerrillas from the Mekong delta after they crossed into Cambodia seeking aid for their armed resistance to Hanoi. Pol Pot also decided to refuse further negotiations with Hanoi. Beginning in early 1977, DK armed forces launched new attacks into Việt Nam.[32]

Cambodian refugees who had fled across the Vietnamese border in 1975 witnessed some of these raids. Vong Heng had taken up residence in the mixed Khmer-Vietnamese village of Ke Mea, in Tây Ninh province. In May or June 1977, Heng recalled two years later, Khmer Rouge forces shelled Ke Mea, killing "hundreds of people" of both ethnic groups. Farther south, in Hà Tiên province, Ly Veasna, who was living "500 meters from the border," reported that in mid-1977 "the Khmer Rouge started the fighting." They attacked nearby Prey Tameang village, killing two hundred civilians, including ethnic Khmers and Vietnamese, and then raided Veasna's village of Ấp Sasê. "When the Khmer Rouge crossed the border, everybody ran and grabbed their children and all ran into their houses. But the Khmer Rouge came into our village and burnt down houses and burnt goods, and killed about twenty people who were not able to run away."[33] Inside Cambodia at this same time, the DK regime launched a genocidal campaign to exterminate all ten to twenty thousand ethnic Vietnamese still remaining in Cambodia. A report soon reached Bangkok that in late May 1977, "500 ethnic Vietnamese families were rounded up and many executed in the central province of Kampong Cham, possibly as a security precaution."[34] By the next year the DK regime was massacring hundreds of thousands of ethnic Cambodians for allegedly possessing "Vietnamese heads on Khmer bodies" (*kbal yuon khluon khmaer*).[35]

Soon after the 1977 Cambodian attacks into Việt Nam, Beijing explicitly backed the DK regime against Hanoi and privately informed both sides of its policy.[36] In September 1977, Beijing publicly welcomed Pol Pot on a triumphant visit to China. The next month Hanoi closed down Chinese-language schools in the South.[37] Brutal DK military units continued to massacre thousands of Vietnamese and ethnic Khmer farmers in more than a year of cross-border raids.[38] In all, Việt Nam claims to have lost thirty thousand civilian and military personnel killed during this border war with Cambodia in 1977 and 1978.[39] When Hanoi retaliated in late 1977, DK severed diplomatic relations with Việt Nam, and China publicly blamed Hanoi for the war. The border fighting intensified. By June 1978, three quarters of a million Vietnamese had fled their homes near the border for safety deeper inside the country, and by late 1978, some 350,000 Khmer refugees had fled from Cambodia into Việt Nam.[40]

EXODUS

Yet the coming refugee exodus from Việt Nam would be even larger. As a full-scale war loomed and Beijing's propaganda support for DK intensified, many of northern Việt Nam's Hoa people felt caught between China and Việt Nam. From March 1978 Hanoi began to give Hoa the choice of either adopting Vietnamese citizenship or departing the country. Between April and July 1978, some 160,000 ethnic Chinese took to the sea in boats or crossed overland into China. In May-June Beijing ended its aid program to Việt Nam, then in July Hanoi began encouraging Hoa to leave the country or move to NEZs, and by December 1978 the total number of Hoa refugees reached two hundred thousand.[41] This second large exodus from postwar Việt Nam comprised mostly ethnic Chinese workers and fisherfolk from the North. But others fled from the South, as journalist Barry Wain reported: "The human deluge hit Southeast Asia in the second half of 1978 along with a freakish series of tropical storms."[42] In 1978 ethnic Vietnamese comprised 29 percent of the refugees arriving by boat on the Malaysian island of Pulau Bidong. Vietnamese officials frequently charged many refugees extortionate fees for exit permits. The Hong Kong weekly *Far Eastern Economic Review* estimated that the Vietnamese government made about $115 million from these charges during 1978.[43]

In December 1978 Vietnamese forces invaded Cambodia. They overthrew the Pol Pot regime on January 7, 1979, and set up a new communist-led Cambodian government, made up of Hanoi's Khmer allies and some of the Cambodian refugees who had fled to Việt Nam in 1976–78. The Vietnamese army brought the accelerating genocide in Cambodia to a sudden end. However, China responded in February 1979 with its own large-scale conventional invasion of northern Việt Nam. That was less successful; the Chinese forces withdrew after suffering sixty thousand casualties.[44]

Hanoi's response, beginning on the second day of China's invasion, was to again increase its pressure on ethnic Chinese residents of Việt Nam to leave the country. One of them, a former PAVN major, recalled in a refugee camp a few months later: "In 1952 I was with Hồ Chí Minh in Việt Bắc, in 1954 with Võ Nguyên Giáp at Điện Biên Phủ. But all the same, at a time when Việt Nam was being threatened by China, the Vietnamese no longer dared have Hoa people in their military. After China's invasion they feared a second attack, this time with Hanoi as its objective, and so on February 18 [1979] they began expelling us overseas."[45] Now tens of thousands more Chinese from all over Việt Nam took to the seas. In the hope of being allowed to settle somewhere else, many other Vietnamese joined the exodus.

By mid-1979 the proportion of ethnic Vietnamese among the refugees reaching the island of Pulau Bidong had risen to 52 percent. A total of 240,000 refugees had reached China, and more than 160,000 more were housed in refugee camps in Hong Kong, Malaysia, and Indonesia. Including the refugees already resettled in the United States, France, Canada, Australia, and Europe, a million Vietnamese were living in exile. Many thousands more had perished in small boats on the South China Sea.[46] One vessel, carrying among others seven year-old Lâm Hiệp and her family, drifted helplessly for twenty-five days without food and water while brutal Thai fishermen attacked the boat and its passengers no fewer than twenty-seven times.[47]

"Australia's first boat people" sailed into that country's northern port of Darwin on April 27, 1976. Though apparently "nobody in Australia" had expected refugees to hazard the four-thousand-mile sea voyage, five Vietnamese had successfully piloted a vessel from one end of Southeast Asia to the other. They were "harbingers of first a trickle, then waves of arrivals in the north of Australia by sea." Two more boats came in November-December, carrying 106 Vietnamese. Six months later four boats landed, then more again, and in 1977 the number of these "unassisted" refugee arrivals reached 868. By late 1979, more than two thousand Vietnamese had reached Australia by sea.[48]

Even in their act of departure, the "boat people" demonstrated their Vietnameseness in their own way. Just as Vietnamese history and society combined elements of both local and Chinese culture, its refugees proved no different. On the one hand they followed in the wake of the first "boat people" (*người tàu*)—seventeenth-century Ming refugees who had sailed from China to Đàng Trong. (The Vietnamese word *tàu* means "Chinese" as well as "ship.") By navigating the dangers and distances they did, modern boat people (*thuyền nhân*) demonstrated a traditional Vietnamese command of what the nineteenth-century emperor Minh Mạng's court had termed "the favor of wind and water."[49] But the toll of those lost at sea was very high.

ARMED OPPOSITION IN THE HILLS

When Saigon fell in 1975, FULRO's anticommunist wing resolved to fight on against the victorious PAVN.[50] The holdouts included at least thirty or more uplanders trained by the U.S. Special Forces, including veterans of the 1964 FULRO revolt against the GVN at Ban Mê Thuột in the Central Highlands. Another member, Y-Tlur Eban, had served in 1962–67 as an interpreter for the Special Forces, mostly around Pleiku. The group, comprising mostly Rhadé but also Jarai and Cơ Ho, also mustered at least fifteen former ARVN military officers and twenty RVN civil servants, as well as nurses and schoolteachers. Under the name Dega, a Rhadé term meaning "hill peoples," they fought on in the highlands for several years. They suffered occasional PAVN infantry and air strikes, which killed two or three Dega each time, including in one battle on Highway 19 in the Central Highlands.[51] But their ranks probably swelled with uplanders disaffected by continuing arrivals of thousands of ethnic Vietnamese settlers from the lowlands.

By early 1979, when Vietnamese forces overthrew the DK regime in neighboring Cambodia, former schoolteacher Y Bhuat Eban concluded that the anti-Hanoi cause was hopeless.[52] He led fifty or more Dega civilians west across the border into Cambodia in February 1979. "Our aim was to get to Thailand to contact the Americans and French." After a two-day trek into Cambodia's Mondulkiri province, they met for a day with its DK province chief, Srun, and his staff. "We didn't trust them," Y Bhuat Eban recalled six years later. But he had little choice. For the next year, Khmer Rouge forces escorted the Dega refugees through the jungles across the far north of Cambodia. Forty-six Dega eventually reached a DK armed camp in the Dangrek Mountains on the Cambodian-Thai border. Its commander, Pol Pot's deputy premier Son Sen, told the refugees that the Vietnamese were their common enemy: "We will fight together, live or die together." But for the next four years, the Khmer Rouge detained the Dega refugees in the camp. According to Y Bhuat Eban, "They planted mines all around our camp." Mine explosions killed two of the Dega people and wounded two others.[53]

Back in the Central Highlands, life for the Dega rebels still holding out in Việt Nam was harsh. "Sometimes we had to steal villagers' crops," or survive on animal flesh, Y Bhuat Eban recalled of his experience in 1975–79. Sil Be, another Rhadé former schoolteacher who stayed a year longer in the Highlands, said, "The game were our friends, the villages were our enemies." Remnant DK forces still holding out in Cambodia's upland northeast struck across the border into Việt Nam in November 1979; they too assaulted a Dega unit, killing a young woman. Then, near Đà Lạt in 1980, PAVN troops captured a large force of seventy Dega trying to reach the coast to escape Việt Nam by sea. Now Cambodia was the only way out. In 1980 and 1981 four more Dega parties left the Central Highlands and hiked across Cambodia, mostly under Khmer Rouge guard, to join Y Bhuat Eban and the others confined near the Thai border. Sil Be's hundred-strong group left Việt Nam in 1980 and finally reached the camp in 1982. The last group of fifty Dega arrived in March 1984. "The Khmer Rouge held many of us almost as prisoners," Y Bhuat Eban said; "for four years we were cut off from all other relations." Their isolation ended with a PAVN offensive along the Thai border in late 1984–early 1985. "Luckily the Vietnamese came and attacked all the Khmer Rouge bases." The Khmer Rouge fled first, taking two of the Dega and possibly killing them. Finally, "we had the chance to flee, last of all." More than two hundred Dega, mostly Rhadé, managed to cross into Thailand in January 1985. That June, Y Bhuat Eban said, they collectively decided to end their struggle against Hanoi. "The war is over. We would like a peaceful life," Y-Tlur Eban told the *New York Times*.[54]

In Hanoi the next year, Trường Chinh asserted that PAVN had "wiped out and routed a major part of the FULRO reactionaries in the Tây Nguyên [Central Highlands], arrested many other reactionary groups and captured many spies and scouts."[55] The last four hundred FULRO fighters and their families crossed into northeastern Cambodia and remained in hidden camps in the hills there. United Nations peacekeepers airlifted them out in 1992.[56] Many resettled successfully in North Carolina.

STRUGGLES FOR DOMESTIC REFORM

Despite Hanoi's 1975 victory, the Vietnamese economy only very slowly recovered from the war. The government's key challenge was to promote agricultural productivity in the postwar South, especially its Mekong delta rice basket. Although Cochinchina's longer period of French colonial rule had fostered concentration of its rural landholdings into few hands, from 1953 to 1971 successive Việt Minh, NLF, and RVN land reforms, and the war's massive population dislocations, all ensured that most of the farmers still cultivating in the Mekong delta now owned their own land. Landlordism had almost disappeared and a new middle class accounted for 70 percent of the delta's rural population.[57] Middle peasants, Ngo Vinh Long writes, now "owned 80 percent of the cultivated surface, 60 percent of the total farm equipment, and over 90 percent of the draft animals."[58] It remained to be seen whether the triumphant communists would nevertheless attempt a reprise of either the violent 1954–56 northern land reform campaign or the subsequent collectivization of northern agriculture, neither of which was likely to be productive in the more lightly populated rural south, with its now much less polarized agrarian structure.

In mid-1975 Hanoi transferred COSVN's General Trần Văn Trà to the north. Two other veteran underground wartime activists in the VWP's southern branch took responsibility for Hồ Chí Minh City. Resuming a position he had occupied from 1946 to 1957, Nguyễn Văn Linh became the first postwar secretary of the party committee for Hồ Chí Minh City.

A secret member of the VWP Politburo since 1967, Linh was once again Hanoi's leading official in the South, as he had been from 1957 to 1964.[59] Another southern communist veteran, Võ Văn Kiệt, born in Vĩnh Long in 1922, had followed in Linh's footsteps as underground secretary of the Saigon party committee for the latter years of the war. With victory in 1975, Kiệt exchanged his party post for an administrative role as chair of the Hồ Chí Minh City people's committee. He ran the municipality while working closely with Linh there.[60] In addition, the noncommunist newspaper *Tin Sáng* enjoyed the patronage of Trần Bạch Đằng, another senior southern party official who had served as Võ Văn Kiệt's assistant during the war and maintained contacts with Saigon opposition figures like *Tin Sáng*'s editor Ngô Công Đức. The new government also permitted a small independent monthly magazine, *Đối Diện* (Face to face) and two Catholic weeklies that hewed closely to Hanoi's policies.[61]

The party's Fourth Congress in December 1976 attempted to unite the VCP around a radical five-year economic plan. It reelected Linh to the CC and publicly disclosed his membership of the Politburo. He also took over the CC's Commission for Socialist Transformation.[62] But Linh soon clashed with the dominant party leaders in Hanoi, led by Lê Duẩn, Lê Đức Thọ, Tố Hữu, and Trường Chinh. He disagreed with their plans for rapid nationalization of the southern economy. He favored a larger continuing role for private businesses and argued against quick economic transformation. In November 1977, Linh argued that although socialism involved abolishing "all exploitation and all anarchistic competition and production of the capitalist regime," nevertheless managerial, technical, and production workers should be "cultivated and developed," and small and middle businesses converted to socialism by easy stages.[63] Brought up in the South, able to read Chinese and French, and having served for a decade as party secretary for Saigon–Chợ Lớn, Linh likely harbored a greater appreciation of the potential of Chợ Lớn's ethnic Chinese firms to contribute to southern and national economic development.[64]

The Communist Party internal conflict soon came to a head. In 1977 its first attempts at collectivization of peasant agriculture in the south "foundered in the face of middle peasant resistance."[65] In early 1978 Linh was dismissed, supposedly for incompetence, both as party secretary for Hồ Chí Minh City and as head of the CC Commission for Socialist Transformation. This was Linh's third demotion at the hands of Lê Duẩn, after successive wartime demotions as COSVN chief in 1964 and 1967. Fellow reformer Võ Văn Kiệt succeeded Linh as Hồ Chí Minh City party secretary. But a conservative antireformer, Đỗ Mười, took charge of the socialist transformation of trade and industry in the South.[66] Deprived of both his key party posts, Linh was sidelined to less important united front and trade union positions. He began to busy himself "attending overseas conferences and establishing international contacts."[67]

Apart from his unpalatably gradualist economic views, Nguyễn Văn Linh had probably also taken some blame in Hanoi for the murderous 1977–78 Cambodian attacks across the frontier into southern Việt Nam—just as the party had earlier demoted Trần Văn Trà after Cambodia's mid-1975 border raids.[68] As a leader of the communist war effort in the South in the 1960s and early 1970s, Linh had become the VWP's "chief advisor to the Cambodian Communists" in the spring of 1970. By then he had already concluded regarding Cambodia that "the revolutionary movement there had grown too rapidly and was out of control," with the result that the Vietnamese communists "were forced into action in Cambodia." But Linh had declined to take a hard line with the Khmer Rouge when he was advising them in the early 1970s. He felt compelled to handle them "with kid gloves" and "did his best to hurry along a more independent Khmer Communist structure." In June 1975, after the initial postwar DK attacks into Việt Nam, Linh drove by car from Hồ Chí Minh City to Phnom Penh and met with Pol Pot in an attempt to resolve their differences.[69] By early 1978 it was clear that this conciliatory approach had ended badly, and VCP colleagues may have held Linh partly responsible.

Việt Nam's problems were not susceptible to a sweeping solution. Recommencing in early 1977, Cambodia's cross-border attacks had aggravated the Vietnamese domestic crisis. The 750,000 internal refugees who fled the border areas in 1977–78 left large tracts of cropland uncultivated, while also placing an economic burden on Hồ Chí Minh City. Rice production in the South, having peaked at 6.6 million tons in 1976, fell to 6.0 million in 1977 and 5.5 million in 1978. Meanwhile in the North, from a peak of 7.1 million tons in 1972, output fell steadily from 6.4 million tons in 1976 to 6.0 million in 1980.[70] In the late 1970s, as full-scale war loomed, the VCP had to abandon its 1976–80 five-year plan. But rather than stabilize the economy of the south, it decided to accelerate the revolutionary transformation. In late March 1978 the Hanoi government, presumably in coordination with Đỗ Mười, who had supplanted Linh in Hồ Chí Minh City, decreed the rapid nationalization of all industry and commerce above the family level and attempted to speed the collectivization of southern agriculture with the goal of completing it by 1980.[71]

The VCP's wholesale nationalizations and repression of large private traders forced the closure of thirty thousand southern businesses, many of them Chinese-owned. Along with Việt Nam's two border wars, these measures spurred the flight abroad of 200,000 ethnic Chinese refugees in 1978 and another 271,000 refugees in 1979, nearly half of them ethnic Chinese.[72] The Vietnamese economy continued to deteriorate as production levels fell. Beyond charging extortionate fees for the refugees' exit permits, the government bureaucracy proved unable to take advantage of the mass exodus of private merchants. Nationwide state grain procurements also fell from 1.8 million tons (14 percent of the rice crop) in 1977 to 1.6 million in 1978, and then to 1.4 million (10 percent of the crop) in 1979.[73]

Finally, but only haltingly, the VCP leadership began to back away from its nationalization drive and turn to economic reform. In the third quarter of 1979 the CC met for its sixth plenum, and in September it announced a series of policy initiatives.[74] The new economic policies included various experiments in material incentives: in light industry the introduction of piecework rates, bonuses, and greater managerial autonomy, and in agriculture a set "product contract" (*khoán*) system for family-based producers, along with higher state grain prices and the right to sell a surplus on the free market.[75] In addition, members of agricultural cooperatives could be paid in rice on a piecework basis rather than by the amount of time they worked, and farmers could grow vegetables on uncultivated land or on riceland between harvests, also for sale on the free market. Small private businesses employing twenty to thirty people could sell consumer or export goods on the free market, including transporting and selling southern products in the north.[76] The CC renewed these policies at its ninth plenum in December 1980.

CULTURAL REPRESSION

The reforms met extended resistance and debate, reflecting in part a VCP generational crisis, but also a political contest. The conservatives accepted some economic reforms but became more politically repressive. The year after Linh's demotion his former superior in the wartime south, Lê Duẩn's longtime close ally Phạm Hùng, became SRV minister of the interior, responsible for police and security. The year 1980 saw the demotion of Trần Bạch Đằng, a leading southern party official who had criticized VCP efforts among workers in Hồ Chí Minh City, where Đằng was also the VCP patron of the independent newspaper *Tin Sáng*. The sole independent magazine, *Đối Diện*, closed in late 1980. By 1981 the government had launched a campaign reminiscent of that conducted in the north by Tố Hữu in the late 1950s, against "bad books and noxious music," as well as "decadence," corruption, and black marketeering. In July 1981, Hanoi finally shut down *Tin Sáng*. The reason given was that the paper had reflected the views of "one segment of the masses," but apparently the wrong segment: it had "openly encouraged the backward masses to complain." *Tin Sáng* had allegedly completed its "historic mission." Its time had passed; there was no need for it, the government seemed to be saying: this was a time for "complete unity of will and voice."[77] A mythical Marxist future now ruled the Vietnamese present, as a mythical Confucian past once had. Hồ Chí Minh City's VCP youth newspaper recruited some of *Tin Sáng*'s former reporters, but its key voice fell silent.[78]

The cultural repression extended to fiction as well. Dương Thu Hương, a former member of a PAVN women's unit who had fought in the Central Highlands for seven years and then taken part in the final takeover of Saigon, returned north in 1977 and became a writer. During the 1979 Chinese invasion, Hương covered the fighting from the front lines, the first woman combatant to do so. In the late 1970s she wrote a screenplay for the Hanoi Fiction Film studio, entitled *Đất của những dây trường xuân* (Land of the flowers of eternal spring). When the script was adapted as a satirical play, government censors banned it. She protested publicly, and in 1982 the government imposed a three-year official ban on her work, during which time none of Dương Thu Hương's short stories or plays were published.[79]

Within the VCP, fierce debate was raging, and cultural dissidents played a role. In June 1981 Nguyễn Khắc Viện, the founding editor of Hanoi's *Vietnamese Studies*, attacked VCP conservatives such as Trường Chinh for their "hasty, leap-forward mentality" and disastrous economic planning based on the "Chinese Great Leap Forward" of the late 1950s. In addition Viện not only targeted Lê Duẩn's top ally, Lê Đức Thọ, protesting that Thọ's party organization commission had "encroached on the powers of the government" of premier Phạm Văn Đồng; he even implicitly criticized Duẩn himself when he complained that "the party committees have monopolized everything." Viện called for "important changes on all fronts" and wondered "why those high-ranking individuals who have made mistakes have not been punished."[80] The battle was joined. The CC's ninth plenum had resolved that the Fifth Party Congress would be held in "the last quarter of 1981," but in November of that year, after a "marathon" twenty-six-day tenth plenum, the CC postponed the congress to March 1982, and two further plenums were held before it finally met.[81] Also in late 1981, in a further sign that the intraparty contest continued, Nguyễn Văn Linh quietly returned as secretary of the Hồ Chí Minh City party committee.[82] By March 1982 the outgoing editor of the VCP newspaper *Nhân Dân*, Hoàng Tùng, was hinting at a compromise when he urged the party to "rejuvenate" the Politburo but "only gradually and slowly."[83]

The party congress later that month held to a path of gradual reform.[84] But it dithered on its leadership. When the congress assembled, Nguyễn Văn Linh won reelection to the CC, but, in what seems to have been a compromise between reformers and hard-liners, he lost his previous positions in the Politburo and CC Secretariat.[85] Linh, whom Lê Duẩn had first demoted in 1964, then again 1967, and most recently in 1978, suffered a fourth demotion—his "second temporary eclipse" of the postwar period. In his place Tố Hữu, the longtime cultural apparatchik and hard-liner, gained promotion to the Politburo.[86] And Lê Đức Thọ's younger brother Mai Chí Thọ, who apparently still shared the hard-line approach, was appointed to chair the Hồ Chí Minh City Municipal Committee, alongside Linh.[87]

Nevertheless, as party secretary, Linh was quietly initiating changes in Hồ Chí Minh City. He is said to have "personally ordered the release of capitalist Le Cong Thanh," who went on to become a leading flashlight manufacturer.[88] Around the same time the city gave a businesswoman, Mrs. Nguyễn Thị Thi, "permission to experiment with capitalist-style business techniques" for her Hồ Chí Minh City Food Company. She contacted Châu Hồng, a local ethnic Chinese who had operated a textile mill, a knitting factory, and several bakeries until police seized them in March 1978. Arrested that October, he spent ten months under detention and two years laboring on farms in the Mekong delta. Hồng then returned to Hồ Chí Minh City, and in late 1981, he recalled seven years later, "Mrs. Thi encouraged me to reopen my bakery.... She knew I had been ill-treated and provided me with materials to increase my production." He later expanded his business to three bakeries. But his textile mill and knitting factory remained shuttered.[89]

The 1982 Party Congress recognized a need for new policies. It shelved the VCP's projected five-year plan for 1981–85, just as it had abandoned that of 1976–80. Lê Duẩn presented the CC's report, conceding that "mistakes of the party and state agencies, from national down to grassroots level," were among "the main causes leading to, or aggravating, the economic and social difficulties in the past years." The CC undertook "severe self-criticism." Since the 1976 Fourth Congress, party leaders had already canceled the membership of eighty-six thousand "corrupt and degenerate" party members, 5 percent of the total, including as many as one-third of those holding posts at the provincial or lower levels. Lê Đức Thọ also denounced "certain Maoist elements who have betrayed the Party," and many VCP officials considered pro-Chinese were now purged; slightly more northerners than southerners gained senior posts.[90]

However, at the top level of the VCP, the generation of veteran revolutionaries stayed in place. Lê Đức Thọ informed the Fifth Congress that "nearly 100 percent" of CC members, and more than 62 percent of the members of provincial and city party committees, had first joined the party in the years before 1954.[91] Younger, more junior and more technocratic cadres remained in the wings. However, broad, longer-term changes were afoot. The congress expelled thirty-nine CC members (including General Trần Văn Trà) and demoted six of the Politburo's seventeen members, including General Võ Nguyên Giáp as well as Nguyễn Văn Linh, but it also dropped five of the nine members of the Party Secretariat, a body long dominated by General Secretary Lê Duẩn.[92] Moreover, two of the new full members of the Politburo were Linh's southern ally Võ Văn Kiệt and fellow reformist Nguyễn Cơ Thạch, a former ambassador to India who had risen to become SRV foreign minister in 1980. Võ Văn Kiệt became deputy prime minister under the aging centrist Phạm Văn Đồng, prime minister since 1955.[93] On a more general level, two groups of CC members were slowly diminishing in number: senior and central party officials were losing ground to provincial and secondary-level cadres, and military leaders were increasingly outnumbered by civilians.[94] The VCP was reaching deeper into its ranks and turning away from a militarized politics.

RESTORING "MOUNTAINS AND RIVERS"

Most importantly, the post-1979 economic reforms remained in place, and their impact on both agricultural and industrial production was substantial. The 1981–82 rice harvest was reportedly a record 16 million tons, one-third above late 1970s levels. Offering higher prices and private incentives under the product contract system, the state was able to procure 2.9 million tons in 1982, double the 1979 level and by far the highest since 1974. State procurements increased again in both 1983 and 1984, reaching as high as 3.9 million tons (22 percent of the crop).[95]

One of the reasons for this rural economic productivity was that the Vietnamese peasantry had rebuffed the VCP's agricultural collectivization campaign in both north and south. Northern peasants had become disillusioned with the party's attempts from 1974 to 1978 to enlarge and strengthen collectivization, which one group of villagers called yet another "rearranging of the mountains and the rivers." Northerners had begun to undermine the cooperatives from within. The introduction during the 1970s of high-yielding varieties of rice made their task easier. Between the two annual rice crops, the new varieties' quicker maturation time allowed a third "winter season" (November–January) for secondary crops such as corn, cassava, potatoes, and beans. Cooperatives quietly assigned more of their land to individual families, and by early 1979 this had become the most common arrangement throughout northern Việt Nam during the winter season. But it had also begun to spread to rice cultivation. In two northern provinces the proportion of cooperative riceland being farmed privately had already reached 5–6 percent in 1977–78, and in parts of a third province in 1978, 25 percent. Many cooperatives in the north already resorted to "sneaky contracts" (*khoán chui*) in which households farmed many of the paddy fields. This practice had first appeared in Hải Phòng as early as 1962, but it proliferated from 1976 to 1979, when product contracts finally became legal. Cooperative farmers also reduced the size of their collective units and assigned the land to smaller groups. The average size of the "production brigades" in the Red River delta fell by 30 percent from 1979 to 1980.[96]

Beginning in the late 1970s, then, what Benedict Kerkvliet calls "everyday political practices" of villagers in the Red River delta successfully pressured the government into "giving up on collective farming and allowing family farming instead." During the 1980s, the collectives in northern Việt Nam were simply dismantled. They "collapsed without social upheaval, without violence, without a change in government, without even organized opposition."[97] Spontaneous peasant foot-dragging had brought down the cooperative farm system.

In the rural South, the middle-peasant majority also resisted the encroaching cooperativization and quickly abandoned it once the contract system began. In the Mekong delta, a group of farmers in Bến Tre province vented their opposition by burning down a model cooperative building in 1979.[98] By that year, thirteen thousand lower-level production teams and no more than several hundred cooperatives had been established in the delta. Fewer than a third of those units still operated a year later. In 1980–81 less than 5 percent of rural southern delta households were members of cooperatives (farming 200–300 ha of land apiece), and a total of only about 24.5 percent were members of either cooperatives or lower-level production collectives (farming 30–50 ha). The latter percentage increased to only 25.1 percent in 1984, although the number of collectives tripled, indicating they were becoming much smaller, as in the north.[99] By 1985, despite much communist mismanagement, most Vietnamese peasants in north and south were farming individually, producing more and more for the free market, and the country had become almost self-sufficient in rice. Provinces were authorized to export their produce directly rather than through central state bodies.[100]

After the disastrous 1978 nationalizations, the partial reforms permitted industry to begin to recover too. State industrial enterprises were allowed to buy their own raw materials, determine wages, offer bonuses, and sell their produce. Industrial growth rose by 12 percent in 1982 and thereafter by about 10 percent annually. Hồ Chí Minh City's municipal government sponsored private export-import firms and engaged in "joint export-import business" with three Mekong delta provinces (Minh Hải, An Giang, and Kiên Giang). Many new private manufacturers and small traders also went into business. The free market soon accounted for almost 70 percent of the goods in circulation. The average enterprise was small; in 1983, two million petty traders controlled 60 percent of the country's retail commerce.[101]

Yet these beginnings of Việt Nam's economic recovery occurred in the teeth of continuing official opposition. In October 1982, the military magazine *Tạp Chí Quân Đội Nhân Dân* (People's Army review) published an analysis on the security situation in the South and warned of many enemies there: former RVN and ARVN personnel, ethnic Chinese, and "reactionaries under the cover of religion." Three months later the VCP's official journal *Tạp Chí Cộng Sản* (Communist review) lambasted the party leaders in the South for allegedly ignoring Hanoi's directives and moving too slowly against capitalists. By the second half of 1983, official press attacks on "right-leaning" southern leaders and their "economism" gathered force. Much of the critique emanated from Trường Chinh, whereas Lê Duẩn and Phạm Văn Đồng reportedly backed economic reforms.[102] But retired General Trần Văn Trà, dropped from the CC the previous year, took up the cause of political reform. He founded the "Club of Former Resistance Fighters" in Hồ Chí Minh City. Intended as a "pressure group" within the party, it soon set up branches in nearby southern provinces. Lê Đức Thọ complained in 1984 that VCP members "speaking in a disorderly manner outside the [party] conference is a violation of discipline. Only within the organization do we have freedom to speak." The next year Hanoi ignored requests from the Club of Former Resistance Fighters for official recognition of their organization.[103]

Nevertheless the official denunciations of "right-leaning" southerners slowed from November 1983, when Lê Duẩn attended a meeting of the Hồ Chí Minh City party committee. He praised its "significant progress" in transforming the southern metropole from a city that had "indulged in a luxurious and hedonistic lifestyle serving the rulers and exploiters" into what he now called "a productive city belonging to and serving the working people."[104] Duẩn's intervention may have moved the ground under the feet of the hard-liners. The next year Võ Văn Kiệt was able to publicly acknowledge and take seriously the "dislike" of socialist transformation "shown by honest people" who had "previously contributed to the victory." Kiệt explained that "the natural and historical conditions in the South" favored "small entrepreneurs," whose numbers, economic role, and influence were significant. During the transition to socialism, he added, they must be ensured a "proper livelihood" and the maintenance of their "private business network."[105]

Changes were afoot. In 1985, as party secretary of Hồ Chí Minh City, Nguyễn Văn Linh wrote a letter in support of the formation of the Club of Former Resistance Fighters, and in midyear, the CC's eighth plenum restored him to the Politburo position he had lost three years earlier.[106] Linh commenced his third ascent of the party ladder since his 1941–45 prison term on Poulo Condore (from which he helped Lê Duẩn escape). It was around mid-1985, ethnic Chinese in Chợ Lớn recounted three years later, that "Hanoi began gradually softening its suspicions" toward Chinese.[107]

The rise to power of Mikhail Gorbachev in the Soviet Union in March 1985 also nourished hopes of reform in communist countries. But its impact on Hanoi at this early point is difficult to discern. Already life for the mass of farmers in Việt Nam had slowly improved, exports had risen, and in some instances the cultural atmosphere was beginning to ease slightly. After three years of censorship of her work, in 1985 the playwright Dương Thu Hương finally managed to publish her first short story, along with her first novel, *Hành trình ngày thơ ấu* (Itinerary of childhood), which quickly became a bestseller.[108]

But many problems remained that the Hanoi government still seemed unable to resolve. Việt Nam's foreign debt had almost doubled, from US$3 billion in 1981 to $6 billion in 1985.[109] In that year China threatened another full-scale invasion. Vietnamese military spending was estimated to still account for one-fifth of the country's gross domestic product.[110] In September 1985, the anti-reform deputy premier Tố Hữu sponsored a currency revaluation involving the replacement of old banknotes with new ones of lesser denominations. Inflation immediately soared from 50 to 350 percent annually. In December, the usually quiescent National Assembly sent a protest delegation, led by southerner Mme. Ngô Bá Thành, to the SRV prime minister, Phạm Văn Đồng, demanding an apology for this disaster. Tố Hữu was sacked, but the runaway inflation he had unleashed reached 700 percent during 1986.[111]

The disgrace of Tố Hữu facilitated the continuing ascent of Nguyễn Văn Linh in the party hierarchy. Seven months after rejoining the Politburo, in January 1986 Linh also became a permanent member of the CC Secretariat, Lê Duẩn's former fiefdom.[112] From this position he proceeded with a new push for reform. Linh used his national VCP posts both to bring Hanoi's policy into line with the southern-based reformers and to woo the same southern constituencies that *Tạp Chí Quân Đội Nhân Dân* had targeted as subversive in 1982.

Lê Duẩn died in July 1986, aged seventy-eight. His temporary replacement as general secretary was the seventy-nine-year-old Trường Chinh. Around the same time, Linh left his post in Hồ Chí Minh City and moved north to work at the central party level in Hanoi.[113] This northerner who had worked in the South since 1929 stepped into the shoes of Lê Duẩn, a southerner based in the north since 1957. Then, Duẩn had brought north a southern policy of armed resistance to the United States and GVN. Now, Linh headed north with a southern policy of economic reform. And like Duẩn, he gained backing from Lê Đức Thọ.[114]

Linh began to focus Hanoi's attention on unleashing the South's economic potential. In August 1986 the CC Secretariat and the national government's Council of Ministers both met with representatives of the Hồ Chí Minh City party committee and of southern provinces. At that meeting the central party and government agreed to ensure the "supply in full" of the monthly quantity of grain needed for the rations of southern urban and industrial workers, including "grain sold at state-established prices to wage-earners and those who have signed bilateral contracts with the state, and grain sold to people at commercial prices." As a long-term measure, the CC Secretariat also "suggested" that the government "should assign the grain supply for Hồ Chí Minh City to some provinces in the Mekong river delta." With the south self-sufficient in rice, it appeared that it had now obtained Hanoi's guarantee of both its own subsistence and an increasing economic autonomy. The VCP Politburo "named Hồ Chí Minh City as an industrial, scientific, and technical centre in the region."[115]

By the time Nguyễn Văn Linh returned south to address the fourth congress of the Hồ Chí Minh City party branch in October 1986, he was able to demonstrate an emerging consensus within the VCP backing reforms based on proposals from its southern branch. In the face of "the severe and burning nature of the problems posed for our party and people," Linh reported to his southern former party associates that despite continuing "intramural struggle," the CC Secretariat and Politburo had adopted "most" of the "proposals made by the [Hồ Chí Minh] city party committee." On "the most pressing issue that involves life at present," Linh announced that the Secretariat "subscribes to the city's views on improving the diet of cadres and the people." He also revealed that the Secretariat now "agrees with the city's proposals on the foreign exchange rate and customs policy concerning goods sent from abroad," as well as "with the essence of the cultural and social welfare tasks set forth by the city's party committee." He added that the VCP Politburo, for its part, had "just reached a conclusion" that "the city's ideas on the transformation of industry, small industry, handicrafts, trade and agriculture reflect many points that are consistent with the party's outlook."[116]

Linh then turned his attention to large social groups that the VCP leadership had long distrusted. He told the Hồ Chí Minh City party congress that most of the intellectuals "who once worked for the former regime" and had remained in Việt Nam had "shown over the past 10 years and more that they want to contribute their efforts to national construction." Therefore, he concluded, "We should not distinguish between old and new intellectuals from now on." And for ethnic Vietnamese "who used to work for the former regime," Linh advocated applying "satisfactory polices so that they may rid themselves of the conviction that they are being discriminated against and, especially, may foresee their children's future under the socialist regime."[117]

Next, Linh said that "most" of "the Catholics, including those who migrated" from North to South in 1954, were "patriotic working people." They needed government policies "to help them find employment, to care for their material and spiritual life and to heighten their political awareness so that they may become increasingly attached to the common cause and live in harmony with the national community." As for Catholic priests, Linh went on, "We should actively maintain close contact to help good ones to discharge their responsibilities toward religion and life, in the interests of God and the fatherland." On the other hand, he warned that the VCP still needed to "maintain vigilance" and to "unmask and punish severely reactionary elements." In a briefer reference to Việt Nam's ethnic Chinese "Hoa people," Linh urged the congress to "settle this question on the basis of the party's class viewpoint" and to train "cadres from among the Hoa people to accomplish the task of motivating them."[118]

In his conclusion, Linh related the economic crisis to political ideology and VCP behavior. "The serious consequences of the errors in economic management cannot be overcome quickly." At the same time, he added, "no one can deny" that the Vietnamese Communist Party had finally declared "war on a mechanism that is characterized by bureaucratic centralism, state subsidization, conservatism and sluggishness."[119]

Trường Chinh's final report that December, at the opening session of the VCP's Sixth Party Congress, was even more dramatic. Standing down as General Secretary for the second time, Trường Chinh stated: "We frankly analyze and bravely admit the serious and long-lasting shortcomings and mistakes. . . . The main ideological factors leading to such mistakes consist of subjectivism, idealism, simplistic thinking and action, impatience, yielding to one's own wishes, the tendency to leave everything afloat and to relax.... Responsibility for these shortcomings and mistakes rests first of all with the Party Central Committee, the Political Bureau, the Secretariat, and with the Council of Ministers. The Party Central Committee would like to seriously criticize itself."[120]

Once again six members of the ruling Politburo, nearly half of its membership, stepped down at the Sixth Congress, making twelve departures since 1981—minus the returning Linh. Trường Chinh, Lê Đức Thọ, and Tố Hữu all retired from the Politburo; of Lê Duẩn's former close allies there only Phạm Hùng remained. The centrist Phạm Văn Đồng also left the Politburo, but to ensure a transition in the government he stayed on as an interim prime minister. Even more significant, the generational and sectoral personnel turnovers that began on a small scale in 1982 had rapidly accelerated. In 1982, nearly all CC members had joined the party before 1954; fully 68 percent of the new CC had been promoted to that body only since 1982.[121] And the diminution of senior and central party officials and military officers continued: from 69 and 16 percent, respectively, in 1976, down to 43 and 7 percent in 1986. In that same decade the proportion of provincial and secondary party officials in the CC nearly doubled, from 26 to 49 percent.[122] The VCP had transitioned to a new party leadership with a younger and wider political base. Nguyễn Văn Linh was now its only remaining senior veteran leader. He had joined Hồ Chí Minh's Revolutionary Youth League in 1929.[123] He now became the VCP's secretary general, ahead of his wartime superior Phạm Hùng, who was now deputy party secretary and would become prime minister in June 1987. Linh announced: "Let the people know, discuss, work and control," and he urged party members to "fight bureaucracy, authoritarianism, and bullying of the masses."[124]

Reformers emerged from the 1986 Sixth Congress occupying the first-, third-, fifth-, and eighth-ranking positions in the VCP hierarchy, among the Politburo's thirteen full members and one alternate member.[125] Four of the top five were southerners, and three of those were reformers. Born in the North in 1915, Nguyễn Văn Linh had spent nearly all his life in the South. The number two in the party hierarchy, Interior Minister Phạm Hùng, was a southerner but was not known as a reformer. The third-ranking party leader, Võ Chí Công, was both a southerner and a reformer, as was the fifth-ranking Võ Văn Kiệt, deputy prime minister. Foreign minister and reformer Nguyễn Cơ Thạch occupied the eighth position in the hierarchy. With these men, Linh was now leading the party and setting policies for the country. One policy was encapsulated by another slogan heard at the Sixth

Congress: "The North won the war, the South must manage the economy."[126] A degree of national reconciliation was finally on the horizon.

ĐỔI MỚI

The VCP-dominated elections for the National Assembly held in February 1987 still permitted no opposition parties but involved more contending candidates and more spirited debates than before. Nguyễn Văn Linh termed this a step "in the direction of the democratization of political life." Another southern communist leader who supported Linh's campaign for *đổi mới* ("renovation") was Trần Bạch Đằng, the former patron of *Tin Sáng* newspaper, who was considered "perhaps the most prominent independent-minded intellectual in the VCP." He argued in 1988 that "the working class" itself should "control its general staff [the VCP]," which he said "can easily become detached from its class nature." Đằng complained that in Việt Nam "freedom of opinion is not respected, and open expression is still more restrained," further weakening the voice of the working class.[127]

The new leadership began to implement *đổi mới* in the economy and daily life. Phạm Hùng became premier in June 1987 and now surprised observers as "an active champion of economic reform."[128] In July, several Chợ Lớn residents related the next year, Nguyễn Văn Linh met with ethnic Chinese representatives in Hồ Chí Minh City and told them they would be "protected by the court of law."[129] That year the government removed constraints on private sector trade and transportation, which along with the easing of personal travel restrictions contributed to what historian Li Tana called "a massive decentralization of power."[130] During a 1988 visit to Việt Nam, expatriate scholar Huỳnh Kim Khánh noted that the new policy of *đổi mới* "does make a difference in daily life." In 1986, he wrote, "a bus trip from Hồ Chí Minh City to Ban Mê Thuột took up to two full days," with a passenger's baggage searched eight to twelve times. "Today, without checkpoints, the same trip takes 14 to 16 hours."[131] All this led to more population mobility. State-organized migration to New Economic Zones continued, relocating four million laborers from northern and central to southern Việt Nam from 1976 to 1992. Large numbers, especially northerners, migrated south spontaneously. From 1989 to 1992 some fifty thousand people, including members of northern ethnic minorities, migrated south to Lâm Đồng province alone, joining the 150,000 organized immigrants from Hanoi and elsewhere who had been resettled there.[132]

Nguyễn Văn Linh also oversaw the complete Vietnamese military withdrawal from Cambodia and Việt Nam's acceptance into the Association of

Southeast Asian Nations (ASEAN). From a high of 224,000 troops after the overthrow of the Pol Pot regime in 1979, PAVN force levels in Cambodia had fallen gradually to 150,000 in 1983 and 120,000 in 1987. The pace then accelerated, and the last fifty thousand troops withdrew in 1989, leaving the country to the newly proclaimed State of Cambodia (SOC) regime, led by premier Hun Sen. The ten-year occupation had cost PAVN twenty-five thousand troops killed, mostly at the hands of remnant Khmer Rouge forces based in Thailand.[133] But PAVN had also successfully trained a substantial SOC military force that now held Cambodia on its own.[134] Hanoi demobilized half of Việt Nam's armed forces, reducing their numbers from 1.5 million in 1987 to 750,000 in 1990.[135] Both the SRV and SOC, along with the United States, China, Russia and France, signed the 1991 Paris Agreement that ended the international "Cambodia question." In 1994 the United States recognized Việt Nam and established an embassy in Hanoi. The next year Việt Nam joined ASEAN, as did Cambodia and Laos.

Meanwhile in 1987–88, China expanded into the Spratley Islands in the South China Sea, occupying six coral reefs and destroying three Vietnamese ships. In one incident, Chinese ships machine-gunned to death sixty-four Vietnamese soldiers standing exposed knee-deep on Johnson Reef.[136] Despite these bloody clashes and continuing tensions with China, Việt Nam's military expenditures fell from 20 percent of GDP in 1985 to 2.5 percent (on an exchange rate basis) in 1998, and remained at the same level in 2005.[137]

The domestic political and cultural relaxation continued into the late 1980s, but then stagnated.[138] In January 1988 Linh announced that Hanoi would free all remaining political detainees, who would also be allowed to emigrate if they wished. The next month 3,820 prisoners gained release, though at least 159 others did not.[139] One of those released was Nguyễn Công Giân, a former ARVN officer who had spent thirteen years in a northern reeducation camp. He was the brother of the imprisoned Hanoi poet Nguyễn Chí Thiện, whom the authorities finally freed in 1991 after twelve years of detention without trial. Separated for forty-one years, the brothers reunited when they emigrated to the United States in the mid-1990s.[140]

Meanwhile the Vietnamese press became freer, and parts of it were emboldened by Linh's encouragement to expose official abuses and propose reforms by "speaking straight, speaking the truth" (*nói thẳng nói thật*). However in 1988 only 30 of the country's 253 newspapers and periodicals took the opportunity to participate in campaigns for *đổi mới*; even the VCP daily *Nhân Dân* was not one of them.[141] The first private university, Thăng Long University in Hanoi, opened its doors in February 1989, and the first private secondary school started up in Hồ Chí Minh City that September.[142]

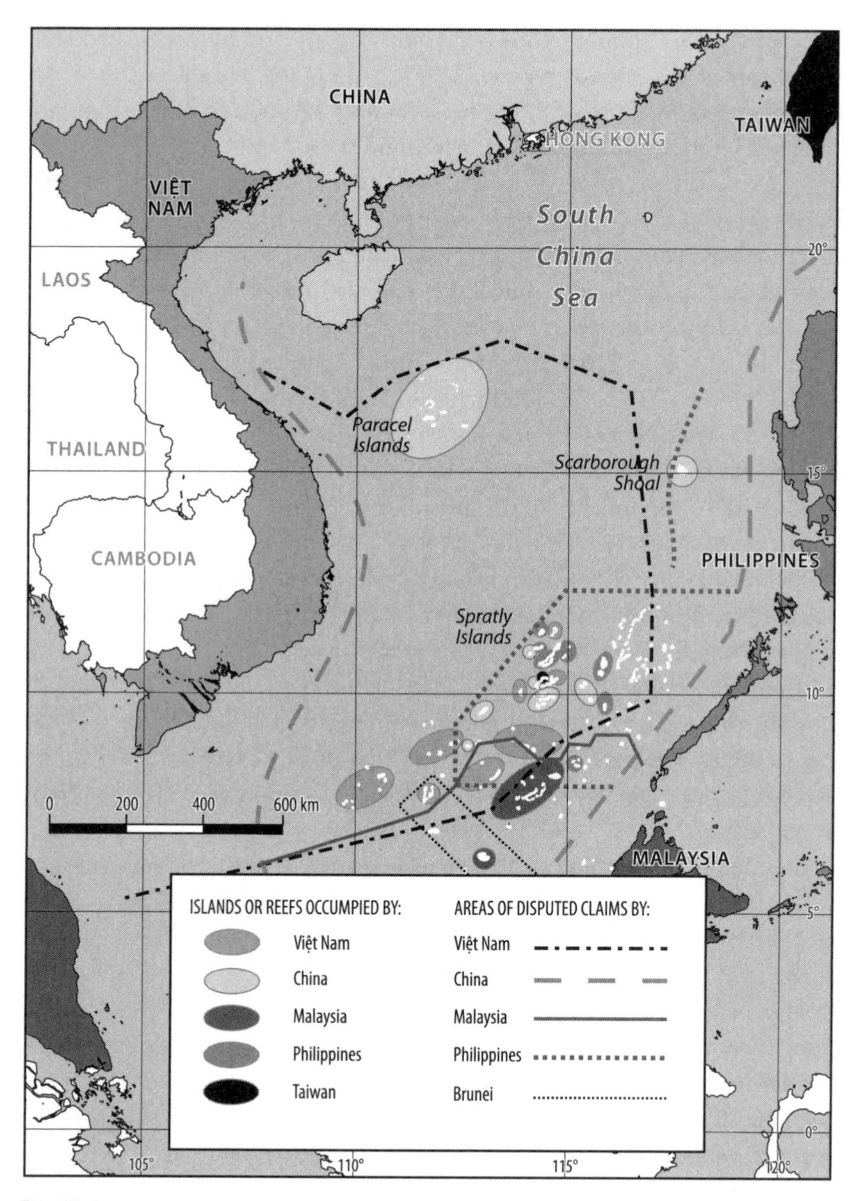

Fig. 11.1
Conflicting claims to the South China Sea.

To a limited extent Việt Nam's *đổi mới* resembled the example of Gorbachev's glasnost (openness) and perestroika (restructuring). A reformist intellectual in Việt Nam commented: "Had it not been for the reforms that we have seen in the Soviet Union, Vietnam might not have dared to embark on *đổi mới*."[143]

In the South in late 1988, the Club of Former Resistance Fighters supported Việt Nam's "first known demonstrations since 1975," when farmers with various land grievances, "waving banners and placards, paraded through the streets of Hồ Chí Minh City and southern provincial capitals." Six months later, the club had twelve branches with ten thousand members in Hồ Chí Minh City and affiliated clubs in seven southern provinces. One of its seven leaders spoke out anonymously in favor of "human freedom—freedom of the press, freedom of assembly, freedom to speak out, freedom to demonstrate." The club's journal, *Truyền thống kháng chiến* (Tradition of resistance), published criticisms of the VCP's lack of openness and failure to resolve social problems, and conservatives in the CC and Politburo attempted to stop the journal's publication.[144] But Nguyễn Văn Linh met informally with members of the club in January 1990. Two months later the government officially recognized the club as the Việt Nam Veterans Association.[145]

The cultural opening in Việt Nam was significant, but less dramatic and thoroughgoing than in Gorbachev's Soviet Union.[146] After 1985 the former screenwriter Dương Thu Hương emerged as one of the country's leading novelists. Her writing recalled the critical realism of Vũ Trọng Phụng written in the Hanoi of the 1930s.[147] The clipped portraits of "sidewalk" Hanoi in her second novel, *Beyond Illusions* (*Bên Kia Bờ Ảo vọng*), were as vivid as Phụng's urban scenes: "The two women turned a corner and arrived at a back alley. There was no sign, not even an arrow to mark the spot. Lan guided her through the street. They passed several *chè* pudding stalls, where groups of the city's black marketers were squatted down to eat. They slid under a low door, through a back entrance, and climbed up a crumbling staircase in the dark."[148] Yet Hương was equally at home in the aquatic environment of rural north Việt Nam: "Water buffalo nuzzled the water, shattering the sun's reflections into a thousand shards of light. As they watched, the boatman's arms slowly darkened, silhouetted against the scarlet backdrop of the water. Each slice of the oar seemed to release waves of blood, as if gushing from the throat of some sacrificed beast. The luminous glow of sunset flickered out and the surface of the water turned to the deep purple of the water lilies."[149]

Beyond Illusions appeared in Hanoi in 1987, breaking new ground both in its characters' exploration of illicit sexual relations and in its recounting of the repression of literary freedom during the *Nhân Văn Giai Phẩm* affair of 1955–58. The novel sold out all sixty thousand copies in two weeks, was reprinted, and sold another forty thousand. Nguyễn Văn Linh personally championed Hương as a VCP member and protégée; she won prizes and official patronage.[150]

CULTURAL AND POLITICAL LIMITS

Suddenly, however, the cultural climate began to deteriorate.[151] In 1988 Dương Thu Hương published her third novel, *Paradise of the Blind* (*Những Thiên Đường Mù*). This was a vivid account of North Việt Nam's land reform campaign of the mid-1950s, which, she wrote, "ripped through the village like a squall, devastating fields and rice paddies, sowing only chaos and misery in its wake." *Paradise of the Blind* sold more than a hundred thousand copies. Then the government banned it.[152] Phạm Hùng had died in March 1988, but Tố Hữu and Trường Chinh (until his death in an accident that October) remained active, and both men no doubt resented the specific topics Hương had chosen for her riveting fictional exposés. In 1990 the VCP expelled her from the party. Hương complained that Việt Nam was a "dictatorship of the bureaucracy." Nguyễn Văn Linh even denounced her as "the dissident slut," and she was jailed for seven months in 1991 before international pressure led to her release. In 1994 Hương visited Paris to receive a French national award, but on her return to Việt Nam the next year, the government revoked her passport. It also banned her next two novels. She spent a decade in Hanoi as an internal exile but kept writing, and her books were published abroad.[153] Finally in 2006 she left Việt Nam to live in Paris, where she published *Đỉnh Cao Chói Lọi*, which also appeared in French as *Au zénith*. Dương Thu Hương remains the most popular writer in the very large Vietnamese diaspora, and possibly at home as well.

The cultural crackdown from the late 1980s on seems to have been a result of a political compromise made within the VCP in 1988. The proponents of change still faced entrenched power. The four leading reformers in the Politburo—Nguyễn Văn Linh, Võ Chí Công, Võ Văn Kiệt, and Nguyễn Cơ Thạch—still needed the support of Phạm Hùng, Mai Chí Thọ, and Đỗ Mười. From 1986 they received this support, though not on all issues. Võ Chí Công became the SRV's president in 1987, and when Premier Phạm Hùng died in 1988, the reformist deputy premier Võ Văn Kiệt became acting premier. He was expected to succeed Hùng. But criticisms of resurgent inflation and a regional food shortage made it difficult for

Kiệt to muster sufficient votes in the National Assembly.[154] Delegates had their "first experience in real debate on issues of concern," and "actually questioned, and berated, cabinet ministers for governmental failings." The premiership was then decided by "the first real election with several candidates" that the National Assembly had undertaken. Winning 60 percent of the votes, the conservative Đỗ Mười outpolled Kiệt and became prime minister in June 1988.[155] Like Hùng before him, Mười and other conservatives were prepared to support economic *đổi mới* but not political democracy.

The limits of reform had now been defined. As Linh put it in September 1989, "Democratisation is now essentially directed at the economic domain. It is not our policy to hasten renovation of the political system while preparations are still inadequate. Neither is it our intention to effect limitless democratization."[156] This compromise stuck. Reformist foreign minister Nguyễn Cơ Thạch, who favored closer ties with the United States, also denounced "the Chinese policy criticizing the restructuring in the Soviet Union," but at the Seventh Party Congress in June 1991, in a gesture to China, the VCP removed Thạch from the Politburo and CC.[157] At the same time Nguyễn Văn Linh, aged seventy-six, retired and stepped down as party secretary. The conservative Đỗ Mười succeeded him, while the reformer Võ Văn Kiệt stepped into Mười's shoes as premier until both men retired in 1997.

These political compromises demoralized several party reformers. In late 1989 Bùi Tín, the PAVN colonel who took the RVN surrender in Saigon on April 30, 1975, then became a journalist and deputy editor of the VCP daily *Nhân Dân*, defected to France. Tín urged Việt Nam to embrace "real democratization and opening."[158] And in early 1991 the Hanoi historian Nguyễn Khắc Viện, who a decade earlier had criticized the then VCP leaders, penned a semi-open letter to the founding president of the National Liberation Front, Nguyễn Hữu Thọ, who in 1975 had become president of the nationwide Fatherland Front. Viện now appealed for "freedom of the press, freedom of thought," and "freedom of association to organize activities outside the confines" of the administration. The seventy-seven-year-old historian added: "People in the advanced capitalist countries have over the past 200 years continuously struggled to realize the present regimes, which we have misnamed as 'bourgeois democracy'; the freedoms, the social welfare that exist were not bestowed by the bourgeoisie, but were attained through popular struggles; 'popular democracy' would be a more correct term. Thus, progress can be seen."[159]

Nguyễn Khắc Viện devoted his final years to developing a field of child psychology in Việt Nam. He died in 1997.

ECONOMIC TAKE-OFF

Under the administration of Nguyễn Văn Linh and other proponents of *đổi mới*, the Vietnamese economy took off, beginning with their reduction of inflation from 700 percent in 1986 to 184 percent in 1988 and 32 percent in 1989.[160] In 1988 Hanoi also introduced a foreign investment code that allowed "100% foreign ownership, the right to repatriate profits, foreign management control over joint ventures, and a guarantee against nationalization." The next year the Vietnamese government put an end to central planning and to most subsidies for state enterprises, inaugurated a single price system, floated the Vietnamese currency, and permitted the purchase and sale of gold.[161]

The 1986 Sixth Party Congress had singled out for special attention the three sectors of agriculture, consumer goods, and exports. In April 1988 the CC issued Decree no. 10, which called for the decentralization of production. By year's end the Council of Ministers had also issued four ordinances (nos. 169–71 and 193). These ended all subsidies to state enterprises, including subsidized grain rations for employees; assigned farmers possession of their land on long-term renewable leases; replaced the contract system of state procurements with a land tax; and privatized the marketing of inputs and outputs. The privatization of agriculture also included returning confiscated land to its former owners, while absentee landlords were prohibited from reacquiring their former estates. This package of reforms favored individual farmers and led to an "instant" rise in agricultural productivity. Then in July 1993, the National Assembly passed a new land law that ended the collective ownership of land and divided it among villagers, who received individual farm plots with twenty-year tenure that included the right to sell, exchange, lease, and bequeath the land to heirs or use it as collateral to raise bank loans.[162]

Rice production rose dramatically. From the previous national record of 17.5 million tons in 1984, the annual production of milled rice reached 27.4 million tons in 2013. After a decade of postwar struggle for self-sufficiency, Việt Nam became one of the world's three leading rice exporters, with shipments increasing from 100,000 tons in 1988 to 1.5 million tons in 1989 and 7.4 million tons in 2013.[163] Việt Nam signed a trade agreement with the United States in 1999 and joined the World Trade Organization in 2007, becoming the world's third-most attractive country for foreign direct investment (after China and India).[164] Despite a post-2000 slowdown in Việt Nam's economic growth, from 2011 to 2016 its GDP resumed growth at rising rates of 5.0–6.5 percent per year.[165] The high foreign exchange income and international investment transformed the economy and, increasingly, individual lifestyles. Vietnamese high-technology exports, which the World Bank valued at zero U.S. dollars in 2004, earned $9 billion in 2011.[166] As for the spread of consumer goods in Việt Nam, one indicator is the rapid increase in internet usage, from 121,000 Vietnamese users in 2000 to 23 million users in 2009.[167] Vietnamese bloggers quickly entered the political equation.

CONTEMPORARY CHALLENGES

In the Mekong delta in 1997, the Cao Đài sect obtained official government recognition as a religion. In July 1999 half a million Hòa Hảo believers gathered in An Giang, also with official approval. The following years saw similar Hòa Hảo religious assemblies. But popular feelings were mixed, as Philip Taylor observed: "Even though many people welcomed this return of the right to associate, some lamented the festival's commercialisation and pallor," linking it to a loss of "self-pride and identity as a result of the political restriction of the religion."[168]

The VCP, however, demonstrated its continuing political domination by renewed arrests of Hòa Hảo activists. Two Hòa Hảo Buddhists immolated themselves in protest in 2005; two years later four more were sentenced to two to six years jail for "causing public disorder." As for the Theravada Buddhists in the delta, five ethnic Khmer monks received similar sentences for participating in a 2007 peaceful protest of two hundred Khmer monks in Sóc Trăng province, appealing for greater religious freedom.[169] And in the Central Highlands, even though FULRO has disbanded, Montagnard Protestants continue to attract the distrust and persecution of Vietnamese authorities.[170] In 2015 an exiled dissident, Cù Huy Hà Vũ, who was released from jail the previous year after serving three years for "conducting propaganda against the state," estimated that there were "two hundred prisoners of conscience in Việt Nam."[171]

A leading expert on contemporary Việt Nam, Carlyle Thayer, concluded in 2010 that "Vietnam is clearly liberalizing but not fully democratizing." Political tensions were increasing, with "potentially far-reaching implications for continued one-party rule." The future, Thayer went on, "is likely to witness multiple sites of contestation," both inside and outside the party as well as in the National Assembly, "as party dissidents and non-party political activists press their reform agendas."[172] This prediction proved accurate. The government once again cracked down. From January to May 2013 alone, fifty Vietnamese bloggers and activists were convicted in political trials, more than the total number convicted in 2012. Vietnamese scholar Lê Hồng Hiệp also reported the appearance of several new groups to challenge the VCP. "Group 72," comprising prominent intellectuals and retired top officials, including a former minister of justice, "took advantage of the opportunity offered by the public consultation on the draft revised Constitution to demand a wide range of political reforms such as the abolishment of Article 4," on the VCP's monopoly of power. The Civil Society Forum, founded in September 2013, was another "attempt by dissidents to mobilize forces to officially challenge the Party." Within the VCP itself, "a senior group led by veteran party member Lê Hiếu Đằng called for the establishment of a new political party" to contest the VCP's monopoly. "And in a widely publicized interview in October 2013, former vice minister of science and technology Chu Hảo and National Assembly deputy Dương Trung Quốc openly called for political reforms towards greater democracy."[173]

Fueling dissent is the extensive governmental corruption that seems to have increased as the economy has expanded. In 2010 Transparency International (TI) ranked Việt Nam tenth among the twenty-one Asian countries for "control of corruption." Five years later, however, TI's Corruption Perceptions Index ranked Việt Nam as the ninth most corrupt of the twenty-one Asian countries, having overtaken Indonesia, the Philippines, and China in the perceived level of corruption.[174] Significant corruption is thought to be linked to official appropriation or seizure of land for development by private investors.[175]

Much of the dissent, especially online and outside the party, also stems from a widespread perception that Hanoi has long gone too far to appease Chinese territorial ambitions in the South China Sea. Eight years after normalizing relations with China in 1991, Việt Nam signed a land border agreement with it. The two countries demarcated their land frontier in 2008 and also reached an agreement on part of their sea border, in the Gulf of Tonkin. Việt Nam's president Trương Tấn Sang visited Beijing in 2013, and Chinese premier Li Keqiang paid a return visit to Hanoi.[176] However, none of this ended China's occupation of the Paracel Islands or its expansion further south into the South China Sea, where Việt Nam has long claimed the Spratley Islands and still occupies most of them.

Vietnamese public outrage boiled over in May 2014. The China National Offshore Oil Corporation towed a giant oil rig into disputed waters 150 miles from Việt Nam's coast. Vietnamese and Chinese vessels squared off, and both sides accused each other of attacking their ships. Protests against China's deployment of the rig erupted in nearly every province of Việt Nam, while "Vietnamese users of social media, particularly Facebook and blogs, widely denounced the Chinese action."[177] Beijing's action had struck a raw nerve, and Hanoi briefly lost control of Việt Nam's response when violent mobs sacked installations of China-owned companies there, even including some belonging to Taiwan, and killed five Chinese citizens.[178] Beijing withdrew its rig from the disputed area on July 15 but maintained its claims. Three months later a Vietnamese fishing boat captain reported a seaborne attack from a Chinese surveillance vessel near the Paracels. "Six people in camouflaged uniforms approached my vessel in a canoe with guns and cudgels," he said. The Chinese crew threw overboard two tons of sea spinach his boat had harvested in the previous three weeks; he estimated his losses at about four thousand dollars. Carlyle Thayer commented: "Vietnamese fishermen are going out into the Paracel waters with the backing and support of the Vietnamese government to assert their sovereignty.... That is going to put them in direct conflict with the Chinese. China is not backing down.... Both China and Vietnam are using fishing boats to advance sovereignty claims."[179] However, despite recent purchases of Russian advanced jet fighters, submarines, and frigates, Việt Nam remained heavily outgunned by China's military.[180] In February 2016, China deployed two batteries of eight HQ-9 air defense missile launchers and a radar system on Woody Island in the Paracels.[181] In addition, many Vietnamese dissidents increasingly made the Hanoi government the target of their more vehement opposition to Beijing's maritime claims.[182]

The United States, for its part, had long expressed concerns at China's apparent effort to take control of the strategic South China Sea trade corridor, vital to Japan's supply of Middle East oil.[183] The Obama administration's 2009–10 "pivot to Asia" aimed in part to shore up the U.S. diplomatic position in Southeast Asia and those of its allies there. Like Việt Nam, the Philippines, Malaysia, and Indonesia were also experiencing varying degrees of tension with China over its South China Sea claims. In 2013, Việt Nam's diplomatic representative Lê Lương Minh assumed the post of secretary general of ASEAN. Two years later ASEAN issued a joint statement of concern over the crisis in the South China Sea. After the Philippines appealed to the Permanent Court of Arbitration in The Hague, China simply denounced the court's July 2016 ruling, which found "no legal basis for any Chinese historic rights, or sovereign rights and jurisdiction... in the waters of the South China Sea" that China claims, beyond the mutual rights provided for in the UN Convention on the Law of the Sea.[184]

Meanwhile Washington hosted SRV president Trương Tấn Sang on a visit to the United States, now Việt Nam's largest export market, and the U.S. elevated its relationship with Việt Nam to the level of a "comprehensive partnership."[185] In October 2014, Washington informed Hanoi that it would sell Việt Nam nonlethal weapons.[186] The two governments began talks to supply Hanoi with Lockheed P-3 Orion long-range sonar-equipped maritime patrol aircraft, and possibly air and maritime surveillance radars, communications equipment, and coast guard ships. Meanwhile, a U.S. Pew Research poll found that 76 percent of Vietnamese had a favorable view of the United States, while only 16 percent had a favorable opinion of China.[187] And Việt Nam had become America's largest Southeast Asian trading partner, with annual two-way trade of US$35 billion, projected to reach $57 billion by 2020. President Obama hosted VCP general secretary Nguyễn Phú Trọng at the White House in July 2015.[188]

Vietnamese communists convincingly defeated large French and U.S. armies and unified their country. Then, after a decade of mismanagement and more wars, including a Chinese invasion, they fostered a robust new economy and permitted the sporadic beginnings of a cultural opening. The country entered a new era. The final passing from the scene of the VCP's founding revolutionary generation was marked by the death in 2013 of General Võ Nguyên Giáp, the victor of Điện Biên Phủ, at the age of 102. Will his generation's party successors eventually allow the citizens of an independent, unified, twenty-first-century Việt Nam to make the most of their achievements of postwar peace and economic development? That question may not be answered until a lasting peace is achieved between China and Việt Nam. But communism's vision of the future has so far shown that it is unlikely to succeed where Confucianism's vision of the past has faded.

Epilogue

The major historical themes of this book are still present in contemporary Vietnamese life, but like other phenomena they sometimes appear cloaked in myth or masquerading as "national" history. Currently their historical forms are changing more rapidly than in previous centuries or millennia. The polyethnic character of Việt Nam remains a factor in resurgent religious diversity and innovations often entwined with the changing status of women. Family and genealogical concerns manifest themselves in continuing kinship links between overseas Vietnamese and those who live in the country. Challenging environmental and regional issues shape politics and policy perhaps more than ever. Long a crossroads of civilizations, Việt Nam today is on the cutting edge of globalization.

The past three millennia of Vietnamese history began in prehistory with the emergence in the northern delta of Lạc chiefdoms that gradually came to adopt the Chinese ethnonym Yuè (Việt) and imperial techniques of governance. On the central coast and in the southern Mekong delta, Cham and Khmer realms incorporated Hindu rituals and kingship. All three were wet-rice societies that flourished at water-level. For the Lạc in the Red River delta, monsoon rainfall, inland and coastal tides, water control techniques, and aquatic motifs all played leading socioeconomic and cultural roles. Perhaps in the context of rites that linked water with fertility, there is evidence of some Lạc women playing influential political roles.

In contemporary Việt Nam, scholars have noted a remarkable social phenomenon, the post–*đổi mới* "upsurge" in religious practice, including not only conventional religions (still subject to surveillance and repression) but rapidly rising "goddess worship."[1] In the north, the resurgent cult of the sixteenth-century deity Princess Liễu Hạnh is an example. In Nam Định province, her cult's original site, home of a "superstitious" festival that Hanoi had attempted to abolish in 1975 but was still visited by thousands of people in 1983, "experienced a rebirth" in the 1990s. The festivals resumed in 1995 and in 1998 were granted official permission to continue. Historian Olga Dror attended in 2001: "I was overwhelmed by the number of people who came to participate in the festival and by the profusion of colors. The combination of communist-style officials and the carnival-like celebration of a religious cult seemed surreal."[2] Another researcher concluded that the most popular new religious movement in Việt Nam is the worship of Hồ Chí Minh as the "Jade Buddha," a cult founded in the 1990s by a woman from Hải Phòng.[3]

Something similarly eclectic was happening in the south. Anthropologist Philip Taylor reports that a group of goddesses "has been on the ascendant in southern Vietnam since the mid-1980s as focal points of mass pilgrimages," especially attracting women who work in marketing and business. This phenomenon in turn gave rise to much of "the enormous commentary on feminine gender" that came with the recent changes in Việt Nam.[4] An example is the cult of Bà Chúa Xứ (the Princess of the Realm), a Mekong delta local protective spirit long favored by indigenous Khmer and Chinese and then adopted by Vietnamese settlers who associated her with the queen bee (*ong chúa*) and built small shrines to her at which they made offerings of honey and prayed for fertility, health, and prosperity.[5] During the 1990s, however, the shrine housing a statue of Bà Chúa Xứ at Vĩnh Tế in the Seven Mountains region on the Cambodian-Vietnamese border became "the most visited religious site in southern Vietnam," with over a million visitors each year, mostly women. The statue is in fact a first-millennium Khmer stone sculpture of the Hindu god Siva, now rendered as a Vietnamese female. Most of her contemporary pilgrims are modern Vietnamese commercial women. As Taylor explains, "The meanings read into goddesses are hot contemporary issues: they go to deeper structures of identity, belonging, feeling, memory, and social experience."[6] Yet some of the contemporary practices of this ascendant goddess cult also resemble the traditional if not ancient associations of Vietnamese women with cultural syncretism, authority, and trade.

The Hanoi government and tourist market have gone much further. They have done their best to exploit the rise of these goddess cults as somehow representing the reassertion of a timeless Vietnamese ethnic identity. Princess Liễu Hạnh is linked with the first-century Trưng sisters as a reminder of a long-term continuity in gender relations, national culture, and resistance to invaders.[7] Yet little continuity exists. As this book shows, the legacy of the Trưng sisters and their Lạc Việt society hardly persisted in the late first millennium. By the early modern era the evidence for bilateral gender relations and a role for women leaders considerably diminished, reduced to vestiges of presumably archaic popular practices often spurned by the contemporary scholarly elite and barely detectable in the written sources they have bequeathed us.[8] Though the prominence of women in trade and literature did persist, in the second millennium many Vietnamese saw Confucian patriarchal models as equally indigenous and authentic, if not more rational and "civilized."

Only in the twentieth century did the position of women gradually begin to approach equality, and in the twenty-first there remains some way to go. The United Nations has recently credited Việt Nam with achieving low maternal mortality, along with high access to education for Vietnamese women and one of the world's highest female labor force participation rates. "On most gender indicators Viet Nam compares positively in international rankings, especially compared to other countries in the Asia-Pacific region."[9]

The country's postwar record on gender issues is promising but inconsistent. Việt Nam's National Assembly, for instance, had its highest percentage of women (32 percent) in 1975, but the ruling VCP Politburo included no women. After 1975, the proportion of women in the National Assembly fell to 18 percent—until the advent of *đổi mới*. After 1987 it rose again, and by 1997 Việt Nam reached the top ten countries in the world with the highest proportion of women in their parliaments. Its proportion peaked in 2002, at 27 percent. But over the next decade Việt Nam fell to forty-fourth place worldwide. In 2012 women made up 24 percent of the members of Việt Nam's National Assembly (women comprised 19 percent of the US Congress in 2014). Other gender indicators for Việt Nam continued to improve. According to UN figures, "In 2008, female literacy rates in Viet Nam exceeded 90%, access to health care was at 85% and women accounted for 47% of the skilled workforce." In 2011, Việt Nam "ranked 1st in Asia and 13th in the world on women's labour force participation."[10]

The VCP's Eleventh Congress, held in 2011, appointed to the Politburo its first ever female member, Tòng Thị Phóng, who had risen to become a deputy chairwoman of the National Assembly. Two years later she was joined by Nguyễn Thị Kim Ngân, minister of labor, war invalids, and social affairs and deputy chairwoman of the National Assembly. From having been ranked by the party in 2011 in only ninetieth place among the 175 full members of the Central Committee, Ngân also rose quickly to become the second woman member of the sixteen-person Politburo.[11] Both women were born in 1954, the year of the victory at Điện Biên Phủ. As elsewhere, however, the relationship between individual women assuming top leadership roles and the general advancement of women's rights remains unclear.[12]

It would be wrong to essentialize the status of women in Vietnamese society. Their position throughout the history of Việt Nam has been a case neither of a persistence of an ancient equality nor of a linear upward progression. Like other features of Vietnamese society, women's status has changed over the centuries in different, sometimes even contradictory ways, in response to diverse outside pressures—for instance, Chinese rule and French colonization—and to Vietnamese domestic adaptations of external religious, cultural, and political influences, such as Buddhism, Confucianism, Catholicism, communism, and human rights.

The importance of water may be a more enduring element of Việt Nam's environment and traditional culture. "Water" still provides the Vietnamese word for "country" (*nước*). But transformative changes have occurred. The agricultural and mechanical revolutions of the second half of the twentieth century and the restoration "of mountains and rivers" that could characterize the rural productivity of the *đổi mới* era have greatly reduced the traditional Vietnamese dependence on a centuries-long uneasy command of water for irrigation, even though floods and typhoons still demand constant attention to water control and drainage. During the 2010 severe drought, for instance, the government was able to provide relief to farmers by releasing water from dams and installing pumps.[13]

Vietnamese may soon value water even more. Climate change threatens the Mekong River "at both source and mouth," the *Economist* magazine warned in 2011. "As glaciers shrink in the Tibetan Himalayas from where the river springs, so will the snow melt that helps to feed it; as sea levels rise, salination will worsen in the Mekong delta." Việt Nam's upstream neighbors compound its problem. By 2011 China had built four dams on the Mekong's northern reaches, begun constructing a fifth, and planned three more; south of the Chinese border, eleven additional dams on the Mekong main stem are planned in Thailand, Laos, and Cambodia. The environmental implications are serious. "The flows of fertile sediment that have for centuries sustained farmers along the Mekong's banks will diminish. Species of fish that have provided livelihoods and protein for millions of people (some 60m live in the lower Mekong basin) are unlikely to survive the obstacles to their migrations." Việt Nam, joined by the Mekong River Commission and environmental groups, opposed further dams but proved unable to delay construction.[14] The dams' blockage of the flow of fresh water downstream into Việt Nam threatens to allow a higher rate of seawater encroachment there, putting coastal crop cultivation at great risk. China remains "the Mekong's biggest threat," according to the *Economist*.[15]

Before his death in 2008 at the age of eighty-six, former premier Võ Văn Kiệt expressed concern about the impact on Việt Nam of global warming and more frequent droughts, and he called attention to the need to adapt to the consequent rise in sea levels.[16] The drought two years later brought the Red River to its lowest level since the compilation of records began in 1902. It "turned sections of the normally bustling river into sand dunes" and halted its ship traffic. "Never before has the water been so low that most ships cannot move," said river boat proprietor Nguyễn Mạnh Khoa of Phú Thọ. In the Mekong delta, saltwater from the South China Sea "contaminated communities" thirty-eight miles inland, twice as far as in the past. "Salinization has been a pattern in the Mekong Delta the last 30 to 50 years, but things are getting worse every year due to climate change," said Phạm Văn Dư of the agriculture ministry. He estimated that ha of riceland there were threatened.[17]

Vietnamese have responded with traditional adaptive skills. As the seawater has encroached, they have expanded aquaculture in its wake. Involving both new shrimp ponds and mangrove reforestation, the area devoted to aquaculture "skyrocketed" in 2000–2010, from 641,900 ha to more than a million. Most of the increase was due to shrimp farming, over an area that nearly doubled to 645,000 ha, especially in the Mekong delta. In Thanh Hóa province on the north-central coast, too, farmers converted their rice paddies to shrimp farms, which expanded there from 10,600 ha to 13,900 ha in the decade 2000–2010. With soil and crops in the Mekong delta suffering damage from saltwater intrusion, some farmers there turned to genetically modified rice varieties that are more tolerant of flooding and saltwater. Speaking of encroaching salinization, an agricultural expert said in 2011: "It's like a slow poisoning, and now it's increasing, moving up the rivers." He added: "It has a long-term impact, and there's no solution. Nobody can stop the saline water, but we just have to adapt."[18]

In addition, the large population of the Mekong delta, twenty million people in 2014 (an exponential rise from around three million in 1930), compounds the problem. Việt Nam's historical "frontier," a thinly populated Mekong delta, can no longer offer available land to absorb surplus populations from farther north. Indeed, the southern delta has probably already exceeded its capacity to sustain its existing inhabitants. Since the 1960s alone, more than a million freshwater wells have been drilled there.[19] Overexploitation of aquifers in the delta has seriously reduced groundwater levels, risking land subsidence (of up to one meter by 2050) that threatens to exacerbate the growing impact of the rising sea levels.[20] UN sources warned in 2011: "If sea levels rise by one metre—the low end of climate scientists' projections of a one- to two-metre rise by 2100—an estimated

1.7 million hectares would be inundated, or 5.3 percent of Vietnam's land area. Most of this threatened land (82 percent) is in the Mekong Delta, where millions of people would be displaced."[21] In the 2016 drought, river water reaching the mouth of the Mekong fell to its lowest levels in ninety years, and incoming saltwater was "creeping through the farmland like damp up a wall."[22] Rising sea levels and reductions in the land available for rice growing indicate a projected 5.6 percent decline in rice production in the Mekong delta by 2030 and 2.2 percent in the Red River delta. By 2050 the country could experience an overall decline of 20 percent.[23] Water and water control will remain as important to Việt Nam's future as they have been throughout its long history.

Endangered species are another sector of Việt Nam's traditional ecology under escalating global pressure. The highly prized traditional medicine made from rhinoceros horn is one example. *Time* magazine reported that in 2010 "what may have been Vietnam's last rhino was killed in a national park. Its horn was hacked off its face."[24] The extinction of the once common Javan rhinoceros within Việt Nam has only fueled the globalization of local demand and illicit supply of rhino horn, which is prohibited by the 1993 Convention on International Trade in Endangered Species. An international smuggling trade has grown up that parallels Việt Nam's increasing role in more conventional global markets since its normalization of relations with the United States in 1995. In South Africa in 2010 "three Vietnamese were arrested at the Johannesburg airport with twenty-four pieces of rhino horn," and just a few months later "a Vietnamese man and woman were detained at the Pretoria airport trying to sneak out four unlicensed horns from animals they had shot during a trophy hunt." African rhinoceros horn fetched $350 per gram in a traditional pharmacology store in Hanoi's Lãn Ông Street. A factory on the city's outskirts run by the new Thiên Đức Company manufactures electronic grinding machines "to hold and pulverize chunks of rhino horn."[25]

Globalization is, of course, nothing new in Việt Nam. Since the arrival of Buddhism, Hinduism, and Confucianism two millennia ago, and even after the French invasion commenced in 1859, some Vietnamese have been open and receptive to distant international influences—from Chinese characters to the *quốc ngữ* script, from Catholicism and colonialism to communism. From the Great Depression to World War Two and global decolonization, Vietnamese have responded in different ways that have linked local and transnational issues. What began in the late 1950s as a civil war within South Việt Nam, for instance, then escalated with US and North Vietnamese involvement to an American-Vietnamese conflict with global reverberations.

The war and its outcome also produced a global diaspora of Vietnamese refugees, continuing another theme of Vietnamese history: mobility and migration. Along with longstanding Vietnamese resident (*Việt Kiều*) populations in Cambodia, Laos, and Thailand, an additional three million overseas Vietnamese (*Người Việt Hải Ngoại*) live in the United States, France, Australia, Taiwan, Canada, Germany, South Korea, Japan, the Czech Republic, Malaysia, Britain, Poland, China, Norway, the Netherlands, Sweden, Belgium, and Russia. By 2008, Vietnamese living abroad contributed, via their families, more than $7 billion in remittances to Việt Nam's economy, compared to $5 billion in pledges by international donors for official development assistance. And by 2010, every year half a million Vietnamese living abroad were returning to Việt Nam for a visit. Nguyễn Quí Đức, a refugee who had become an American radio host and written a memoir, *Where the Ashes Are*, then became a bar owner and art curator in Hanoi. He explained his return to Việt Nam: "Home is where there's a sense of connection, of family, of community"—illustrating yet another theme of this book.[26] The importance of family, locality, and the sites of one's ancestors appears undiminished.

This chronological narrative of the history of the different peoples who have lived in the three major lowland regions of Việt Nam and in its uplands over the past three thousand years or more has set out to highlight their relationships with these regions' landscapes, water resources, and climatic conditions; their changing cultures and religious traditions; and their interactions with their neighbors in China and Southeast Asia. Its key themes have included the central importance of riverine and maritime communications, the dramatic impact of changing weather patterns from ancient to medieval and modern times, ecological and economic transformations, and linguistic and literary changes. The country's long experience of regional diversity, polyethnic populations, and a multireligious heritage that ranges from local spirit cults to the influences of Buddhism, Daoism, Confucianism, and Catholicism makes for a vividly pluralistic culture, which in turn overseas Vietnamese are recreating across the globe.[27]

The arcs of Vietnamese history also include the rise and fall of different political formations, from chiefdoms to Chinese provinces, from independent kingdoms to divided regions, civil wars, French colonies, and modern republics. In the twentieth century alone anticolonial nationalism; the worldwide depression; Japanese, British, and Chinese occupations; a French attempt at reconquest; Vietnamese anticolonial resistance; civil war; the American-Vietnamese conflict; and the 1975 communist victory all set the scene for the making of contemporary Việt Nam. Rapid economic growth in recent decades has transformed this one-party state into a global trading nation. Yet its environmental context and rich history still cast long shadows. Just as Đại Việt's conquest of Champa from the fifteenth to the nineteenth centuries did not alter the latter region's seaborne and commercial orientation, inherited by its successor southern polity of Đàng Trong, so the 1975 communist military victory in the south did not prevent that region's more commercial and global orientation from sweeping the communist north in turn.

On May 23, 2016, US president Barack Obama arrived in Hanoi for a state visit. There he announced: "The United States is fully lifting the ban on the sale of military equipment to Vietnam that has been in place for some 50 years."[28] Việt Nam, along with other members of the Association of Southeast Asian Nations, is involved in a tense territorial standoff in the South China Sea, once again as a rival of China but this time also as a "comprehensive partner" of the United States. If its political independence, economic prosperity, and geographical unity seem assured, Việt Nam's regional security, environmental integrity, and prospects for democracy all remain unresolved.

NOTES

PREFACE

1. Vũ Văn Mẫu, Saigon, January 31, 1975, in Ben Kiernan,"Vietnamese Democracy: An Interview with Senator Vũ Văn Mẫu," *Tharunka*, March 26, 1975, 7.
2. See, e.g., http://cseas.yale.edu/huynh-sanh-thong.

INTRODUCTION

1. Trịnh Hoài Đức, *Gia Định Thành Thông Chí* (1820), in *Gia-Dinh-Thung-Chi*, trans. G. Aubaret (Paris: Imprimerie Impériale, 1863), 111.
2. See Phạm Ngọc Điệp's sketch in Trương Bửu Lâm, *A Story of Việt Nam* (Denver: Outskirts, 2010), 4.
3. Alexander Barton Woodside, *Vietnam and the Chinese Model: A Comparative Study of Vietnamese and Chinese Government in the First Half of the Nineteenth Century* (Cambridge, MA: Harvard University Press, 1971), 16–17; Choi Byung Wook, *Southern Vietnam under the Reign of Minh Mang (1820–1841): Central Policies and Local Response* (Ithaca, NY: Cornell Southeast Asia Program, 2004), 42; George Dutton, *The Tây Sơn Uprising: Society and Rebellion in Eighteenth-Century Vietnam* (Honolulu: University of Hawai'i Press, 2006), 206–8; David Biggs, *Quagmire: Nation-Building and Nature in the Mekong Delta* (Seattle: University of Washington Press, 2010), 59–60.
4. David W. P. Elliott, *The Vietnamese War: Revolution and Social Change in the Mekong Delta 1930–1975*, 2 vols. (Armonk, NY: M. E. Sharpe, 2003), 1:4.
5. Jerome Coffee, a deputy sheriff from Alabama, before his December 1985 loss to Jeff Fenech in Sydney.
6. George H. W. Bush, *New York Times*, March 2, 1991.
7. Maureen Dowd, "Ozone Man Sequel," *New York Times*, Feb. 28, 2007.
8. Fredrik Logevall and Gordon M. Goldstein, "Will Syria Be Obama's Vietnam?," *New York Times*, Oct. 8, 2014; "Is the Syria Conflict Like Vietnam?," and "The Vietnam War Still Sets Off a Battle in America," letters to the editor, *New York Times*, Oct. 10 and 20, 2014.
9. Thomas L. Friedman, "ISIS and Vietnam," *NYT*, Oct. 29, 2014; "A Deepening Partnership with Vietnam," *NYT* editorial, Oct. 25, 2014.
10. "Obama Backs Vietnam in South China Sea Dispute with Beijing," *Guardian*, May 24, 2016, available online at http://www.theguardian.com/world/2016/may/24/obama-backs-vietnam-in-south-china-sea-dispute-with-beijing (accessed May 25, 2016).
11. Ha Van Tan, "Inscriptions from the Tenth to Fourteenth Centuries Recently Discovered in Viet Nam," in *Essays into Vietnamese Pasts*, ed. K. W. Taylor and J. K. Whitmore (Ithaca, NY: Cornell Southeast Asia Program, 1995), 51–2.

12. Gia Long, "Naming the Country Viet Nam (1804)," in *Sources of Vietnamese Tradition*, ed. George E. Dutton, Jayne S. Werner, and John K. Whitmore (New York: Columbia University Press, 2012), 258–59.
13. Woodside, *Vietnam and the Chinese Model*, 120; Liam Kelley, "How Việt Nam Became Việt Nam," *Le Minh Khai's SEAsian History Blog*, Aug. 26, 2013, https://leminhkhai.wordpress.com/2013/08/26/how-viet-nam-became-viet-nam/ (accessed June 29, 2015).
14. Nguyễn Mạnh Hà, "Les problèmes politiques auxquels sont affrontés les pays du Tiers-Monde. Exemple et cas limite: Le Vietnam," in *Le Tiers-Monde l'Occident et l'Eglise* (Paris: Cerf, 1967), 213.
15. Trần Huy Liệu, "Giỗ tổ Hùng Vương," *Tập San Nghiên Cứu Văn Sử Địa* 17 (May 1956): 1, quoted in Haydon Cherry, "Unearthing Viet Nam: Archaeology and the Making of a Nation" (MA thesis, Department of History, National University of Singapore, 2004), 1; Cherry, "Digging up the Past: Prehistory and the Weight of the Present in Vietnam," *Journal of Vietnamese Studies* 4, no. 1 (Winter 2009): 84, 108.
16. Keith Weller Taylor, *The Birth of Vietnam* (Berkeley: University of California Press, 1983), xix–xx.
17. Taylor, *A History of the Vietnamese* (Cambridge, U.K: Cambridge University Press, 2013); Taylor, "Author's Response," *Sojourn* 29, no. 3 (2014): 749.
18. Stephen O'Harrow, quoted in Taylor, *History*, 29; O'Harrow, "Men of Hu, Men of Han, Men of the Hundred Man: The Biography of Sĩ Nhiêp and the Conceptualization of Early Vietnamese Society," *Bulletin de l'Ecole Française d'Extrême-Orient* (henceforth cited as *BEFEO*) 75 (1986): 250–51, 258; O'Harrow, "Nguyen Trai's 'Binh Ngo Dai Cao' of 1428: The Development of a Vietnamese National Identity," *Journal of Southeast Asian Studies* 10, no. 1 (March 1979): 173.
19. Keith Taylor, "The Construction and Deconstruction of Vietnamese History," presentation to Yale Council on Southeast Asia Studies, Dec. 11, 1991; also Taylor, *History*.
20. Cherry, "Unearthing Viet Nam," 10–14, citing Liam Kelley, 13, and Cherry, pers. comm., June 20, 2015. See also Liam Kelley, *Beyond the Bronze Pillars: Envoy Poetry and the Sino-Vietnamese Relationship* (Honolulu: University of Hawai'i Press, 2005).
21. See, e.g., K. W. Taylor, "Surface Orientations in Vietnam: Beyond Histories of Nation and Religion," *Journal of Asian Studies* 75, no. 4 (Nov. 1998), 949–78.
22. Biggs, *Quagmire*, 61.
23. See Bruce M. Lockhart, "Colonial and Post-Colonial Constructions of 'Champa,'" in *The Cham of Vietnam: History, Society and Art*, ed. Lockhart and Trần Kỳ Phương (Singapore, NUS Press, 2011), 33–34.
24. On "deep history," see Jo Guldi and David Armitage, *The History Manifesto* (Cambridge, UK: Cambridge University Press, 2014), 8, 86, 118–19, 3, 5, 125, 86–87, 120–21.
25. Huỳnh Sanh Thông, "Live by Water, Die for Water (*Sống vì nước, chết vì nước*): Metaphors of Vietnamese Culture and History," *Vietnam Review* 1 (Autumn-Winter 1996), at 121, 152–53.
26. Huỳnh Sanh Thông, "The Vietnamese Worldview: Water, Water Everywhere," *Vietnam Review* 2 (Spring-Summer 1997), 16.
27. Charles Wheeler, "Re-Thinking the Sea in Vietnamese History: Littoral Society in the Integration of Thuận-Quảng, Seventeenth-Eighteenth Centuries," *Journal of Southeast Asian Studies* 37, no. 1 (2006), 124, 126.
28. Chou Ch'u-fei (1170s), quoted in John K. Whitmore, "'Elephants Can Actually Swim': Contemporary Chinese Views of Late Ly Dai Viet," in *Southeast Asia in the 9th to 14th Centuries*, ed. David G. Marr and A.C. Milner (Singapore: Institute of Southeast Asian Studies, 1986), 123.

29. Samuel Baron, "A Description of the Kingdom of Tonqueen," in *Views of Seventeenth-Century Vietnam: Christoforo Borri on Cochinchina and Samuel Baron on Tonkin*, ed. Olga Dror and K. W. Taylor (Ithaca, NY: Southeast Asia Program Publications, Southeast Asia Program, Cornell University, 2006), 217, 204–5, 224.
30. Gerald Norris, ed., *William Dampier: Buccaneer Explorer* (London: Folio, 1994), 139, 151–2.
31. Norris, *William Dampier*, 152.
32. Ma Huan, *Ying-Yai Sheng-Lan, "The Overall Survey of the Ocean's Shores" [1433]*, ed. J. V. G. Mills (Bangkok: White Lotus, 1997), 81.
33. Pierre-Yves Manguin, "Etudes Cam, IV: Une relation ibérique du Campa en 1595," *BEFEO* 70 (1981): 256n2.
34. Christoforo Borri, "An Account of Cochin-China in Two Parts" (London, 1732), in Dror and Taylor, *Views of Seventeenth-Century Vietnam*, 95–96, 106, 103.
35. Biggs, *Quagmire*, 14–15.
36. Manguin, "Etudes Cam, IV," 256n2.
37. Lê Quý Đôn, "Miscellaneous Nguyễn Records Seized in 1775–76," trans. Li Tana, in *Southern Vietnam under the Nguyễn: Documents on the Economic History of Cochinchina (Đàng Trong), 1602–1777*, ed. Li Tana and Anthony Reid (Singapore: ASEAN Economic Research Unit, Institute of Southeast Asian Studies, 1993), 126.
38. Trịnh Hoài Đức, *Gia Định Thành Thông Chí* (1820), translation in Dutton, Werner, and Whitmore, *Sources*, 271, 297, 299.
39. Ngo Vinh Long, "The Tet Offensive and Its Aftermath, Part 3," *Indochina Newsletter* 60 (Nov.–Dec. 1989), 4.
40. O. W. Wolters, *Two Essays on Đại-Việt in the Fourteenth Century* (New Haven, CT: Yale Southeast Asia Program, 1988), 11.
41. C. Michele Thompson, "Setting the Stage: Ancient Medical History of the Geographical Space that is Now Vietnam," in *Southern Medicine for Southern People*, ed. Laurence Monnais, C. Michele Thompson, and Ayo Wahlberg (Newcastle, UK: Cambridge Scholars, 2012), 33.
42. Borri, "An Account of Cochin-China," 112.
43. Gerald Hickey, *Sons of the Mountains: Ethnohistory of the Vietnamese Central Highlands to 1954* (New Haven, CT: Yale University Press, 1982), 188.
44. Michael Vickery, *Champa Revised* (Singapore: Asia Research Institute, 2005), 8.
45. Nguyễn Đình Hòa, "Chữ Nôm: The Demotic System of Writing in Vietnam," *Journal of the American Oriental Society* 79, no. 4 (1959): 271; C. Michele Thompson, "Scripts, Signs, and Swords: The Viet Peoples and the Origins of Nom," *Sino-Platonic Papers* 101 (March 2000): 11; Keith Weller Taylor, *The Birth of Vietnam* (Berkeley: University of California Press, 1983), 334, 351.
46. Taylor and Whitmore, *Essays*, 6; Haydon Cherry, pers. comm, March 15, 2007. See also Cherry, "Unearthing Viet Nam."
47. Michael Churchman notes "a fairly stable group of people in Jiaozhi throughout the Han–Tang period who spoke Austroasiatic languages ancestral to modern Vietnamese." See "Before Chinese and Vietnamese in the Red River Plain: The Han-Tang Period," *Chinese Southern Diaspora Studies* 4 (2010): 36.
48. Stephen O'Harrow, "From Co-loa to the Trung Sisters' Revolt: Vietnam as the Chinese Found It," *Asian Perspectives* 22, no. 2 (1979): 140–64.
49. Phạm Quỳnh, quoted by Alexander B. Woodside, "The Historical Background," in Nguyen Du, *The Tale of Kieu*, trans. Huỳnh Sanh Thông (New Haven, CT: 1983), xxxix.
50. Woodside, *Vietnam and the Chinese Model*, 44.

51. Min-Sheng Peng et al., "Tracing the Austronesian Footprint in Mainland Southeast Asia: A Perspective from Mitochondrial DNA," *Molecular Biology and Evolution* 27, no. 10 (2010): 2428, 2417, 2427.
52. Hồ Trung Tú, *Có 500 năm như thế: bản sắc Quảng Nam từ góc nhìn phân kỳ lịch sử* (Hanoi: Thời đại, 2011).
53. Trần Đức Anh Sơn, pers. comm., April 2016.
54. Victor B. Lieberman, *Strange Parallels: Southeast Asia in Global Context, c. 800–1830*, vol. 1, *Integration on the Mainland* (New York: Cambridge University Press, 2003), ch. 4.
55. Hippolyte Le Breton, *Le Vieux An-Tinh*, in *Bulletin des Amis du vieux Hué* 3–4, 1936 (repr. Hanoi: Ecole Française d'Extrême-Orient, 2001), 290–91.
56. Biggs, *Quagmire*, 62–65.
57. Wheeler, "Re-Thinking the Sea," 128, 124, 126.
58. Lockhart, "Colonial and Post-Colonial Constructions of 'Champa,'" 28–30.
59. K. W. Taylor, "Surface Orientations in Vietnam: Beyond Histories of Nation and Region," *Journal of Asian Studies* 57, no. 4 (Nov. 1998): 950 (map), 954.
60. Taylor and Whitmore, *Essays*, 9, 5, 6, 7.
61. "South China Sea: Beijing plans military drills running up to court ruling," *Guardian*, July 3, 2016, available online at http://www.theguardian.com/world/2016/jul/03/south-china-sea-beijing-plans-military-drills-running-up-to-court-ruling (accessed July 3, 2016).

CHAPTER 1

1. Fernand Braudel, *Memory and the Mediterranean* (New York: Knopf, 2001), 18.
2. Nguyễn Đình Hòa, "*Chữ nôm*: The Demotic System of Writing in Vietnam," *Journal of the American Oriental Society* 79, no. 4 (Oct.-Dec. 1959): 271; for 14th-century sources, see E. S. Ungar, "From Myth to History: Imagined Polities in 14th Century Vietnam," in *Southeast Asia in the 9th to 14th Centuries*, ed. D. G. Marr and A. C. Milner (Canberra: Australian National University, 1986), 178.
3. Quoted in Cyprian Broodbank, *The Making of the Middle Sea: A History of the Mediterranean from the Beginning to the Emergence of the Classical World* (New York: Oxford University Press, 2013), 21.
4. Eleanor Jane Sterling, Martha Maud Hurley, and Le Duc Minh, *Vietnam: A Natural History* (New Haven, CT: Yale University Press, 2006), 10, 72, 157.
5. For another example, see Anne Ross, *Pagan Celtic Britain* (Chicago: Academy, 1967), 46–48, 140–41, 455.
6. Huỳnh Sanh Thông, "The Vietnamese Worldview: Water, Water Everywhere," *Vietnam Review* 2 (1997): 16–97; Huỳnh Sanh Thông, *The Golden Serpent: How Humans Learned to Speak and Invent Culture* (Hamden, CT: Huỳnh Sanh Thông, 1999), 25.
7. Charles Higham, *Early Cultures of Mainland Southeast Asia* (Bangkok: River, 2002), 8, 36.
8. Stephen Oppenheimer, *Eden in the East: The Drowned Continent of Southeast Asia* (London: Phoenix, 1998), 62, 68 (fig. 10); Jennifer Holmgren, *Chinese Colonisation of Northern Vietnam: Administrative Geography and Political Development in the Tongking Delta, First to Sixth Centuries A.D.* (Canberra, Australian National University, 1980), 25; Charles Higham, "The Later Prehistory of Mainland Southeast Asia," *Journal of World Prehistory* 3, no. 3 (1989): 260.
9. Hippolyte Le Breton, *Le Vieux An-Tinh*, in *Bulletin des Amis du vieux Hué* 3–4, 1936 (repr. Hanoi, Ecole Française d'Extrême-Orient, 2001), 226.
10. Van Lap Nguyen, Thi Kim Oanh Ta, and Masaaki Tateishi, "Late Holocene Depositional Environments and Coastal Evolution of the Mekong River Delta,"

Journal of Asian Earth Sciences 18 (2000): 437 (fig. 5); David Biggs, *Quagmire: Nation-Building and Nature in the Mekong Delta* (Seattle: University of Washington Press, 2010), 14.

11. Trần Quốc Vượng, ed., *Việt sử lược* (Hanoi: Văn Sử Địa, 1960), 45n1d, 80n2.
12. M. Ganis (?), Résident à Sơn Tây, "Rapport commercial, Industriel et agricole, mois de septembre 1886," September 30, 1886, Archives Nationales d'Outre-Mer (ANOM), Aix-en-Provence, Fonds de la Résidence Supérieure du Tonkin, Nouveaux Fonds (RSTNF), 7005, 5–6. All translations are mine unless otherwise noted.
13. Émile Gaspardone, "Champs *Lo* et Champs *Hiong*," *Journal Asiatique* 243 (1955): 474n5; Holmgren, *Chinese Colonisation*, 177–79; Keith W. Taylor, *The Birth of Vietnam* (Berkeley: University of California Press, 1983), 12.
14. Huỳnh Sanh Thông, *The Heritage of Vietnamese Poetry* (New Haven, CT: Yale, 1979), 217.
15. Nishimura Masanari, "Settlement Patterns on the Red River Plain from the Late Prehistoric Period to the 10th Century AD," *Indo-Pacific Prehistory Association Bulletin* 25 (2005): 99.
16. M. Ganis (?), Résident à Sơn Tây, "Rapport commercial industriel et agricole (mois d'octobre 1886)," ANOM, RSTNF 7005, 14–15.
17. Gerald Norris, ed., *William Dampier: Buccaneer Explorer* (London: Folio, 1994), 139.
18. Ganis, "Rapport commercial industriel et agricole (mois d'octobre 1886)," 15.
19. Stephen O'Harrow, "From Co-loa to the Trung Sisters' Revolt: Vietnam as the Chinese Found It," *Asian Perspectives* 22, no. 2 (1979): 152; Taylor, *Birth*, 4.
20. Huỳnh, *Heritage*, 218.
21. Holmgren, *Chinese Colonisation*, 28, map 2:4; Taylor, *Birth*, 2, map 1.
22. I am grateful to the late Huỳnh Sanh Thông for drawing this to my attention.
23. Higham, *Early Cultures*, 30–35; Nguyen Khac Su, "Northern Vietnam from the Neolithic to the Han Period: Part I, The Neolithic Cultures of Vietnam," in *Southeast Asia: From Prehistory to History*, ed. Ian Glover and Peter Bellwood (London: RoutledgeCurzon, 2004), 179.
24. Nguyen, "Northern Vietnam, Part I," 180.
25. Oppenheimer, *Eden*, 134–39; Nguyen, "Northern Vietnam, Part I," 180.
26. Higham, *Early Cultures*, 35–36.
27. Marc Oxenham et al., "Health and the Experience of Childhood in Late Neolithic Viet Nam," *Asian Perspectives* 47, no. 2 (2008): 190, citing K. S. Nguyen, M. H. Pham, and T. T. Tong, "Northern Vietnam from the Neolithic to the Han Period," in Glover and Bellwood, *Southeast Asia*, 177–201.
28. Higham, *Early Cultures*, 84–85; David Christian, *Maps of Time: An Introduction to Big History* (Berkeley: University of California Press, 2004), 218, 221; Oppenheimer, *Eden*, 71, 476.
29. Oppenheimer, *Eden*, 18, 62, 80, 477.
30. Nguyen, "Northern Vietnam, Part I," 181–82.
31. Nguyen, "Northern Vietnam, Part I," 183–85.
32. Wolfram Eberhard, *The Local Cultures of South and East China* (Leiden: Brill, 1968), 435.
33. Henri Maspero, "Études d'histoire d'Annam: IV, Le royaume de Van-Lang," *BEFEO* 18, no. 3(1918): 9n2.
34. Taylor, *Birth*, 9; Oppenheimer, *Eden*, 63.
35. Charles Higham, *The Bronze Age of Southeast Asia* (Cambridge, UK: Cambridge University Press, 1996), 108–9; P. Boriskovskii, "Vietnam in Primeval Times—Chapter VII," *Soviet Anthropology and Archeology* 9, no. 3 (1970–71): 228–35; Holmgren, *Chinese Colonisation*, 7.

36. Taylor, *Birth*, 7; Boriskovskii, "Vietnam in Primeval Times," 227.
37. Pham Minh Huyen, "Northern Vietnam from the Neolithic to the Han Period: Part II, The Metal Age," in Glover and Bellwood, *Southeast Asia*, 190; Hoang Xuan Chinh and Bui Van Tien, "The Dongson Culture and Cultural Centers in the Metal Age in Vietnam," *Asian Perspectives* 23 (1980): 56; Higham, *Bronze Age*, 88, and *Early Cultures*, 86–90.
38. Pham, "Northern Vietnam, Part II," 189–90, 192.
39. Higham, "Later Prehistory," 253–54, 276–78; Boriskovskii, "Vietnam in Primeval Times," 231.
40. Charles Higham and Tracey L.-D. Lu, "The Origins and Dispersal of Rice Cultivation," *Antiquity* 72, no. 278 (Dec. 1998): 874.
41. Oxenham et al., "Health and the Experience of Childhood," 191; Higham and Lu, "Origins and Dispersal of Rice," 874.
42. Judith Cameron, "Textile Crafts in the Gulf of Tongking: The Intersection between Archaeology and History," in *The Tongking Gulf through History*, ed. Nola Cooke, Li Tana, and James A. Anderson (Philadelphia: University of Pennsylvania Press, 2011): 28–30, and Li Tana, "Introduction," in Cooke, Tana, and Anderson, *Tongking Gulf through History*, 6.
43. Hoang and Bui, "Dongson Culture," 56; Taylor, *Birth*, 4; Higham, "Later Prehistory," 253, 261; Pham Minh Huyen, "Northern Vietnam, Part II," 190. See also Haydon Cherry, "Unearthing Viet Nam: Archaeology and the Making of a Nation" (MA thesis, National University of Singapore, 2004), ch. 4; and Cherry, "Digging Up the Past: Prehistory and the Weight of the Present in Vietnam," *Journal of Vietnamese Studies* 4, no. 1 (2009): 84–144.
44. Pham, "Northern Vietnam, Part II," 190.
45. Hoang and Bui, "Dongson Culture," 57, 63n; Higham, "Later Prehistory," 253, 261.
46. Pham, "Northern Vietnam, Part II," 192; Taylor, *Birth*, 12.
47. Braudel, *Memory and the Mediterranean*, 97; Higham, "Later Prehistory," 278, 239, 255, 257; Taylor, *Birth*, 22.
48. Hoang and Bui, "Dongson Culture," 57.
49. Pham, "Northern Vietnam, Part II," 192.
50. O'Harrow, "From Co-loa," 142; Pierre Gourou, *Les paysans du delta Tonkinois* (Paris: Les Éditions d'Art et d'Histoire, 1936), translated by Richard R. Miller as *The Peasants of the Tonkin Delta: A Study of Human Geography* (New Haven, CT: Human Relations Area Files, 1955), 1:59–64; Clifford Geertz, *Agricultural Involution: The Process of Agricultural Change in Indonesia* (Berkeley: University of California Press, 1963), 31.
51. Higham, "Later Prehistory," 272–73; Taylor, *Birth*, 35; Christian Lentz, pers. comm.
52. Pham, "Northern Vietnam, Part II," 193, 195.
53. Nam C. Kim, "Lasting Monuments and Durable Institutions: Labor, Urbanism, and Statehood in Northern Vietnam and Beyond," *Journal of Archaeological Research* 21, no. 1 (March 2013): fig. 1; Pham, "Northern Vietnam, Part II," 195, 197, 199, 201.
54. Taylor, *Birth*, 4, 7; Higham, "Later Prehistory," 262.
55. Nam C. Kim, Lai Van Toi, and Trinh Hoang Hiep, "Co Loa: An Investigation of Vietnam's Ancient Capital," *Antiquity* 84 (2010): 1025–26.
56. Pham, "Northern Vietnam, Part II," 199.
57. Richard Pearson, "Dong-So'n and Its Origins," *Zhong yang yan jiu yuan min zu xue yan jiu suo ji kan* (*Bulletin of the Institute of Ethnology, Academia Sinica*) 13 (1962): 32, 34; Boriskovskii, "Vietnam in Primeval Times," 261.

58. Pham, "Northern Vietnam, Part II," 195; Boriskovskii, "Vietnam in Primeval Times," 231; Taylor, *Birth*, 9.
59. Pearson, "Dong-So'n and Its Origins," 45.
60. Pham, "Northern Vietnam, Part II," 201.
61. Barry Cunliffe, *Europe between the Oceans, 9000 BC–AD 1000* (New Haven, CT: Yale, 2008), 146–47.
62. Hoang and Bui, "Dongson Culture," 58; Pham, "Northern Vietnam, Part II," 201.
63. Pearson, "Dong-So'n and Its Origins," 27–34, 30.
64. Nam, Lai, and Trinh, "Co Loa," 1012.
65. Ambra Calo, *Trails of Bronze Drums across Early Southeast Asia* (Singapore: Institute of Southeast Asian Studies, 2014), 38, fig. 2.1; Han Xiaorong, "The Present Echoes of the Ancient Bronze Drum: Nationalism and Archaeology in Modern Vietnam and China," *Explorations in Southeast Asian Studies* 2, no. 2 (Fall 1998): 14, 1, 3–5, 10, 12.
66. *Dong Son Drums in Viet Nam* (Hanoi: Viet Nam Social Science Publishing House, 1990), documents 144 of these drums of "Heger type 1," 246–52, 262; Pham, "Northern Vietnam, Part II," 200, indicates "more than 200 . . . found in northern Vietnam"; Ambra Calo says about three hundred have been found throughout Việt Nam. *Trails of Bronze Drums*, 38, 96, 107–8, and maps, figs. 2.1, 3.1.
67. Holmgren, *Chinese Colonisation*, 19.
68. Higham, "Later Prehistory," 261; Hoang and Bui, "Dongson Culture," 58.
69. Nam C. Kim, *The Origins of Ancient Vietnam* (Oxford: Oxford University Press, 2015).
70. Nam, Lai, and Trinh, "Co Loa," 1014, 1023, 1026; Kim, "Cổ Loa: A Site of Manifold Significance," *Arts du Vietnam* 2015, 70; Kim, *Origins*, 206–8; Higham, *Bronze Age*, 122; Higham, "Later Prehistory," 260–61; Holmgren, *Chinese Colonisation*, 37.
71. Trần Quốc Vượng, "Cổ Loa: Những kết quả nghiên cứu vừa qua và những triển vọng tới," *Khảo cổ học* 3–4 (1969): 108 (map), 113; Marilynn Larew, "Thục Phán, Cao Tông, and the Transfer of Military Technology in Third Century BC Việt Nam," *East Asian Science, Technology, and Medicine* 21 (2003): 15.
72. Higham, "Later Prehistory," 261–62, 264.
73. Calo, *Trails of Bronze Drums*, 47; C. Michele Thompson, *Scripts, Signs, and Swords: The Việt Peoples and the Origins of Nôm*, Sino-Platonic Papers 101 (March 2000), http://www.sino-platonic.org/complete/spp101_vietnamese_chu_nom.pdf (accessed June 12, 2015), 63, and appendix, 72.
74. Nam, Lai, and Trinh, "Co Loa," 1024–25.
75. Higham, "Later Prehistory," 279, 239, 264, 267.
76. Taylor, *Birth*, 24, 35; Higham, "Later Prehistory," 273–75.
77. Pham, "Northern Vietnam, Part II," 201, 199.
78. Hoang and Bui, "Dongson Culture," 64; Higham, "Later Prehistory," 260–61; Higham, *Bronze Age*, 122.
79. Calo, *Trails of Bronze Drums*, 40.
80. Higham, *Bronze Age*, 111–16; Higham, "Later Prehistory," 260–62; Taylor, *Birth*, 7.
81. Higham, "Later Prehistory," 262; Pearson, "Dong-So'n and Its Origins," 30.
82. Oppenheimer, *Eden*, 100, 138–39, 313.
83. "Crocodiles," *China Review* 7, no. 5 (March-April 1879): 351. An alligator sighted in the Yangzi region in 1879 was "said to presage a great rise in the river this year." *Shanghai Courier*, March 11, 1879, translation of an article in *Shen Pao*, quoted in A. A. Fauvel, "Alligators in China," *Journal of the North-China Branch of the Royal Asiatic Society*, n.s., 13 (1879).

84. Hoang and Bui, "Dongson Culture," 59.
85. *Dong Son Drums in Viet Nam*, 22–23, 205; Calo, *Trails of Bronze Drums*, 40–41. A crocodile appears on a first-century bronze halberd held at the National Museum of Vietnamese History, Hanoi; Nancy Tingley, *Arts of Ancient Vietnam: From River Plain to Open Sea* (New York: Asia Society, 2009), 64. A chest plate depicting a crocodile was found in Ninh Bình: "The Thematic Exhibition on Dong Son Culture," Talk Vietnam, Dec. 5, 2014, http://www.talkvietnam.com/2014/12/the-thematic-exhibition-on-dong-son-culture/ (accessed Sept. 5, 2015).
86. Edward H. Schafer, *The Vermilion Bird: T'ang Images of the South* (Berkeley: University of California Press, 1967), 32.
87. Sterling, Hurley, and Le, *Vietnam: A Natural History*, 300.
88. Guangdong had a "colony of crocodiles" in the Tang era (618–905). Schafer, *Vermilion Bird*, 217–18, 30, 128. The Chinese alligator has lived in Yangzi River flood lands for six thousand years. Huang Chu-chien, "The Ecology of the Chinese Alligator and Changes in its Geographical Distribution," in *Crocodiles: Proceedings of the 5th Working Meeting of the Crocodile Specialist Group* (Gland, Switzerland: International Union for Conservation of Nature and Natural Resources, 1982), 54–62.
89. David Chuenyuan Lai, "The Dragon in China," http://www.cic.sfu.ca/cchf/dragonInChina.html (accessed Sept. 21, 2008).
90. Nguyễn Khắc-Kham, "*Chữ nôm* or the Former Vietnamese Script and its Past Contributions to Vietnamese Literature," *Area and Culture Studies* 24 (1974): 1; Thomas Hodgkin, *Vietnam: The Revolutionary Path* (London: Macmillan, 1981), 49.
91. Fauvel, "Alligators in China," 19, 30, 6–8, 10–14; "Takashima (1955) reports three crocodiles from Japanese territory; one from Iwo Jima (in 1744), one from . . . the northern end of the Ryukyu Islands (in 1800), and a third from . . . Honshu. All three were presumably specimens of *C. porosus* [saltwater crocodile]. . . . The continued presence of *C. porosus* in southern China remains to be verified." "Crocodylus porosus," http://www.flmnh.ufl.edu/natsci/herpetology/act-plan/cporo.htm accessed Sept. 21, 2008). See also Huang, "Ecology of the Chinese Alligator," 91–102.
92. Taylor, *Birth*, 8–9.
93. Mark Alves, "Linguistic Research on the Origins of the Vietnamese Language: An Overview," *Journal of Vietnamese Studies* 1, nos. 1–2 (Feb.-Aug. 2006): 123.
94. Alexander B. Woodside, *Vietnam and the Chinese Model* (Cambridge, MA: Harvard University Press, 1971), 50. Vietnamese words for "rice" include the Sino-Vietnamese term *mê*; *lúa* (the plant unharvested), a possible cognate to the Khmer *srauv*; and *gạo* (rice husked but uncooked), close to Thai *kao* and a possible cognate for Khmer *nkor*. Eric Henry adds *thóc* (rice harvested but unhusked); *cơm* (cooked and ready to eat); glutinous rice *nếp* (when uncooked), a possible cognate for Khmer *domnaeup*; and *xôi* (cooked sticky rice).
95. Nguyễn Tài Cẩn, "12-Century History of the Vietnamese Language: Essay on the Delimitation of Periods," *Vietnamese Studies* 3 (1999): 14.
96. Heinz-Jürgen Pinnow, *Versuch einer historischen Lautlehre der Kharia-Sprache* (Wiesbaden, Germany: O. Harrassowitz, 1959); see also Patricia Donegan and Davis Stampe's website on Austroasiatic languages at http://www.ling.hawaii.edu/austroasiatic/ (accessed June 17, 2014).
97. Gérard Diffloth, "An Appraisal of Benedict's Views on Austroasiatic and Austro-Thai Relations" (Center for Southeast Asian Studies, Kyoto University, Discussion Paper no. 82, March 1976), 3.

98. Gérard Diffloth, "The Contribution of Linguistic Palaeontology to the Homeland of Austro-Asiatic," in *The Peopling of East Asia: Putting Together Archaeology, Linguistics, and Genetics*, ed. L. Sagart, R. Blench, and A. Sanchez-Mazas (London: Routledge, 2005), 77–80.
99. Alves, "Linguistic Research," 113.
100. Taylor, *Birth*, 1, 10; Eric Henry, pers. comm., April 30, 2007.
101. Taylor, *Birth*, 10–12.
102. Huỳnh Sanh Thông, "Live by Water, Die for Water (*Sống vì nước, chết vì nước*): Metaphors of Vietnamese Culture and History," *Vietnam Review* 1 (Autumn-Winter 1996): 139.
103. Li Daoyuan, *Shui Jing Zhu*, annotated by Yang Shoujing and Xiong Huizhen (Nanjing: Jiangsu guji chubanshe, 1989), 37:3042–43. Jennifer Holmgren offers a slightly different translation: "This area formed the fields of the Lo [Lạc]. Here, agricultural labor followed the rise and fall of the tides. Because the people cultivated the fields, they were called the Lo people." *Chinese Colonisation*, 37n20, 8n4, citing Li, *Shui Jing Zhu*, 37:62.
104. Taylor, *Birth*, 6, 10, 42, 307, appendices A, B.
105. Taylor, *Birth*, 307; Gaspardone, "Champs *Lo* et Champs *Hiong*," 473. On dating the *Kuang chou chi*: 467n4, and Edward H. Schafer, "Rosewood, Dragon's Blood, and Lac," *Journal of the American Oriental Society* 77, no. 2 (1957): 135n67. The quotation from the *Jiaozhou waiyu ji* is in Li, *Shui Jing Zhu*, 37:62, translated in Holmgren, *Chinese Colonisation*, 37n20.
106. Nguyen, "Northern Vietnam, Part I," 183.
107. James R. Chamberlain, "The Origin of the Sek: Implications for Tai and Vietnamese History," *Journal of the Siam Society* 86 (1998): 37, 40, 41, 34.
108. Jerry Norman and Tsu-lin Mei, "The Austroasiatics in Ancient South China: Some Lexical Evidence," *Monumenta Serica* 32 (1976): 274–301. Twelve Mon-Khmer languages are spoken in southern China today: see the Ethnologue webpage on Mon-Khmer, http://www.ethnologue.com/subgroups/mon-khmer-1 (accessed June 23, 2016).
109. Norman and Mei, "Austroasiatics," 274–75, 277–99.
110. Taylor, *Birth*, 16; Chamberlain, "Origin of the Sek," 46n18.
111. Gérard Diffloth, "Linguistic Prehistory from a Mon-Khmer Perspective" (paper presented at the conference The High Bronze Age of Southeast Asia and South China, Hua Hin, 1991), cited in James R. Chamberlain, "The Black Tai Chronicle of Muong Muay, Part I: Mythology," *Mon-Khmer Studies* 21 (1992): 22.
112. Chamberlain, "Origin of the Sek," 35, 37; "The Vietic Branch, SEAlang, http://sealang.net/mk/vietic.htm# (accessed July 18, 2008).
113. See Paul Sidwell, "Mon-Khmer Languages Working Family Tree," SEAlang, http://sealang.net/monkhmer, http://sealang.net/mk/lexical_sources-1.htm, and "Austro-Asiatic, Mon-Khmer," Ethnologue, http://www.ethnologue.com/show_family.asp?subid=90152 (both accessed Oct. 17, 2008); Taylor, *Birth*, 43, 7–8; Nguyen Dang Thuc, *The Origins of the Vietnamese People*, Vietnam Culture Series 10 (Saigon: Directorate of Cultural Affairs, Ministry of State in Charge of Cultural Affairs, n.d.), cites linguistic affiliations of "the Au-Lac people" with Rhadé (27).
114. Alves, "Linguistic Research," 104; La Vaughn H. Hayes, "Vietic and Việt-Mường: A New Subgrouping in Mon-Khmer," *Mon-Khmer Studies* 21 (1992): 219.
115. Norman and Mei, "Austroasiatics," cited in Eric Henry, "The Submerged History of Yuè," *Sino-Platonic Papers* 176 (May 2007): 16n28.
116. Alves, "Linguistic Research," 110.

117. Norman and Mei, "Austroasiatics" 284ff.; Eric Henry, pers. comm., May 13 and 14, 2007.
118. David Thomas, "A Note on the Branches of Mon-Khmer," *Mon-Khmer Studies* 5 (1973): 139–41.
119. See for instance Oppenheimer, *Eden*, 135.
120. Chamberlain, "Origin of Sek," 27, 37, 35.
121. Nguyen Quang Hong, remarks at the Nom Studies Workshop, Yale University, April 18, 2008.
122. Chamberlain, "Origin of Sek," 44. Chamberlain's bibliography omits Norman and Mei, "Austroasiatics."
123. Alves, "Linguistic Research," 111.
124. O. W. Wolters, *Two Essays on Đại Việt in the Fourteenth Century* (New Haven, CT: Council on Southeast Asia Studies, 1988), 13, citing Tsu-lin Mei.
125. Chamberlain, "Origin of the Sek," 34.
126. Diffloth, "Contribution of Linguistic Palaeontology," 79.
127. Hayes, "Vietic and Việt-Mường," 218–20.
128. Alves, "Linguistic Research," 113, 122.
129. Hayes, "Vietic and Việt-Mường," 216.
130. Henry, "Submerged History of Yuè," 7, 21, 17, 4; Norman and Mei, "Austroasiatics," 277.
131. Cameron, "Textile Crafts in the Gulf of Tongking," 37.
132. Léonard Aurousseau, "La première conquête chinoise des pays annamites (IIIe siècle avant notre ère)," *BEFEO* 23 (1923): 262–63. Hayes, "Vietic and Việt-Mường," 216n11, suggests this may have occurred around 1000 BCE.
133. Taylor, *Birth*, 43; Chamberlain, "Origin," 46n18.
134. Brian Sykes, *Saxons, Vikings, and Celts: The Genetic Roots of Britain and Ireland* (New York: Norton, 2006), 287, 231; Taylor, *Birth*, 17.
135. Kwang-chih Chang and Ward H. Goodenough, "Archaeology of Southeastern Coastal China and Its Bearing on the Austronesian Homeland," in *Prehistoric Settlement of the Pacific*, ed. Ward Goodenough, Transactions of the American Philosophical Society 86, pt. 5 (Philadelphia: American Philosophical Society, 1996), 48; Henry, "Submerged History of Yuè," 6–8; David Hawkes, "General Introduction," in *Songs of the South: An Anthology of Ancient Chinese Poems by Qu Yuan and Other Poets* (New York: Penguin, 1985), 20.
136. *Yüeh chüeh-shu* 8.8a–b, cited in H. S. Levy, "T'ang Women of Pleasure," *Sinologica* 8, no. 2 (1964): 109.
137. Wang Gungwu, *The Nanhai Trade: A Study of the Early History of Chinese Trade in the South China Sea* (Kuala Lumpur: Malayan Branch of the Royal Asiatic Society, 1958), 3.
138. *Chan-Kuo T'se* [*Zhanguoce*], trans. J. I. Crump (Oxford: Clarendon, 1970), 135.
139. Aurousseau, "La première conquête," 252–53, 262–63; Taylor, *Birth*, 16.
140. Aurousseau, "La première conquête," 259.
141. Erica Fox Brindley, *Ancient China and the Yue* (Cambridge, UK: Cambridge University Press, 2015), 54–59; Chang and Goodenough, "Archaeology," 43, 46, 48, 53; Chamberlain, "Origin," 46n18.
142. Taylor, *Birth*, 43, citing Norman and Mei, "Austroasiatics."
143. Eric Henry, "Yue Chronology," Warring States Working Group e-mail list, Feb. 11, 2007. Henry kindly supplied translations of documentation for his finding. He cites Yang Shanqun, *Gou Jian* (Taibei: Taibei Xian Zhonghe Shi, 1991).
144. Henry, "Submerged History of Yuè," 3, 12, 13, 17.

145. *Wu Yüeh Ch'un-ch'iu*, 232, quoted in Wang, *Nanhai Trade*, 4.
146. Mark Elvin, *The Retreat of the Elephants: An Environmental History of China* (New Haven, CT: Yale University Press, 2004), 12.
147. Eberhard, *Local Cultures*, 355, 356, 362, 349; Hawkes, *Songs of the South*, 342.
148. Taylor, *Birth*, 1, 10; Eric Henry, pers. comm., April 30, 2007.
149. Edward H. Schafer, *The Vermilion Bird: T'ang Images of the South* (Berkeley: University of California Press, 1967), 10, 221.
150. Eberhard, *Local Cultures*, 363–65, 366–67, 373, 368.
151. Laurence A. Schneider, *A Madman of Ch'u: The Chinese Myth of Loyalty and Dissent* (Berkeley: University of California Press, 1980), 148, 150.
152. James Legge, quoted in Schneider, *Madman of Ch'u*, 143.
153. O'Harrow, "From Co-loa," 142, 151; Kim, *Origins*, chs. 9, 10.
154. Holmgren, *Chinese Colonisation*, 19–20.
155. Huynh, *Golden Serpent*, 20.
156. Henri Maspéro, "Études d'histoire d'Annam," *BEFEO* 18, no. 3 (1918): 10n7; Holmgren, *Chinese Colonisation*, 19–20.
157. Taylor, *Birth*, 75–77.
158. Huynh, *Golden Serpent*, 9–25.
159. Gerald Hickey, *Sons of the Mountains: Ethnohistory of the Vietnamese Central Highlands to 1954* (New Haven, CT: Yale University Press, 1982), 62–63. For comparable multidisciplinary work on ancient Britons, see Ross, *Pagan Celtic Britain*, 25–26, 143.
160. Karl Gustav Izikowitz, *Lamet: Hill Peasants in French Indochina* (Göteborg, Sweden: Etnologisker Studier, 1951), 20, 206–8, 99.
161. Izikowitz, *Lamet*, 22, 305, 116–18, 330, 347, 102.
162. Hickey, *Sons of the Mountains*, 186–87, 449; Anthony Reid, *Southeast Asia in the Age of Commerce 1450–1680*, vol. 1, *The Lands Below the Winds* (New Haven, CT: Yale University Press, 1988), 119.
163. Calo, *Trails of Bronze Drums*, 179.
164. "Gongs are an important aspect of all the upland groups around here . . . well recorded in French sources." Jonathan Padwe, pers. comm., February 25 and December 15, 2006, and March 11, 2007.
165. O'Harrow, "From Co-loa," 152–53; Taylor, *Birth*, 28–29n133.
166. Taylor, *Birth*, 12, 30; Gaspardone suggests the term Hùng/Hiong appeared only in the Song era, "Champs *Lo* et Champs *Hiong*," 472; Chamberlain, "Origins," 38.
167. Maspero, "Études d'histoire d'Annam," 7. See also Huỳnh, "Live by Water, Die for Water," 140, and Liam C. Kelley, "The Biography of the Hồng Bàng Clan as a Medieval Vietnamese Invented Tradition," *Journal of Vietnamese Studies* 7, no. 2 (Summer 2012): 87–130.
168. Ngô Sĩ Liên, *Đại Việt Sử-Ký Toàn Thư* (Saigon: Tân Việt, 1964), 59ff.; Gaspardone, "Champs *Lo* et Champs *Hiong*," 473; Li, *Shui Jing Zhu*, 37:3042, quoting *Jiaozhou waiyu ji* (A record of a region beyond Jiao prefecture), trans. Jinping Wang; Taylor, *Birth*, 13, 20–21; Maspero, "Bulletin Critique," 393.
169. Taylor, *Birth*, 15.
170. Michael Vickery, "Champa Revised" (Asia Research Institute, Singapore, Working Paper 37, 2005), 14.
171. Nguyen, "Northern Vietnam, Part I," 185–88.
172. A. Debay, "Étude sur les Régions centrales du Massif Annamitique," March 1899, Archives Nationales D'Outre-Mer (ANOM), Aix-en-Provence, France, Gouvernement Général de l'Indochine, 5979, 1–2.

173. Nguyen, "Northern Vietnam, Part I," 185–88.
174. Pierre-Yves Manguin, quoted in Michael Vickery, "Funan Reviewed: Deconstructing the Ancients," *BEFEO* 90–91 (2003–4): 110–11.
175. Wang, *Nanhai Trade*, 4–5, 8–9.
176. Wang, *Nanhai Trade*, 38; Vickery, "Funan Reviewed," 111.
177. Dougald J. W. O'Reilly, *Early Civilizations of Southeast Asia* (New York: Altamira, 2007), 94, 129, 134; Graham Thurgood, *From Ancient Cham to Modern Dialects: Two Thousand Years of Language Contact and Change*, Oceanic Linguistics Special Publication 28 (Honolulu: University of Hawai'i Press, 1999), 16; Vickery, "Champa Revised," 15, 13.
178. Ian W. Mabbett, "Buddhism in Champa," in Marr and Milner, *Southeast Asia in the 9th to 14th Centuries*, 308n11.
179. O'Reilly, *Early Civilizations of Southeast Asia*, 129, 134; Calo, *Trails of Bronze Drums*, 43.
180. Andreas Reinecke, "Ancient Gold and Silver Jewelry and the Beginnings of Gold Working in Mainland Southeast Asia," in *Gold in Early Southeast Asia*, ed. Ruth Barnes, Emma Natalya Stein, and Benjamin Diebold (New Haven, CT: Yale Southeast Asia Studies, 2015), 151, 153.
181. William A. Southworth, "The Coastal States of Champa," in Glover and Bellwood, *Southeast Asia*, 212–13.
182. Graham Thurgood, "Language Contact and the Directionality of Internal Drift: The Development of Tones and Registers in Chamic," *Language* 72, no. 1 (March 1996): 1–2, 22–24.
183. Thurgood, *From Ancient Cham to Modern Dialects*, 61; Thurgood, "Language Contact," 1–5, 27.
184. Gérard Diffloth, quoted in Vickery, "Champa Revised," 16.
185. O'Reilly, *Early Civilizations of Southeast Asia*, 92.
186. Miriam T. Stark, et al., "Results of the 1995–1996 Archaeological Field Investigations at Angkor Borei, Cambodia," *Asian Perspectives* 83, no. 1 (Spring 1999): 26.
187. Pierre-Yves Manguin, quoted in Vickery, "Funan Reviewed," 110–11; Wang, *Nanhai Trade*, 21–24.

CHAPTER 2

1. *Chan-Kuo T'se* [*Zhanguoce*], trans. J. I. Crump (Oxford: Clarendon, 1970), 302, 299. Dating *Zhanguoce* to 230–221 BCE, Léonard Aurousseau, "La première conquête chinoise des pays annamites (IIIe siècle avant notre ère)," *BEFEO* 23 (1923): 247n1, quotes k. 6, fo 21 ro: "The people of Ngeou-Yüeh [*V.* Âu-Việt] cut their hair, tattoo their bodies, cross their arms, and tie up their clothes to the left."
2. Wang Gungwu, *The Nanhai Trade: A Study of the Early History of Chinese Trade in the South China Sea* (Kuala Lumpur: Malayan Branch of the Royal Asiatic Society, 1958), 4–5, 8–9.
3. *Huáinánzǐ* (1804 ed.), k. 18, fo 18 ro, col. 2–10, translated into French in Aurousseau, "La première conquête," 172–76.
4. Jennifer Holmgren, *Chinese Colonisation of Northern Vietnam: Administrative Geography and Political Development in the Tongking Delta, First to Sixth Centuries A.D.* (Canberra: Australian National University, 1980), 173.
5. C. Michele Thompson, *Scripts, Signs, and Swords: The Việt Peoples and the Origins of Nôm*, Sino-Platonic Papers 101 (March 2000), http://www.sino-platonic.org/complete/spp101_vietnamese_chu_nom.pdf (accessed June 13, 2015), 48–54.
6. Thompson, *Scripts, Signs, and Swords*, 58.

7. Rafe de Crespigny, "Two Maps from Mawangdui," *Cartography* 11, no. 4 (September 1980): 213, 221.
8. C. Michele Thompson, "Medical Exchanges between the Han and the Viet c. 300 BCE–1389 CE," presentation to Council on Southeast Asia Studies, Yale University, Dec. 12, 2007.
9. Thompson, *Scripts, Signs and Swords*, 56, 59–60, 63.
10. Li, *Shui Jing Zhu*, annotated by Yang Shoujing and Xiong Huizhen (Nanjing: Jiangsu guji chubanshe, 1989), 37:3042–43, translation by Jinping Wang; Thompson, *Scripts, Signs and Swords*, 63, and appendix, 72.
11. *Lüshi chunqiu*, quoted in G. Sukhu, "Monkeys, Shamans, Emperors, and Poets: The *Chuci* and Images of Chu during the Han Dynasty," in *Defining Chu: Image and Reality in Ancient China*, ed. C. A. Cook and J. S. Major (Honolulu: University of Hawai'i Press, 1999), 149.
12. Aurousseau, "La première conquête," 249n6, quoting *Huai nan tzu* (135 BCE).
13. *Huáinánzǐ*, k. 18, fo 18 ro, col. 2–10, translated into French in Aurousseau, "La première conquête," 172–76. I thank Joanna Waley-Cohen for help with the Chinese characters. See also Eric Henry, "The Submerged History of Yuè," *Sino-Platonic Papers* 176 (2007): 15–16.
14. Aurousseau, "La première conquête," 206, citing *Ts'ien Han chou*, k. 64, fo 3 ro, col. 11.
15. *Huáinánzǐ* (Sìbú Bèiyào ed.), 18, 16a–16b, cited in Henry, "Submerged History of Yuè," 16; see also Keith W. Taylor, *The Birth of Vietnam* (Berkeley: University of California Press, 1983), 18.
16. *Shi ji*, 6, 17a, cited in Wang, *Nanhai Trade*, 10, and in Pan Ku, *History of the Former Han Dynasty* [*Han shu*], trans. H. H. Dubs (Baltimore: American Council of Learned Societies, 1938), 1:133n3, citing *SC* (*Mh* II, 168); *Huáinánzǐ*, k. 18, fo 18 ro, col. 2–10, translated into French in Aurousseau, "La première conquête," 172–76.
17. Aurousseau, "La première conquête," 181, citing *Che-ki*, k. 6, fo 17 ro, col. 5, and k. 48, fo 5 ro, col. 3.
18. Chun-shu Chang, *The Rise of the Chinese Empire: Nation, State and Imperialism in Early China, c.1600 B.C.–A.D. 8* (Ann Arbor: University of Michigan Press, 2007), 340.
19. Wang, *Nanhai Trade*, 5.
20. Henri Maspero, "Bulletin Critique," review of Aurousseau, "La première conquête," *T'oung Pao*, 2nd ser., 23 (1924): 388–89.
21. Maspero, "Bulletin Critique," 390–91.
22. Quoted in Charles Holcombe, *The Genesis of East Asia, 221 B.C.–A.D. 907* (Honolulu: University of Hawai'i Press, 2001), 148–49.
23. Pan, *History of the Former Han*, 1:102–3 (*Han-shu* [*HS*] 1B:4a–b).
24. Pan, *History of the Former Han*, 1:181 (*HS* 2:4b); Hans Bielenstein, "The Restoration of the Han Dynasty, Vol. III, The People," *Bulletin of the Museum of Far Eastern Antiquities* 39 (1967): 2, 57–58, says Tung-ou was also known as Tung-hai; Taylor, *Birth*, 15.
25. Pan, *History of the Former Han*, 1:133–34 (*HS* 1B:19a).
26. Holcombe, *Genesis*, 149; Eric Henry kindly provided his translation of these passages from *Shi ji*, "Lù Jia Zhuàn."
27. Henry, translation of *Shi ji*, "Lù Jia Zhuàn." Stephen O'Harrow quotes *Shi ji*, ch. 97: "no more than a hundred thousand, barbarians all of them, squeezed between mountain and sea" (O'Harrow, "From Co-loa to the Trung Sisters' Revolt: Vietnam as the Chinese Found It," *Asian Perspectives* 22, no. 2 [1979]: 144).

28. Eric Henry's translation of *Shi ji*, "Lù Jia Zhuàn."
29. Pan, *History of the Former Han*, I, 141, 181 (*HS* 1B:21b; 2:4b); 200 (*HS* 3:5a).
30. Crespigny, "Two Maps from Mawangdui," 213, 221.
31. Bielenstein, "Restoration of the Han Dynasty," 58.
32. Aurousseau, "La première conquête," 254–59; Maspero, "Bulletin Critique," 391; Taylor, *Birth*, 23–25.
33. Émile Gaspardone, "Champs *Lo* et Champs *Hiong*," *Journal Asiatique* 243 (1955): 473; Li, *Shui Jing Zhu*, 37:3042, quoting *Jiaozhou waiyu ji* (A record of a region beyond Jiao prefecture), trans. Jinping Wang; Maspero, "Bulletin Critique," 392.
34. Quoted in Nguyen Dang Thuc, *The Origins of the Vietnamese People* (Saigon: Directorate of Cultural Affairs, Ministry of State in Charge of Cultural Affairs, n.d.), 23.
35. *Han shu* 95, 9b, quoted in Wang, *Nanhai Trade*, 13.
36. Pan, *History of the Former Han*, 1:273 (*HS* 4:21b).
37. Pan, *History of the Former Han*, 2:32 (*HS* 6:3b).
38. Bielenstein, "Restoration of the Han Dynasty," 58.
39. Maspero, "Bulletin Critique," 391–92; Taylor, *Birth*, 24, 26; Bielenstein, "Restoration of the Han Dynasty," 58; Minh Chi, Hà Văn Tấn, and Nguyễn Tài Thư, *Buddhism in Vietnam: From Its Origins to the 19th Century* (Hanoi: Thế Giới, 1999), 14, 16, 9.
40. Bielenstein, "Restoration of the Han Dynasty," 58; Chun-shu Chang, *The Rise of the Chinese Empire*, vol. 1, *Nation, State, and Imperialism in Early China, c. 1600 B.C.–A.D. 8* (Ann Arbor: University of Michigan Press, 2007), 60, 342–43.
41. Holcombe, *Genesis*, 147–48.
42. Chang, *Rise of the Chinese Empire*, 1:343; *Annam chí lược* 5.113, quoted in Holcombe, *Genesis*, 148.
43. Pan, *History of the Former Han*, 2:34 (*HS* 6:4a).
44. Eric Henry, "Nán Yuè (Nam Việt) Lineage Chart, 203–111 BCE," 2008. I am grateful to Henry for this unpublished report of his 2008 visit to the tomb of Zhào Mò (r. 137–122 BCE), excavated in 1983.
45. Wang, *Nanhai Trade*, 21, 23, 20.
46. Li, *Shui Jing Zhu*, 37:3042–43, trans. Jinping Wang.
47. Wang, *Nanhai Trade*, 14.
48. Bielenstein, "Restoration of the Han Dynasty," 59. See also Chang, *Rise of the Chinese Empire*, 1:240–41.
49. O'Harrow, "From Co-loa," 152–53; Taylor, *Birth*, 28–29.
50. Li, *Shui Jing Zhu*, 37:3042–43, trans. Jinping Wang.
51. O'Harrow, "From Co-loa," 152–53; Taylor, *Birth*, 28–29.
52. Fan Ye, *Hou Han shu* 24/14, 839–40; Li Daoyuan, *Shui Jing Zhu*, 37:3046; Henri Maspero, "Etudes d'histoire d'Annam," *BEFEO* 18, no. 3 (1918): 11.
53. Li, *Shui Jing Zhu*, 37:3042–43.
54. Li, *Shui Jing Zhu*, 37:3045–46, quoting the *Jiaozhou waiyu ji* (tr. Jinping Wang).
55. Tong Trung Tin, "Northern Vietnam from the Neolithic to the Han Period: Part III, Archaeological Aspects of Han Dynasty Rule in the Early First Millennium AD," in *Southeast Asia from Prehistory to History*, ed. Ian Glover and Peter Bellwood (London: Routledge, 2004), 202.
56. Wang, *Nanhai Trade*, 17.
57. Sima Qian, *Shi ji*, 30, 9a–b, quoted in Ying-shih Yü, *Trade and Expansion in Han China: A Study in the Structure of Sino-Barbarian Economic Relations* (Berkeley: University of California Press, 1967), 80, 81.
58. Wang, *Nanhai Trade*, 17; Taylor, *Birth*, 30.

59. Han Yü, writing in 819 CE, quoted in Edward H. Schafer, *The Vermilion Bird: T'ang Images of the South* (Berkeley: University of California Press, 1967), 217.
60. Nguyen Phuc Long, "Les nouvelles recherches archaéologiques au Vietnam," *Arts asiatiques* 31 (1975): 14, cited in O. W. Wolters, "Historians and Emperors in Vietnam and China," in *Perceptions of the Past in Southeast Asia*, ed. Anthony Reid and David Marr (Singapore: Heinemann, 1979), 71n3.
61. Bui Quang Trung, "Le soulèvement des Soeurs Trưng à travers les texts et le folklore vietnamien," *Bulletin de la Sociéte des Études Indochinoises de Saigon*, n.s., 36, no. 1 (1961): 73; Schafer, *Vermilion Bird*, 32; Taylor, *Birth*, 26; Maurice Durand, "Cu'o'ng-Muc quyen II, traduction et notes accompagnées du texte," *BEFEO* 47 (1953): 371–72.
62. Sima Qian, *Shi ji* ("Records of the Historian"), ch. 129, quoted in Rafe de Crespigny, *Generals of the South: The Foundation and Early History of the Three Kingdoms State of Wu* (Canberra: Australian National University, Faculty of Asian Studies, 1990), 4.
63. *Hou Han Shu*, quoted in Nguyen, *Origins of the Vietnamese*, 23–24.
64. *Hou Han Shu*, quoted in Nguyen, *Origins of the Vietnamese*, 23–24.
65. Wang, *Nanhai Trade*, 17.
66. Tong, "Northern Vietnam from the Neolithic" 202.
67. Hans Bielenstein, "The Census of China during the Period 2–742 A.D.," *Bulletin of the Museum of Far Eastern Antiquities* 19 (1948): 125–63, esp. plates 2, 8; Li Tana, "Introduction," in *The Tongking Gulf Through History*, ed. Nola Cooke, Li Tana, and James A. Anderson (Philadelphia, University of Pennsylvania Press, 2011), 7, 40–42; O'Harrow, "From Co-loa," 156; Wang, *Nanhai Trade*, 17–18; Holmgren, *Chinese Colonization*, 64, table 3:1; Taylor, *Birth*, table 1, 55.
68. Confucius, *The Analects of Confucius*, trans. Arthur Waley (New York: Vintage, 1938), 17:27.
69. Holcombe, *Genesis*, 27.
70. Bielenstein, "Restoration of the Han Dynasty," 62; Holmgren, *Chinese Colonisation*, 11n22.
71. Quoted in Mark Edward Lewis, *The Early Chinese Empires: Qin and Han* (Cambridge, MA: Harvard University Press, 2007), 13.
72. Quoted in Lewis, *Early Chinese Empires*, 15.
73. Hisayuki Miyakawa, "The Confucianization of South China," in *The Confucian Persuasion*, ed. Arthur Wright (Stanford, CA: Stanford University Press, 1960), 31.
74. Quotation in Lê Tắc, *Annam chí lược*; French translation by Camille Sainson, *Ngann-Nann-Tche-Luo: Mémoires sur l'Annam* (Beijing: Imprimerie des Lazaristes au Pe-T'ang, 1896), 529.
75. *Hou Han Shu*, quoted in Holmgren, *Chinese Colonisation*, 5–6; Miyakawa, "Confucianization," 31.
76. *Hou Han Shu*, quoted in Holmgren, *Chinese Colonisation*, 5–6; Miyakawa, "Confucianization," 31. On Lingnan, see Holcombe, *Genesis*, 27, 145.
77. Quoted in Holmgren, *Chinese Colonisation*, 6.
78. Wang, *Nanhai Trade*, 24.
79. *Hou Han Shu*, ch. 106, quoted in O'Harrow, "From Co-loa," 159–60; *Hou Han-shu*, "The Account of the Southern Man," quoted in Holmgren, *Chinese Colonisation*, 6, 10.
80. Ying-shih Yü, *Trade and Expansion in Han China*, 81–82.
81. *Hou Han shu* (Beijing: Zhonghua Shuju, 1973), 86/76:2836–37, 1:62.
82. Wang, *Nanhai Trade*, 24.
83. Bielenstein, "Restoration of the Han Dynasty," 2, 62.

84. Holmgren, *Chinese Colonization*, 4.
85. Li, *Shui Jing Zhu*, 37:3042–43.
86. *Hou Han Shu*, 86/76:9b–10a and 24/14:12a, and Li, *Shui Jing Zhu*, 37:62, all cited in Holmgren, *Chinese Colonisation*, 10–11, 21; see also Li, *Shui Jing Zhu*, 37:3042–43.
87. *Hou Han Shu*, ch. 54, quoted in O'Harrow, "From Co-loa," 160; Holmgren, *Chinese Colonisation*, 4, 10.
88. Taylor, *Birth*, 38.
89. Alexander B. Woodside, *Vietnam and the Chinese Model* (Cambridge, MA: Harvard University Press, 1971), 46; Taylor, *Birth*, 38–39.
90. Li, *Shui Jing Zhu*, 37:3042–44.
91. *Hou Han shu*, 1:66; Holmgren, *Chinese Colonisation*, 11; Taylor, *Birth*, 37–38.
92. Fan, *Hou Han shu* 24/14:838–39.
93. *Hou Han shu*, 86/76:2836–37.
94. Li, *Shui Jing Zhu*, 37:3042–44; Taylor, *Birth* 38.
95. *Hou Han-shu*, 86/76:2837; Li, *Shui Jing Zhu*, 37:3051.
96. Holmgren, *Chinese Colonisation*, 15.
97. *Hou Han shu*, 1:69, and 86/76:2836–37.
98. Li, *Shui Jing Zhu*, 37:3044.
99. Fan Ye, *Hou Han shu* 24/14:838–39; *Hou Han shu*, 22:781.
100. Li, *Shui Jing Zhu*, 37:3051.
101. Holmgren, *Chinese Colonisation*, 12–14; Li, *Shui Jing Zhu*, 37:3047.
102. Fan Ye, *Hou Han shu* 24/14:838–39; Holmgren, 12; Taylor, *Birth*, 38–40.
103. "Ma Yuan: Letter to His Nephews Ma Yan and Ma Dun," trans. H. Frankel, *Renditions* 41–42 (1994): 4–6.
104. Fan Ye, *Hou Han shu* 24/14:838–39.
105. Li, *Shui Jing Zhu*, 37:3043–44; Fan Ye, *Hou Han shu* 24/14, 838–39.
106. *Hou Han shu*, 22:781.
107. Fan Ye, *Hou Han shu* 24/14:838–39; Hou Han-shu, 86/76:2837.
108. Li, *Shui Jing Zhu*, 37:3051.
109. Fan Ye, *Hou Han shu* 24/14:839–40; Li, *Shui Jing Zhu*, 37:3051.
110. Ambra Calo, *Trails of Bronze Drums across Early Southeast Asia* (Singapore: Institute of Southeast Asian Studies, 2014), 42–43; *Hou Han-shu*, 86/76:2837.
111. Li, *Shui Jing Zhu*, 37:3051.
112. Fan Ye, *Hou Han shu* 24/14:839–40; Hou Han-shu, 86/76:2837.
113. Fan Ye, *Hou Han shu* 24/14:838–40.
114. Holmgren, 12–13; Taylor, *Birth*, 40–41, citing *Hou Han-shu*.
115. Frankel, "Ma Yuan," 6.
116. Fan Ye, *Hou Han shu* 24/14:839–40; Li, *Shui Jing Zhu*, 37:3046.
117. Fan Ye, *Hou Han shu* 24/14:839–40; Holmgren, *Chinese Colonisation*, 16, cites 24/14:14a.
118. Thompson, *Scripts, Signs, and Swords*, 63, and appendix, 72; Calo, *Trails of Bronze Drums*, 73.
119. Bielenstein, "Restoration of the Han Dynasty," 65.
120. Holmgren, *Chinese Colonisation*, 17, quoting Ngô Sĩ Liên's 1479 text *Đại Việt sử ký toàn thư* 3:1b–2b.
121. Fan Chuo [Fan Ch'o], *Man Shu* ("Book of the Southern Barbarians"), originally entitled "Record of Yunnan," (860–73 CE), trans. G. H. Luce, ed. G. P. Oey (Cornell Southeast Asia Program Data Paper 44, Ithaca, NY, 1961), 4; Wolfram Eberhard, *The Local Cultures of South and East China* (Leiden: Brill, 1968), 369.

122. Lê Tắc, *Annam chí lược*, in *The World of Southeast Asia*, ed. H. J. Benda and J. A. Larkin (New York: Harper & Row, 1967), 48.
123. Holmgren, *Chinese Colonisation*, 11n22, 17–19, 21.
124. See map, "The Later Han Empire in 189 AD," in vol. 2 of Sima Guang, *To Establish Peace: Being the Chronicle of Later Han for the Years 189 to 220 AD, as recorded in Chapters 59 to 69 of the Zizhi tongjian of Sima Guang*, trans. Rafe de Crespigny (Canberra: Faculty of Asian Studies, Australian National University, 1996).
125. Fan Ye, *Hou Han shu* 24/14:846.
126. Holmgren, *Chinese Colonisation*, 171–72.
127. Holmgren, *Chinese Colonisation*, 172.
128. Tong, "Northern Vietnam from the Neolithic," 203.
129. Wang, *Nanhai Trade*, 21, 29–30, 26.
130. Wang, *Nanhai Trade*, 22–24, 20; Taylor, *Birth*, 61.
131. Dougald J. W. O'Reilly, *Early Civilizations of Southeast Asia* (New York: Altamira, 2007), 129.
132. Taylor, *Birth*, 65, 60–61.
133. William A. Southworth, "The Coastal States of Champa," in Glover and Bellwood, *Southeast Asia*, 216; Taylor, *Birth*, 60–61.
134. *Hou Han shu*, 1:268; Wang, *Nanhai Trade*, 26.
135. *Hou Han shu*, 1:268, 1:276; Taylor, *Birth*, 61–64.
136. Bielenstein, "Census of China," plate 3.
137. Minh, Hà, and Nguyễn, *Buddhism in Vietnam*, 15; Taylor, *Birth*, 31, map 3; Philippe Papin, *Histoire de Hanoi* (Paris: Fayard, 2004), 40, says Luy Lâu and Long Yuan (later Long Biên) form a single site.
138. Taylor, *Birth*, 64–66; Holmgren, *Chinese Colonisation*, 68–69.
139. Wang, *Nanhai Trade*, 28, 119.
140. Southworth, "Coastal States," 216; Wang, *Nanhai Trade*, 120; Michael Vickery, "Champa Revised" (Asia Research Institute, Singapore, Working Paper 37, 2005), 11, 17.
141. *Hou Han shu*, 61:14a, quoted in Wang, *Nanhai Trade*, 25. See also Ssu-ma Kuang, *The Last of the Han, Being the Chronicle of the Years 181–220 A.D. as Recorded in Chapters 58–68 of the Tzu-chich t'ung-chien of Ssu-ma Kuang*, trans. Rafe de Crespigny, Centre of Oriental Studies Monograph 9 (Canberra: Australian National University, 1969), ch. 58, 15.
142. *Hou Han shu*, 71:2308, "The Biography of Zhu Jun."
143. Ssu-ma, *Last of the Han*, ch. 58, 1, 361n.3; Sima, *Emperor Huan and Emperor Ling: Being the Chronicle of Later Han for the Years 157 to 189 AD as recorded in Chapters 54 to 59 of the Zizhi tongjian of Sima Guang*, trans. Rafe de Crespigny (Canberra: Faculty of Asian Studies, Australian National University, 1989), 145; see also Taylor, *Birth*, 67–68.
144. *Hou Han shu*, 71:2308; Wang, *Nanhai Trade*, 27.
145. Sima, *Emperor Huan and Emperor Ling*, 145; *Hou Han shu*, 1, 340.
146. Ssu-ma, *Last of the Han*, ch. 58, 1; *Hou Han shu*, 71:2308.
147. Ssu-ma, *Last of the Han*, ch. 58, 1; *Hou Han shu*, 71:2308–309.
148. *Hou Han shu*, 1, 345.
149. Ssu-ma Kuang, *Last of the Han*, ch. 58, 1. See Taylor, *Birth*, 67–68; *Hou Han shu*, 71:2309.
150. *Hou Han shu*, 71:2309; Taylor, *Birth*, 71; *Hou Han shu*, 86:2839.
151. *Hou Han shu*, 1:349.
152. Ssu-ma Kuang, *Last of the Han*, ch. 58, 15–16.

153. Mou Bo, "Beliefs in the South (ca. 200)," translated in Taylor, *Birth*, 81, reprinted in *Sources of Vietnamese Tradition*, ed. George E. Dutton, Jayne S. Werner, and John K. Whitmore (New York: Columbia University Press, 2012), 16.
154. Holmgren, *Chinese Colonisation*, 173, 72; Taylor, *Birth*, 70–80; Wang, *Nanhai Trade*, 27. Shi Xie's accession date of 177 is from Claudine Salmon, "Tang-Viet Society as Reflected in a Buddhist Bell Inscription from the Protectorate of Annam (798)," in *Guangdong: Archaeology and Early Texts*, ed. Shing Müller, Thomas O. Höllmann, and Putao Gui (Wiesbaden, Germany: Harrassowitz Verlag, 2004), 200.
155. Chen Shou, "Scholarship in the South (297)," trans. Liam Kelley, in Dutton, Werner, and Whitmore, *Sources*, 17.
156. Ssu-ma, *Last of the Han*, ch. 66, 280–81; Sima, *To Establish Peace*, 2:419.
157. Minh, Hà, and Nguyễn, *Buddhism in Vietnam*, 15; Taylor, *Birth*, 73; Rafe de Crespigny, in Sima, *To Establish Peace*, 2:420n38.
158. Letter from Viên Huy to minister Tuân Húc, from the book *Ngô Chí*, quoted in Minh, Hà, and Nguyễn, *Buddhism in Vietnam*, 11.
159. Li, *Shui Jing Zhu*, 37:3047; Taylor, *Birth*, 73.
160. Sima, *To Establish Peace*, 2:419–20; Wang, *Nanhai Trade*, 33.
161. *Shui Zhing Chu* 49 (Wu 4), 11b–12a, quoted in Holmgren, *Chinese Colonisation*, 75.
162. Wang, *Nanhai Trade*, 40.
163. Taylor, *Birth*, 86–89; Wang, *Nanhai Trade*, 32; Holmgren, *Chinese Colonisation*, 173.
164. Holmgren, *Chinese Colonisation*, 85–86, 3 (map 1).
165. Liu Hsi, *Shih ming*, quoted in Taylor, *Birth*, 77.
166. T'ao Chi and Hsieh Tsung, both quoted in Hisayuki Miyakawa, "Confucianization of South China," in Wright, *Confucian Persuasion*, 31–32.
167. Lê Thành Khôi, *Histoire du Vietnam des origines à 1858* (Paris: Sudestasie, 1981), 98.
168. Huỳnh Sanh Thông, "Live by Water, Die for Water (*Sống vì nước, chết vì nước*): Symbols and Metaphors of Vietnamese Culture" (1991), unpublished manuscript, 3; also Huỳnh Sanh Thông, "Live by Water, Die for Water (*Sống vì nước, chết vì nước*): Metaphors of Vietnamese Culture and History," *Vietnam Review* 1 (1996): 121–53, and "The Vietnamese Worldview: Water, Water Everywhere," *Vietnam Review* 2 (1997): 21.
169. Calo, *Trails of Bronze Drums*, 105n7, 107–10.
170. Viên Huy to Tuân Húc, from the *Ngô Chí*, quoted in Minh, Hà, and Nguyễn, *Buddhism in Vietnam*, 11.
171. Taylor, *Birth*, 81–83.
172. Huỳnh, "Vietnamese Worldview," 21.
173. Minh, Hà, and Nguyễn, *Buddhism in Vietnam*, 10–11, 24–25.
174. Cuong Tu Nguyen, *Zen in Medieval Vietnam: A Study and Translation of the* Thien Uyen Tap Anh (Honolulu: University of Hawai'i Press, 1997), 129.
175. Minh, Hà, and Nguyễn, *Buddhism in Vietnam*, 10, 7, 18–19; Taylor, *Birth*, 80.
176. Minh, Hà, and Nguyễn, *Buddhism in Vietnam*, 28.
177. Salmon, "Tang-Viet Society," 201; Minh, Hà, and Nguyễn, *Buddhism in Vietnam*, 31.
178. Huệ Hạo, *Cao Tăng Truyện*, quoted in Minh, Hà, and Nguyễn, *Buddhism in Vietnam*, 29.
179. Andreas Reinecke, "Ancient Gold and Silver Jewelry and the Beginnings of Gold Working in Mainland Southeast Asia," in *Gold in Early Southeast Asia*, ed. Ruth Barnes, Emma Natalya Stein, and Benjamin Diebold (New Haven, CT: Yale Southeast Asia Studies, 2015), 152–53, and map, 126.

180. Southworth, "Coastal States," 216; Wang, *Nanhai Trade*, 120; Vickery, "Champa Revised," 11, 17.
181. Southworth, "Coastal States," 219–20; Vickery, "Champa Revised," 7.
182. Michael Vickery, *Society, Economics, and Politics in Pre-Angkor Cambodia: The 7th–8th Centuries* (Tokyo: Toyo Bunko, 1998), 48–51, 203–204; "Champa Revised," 21, 17.
183. Reinecke, "Ancient Gold and Silver," 154–56, map, 126.
184. Michael Vickery, "Funan Reviewed: Deconstructing the Ancients," *BEFEO* 90–91 (2003–4): 105, 108, 110, 111.
185. Wang, *Nanhai Trade*, 38; Vickery, "Funan Reviewed," 111–12.
186. Jean Boisselier, quoted in Vickery, "Funan Reviewed," 119–20, 124; O'Reilly, *Early Civilizations of Southeast Asia*, 97; Reinecke, "Ancient Gold and Silver," 152–53.
187. Vickery, "Funan Reviewed," 114.
188. Wang, *Nanhai Trade*, 38; Vickery, "Funan Reviewed," 107, 112, 108.
189. Wang, *Nanhai Trade*, 120, 51, 53; Vickery, "Funan Reviewed," 112, 114–15, 122, 133n136.
190. Vickery, "Funan Reviewed," 115.
191. George Coedès, "La plus ancienne inscription en langue cham," in *A Volume of Eastern and Indian Studies presented to Professor F. W. Thomas*, ed. S. M. Katre and P. K. Gode, eds. (Bombay: Karnatak, 1939), 46–49; Vickery, "Champa Revised," 8.
192. Southworth, "Coastal States," 219.
193. Coedès, "La plus ancienne inscription," 49.
194. Louis Finot, "Notes d'Épigraphie I: Deux nouvelles inscriptions de Bhadravarman Ier, roi de Champa," *BEFEO* 2 (1902): 185–87, reprinted in Claude Jacques, comp., *Études épigraphiques sur le pays cham* (Paris: EFEO, 1995), 1–7.
195. Finot, "Notes d'Épigraphie I," 189.
196. Emmanuel Guillon, *Hindu-Buddhist Art of Vietnam: Treasures from Champa*, (Trumbull, CT: Weatherhill, c. 2001), 68, indicates a total of 210 inscriptions of Champa dating from the fourth to the fifteenth centuries; Vickery, "Champa Revised," 8, suggests that about thirty Cham inscriptions postdate 1263.
197. Holmgren, *Chinese Colonisation*, 175, 174, 177, 80–81, 100–101, 112–13.
198. Taylor, *Birth*, 89–90.
199. Lê Tắc, *Annam chí lược*, 148, in Sainson, *Ngann-Nann-Tche-Luo*, 525. Taylor writes (*Birth*, 90n18) that this account of Triệu "is based on Vietnamese documentation familiar to Lê Tắc" and that the citation in Ngô Sĩ Liên's 1479 *Đại Việt sử ký toàn thư ngoại kỷ* is "identical." It is thus the only source on Triệu Ẩu, who is ignored in the mid-fourteenth-century text *Việt sử lược* (I, 5b); Trần Quốc Vượng, ed. *Việt sử lược* (Hanoi: Văn Sử Địa, 1960), 24.
200. Taylor, *Birth*, 90–91; Wang, *Nanhai Trade*, 34.
201. *Jin shu* 57, quoted in Southworth, "Coastal States," 218.
202. Southworth, "Coastal States," 218–19.
203. Holmgren, *Chinese Colonisation*, 173; Wang, *Nanhai Trade*, 35.
204. *Jin shu* 97, 9a, quoted in Wang, *Nanhai Trade*, 40.
205. Wang, *Nanhai Trade*, 35–37; Holmgren, *Chinese Colonisation*, 173.
206. Wang, *Nanhai Trade*, 37, 41, 48, 120; Holmgren, *Chinese Colonisation*, 173.
207. Southworth, "Coastal States," 220–21; Wang, *Nanhai Trade*, 52, 58, 90–91, 120–21.
208. Wang, *Nanhai Trade*, 48–49, 53, 58, 61.
209. Holmgren, *Chinese Colonisation*, 115–19, 121, 129–30, 172; Wang, *Nanhai Trade*, 72–73.
210. Taylor, *Birth*, 131, 86.

CHAPTER 3

1. Edward H. Schafer, *The Vermilion Bird: T'ang Images of the South* (Berkeley: University of California Press, 1967), 224–28; Li Tana, "Swamps, Lakes, Rivers and Elephants: A Preliminary Attempt towards an Environmental History of the Red River Delta, c. 600–1400," *Water History* 7 (2015): 200–202.
2. Li, "Swamps, Lakes, Rivers and Elephants," 201, quoting *Đại Việt sử ký toàn thư*.
3. Jennifer Holmgren, *Chinese Colonisation of Northern Vietnam: Administrative Geography and Political Development in the Tongking Delta, First to Sixth Centuries A.D.* (Canberra: Australian National University, 1980), 136; Michael Vickery, "Champa Revised" (Asia Research Institute, Singapore, Working Paper 37, 2005), 23.
4. Lê Thành Khôi, *Histoire du Viêt Nam des origines à 1858* (Paris: Sudestasie, 1981), 113; Holmgren, *Chinese Colonisation*, 57–58, 136.
5. Keith W. Taylor, *The Birth of Vietnam* (Berkeley: University of California Press, 1983), 135–36, 140.
6. Maurice Durand, "La dynastie des Lý antérieurs d'après le *Viet Dien U Linh Tap*," *BEFEO* 44, no. 2 (1954): at 438–39; Taylor, *Birth*, 136.
7. Charles Holcombe, *The Genesis of East Asia, 221 B.C.–A.D. 907* (Honolulu: University of Hawai'i Press, 2001), 156–57; Taylor, *Birth*, 139.
8. Lê, *Histoire du Viêt Nam*, 107.
9. Durand, "La dynastie des Lý antérieurs," 440–41; Vickery, "Champa Revised," 21.
10. Taylor, *Birth*, 142–43; Durand, "La dynastie des Lý antérieurs," 443.
11. Holcombe, *Genesis of East Asia*, 156–57.
12. André-G. Haudricourt, "De l'origine des tons en viêtnamien," *Journal Asiatique* 242 (1954): 75, 81 (table).
13. La Vaughn H. Hayes, "Vietic and Việt-Mường: A New Subgrouping in Mon-Khmer," *Mon-Khmer Studies* 21 (1992): 219, 220. He dates it to c. 570 CE plus or minus 250 years.
14. Taylor, *Birth*, 140.
15. Wang Gungwu, *The Nanhai Trade: A Study of the Early History of Chinese Trade in the South China Sea* (Kuala Lumpur: Malayan Branch of the Royal Asiatic Society, 1958), 33–34.
16. *Sui shu*, translated in Geoff Wade, "Lady Sinn and the Southward Expansion of China in the Sixth Century," in *Guangdong: Archaeology and Early Texts (Zhou-Tang)*, ed. Shing Müller, Thomas O. Höllmann, and Putao Gui. (Wiesbaden, Germany: Harrassowitz, 2004) 131, 141–42.
17. Wade, "Lady Sinn," 132–33, quoting the "Nan-man" section of the *Sui shu* and the *Account of Geography*.
18. Schafer, *Vermilion Bird*, 224.
19. Wade, "Lady Sinn," 132, 142, 144, 145–48, 135.
20. Hans Bielenstein, "The Census of China during the Period 2–742 A.D.," *Bulletin of the Museum of Far Eastern Antiquities* 19 (1948): plate 5.
21. Bielenstein, "Census of China," plate 5.
22. Michael Vickery, "Funan Reviewed: Deconstructing the Ancients," *BEFEO* 90–91 (2003–4): 115.
23. Holcombe, *Genesis of East Asia*, 160.
24. Keith Taylor, "Authority and Legitimacy in Eleventh-Century Vietnam," in *Southeast Asia in the 9th to 14th Centuries*, ed. David G. Marr and A. C. Milner (Singapore: ISEAS, 1986), 157.
25. Taylor, *Birth*, 139–40, 156.

26. Cuong Tu Nguyen, *Zen in Medieval Vietnam: A Study and Translation of the Thien Uyen Tap Anh* (Honolulu: University of Hawai'i Press, 1997), 11, 12. For a similar fifth-century assessment, see Taylor, *Birth*, 155.
27. Nguyen, *Zen in Medieval Vietnam*, 339–40n33.
28. Nguyen, *Zen in Medieval Vietnam*; Taylor, *Birth*, 156ff.
29. Minh Chi, Hà Văn Tấn, and Nguyễn Tài Thư, *Buddhism in Vietnam: From Its Origins to the 19th Century* (Hanoi: Thế Giới, 1999), 35–39. For a different translation, see Nguyen, *Zen in Medieval Vietnam*, 164–65.
30. Nguyen, *Zen in Medieval Vietnam*, 165–66.
31. Phan Van Cac et Claudine Salmon, eds., *Épigraphie en chinois du Viêt Nam*, vol. 1, *De l'occupation chinoise à la dynastie des Lý* (Paris: École Française d'Extrême-Orient, 1998), 1–2.
32. Nguyen, *Zen in Medieval Vietnam*, 334–35.
33. Nguyen, *Zen in Medieval Vietnam*, 335–36.
34. Nguyen, *Zen in Medieval Vietnam*, 336–37.
35. Marc S. Abramson, *Ethnic Identity in Tang China* (Philadelphia: University of Pennsylvania Press, 2008), xxi, viii, 52–82.
36. "Inscription de la cloche de Thanh Mai (798)," in Phan and Salmon, *Épigraphie en chinois du Viêt Nam*, 13–14.
37. Claudine Salmon, "Tang-Viet Society as Reflected in a Buddhist Bell Inscription from the Protectorate of Annam (798)," in Müller, Höllmann, and Gui, *Guangdong*, 196; Phan and Salmon, *Épigraphie en chinois du Viêt Nam*, 14.
38. Salmon, "Tang-Viet Society," 203.
39. Salmon, "Tang-Viet Society," 203–5, 209.
40. Salmon, "Tang-Viet Society," 204–5, 207.
41. Phan and Salmon, *Épigraphie en chinois du Viêt Nam*, 14; Salmon, "Tang-Viet Society," 204, 209.
42. Salmon, "Tang-Viet Society," 197–99, 211.
43. Lê, *Histoire du Viêt Nam*, 116; Taylor, *Birth*, 217–18.
44. Taylor, *Birth*, 198.
45. Taylor, *Birth*, 218–19.
46. Yumio Sakurai, cited in Keith Taylor, "Authority and Legitimacy in 11th Century Vietnam," in *Southeast Asia in the 9th to 14th Centuries*, ed. D. G. Marr and A. S. Milner (Canberra: Australian National University, 1986), 139–40; Taylor, *Birth*, 173, 175, 181, 209.
47. Kenneth R. Hall, *Maritime Trade and State Development in Early Southeast Asia* (Honolulu, University of Hawai'i Press, 1985), 180.
48. Wang, *Nanhai Trade*, 62.
49. Vickery, "Funan Reviewed," 134.
50. Wang, *Nanhai Trade*, 51, 53, 121–22.
51. Vickery, "Funan Reviewed," 131–36.
52. Wang, *Nanhai Trade*, 64, 122; Taylor, *Birth*, 165.
53. Wang, *Nanhai Trade*, 91, 122–23.
54. Vickery, "Champa Revised," 11, 17, 28.
55. Wang, *Nanhai Trade*, 122; Vickery, "Champa Revised," 25–26, 28.
56. Vickery, "Champa Revised," 5, 8; Anon., *Mỹ Sơn Sanctuary* (Ho Chi Minh City: Nhà xuất bản Lao động, 2005).
57. Taylor, *Birth*, 188–89.
58. Huỳnh Sanh Thông, *The Heritage of Vietnamese Poetry* (New Haven, CT: Yale University Press, 1979), 221.

59. Lê, *Histoire du Viêt Nam*, 119; Taylor, *Birth*, 248.
60. Holcombe, *Genesis of East Asia*, 160; Keith Taylor, "The Rise of Dai Viet and the Establishment of Thang-long," in *Explorations in Early Southeast Asian History: The Origins of Southeast Asian Statecraft*, ed. K. R. Hall and J. K. Whitmore, Papers on South and Southeast Asia 11 (Ann Arbor: Center for South and Southeast Asian Studies, University of Michigan, 1976) 151–53.
61. *History of Đại Việt*, quoted in Minh, Hà, and Nguyễn, *Buddhism in Vietnam*, 15–16.
62. Holcombe, *Genesis of East Asia*, 160.
63. Quoted in Taylor, "Rise of Dai Viet," 153.
64. Charles Holcombe, "Early Imperial China's Deep South: The Viet Regions through Tang Times," *T'ang Studies* 15–16 (1997): 125–56. See also Michael Churchman, "Before Chinese and Vietnamese in the Red River Plain: The Han-Tang Period," *Chinese Southern Diaspora Studies* 4 (2010): 25–37.
65. Salmon, "Tang-Viet Society," 208.
66. Fan Ch'o [Fan Chuo], *The Man Shu: Book of the Southern Barbarians*, trans. G. H. Luce, ed. G. P. Oey, Cornell University Southeast Asia Program Data Paper 44 (Ithaca, NY: Southeast Asia Program, Dept. of Far Eastern Studies, Cornell University, 1961), 4.
67. Charles Backus, *The Nan-chao Kingdom and T'ang China's Southwestern Frontier* (New York: Cambridge University Press, 1981), 111, map 7; Fan, *Man Shu*, 4–5, 59, map following p. 117.
68. Fan, *Man Shu*, 4, 51–52.
69. Fan, *Man Shu*, 33, 1, 59, map following p. 117.
70. Fan, *Man Shu*, 26, 23; Backus, *Nan-chao Kingdom*, 61, map 4, 50–52.
71. "Customs, Practices and Folk Laws of 'Lo Lo' Ethnic Group," Vets with a Mission, http://www.vwam.com/vets/tribes/lolo.html (accessed Sept. 15, 2008).
72. Fan, *Man Shu*, 102.
73. Backus, *Nan-chao Kingdom*, 61, 51.
74. Fan, *Man Shu*, 33; Backus, *Nan-chao Kingdom*, 64, 69.
75. Fan, *Man Shu*, 33–34, 37, 51.
76. Fan, *Man Shu*, 105, 34, 28, 68, 5; Backus, *Nan-chao Kingdom*, 76.
77. Backus, *Nan-chao Kingdom*, 167n16; Fan, *Man Shu*, 35.
78. Fan, *Man Shu*, 28, 105–6, 94.
79. Fan, *Man Shu*, 52–53, 85.
80. Fan, *Man Shu*, 36–37.
81. Fan, *Man Shu*, 4, 34, 86; James Anderson, *The Rebel Den of Nùng Trí Cao: Loyalty and Identity along the Sino-Vietnamese Frontier* (Seattle: University of Washington Press, 2007), ch. 2.
82. Fan, *Man Shu*, 45–46.
83. Fan, *Man Shu*, 34, 45; Backus, *Nan-chao Kingdom*, 132.
84. Fan, *Man Shu*, 45; Backus, *Nan-chao Kingdom*, 132.
85. Fan, *Man Shu*, 34, 45, 5; Taylor, *Birth*, 240–41.
86. Fan, *Man Shu*, 87.
87. Taylor, *Birth*, 240, 173; Backus, *Nan-chao Kingdom*, 133; Holmgren, *Chinese Colonisation*, 133.
88. Fan, *Man Shu*, 4, 34.
89. Backus, *Nan-chao Kingdom*, 133, 135.
90. Fan, *Man Shu*, 93, 34–35.
91. Fan, *Man Shu*, 45–46.
92. Fan, *Man Shu*, 99, 35, 45–46.

93. Fan, *Man Shu*, 86–87, 34–35.
94. Backus, *Nan-chao Kingdom*, 138.
95. Fan, *Man Shu*, 44, 40–41.
96. Fan, *Man Shu*, 38, 40.
97. Fan, *Man Shu*, 39.
98. Fan, *Man Shu*, 91.
99. Fan, *Man Shu*, 41.
100. Fan, *Man Shu*, 28–29.
101. Fan, *Man Shu*, 41–42, 35, 98.
102. Taylor, *Birth*, 245; Fan, *Man Shu*, 41.
103. Fan, *Man Shu*, 41, introduction by G. H. Luce.
104. Fan, *Man Shu*, 41–42.
105. Fan, *Man Shu*, 98; Backus, *Nan-chao Kingdom*, 111, map 7; Taylor, *Birth*, 197, map 8.
106. Fan, *Man Shu*, 93–94, 98, 107.
107. Backus, *Nan-chao Kingdom*, 139.
108. *Ngann-Nann-Tche-Luo: Mémoires sur l'Annam* [Lê Tắc, *An Nam chí lược*], trans. Camille Sainson (Beijing: Imprimerie des Lazaristes au Pe-T'ang, 1896), 403.
109. Fan, *Man Shu*, 8 (dating on 58, 99).
110. Lê, *Ngann-Nann-Tche-Luo*, 374.
111. Backus, *Nan-chao Kingdom*, 142–43.
112. Ken Gardiner, "Vietnam and Southern Han: Part I," *Papers on Far Eastern History* 23 (March 1981): at 77; Anderson, *Rebel Den of Nùng Trí Cao*, 38.
113. Taylor, *Birth*, 251–52.
114. Taylor, "Rise of Đại Việt," 153–54.
115. Gardiner, "Vietnam and Southern Han: Part I," 66.
116. Gardiner, "Vietnam and Southern Han: Part I," 76n22.
117. Holcombe, *Genesis of East Asia*, 160; Gardiner, "Vietnam and Southern Han: Part I," 74–75.
118. Taylor, *Birth*, 258–59; Gardiner, "Vietnam and Southern Han: Part I," 78–82; Taylor, "Rise of Đại Việt," 154.
119. John D. Phan, "Re-Imagining 'Annam:' A New Analysis of Sino-Viet-Muong Linguistic Contact," *Chinese Southern Diaspora Studies* 4 (2010): 3–25.
120. Minh, Hà, and Nguyễn, *Buddhism in Vietnam*, 32.
121. Nguyễn Khắc-Kham, "Chữ nôm or the Former Vietnamese Script and Its Past Contributions to Vietnamese Literature," *Area and Culture Studies* 24 (1974): 1–2, citing Nguyễn Văn Tố, "Phan Kế Bính Việt Hán Văn Khảo," *BEFEO* 30, nos. 1–2 (1930) 141–46; Dương Quảng Hàm, *Việt Nam Văn-Học Sử-Yếu*, in lần thứ bảy (Saigon: Bộ Quốc Gia Giáo Dục, 1960), 101.
122. Nguyễn Đình Hoà, "Chữ' Nôm, the Demotic System of Writing in Vietnam," *Journal of the American Oriental Society* 79, no. 4 (1959): 271.
123. Ha Van Tan, "Inscriptions from the Tenth to Fourteenth Centuries Recently Discovered in Viet Nam (July 1991)," in *Essays into Vietnamese Pasts*, ed. K. W. Taylor and John K. Whitmore (Ithaca, NY: Cornell Southeast Asia Program, 1995), 51–58.
124. Ken Gardiner, "Vietnam and Southern Han: Part II," *Papers on Far Eastern History* 28 (Sept. 1983): 25–27.
125. Gardiner, "Vietnam and Southern Han: Part I," 97, 98n68, 102; "Part II," 29, 31, 40–42; Taylor, "Rise of Đại Việt," 155.
126. Taylor, "Rise of Đại Việt," 155–56; Gardiner, "Vietnam and Southern Han: Part II," 43, 46–47.

127. Taylor, "Rise of Đại Việt," 156.
128. Lê Tắc, *Ngann-Nann-Tche-Luo*, 3–4, 8–11, 219.
129. Lê Tắc, *Ngann-Nann-Tche-Luo*, 218–19.
130. Anon., *Việt sử lược*, 1:14b; *quốc ngữ* edition, *Việt sử lược*, ed. Trần Quốc Vượng (Hanoi: Văn Sử Địa, 1960), 41. English translation by Đỗ Ngọc Bích.
131. Lê Tắc, *Ngann-Nann-Tche-Luo*, 219.
132. *Việt sử lược*, 41.
133. Lê Tắc, *Ngann-Nann-Tche-Luo*, 219.
134. *Việt sử lược*, 1:14b 41n2 in *quốc ngữ* edition.

CHAPTER 4

1. Hà Văn Tấn, "Inscriptions from the Tenth to Fourteenth Centuries Recently Discovered in Việt Nam (July 1991)," in *Essays into Vietnamese Pasts*, ed. K. W. Taylor and John K. Whitmore (Ithaca, NY: Cornell Southeast Asia Program, 1995), 51–52.
2. James Anderson, *The Rebel Den of Nùng Trí Cao: Loyalty and Identity along the Sino-Vietnamese Frontier* (Seattle: University of Washington Press, 2007), 75.
3. Keith W. Taylor, *The Birth of Vietnam* (Berkeley: University of California Press, 1983), 177–81, 267–71; Taylor, "The Rise of Đại Việt and the Establishment of Thăng-long," in *Explorations in Early Southeast Asian History: The Origins of Southeast Asian Statecraft*, ed. K. R. Hall and J. K. Whitmore, Papers on South and Southeast Asia 11 (Ann Arbor: Center for South and Southeast Asian Studies, University of Michigan, 1976), 149; and Taylor, "The 'Twelve Lords' in Tenth-Century Vietnam," *Journal of Southeast Asian Studies* 14, no. 1 (March 1983): 61–62.
4. *Ngann-Nann-Tche-Luo: Mémoires sur l'Annam* [Lê Tắc, *An Nam chí lược*], trans. Camille Sainson (Beijing: Imprimerie des Lazaristes au Pe-T'ang, 1896), 50; Taylor, *Birth*, 180–81; La Vaughn H. Hayes, "Vietic and Việt-Mường: A New Subgrouping in Mon-Khmer," *Mon-Khmer Studies* 21 (1992): 211–28; Nguyễn Phú Phong, *Le Parler Nguồn: Langue d'une minorité ethnique des hautes vallées du Sông Gianh, Quảng Bình—Việt Nam* (Paris: Université Paris 7, 1997).
5. In *An Nam chí lược*, Lê Tắc says that Lê Văn Hưu revised Trần Chu Phố's *Việt Chí* to produce *Đại Việt sử ký*. Cuong Tu Nguyen, *Zen in Medieval Vietnam: A Study and Translation of the* Thiền Uyển Tập Anh (Honolulu: University of Hawai'i Press, 1997), 217, and Keith Taylor, "Some Thoughts on the Lý Dynasty," *Vietnam Social Sciences* 1, nos. 1–2 (1988): 120–21.
6. Sainson, *Ngann-Nann-Tche-Luo* [*An Nam chí lược*], 16, 3–4, 8–11, 127.
7. Translations in Lý Tế Xuyên, *Departed Spirits of the Viet Realm*, trans. K. W. Taylor, Brian Ostrowski, and Brian Zottoli, at http://www.einaudi.cornell.edu/southeastasia/outreach/resources/departed/departed.html (accessed May 16, 2010); Nguyen, *Zen in Medieval Vietnam*, 3, 103–205.
8. K. W. Taylor, "Voices Within and Without: Tales from Stone and Paper about Đỗ Anh Vũ (1114–1159)," in Taylor and Whitmore, *Essays*, 75–76.
9. Quang Phu Van kindly provided translations for pre-1200 titles. The list is compiled from Trần Quốc Vượng, "The Legend of Ông Dóng," in Taylor and Whitmore, *Essays into Vietnamese Pasts*, 21–22; Trần, ed., *Việt sử lược* (Hanoi, Văn Sử Địa, 1960); Nguyen, *Zen in Medieval Vietnam*, 66–67, 215–25; Nguyễn Quang Hồng, "Ba thứ chữ trong lịch sử ngữ văn Việt Nam" (Three types of script in the history of Vietnamese language and literature), available online at http://www.temple.edu/vietnamese_center/nomstudies/three_scripts_in_Vietnam.pdf (accessed May 16, 2010) 3; K. Taylor, "Authority and Legitimacy in 11th Century Vietnam," in Marr and Milner, *Southeast Asia in the 9th to 14th*

Centuries, 144–47; E. S. Ungar, "From Myth to History: Imagined Polities in 14th Century Vietnam," in Marr and Milner, *Southeast Asia in the 9th to 14th Centuries*, 178; Lê Tắc, *Ngann-Nann-Tche-Luo*; K. Taylor, "Some Thoughts on the Lý Dynasty,", and "Looking Behind the Vietnamese Annals"; Lý, *Departed Spirits of the Viet Realm*.

10. Nguyen, *Zen in Medieval Vietnam*, 210, 251–54.
11. Hà, "Inscriptions," 52–57; Huỳnh Sanh Thông, *The Heritage of Vietnamese Poetry* (New Haven, CT: Yale University Press, 1979); Nguyễn Khắc Viện and Hữu Ngọc, *Vietnamese Literature* (Hanoi: Red River, c. 1986).
12. Võ Thu Tịnh, "Chữ Nôm, The Early Script of Viet Nam," http://www.vothutinh.net/English/chunom.htm (accessed May 14, 2010).
13. Nguyễn Quang Hồng, "Ba thứ chữ trong lịch sử ngữ văn Việt Nam" (unpublished paper), states that the bilingual Hán-Nôm text *Phật thuyết đại báo phụ mẫu ân trọng kinh* "could not have been later than the twelfth century" (3), a view he reiterated in a presentation to the Nôm Studies Workshop, Yale University, April 18, 2008. See also Nguyễn Quang Hồng, "Một số vấn đề và khía cạnh nghiên cứu chữ Nôm," *Thời đại mới* 5 (July 2005): 2–3, http://www.tapchithoidai.org/ThoiDai5/200505_NguyenQuangHong_1.pdf (accessed May 12, 2010); Nguyễn Tài Cẩn, "Some Issues in Nôm Studies," Temple University Conference on Nôm Studies, April 2008, 3–6, http://www.temple.edu/vietnamese_center/nomstudies/issues_in_nom_studies.pdf (accessed May 13, 2010); Taylor, "Authority," 144.
14. Historical linguists date the separation of Vietnamese and Mường to the period 950–1280 or 1090–1420 (Hayes, "Vietic and Việt-Mường," 219); Nguồn is thought to have separated from Vietnamese in the early fifteenth century (Nguyễn Phú Phong, *Le Parler Nguồn*, 9, 20). See also John D. Phan, "Re-Imagining 'Annam': A New Analysis of Sino-Viet-Muong Linguistic Contact," *Chinese Southern Diaspora Studies* 4 (2010): 3–25.
15. André-G. Haudricourt, "De l'origine des tons en viêtnamien," *Journal Asiatique* 242 (1954): 71–72, 81.
16. In his presentation to the Nôm Studies Workshop, Yale University, April 18, 2008, Nguyễn Quang Hồng noted that the Buddhist text *Phật thuyết đại báo phụ mẫu ân trọng kinh*, which he dates to the twelfth century or earlier, contains "hundreds" of disyllabic words, many more for instance than in Trần Nhân-Tông's thirteenth-century poems. Nguyễn Quang Hồng, "Ba thứ chữ trong lịch sử ngữ văn Việt Nam," http://www.temple.edu/vietnamese_center/nomstudies/three_scripts_in_Vietnam.pdf (accessed May 16, 2010), 3. Hayes concurs that "the Việt-Mường languages were also disyllabic to some degree in the not too remote past" ("Vietic and Việt-Mường," 219).
17. Victor Lieberman, *Strange Parallels: Southeast Asia in Global Context, c. 800–1830*, vol. 1, *Integration on the Mainland* (New York: Cambridge University Press, 2003), 49, and vol. 2, *Mainland Mirrors* (2009), 79–83.
18. Brendan M. Buckley et al., "Climate as a Contributing Factor in the Demise of Angkor," *Proceedings of the National Academy of Sciences* 107 (2010): supplemental material, fig. S3, available online at http://www.pnas.org/content/107/15/6748.short.
19. Trần Quốc Vượng, ed., *Việt sử lược* (Hanoi: Văn Sử Địa, 1960), 1:16b, 17b (pp. 50, 56), trans. Đỗ Ngọc Bích.
20. Anderson, *Rebel Den of Nùng Trí Cao*.
21. Taylor, *Birth*, 269, citing Lý Tế Xuyên, *Việt Điện u linh tập* (1329), 6–7. For a different version, see Taylor, Ostrowski, and Zottoli, *Departed Spirits of the Viet Realm*.

22. Trần, *Việt sử lược*, 41n2, trans. Đỗ Ngọc Bích.
23. Trần, *Việt sử lược*, 1:14b–15a (pp. 42–43).
24. Trần, *Việt sử lược*, 1:15b (p. 43).
25. Sainson, *Ngann-Nann-Tche-Luo*, 421.
26. Trần, *Việt sử lược*, 1:16a–b (pp. 48–49).
27. O. W. Wolters, *History, Culture and Region in Southeast Asian Perspectives* (Ithaca, NY: Cornell Southeast Asia Program, 1999), 18–19.
28. Trần, *Việt sử lược*, 1:16a (p. 48). The fifteenth-century account of Ngô Sĩ Liên gives Bộ Lĩnh a more prolonged and orthodox Confucian heritage, asserting that his father had not only been governor of Hoan and "close aide" of Dương Đình Nghệ but later even a follower of Ngô Quyền, and that at his death his widow had taken their son "and several servants" to live by the temple (*Đại Việt sử ký toàn thư*, Bản kỷ, 1:1a, cited in Trần, *Việt sử lược*, 48n4.) But Bộ Lĩnh was born c. 924 (Trần, *Việt sử lược*, 52), and both texts agree that he was "small," "a child," when his father died. It is hard to see the father outliving Dương Đình Nghệ (d. 937) to serve Ngô Quyền, who took power in 939 when Bộ Lĩnh was already aged fifteen.
29. Trần, *Việt sử lược*, 1:15a (p. 43).
30. Trần, *Việt sử lược*, 1:15b (p. 43).
31. Li T'ao, *Hsü tzu-chih t'ung-chien ch'ang-bien*, quoted in Taylor, "Twelve Lords, 48–49.
32. Trần, *Việt sử lược*, 1:15b (pp. 44, 47, 49); Taylor, "Twelve Lords," 56–57.
33. Taylor, *Birth*, 278.
34. Keith Taylor, "The Rise of Đại Việt and the Establishment of Thăng-long," in Hall and Whitmore, *Explorations in Early Southeast Asian History*, 159.
35. Ngô Sĩ Liên, *Đại Việt sử ký toàn thư*, Ngoại kỷ (1479), 5:26a, translated in Taylor, "Twelve Lords," 57; Trần, *Việt sử lược*, 49n6.
36. Trần, *Việt sử lược*, 1:16b (p. 50); Taylor, "Rise," 159–60; James Anderson, *The Rebel Den of Nùng Trí Cao: Loyalty and Identity along the Sino-Vietnamese Frontier* (Seattle: University of Washington Press, 2007), 44.
37. Taylor, *Birth*, 280.
38. Trần, *Việt sử lược*, 1:16b (p. 50); Taylor, *Birth*, 280–81; K. W. Taylor, "Looking Behind the Vietnamese Annals: Lý Phật Mã (1028–54) and Lý Nhật Tôn (1054–72) in the *Việt sử lược* and the *Toàn Thư*," *Vietnam Forum* 7 (1986): 59.
39. Lê Văn Hưu, *Đại Việt sử ký* (1272), excerpt in Ngô Sĩ Liên, *Đại Việt sử ký toàn thư* (Bản kỷ), (Hanoi: Khoa Học Xã Hội, 1967), 154, trans. Đỗ Ngọc Bích.
40. Trần, *Việt sử lược*, 1:16b (p. 50).
41. Ngô, *Đại Việt sử ký toàn thư*, Bản kỷ (1479), 1:8a–b, translated in Taylor, "Twelve Lords," 59.
42. Taylor, "Authority," 142; Sainson, *Ngann-Nann-Tche-Luo*, 45.
43. Trần, *Việt sử lược*, 1:17a (p. 50).
44. Sainson, *Ngann-Nann-Tche-Luo*, 422.
45. Trần, *Việt sử lược*, 1:17a, 18b (pp. 51, 54), trans. Quang Phu Van.
46. Taylor, "Authority," 148, 151; Taylor, *Birth*, 281–83.
47. Lê Văn Hưu, *Đại Việt sử ký* (1272), excerpt in Ngô, *Đại Việt sử ký toàn thư*, 155.
48. Taylor, *Birth*, 283.
49. Taylor, "Authority," 150.
50. Sainson, *Ngann-Nann-Tche-Luo*, 422.
51. Hà, "Inscriptions," 52, 51–53.
52. Hà, "Inscriptions," 52.
53. Trần, *Việt sử lược*, 1:17b, 18b (pp. 52, 54).
54. Ngô Sĩ Liên, *Đại Việt sử ký toàn thư*, Bản kỷ (1479), 1: 8a–b, translated in Taylor, "Twelve Lords," 59.

55. Sainson, *Ngann-Nann-Tche-Luo*, 132–33, 424.
56. Text in Sainson, *Ngann-Nann-Tche-Luo*, 263–67.
57. Trần, *Việt sử lược*, 1:18b–19a (p. 55).
58. Sainson, *Ngann-Nann-Tche-Luo*, 178n6, 220.
59. Trần, *Việt sử lược*, 1:18b (pp. 54–55n2).
60. Trần, *Việt sử lược*, 1:18b–19a (p. 56).
61. Sainson, *Ngann-Nann-Tche-Luo*, 220–21; Trần, *Việt sử lược*, 1:18b–19a (p. 56).
62. Trần, *Việt sử lược*, 1:18b–19b (p. 56).
63. Sainson, *Ngann-Nann-Tche-Luo*, 423–26.
64. Taylor, "Authority," 148, 151, 152, 155; Taylor, "Some Thoughts on the Lý Dynasty," 126.
65. Sainson, *Ngann-Nann-Tche-Luo*, 179–80.
66. Sung Hao, quoted in John K. Whitmore, "'Elephants Can Actually Swim': Contemporary Chinese Views of Late Ly Dai Viet," in *Southeast Asia in the 9th to 14th Centuries*, ed. David G. Marr and A. C. Milner (Singapore: ISEAS, 1986) 119.
67. Ngô Sĩ Liên, *Đại Việt sử ký toàn thư*, Bản kỷ, 166, 168, cited in the translation in Taylor, "Rise," 168.
68. Sainson, *Ngann-Nann-Tche-Luo*, 180.
69. Trần, *Việt sử lược*, 1:20a–b, 21a (pp. 58–60, 59n2, 71n2).
70. Trần, *Việt sử lược*, 1:21a–22a (pp. 61–62).
71. Taylor, "Rise," 170.
72. Trần, *Việt sử lược*, 1:22a (p. 63).
73. Trần, *Việt sử lược*, 1 I:2a (p. 68); Taylor, "Authority," 157; Huỳnh, *Heritage*, 262.
74. Trần, *Việt sử lược*, 1 I:2b (p. 70); William J. Duiker, *Historical Dictionary of Vietnam*, 2nd ed. (Lanham, MD: Scarecrow, 1998), 91.
75. O. W. Wolters, "Lê Văn Hưu's Treatment of Lý Thần Tôn's Reign (1127–1137)," in *Southeast Asian History and Historiography*, ed. C. D. Cowan and O. W. Wolters (Ithaca, NY: Cornell University Press, 1976), 204.
76. Fan Shih-hu, *Kuei Hai Yu Heng Chih*, excerpted in Ma Duanlin, *Wen-hsien T'ung-k'ao*, translated into French by Hervey de Saint-Denys as *Ethnographie des peuples étrangers à la Chine*, vol. 2 (Genève: H. Georg, 1883), 351–52.
77. Trần, *Việt sử lược*, 1:20b 2:1a–3:5a (pp. 59; 64–143).
78. Trần, *Việt sử lược*, 1:19b–20a, 2:5b–19b (pp. 56–7; 79–120).
79. Wolters, "Lê Văn Hưu's Treatment," 210–12.
80. Trần, *Việt sử lược*, 2:2b, 10a (pp. 69, 84n1, citing *Đại Việt sử ký toàn thư*, 94); Taylor, "Rise," 173, 175.
81. *Đại Việt sử ký toàn thư* 1:32a, 2:11b, translated in Taylor, "Authority," 162, 150.
82. Sainson, *Ngann-Nann-Tche-Luo*, 488; Taylor, "Authority," 151, 165.
83. *Đại Việt sử ký toàn thư* 2:36a, quoted in Taylor, "Authority," 163.
84. Li Tana, "Swamps, Lakes, Rivers and Elephants: A Preliminary Attempt Towards an Environmental History of the Red River Delta, c. 600–1400," *Water History* 7 (2015): 204, 209–10.
85. Taylor, "Rise," 170–71.
86. *Đại Việt sử ký toàn thư* 190–91, translated in Taylor, "Rise," 173.
87. Taylor, "Rise," 174.
88. Trần, *Việt sử lược*, 2:5b (p. 79).
89. Taylor, "Rise," 175–76, 178.
90. *Đại Việt sử ký toàn thư* 190–91, translated in Taylor, "Rise," 173.
91. Taylor, "Authority," 168, and "Rise," 173.

92. Trần, "Legend," 23–25.
93. Trần, *Việt sử lược*, 2:3b (p. 74).
94. Trần, "Legend," 23–25.
95. Taylor, "Some Thoughts on the Lý Dynasty," 127.
96. Taylor, "Authority," 158–59.
97. Trần, "Legend," 23–25; Taylor, "Authority," 158.
98. Trần, "Legend," 26n35; Taylor, "Authority," 161, 158.
99. Taylor, "Authority," 165, and "Rise," 175.
100. Taylor, "Authority," 160; Trần, "Legend," 25.
101. Taylor, "Authority," 160.
102. Taylor, "Rise," 177–78, and "Authority," 167.
103. Richard Miles, *Carthage Must be Destroyed* (London: Penguin, 2010), 159.
104. Taylor, "Rise," 177–78.
105. Trần, *Việt sử lược*, 2:11b (p. 98).
106. Trần, "Legend," 27, 41.
107. Taylor, "Rise," 171, 173, 179.
108. Whitmore, "Elephants," 126; Taylor, "Rise," 179.
109. Trần, *Việt sử lược*, 2:11a (p. 96).
110. Whitmore, "Elephants," 126; Nola Cooke, "Nineteenth-Century Vietnamese Confucianization in Historical Perspective: Evidence from the Palace Examination (1463–1883)," *Journal of Southeast Asian Studies* 25, no. 2 (Sept. 1994): 289; Huỳnh, *Heritage*, 250.
111. Taylor, "Authority," 162–63.
112. Anderson, *Rebel Den of Nùng Trí Cao*, 7, 68, 79–82.
113. *Đại Việt sử ký toàn thư* 2:25b, quoted in Trần, ed., *Việt sử lược*, 82n3.
114. Taylor, "Rise," 176–77.
115. Wolters, "Lê Văn Hưu's Treatment," 216n67.
116. Taylor, "Rise," 177.
117. Wolters, "Lê Văn Hưu's Treatment," 217–18.
118. Taylor, "Rise," 179, and "Authority," 153.
119. Taylor, *Birth*, 281, "Looking Behind the Vietnamese Annals," 59, and "Voices," 59.
120. Taylor, "Authority," 150.
121. Taylor, "Rise," 180; "Authority," 161, 154.
122. Trần, "Legend," 21.
123. Trần, *Việt sử lược*, 1:16b, 18b, 2:2b, 5b (pp. 49, 54, 70, 78–79).
124. *Đại Việt sử ký toàn thư* 2:19a, cited in Taylor, "Authority," 148.
125. Kenneth R. Hall, *Maritime Trade and State Development in Early Southeast Asia* (Honolulu: University of Hawai'i Press, 1985), 173, 184.
126. Trần, *Việt sử lược*, 2:2b, 3a (pp. 72–73). The later Khmer missions arrived in 1025, 1039, and 1056; Trần, *Việt sử lược*, 2:4a, 7a, 10a (pp. 75, 83, 95).
127. Trần, *Việt sử lược*, 2:13b, 14a, 15a (pp. 104, 105, 107).
128. Fan Shih-hu, *Kuei Hai Yu Heng Chih*, excerpted in Ma, *Ethnographie des peoples étrangers*, 351–52.
129. Quoted in Taylor, "Looking Behind the Vietnamese Annals," 59–60.
130. Sainson, *Ngann-Nann-Tche-Luo*, 221–22.
131. Taylor, "Authority," 153–55.
132. Sainson, *Ngann-Nann-Tche-Luo*, 222–23, 136–40; Fan Shih-hu, *Kuei Hai Yu Heng Chih*, in Ma, *Ethnographie des peuples étrangers*, 350; Trần, *Việt sử lược* 2:14b (p. 106).
133. Fan Shih-hu, *Kuei Hai Yu Heng Chih*, in Ma, *Ethnographie des peuples étrangers*, 351.
134. Trần, *Việt sử lược*, 2:16b (p. 111).

135. Huỳnh, *Heritage*, 3; for a different translation, see K. W. Taylor, "Will over Fate: Nationalism's Appropriation of a Poem," *Tieng vong* 4 (1989): 10–13.
136. Sainson, *Ngann-Nann-Tche-Luo*, 273–76.
137. Trần, *Việt sử lược*, 2:17b, 18a, 18b (pp. 115, 116, 117).
138. Trần, *Việt sử lược*, 2:17a (p. 51); Taylor, "Authority," 151–52, and "Some Thoughts on the Lý Dynasty," 126.
139. Taylor, "Authority," 145, 147–48, 155, and "Voices," 62; O. W. Wolters, *Two Essays on Đại-Việt in the Fourteenth Century* (New Haven, CT: Council on Southeast Asia Studies, Yale Center for International and Area Studies, 1988), 32.
140. Taylor, "Voices," 62, and "Authority," 153.
141. O. W. Wolters, "Possibilities for a Reading of the 1293–1357 Period in the Vietnamese Annals," in Marr and Milner, *Southeast Asia in the 9th to 14th Centuries*, 374.
142. Taylor, "Authority," 154, 151, 155.
143. Taylor, "Authority," 152, 165–66.
144. Wolters, "Lê Văn Hưu's Treatment," 209.
145. Taylor, "Authority," 152–53, 155.
146. Wolters, "Lê Văn Hưu's Treatment," 219; Taylor, "Authority," 153, and "Voices," 75.
147. Taylor, "Authority," 156, 170.
148. Wolters, "Lê Văn Hưu's Treatment," 222, 209.
149. Taylor, "Voices," 75; Wolters, "Lê Văn Hưu's Treatment," 223.
150. Hà, "Inscriptions," 52, 53–54.
151. Trần, *Việt sử lược*, 3:3a (p. 139).
152. Hà, "Inscriptions," 54.
153. Đỗ Anh Vũ inscription (1159), translated in Taylor, "Voices," 62, 64.
154. Hà, "Inscriptions," 54; Taylor, "Voices," 62–64, 71, 79 (chart); Wolters, "Lê Văn Hưu's Treatment," 220.
155. Trần, *Việt sử lược*, 3:1a (p. 132).
156. Wolters, "Lê Văn Hưu's Treatment," 220.
157. Trần, *Việt sử lược*, 2:18b–22a (pp. 117–27); Taylor, "Voices," 65, n.22.
158. Trần, *Việt sử lược*, 2:22b–23a (pp. 127–29); Wolters, "Lê Văn Hưu's Treatment," 220n103.
159. Trần, *Việt sử lược*, 3:1a,b (p. 133).
160. Wolters, "Lê Văn Hưu's Treatment," 220.
161. Taylor, "Voices," 63, 66–67.
162. Trần, *Việt sử lược*, 3:1b (p. 134).
163. Đỗ Anh Vũ inscription, translated in Taylor, "Voices," 65.
164. Taylor, "Authority," 152; Đỗ Anh Vũ inscription, translated in Taylor, "Voices," 65.
165. Wolters, "Lê Văn Hưu's Treatment," 206–7.
166. Đỗ Anh Vũ inscription, translated in Taylor, "Voices," 66; Whitmore, "Elephants," 122, 128.
167. Đỗ Anh Vũ inscription, translated in Taylor, "Voices," 66–67, 69–70.
168. Trần, *Việt sử lược*, 3:3b, 4a (pp. 140, 141–42).
169. *Đại Việt sử ký toàn thư*, translated in Taylor, "Voices," 71–72.
170. Trần, *Việt sử lược*, 3:4a, b (pp. 141–43); *Đại Việt sử ký toàn thư*, translated in Taylor, "Voices," 72–73.
171. Taylor, "Voices," 69–70.
172. Nguyễn Văn Thái and Nguyễn Văn Mừng, *A Short History of Viet-Nam* (Saigon: Times Publishing, 1958), 85.

173. Taylor, "Voices," 75.
174. James A. Anderson, "The *ANCL* as Common Ground: Le Tac's Private History and its Sino-Vietnamese Audience," American Historical Association's 115th Annual Meeting, Boston, Jan. 4–7, 2001, 11.
175. Fan Shih-hu, *Kuei Hai Yu Heng Chih*, in Ma, *Ethnographie des peuples étrangers*, 360–61.
176. Sainson, *Ngann-Nann-Tche-Luo*, 45; Taylor, "Authority," 142.
177. Fan Shih-hu, *Kuei Hai Yu Heng Chih*, in Ma, *Ethnographie des peuples étrangers*, 357, 353–54; Whitmore, "Elephants," 120–21.
178. Fan Shih-hu, *Kuei Hai Yu Heng Chih*, in Ma, *Ethnographie des peuples étrangers*, 363–65.
179. Fan Shih-hu, *Kuei Hai Yu Heng Chih*, in Ma, *Ethnographie des peuples étrangers*, 355.
180. *Chau Ju-Kua: His Work on the Chinese and Arab Trade in the Twelfth and Thirteenth Centuries, Entitled Chu-fan-chï*, trans. F. Hirth and W. W. Rockhill (1911, repr. New York: Paragon, 1966), 45.
181. Hà, "Inscriptions," 55–56.
182. Wolters, "Lê Văn Hưu's Treatment," 226, 216.
183. Taylor, "Voices," 75.
184. O. W. Wolters, "Narrating the Fall of the Lý and the Rise of the Trần Dynasties," *Asian Studies Association of Australia Review* 10, no. 2 (November 1986): 25.
185. Nguyễn and Nguyễn, *Short History of Viet-Nam*, 86.
186. Nguyen, *Zen in Medieval Vietnam*, 402–3.
187. Po Dharma, *Le Pāṇḍuraṅga (Campa) 1802–1835: Ses rapports avec le Vietnam*, vol. 1, Paris, EFEO, 1981), 60–61, cited in Bruce M. Lockhart, "Colonial and Post-Colonial Constructions of 'Champa,'" in *The Cham of Vietnam: History, Society and Art*, ed. Lockhart and Trần Kỳ Phương (Singapore: NUS Press, 2011), 28–29.
188. Wolters, "Lê Văn Hưu's Treatment," 224, and "Narrating the Fall of the Lý," 29–30.
189. Nguyễn and Nguyễn, *Short History of Viet-Nam*, 87.
190. Wolters, "Narrating the Fall of the Lý," 25–30.
191. Nguyễn and Nguyễn, *Short History of Viet-Nam*, 88.
192. William Duiker, *Historical Dictionary of Vietnam*, 2nd ed. (Lanham, MD, Scarecrow, 1998), 249.
193. Lê Thành Khôi, *Histoire du Viêt Nam des origines à 1858* (Paris: Sudestasie, 1981), 117–18; Cuong T. Nguyen, "Rethinking Vietnamese Buddhist History: Is the *Thiền Uyển Tập Anh* a 'Transmission of the Lamp' Text?," in Taylor and Whitmore, *Essays*, 82n2.
194. Wolters, *Two Essays*, 32, 50n108.
195. Taylor, "Authority," 155; O. W. Wolters, "Historians and Emperors in Vietnam and China: Comments Arising out of Le Van Huu's History, Presented to the Tran court in 1272," in *Perceptions of the Past in Southeast Asia*, ed. Anthony Reid and David Marr (Singapore: Heinemann, 1979) 78.
196. Cooke, "Nineteenth-Century Vietnamese Confucianization," 276; Lê, *Histoire du Viêt Nam*, 176.
197. Lê, *Histoire du Viêt Nam*, 174–75.
198. Wolters, "Lê Văn Hưu's Treatment," 224.
199. Nguyễn and Nguyễn, *Short History of Viet-Nam*, 98.
200. Wolters, "Narrating the Fall of the Lý," 30, and "Lê Văn Hưu's Treatment," 224–25.
201. Buckley et al., "Climate as a Contributing"; table S2 of the supplemental online material, is at http://www.pnas.org/content/early/2010/03/22/0910827107/suppl/DCSupplemental. The nine very high rainfall years from 1250 to 1325 were 1257, 1258, 1274–76, 1279, 1283, 1316, and 1322.

202. Li, "Swamps, Lakes, Rivers and Elephants," 207.
203. Wolters, "Narrating the Fall of the Lý and the Rise of the Trần," 30.
204. Lieberman, *Strange Parallels*, vol. 1, 368.
205. O. W. Wolters, "On Telling a Story of Vietnam in the Thirteenth and Fourteenth Centuries," in Wolters, *Early Southeast Asia: Selected Essays*, ed. Craig Reynolds (Ithaca, NY: Cornell Southeast Asia Program, 2008), 227.
206. Lieberman, *Strange Parallels*, vol. 1, 360–61, 368, 371; John K. Whitmore, *Vietnam, Hồ Quý Ly, and the Ming, 1371–1421* (New Haven, CT: Yale Council on Southeast Asia Studies, 1985), 138n14; Wolters, *Two Essays*, 46n39.
207. Yu Insun, "Lê Văn Hưu and Ngô Sĩ Liên: A Comparison of Their Perception of Vietnamese History," in *Việt Nam: Borderless Histories*, ed. Nhung Tuyet Tran and Anthony Reid (Madison: University of Wisconsin Press, 2005), 54.
208. Sainson, *Ngann-Nann-Tche-Luo*, 140.
209. *Chau Ju-Kua: His Work on the Chinese and Arab Trade*, 45–46; Whitmore, "Elephants," 119.
210. Wolters, "On Telling a Story of Vietnam ," 225.
211. Anderson, "*ANCL*," 11.
212. Sainson, *Ngann-Nann-Tche-Luo*, 182–83; Anderson, "*ANCL*," 6.
213. Sainson, *Ngann-Nann-Tche-Luo*, 184.
214. Anderson, "*ANCL*," 6; Sainson, *Ngann-Nann-Tche-Luo*, 185–86.
215. Sainson, *Ngann-Nann-Tche-Luo*, 5, 188, 473–75; Anderson, "*ANCL*," 7.
216. Nguyễn and Nguyễn, *Short History of Viet-Nam*, 111–20; Sainson, *Ngann-Nann-Tche-Luo*, 189, 473–75; Anderson, "*ANCL*," 7–8.
217. Wolters, "On Telling a Story of Vietnam ," 225.
218. Anderson, "*ANCL*," 4–5; Yu, "Lê Văn Hưu," 47.
219. Wolters, "Historians," 78; Nguyen, *Zen in Medieval Vietnam*, 341n44.
220. Wolters, "Historians," 79, 69–70, 77.
221. Sainson, *Ngann-Nann-Tche-Luo*, 519.
222. Wolters, "Historians," 69–70. Insun Yu states that the then reigning emperor Trần Thánh Tông (r. 1258–78), not his father, Trần Thái Tông, commissioned the *Đại Việt Sử Ký*. "Lê Văn Hưu," 46.
223. Wolters, "Historians," 73–74, 77, 85, 87–88, 86–87.
224. Lê Văn Hưu, *Đại Việt Sử Ký*, excerpt in Ngô Sĩ Liên, *Đại Việt Sử Ký Toàn Thư (Ngoại Kỷ)* (Saigon: Tân Việt, 1964), 131.
225. Lê Văn Hưu, *Đại Việt Sử Ký*, excerpt in Ngô, *Đại Việt Sử Ký Toàn Thư (Ngoại Kỷ)*, 304; Wolters, "Historians," 74.
226. Lê Văn Hưu, *Đại Việt Sử Ký*, excerpt in Ngô Sĩ Liên, *Đại Việt Sử Ký Toàn Thư (Bốn Tập)* (Hanoi: Nhà Xuất Bản Khoa Học Xã Hội, 1967), 154 (*Bản Kỷ*); Wolters, "Historians," 74.
227. Wolters, "Historians," 75–76; Lê Văn Hưu, *Đại Việt Sử Ký*, excerpt in Ngô, *Đại Việt Sử Ký Toàn Thư (Bốn Tập)*, 188 (*Bản Kỷ*).
228. Lê Văn Hưu, *Đại Việt Sử Ký*, excerpt in Ngô, *Đại Việt Sử Ký Toàn Thư (Bốn Tập)*, 191–92 (*Bản Kỷ*).
229. Wolters, "Historians," 73, 75.
230. Wolters, "Historians," 78, "Possibilities for a Reading," 374.
231. Cooke, "Nineteenth-Century Vietnamese Confucianization," 276.
232. Yu, "Lê Văn Hưu," 48.
233. Alexander B. Woodside, *Vietnam and the Chinese Model* (Cambridge, MA: Harvard University Press, 1971), 15.
234. The next extant text in *chữ nôm* is dated to 1343. Nguyễn Quang Hồng, "Earliest Evidence of Nôm Ideograms in Recorded History," presentation to Nôm Studies

Workshop, Yale University, April 18, 2008; Nguyen Dinh Hoa, "Chu Nom: The Demotic System of Writing in Vietnam," *Journal of the American Oriental Society* 79, no. 4 (Oct.-Dec. 1959): 270–74, 271. See also Nguyễn Khắc-Kham, "Chữ nôm or the Former Vietnamese Script and Its Past Contributions to Vietnamese Literature," *Area and Culture Studies* 24 (1974).

235. Nguyễn-Thuyên, "Văn-tế cá-sấu," in Dương Đình Khuê, *Les chefs d'oeuvre de la littérature vietnamienne* (Saigon: Kim lai Ấn-quán, 1966), 36–37.
236. Liam C. Kelley, "The Biography of the Hồng Bàng Clan as a Medieval Vietnamese Invented Tradition," *Journal of Vietnamese Studies* 7, no. 2 (Summer 2012): 87–130.
237. Wolters, "On Telling a Story of Vietnam ," 227, 230.
238. Wolters, "Historians," 83–84.
239. Yu, "Lê Văn Hưu," 64.
240. Nguyễn Quang Hồng, "Three Writing Systems in the Vietnamese Philology," presentation to Department of East Asian Languages and Civilizations, Harvard University, April 17, 2008. For a translation, see http://www.cla.temple.edu/vietnamese_center/nomstudies/three_writing_systems_in_Vietnam.pdf.
241. "Zen Master Trần Nhân Tông: His Teachings and Literature," translated with notes by Phan Minh Trị, http://hoangphap.info/Page.aspx?ArticleID=2748&SubID=0&ID=6 .
242. Wolters, "On Telling a Story of Vietnam," 228.
243. Anderson, "*ANCL*," 5.
244. Sainson, *Ngann-Nann-Tche-Luo*, 12–13, 16–17, 473–75, 551, 552–54.
245. Sainson, *Ngann-Nann-Tche-Luo*, 8–11, 127, 17.
246. Lê Tắc, *An nan zhi lue*, 5.113, quoted in Charles Holcombe, *The Genesis of East Asia, 221 B.C.–A.D. 907* (Honolulu: University of Hawai'i Press, 2001), 148.
247. Sainson, *Ngann-Nann-Tche-Luo*, 549; Anderson, "*ANCL*," 16, citing Lê Tắc and Wu Shanqing, *Annan zhi lue* (Beijing: Zhonghua, 1995), 432.
248. Sainson, *Ngann-Nann-Tche-Luo*, 304–306, 476, 536, 205–6, 524–25.
249. Lý, *Departed Spirits of the Việt Realm*, 1–2, 22–26, iii.
250. Nguyen, *Zen in Medieval Vietnam*, 3, 215, 103–205.
251. Wolters, "Possibilities for a Reading," 377.
252. Lê, *Histoire du Viêt Nam*, 175. For other translations, see Nguyễn Khắc Viện, *Tradition and Revolution in Vietnam* (Berkeley, CA: Indochina Resource Center, 1974), 29.
253. Viện Việt-Học (Institute of Vietnamese Studies) History Forum, Trịnh Quốc Thiên, tr., http://www.viethoc.org/phorum/read.php?10,31679,31953,quote=1 (accessed Feb. 18, 2011).
254. Nguyễn Khắc Viện, *Tradition and Revolution*, 29; Wolters, *Two Essays*, 17–18.
255. Wolters, "Possibilities for a Reading," 377; Huỳnh, *Heritage*, 289.

CHAPTER 5

1. O. W. Wolters, "On Telling a Story of Vietnam in the Thirteenth and Fourteenth Centuries," in his *Early Southeast Asia: Selected Essays*, ed. Craig Reynolds (Ithaca, NY: Cornell Southeast Asia Program, 2008), 226; Wolters, *Two Essays on Đại-Việt in the Fourteenth Century* (New Haven, CT: Yale Southeast Asia Studies, 1988), 36; John K. Whitmore, "Chu Văn An and the Rise of 'Antiquity' in Fourteenth-Century Đại Việt," *Vietnam Review* 1 (1996): 60.
2. Wolters, *Two Essays*, xii, and "On Telling," 232; John K. Whitmore, "Queen Mother: The Origin of Family Politics in Early Modern Việt Nam," in *Le Việt Nam au feminin*, ed. G. Bousquet and N. Taylor (Paris: Indes Savantes, 2005), 43.

3. Brendan Buckley et al., "Climate as a Contributing Factor in the Demise of Angkor, Cambodia," *Proceedings of the National Academy of Sciences* 107, no. 15 (2010): 6748–52, available online at http://www.pnas.org/content/107/15/6748.full.pdf+html, noting "a multidecadal scale period of weakened monsoon in the mid to late fourteenth century" (6748). See also fig. 3 and supplemental online material, fig. S1, and table S2, again noting droughts "in the mid 1300s": http://www.pnas.org/content/early/2010/03/22/0910827107/suppl/DCSupplemental.
4. Li Tana, "Towards an Environmental History of the Eastern Red River Delta, Vietnam, c. 900–1400," *Journal of Southeast Asian Studies* 45 (2014): 315, 332–33, 337; Li, "Swamps, Lakes, Rivers and Elephants: A Preliminary Attempt towards an Environmental History of the Red River Delta, c. 600–1400," *Water History* 7 (2015): 201–2, 204–6.
5. Nguyễn Quang Hồng, "Earliest Evidence of Nôm Ideograms in Recorded History," Nôm Studies Workshop, Yale University, April 18, 2008; Nguyễn Đình Hoà, "Chữ Nôm: The Demotic System of Writing in Vietnam," *Journal of the American Oriental Society* 79, no. 4 (Oct.–Dec. 1959): 270–74, 271; Nguyễn Khắc-Kham, "*Chữ nôm* or the Former Vietnamese Script and Its Past Contributions to Vietnamese literature," *Area and Culture Studies* 24 (1974).
6. C. Michele Thompson, "Tuệ Tĩnh 1330–?," in *Dictionary of Medical Biography*, ed. W. F. Bynum and H. Bynum (Westport, CT: Greenwood, 2007), 1243–44; see also Laurence Monnais, C. Michele Thompson, and Ayo Wahlberg, eds., *Southern Medicine for Southern people: Vietnamese Medicine in the Making* (Newcastle upon Tyne, UK: Cambridge Scholars, 2012).
7. John K. Whitmore, *Vietnam, Hồ Quý Ly, and the Ming, 1371–1421* (New Haven, CT: Yale Southeast Asia Studies, 1985), 24ff., 40–42, 151n30; E. S. Ungar, "From Myth to History: Imagined Polities in 14th Century Vietnam," in *Southeast Asia in the 9th to 14th Centuries*, ed. David G. Marr and A.C. Milner (Canberra: Australian National University, 1986): 184.
8. Trương Bửu Lâm, *A Story of Việt Nam* (Denver: Outskirts, 2010), 84; Nguyễn Đình Hoà, "Chữ Nôm," 273.
9. Whitmore, *Vietnam, Hồ Quý Ly*, 138n14.
10. O. W. Wolters, "Phạm Sư Mạnh's Poems Written While Patrolling the Vietnamese Northern Border in the Middle of the Fourteenth Century," in Wolters, *Early Southeast Asia*, 210–24; Wolters, "Celebrating the Educated Official: A Reading of Some of Nguyễn Phi Khanh's Poems," *Vietnam Forum* 2 (1983): 89.
11. Maurice Durand and Nguyễn Trần Huân, *Introduction à la littérature vietnamienne* (Paris: G. P. Maisonneuve & Larose, 1969), 63, tr. Whitmore, *Vietnam, Hồ Quý Ly*, 165.
12. See Keith Taylor, *The Birth of Vietnam* (Berkeley: University of California Press, 1983), 349–59; Haydon L. Cherry, "Unearthing Việt Nam: Archaeology and the Making of a Nation" (M.A. thesis, National University of Singapore, 2004), 22–35; Jennifer Holmgren, *Chinese Colonisation of Northern Vietnam* (Canberra: Australian National University, 1980), 180–81; Wolters, *Two Essays*, 49n77, 52n120. See Vũ Quỳnh, comp., *Lĩnh Nam chích quái liệt truyện* [Arrayed tales of selected oddities from south of the passes], trans. Liam C. Kelley et al., Việt Texts, https://sites.google.com/a/hawaii.edu/viet-texts/lncqlt (accessed July 13, 2015).
13. Compiled from Ungar, "From Myth to History," 178; E. S. Ungar, "Vietnamese Leadership and Order: Đại Việt under the Lê Dynasty (1428–1459)" (PhD diss., Cornell University, 1983); Keith Taylor, "Some Thoughts on the Lý Dynasty," *Vietnam*

Social Sciences 1, nos. 1–2 (1988): 121; Thompson, "Tuệ Tĩnh,"; Cuong Tu Nguyen, *Zen in Medieval Vietnam* (Honolulu: University of Hawai'i Press, 1997), 236–41, 210, 249–54; *Vietnamese Literature*, 233–50; Whitmore, *Vietnam, Hồ Quý Ly*, ix–x, 198–99; Huỳnh, *Heritage of Vietnamese Poetry*, 303, 278; Nguyễn Văn Nguyên, *Tấu, Biểu Đấu Tranh Ngoại Giao Của Nguyễn Trãi; Les Documents diplomatiques rédigés par Nguyễn Trãi au XVe siècle* (Hanoi: EFEO, 2003), 101ff.; Cherry, *Unearthing Việt Nam*, 147–52; Lê Thành Khôi, *Histoire et anthologie de la littérature viêtnamienne des origines à nos jours* (Paris: Indes Savantes, 2008); Stephen O'Harrow, "Nguyen Trai's 'Binh Ngo Dai Cao' of 1428: The Development of a Vietnamese National Identity," *Journal of Southeast Asian Studies* 10, no. 1 (March 1979): 159–74; Nguyễn and Tạ, *Lê Code*, vol. 1; O. W. Wolters, "Possibilities for a Reading of the 1293–1357 Period in the Vietnamese Annals," in Marr and Milner, *Southeast Asia in the 9th to 14th Centuries*, 370; Wolters, *Two Essays*, 165–66.

14. *Đại Việt sử ký toàn thư*, quoted in Jean Chesneaux, *The Vietnamese Nation: Contribution to a History*, trans. Malcolm Salmon (Sydney: Current Books, 1966), 25; Wolters, *Two Essays*, 16.
15. Lê Thành Khôi, *Histoire du Viêt Nam des origines à 1858* (Paris: Sudestasie, 1981), 195, 404; Nguyễn Ngọc Huy and Tạ Văn Tài, *The Lê Code: Law in Traditional Vietnam* (Athens, OH: Ohio University Press, 1987), 3:180, 211.
16. Wolters, "On Telling," 231, O. W. Wolters, "Possibilities for a Reading of the 1293–1357 Period in the Vietnamese Annals," in Marr and Milner, *Southeast Asia in the 9th to 14th Centuries*, 369, 382–83, 398, and *Two Essays*, 16–17; Whitmore, *Vietnam, Hồ Quý Ly*, 30.
17. John K. Whitmore, "The Two Great Campaigns of the Hồng-đức Era (1460–97) in Đại Việt," *Southeast Asia Research* 12, no. 1 (2004): 121; Lê Thành Khôi, *Histoire du Viêt Nam*, 195–96; Thomas Hodgkin, *Vietnam: The Revolutionary Path* (London: Macmillan, 1981), 51; Wolters, *Early Southeast Asia*, 214–15; E. S. Ungar, "Vietnamese Leadership and Order: Đại Việt under the Lê Dynasty (1428–1459)" (PhD diss., Cornell University, 1983), 21.
18. Wolters, "Possibilities," 383, 391.
19. Wolters, "Celebrating," 89, 92–93, and "Possibilities," 389; Whitmore, *Vietnam, Hồ Quý Ly*, 34.
20. Wolters, *Two Essays*, xii, and "Possibilities," 397, 399; Whitmore, *Vietnam, Hồ Quý Ly*, 8–9.
21. Whitmore, "Two Great Campaigns," 119, 121; Lê Thành Khôi, *Histoire du Viêt Nam*, 193–94.
22. Georges Maspero, *Le Royaume de Champa* (Paris: G. Van Oest, 1928), 203–17.
23. Whitmore, *Vietnam, Hồ Quý Ly*, 11, 145.
24. Lê Thành Khôi, *Histoire du Viêt Nam*, 196; Whitmore, *Vietnam, Hồ Quý Ly*, 11, 17–20, 22, 30; Whitmore, "Two Great Campaigns," 120–21; Maspero, *Royaume de Champa*, 206–17; Hodgkin, *Vietnam*, 51.
25. Victor Lieberman, *Strange Parallels: Southeast Asia in Global Context c. 800–1830* (New York: Cambridge University Press, 2003), 1:368–69; Sun Laichen, "Ming-Southeast Asian Overland Interactions, 1368–1644" (PhD diss., University of Michigan, 2000), 71.
26. Whitmore, *Vietnam, Hồ Quý Ly*, 3, 139–40, 20.
27. Whitmore, *Vietnam, Hồ Quý Ly*, 31, 38, 68.
28. Whitmore, "Chu Văn An," 50–61; Wolters, "Possibilities," 374, 392, 394, and *Two Essays*, 4–5.
29. Whitmore, "Chu Văn An," 55–56.

30. Huỳnh Sanh Thông, *The Heritage of Vietnamese Poetry* (New Haven, CT: Yale University Press, 1979), 285; Wolters, "Phạm Sư Mạnh's Poems," 212, 219, and "Possibilities," 392–93.
31. Huỳnh, *Heritage*, 275.
32. Whitmore, "Chu Văn An," 54–56.
33. Wolters, "Phạm Sư Mạnh's Poems," 214–15; Whitmore, *Vietnam, Hồ Quý Ly*, 22.
34. Nguyễn and Tạ, *Lê Code*, 2:166; Wolters, "Possibilities," 398.
35. Thompson, "Tuệ Tĩnh 1330–?," 1243–44.
36. Whitmore, "Chu Văn An," 52–57.
37. Wolters, *Two Essays*, 23, and "Phạm Sư Mạnh's Poems," 214–16.
38. Wolters, *Two Essays*, 22–23; Taylor, *Birth*, 19–20.
39. Wolters, "Phạm Sư Mạnh's Poems," 222–24.
40. Wolters, "Phạm Sư Mạnh's Poems," 216, 217.
41. See chapter 1 of this volume (p. 53).
42. Wolters, "Possibilities," 394; Whitmore, *Vietnam, Hồ Quý Ly*, 7.
43. Nguyễn Khắc Viện, *Tradition and Revolution in Vietnam* (Berkeley, CA: Indochina Resource Center, 1974), 28.
44. Wolters, *Two Essays*, 18.
45. Wolters, "Possibilities," 384; Wolters, *Two Essays*, 32.
46. Whitmore, "Chu Văn An," 58; Wolters, "Celebrating," 86.
47. O. W. Wolters, "Chu Văn An: An Exemplary Retirement," *Vietnam Review* 1 (Autumn-Winter 1996): 62.
48. Whitmore, *Vietnam, Hồ Quý Ly*, 6.
49. Wolters, *Two Essays*, 20–22; Whitmore, "Chu Văn An," 51, 56–57.
50. Wolters, *Two Essays*, 24.
51. See chapter 1 and Liam C. Kelley, "The Biography of the Hồng Bàng Clan as a Medieval Vietnamese Invented Tradition," *Journal of Vietnamese Studies* 7, no. 2 (Summer 2012): 87–130.
52. Trần Quốc Vượng, ed., *Việt sử lược* (Hanoi: Văn Sử Địa, 1960), 14; Henri Maspero, "Études d'histoire d'Annam: IV, Le royaume de Van-Lang," *BEFEO* 18, no. 3 (1918): 7; Wolters, *Two Essays*, 25–26.
53. Bùi Quang Tung and Nguyễn Hương, trans., *Le Đại Việt et ses voisins, d'après le Đại Việt Sử Ký Toàn Thư* (Paris: L'Harmattan, 1990), 52; O. W. Wolters, *History, Culture and Region in Southeast Asian Perspectives*, rev. ed. (Ithaca, NY: Cornell Southeast Asia Program, 1999), 52–53.
54. Nguyễn Thế Anh, "The Vietnamization of the Cham Deity Pô Nagar," in *Essays into Vietnamese Pasts*, ed. K. W. Taylor and John K. Whitmore (Ithaca, NY: Cornell Southeast Asia Program, 1995): 46.
55. Whitmore, *Vietnam, Hồ Quý Ly*, 32, 75–77.
56. A. B. Woodside, "Early Ming Expansionism (1406–1427): China's Abortive Conquest of Vietnam," *Papers on China* 16–17 (1962–63): 6.
57. Whitmore, *Vietnam, Hồ Quý Ly*, 26.
58. Thompson, "Tuệ Tĩnh 1330–?," 1243–44.
59. Sun, "Ming-Southeast Asian Overland Interactions, 1368–1644," 5–7n15, 55–58.
60. John K. Whitmore, "The Last Great King of Classical Southeast Asia: 'Che Bong Nga' and Fourteenth Century Champa," paper presented at the Asia Research Institute, Singapore, 2004.
61. Maspero, *Royaume de Champa*, 219; Whitmore, *Vietnam, Hồ Quý Ly*, 30–32.
62. Woodside, "Early Ming Expansionism," 9.
63. Wolters, "Celebrating," 87, 94, 83, 95.

64. Whitmore, *Vietnam, Hồ Quý Ly*, 38, 12, 21; Wolters, *Two Essays*, 32.
65. Lê Thành Khôi, *Histoire du Viêt Nam*, 196; Whitmore, *Vietnam, Hồ Quý Ly*, 27, 52.
66. Wolters, "Celebrating," 87; Whitmore, *Vietnam, Hồ Quý Ly*, 49–50, 58–59, 39–43, 34–35.
67. Wolters, *Two Essays*, 29; Whitmore, *Vietnam, Hồ Quý Ly*, 41–42.
68. Whitmore, *Vietnam, Hồ Quý Ly*, 44–46, 52.
69. Whitmore, *Vietnam, Hồ Quý Ly*, 63.
70. Nguyễn and Tạ, *Lê Code*, 2:204; Lê Thành Khôi, *Histoire du Viêt Nam*, 196–97, 403.
71. Whitmore, *Vietnam, Hồ Quý Ly*, 70, 166.
72. Lê Thành Khôi, *Histoire du Viêt Nam*, 197–98; Wolters, "Celebrating," 97n15.
73. Sun, "Ming-Southeast Asian," 68–69; Lê Thành Khôi, *Histoire du Viêt Nam*, 198.
74. Lê Thành Khôi, *Histoire du Viêt Nam*, 198; Whitmore, *Vietnam, Hồ Quý Ly*, 42–43; see also *Lê Code*, article 288; Nola Cooke, "Nineteenth-Century Vietnamese Confucianization in Historical Perspective: Evidence from the Palace Examination (1463–1883)," *Journal of Southeast Asian Studies* 25, no. 2 (Sept. 1994): 276.
75. Whitmore, *Vietnam, Hồ Quý Ly*, 42, 152n33, 66, 139n16.
76. Wolters, "Celebrating," 96; Whitmore, *Vietnam, Hồ Quý Ly*, 66.
77. Whitmore, *Vietnam, Hồ Quý Ly*, 68, 45, 53–54, 61, 71–75; Lê Thành Khôi, *Histoire du Viêt Nam*, 196–97; Sun, "Ming-Southeast Asian," 72; Wolters, "Celebrating," 88, 101n98.
78. Whitmore, *Vietnam, Hồ Quý Ly*, 43, 74–76; Lieberman, *Strange Parallels*, 1:379–80.
79. Whitmore, *Vietnam, Hồ Quý Ly*, 88, 93, 149n24.
80. Buckley et al., "Climate," notes "a shorter though at times more severe drought in the early fifteenth century" (6748); see also fig. 3, supplemental online material, fig. S1, and table S2, noting a drought "in the early 1400s," http://www.pnas.org/content/early/2010/03/22/0910827107/suppl/DCSupplemental.
81. Whitmore, *Vietnam, Hồ Quý Ly*, 72.
82. Woodside, "Early Ming Expansionism," 11–12; Whitmore, *Vietnam, Hồ Quý Ly*, 85ff.
83. Sun Laichen, "Chinese Gunpowder Technology and Đại Việt, ca. 1390–1497," in *Việt Nam: Borderless Histories*, ed. Nhung Tuyet Tran and Anthony Reid (Madison: University of Wisconsin Press, 2006), 72–120.
84. John K. Whitmore, "Literati Culture and Integration in Dai Viet, c. 1430–c. 1840," *Modern Asian Studies* 31, no. 3 (1997): 669, 671, 673.
85. Woodside, "Early Ming Expansionism," 14; Wolters, "Celebrating," 79.
86. Woodside, "Early Ming Expansionism," 22–23.
87. Whitmore, *Vietnam, Hồ Quý Ly*, 65, 123; Cooke, "Nineteenth-Century Vietnamese Confucianization," 279.
88. Woodside, "Early Ming Expansionism," 22, 24–27.
89. Whitmore, *Vietnam, Hồ Quý Ly*, 100–104; Hodgkin, *Vietnam*, 56.
90. Woodside, "Early Ming Expansionism," 16–19.
91. Woodside, "Early Ming Expansionism," 13, 18, 21, 28–29.
92. Sun, "Ming-Southeast Asian," 60–64; Woodside, "Early Ming Expansionism," 30; Whitmore, *Vietnam, Hồ Quý Ly*, 85, 91.
93. Ungar, "Vietnamese Leadership and Order," 71; Hodgkin, *Vietnam*, 58–59.
94. Quoted in Hodgkin, *Vietnam*, 64; Ungar, "Vietnamese Leadership and Order," 72.
95. Esta Ungar, "Origins of Ideology and Nation: A Vietnamese Alternative to the Chinese Tributary System," paper presented to the Cornell Vietnam Seminar, "Vietnam: Responses to Foreign Intervention," Ithaca, NY, Oct. 3, 1979, 11–12.
96. Sun, "Ming-Southeast Asian," 65–66.

97. Woodside, "Early Ming Expansionism," 2; quoted in Hodgkin, *Vietnam*, 59.
98. *Vietnamese Literature* (Hanoi, 1986), 238. Different translations may be found in Nguyen Do and Paul Hoover, eds., *Beyond the Court Gate: Selected Poems of Nguyen Trai* (Denver: Counterpath, 2010), 150–56, and Hodgkin, *Vietnam*, 60.
99. Huỳnh, *Heritage*, 77 (no. 181); Paul Schneider, ed., *Nguyen Trai et son receuil de poèmes en langue nationale* (Paris: CNRS, 1987), 143 (no. 74).
100. Nguyễn and Tạ, *Lê Code*, 2:202; Anne-Valérie Schweyer, *Le Viêtnam ancien* (Paris: Belles Lettres, 2005), 46, 73.
101. Whitmore, *Vietnam, Hồ Quý Ly*, e.g., 37, 66.
102. Li Tana, *Nguyễn Cochinchina: Southern Vietnam in the Seventeenth and Eighteenth Centuries* (Ithaca, NY: Cornell Southeast Asia Program, 1998), 12.
103. Sun, "Ming-Southeast Asian," 65–68, 279.
104. Buckley, "Climate,", 6748, fig. 3, and supplemental online material, table S2: http://www.pnas.org/content/early/2010/03/22/0910827107/suppl/DCSupplemental; Sun, "Ming-Southeast Asian," 273–74.
105. *Lam sơn thực lục*, quoted in Alexander B. Woodside, *Vietnam and the Chinese Model* (Cambridge, MA: Harvard University Press, 1971), 21.
106. Nguyễn Trãi, *Dư địa chí*, trans. John K. Whitmore, excerpted in George E. Dutton, Jayne S. Werner, and John K. Whitmore, eds., *Sources of Vietnamese Tradition* (New York: Columbia University Press, 2012), 138–39; see also John K. Whitmore, "Colliding Peoples: Tai/Viet Interactions in the 14th and 15th Centuries," unpublished manuscript, 7, and Lieberman, *Strange Parallels*, 1:380n111.
107. Whitmore, *Vietnam, Hồ Quý Ly*, 65, 67.
108. Cooke, "Nineteenth-Century Vietnamese Confucianization," 277, 279.
109. Nguyễn and Tạ, *Lê Code*, 2:170; see also 1:178–9, including articles 288–94.
110. *Lê Code*, 1:217, article 429, 2:250.
111. Quoted in Hodgkin, *Vietnam*, 60–61.
112. Nguyễn and Tạ, *Lê Code*, 1:192 (article 347).
113. Li, *Nguyễn Cochinchina*, 171 (estimating 1.86 million in 1417); Whitmore, *Vietnam, Hồ Quý Ly*, 106, cites a 1408 Ming estimate of Jiaozhi's population at three million "pacified," plus two million "captive barbarians."
114. Nguyễn and Tạ, *Lê Code*, 2:167, 190–91.
115. Nguyễn and Tạ, *Lê Code*, 1:24, 39n149, 191–98 (articles 342–73), 2:189.
116. Nguyễn and Tạ, *Lê Code*, 1:196 (articles 363–65).
117. Whitmore, "Literati Culture," 667.
118. Nguyễn Văn Thái and Nguyễn Văn Mừng, *A Short History of Viet-Nam* (Saigon: Times Publishing, 1958), 158.
119. Lê Thành Khôi, *Histoire du Việt Nam des origines à 1858* (Paris: Sudestasie, 1981), 222, 239–40; Woodside, "Early Ming Expansionism," 18–21.
120. Quoted in Hodgkin, *Vietnam*, 64.
121. Schweyer, *Viêtnam ancien*, 46; cf. Maspero, *Royaume de Champa*, 221, 226.
122. Ma Huan, *Ying-Yai Sheng-Lan, "The Overall Survey of the Ocean's Shores" [1433]*, ed. J. V. G. Mills (Bangkok: White Lotus, 1997), 77.
123. Ma, *Ying-Yai Sheng-Lan*, 79, 81–82, 85, 83.
124. Ma, *Ying-Yai Sheng-Lan*, 80, 82–84.
125. A. Cabaton, "Indochina," in *Encyclopaedia of Islam*, 2nd ed. (Leiden: Brill, 1986), 1210–12.
126. Lê, *Histoire du Việt Nam*, 194; Pierre-Yves Manguin, "Etudes Cam, IV: Une relation ibérique du Campa en 1595," *Bulletin de l'Ecole française d'Extrême-Orient* 70 (1981): 254.

127. Ma, *Ying-Yai Sheng-Lan*, 79–80, 83–84, 79n5; George Coedès, *The Indianized States of Southeast Asia*, ed. Walter F. Vella, trans. Susan Brown Cowing (Honolulu: East-West Center, 1968), 238.
128. Schweyer, *Viêtnam ancien*, 46.
129. Maspero, *Royaume de Champa*, 237.
130. Sun, "Ming-Southeast Asian," 260, 72.
131. Nguyễn and Tạ, *Lê Code*, 1:203 (articles 388–89), 2:219.
132. Nguyễn and Tạ, *Lê Code*, (articles 374–387), 1:39n151, 2:204, 208.
133. Woodside, *Vietnam and the Chinese Model*, 45–46.
134. Nguyễn and Tạ, *Lê Code*, 1:199.
135. Nhung Tuyet Tran, "Beyond the Myth of Equality: Daughters' Inheritance Rights in the Lê Code," in *Việt Nam: Borderless Histories*, ed. Nhung Tuyet Tran and Anthony Reid (Madison: University of Wisconsin Press, 2005), 121–44.
136. O. W. Wolters, "What Else May Ngo Si Lien Mean? A Matter of Distinctions in the Fifteenth Century," in *Sojourners and Settlers: Histories of Southeast Asia and the Chinese*, ed. Anthony Reid (Sydney: Allen & Unwin, 1996), 94n2.
137. Li, *Nguyễn Cochinchina*, 21; Cooke, "Nineteenth-Century Vietnamese Confucianization," 280; John K. Whitmore, "Cartography in Vietnam," in *The History of Cartography*, ed. J. B. Harley and David Woodward, vol. 2, Book 2 (Chicago: University of Chicago Press, 1994), 478–508.
138. Whitmore, "Two Great Campaigns," 122–23; Lieberman, *Strange Parallels*, 1:384; Nguyễn and Tạ, *Lê Code*, 2:170, 1:178–79 (articles 288–89).
139. John K. Whitmore, "*Chung-hsing* and *Cheng-t'ung* in Texts of and on Sixteenth Century Việt Nam," in Taylor and Whitmore, *Essays*, 118; Cooke, "Nineteenth-Century Vietnamese Confucianization," 277.
140. Cooke, "Nineteenth-Century Vietnamese Confucianization," 275–78, 281.
141. Lê, *Histoire du Việt Nam*, 236; Cooke gives slightly different figures: 501 *tien si* graduates in 1463–97 out of a total of 2,269 from 1463–1883 ("Nineteenth-Century Vietnamese Confucianization," 275, 277).
142. Cooke, "Nineteenth-Century Vietnamese Confucianization," 277–78.
143. Lê, *Histoire du Việt Nam*, 225, 231; Cooke, "Nineteenth-Century Vietnamese Confucianization," 281; Ungar, "Origins of Ideology and Nation," 16, quoting an inscription left by Lê Lợi in the 1430s.
144. Nguyễn and Tạ, *Lê Code*, 1:203, article 388; 2:225.
145. Nguyễn and Tạ, *Lê Code*, 1:204, article. 391; 2:222, 227; 2:204, 219, 222.
146. Nguyễn and Tạ, *Lê Code*, 1:183 (article 308), 2:174.
147. Anthony Reid, *A History of Southeast Asia: Critical Crossroads* (London: Wiley Blackwell, 2015), 24.
148. Nguyễn and Tạ, *Lê Code*, 1:186 (article 321), 2:180; 1:233 (article 482), 2:270.
149. Nguyễn and Tạ, *Lê Code*, 1:186 (article 324); 2:181.
150. See, e.g., Nha Trang Pensinger, "Women in Vietnamese Folklore" (1992), *The Viet Nam Literature Project*, http://vietnamlit.org/nhatrang/women.html, currently offline but being restored: see http://vietnamlit.org/wiki/index.php?title=Cong_Huyen_Ton_Nu_Nha_Trang (accessed Sept. 23, 2016).
151. Nguyễn and Tạ, *Lê Code*, 1:109–10 (article 2), 2:21–2.
152. Ngô Vĩnh Long, *Before the Revolution: Vietnamese Peasants under the French* (Cambridge, MA: MIT Press, 1973), 5–6; Lê, *Histoire du Việt Nam*, 222; Hodgkin, *Vietnam*, 62.
153. Ngô Vĩnh Long, *Before the Revolution*, 6; Hodgkin, *Vietnam*, 62.
154. Nguyễn and Tạ, *Lê Code*, 1:187 (article 327); 214 (article 419).

155. Nguyễn and Tạ, *Lê Code*, 1:224 (article 464); 1:232 (article 480).
156. Nguyễn and Tạ, *Lê Code*, 1:234–5 (articles 490, 486).
157. Whitmore, "Literati Culture," 676.
158. Cooke, "Nineteenth-Century Vietnamese Confucianization," 278–79.
159. Lê, *Histoire du Việt Nam*, 236; Hodgkin, *Vietnam*, 67.
160. Cooke, "Nineteenth-Century Vietnamese Confucianization," 293.
161. Quoted in Whitmore, "Literati Culture," 676; Hodgkin, *Vietnam*, 66.
162. Sun, "Ming-Southeast Asian," 273–74; Woodside, *Vietnam and the Chinese Model*, 20.
163. Lê Thành Khôi, *Histoire du Viêt Nam*, 241; Yu Insun, "Lê Văn Hưu and Ngô Sĩ Liên: A Comparison of Their Perception of Vietnamese History," in Tran and Reid, *Việt Nam*, 46; Kelley, "Biography of the Hồng Bàng Clan."
164. Liam Kelley, "The Unimportance of Bronze Drums in Việt History," *Le Minh Khai's SEAsian History Blog*, Sept. 15, 2013, https://leminhkhai.wordpress.com/2013/09/15/the-unimportance-of-bronze-drums-in-viet-history (accessed July 23, 2015).
165. Livia Kohn, *God of the Dao: Lord Lao in History and Myth* (Ann Arbor, MI: Center for Chinese Studies, 1998), 237ff., and see also 8–12, 19–21, 35.
166. Whitmore, "Two Great Campaigns," 123.
167. Geoff Wade, trans., "The Ming shi Account of Champa" (Asia Research Institute, National University of Singapore, Working Paper no. 3, June 2003), 11–12.
168. Whitmore, "Two Great Campaigns," 125, 129; Sun, "Ming-Southeast Asian," 67.
169. Whitmore, "Two Great Campaigns," 125, 129; Wade, "Ming shi Account of Champa," 12.
170. Sun, "Ming-Southeast Asian," 279.
171. Maspero, *Royaume de Champa*, 237; 1470 edict in Dutton, Werner, and Whitmore, *Sources of Vietnamese Tradition*, 140; Whitmore, "Two Great Campaigns," 128, 126.
172. Sun, "Ming-Southeast Asian," 277, 262, 279; Whitmore, "Two Great Campaigns," 125, 128–29; Lê Thành Khôi, *Histoire du Viêt Nam*, 243.
173. *Đại Việt Sử Ký Toàn Thư*, xii, 62a, cited in Maspero, *Royaume de Champa*, 237–38.
174. Wade, "Ming shi Account of Champa," 12–13.
175. *Đại Việt Sử Ký Toàn Thư*, xii, 63a, b, cited in Maspero, *Royaume de Champa*, 238, no. 6, 239, no. 1.
176. Lê Thành Khôi, *Histoire du Viêt Nam*, 239.
177. Bùi and Nguyễn, *Le Đại Việt et ses voisins*, 90; John K. Whitmore, "New View," 70, quoted in Lieberman, *Strange Parallels*, 1:379n111.
178. Whitmore, "Two Great Campaigns," 130; Chesneaux, *Vietnamese Nation*, 29.
179. Wade, "Ming shi Account of Champa," 14–15.
180. Sun, "Ming-Southeast Asian," 261; Whitmore, "Two Great Campaigns," 133.
181. Whitmore, "Two Great Campaigns," 132–33; Sun, "Ming-Southeast Asian," 265.
182. Sun, "Ming-Southeast Asian," 262–63, 266; Whitmore, "Two Great Campaigns," 133.
183. *Đại Việt Sử Ký Toàn Thư*, 2:835, quoted in Sun, "Ming-Southeast Asian," 266–67.
184. Li, *Nguyễn Cochinchina*, 171, table 4.
185. Li Tana and Anthony Reid, eds., *Southern Vietnam under the Nguyễn: Documents on the Economic History of Cochinchina (Đàng Trong), 1602–1777* (Canberra: Economic History of Southeast Asia Project, Research School of Pacific Studies, Australian National University, 1993), 1.
186. Whitmore, "*Chung-hsing* and *Cheng-t'ung*," 118.

187. Nguyễn Thế Anh, "Vietnamization of the Cham Deity," 46.
188. Cooke, "Nineteenth-Century Vietnamese Confucianization," 282.
189. Bùi and Nguyễn, *Le Đại Việt et ses voisins*, 90; William Duiker, *Historical Dictionary of Vietnam*, 2nd ed. (Lanham, MD: Scarecrow, 1998), 132.
190. Whitmore, "*Chung-hsing* and *Cheng-t'ung*," 120.
191. Bùi and Nguyễn, *Le Đại Việt et ses voisins*, 90–91; Nguyễn Thế Anh, "Vietnamization of the Cham Deity," 46.
192. Lê Thành Khôi, *Histoire du Viêt Nam*, 243–44; Maspéro, *Royaume du Champa*, 240; Wade, "Ming shi Account of Champa," 13–14; Po Dharma, *Le Pāṇḍuraṅga (Campā), 1802–1835. Ses rapports avec le Vietnam* (Paris: EFEO, 1987), 62–63.
193. Buckley et al., "Climate," table S2: http://www.pnas.org/content/early/2010/03/22/0910827107/suppl/DCSupplemental.
194. Whitmore, "*Chung-hsing* and *Cheng-t'ung*," 118.
195. Lê Thành Khôi, *Histoire du Viêt Nam*, 246.
196. Joseph Buttinger, *A Dragon Defiant: A Short History of Vietnam* (New York: Praeger, 1972), 48.
197. John K. Whitmore, "Mac Dang-dung," in *Dictionary of Ming Biography, 1368–1644*, ed. L. Carrington Goodrich (New York: Columbia University Press, 1976), 1030–31.
198. Cooke, "Nineteenth-Century Vietnamese Confucianization," 289n103.
199. Quoted in Whitmore, "*Chung-hsing* and *Cheng-t'ung*," 119.
200. Lê Tung, *Việt Giám Thông Khảo Tổng Luận*, quoted in Whitmore, "*Chung-hsing* and *Cheng-t'ung*," 121.
201. *Đại Việt Sử Ký Toàn Thư (Thực Lục)*, 2:814–15, quoted in Whitmore, "*Chung-hsing* and *Cheng-t'ung*," 127.
202. Dương Văn An, *Ô Châu Cận Lục*, quoted in Whitmore, "*Chung-hsing* and *Cheng-t'ung*," 123.
203. Whitmore, "Mac Dang-dung," 1031; Lê Thành Khôi, *Histoire du Viêt Nam*, 247; Cooke, "Nineteenth-Century Vietnamese Confucianization," 289–92; Huỳnh, *Heritage*, 250.
204. *Đại Việt Sử Ký Toàn Thư (Thực Lục)* 2:814–15, quoted in Whitmore, "*Chung-hsing* and *Cheng-t'ung*," 127.
205. Lê Quý Đôn, quoted in Nguyễn and Tạ, *Lê Code*, 1:49–50.
206. Whitmore, "Mac Dang-dung," 1031.
207. Whitmore, "Mac Dang-dung," 1029–32, and "*Chung-hsing* and *Cheng-t'ung*," 122–23.
208. Whitmore, "Mac Dang-dung," 1033–34.
209. Quoted in Kathlene Baldanza, "The Ambiguous Border: Early Modern Sino-Viet relations" (PhD diss., University of Pennsylvania, 2010), 111. See also Baldanza, "Perspectives on the Mac Surrender of 1540," *Asia Major* 27, no. 2 (Nov. 2014): 127–59.
210. Whitmore, "Mac Dang-dung," 1034.
211. Luo Yuejiong, *Xian bin lu* (Beijing: Zhonghua, 1983), 132, quoted in Baldanza, "Ambiguous Border," 36.
212. Whitmore, "Mac Dang-dung," 1035; Whitmore, "*Chung-hsing* and *Cheng-t'ung*," 123.
213. Whitmore, "Literati Culture," 670.
214. Huỳnh, *Heritage*, 281–82; Nguyễn Bỉnh Khiêm, "The Three Teachings," in Dutton, Werner, and Whitmore, *Sources of Vietnamese Tradition*, 124, 114–15.
215. Lê Thành Khôi, *Histoire du Viêt Nam*, 225.
216. Huỳnh, *Heritage*, 235, 51–52. On Nguyễn Bỉnh Khiêm (1491–1585), see also Keith W. Taylor, "Nguyen Hoang and the Beginning of Vietnam's Southward

Expansion," in *Southeast Asia in the Early Modern Era: Trade, Power, and Belief*, ed. Anthony Reid (Ithaca, NY: Cornell University Press, 1993), 46.

217. Nguyễn and Tạ, *Lê Code*, 1:18.
218. Taylor, "Nguyen Hoang," 43; Whitmore, "Mac Dang-dung," 1035.
219. Nola Cooke, "Nineteenth-Century Vietnamese Confucianization," 300n143.
220. *Đại Việt sử ký toàn thư*, quoted in Li, *Nguyễn Cochinchina*, 163.
221. Li, *Nguyễn Cochinchina*, 11; Li and Reid, *Southern Vietnam under the Nguyễn*, 4, 2; Taylor, "Nguyen Hoang," 43, 45–46; see also Dutton, Werner, and Whitmore, *Sources of Vietnamese Tradition*, 155–59.
222. Cooke, "Nineteenth-Century Vietnamese Confucianization," 282; Taylor, "Nguyen Hoang," 45–47.

CHAPTER 6

1. Li Tana, *Nguyễn Cochinchina: Southern Vietnam in the Seventeenth and Eighteenth Centuries* (Ithaca, NY: Cornell Southeast Asia Program, 1998), 163.
2. George Dutton, *The Tây Sơn Uprising: Society and Rebellion in Eighteenth-Century Vietnam* (Honolulu: University of Hawai'i Press, 2006).
3. Samuel Baron, "A Description of the Kingdom of Tonqueen," in *Views of Seventeenth-Century Vietnam: Christoforo Borri on Cochinchina and Samuel Baron on Tonkin*, ed. Olga Dror and K. W. Taylor (Ithaca, NY: Cornell Southeast Asia Program, 2006), 241, 244 (see also 128n8); G. Norris, ed., *William Dampier: Buccaneer Explorer* (London: Folio, 1994), 164; K. W. Taylor, "The Literati Revival in Seventeenth-Century Vietnam," *Journal of Southeast Asian Studies* 18, no. 1 (March 1987): 2–3; Nguyễn Thế Anh, "State and Civil Society under the Trịnh Lords in Seventeenth Century Vietnam," in *La Société civile face à l'état dans les traditions chinoise, japonaise, coréenne et vietnamienne*, ed. L. Vandermeersch (Paris: Ecole française d'Extrême-Orient, 1994), 368; Li Tana and Anthony Reid, eds., *Southern Vietnam under the Nguyễn: Documents on the Economic History of Cochinchina (Đàng Trong), 1602–1777* (Singapore: Institute of Southeast Asian Studies, 1993), 127.
4. Thomas Hodgkin posed this question in his *Vietnam: The Revolutionary Path* (London: Macmillan 1981), 68.
5. Norris, *William Dampier*, 151, 154–55.
6. Brendan Buckley et al., "Climate as a Contributing Factor in the Demise of Angkor, Cambodia," *Proceedings of the National Academy of Sciences* 107, no. 15 (2010): 6748–52, available online at http://www.pnas.org/content/107/15/6748.full.pdf+html, supplemental online table S2: http://www.pnas.org/content/early/2010/03/22/0910827107/suppl/DCSupplemental.
7. Li, *Nguyễn Cochinchina*, 162–63, 171–72.
8. Buckley et al., "Climate," table S2.
9. Lê Thành Khôi, *Histoire du Việt Nam des origines à 1858* (Paris: Sudestasie, 1981), 246; Nguyễn, "State and Civil Society," 379.
10. Li and Reid, *Southern Vietnam under the Nguyễn*, 1; Li, *Nguyễn Cochinchina*, 162–63.
11. Keith W. Taylor, "Nguyen Hoang and the Beginning of Vietnam's Southward Expansion," in *Southeast Asia in the Early Modern Era: Trade, Power, and Belief*, ed. Anthony Reid (Ithaca, NY: Cornell University Press, 1993), 45.
12. Li and Reid, *Southern Vietnam under the Nguyễn*, 3.
13. Li, *Nguyễn Cochinchina*, 59–61; Taylor, "Nguyen Hoang," 50n10.
14. Chen Ching-ho, "On the Rules and Regulations of the Duong-thuong Hoi-quan at Faifo (Hoi-An), Central Vietnam," *Southeast Asian Archives* 2 (July 1969): 149.

See also Charles Wheeler, "Cross-cultural Trade and Trans-regional Networks in the Port of Hoi An: Maritime Vietnam in the Early Modern Era" (PhD diss., Yale University, 2001).

15. Nguyễn, "State and Civil Society," 367; Li, *Nguyễn Cochinchina*, 11n3.
16. Li, *Nguyễn Cochinchina*, 162–63.
17. Quoted in John K. Whitmore, "*Chung-hsing* and *Cheng-t'ung* in Texts of and on Sixteenth Century Việt Nam," in *Essays into Vietnamese Pasts* (Ithaca, NY: Cornell Southeast Asia Program, 1995), ed. K. W. Taylor and John K. Whitmore, 131.
18. Li, *Nguyễn Cochinchina*, 162–63; Taylor, "Nguyen Hoang," 45, 53.
19. Li, *Nguyễn Cochinchina*, 105.
20. Taylor, "Nguyen Hoang," 43, 48–50, 65; Li, *Nguyễn Cochinchina*, 105.
21. *Đại Việt sử ký toàn thư*, Bản kỷ 16, p. 869, and *Đại Nam thực lục* 1:14, quoted in Taylor, "Nguyen Hoang," 51–52.
22. *Đại Việt sử ký toàn thư*, Bản kỷ 16, p. 868, quoted in Taylor, "Nguyen Hoang," 49.
23. Li, *Nguyễn Cochinchina*, 60; *Đại Nam thực lục* 1:13–14, quoted in Taylor, "Nguyen Hoang," 50n10.
24. *Đại Việt sử ký toàn thư*, Bản kỷ 16, p. 868, quoted in Taylor, "Nguyen Hoang," 49; Li, *Nguyễn Cochinchina*, 60.
25. Pierre-Yves Manguin, *Les Portugais sur les côtes du Việt-Nam et du Campā* (Paris: Ecole française d'Extrême-Orient, 1972), 184–87; Li, *Nguyễn Cochinchina*, 72.
26. Li, *Nguyễn Cochinchina*, 60; Li and Reid, *Southern Vietnam*, 8–10, 17–18.
27. *Đại Nam thực lục* 1:8, 12, and 21, quoted in Taylor, "Nguyen Hoang," 49–50, 63.
28. Taylor, "Nguyen Hoang," 62.
29. Nola Cooke, "Nineteenth-Century Vietnamese Confucianization in Historical Perspective: Evidence from the Palace Examination (1463–1883)," *Journal of Southeast Asian Studies* 25, no. 2 (Sept. 1994): 283–84; Taylor, "Nguyen Hoang," 62.
30. Li, *Nguyễn Cochinchina*, 46; Cooke, "Nineteenth-Century Vietnamese Confucianization," 283–84, 306.
31. Lê, *Histoire*, 292–93; Cooke, "Nineteenth-Century Vietnamese Confucianization," 283.
32. Cooke, "Nineteenth-Century Vietnamese Confucianization," 300, table 1.
33. R. B. Smith, "England and Vietnam in the Fifteenth and Sixteenth Centuries," in *Southeast Asian History and Historiography: Essays Presented to D. G. E. Hall*, ed. C. D. Cowan and O. W. Wolters (Ithaca, NY: 1976), 240; Lê, *Histoire*, 292.
34. *Đại Việt Sử Ký Toàn Thư*, 9:10b–11a, quoted in Taylor, "Literati Revival," 4; Nguyễn, "State and Civil Society," 372.
35. Alexander B. Woodside, *Vietnam and the Chinese Model* (Cambridge, MA: Harvard University Press, 1971), 2; Nguyễn, "State and Civil Society," 368; Mary Elizabeth Berry, *Hideyoshi* (Cambridge, MA: Harvard University Press, 1982), 12.
36. Nguyễn, "State and Civil Society," 369–71, 373; Lê, *Histoire*, 257–58; Taylor, "Literati Revival," 4, 7; John K. Whitmore, "Literati Culture and Integration in Dai Viet, c. 1430–c. 1840," *Modern Asian Studies* 31, no. 3 (1997): 672.
37. Li, *Nguyễn Cochinchina*, 60–63, 61n10, 64–65.
38. Anthony Reid, *Southeast Asia in the Age of Commerce, 1450–1680*, vol. 1, *The Lands Below the Winds* (New Haven, CT: Yale University Press, 1988), 99; Li, *Nguyễn Cochinchina*, 63; Hoang Anh Tuan, *Silk for Silver: Dutch-Vietnamese Relations, 1637–1700* (Leiden: Brill, 2007).
39. Li, *Nguyễn Cochinchina*, 64.
40. Li and Reid, *Southern Vietnam*, 10; Dror and Taylor, *Views*, 31.
41. Chen, "Rules and Regulations," 148–49.
42. Li, *Nguyễn Cochinchina*, 68, 62, 84, 79–81; Li and Reid, *Southern Vietnam*, 3.

43. "A Japanese Resident's Account," in Li and Reid, *Southern Vietnam*, 31–32; Li, *Nguyễn Cochinchina*, 68.
44. Dror and Taylor, *Views*, 75–76, 202n12.
45. Baron, "Kingdom of Tonqueen," 191, 204, 202.
46. Christoforo Borri, "An Account of Cochin-China," in Dror and Taylor, *Views*, 107, 132–36; Baron, "Kingdom of Tonqueen," 181, 210–11, 215, 247.
47. Li, *Nguyễn Cochinchina*, 62, 61n11, 73–74.
48. Taylor, "Literary Revival," 9.
49. Li, *Nguyễn Cochinchina*, 68, 85.
50. Phan Phát Huồn, *History of the Catholic Church in Việt Nam*, vol. 1, *1533–1960* (Long Beach, CA: Cứu Thế Tùng Thư, 2000), 19–35; Manguin, *Portugais*, 187; Li and Reid, *Southern Vietnam*, 10.
51. Dror and Taylor, *Views*, 31–32n72.
52. Buckley et al., "Climate," table S2; Borri, "Account of Cochin-China," 142–44, 32–33.
53. Borri, "Account of Cochin-China," 145.
54. Dror and Taylor, *Views*, 32–33, 93n10.
55. Micheline Lessard, "Curious Relations: Jesuit Perceptions of the Vietnamese," in Taylor and Whitmore, *Essays*, 142.
56. Lessard, "Curious Relations," 142; Manguin, *Portugais*, 201; Woodside, *Vietnam and the Chinese Model*, 262.
57. Phan Phát Huồn, *History of the Catholic Church in Việt Nam*, 1:59.
58. Lessard, "Curious Relations," 142; Nguyễn, "State and Civil Society," 376.
59. Cooke, "Nineteenth-Century Vietnamese Confucianization," 295n120.
60. Nola Cooke, "Strange Brew: Global, Regional and Local Factors Behind the 1690 Prohibition of Christian Practice in Nguyễn Cochinchina," *Journal of Southeast Asian Studies* 39, no. 3 (Oct. 2008): 395; Cooke, "Nineteenth-Century Vietnamese Confucianization," 295n120.
61. Woodside, *Vietnam and the Chinese Model*, 262; Lessard, "Curious Relations," 147.
62. Alexandre de Rhodes, *Cathechismvs pro ijs, qui volunt suscipere baptismvm in octo dies diuisus: Phép giảng tám ngày . . .* (Rome: Typis sacræ Congregationis de propaganda fide, 1651[?]); *Histoire du royaume de Tunquin*, Lyon, 1651; *Từ điển Annam-Lusitan-Latinh: thường gọi từ điển Việt-Bồ-La*, trans. Thanh Lãng, Hoàng Xuân Việt, Đỗ Quang Chính (Hồ Chí Minh City: Khoa học xã hội, 1991).
63. Borri, "Account of Cochin-China," 115.
64. Domingo Fernández Navarrete, *The Travels and Controversies of Friar Domingo Navarrete, 1618–1686*, ed. J. S. Cummins (Cambridge, UK: Hakluyt Society, 1962), 2:268.
65. Da Shan, "A Chinese Buddhist Report, 1694–5," in Li, *Southern Vietnam under the Nguyễn*, 55, 58.
66. Alexander Woodside, "Central Vietnam's Trading World in the Eighteenth Century as Seen in Lê Quý Đôn's 'Frontier Chronicles,'" in Taylor and Whitmore, *Essays*, 164, 166.
67. Borri, "Account of Cochin-China," *Views*, 126; Baron, "Kingdom of Tonqueen," 218–20.
68. Lessard, "Curious Relations," 154–55, 149–50.
69. Norris, *William Dampier*, 108, 155–56.
70. Pierre-Yves Manguin, "The Introduction of Islam into Champa," in *The Propagation of Islam in the Indonesian-Malay Archipelago*, ed. Alijah Gordon (Kuala Lumpur: Malaysian Sociological Research Institute, 2001), 306–7; Manguin, *Portugais*, 236.
71. Li, *Nguyễn Cochinchina*, 62–63; Chen, "Rules and Regulations," 149.

72. Manguin, "Introduction of Islam," 300–301, 303–304.
73. Taylor, "Literati Revival," 5, 9; Li, *Nguyễn Cochinchina*, 37–38, 40.
74. Borri, "Account of Cochin-China," 129–30.
75. Po Dharma, *Le Pāṇḍuraṅga (Campā), 1802–1835: Ses rapports avec le Vietnam* (Paris: Ecole française d'Extrême-Orient, 1987), 1:64.
76. Borri, "Account of Cochin-China," 129n11.
77. Dutton, *Tây Sơn Uprising*, 20–21; Li, *Nguyễn Cochinchina*, 11, 44; Léopold Cadière, "Le mur de Đồng Hới," *BEFEO* 6 (1906): 87–254.
78. Choi Byung Wook, *Southern Vietnam under the Reign of Minh Mang, 1820–1841: Central Policies and Local Response* (Ithaca, NY: Cornell Southeast Asia Program, 2004), 165; Li, *Nguyễn Cochinchina*, 27.
79. Li, *Nguyễn Cochinchina*, 32; Li and Reid, *Southern Vietnam*, 35n3; Pierre-Yves Manguin, "Etudes Cam, IV: Une relation ibérique du Campa en 1595," *BEFEO* 70 (1981): 260; Po, *Pāṇḍuraṅga*, 63–66.
80. Li, *Nguyễn Cochinchina*, 28.
81. Buckley et al., "Climate," table S2.
82. "The Nguyễn Chronicle to 1777," in Li and Reid, *Southern Vietnam*, 132; Li, *Nguyễn Cochinchina*, 84.
83. Navarrete, *Travels*, 2:381.
84. "Japanese Resident's Account," in Li and Reid, *Southern Vietnam*, 30–31.
85. Navarrete, *Travels*, 2:381.
86. "Japanese Resident's Account," 30–31; cf. Lê, *Histoire*, 263.
87. Li, *Nguyễn Cochinchina*, 41.
88. Navarrete, *Travels*, 2:381; Taylor, "Literati Revival," 5.
89. Norris, *William Dampier*, 166; Baron, "Kingdom of Tonqueen," 212.
90. Navarrete, *Travels*, 2:381; Baron, "Kingdom of Tonqueen," 241.
91. Pierre-Yves Manguin, "L'Introduction de l'Islam au Champa," *BEFEO* 66 (1979): 271.
92. Manguin, "Introduction of Islam," 302.
93. Marcel Ner, "Les Musulmans de l'Indochine française," *BEFEO* 41 (1941): 154; A. Cabaton, "Indochina," *Encyclopedia of Islam*, 2nd ed. (Leiden: Brill, 1986).
94. Manguin, "Introduction of Islam," 302, 307; Po, *Pāṇḍuraṅga*, 66.
95. Li, *Nguyễn Cochinchina*, 32; Li and Reid, *Southern Vietnam*, 39; Po, *Pāṇḍuraṅga*, 1:68–69; Victor Lieberman, *Strange Parallels: Southeast Asia in Global Context, c. 800–1830*, vol. 1, *Integration on the Mainland* (New York: Cambridge University Press, 2003), 411.
96. D. G. E. Hall, *A History of South-East Asia* (London: Macmillan, 1985), 462; Lieberman, *Strange Parallels*, 1:412.
97. Po, *Pāṇḍuraṅga*, 1:70–71.
98. Mak Phoeun, trans., *Chroniques royales du Cambodge (de 1594 à 1677)* (Paris: Ecole française d'Extrême-Orient, 1981), 94, 106, 120.
99. Michael Vickery, review of *Histoire du Cambodge de la fin du XVIe siècle au début du XVIIIe* by Mak Phoeun, *BEFEO* 83 (1996): 407.
100. Mak Phoeun, *Histoire du Cambodge de la fin du XVIe siècle au début du XVIIIe* (Paris: Ecole française d'Extrême-Orient, 1995), 177–83; Mak Phoeun, *Chroniques royales*, 180, 334–36, 185–90, 342.
101. Mak Phoeun, *Histoire*, 273.
102. Mak Phoeun, *Chroniques royales*, 191, 359, 354, 195, 368–70.
103. Mak Phoeun, *Histoire*, 294ff.; Manguin, *Portugais*, 205; Vickery, review of Mak Phoeun, *Histoire*, 415, 409.

104. Mak Phoeun, *Histoire*, 323–26; 294–410 dates the first five Vietnamese military interventions in Cambodia at 1658–59, 1673–79, 1682–88, 1688–90, and 1699–1700.
105. Li, *Nguyễn Cochinchina*, 16, 46–47.
106. Woodside, *Vietnam and the Chinese Model*, 2; Norris, *William Dampier*, 163–64; "Description of Cochinchina, 1749–50," in Li and Reid, *Southern Vietnam under the Nguyễn*, 68.
107. Dutton, *Tây Sơn Uprising*, 95, 249nn133–34.
108. Woodside, "Central Vietnam's Trading World," 170.
109. Liam Kelley, *Beyond the Bronze Pillars: Envoy Poetry and the Sino-Vietnamese Relationship* (Honolulu: University of Hawai'i Press, 2005), e.g., 43–50.
110. Nguyễn Phú Phong, *Questions de linguistique vietnamienne: Les classificateurs et les déictiques* (Paris: Ecole française d'Extrême-Orient, 1995), 237–38, 268.
111. Cooke, "Nineteenth-Century Vietnamese Confucianization," 283; Li, *Nguyễn Cochinchina*, 46.
112. Da Shan, "A Chinese Buddhist Report, 1694–5," in Li, *Southern Vietnam under the Nguyễn*, 56.
113. Li, *Nguyễn Cochinchina*, 104–5.
114. Da Shan, "A Chinese Buddhist Report, 1694–5," in Li, *Southern Vietnam under the Nguyễn*, 58–59.
115. Li, *Nguyễn Cochinchina*, 69–71; "Miscellaneous Nguyễn Records Seized in 1775–76," in Li, *Southern Vietnam under the Nguyễn*, 116; Woodside, "Central Vietnam's Trading World," 162.
116. Woodside, "Central Vietnam's Trading World," 164, 166.
117. Cooke, "Nineteenth-Century Vietnamese Confucianization," 300, table 1; Taylor, "Literati Revival," 7–9.
118. Nguyễn, "State and Civil Society," 375; Taylor, "Literati Revival," 12–15.
119. Lê, *Histoire*, 271.
120. Jean Chesneaux, *The Vietnamese Nation: Contribution to a History*, trans. Malcolm Salmon (Sydney: Current, 1966), 39.
121. Whitmore, "Literati Culture," 672, 678, 679.
122. Li, *Nguyễn Cochinchina*, 172, 68 (table 2).
123. Norris, *William Dampier*, 141, 149; Baron, "Kingdom of Tonqueen," 191, 202.
124. Nguyễn, "State and Civil Society," 379; Taylor, "Literati Revival," 18; Li, *Nguyễn Cochinchina*, 163.
125. Buckley et al., "Climate," table S2.
126. Baron, "Kingdom of Tonqueen," 191, 205; Norris, *William Dampier*, 148, 151.
127. Woodside, "Central Vietnam's Trading World," 164.
128. Cooke, "Nineteenth-Century Vietnamese Confucianization," 300, Table 1; Taylor, "Literati Revival," 2, 21.
129. Taylor, "Literati Revival," 13–22; Nguyễn, "State and Civil Society," 379.
130. Buckley et al., "Climate," table S2; Li, *Nguyễn Cochinchina*, 172.
131. Quoted in Philippe Langlet, *L'Ancienne Historiographie d'état au Vietnam*, vol. 2 (Paris: Ecole française d'Extrême-Orient, 1985), 1.
132. Charles B. Maybon, *Histoire moderne du pays d'Annam (1592–1820)* (Paris: Typographie Plon-Nourrit, 1919), 69.
133. Li, *Nguyễn Cochinchina*, 69.
134. Lê, *Histoire*, 303–306; Nguyễn, "State and Civil Society," 379.
135. Li, *Nguyễn Cochinchina*, 163–64; Lê, *Histoire*, 305.
136. Li, *Nguyễn Cochinchina*, 163–65.

137. Lê, *Histoire*, 304.
138. Nguyễn Ngọc Huy and Tạ Văn Tài, *The Lê Code: Law in Traditional Vietnam* (Athens, OH: Ohio University Press, 1987), vol. 2:196.
139. Lê, *Histoire*, 272, 304.
140. Whitmore, "Literati Culture," 680; Lê, *Histoire*, 304.
141. Lê, *Histoire*, 259–60, 270–72, 303–4; Whitmore, "Literati Culture," 681.
142. Whitmore, "Literati Culture," 681–82.
143. Nguyễn, "State and Civil Society," 377–80; Lê, *Histoire*, 258n10.
144. Li, *Nguyễn Cochinchina*, 171, table 4.
145. Lê, *Histoire*, 271, 304.
146. Nguyễn, "State and Civil Society," 371.
147. Lê, *Histoire*, 258.
148. Lê, *Histoire*, 259.
149. Cooke, "Nineteenth-Century Vietnamese Confucianization," 300, table 1.
150. Nguyễn, "State and Civil Society," 380.
151. Lê, *Histoire*, 292–93; Whitmore, "Literati Culture," 673–74.
152. Alexander Woodside, "Conceptions of Change and of Human Responsibility for Change in Late Traditional Vietnam," in *Moral Order and the Question of Change: Essays on Southeast Asian Thought*, ed. David K. Wyatt and Alexander Woodside (New Haven, CT: Yale University Southeast Asia Studies, 1982), 142–43.
153. Lê Quý Đôn, *Kiến Văn Tiểu Lục* (A small record of things seen and heard), 107, quoted in Olga Dror, *Cult, Culture and Authority: Princess Liễu Hạnh in Vietnamese History* (Honolulu: University of Hawai'i Press, 2007), 40–41.
154. Lê, *Histoire*, 292, 305; Dutton, *Tây Sơn Uprising*, 23.
155. Buckley et al., "Climate," table S2; Whitmore, "Literati Culture," 682.
156. George E. Dutton, Jayne S. Werner, and John K. Whitmore, eds., *Sources of Vietnamese Tradition* (New York: Columbia University Press, 2012), 205–8; Dutton, *Tây Sơn Uprising*, 23; Li, *Nguyễn Cochinchina*, 164–65; Lê, *Histoire*, 326.
157. "Description of Cochinchina, 1749–50," in Li and Reid, *Southern Vietnam*, 67.
158. Li, *Nguyễn Cochinchina*, 164.
159. Buckley et al., "Climate," 6750, fig. 2, fig. S1, table S2; Dan Penny, pers. comm., Nov. 2, 2009.
160. Masaki Sano, Brendan M. Buckley, and Tatsuo Sweda, "Tree-Ring Based Hydroclimate Reconstruction over Northern Vietnam from *Fokienia hodginsii*: Eighteenth Century Mega-Drought and Tropical Pacific Influence," *Climate Dynamics* 33 (2009): 331, 336 (fig. 5), 339.
161. Li, *Nguyễn Cochinchina*, 166; Buckley et al., "Climate," table S2.
162. Choi, *Southern Vietnam under the Reign*, 38–39, 165; Maurice Durand, *Histoire des Tây Sơn* (Paris: Indes Savantes, 2006), 44.
163. Mak Phoeun, *Histoire*, 294–410, lists five Vietnamese military interventions to 1700; Lieberman, *Strange Parallels* 1:411, says there were thirteen by 1772.
164. Pierre du Puy du Fayet, Jean de Antoine de la Court, and Charles Gouge, to the Directors, Missions Etrangères de Paris [136], July 26, 1732, vol. 739, 925–30, translated by Nola Cooke, who kindly supplied her detailed notes from the MEP archives, Paris. See also Lieberman, *Strange Parallels*, 1:412.
165. Khin Sok, *Le Cambodge entre le Siam et le Vietnam (de 1775 à 1860)* (Paris: Ecole française d'Extrême-Orient, 1991, 36.
166. Mak Phoeun, "La frontière entre le Cambodge et le Viêtnam du XVIIe siècle à l'instauration du protectorat français présentée à travers les chroniques royales khmères," in *Les Frontières du Vietnam*, ed. P.-B. Laffont (Paris: Harmattan, 1989), 139–40.

167. Yumio Sakurai and Takako Kitagawa, "Ha Tien or Banteay Meas in the Time of the Fall of Ayutthaya," in *From Japan to Arabia: Ayutthaya's Maritime Relations with Asia*, ed. Kennon Breazeale (Bangkok: Toyota Thailand Foundation, 1999), 160.
168. M. Piguel à Mgr. Lefebvre, April 8, 1751, in Adrien Launay, *Histoire de la Mission de Cochinchine 1658–1823, Documents Historiques*, vol. 2, *1728–1771* (Paris: C. Douniol & Retaux, 1924), 368.
169. M. d'Azema à M. de Noëlène, quoted in M. J.-B. Maigrot à Mgr. de Martiliat, Sept. 16, 1751, and d'Azema aux Directeurs du Séminaire des M.-E., Cambodge, June 20, 1757, in Launay, *Histoire de la Mission de Cochinchine*, 2: 2:366, 370; Khin, *Cambodge entre le Siam et le Vietnam*, 37.
170. D'Azema à De Noëlène, undated, and Piguel à Lefebvre, April 8, 1751, and D'Azema aux Directeurs du Séminaire des M.-E., Cambodge, June 20, 1757, in Launay, *Histoire*, 365–66, 368, 370–71.
171. Li, *Nguyễn Cochinchina*, 153, 157.
172. Li, *Nguyễn Cochinchina*, 90–98.
173. Li, *Nguyễn Cochinchina*, 158, 71; "Miscellaneous Nguyễn Records," in Li and Reid, *Southern Vietnam*, 116.
174. Woodside, "Central Vietnam's Trading World," 166.
175. Choi, *Southern Vietnam under the Reign*, 38–39.
176. Li, *Nguyễn Cochinchina*, 142–44, 158.
177. "Miscellaneous Nguyễn Records," in Li and Reid, *Southern Vietnam*, 101–102.
178. "Nguyễn Chronicle to 1777," in Li and Reid, *Southern Vietnam*, 132; Dutton, *Tây Sơn Uprising*, 25–26.
179. Dutton, *Tây Sơn Uprising*, 36–38.
180. Li, *Nguyễn Cochinchina*, 134–35, 136–38, 135, 149; Dutton, *Tây Sơn Uprising*, 24, 91.
181. Dutton, *Tây Sơn Uprising*, 38.
182. Po, *Le Pāṇḍuraṅga (Campā)*, 1:68–75.
183. Durand, *Histoire des Tây Sơn*, 45–46.
184. Dutton, *Tây Sơn Uprising*, 240n60.

CHAPTER 7

1. Victor Lieberman, *Strange Parallels: Southeast Asia in Global Context, c. 800–1830*, vol. 1, *Integration on the Mainland* (New York: Cambridge University Press, 2003), 1–2.
2. Alexander B. Woodside, *Vietnam and the Chinese Model: A Comparative Study of Nguyễn and Ch'ing Civil Government in the First Half of the Nineteenth Century* (Cambridge, MA: Harvard University Press, 1971), 59.
3. George Dutton, *The Tây Sơn Uprising: Society and Rebellion in Eighteenth-Century Vietnam* (Honolulu: University of Hawai'i Press, 2006), 1–2.
4. Li Tana, *Nguyễn Cochinchina: Southern Vietnam in the Seventeenth and Eighteenth Centuries* (Ithaca, NY: Cornell Southeast Asia Program, 1998), 148; Dutton, *Tây Sơn*, 116.
5. Dutton, *Tây Sơn*, 39, 78–82; Lê Thành Khôi, *Le Viêt-Nam: Histoire et civilization* (Paris: Minuit, 1955), 297.
6. Dutton, *Tây Sơn*, 210; Li, *Nguyễn Cochinchina*, 138.
7. Dutton, *Tây Sơn*, 1, 39–40.
8. Lê, *Viêt-Nam*, 297–98, map 13, p. 527; Dutton, *Tây Sơn*, 132, 80.
9. Lê, *Viêt-Nam*, 298.
10. Choi Byung Wook, *Southern Vietnam under the Reign of Minh Mang, 1820–1841: Central Policies and Local Response* (Ithaca, NY: Cornell Southeast Asia Program, 2004), 33.

11. Dutton, *Tây Sơn*, 91–92, 206–208; Po Dharma, "À propos de l'exil d'un roi cam au Cambodge," *BEFEO* 72 (1983): 259–61.
12. Po Dharma, *Le Pāṇḍuraṅga (Campā), 1802–1835. Ses rapports avec le Vietnam* (Paris: Ecole française d'Extrême-Orient, 1987), 1:85; Dutton, *Tây Sơn*, 208.
13. Choi, *Southern Vietnam*, 38.
14. Dutton, *Tây Sơn*, 183ff.
15. Lê, *Viêt-Nam*, 298–99.
16. Dutton, *Tây Sơn*, 94; Lê, *Viêt-Nam*, 299.
17. Woodside, *Vietnam*, 29.
18. Lê, *Viêt-Nam*, 299–300; Dutton, *Tây Sơn*, 45.
19. Lê, *Viêt-Nam*, 300–302.
20. Li, *Nguyễn Cochinchina*, 144.
21. Lê, *Viêt-Nam*, 301–2.
22. Lê, *Viêt-Nam*, 302–4; Dutton, *Tây Sơn*, 2, 47, 79–80.
23. Dutton, *Tây Sơn*, 47–49.
24. Dutton, *Tây Sơn*, 47–49, 110–13, 209.
25. Nola Cooke, "The Myth of the Restoration: Dang-Trong Influences in the Spiritual Life of the Early Nguyen Dynasty (1802–47)," in *The Last Stand of Asian Autonomies: Responses to Modernity in the Diverse States of Southeast Asia and Korea, 1750–1900*, ed. Anthony Reid (New York: St. Martin's, 1997), 278.
26. Dutton, *Tây Sơn*, 232, 48; Lê, *Viêt-Nam*, 307.
27. Emperor Minh Mạng in the late 1830s, quoted in Woodside, *Vietnam*, 24.
28. "Nguyễn Huệ's Address to the Army (1789)," translated in Trương Bửu Lâm, *Patterns of Vietnamese Response to Foreign Intervention: 1858–1900*, Southeast Asia Studies Monograph 11 (New Haven, CT: Southeast Asia Studies, Yale University, 1967), 63–65.
29. Dutton, *Tây Sơn*, 49; Lê, *Viêt-Nam*, 308.
30. Dutton, *Tây Sơn*, 47.
31. Lê, *Viêt-Nam*, 308.
32. Maurice Durand, *Histoire des Tây Sơn* (Paris: Indes Savantes, 2006), 108–12; Lê, *Viêt-Nam*, 313–14; Choi, *Southern Vietnam*, 84ff.
33. Dutton, *Tây Sơn*, 209–10.
34. Lê, *Viêt-Nam*, 317.
35. Woodside, *Vietnam*, 16–17; Lê, *Viêt-Nam*, 316; Dutton, *Tây Sơn*, 51–52.
36. Dutton, *Tây Sơn*, 50; Lê, *Viêt-Nam*, 309–10.
37. Maurice Durand, *L'Oeuvre de la poétesse vietnamienne Hồ Xuân Hương: Textes traduction et notes* (Paris: Ecole française d'Extrême-Orient, 1968), 7.
38. Lê, *Viêt-Nam*, 318; Dutton, *Tây Sơn*, 51–52.
39. Dutton, *Tây Sơn*, 206–8.
40. Po, *Pāṇḍuraṅga*, I, 73–74; Po, "À propos de l'exil d'un roi cam," 260–63; Lê, *Viêt-Nam*, 318.
41. Lê, *Viêt-Nam*, 318–22; Dutton, *Tây Sơn*, 54.
42. "Nguyễn Huệ's Address to the Army (1789)," in Trương Bửu Lâm, *Patterns of Vietnamese Response*, 64.
43. Woodside, *Vietnam*, 46; Jean Chesneaux, *The Vietnamese Nation: Contribution to a History*, trans. Malcolm Salmon (Sydney: Current Books, 1966), 43.
44. Dutton, *Tây Sơn*, 51–53, 57–58, 111, 123–26, 194–95.
45. Dutton, *Tây Sơn*, 78–80.
46. Dutton, *Tây Sơn*, 113, 166; Lê, *Viêt-Nam*, 322.
47. Choi, *Southern Vietnam*, 42; Woodside, *Vietnam*, 16–17.
48. Dutton, *Tây Sơn*, 55–56.

49. Lê, *Viêt-Nam*, 321; Dutton, *Tây Sơn*, 55–56.
50. Quoted in Thomas Hodgkin, *Vietnam: The Revolutionary Path* (London: Macmillan, 1981), 98.
51. John Balaban, *Spring Essence: The Poetry of Hồ Xuân Hương* (Port Townsend, WA: Copper Canyon, 2000), 121.
52. Durand, *L'Oeuvre de la poétesse*, 2, 3; Lê Thành Khôi writes of "l'étonnante Hồ Xuân Hương," *Viêt-Nam*, 310; Balaban, *Spring Essence*, 6–7, 15n9.
53. Balaban, *Spring Essence*, 13, 15n3.
54. Woodside, *Vietnam*, 47; Hồ Xuân Hương, "Young Scholars," translated in Balaban, *Spring Essence*, 79.
55. Hồ Xuân Hương, "The Condition of Women," translated in Balaban, *Spring Essence*, 73.
56. Balaban, *Spring Essence*, 6.
57. Hồ Xuân Hương, "On Being a Concubine," translated in Huỳnh Sanh Thông, *The Heritage of Vietnamese Poetry* (New Haven, CT: Yale University Press, 1979), 100, 248. A different translation is "On Sharing a Husband," in Balaban, *Spring Essence*, 35.
58. Hồ Xuân Hương, "Buddhist Nun," and "The Lustful Monk," translated in Balaban, *Spring Essence*, 83, 85, 91, 125.
59. Hồ Xuân Hương, "Poking Fun at a Bonze," translated in Huỳnh Sanh Thông, *Heritage*, 184.
60. Hồ Xuân Hương, "Trấn Quốc Temple," translated in Balaban, *Spring Essence*, 93, 126.
61. Hồ Xuân Hương, "Weaving at Night," and "Swinging," translated in Balaban, *Spring Essence*, 49, 55.
62. Woodside, *Vietnam*, 47.
63. Hồ Xuân Hương, "Jackfruit," translated in Huỳnh Sanh Thông, *Heritage*, 99.
64. Hồ Xuân Hương, "Spring-Watching Pavilion," "Country Scene," and "Confession (III)," translated in Balaban, *Spring Essence*, 115, 113, 31.
65. Hữu Ngọc et Françoise Corrèze, *Hồ Xuân Hương, ou le voile déchiré* (Hanoi: Fleuve Rouge, 1984), quoted in Balaban, *Spring Essence*, 15n7; Balaban, *Spring Essence*, 15n7.
66. Hồ Xuân Hương, "Snail," translated in Huỳnh Sanh Thông, *Heritage*, 99.
67. Durand, *L'Oeuvre de la poétesse*, 2.
68. Hồ Xuân Hương, "Snail," translated in Huỳnh Sanh Thông, *Heritage*, 99.
69. Durand, *L'Oeuvre de la poétesse*, 6, 8.
70. Cooke, "Myth of the Restoration," 271.
71. Woodside, *Vietnam*, 67, 27; George E. Dutton, Jayne S. Werner, and John K. Whitmore, eds., *Sources of Vietnamese Tradition* (New York: Columbia University Press, 2012), 323; Alexander B. Woodside, "The Historical Background," in Nguyễn Du, *The Tale of Kiều*, trans. Huỳnh Sanh Thông (New Haven, CT: Yale University Press, 1983), xvi.
72. Woodside, *Vietnam*, 38.
73. Woodside, *Vietnam*, 17; Cooke, "Myth of the Restoration," 272–73, 278.
74. See, e.g., Liam Kelley, "How Việt Nam Became Việt Nam," *Le Minh Khai's SEAsian History Blog*, Aug. 26, 2013, https://leminhkhai.wordpress.com/2013/08/26/how-viet-nam-became-viet-nam/.
75. Gia Long, "Naming the Country Viet Nam (1804)," in Dutton, *Sources*, 258–59.
76. Christopher E. Goscha, *Vietnam or Indochina? Contesting Concepts of Space in Vietnamese Nationalism, 1887–1954* (Copenhagen: Nordic Institute of Asian Studies, 1995), 13–14.
77. Woodside, *Vietnam*, 18; Cooke, "Myth of the Restoration," 271, 284.

78. Woodside, *Vietnam*, 54, 135–36, 93, and "Historical Background," in Nguyễn Du, *Tale of Kiều*, xvi. See also Nola Cooke, "Southern Regionalism and the Composition of the Nguyễn Ruling Elite," *Asian Studies Review* 23, no. 2 (June 1999): 205–31.
79. Woodside, *Vietnam*, 36–37, 25.
80. Nguyễn Du, *Tale of Kiều*, xxi.
81. Nguyễn Du, *Tale of Kiều*, xiv, xx, 165.
82. Nguyễn Du, *Tale of Kiều*, xxii, xxxvii–xxxviii, 149–51.
83. Bà Huyện Thanh Quan, "The Wife of the Subprefect of Thanh Quan," in Nguyễn Khắc Viện and Hữu Ngọc, *Vietnamese Literature* (Hanoi: Red River, n.d.), 374; I use the translation in Woodside, *Vietnam*, 75.
84. Articles 143–44 of the Nguyễn Code, quoted in Chesneaux, *Vietnamese Nation*, 61.
85. Woodside, *Vietnam*, 48, 79.
86. Woodside, *Vietnam*, 237–39, 16–17.
87. Woodside, *Vietnam*, 81, 18.
88. John White, *A Voyage to Cochin China* (London: Longman, Hurst, Rees, Orme, Brown, & Green, 1824), 264–65.
89. Cooke, "Myth of the Restoration," 272, 279–80, 282.
90. Woodside, *Vietnam*, 134, 220.
91. Lieberman, *Strange Parallels*, 1:412.
92. Woodside, *Vietnam*, 16–17, 243–44; Choi, *Southern Vietnam*, 42.
93. D. P. Chandler, *A History of Cambodia* (Boulder, CO: Westview, 1983), 118; Chandler, "Cambodia before the French: Politics in a Tributary Kingdom, 1794–1848," (PhD diss., University of Michigan, 1973), 91.
94. Choi, *Southern Vietnam*, 34; Lieberman, *Strange Parallels*, 1:427; Chandler, *History*, 116, 119.
95. Woodside, *Vietnam*, 248, 244; Chandler, *History*, 114, 119–20.
96. Chandler, "Cambodia before the French," 90.
97. Goscha, *Vietnam or Indochina?*, 14; Woodside, *Vietnam*, 248; Choi, *Southern Vietnam*, 53.
98. Choi, *Southern Vietnam*, 34–35; Chandler, "Cambodia Before the French," 90, 93; Woodside, *Vietnam*, 248; Lê Thành Khôi, *Histoire du Viêt Nam des origines à 1858* (Paris: Sudestasie, 1981), 363.
99. D. P. Chandler, "An Anti-Vietnamese Rebellion in Early Nineteenth Century Cambodia: Pre-colonial Imperialism and a Pre-Nationalist Response," *Journal of Southeast Asian Studies* 6, no. 1 (1975): 16–24, 17.
100. Bâtum Baramey Pich, *Sastra voat Kroch khum Kroch srok Prey Chhô khêt Kâmpung Cham* [1869?] ("Manuscript of Kroch pagoda, Kroch subdistrict, Prey Chhor district, Kompong Cham province"), text and translation of an 1875 copy, in Khin Sok, *L'Annexion du Cambodge par les Vietnamiens au XIXe siècle d'après les deux poèmes du Vénérable Bâtum Baramey Pich* (Paris: You-Feng, 2002), 203, 52.
101. John Crawfurd, *Journal of an Embassy from the Governor General of India to the Courts of Siam and Cochinchina*, 587, cited in Chandler, "Anti-Vietnamese Rebellion," 18n15.
102. Chandler, "Anti-Vietnamese Rebellion," 18.
103. *Sastra voat Kroch khum Kroch srok Prey Chhô khêt Kâmpung Cham*, in Khin, *L'Annexion*, 55–56; Chandler, "Anti-Vietnamese Rebellion," 17–21.
104. Chandler, "An Anti-Vietnamese Rebellion," 21–22; Chandler, *History*, 120–21.
105. Chandler, "Anti-Vietnamese Rebellion," 22–24.
106. C. Michele Thompson, *Vietnamese Traditional Medicine: A Social History* (Singapore: NUS Press, 2015), 49–50.

107. Quoted in Mai Khắc Ứng, *Chính Sách Khuyến Nông Dưới Thời Minh Mạng* [Emperor Minh Mạng's agriculture encouraging policy] (Hanoi: Văn hóa thông tin, 1996), 129, 133 (trans. Mai Bui Dieu Linh).
108. Woodside, *Vietnam*, 37, 54–55, 135, 57, 194–95; Po, *Pāṇḍuraṅga*, 1:90–96, 153–64; Masaya Shiraishi, "State, Villagers, and Vagabonds: Vietnamese Rural Society and the Phan Bá Vành Rebellion," in *History and Peasant Consciousness in Southeast Asia*, ed. Andrew Turton and Shigeharu Tanabe (Osaka: National Museum of Ethnology, 1984), 345–400.
109. Thompson, *Vietnamese Traditional Medicine*, 52–53.
110. Minh Mạng, "Comments Regarding Christianity (1839)," in Dutton, *Sources*, 325–28.
111. Jacob Ramsay, *Mandarins and Martyrs: The Church and the Nguyen Dynasty in the Early Nineteenth Century* (Stanford, CA: Stanford University Press, 2008), 68, 67.
112. Woodside, *Vietnam*, 134, 55, 27; Lê, *Histoire*, 369; Choi, *Southern Vietnam*, 130n5.
113. Woodside, *Vietnam*, 135.
114. Cooke, "Myth of the Restoration," 285–86, 288–89; Woodside, *Vietnam*, 29–30.
115. Woodside, *Vietnam*, 167.
116. Choi, *Southern Vietnam*, 45–47, 60–66; 152–53, 84–87.
117. See, e.g., Minh Mạng, "Edict to the Literati and Commoners (1835)," in Dutton, *Sources*, 280–84.
118. Choi, *Southern Vietnam*, 95, 151–53, 141; Woodside, *Vietnam*, 249; Chandler, "Anti-Vietnamese Rebellion," 20n32; Puanthong Rungswasdisab, "War and Trade: Siamese Interventions in Cambodia, 1767–1851" (PhD diss., University of Wollongong, 1995).
119. Choi, *Southern Vietnam*, 96; Po, *Le Pāṇḍuraṅga*, 124; Lieberman, *Strange Parallels*, 430. According to a later account, France annexed Champa's last provinces to its Cochinchina colony in 1883. E. Aymonier, *Excursions et reconnaissances* 10 (June 1883).
120. Choi, *Southern Vietnam*, 137–38.
121. Chesneaux, *Vietnamese Nation*, 51.
122. Chesneaux, *Vietnamese Nation*, 62–63.
123. Mai, *Chính Sách Khuyến Nông Dưới Thời Minh Mạng*, ch. 5, 459.
124. Mai, *Chính Sách Khuyến Nông Dưới Thời Minh Mạng*, 401.
125. Choi, *Southern Vietnam*, 175, 182–86.
126. David Biggs, *Quagmire: Nation-Building and Nature in the Mekong Delta* (Seattle: University of Washington Press, 2010), 68.
127. Phan Phương Thảo, *Land Equalization in 1839 in Bình Định Seen from the Land Records* (Hanoi: Thế Giới, 2009), 39–44, 157–59.
128. *Catalogue of the Imperial Archives of the Nguyễn Dynasty*, vol. 2, *The 6th and 7th Years of Minh Mạng Reign (1825–1826), Tomes 11–20* (Hanoi: Thế Giới, 2000), 567–68.
129. Mai, *Chính Sách Khuyến Nông Dưới Thời Minh Mạng*, 268–69.
130. Woodside, *Vietnam*, 283.
131. Woodside, *Vietnam*, 13–14; Chandler, *History*, 127.
132. Cooke, "Myth of the Restoration," 286–88.
133. Woodside, *Vietnam*, 14.
134. Woodside, *Vietnam*, 249; Lê, *Histoire*, 364.
135. "Chotmaihet kieokap khmen lae yuan," in *Prachum Pongsawadan*, part 68, vol. 41 (Bangkok: Khurusapha, 1969), 244, trans. Puangthong Rungwasdisab Pawakapan; Rungswasdisab, "War and Trade," 144.

136. Bâtum Baramey Pich, *Sastra voat Kroch*, in Khin, *L'Annexion*, 235, 238.
137. Chandler, "Cambodia before the French," 114–15.
138. Bâtum Baramey Pich, *Sastra voat Kroch*, in Khin, *L'Annexion*, 250.
139. Pich, *Sastra voat Kroch*, in Khin, *L'Annexion*, 245; Rungswasdisab, "War and Trade," 144–45.
140. Chandler, *History*, 122–23; Lê, *Histoire*, 363; Woodside, *Vietnam*, 121, 1, 249–50.
141. Choi, *Southern Vietnam*, 132; Minh Mạng, "Naming the Country Đai Nam (1838)," in Dutton, *Sources*, 259–60.
142. Pich, *Sastra lbaoeuk rôba khsat*, in Khin, *L'Annexion*, 333.
143. Chandler, *History*, 124.
144. *Zhenxi fengtu ji* [The customs of Trấn Tây], ms. dating from c. 1840, English translation kindly provided by Li Tana, 6.
145. Woodside, *Vietnam*, 145.
146. *Zhenxi fengtu ji*, trans. Li Tana, 6.
147. Chandler, *History*, 126.
148. Chandler, *History*, 126–27.
149. Woodside, *Vietnam*, 145, 250.
150. *Đại Nam thực lục chính biên, đệ nhị kỷ* [Primary compilation of the veritable records of the second reign of Đại Nam] 14 (1836), vol. 18, Book 176, 342 (cited as *DNTL* 2, 176:12–12b) (Hanoi: Nhà Xuất bản Khoa học xã hội, 1967), translated by Vy Vu. On the Chams, see *Đại Nam thực lục chính biên, đệ nhị kỷ*, Book 121 (*DNTL* 2, 121:28). Both cited in Woodside, *Vietnam*, 250.
151. *Đại Nam thực lục chính biên, đệ nhị kỷ*, vol. 18, Book 176, 342, trans. by Vy Vu.
152. *Đại Nam thực lục chính biên, đệ nhị kỷ* 11 (1834), vol. 15, Book 138, 297 (cited as *DNTL* 2, 138:27, in Woodside, *Vietnam*, 254) (Hanoi: Nhà Xuất bản Khoa học, 1965), trans. Vy Vu.
153. *Đại Nam thực lục chính biên, đệ nhị kỷ*, vol. 18, Book 176, 342; Chandler, *History*, 129.
154. *Đại Nam thực lục chính biên, đệ nhị kỷ*, vol. 15, Book 138, 297, trans. Vy Vu.
155. Woodside, *Vietnam*, 251; Chandler, *History*, 127–28.
156. *Zhenxi fengtu ji* [The customs of Trấn Tây], trans. Li Tana, 6–7.
157. Chandler, *History*, 122, 124–25.
158. Trudy Jacobsen, *Lost Goddesses: The Denial of Female Power in Cambodian History* (Copenhagen: NIAS, 2008), 22–27, 112–17.
159. Pich, *Sastra lbaoeuk rôba khsat*, in Khin, *L'Annexion*, 334–39.
160. Chandler, *History*, 128–29.
161. Pich, *Sastra lbaoeuk rôba khsat*, in Khin, *L'Annexion*, 340–41.
162. Chandler, *History*, 130, 127, 125, 129–31.
163. *Zhenxi fengtu ji*, trans. Li Tana, p. 1.
164. Choi, *Southern Vietnam*, 180, 178, 176, 188, 171n27.
165. Choi, *Southern Vietnam*, 187, 189, 178–79, 171, 190; Woodside, *Vietnam*, 147–49.
166. Chandler, *History*, 128–30; Pich, *Sastra lbaoeuk rôba khsat*, in Khin, *L'Annexion*, 341.
167. Chandler, "Cambodia before the French," 153–54; Chandler, *History*, 132.
168. Chandler, *History*, 127–28, 132–33.
169. "Chotmaihet kieokap khmen lae yuan," in *Prachum Pongsawadan*, part 68, vol. 42, 244 (1840), trans. Puangthong Rungwasdisab Pawakapan.
170. Chandler, *History*, 132.
171. P. J. Honey, in P. J. B. Trương-Vĩnh-Ký, *Voyage to Tonking in the Year Ất-Hợi* (1876) (London: School of Oriental and African Studies, 1982), 75n52.
172. J. B. Granjean, Bangkok, Jan. 20, 1842, excerpted in Khin, *L'Annexion*, 82n1.
173. Chandler, *History*, 134.

174. Auguste Pavie, "Excursion dans le Cambodge et le Royaume de Siam," *Excursions et Reconnaissances*, 7, no. 18 (1884): 405; C.-E. Bouillevaux, *Voyage dans l'Indochine, 1848–1856* (Paris: Victor Palmé, 1858), 181. See Nola Cooke and Li Tana, *Water Frontier: Commerce and the Chinese in the Lower Mekong Region, 1750–1880* (New York: Rowman & Littlefield, 2004), 155n42.
175. Rungswasdisab, "War and Trade," 151, 154.
176. *Chotmaihet Rama III*, quoted in Chandler, *History*, 134–35.
177. Quoted in Khin, *L'Annexion*, 87.
178. Chandler, *History*, 135; Khin, *L'Annexion*, 88, 90.
179. Cooke, "Southern Regionalism," 217; Cooke, "Myth of the Restoration," 285–86, 289–90.
180. Cooke, "Myth of the Restoration," 290; Woodside, *Vietnam*, 305n25.
181. Trương Bửu Lâm, *Patterns of Vietnamese Response*, 38n40; Cooke, "Myth of the Restoration," 290.
182. Minh Mạng, "Policy for Trading with Europeans (1840)," in Dutton, *Sources*, 275–76.
183. Nguyễn Điền, "Vietnamese Response to French Conquest, 1858–1885" (honors thesis, Australian National University, 1971), 4; Honey, "Historical Background," 19, 75n52; Woodside, *Vietnam*, 93.
184. Quoted in Nguyễn Điền, "Vietnamese Response to French Conquest," 9.
185. Honey, "Historical Background," 20, 75n53.
186. Pierre Brocheux and Daniel Hémery, *Indochina: An Ambiguous Colonization, 1858–1954* (Berkeley: University of California Press, 2009), 19.
187. Père Huc, Jan. 1857 note to the emperor, quoted in Hodgkin, *Vietnam*, 124.
188. Honey, "Historical Background," 20.
189. Archives Nationales d'Outre-Mer (ANOM), Aix-en-Provence, Gouvernement Général de l'Indochine (GGI) 13015, consul Kergaradec to Governor of Cochinchina, Hanoi, Sept. 1, 1879, 3–4.
190. Nguyễn Thế Anh, *Kinh tế và Xã hội Việt Nam dưới các vua triều Nguyễn* (Saigon: Lửa Thiêng, 1971), 127–28, cited in Nguyễn Điền, "Vietnamese Response to French Conquest," 5–6.
191. Translated in Nguyễn Điền, "Vietnamese Response to French Conquest," 5.
192. Trương-Vĩnh-Ký, *Voyage to Tonking*, 115, 4.
193. Martin J. Murray, *The Development of Capitalism in Colonial Indochina, 1870–1940* (Berkeley: University of California Press, 1980), 54, 58.

CHAPTER 8

1. For use of the term "barbarians," see Nguyễn Đình Chiểu (1822–1888), "Elegy for Those Who Fought Righteously at Can Giuoc (1861)," in Trương Bửu Lâm, *Patterns of Vietnamese Response to Foreign Intervention: 1858–1900* (New Haven, CT: Yale Southeast Asia Studies, 1967), 68, 70, and Anonymous, "An Appeal to Resist the French (1864)," in Lâm, *Patterns*, 79.
2. Mike Davis, *Late Victorian Holocausts: El Niño Famines and the Making of the Third World* (London: Verso, 2001), 273.
3. For the dendrochronological evidence from southern Việt Nam, see Brendan Buckley et al., "Climate as a Contributing Factor in the Demise of Angkor, Cambodia," *Proceedings of the National Academy of Sciences* 107, no. 15 (2010): 6748–52, available online at http://www.pnas.org/content/107/15/6748.full .pdf+html, supplemental online material, fig. S1, table S2 at http://www.pnas.org/ content/early/2010/03/22/0910827107/suppl/DCSupplemental. For evidence

from northern Việt Nam, see Masaki Sano, Brendan M. Buckley, and Tatsuo Sweda, "Tree-Ring Based Hydroclimate Reconstruction over Northern Vietnam from *Fokienia hodginsii*: Eighteenth Century Mega-drought and Tropical Pacific Influence," *Climate Dynamics* 33 (2009): 331, 337.

4. Davis, *Late Victorian Holocausts*, 273, 271 (table 8.8), 7 (table P1), 25ff., 119.
5. Trần Tế Xương, "Drought," in *The Heritage of Vietnamese Poetry*, ed. Huỳnh Sanh Thông (New Haven, CT: Yale University Press, 1979), 210, 272, 288. For a different translation, see Huỳnh Sanh Thông, "Live by Water, Die for Water (*Sống vì nước, chết vì nước*): Metaphors of Vietnamese Culture and History," *Vietnam Review* 1 (1996): 151.
6. Jean Chesneaux, *The Vietnamese Nation: Contribution to a History*, trans. Malcolm Salmon (Sydney: Current Books, 1966), 77.
7. Martin J. Murray, *The Development of Capitalism in Colonial Indochina, 1870–1940* (Berkeley: University of California Press, 1980), 418, 422.
8. Bonard to the Minister of the Colonies, Saigon, Aug. 16, 1862, and La Grandière to Minister of the Colonies, Saigon, Sept. 29, 1864, both quoted in Milton E. Osborne, *The French Presence in Cochinchina and Cambodia: Rule and Response, 1859–1905* (Ithaca, NY: Cornell University Press, 1969), 38, 99.
9. Pierre Brocheux and Daniel Hémery, *Indochina: An Ambiguous Colonization, 1858–1954* (Berkeley: University of California Press, 2009), 56.
10. Nguyen Thanh Nha, *Tableau économique du Vietnam aux XVIIe et XVIIIe siècles* (Paris: Cujas, 1970), 44, cited in Murray, *Development of Capitalism*, 610n212 (cf. 418, table 8.2).
11. Chesneaux, *Vietnamese Nation*, 81; Brocheux and Hémery, *Indochina*, 253–54.
12. C. Michele Thompson, "A Pox on Tự Đức: The Social and Political Effects of Smallpox on the House of Nguyễn," Yale Southeast Asia Council seminar, Feb. 20, 2013.
13. Lâm, *Patterns*, 19, 42n81.
14. David G. Marr, *Vietnamese Anticolonialism, 1885–1925* (Berkeley: University of California Press, 1971), 52–53.
15. David G. Marr, *Vietnamese Tradition on Trial, 1920–1945* (Berkeley: University of California Press, 1981), 33–34.
16. P. J. B. Trương-Vĩnh-Ký, *Voyage to Tonking in the Year Ất-Hợi*, ed. P. J. Honey (London: School of Oriental and African Studies, 1982), 62n14.
17. Nguyễn Điền, "Vietnamese Response to French Conquest, 1858–1885" (honors thesis, Australian National University, 1971), 19.
18. Nguyễn Điền, "Vietnamese Response," 39–40.
19. Quoted in Osborne, *French Presence*, 65–66.
20. Lorraine Marion Paterson, "Tenacious Texts: Vietnam, China, and Radical Cultural Intersections, 1890-1930" (PhD diss., Yale University, 2006), 31, 36; Nguyễn Điền, "Vietnamese Response," 41–42.
21. Nguyễn Trường Tộ, "Memorial on the Great Position under Heaven" (1866), in Lâm, *Patterns*, 90–91.
22. "An Appeal to Resist the French (1864)," in Lâm, *Patterns*, 78.
23. Quoted in Paul Mus, *Viêt Nam: Sociologie d'une guerre* (Paris: Seuil, 1952), 224, citing Contre-Amiral Reveillère, "Nationalisme Annamite," *Revue Indochinoise*, June 9, 1902; also Jean Chesneaux, "Stages in the Development of the Vietnam National Movement, 1862–1940," *Past and Present* 7 (1955): 65.
24. Nguyễn Điền, "Vietnamese Response," 39–41; Lâm, *Patterns*, 18.
25. Nguyễn Điền, "Vietnamese Response," 20, 10, 21; Lâm, *Patterns*, 89.

26. Hoàng Diệu, "Farewell Apologies to the King," in Lâm, *Patterns*, 109–15.
27. Lâm, *Patterns*, 39n46, 81.
28. Tôn Thọ Tường and Phan Văn Trị, "Collaboration vs. Resistance (ca. 1866)," in Lâm, *Patterns*, 81–86.
29. Phan Thanh Giản and Trương Công Định, "After the Peace Treaty (1863)," in Lâm, *Patterns*, 74.
30. Nguyễn Điền, "Vietnamese Response," 7.
31. Nguyễn Đình Chiểu, "Elegy for Those Who Fought Righteously," in Lâm, *Patterns*, 68–69, 71–72.
32. Lâm, *Patterns*, 67.
33. Nguyễn Điền, "Vietnamese Response," 32–33.
34. Nguyễn Điền, "Vietnamese Response," 33–34, 7–8, 14; Lâm, *Patterns*, 38n40.
35. Nguyễn Điền, "Vietnamese Response," 19, 26, 40, 42; Lâm, *Patterns*, 18.
36. Nguyễn Trường Tộ, "Memorial on Eight Reforms Urgently Needed" (1868), in Lâm, *Patterns*, 94, 99; Paterson, "Tenacious Texts," 33.
37. Nguyễn Trường Tộ, "Memorial on Eight Reforms," 92–93, 97; Paterson, "Tenacious Texts," 33, 28–30, 36.
38. Nguyễn Trường Tộ, "Memorial on Eight Reforms," 93, 101, 94.
39. Brocheux and Hémery, *Indochina*, 21–22, 30ff.; Milton E. Osborne, *River Road to China: the Mekong River Expedition 1866–1873* (New York: Liveright, 1975); Murray, *Development*, 54–55.
40. Archives Nationales d'Outre-Mer (henceforth ANOM), Aix-en-Provence, Indochine, Gouvernement-Général de l'Indochine (GGI) 12990, consul Kergaradec to Governor of Cochinchina, Hanoi, Jan. 5, 1876, esp. 1–2, 3–5, 7–9; Brocheux and Hémery, *Indochina*, 32.
41. Brocheux and Hémery, *Indochina*, 28–29; P. J. Honey, "The Historical Background," in Trương-Vĩnh-Ký, *Voyage*, 22.
42. Nguyễn Điền, "Vietnamese Response," 34–35, citing French officer Harmand, from Hanoi, January 15, 1874, and Philastre to Dupré, from Hanoi, January 4, 1874.
43. P. Trương-Vĩnh-Ký, "Rapport à l'Amiral" (April 28, 1876), in *Voyage*, 123; Honey, "Historical Background," 24.
44. Nguyễn Điền, "Vietnamese Response," 35, 38n25; Honey, "Historical Background," 23; Brocheux and Hémery, *Indochina*, 29.
45. Nguyễn Điền, "Vietnamese Response," 35; Chesneaux, *Vietnamese Nation*, 86; Honey, "Historical Background," 25, 23–24; P. Trương-Vĩnh-Ký, "Rapport à l'Amiral," in *Voyage*, 124.
46. Brocheux and Hémery, *Indochina*, 29, 43; Honey, "Historical Background," 25.
47. P. Trương-Vĩnh-Ký, "Rapport à l'Amiral," in *Voyage*, 123.
48. P. Trương-Vĩnh-Ký, "Rapport à l'Amiral," in *Voyage*, 123–25.
49. ANOM, GGI 12990, "Rapports du consul de France à Hanoi," Kergaradec to Gov. Cochinchina, Hanoi, Jan. 5, 1876, 10, 11.
50. Honey, "Trương-vĩnh-Ký," in *Voyage*, 6–7, 12, 14–18.
51. Honey, "Trương-vĩnh-Ký," 7–8; Osborne, *French Presence*, 96.
52. Honey, "Trương-vĩnh-Ký," 8–9, 14; Osborne, *French Presence*, 93.
53. Philippe M. F. Peycam, *The Birth of Vietnamese Political Journalism: Saigon 1916–1930* (New York: Columbia University Press, 2012), 50–51; Brocheux and Hémery, *Indochina*, 73.
54. Lâm, *Patterns*, 40n59; Honey, "Trương-vĩnh-Ký," 12, 14–16; Peycam, *Birth*, 237n57.

55. Peycam, *Birth*, 238n61, 52; Lê Thành Khôi, *Histoire et anthologie de la littérature vietnamienne des origines à nos jours* (Paris: Indes Savantes, 2008), 441.
56. Osborne, *French Presence*, 98.
57. P. J. Honey, introduction to Trương-Vĩnh-Ký, *Voyage*, 1.
58. Trương-Vĩnh-Ký, *Voyage*, 61, 63, 79–80, 102–103, 107, 110, and map, 126–27; 107, 110.
59. Trương-Vĩnh-Ký, *Voyage*, 79–80, 86n83; Alexandre de Rhodes, *Histoire du royaume de Tunquin* (Lyon, 1651).
60. Trương-Vĩnh-Ký, *Voyage*, 86–87.
61. Trương-Vĩnh-Ký, *Voyage*, 91.
62. Trương-Vĩnh-Ký, *Voyage*, 113.
63. Trương-Vĩnh-Ký, *Voyage*, 61–63.
64. Trương-Vĩnh-Ký, *Voyage*, 64; ANOM, GGI 13015, Kergaradec to Gov. Cochinchina, Hanoi, April 30, 1880, 2; GGI 12990, Kergaradec to Gov. Cochinchina, Hanoi, Jan. 5, 1876, 4.
65. Trương-Vĩnh-Ký, *Voyage*, 65–66, 75–76.
66. Trương-Vĩnh-Ký, *Voyage*, 77–78, 73–74.
67. Trương-Vĩnh-Ký, *Voyage*, 87, 89, 90, 97.
68. Honey, introduction to Trương Vĩnh Ký, *Voyage*, 1–2, 4; Trương Vĩnh Ký, *Voyage*, 85, 92–94.
69. ANOM, GGI 12990, Kergaradec to Gov. Cochinchina, Hanoi, Jan. 5, 1876, 11. M. Ganis (?) had apparently accompanied Kergaradec upriver and ten years later became the first résident at Sơn Tây. He recalled this journey: "I am, after the missionaries, the first European who has penetrated into the Clear River. (We know M. Dupuis has sailed only on the Red River.) Toward the end of 1875 I did about ten miles of it in a gunboat. The country was peaceful and well populated." ANOM, Indochine, Fonds de la Résidence Supérieure du Tonkin, Nouveaux Fonds (RSTNF), 7005, Résident à Sơn Tây, "Rapport commercial, Industriel et agricole, mois de septembre 1886," Sept. 30, 1886, 18.
70. ANOM, GGI 12990, Kergaradec to Gov. Cochinchina, Hanoi, Jan. 5, 1876, 6–7.
71. Trương Vĩnh Ký, *Voyage*, 92, 99–100, 123.
72. ANOM, GGI 13064, "Rapports du consul de France à Qui Nhơn," Nov. 5–Dec. 15, 1876, to Gov. Cochinchina, Thị Nại, Nov. 5, 1876, 4, 6–7.
73. ANOM, Indochine, GGI 13114, Royaume d'Annam, Consulat de Quinhon, "Rapport sur le poste de Qui-Nhon," June 10, 1883, 15, 16.
74. Buckley et al., "Climate as a Contributing Factor," table S2.
75. ANOM, GGI 13015, Kergaradec to Gov. Cochinchina, Hanoi, Sept. 1, 1879, 2–3; April 30, 1880.
76. ANOM, GGI 13041, Kergaradec to Gov. Cochinchina, Hanoi, Sept. 3, 1880; Huỳnh, Gouverneur-général de Hanoi et Ninh Bình, to Kergaradec, "Tự Đức, 33e année, 7e mois, 27e jour."
77. ANOM, Indochine, Résidence Supérieure de Tonkin (RST), Nouveaux Fonds (NF), 7005, M. Ganis (?), Résident de Sơn Tây, Oct. 1886, "Rapport commercial industriel et agricole (mois d'octobre 1886)," 3.
78. ANOM, GGI 13059, "Rapports du consul de France à Hanoi," April 15–Dec. 31, 1882, Kergaradec to Gov. Cochinchina, Hanoi, April 16, 1882, 2, 3.
79. Marr, *Vietnamese Anticolonialism*, 41.
80. ANOM, GGI 13059, Kergaradec to Gov. Cochinchina, Hanoi, April 26, 1882, 1, 3.
81. Brocheux and Hémery, *Indochina*, 42–64; Charles Fourniau, *Annam-Tonkin 1885–1896: Lettrés et paysans vietnamiens face à la conquête coloniale* (Paris: L'Harmattan, 1989).

82. Brocheux and Hémery, *Indochina*, 43; ANOM, GGI 12697, "Rapports du chargé d'affaires à Huế," Jan. 15–April 4, 1883, Rivière to Rheinart, March 19, 1883, 1–3.
83. ANOM, GGI 12697, "Rapports du chargé d'affaires à Huế," Jan. 15–April 4, 1883, Rheinart to Gov. Cochinchina, April 4, 1883, 1.
84. ANOM, GGI 12697, "Rapports du chargé d'affaires à Huế," Jan. 15–April 4, 1883, Rheinart to Gov. of Cochinchina, April 4, 1883, 1, 4, 8.
85. Brocheux and Hémery, *Indochina*, 44.
86. ANOM, GGI 13114, Royaume d'Annam, Consulat de Quinhon, "Rapport sur le poste de Qui-Nhon," June 10, 1883, 9, 15, 16.
87. ANOM, GGI 12979, Protectorat de l'Annam et du Tonkin, "Rapports du Résident de France à Huế," Résident Luc Hampreaux (?) to Gov. Cochinchina, "Situation politique en Annam," Huế, Jan. 7, 1884, 1, 3–4.
88. Brocheux and Hémery, *Indochina*, 45.
89. Chesneaux, *Vietnamese Nation*, 88; Brocheux and Hémery, *Indochina*, 43, 44, 47, 49; Marr, *Vietnamese Anticolonialism*, 49–51.
90. Brocheux and Hémery, *Indochina*, 52; Fourniau, *Annam-Tonkin*, 49–54.
91. ANOM, GGI 13114, "Rapport sur le poste de Qui-Nhon," June 10, 1883, 2–5, 6–7, 14.
92. Phan Khoang, *Việt Nam Pháp thuộc sử* (Saigon: Khai-trí, 1961), 363, cited in Nguyễn Điền, "Vietnamese Response," 36; Fourniau, *Annam-Tonkin*, 47, 52.
93. ANOM, GGI 11926, "Soulèvements du Phú Yên et du Bình Định," 1886, Résident Général, Hanoi, to Gov. Cochinchina, télégramme officiel, Jan. 2, 1887, 2; Jan. 3, 1887, Phúyên No. 6, 2.
94. ANOM, GGI 11926, Trần Bá Lộc to director of Interior, Nov. 22, 1886, 1, 2.
95. Fourniau, *Annam-Tonkin*, 68; ANOM, GGI 11926, " Notes sur l'expédition proposée by le Phu Loc pour la soumission du Phu Yen et du Binh Dinh," Nov. 3, 1886, 6pp, and Trần Bá Lộc to director of Interior, Nov. 6, 1886, 1.
96. Fourniau, *Annam-Tonkin*, 65–67; Osborne, *French Presence*, 138, 137.
97. ANOM, GGI 11926, Trần Bá Lộc to director of Interior, Nov. 22, 1886.
98. ANOM, GGI 11926, Trần Bá Lộc to director of Interior, Nov. 6, 1886, 2.
99. ANOM, GGI 11926, Résident Général, Hanoi, to Gov. Cochinchina, Dec. 5, 6, 1886.
100. ANOM, GGI 11926, Résident Général, Hanoi, to Gov. Cochinchina, Dec. 5, 1886, 1–2.
101. ANOM, GGI 11926, Résident Général, Hanoi, to Gov. Cochinchina, Dec. 11, 1886, 1–2.
102. Fourniau, *Annam-Tonkin*, 62; Brocheux and Hémery, *Indochina*, 51.
103. ANOM, GGI 11929, "Soulèvements du Phú Yên et du Bình Định," April–June 1887, Résident Général, Hanoi, to Gov. Cochinchina, May 19, 1887, 5–6.
104. ANOM, GGI 11926, Résident Général, Hanoi, to Gov. Cochinchina, Dec. 18, 1886, 1.
105. ANOM, GGI 11926, Gov. Cochinchina to Résident Général, Hanoi, Dec. 18, 1886, 1–2.
106. ANOM, GGI 11926, Résident Général, Hanoi, to Gov. Cochinchina, Dec. 19, 1886, 1 p.
107. ANOM, GGI 11926, Résident Général, Hanoi, to Gov. Cochinchina, Dec. 29, 1886, 2pp.
108. ANOM, GGI 11926, Gov. Cochinchina to Résident Général, Hanoi, Dec. 29, 1886, 2pp.
109. ANOM, GGI 11926, Résident Général, Hanoi, to Gov. Cochinchina, Jan. 2, 1887, 1, 2.
110. ANOM, GGI 11926, Résident Général, Hanoi, to Gov. Cochinchina, Jan. 3, 1887, 1–3.

111. ANOM, GGI 11926, Gov. Cochinchina to Résident Général, Hanoi, Jan. 5, 1887.
112. ANOM, GGI 11926, Résident Général, Hanoi, to Gov. Cochinchina, Jan. 13, 1887, 3–4.
113. ANOM, GGI 11926, Gov. Cochinchina to Résident Général, Hanoi, Jan. 20, 1887, 1, 2.
114. ANOM, GGI 11926, Gov. Cochinchina to Résident Général, Hanoi, Jan. 20, 1887, 1–2; Jan. 24, 1887, 1–2.
115. ANOM, GGI 11926, Résident Général, Haiphong, to Gov. Cochinchina, Jan. 25, 1887.
116. ANOM, GGI 11926, Résident Général, Haiphong, to Gov. Cochinchina, Jan. 26, 1887, 1–2.
117. Fourniau, *Annam-Tonkin*, 68–69.
118. Fourniau, *Annam-Tonkin*, 69–70; ANOM, GGI 11929, Résident Général, Hanoi, to Gov. Cochinchina, May 19, 1887, 4–5.
119. ANOM, GGI 11929, "Soulèvements du Phú Yên et du Bình Định," April–June 1887, Résident Phú Yên to Gov. Cochinchina, April 2, 1887.
120. ANOM, GGI 11929, Résident Général, Hanoi, to Gov. Cochinchina, May 19, 1887, 5.
121. ANOM, GGI 11929, Trần Bá Lộc, "Récapitulation Générale des Soumissions des Chefs rebelles," April 14, 1887.
122. ANOM, GGI 11929, Gov. Cochinchina to Résident Général, Hanoi, April 23, 1887.
123. ANOM, GGI 11929, Bình Định resident to Gov. Cochinchina, June 21, 1887, 3.
124. Fourniau, *Annam-Tonkin*, 70.
125. ANOM, GGI 11929, "Liste des chefs rebelles de la province Binh Dinh condamnés à mort par les autorités provinciales, exécutés," Vũng Lắm (Phú Yên), June 11, 1887 (seventeen named, including Mai Xuân Thưởng); "Liste des chefs rebelles des provinces du Bình Định et du Phú Yên, condamnés à mort par les autorités provinciales et exécutés les 12 et 13 juin 1887" (ten named), dated June 20, 1887.
126. ANOM, GGI 11929, Bình Định resident to Gov. Cochinchina, June 21, 1887, 1; Gov. Cochinchina to Résident Général, Hanoi, June 25, 1887.
127. Fourniau, *Annam-Tonkin*, 71.
128. ANOM, GGI 11929, Trần Bá Lộc report dated June 9, 1887, 2.
129. George Dutton, *The Tây Sơn Uprising: Society and Rebellion in Eighteenth-Century Vietnam* (Honolulu: University of Hawai'i Press, 2006), 93.
130. Fourniau, *Annam-Tonkin*, 65–67.
131. ANOM, GGI 11929, Bình Định resident to Gov. Cochinchina, June 21, 1887, 3–4.
132. Osborne, *French Presence*, 138.
133. Fourniau, *Annam-Tonkin*, passim; Marr, *Vietnamese Anticolonialism*, ch. 3; Brocheux and Hémery, *Indochina*, 50, 44; Marr, *Vietnamese Anticolonialism*, 46.
134. ANOM, RST NF, 7005, Ganis, Résident de Sơn Tây, Oct. 1886, "Rapport commercial industriel et agricole," 3–4; Brocheux and Hémery, *Indochina*, 253–54.
135. Brocheux and Hémery, *Indochina*, 56–57, 52.
136. ANOM, GGI 11929, Trần Bá Lộc's report dated June 9, 1887, 3.
137. Nola Cooke, "The Myth of the Restoration: Dang-Trong Influences in the Spiritual Life of the Early Nguyen Dynasty (1802–47)," in *The Last Stand of Asian Autonomies*, ed. Anthony Reid (New York: St. Martin's, 1997), 290.
138. Brocheux and Hémery, *Indochina*, 49, 52; ANOM, GGI, N 5979, A. Debay, "Étude sur les Régions centrales du Massif Annamitique," March 1899, map indicating "Région actuellement insoumise."

139. Vinh Sinh, introduction to *Overturned Chariot: The Autobiography of Phan-Bội-Châu*, trans. Vinh Sinh and Nicholas Wickenden (Honolulu: University of Hawai'i Press, 1999), 4.
140. Marr, *Vietnamese Anticolonialism*, 53, 63, 67; Lâm, *Patterns*, 27, 125.
141. ANOM, GGI 12990, "Rapports du consul de France à Hanoi," Kergaradec to Gov. Cochinchina, Hanoi, Jan. 5, 1876, 10, 11.
142. ANOM, GGI 11926, "Soulèvements du Phú Yên et du Bình Định," 1886, Paulin Vial, Résident Général, Hanoi, to Gov. Cochinchina, Dec. 5, 1886, 3.
143. ANOM, GGI 11926, Résident Général, Hanoi, to Gov. Cochinchina, Jan. 3, 1887, Phúyên No. 6, suite, 3.
144. ANOM, GGI 11926, Résident Général, Hanoi, to Gov. Cochinchina, Dec. 5, 1886, 3.
145. ANOM, GGI 11926, Résident Général, Hanoi, to Gov. Cochinchina, Jan. 3, 1887, Phúyên No. 6, suite, 4; Jan. 13, 1887, 4.
146. ANOM, GGI 11928, "Expédition du Phu Yen et du Binh Dinh," mars 1887, Résident of Phú Yên to Gov. Cochinchina, March 18, 1887, 2–3.
147. ANOM, Résidence supérieure en Annam (RSA), D4, 4279, "Voyage d'études économiques en Annam . . .," M. Dauplay to Résident supérieur à Vientiane, from Saravane, Laos, March 17, 1914, 2.
148. Osborne, *French Presence*, 76–83, 147, 86; Murray, *Development*, 424–26; Brocheux and Hémery, *Indochina*, 73.
149. Murray, *Development*, 423, 58–59.
150. Pierre Brocheux, *The Mekong Delta: Ecology, Economy, and Revolution, 1860–1960* (Madison: Center for Southeast Asian Studies, University of Wisconsin-Madison, 1995), 17–22, 25.
151. For proportions of ethnic Khmers in Cochinchina's provinces, see *Cambodge* (Phnom Penh, 1961), 50, map reprinted in Ben Kiernan, *How Pol Pot Came to Power: Colonialism, Nationalism and Communism in Cambodia, 1930–1975*, 2nd ed. (New Haven, CT: Yale University Press, 2004), xiv.
152. Murray, *Development*, 427; Brocheux, *Mekong Delta*, 25.
153. Jean Delvert, *Le paysan cambodgien* (The Hague: Mouton, 1962), 185, 636–37.
154. Murray, *Development*, 417–18, 449.
155. Buckley, "Climate," table S2.
156. Osborne, *French Presence*, 138; Murray, *Development*, 421, 429.
157. Ngo Vinh Long, *Before the Revolution: The Vietnamese Peasants under the French* (Cambridge, MA: MIT Press, 1973), 15; Murray, *Development*, 411, 422; Yves Henry, *L'Economie agricole de l'Indochine* (Hanoi: Imprimerie d'Extrême-orient, 1932), 43–44, cited in James C. Scott, *The Moral Economy of the Peasant: Rebellion and Subsistence in Southeast Asia* (New Haven, CT: Yale University Press, 1976), 43.
158. Murray, *Development*, 396–97, 421, 429.
159. RST (NF) M04695, "Formation des lais de mer et leur transformation en rizières cultivables (Ninh-Binh)," J. B. Tòng (Nguyễn Bá Tòng), Phát Diệm, to Resident Superior of Tonkin, Yves Chatel, Aug. 1, 1937, 2; Charles Keith, *Catholic Vietnam: A Church from Empire to Nation* (Berkeley: University of California Press, 2012), 51–52.
160. Ngo, *Before the Revolution*, 14, 28; Murray, *Development*, 423.
161. Ngo, *Before the Revolution*, 31; Philippe Papin, *Histoire de Hanoi* (Paris: Fayard, 2004), 251, 253, 256.
162. Peycam, *Birth*, 30.
163. Peycam, *Birth*, 19.
164. Nguyễn Phạm Điền, "Culture and Politics in Vietnam, 1920–1945" (draft PhD thesis submitted to the Australian National University, 1979), 22; Peycam,

Birth, 20; John C. Schafer and Thế Uyên, "The Novel Emerges in Cochinchina," *Journal of Asian Studies* 52, no. 4 (1993): 854–84.

165. Paterson, "Tenacious Texts," 36–37.
166. See, e.g., Phan Châu Trinh, "A New Vietnam Following the Franco-Vietnamese Alliance," in *Phan Châu Trinh and His Political Writings*, ed. and trans. Vinh Sinh (Ithaca, NY: Cornell Southeast Asia Program, 2009), 64, 75, 85 (also "Introduction," 41); Marr, *Vietnamese Anticolonialism*, 121.
167. Marr, *Vietnamese Anticolonialism*, 99, 157; Paterson, "Tenacious Texts," 40–43.
168. Claude Gendre, *Le Dê Thám (1846–1913): Un résistant vietnamien à la colonisation française* (Paris: L'Harmattan, 2009).
169. Phan Bội Châu, *Overturned Chariot*, 47, 51–52.
170. Phan Bội Châu, *Overturned Chariot*, 58; Vinh Sinh, ed., *Phan Bội Châu and the Đông-Du Movement* (New Haven, CT: Yale Council on Southeast Asia Studies, 1988), 58.
171. Phan Bội Châu, *Overturned Chariot*, 59, 61; Vinh Sinh, introduction to Phan Bội Châu, *Overturned Chariot*, 7, and *Phan Bội Châu and the Đông-Du Movement*, 52, 23.
172. Marr, *Vietnamese Anticolonialism*, 87; Vinh Sinh, introduction to *Phan Châu Trinh*, 10.
173. Vinh, *Phan Châu Trinh*, xiii.
174. Marr, *Vietnamese Anticolonialism*, 87; Vinh, introduction to *Phan Châu Trinh*, 45–47.
175. Vinh, introduction to *Phan Châu Trinh*, 15n42, and Phan Châu Trinh, "A New Vietnam Following the Franco-Vietnamese Alliance," in Vinh, *Phan Châu Trinh*, 70, 79–80, 60–61; Marr, *Vietnamese Anticolonialism*, 99.
176. Phan Châu Trinh, "A New Vietnam," in Vinh, *Phan Châu Trinh*, 80.
177. Phan Châu Trinh, "A New Vietnam," 77, 75, 70–71, 76, 77; Phan Bội Châu, *Overturned Chariot*, 76, 66, 75; Marr, *Vietnamese Anticolonialism*, 88.
178. Phan Bội Châu, *Overturned Chariot*, 60, 62–65, 70, 76, 78, 80; cf. Keith, *Catholic Vietnam*, 1–2, 143.
179. Phan Bội Châu, *Overturned Chariot*, 71; Vinh, introduction to Phan Bội Châu, *Overturned Chariot*, 33, and *Phan Châu Trinh*, 57n1.
180. Phan Châu Trinh, "A New Vietnam," 57, 68, 78.
181. Vinh, introduction to *Phan Châu Trinh*, 14–16.
182. Marr, *Vietnamese Anticolonialism*, 173.
183. Phan Bội Châu, *Overturned Chariot*, 74; Phan Châu Trinh, "A New Vietnam," 77.
184. Phan Bội Châu, *Overturned Chariot*, 13, 79, 84–91; Vinh, *Phan Bội Châu and the Đông-Du Movement*, 88.
185. Phan Bội Châu, *The History of the Loss of the Country* (1905), excerpted in *Sources of Vietnamese Tradition*, ed. George E. Dutton, Jayne S. Werner, and John K. Whitmore (New York: Columbia University Press, 2012), 344.
186. Marr, *Vietnamese Anticolonialism*, 152; Vinh, introduction to *Phan Châu Trinh*, 54, and introduction to Phan Bội Châu, *Overturned Chariot*, 32; Shiraishi Masaya, "Phan Bội Châu in Japan," in Vinh, *Phan Bội Châu and the Đông-Du Movement*, 56.
187. Phan Bội Châu, *Overturned Chariot*, 105, 108; Marr, *Vietnamese Anticolonialism*, 128.
188. Vinh, introduction to *Phan Châu Trinh*, 54; Phan Châu Trinh, "A New Vietnam," 75.
189. Phan Châu Trinh, "A New Vietnam," 62, 78.
190. Phan Bội Châu, *Overturned Chariot*, 109, 126; Phan Châu Trinh, "A New Vietnam," 77.
191. Vinh, introduction to *Phan Châu Trinh*, 38–39.

192. Phan Bội Châu, *Overturned Chariot*, 66, 75, 104–109; Phan Châu Trinh, "A New Vietnam," 71–78, 83–84.
193. Phan Bội Châu, *Overturned Chariot*, 140–41; Marr, *Vietnamese Anticolonialism*, 134, 140, 142, 146–55.
194. Vinh, *Phan Bội Châu and the Đông-Du Movement*, 23, and introduction to *Phan Châu Trinh*, 16n50.
195. Trần Mỹ-Vân, *A Vietnamese Royal Exile in Japan: Prince Cường Để, 1882–1951*, (London: Routledge, 2005).
196. See, e.g., Phan Châu Trinh, "Letter to Emperor Khải Định," in Vinh, *Phan Châu Trinh*, 88–89; "Morality and Ethics in the Orient and the Occident," in Vinh, *Phan Châu Trinh*, 107, 117; and "Monarchy or Democracy," in Vinh, *Phan Châu Trinh*, 129–30.
197. Marr, *Vietnamese Anticolonialism*, 169; John K. Whitmore, "Literati Culture and Integration in Dai Viet, c. 1430–c. 1840," *Modern Asian Studies* 31, no. 3 (1997): 669, 671, 673.
198. Marr, *Vietnamese Anticolonialism*, 170; a version written by Phan Khôi is reproduced in Vinh, introduction to *Phan Châu Trinh*, 21–22.
199. Vinh Sinh, introduction to *Phan Châu Trinh*, 20; Phan Châu Trinh, "A New Vietnam," 79, 77, 81.
200. Phan Chu [Châu] Trinh, *A Complete Account of the Peasants' Uprising in the Central Region*, trans. Peter Baugher and Vu Ngu Chieu (Madison: Center for Southeast Asian Studies, University of Wisconsin-Madison, 1983); Marr, *Vietnamese Anticolonialism*, 180–81, 187–93.
201. Marr, *Vietnamese Anticolonialism*, 187, 190–92.
202. Vinh, "Introduction," *Phan Châu Trinh*, 11n31, 26, 25n80; Marr, *Vietnamese Anticolonialism*, 192.
203. Keith, *Catholic Vietnam*, 1–2.
204. Phan Châu Trinh, "A New Vietnam," 72–74, and "Letter to Emperor Khải Định," 87.
205. Phan Châu Trinh, "A New Vietnam," 79.
206. Vinh, introduction to *Phan Châu Trinh*, 24–26; Phan Châu Trinh, "A New Vietnam," 81, 63.
207. Vinh, introduction to *Phan Châu Trinh*, 26–32.
208. Vinh, introduction to *Phan Châu Trinh*, 27, 33–37, 11n31.
209. Phan Châu Trinh, "A New Vietnam," 72, 78; Phan Bội Châu, *Overturned Chariot*, 45.
210. Baugher, introduction to Phan Chu Trinh, *Complete Account of the Peasants' Uprising*, 8.
211. Peycam, *Birth*, 62, 65–66, 240–41, 112; Marr, *Vietnamese Tradition on Trial*, 204–6.
212. Peycam, *Birth*, 80–83.
213. Phan Bội Châu, *Overturned Chariot*, 24, 54n17; Marr, *Vietnamese Anticolonialism*, 209.
214. Vinh Sinh and Nicholas Wickenden, introduction to Phan Bội Châu, *Overturned Chariot*, 4; William J. Duiker, *Ho Chi Minh* (New York: Theia, 2000), 25; Vinh, *Phan Châu Trinh*, 27n83.
215. "Note de la Sûreté d'Annam, 8 mars 1911," document 3 in Daniel Hémery, "Jeunesse d'un colonisé, genèse d'un exil, Ho Chi Minh jusqu'en 1911," *Approches Asie* 11 (1992): 128.
216. Jean Lacouture, *Ho Chi Minh* (Harmondsworth, UK: Penguin, 1968), 17; Duiker, *Ho Chi Minh*, 589n15.

217. Duiker, *Ho Chi Minh*, 50–54; Vinh Sinh, *Phan Châu Trinh*, 29.
218. Marr, *Vietnamese Tradition*, 5; Lacouture, *Ho Chi Minh*, 35.
219. Pierre Brocheux, *Ho Chi Minh: A Biography*, trans. Claire Duiker (Cambridge, UK: Cambridge University Press, 2007), 10–14; Vinh, *Phan Châu Trinh*, 34–35; Sophie Quinn-Judge, *Ho Chi Minh: The Missing Years* (Berkeley: University of California Press, 2002), 16–18, 27–28; Lacouture, *Ho Chi Minh*, 23–29.
220. Phan Châu Trinh, "Letter to Emperor Khải Định," in *Phan Châu Trinh*, 87.
221. Vinh, *Phan Châu Trinh*, ix.
222. Phan Châu Trinh, "Monarchy and Democracy" and "Morality and Ethics in the Orient and the Occident," in Vinh, *Phan Châu Trinh*, 133–36, 106, 110, 113–16.
223. Phan Châu Trinh, "Morality and Ethics in the Orient and the Occident," 115–16, and "Monarchy and Democracy," 125; Vinh, introduction to *Phan Châu Trinh*. 16.

CHAPTER 9

1. Phan Châu Trinh, "Monarchy and Democracy," in *Phan Châu Trinh and His Political Writings*, ed. and trans. Vinh Sinh (Ithaca, NY: Cornell Southeast Asia Program, 2009), 125–39, at 137; Vinh Sinh, introduction to *Phan Châu Trinh*, 55.
2. R. B. Smith, "The Vietnamese Élite of French Cochinchina, 1943," *Modern Asian Studies* 6, no. 4 (1972): 261; David G. Marr, *Vietnam 1945: The Quest for Power* (Berkeley: University of California Press, 1995), 75.
3. David G. Marr, *Vietnamese Tradition on Trial 1920–1945* (Berkeley: University of California Press, 1981), 33; Daniel Hémery, *Révolutionnaires vietnamiens et pouvoir colonial en Indochine: Communistes, trotskystes, nationalistes à Saigon de 1932 à 1937* (Paris: Maspero, 1975), 258.
4. Huỳnh Sanh Thông, "Main Trends of Vietnamese Literature between the Two World Wars," *Vietnam Forum* 3 (Winter-Spring 1984): 3.
5. Huỳnh Kim Khánh, *Vietnamese Communism, 1925–1945* (Ithaca, NY: Cornell University Press, 1982), 36n4; Alexander B. Woodside, *Community and Revolution in Modern Vietnam* (Boston, Houghton Mifflin, 80).
6. Pierre Brocheux and Daniel Hémery, *Indochina: An Ambiguous Colonization, 1858–1954* (Berkeley: University of California Press, 2009), 245.
7. Brocheux and Hémery, *Indochina*, 115.
8. Brendan Buckley et al., "Climate as a Contributing Factor in the Demise of Angkor, Cambodia," *Proceedings of the National Academy of Sciences* 107, no. 15 (2010): 6748–52, available online at http://www.pnas.org/content/107/15/6748.full .pdf+html, supplemental online material, table S2 at http://www.pnas.org/content/early/2010/03/22/0910827107/suppl/DCSupplemental.
9. Peter Zinoman, introduction to Vũ Trọng Phụng, *Dumb Luck*, trans. Nguyễn Nguyệt Cầm and Peter Zinoman (Ann Arbor: University of Michigan Press, 2002), 8.
10. Nguyễn Phạm Điền, "Culture and Politics in Vietnam, 1920–1945" (PhD thesis submitted to the Australian National University, 1979), 22, 46.
11. Philippe M. F. Peycam, *The Birth of Vietnamese Political Journalism: Saigon 1916–1930* (New York: Columbia University Press, 2012), 20; Điền, "Culture and Politics," 21–24, 46.
12. Marr, *Tradition*, 206, 33–44; see Brocheux and Hémery, *Indochina*, 399–400; Zinoman, introduction to Vũ Trọng Phụng, *Dumb Luck*, 8.
13. Marr, *Vietnam 1945*, 75.
14. C. Michele Thompson, *Vietnamese Traditional Medicine: A Social History* (Singapore: NUS Press, 2015), 125.

15. Marr, *Tradition*, 151.
16. Điền, "Culture and Politics," 7–10; Marr, *Tradition*, 164; Christopher E. Goscha, "'The Modern Barbarian': Nguyen Van Vinh and the Complexity of Colonial Modernity in Vietnam," *European Journal of East Asian Studies* 3, no. 1 (2004): 135–69.
17. An example of his work is Phạm Quỳnh, "*Nhân nguyệt vấn đáp*, Dialogue entre l'homme et la lune. Poème annamite traduit," *BEFEO* 11 (1911): 417–23.
18. Phạm Quỳnh, *Nam Phong* 1 (July 1917): 1–5, quoted in Điền, "Culture and Politics," 12–13.
19. Phạm Quỳnh, quoted by Alexander B. Woodside, "The Historical Background," in Nguyễn Du, *The Tale of Kieu*, trans. Huỳnh Sanh Thông (New Haven, CT: Yale University Press, 1983, xxxix.
20. Marr, *Tradition*, 69.
21. Phạm Quỳnh, *Thượng Chi văn tập* (Saigon: Bộ quốc-gia giáo-dục, 1962), 1:83, quoted in Điền, "Culture and Politics," 14.
22. Ralph Smith, *Viet-Nam and the West* (Ithaca, NY: Cornell University Press, 1968), 92–93; Peycam, *Birth*, 81, 92, 67, 248, 28.
23. Peycam, *Birth*, 91; Điền, "Culture and Politics," 101–15; Marr, *Tradition*, 307.
24. Peycam, *Birth*, 236.
25. Khánh, *Vietnamese Communism*, 51, 37; Duiker, *Rise*, 148; Peycam, *Birth*, 186–90.
26. Peycam, *Birth*, 196–97, 200–202, 272n188.
27. Vinh, introduction to *Phan Châu Trinh*, 11–12n31; Marr, *Tradition*, 48n67.
28. Shawn F. McHale, *Print and Power: Confucianism, Communism, and Buddhism in the Making of Modern Vietnam* (Honolulu: University of Hawai'i Press, 2004), 18; Marr, *Tradition*, 49, 51–52.
29. Peycam, *Birth*, 15; Zinoman, introduction to Vũ Trọng Phụng, *Dumb Luck*, 7.
30. John C. Schafer and Thế Uyên, "The Novel Emerges in Cochinchina," *Journal of Asian Studies* 52, no. 4 (1993): 854–84; Neil Jamieson, *Understanding Vietnam* (Berkeley: University of California Press, 1993), 106.
31. Lê Thành Khôi, *Histoire et anthologie de la littérature vietnamienne des origines à nos jours* (Paris: Indes Savantes, 2008), 463; Philippe Papin, *Histoire de Hanoi* (Paris: Fayard, 2001), 275.
32. Zinoman, introduction to Vũ Trọng Phụng, *Dumb Luck*, 18–19; Brocheux and Hémery, *Indochina*, 246.
33. Huỳnh Sanh Thông, "Main Trends of Vietnamese Literature between the Two World Wars," 113.
34. Peter Zinoman, *Vietnamese Colonial Republican: The Political Vision of Vũ Trọng Phụng* (Berkeley: University of California Press, 2014).
35. Zinoman, introduction to Vũ Trọng Phụng, *Dumb Luck*, 8, 15–16, 11, 28n66.
36. Vũ Trọng Phụng, *The Industry of Marrying Europeans*, trans. Thúy Tranviet (Ithaca, NY: Cornell Southeast Asia Program, 2006).
37. Zinoman, introduction to Vũ Trọng Phụng, *Dumb Luck*, 6, 19–20.
38. Huỳnh Sanh Thông, "Live by Water, Die for Water (*Sống vì nước, chết vì nước*): Metaphors of Vietnamese Culture and History," *Vietnam Review* 1 (Autumn–Winter 1996): 152–53.
39. McHale, *Print*, 162, 157, 164, 160–61, 153, 220nn42–43; Marr, *Tradition*, 304n58.
40. Archives Nationales d'Outre-Mer (ANOM), Aix-en-Provence, Cambodge 7F (15)1, Direction de la Sûreté, Rapport annuel 1922–23, 4.
41. Hue-Tam Ho Tai, *Millenarianism and Peasant Politics in Vietnam* (Cambridge, MA: Harvard University Press, 1983).

42. William J. Duiker, *The Rise of Nationalism in Vietnam, 1900–1941* (Ithaca, NY: Cornell University Press, 1976), 152–53; Marr, *Tradition*, 307.
43. Bửu Tín, quoted in McHale, *Print*, 163.
44. Charles Keith, *Catholic Vietnam: A Church from Empire to Nation* (Berkeley: University of California Press, 2012), 139.
45. Keith, *Catholic Vietnam*, 140–43, 178; Peycam, *Birth*, 160, 208–11.
46. Keith, *Catholic Vietnam*, 141, 143.
47. Keith, *Catholic Vietnam*, 112, 107, 109, 169, 161, 170–71.
48. Jayne Susan Werner, *Peasant Politics and Religious Sectarianism: Peasant and Priest in the Cao Dai in Viet Nam* (New Haven, CT: Yale Southeast Asia Studies, 1981).
49. R. B. Smith, "An Introduction to Caodaism: I. Origins and Early History," *Bulletin of the School of Oriental and African Studies* 33, no. 2 (1970): 343–47.
50. Werner, *Peasant Politics*, 6–16; R. B. Smith, "An Introduction to Caodaism: II. Beliefs and Organization," *Bulletin of the School of Oriental and African Studies* 33, no. 3 (1970): 573–89.
51. Smith, "Introduction to Caodaism I," 337–39, and "Introduction to Caodaism II," 578.
52. Werner, *Peasant Politics*, 6, 14; Smith, "Introduction to Caodaism II," 574, 577.
53. Smith, "Introduction to Caodaism I," 338, 339, 348–49, and "Introduction to Caodaism II," 579.
54. Smith, "Introduction to Caodaism I," 338–40, 348–49.
55. Smith, "Introduction to Caodaism I," 340–41, and "Introduction to Caodaism II," 574.
56. Werner, *Peasant Politics*, 7.
57. Smith, "Introduction to Caodaism I," 341.
58. Khy Phanra, "Les origines du caodaisme au Cambodge, 1926–1940," *Mondes Asiatiques* 3 (1975): 315–48; Ben Kiernan, *How Pol Pot Came to Power: Colonialism, Nationalism and Communism in Cambodia, 1930–1975*, 2nd ed. (New Haven, CT: Yale University Press, 2004), 5–7.
59. *Le Khmer*, Aug. 3, 1936; Smith, "Introduction to Caodaism I," 346; Werner, *Peasant Politics*, 75n42; Pierre Bernardini, "L'implantation caodaiste au Cambodge en 1969," in *Actes du XXIXe Congrès international des Orientalistes: Asie du Sud-Est continentale* (Paris: 1976), 1:1–6.
60. Werner, *Peasant Politics*, 4, 72n1; Smith, "Introduction to Caodaism I," 342, 345.
61. Nguyễn An Ninh, *Tôn Giáo* (Saigon: Bảo-Tồn, 1932); Marr, *Tradition*, 442; Werner, *Peasant Politics*, 11, 15.
62. Werner, *Peasant Politics*, 7, 15; Brocheux and Hémery, *Indochina*, 292; Woodside, *Community*, 186.
63. Smith, "Introduction to Caodaism I," 341–42; Werner, *Peasant Politics*, 78n8.
64. Smith, "Introduction to Caodaism I," 342–46; Werner, *Peasant Politics*, 78n8, 75n46; Tai, *Millenarianism*, 87; Douglas Pike, *Viet Cong: The Organization and Techniques of the National Liberation Front of South Vietnam* (Cambridge, MA: MIT Press, 1966), 68.
65. Tai, *Millenarianism*, 95; Werner, *Peasant Politics*, 17–21, 25–31, 33.
66. Alexander Barton Woodside, *Vietnam and the Chinese Model* (Cambridge, MA, Harvard University Press, 1971), 59.
67. Werner, *Peasant Politics*, 32–33.
68. Thai Van Kiem, "Thien-Y-A-Na, or the Legend of Poh Nagar," *Asia* 4 (1954): 408.
69. Werner, *Peasant Politics*, 33–36; Gabriel Gobron, *Histoire et philosophie du Caodaïsme* (Paris: Dervy, 1949), 177.

70. David J. Steinberg, ed., *In Search of Southeast Asia: A Modern History* (Honolulu: University of Hawai'i Press, 1987), 235.
71. Smith, "Vietnamese Elite," 471–73; Martin J. Murray, *The Development of Capitalism in Colonial Indochina, 1870–1940* (Berkeley: University of California Press, 1980), 421.
72. RST (NF) M04695, "Formation des lais de mer et leur transformation en rizières cultivables (Ninh-Binh)," J. B. Tong (Nguyễn Bá Tòng), Phát Diệm, to Cresson, Résident of Ninh Bình, Nov. 1936; J. B. Tong, Phát Diệm, to Résident Supérieur of Tonkin, Yves Chatel, Aug. 1, 1937.
73. Steinberg, *In Search of Southeast Asia*, 235; Joseph Buttinger, *Vietnam: A Dragon Embattled* (New York: Praeger, 1967), 165–66.
74. Brocheux and Hémery, *Indochina*, 122, 260, table 6.2.
75. Buckley et al., "Climate as a Contributing Factor," table S2.
76. Brocheux and Hémery, *Indochina*, 255, 262, 258.
77. Werner, *Peasant Politics*, 33; Brocheux and Hémery, *Indochina*, 261. See also Pierre Brocheux, *The Mekong Delta: Ecology, Economy, and Revolution, 1860–1960* (Madison: University of Wisconsin Center for Southeast Asian Studies, 1995), chs. 2–4.
78. Brocheux and Hémery, *Indochina*, 264; Duiker, *Rise*, 191, 218.
79. Christoph Giebel, *Imagined Ancestries of Vietnamese Communism: Ton Duc Thang and the Politics of History and Memory* (Seattle: University of Washington Press, 2004), ch. 4; Peycam, *Birth*, 24–25; Murray, *Development*, 330.
80. Brocheux and Hémery, *Indochina*, 124, 127; Megan Cook, *The Constitutionalist Party of Cochinchina: The Years of Decline, 1930–1942* (Clayton, Australia: Monash Centre of Southeast Asian Studies, 1977), 49n24.
81. ANOM, Aix-en-Provence, Cambodge 3E 4(4), Rapports politiques trimestriels, April 15, 1927.
82. Brocheux and Hémery, *Indochina*, 128–30; Marr, *Tradition*, 29–30; Haydon Cherry, *Down and Out in Saigon: Stories of the Poor in a Colonial City, 1900–1940* (New Haven, CT: Yale University Press, forthcoming).
83. Tai, *Millenarianism*, 103; Cook, *Constitutionalist Party*, 46; Smith, "Vietnamese Elite," 473.
84. Nguyễn Thị Định, *No Other Road to Take: Memoir of Mrs. Nguyen Thi Dinh*, trans. Mai Elliott (Ithaca, NY: Cornell Southeast Asia Program, 1976), 25–27.
85. Marr, *Tradition*, 30n30; Cook, *Constitutionalist Party*, 49; Cherry, *Down and Out in Saigon*.
86. *Đuốc Nhà Nam*, May 15, 1930, quoted in Ngo Vinh Long, "The Indochinese Communist Party and Peasant Rebellion in Central Vietnam, 1930–31," *Bulletin of Concerned Asian Scholars* 10, no. 4 (Oct.–Dec. 1978): 17; Duiker, *Rise*, 218–19n8.
87. *Echo Annamite*, May 23, 1930, cited in Smith, "Introduction to Caodaism I," 342.
88. Peycam, *Birth*, 67; Cook, *Constitutionalist Party*, 8; Smith, "Vietnamese Elite," 472n10.
89. Jay Carter, "A Subject Elite: The First Decade of the Constitutionalist Party in Cochinchina, 1917–1927," *Việt Nam Forum* 14 (1994): 212, 213–15, 218–20, 214.
90. Brocheux and Hémery, *Indochina*, 254; Carter, "Subject Elite," 226, 222.
91. Cook, *Constitutionalist Party*, 20–21; Carter, "Subject Elite," 211, 221–22; Brocheux and Hémery, *Indochina*, 385.
92. Christopher E. Goscha, *Going Indochinese: Contesting Concepts of Space and Place in French Indochina* (Copenhagen: NIAS Press, 2012), 52–53, 112, 116, 131–33; Carter, "Subject Elite," 223.

93. Smith, "Vietnamese Élite," 467; Marr, *Vietnam 1945*, 47.
94. Carter, "Subject Elite," 219, 229; Smith, *Viet-Nam and the West*, 93.
95. Cook, *Constitutionalist Party*, 20–21; Carter, "Subject Elite," 211, 222, 233–34.
96. Smith, *Viet-Nam and the West*, 95; Cook, *Constitutionalist Party*, 38.
97. Hue-Tam Ho Tai, *Radicalism and the Origins of the Vietnamese Revolution* (Cambridge, MA: Harvard University Press, 1992), 162; Brocheux and Hémery, *Indochina*, 385; Cook, *Constitutionalist Party*, 49.
98. Pierre Brocheux, *Ho Chi Minh: A Biography*, trans. Claire Duiker (Cambridge, UK: Cambridge University Press, 2007), 16.
99. Brocheux, *Ho Chi Minh*, 18, 15–16; Jean Lacouture, *Ho Chi Minh* (London: Pelican, 1969), 39.
100. Phan Bội Châu, *Overturned Chariot: The Autobiography of Phan-Bội-Châu*, trans. Vinh Sinh and N. Wickenden (Honolulu: University of Hawai'i Press, 1999), 260; Khánh, *Vietnamese Communism*, 63–89.
101. Vinh Sinh, introduction to Phan Bội Châu, *Overturned Chariot*, 19–20n11.
102. Phan Bội Châu, *Tiếng dân*, March 24, 1927, quoted in Vinh, *Phan Châu Trinh*, 39.
103. Duiker, *Rise*, 204, 218; Marr, *Tradition*, 374; Khánh, *Vietnamese Communism*, 279n101, 258n57.
104. Khánh, *Vietnamese Communism*, 87–89.
105. Sophie Quinn-Judge, *Ho Chi Minh: The Missing Years* (Berkeley: University of California Press, 2002), ch. 3; Khánh, *Vietnamese Communism*, 88.
106. Duiker, *Rise*, 154, 206, 212; Khánh, *Vietnamese Communism*, 122–23.
107. Khánh, *Vietnamese Communism*, 121, 125n67; Duiker, *Rise*, 218.
108. Khánh, *Vietnamese Communism*, 125n67; Duiker, *Rise*, 156–57, 162, 165.
109. Duiker, *Rise*, 160–64; Brocheux and Hémery, *Indochina*, 316.
110. Marr, *Tradition*, 385.
111. Ngo, "Indochinese Communist Party," 22; Brocheux and Hémery, *Indochina*, 319.
112. Marr, *Tradition*, 332, 385.
113. Edward Miller, *Misalliance: Ngo Dinh Diem, the United States, and the Fate of South Vietnam* (Cambridge, MA: Harvard University Press, 2013), 24–25, 189–90.
114. Special commissioner of the Sûreté at Vinh, declaration in AOM: ICNF, Carton 333, Dos. 2686, cited in Ngo, "Indochinese Communist Party," 27.
115. Brocheux and Hémery, *Indochina*, 317.
116. Duiker, *Rise*, 231–32; Ngo, "Indochinese Communist Party," 23.
117. Duiker, *Rise*, 162, 164–65; Tai, *Radicalism*, 162–64.
118. Bùi Quang Chiêu, *Tribune Indochinoise*, Oct. 19, 1931, quoted in Cook, *Constitutionalist Party*, 49.
119. Ngo, "Indochinese Communist Party," 17.
120. Nguyễn Thị Định, *No Other Road*, 25–27.
121. Duiker, *Rise*, 229; Khánh, *Vietnamese Communism*, 160; Quinn-Judge, *Ho Chi Minh*, 187.
122. Peter Zinoman, *The Colonial Bastille: A History of Imprisonment in Vietnam 1862–1940* (Berkeley: University of California Press, 2001), 300; Khánh, *Vietnamese Communism*, 179; Quinn-Judge, *Ho Chi Minh*, 187–91.
123. Quinn-Judge, *Ho Chi Minh*, 169, 191–95, 201–8, 228–30; Khánh, *Vietnamese Communism*, 174–79.
124. RST (NF) 3000, *L'Avenir du Tonkin*, Aug. 16, 1934, text in Note confidentielle No. 8735/S, Arnoux, Contrôleur Général de la Sûreté, to Résident Supérieur du Tonkin, Hanoi, Aug. 31, 1934.
125. RST (NF) 3000, Résident Supérieur au Tonkin à Messrs. les Administrateurs Résidents de France, Hanoi, Sept. 6, 1934.

126. RST (NF) M04695, J. B. Tòng, Phát Diệm, to Cresson, Résident at Ninh-Binh, Nov. 1936.
127. RST (NF) M04695, J. B. Tòng to Résident Supérieur Yves Chatel, Aug. 1, 1937.
128. RST (NF) M04695, Résident Supérieur Chatel to Nguyễn Bá Tòng, Aug. 13, 1937.
129. Cook, *Constitutionalist Party*, 41ff.
130. Hémery, *Révolutionnaires*, 58–59; Khánh, *Vietnamese Communism*, 201–203.
131. Hémery, *Révolutionnaires*, 253–58; Khánh, *Vietnamese Communism*, 204–205; Duiker, *Rise*, 237–38.
132. Tai, *Millenarianism*, 106.
133. Keith, *Catholic Vietnam*, 205; Brocheux and Hémery, *Indochina*, 328; Khánh, *Vietnamese Communism*, 258n56.
134. Hémery, *Révolutionnaires*, 410–11; Khánh, *Vietnamese Communism*, 225; Pierre Rousset, *Communisme et nationalisme vietnamien* (Paris: Galilée, 1978), 140, 156–57.
135. Brocheux and Hémery, *Indochina*, 333; Duiker, *Historical Dictionary of Vietnam*.
136. Keith, *Catholic Vietnam*, 205–7; Miller, *Misalliance*, 25–26; Brocheux and Hémery, *Indochina*, 386.
137. Khánh, *Vietnamese Communism*, 221–22; Rousset, *Communisme*, 173–79.
138. Cook, *Constitutionalist Party*, 40, 100; Brocheux and Hémery, *Indochina*, 333; Quinn-Judge, *Ho Chi Minh*, 231–32.
139. Hémery, *Révolutionnaires*, 249n2; Brocheux and Hémery, *Indochina*, 386; Duiker, *Rise*, 251.
140. Marr, *Tradition*, 393; Khánh, *Vietnamese Communism*, 222.
141. ANOM, Aix-en-Provence, Résidence Supérieure du Tonkin (RST), 5111, passim; Brocheux and Hémery, *Indochina*, 333, 386.
142. Hémery, *Révolutionnaires*, 249n2.
143. *Ngày Mới* (New day), no. 1, April 19, 1939, French translation in ANOM, RST Nouveaux Fonds (NF) 5228, "Les masses populaires de Hanoi ont choisi leurs trois représentants," 1; Brocheux and Hémery, *Indochina*, 388.
144. ANOM, RST 5111, Yves C. Chatel, Résident Supérieur au Tonkin, to Gouverneur Général de l'Indochine, Hanoi, Dec. 13, 1938, 3; Paul Pujol, Contrôleur Général de la Sûreté, to Résident Supérieur au Tonkin, "Renseignements provenant de Police spéciale Hanoi," Hanoi, Dec. 13, 1938.
145. ANOM, RST 5111, Pujol to Résident Supérieur, "Elections municipales de Hanoi, Scrutin du 4 décembre," Hanoi, Dec. 5, 1938, at 1.
146. ANOM, RST 5111, Chatel to Gouverneur Général, Hanoi, Dec. 13, 1938, 1.
147. ANOM, RST 5111, Pujol to Résident Supérieur, "Elections municipales de Hanoi, Scrutin du 4 décembre," Hanoi, Dec. 5, 1938, 1–2.
148. ANOM, RST 5111, Chatel to Gouverneur Général, Hanoi, Dec. 13, 1938, 2.
149. ANOM, RST, 5111, Pujol, "Renseignements provenant de Police spéciale Hanoi," Hanoi, Dec. 13, 1938, 1.
150. ANOM, RST, 5111, Pujol to Résident Supérieur, Hanoi, Dec. 29, 1938.
151. *Đời nay* (Modern Times), April 20, 1939, French translation in RST NF 5228, "Félicitons les électeurs de Hanoi," 3.
152. ANOM, RST NF 5228, "Elections municipales du 9 avril 1939 et du 16 avril 1939," Saint-Mleux to Gouverneur Général de l'Indochine, Hanoi, April 10, 1939, and Pujol to Résident Supérieur, Hanoi, April 16 and 17, 1939.
153. *Đời nay*, April 20, 1939, 1.
154. Marr, *Tradition*, 393–94; Brocheux and Hémery, *Indochina*, 333.
155. Phan Bội Châu, *Overturned Chariot*, 24, 260n210, 20; Miller, *Misalliance*, 27.
156. Khánh, *Vietnamese Communism*, 49–51; Duiker, *Rise*, 178, 243; Marr, *Tradition*, 307.

157. Khánh, *Vietnamese Communism*, 216–17, 47; Hoàng Văn Đào, *Việt Nam Quốc Dân Đảng: A Contemporary History of a National Struggle 1927–1954*, trans. Huỳnh Khuê (Pittsburgh: RoseDog, 2007[?]), 9, 13–14; Duiker, *Rise*, 155–56; Zinoman, *Colonial Bastille*, 229–30.
158. Brocheux and Hémery, *Indochina*, 331.
159. Nguyễn Thị Định, *No Other Road*, 27–28; Brocheux and Hémery, *Indochina*, 331; Tai, *Millenarianism*, 122.
160. Smith, "Vietnamese Elite," 473.
161. Nancy Wiegersma, *Vietnam: Peasant Land, Peasant Revolution: Patriarchy and Collectivity in the Rural Economy* (London: Macmillan, 1988), 85, 77.
162. Robert L. Sansom, *The Economics of Insurgency* (Cambridge, MA: MIT Press, 1970), 54–55.
163. Cook, *Constitutionalist Party*, 47.
164. Brocheux and Hémery, *Indochina*, 274.
165. RST (NF) 05099, "Décongestionnement du delta tonkinois," Inspecteur des Affaires Politiques et Administratives du Tonkin au Résident Supérieur, "Rapport sur les moyens à résoudre en partie les problèmes de la surpopulation du delta tonkinois," Jan. 26, 1939, 5.
166. Brocheux and Hémery, *Indochina*, 274; Woodside, *Community*, 155.
167. These figures are taken from works by French geographer Pierre Gourou, cited in D. Gareth Porter, *The Myth of the Bloodbath: North Vietnam's Land Reform Reconsidered* (Ithaca, NY: New York, Cornell University, International Relations of East Project, 1972), 9–10.
168. Murray, *Development*, 397.
169. Cook, *Constitutionalist Party*, 48–49; Marr, *Tradition*, 328.
170. Trường Chinh and Võ Nguyên Giáp, *The Peasant Question, 1937–1938*, trans. Christine Pelzer White (Ithaca, NY: Cornell Southeast Asia Program, 1974), 9.
171. Trường Chinh and Võ Nguyên Giáp, *Peasant Question*, 90, 25.
172. Tai, *Millenarianism*, 113, 195n1, 147, 115–17.
173. Tai, *Millenarianism*, vii, 12, 147–50, 115–16, 119, 123, 120–21, 128, 139; Philip Taylor, "Losing the Waterways: The Displacement of Khmer Communities from the Freshwater Rivers of the Mekong Delta, 1945–2010," *Modern Asian Studies* 47, no. 2 (2013): 517, 521, 527–28, 529.
174. Khánh, *Vietnamese Communism*, 250; Brocheux and Hémery, *Indochina*, 335; Marr, *Tradition*, 394.
175. Nguyễn Thị Định, *No Other Road*, 27–28, 31–35.
176. Marr, *Tradition*, 400n87; Khánh, *Vietnamese Communism*, 252–56; Tai, *Millenarianism*, 122.
177. Zinoman, *Colonial Bastille*, 300, 222n99; Khánh, *Vietnamese Communism*, 123n64, 176n77; Duiker, *Ho Chi Minh*, 196–97, 248.
178. Khánh, *Vietnamese Communism*, 251–52.
179. Marr, *Vietnam 1945*, 19–20, 51, 37, 47, 28, 18.
180. Marr, *Vietnam 1945*, 22, 74; Eric Jennings, "Conservative Confluences, 'Nativist' Synergy: Reinscribing Vichy's National Revolution in Indochina, 1940–1945," *French Historical Studies* 27, no. 3 (2004): 635, 604; Jennings, "L'Indochine de l'Amiral Decoux," in *L'Empire colonial sous Vichy*, ed. E. Jennings and J. Cantier (Paris: O. Jacob, 2004).
181. Tai, *Millenarianism*, 114; Marr, *Vietnam 1945*, 21, 83; Werner, *Peasant Politics*, 41, 43.
182. Marr, *Vietnam 1945*, 113, 116n176.

183. Duiker, *Historical Dictionary*; Khánh, *Vietnamese Communism*, 258n57; Marr, *Vietnam 1945*, 180–81, 193.
184. Khánh, *Vietnamese Communism*, 256–60, 275–76; Brocheux, *Ho Chi Minh*, 84; Quinn-Judge, *Ho Chi Minh*, 248–49.
185. Brocheux, *Ho Chi Minh*, 78–79, 81–82; Marr, *Vietnam 1945*, 252–54, 196; Duiker, *Ho Chi Minh*, 270–76.
186. Archimedes L. Patti, *Why Vietnam? Prelude to America's Albatross* (Berkeley: University of California Press, 1980), 47, 49, 53, 55; Marr, *Vietnam 1945*, 253. See also Dixee R. Bartholomew-Feis, *The OSS and Ho Chi Minh: Unexpected Allies in the War against Japan* (Lawrence: University Press of Kansas, 2006).
187. Marr, *Vietnam 1945*, 196; Duiker, *Ho Chi Minh*, 276.
188. Tai, *Millenarianism*, 125, 135; Marr, *Vietnam 1945*, 32–35.
189. Huỳnh Kim Khánh, "The Vietnamese August Revolution Reinterpreted," *Journal of Asian Studies* 30, no. 4 (1971): 776; Khánh, *Vietnamese Communism*, 280.
190. Patti, *Why Vietnam?*, 56–58; Duiker, *Ho Chi Minh*, 282, 287, 292–94; Bartholomew-Feis, *OSS*, 149–53.
191. Miller, *Misalliance*, 30–31; Marr, *Vietnam 1945*, 117.
192. *Tin mới*, March 24, 1945, quoted in Khánh, *Vietnamese Communism*, 297.
193. Khánh, "Vietnamese August Revolution," 765.
194. Marr, *Vietnam 1945*, 84. 467.
195. Tai, *Millenarianism*, 124–32, 142; Marr, *Vietnam 1945*, 134–5 n260.
196. Marr, *Vietnam 1945*, 104–5; Brocheux and Hémery, *Indochina*, 254.
197. Buckley et al., "Climate as a Contributing Factor," table S2; Brocheux and Hémery, *Indochina*, 262; Marr, *Vietnam 1945*, 393.
198. Khánh, *Vietnamese Communism*, 304, 280; Tai, *Millenarianism*, 135–36.
199. Marr, *Vietnam 1945*, 233–34; Brocheux, *Ho Chi Minh*, 91, 93.
200. Marr, *Vietnam 1945*, 66, 239n342.
201. Marr, *Vietnam 1945*, 238, 393; David G. Marr, "Vietnam 1945: A Revolutionary Case Study," unpublished paper in possession of the author.
202. Marr, *Vietnam 1945*, 408–409.
203. Marr, "Vietnam 1945."
204. David G. Marr, "Creating Defense Capacity in Vietnam, 1945–1947," in *The First Vietnam War: Colonial Conflict and Cold War Crisis*, ed. Mark Attwood Lawrence and Fredrik Logevall (Cambridge, MA: Harvard University Press, 2007), 76; Tai, *Millenarianism*, 137.
205. David G. Marr, *Vietnam: State, War and Revolution, 1945–1946* (Berkeley: University of California Press, 2013), 114–16, 186.
206. Marr, *Vietnam 1945*, 537.
207. Maurice Demariaux, *Poulo-Condore, Archipel du Viêtnam: Du bagne historique à la nouvelle zone développement économique* (Paris: L'Harmattan, 1999), 64–65; Marr, *Vietnam 1945*, 469–70; Bunchan Mul, *Kuk Niyobay* [Political prison] (Phnom Penh: 1971), partial translation, "The Umbrella War of 1942," in *Peasants and Politics in Kampuchea, 1942–1981*, ed. Ben Kiernan and Chanthou Boua (London: Zed, 1982) 125.
208. Samuel Adams, "Communism and Cambodia," CIA, Directorate of Intelligence, May 1972 (declassified Feb. 19, 1987), 69; Goscha, *Historical Dictionary*, 370; Marr, *Vietnam 1945*, 469–70; Duiker, *Historical Dictionary*, 142; Bunchan, "Umbrella War of 1942," 125.
209. Marr, "Creating Defense Capacity," 76.
210. Marr, "Creating Defense Capacity," 77.

211. Douglas Gracey, recollection following Melvin Hall, "Aspects of the Present Situation in Indo-China," *Journal of the Central Asiatic Society* 40 (1953): 213–14, quoted in David P. Chandler, "The Kingdom of Kampuchea, March–October 1945," *Journal of Southeast Asian Studies* 17, no. 1 (March 1986): 89.
212. Marr, *Vietnam: State, War and Revolution*, 186.
213. Anthony Barnett, "The Uncrowned King of Cambodia," interview with E. D. Murray, 1982, 1–13, 35–50, at 3–8. Copy in possession of the author.
214. George Rosie, *The British in Vietnam* (London: Panther, 1970), 56–59; Marr, *Vietnam: State, War and Revolution*, 114–18, 186–90.
215. Marr, "Creating Defense Capacity," 77; Tai, *Millenarianism*, 140.
216. Murray interview with Barnett, 6–11.
217. Kiernan, *How Pol Pot Came to Power*, 24, 50–53; Gerald C. Hickey, *Sons of the Mountains: Ethnohistory of the Vietnamese Central Highlands to 1954* (New Haven, CT: Yale University Press, 1982), 379–83, 388–90; Hickey, *Free in the Forest: Ethnohistory of the Vietnamese Central Highlands, 1954–1976* (New Haven, CT: Yale University Press, 1982), 14–15.
218. Gareth Porter, *Vietnam: The Politics of Bureaucratic Socialism* (Ithaca, NY: Cornell University Press, 1993), 14.
219. Marr, *Vietnam 1945*, 434–35, 466; Marr, *Vietnam: State, War and Revolution*, 445–46, 392, 404, 429, 408–10; Tai, *Millenarianism*, 139–40.
220. Marr, *Vietnam: State, War and Revolution*, 266.
221. Marr, *Vietnam: State, War and Revolution*, 454, 94, 418; Stein Tønnesson, *Vietnam 1946: How the War Began* (Berkeley: University of California Press, 2010), 89.
222. Miller, *Misalliance*, 33; Marr, *Vietnam: State, War and Revolution*, 438–39.
223. Marr, *Vietnam: State, War and Revolution*, 61, 216, 96, 661, 420, 402–4, 87–88, 563; Vinh, *Phan Châu Trinh*, 12n31; Marr, *Vietnam 1945*, 440; Tai, *Millenarianism*, 140–43.
224. Tai, *Millenarianism*, 141.
225. Marr, "Creating Defense Capacity," 100–101; Marr, *Vietnam: State, War and Revolution*, 414–28, 96, 94; William J. Duiker, *The Communist Road to Power in Vietnam* (Boulder, CO: Westview, 1981), 127, 135.
226. Tønnesson, *Vietnam 1946*, 126–35; Philippe Devillers, ed., *Paris-Saigon-Hanoi: Les archives de la guerre 1944–1947* (Paris: Gallimard, 1988), 243–58, 261–327.
227. Marr, *Vietnam: State, War and Revolution*, xv, 578.
228. Christopher Goscha, *Vietnam: Un Ètat né de la guerre 1945–1954* (Paris: Armand Colin, 2011); Goscha, ed., *Naissance d'un Etat-parti: Le Viêt Nam depuis 1945* (Paris: Indes Savantes, 2004).
229. Duiker, *Communist Road*, 131; Vinh, *Phan Châu Trinh*, 12n31.
230. Shawn McHale, "Ethnicity, Violence, and Khmer-Vietnamese Relations: The Significance of the Lower Mekong Delta, 1757–1954," *Journal of Asian Studies* 72, no. 2 (May 2013): 367–90, 373–79.
231. Tai, *Millenarianism*, 143–44.
232. Taylor, "Losing the Waterways"; McHale, "Ethnicity, Violence, and Khmer-Vietnamese Relations," 379–80.
233. Marr, *Vietnam: State, War and Revolution*, 428.
234. Duiker, *Communist Road*, 131–32, 134–36.
235. Duiker, *Communist Road*, 139–40, 145, 149, 161; Michael Maclear, *Vietnam: The Ten Thousand Day War* (London: Methuen, 1981), 39; John Prados, *Operation Vulture* (New York: iBooks, 2002), 177–78.

236. Duiker, *Communist Road*, 146, 149–51; Prados, *Operation Vulture*, 10, 179; Maclear, *Vietnam*, 39.
237. Miller, *Misalliance*, 36–41.
238. Thomas L. Ahern, Jr., *CIA and the House of Ngo: Covert Action in South Vietnam, 1954–63* (Washington, DC: CIA, Center for the Study of Intelligence, 2000), declassified Feb. 19, 2009, 21, available online at https://www.cia.gov/library/readingroom/docs/2_CIA_AND_THE_HOUSE_OF_NGO.pdf.
239. Miller, *Misalliance*, 80–81; Ahern, *CIA and the House of Ngo*, 21.
240. Miller, *Misalliance*, 42–46; John C. Donnell, "Politics in South Vietnam: Doctrines of Authority in Conflict" (PhD diss., University of California Berkeley, 1964), 80.
241. Miller, *Misalliance*, 106, 46–47, 94; Donnell, "Politics," 99, 94–95.
242. Ahern, *CIA and the House of Ngo*, 21, 16, 21–22.
243. Duiker, *Communist Road*, 141, 355n25.
244. Duiker, *Communist Road*, 153–56; Tuong Vu, *Paths to Development in Asia: South Korea, Vietnam, China, and Indonesia* (New York: Cambridge University Press, 2010), 103; Bui Tin, *Following Ho Chi Minh: Memoirs of a Vietnamese Colonel* (Honolulu: University of Hawai'i Press, 1995), 14–18, 23–24, 26.
245. Greg Lockhart, *Nation in Arms: The Origins of the People's Army of Vietnam* (Sydney: Allen & Unwin, 1989), 256–59, 263.
246. Philippe Devillers and Jean Lacouture, *End of a War: Indochina, 1954* (New York: Praeger, 1969), 33; Duiker, *Communist Road*, 155, 159, 151; Lockhart, *Nation in Arms*, xii, 263.
247. Duiker, *Communist Road*, 161–62; Lockhart, *Nation in Arms*, 259–63; Bui, *Following Ho*, 22.
248. Maclear, *Vietnam*, 46; Miller, *Misalliance*, 51, 53, 1.
249. Duiker, *Communist Road*, 155, 163.
250. Greg Lockhart, "The Origins of the People's Army of Vietnam: Institutional History" (PhD diss., University of Sydney, 1985), 379; Phan Châu Trinh, "Monarchy and Democracy," in Vinh, *Phan Châu Trinh*, 137.

CHAPTER 10

1. Greg Lockhart, *Nation in Arms: The Origins of the People's Army of Vietnam* (Sydney: Allen & Unwin, 1989), 267; Philippe Devillers and Jean Lacouture, *End of a War: Indochina, 1954* (New York: Praeger, 1969), 86n.
2. Bruce M. Lockhart, *The End of the Vietnamese Monarchy* (New Haven, CT: Yale Southeast Asia Studies, 1993), 172; Edward Miller, *Misalliance: Ngo Dinh Diem, the United States and the Fate of South Vietnam* (Cambridge, MA: Harvard University Press, 2013), 49, 51, 53, 90; François Guillemot, *Dai Viêt, indépendance et révolution au Viêt-Nam: L'échec de la troisième voie, 1938–1955* (Paris: Indes Savantes, 2012).
3. Devillers and Lacouture, *End of a War*, 33, 342–43; Bernard B. Fall, *The Two Viet-Nams* (New York: Praeger, 1963), 290; Miller, *Misalliance*, 89–90.
4. Miller, *Misalliance*, 152, 92–93; Trương Bửu Lâm, *A Story of Việt Nam* (Denver: Outskirts, 2010), 244.
5. Nguyen-Anh-Tuan, *Les forces politiques au Sud Viet-Nam depuis les accords de Genève 1954* (Louvain, Belgium: Offset Frankie, 1967), 85–87; Miller, *Misalliance*, 93–94; Guillemot, *Dai Viêt*.
6. Gerald C. Hickey, *Free in the Forest: Ethnohistory of the Vietnamese Central Highlands, 1954–1976* (New Haven, CT: Yale University Press, 1982), 301; Fall, *Two Viet-Nams*, frontispiece map; Christopher E. Goscha, *Historical Dictionary of the Indochina War, 1945–1954* (Honolulu: University of Hawai'i Press, 2012),

362–63; Lockhart, *End of the Vietnamese Monarchy*, 174; "Ordonnances du Gouvernement Fédéral" (May 27, 1946, May 21, 1951), available online at http://www.mhro.org/wp-content/uploads/2010/10/FRENCH-ORDONNANCE.pdf.

7. Carlyle A. Thayer, *War by Other Means: National Liberation and Revolution in Viet-Nam 1954–60* (Sydney: Allen & Unwin, 1989), 4–5; "General Navarre's Map," in George M. Kahin and John W. Lewis, *The United States in Vietnam* (New York: Dell, 1969), 34; Bernard B. Fall, *Street without Joy*, 4th ed. (London: Pall Mall, 1965), 277; Lockhart, *Nation in Arms*, 265; Fall, *Two Viet-Nams*, 128; Fall, *Viet-Nam Witness 1953–1966* (London: Pall Mall, 1966), 18, 143; P. Brocheux and D. Hémery, *Indochina: An Ambiguous Colonization, 1858–1954* (Berkeley: University of California Press, 2009), 371, map 8.3; Frank Frost, *Australia's War in Vietnam* (Sydney: Allen & Unwin, 1987), 30–37, 52. See also David W. P. Elliott, *The Vietnamese War: Revolution and Social Change in the Mekong Delta, 1930–1975* (Armonk, NY: M. E. Sharpe, 2003), 1:148–58; Miller, *Misalliance*, 88.
8. Miller, *Misalliance*, 198; Thayer, *War by Other Means*, 11, 120, 197n6.
9. Joseph Alsop, "A Man in a Mirror," *New Yorker*, June 25, 1955, quoted in Marilyn Young, *The Vietnam Wars 1945–1990* (New York: HarperCollins, 1991), 55, and Ahern, *Rural Pacification*, 2.
10. David M. Kennedy, *Freedom from Fear: The American People in Depression and War, 1929–1945* (New York: Oxford University Press, 1999), 856–57; Gabriel Kolko, *Vietnam: Anatomy of a War 1940–1975* (London: Allen & Unwin, 1986), 285.
11. George Kennan, Policy Planning Study 23, Feb. 24, 1948, *Foreign Relations of the United States 1948*, vol. 1, Part 2, ed. Ralph R. Goodwin (Washington, DC: Government Printing Office, 1975), 523–26.
12. U.S. Department of State, Office of the Historian, *Milestones 1945–1952*, "Kennan and Containment," https://history.state.gov/milestones/1945-1952/kennan, and "NSC-68, 1950," http://history.state.gov/milestones/1945-1952/NSC68 (accessed April 23, 2014).
13. Kennan to Acheson, Aug. 21, 23, 1950, in Wilson D. Miscamble, *George F. Kennan and the Making of American Foreign Policy, 1947–1950* (Princeton, NJ: Princeton University Press, 1992), 277.
14. Frank Costigliola, introduction to George F. Kennan, *The Kennan Diaries* (New York: Norton, 2014), xxx, 301.
15. National Security Council Statement of Policy (NSC 5405), Jan. 16, 1954, *The Pentagon Papers*, official ed. (Washington, DC: U.S. Government Printing Office, 1971), 9:221–22.
16. Joint Chiefs of Staff Memorandum, March 12, 1954, *Pentagon Papers*, official ed., 9:268.
17. *Pentagon Papers*, official ed., vol. 1, part 1, division i, subdivision D, 2; see Nigel B. Cullen, "Document: America's Vietnam Crimes," *Journal of Contemporary Asia* 13, no. 4 (1983) 508, and references cited.
18. Kolko, *Vietnam*, 84; Dwight D. Eisenhower, *The White House Years*, vol. 1, *Mandate for Change, 1953–1956* (New York: Doubleday, 1963), 372.
19. Ngô Vĩnh Long, "From Polarisation to Integration in Vietnam," *Journal of Contemporary Asia* 39, no. 2 (May 2009): 296; Kahin and Lewis, *United States in Vietnam*, 447; Kolko, *Vietnam*, 82; Noam Chomsky, *American Power and the New Mandarins* (London: Chatto & Windus, 1969), 194.
20. George McT. Kahin, *Intervention: How America Became Involved in Vietnam* (New York: Knopf, 1986), 66–92; Thomas L. Ahern, Jr., *CIA and the House of Ngo: Covert Action in South Vietnam, 1954–63* (Washington, DC: CIA, Center for the Study of Intelligence,

2000), 29–30, 39–40, 118–19; see also Ahern, *The Way We Do Things: Black Entry Operations into North Vietnam, 1961–1964* (Washington, DC: CIA, Center for the Study of Intelligence, 2005). Both declassified Feb. 19, 2009, available online at https://www.cia.gov/library/readingroom/collection/vietnam-histories.

21. James William Gibson, *The Perfect War: The War We Couldn't Lose and How We Did* (New York: Vintage, 1988), 25–27, 327; Nick Turse, *Kill Anything That Moves: The Real American War in Vietnam* (New York: Picador, 2013), 76–79.
22. *The Pentagon Papers*, Gravel ed. (Boston: Beacon Press, 1971), 2:22.
23. Ben Kiernan, "The Vietnam War: Alternative Endings," *American Historical Review* 97, no. 4 (1992): 1126–27.
24. Devillers and Lacouture, *End of a War*, 373; Kahin, *Intervention*, 82.
25. Ahern, *House of Ngo*, 14–15.
26. Ahern, *House of Ngo*, 15, 22–23, 24–25.
27. Miller, *Misalliance*, 51, 53; Ahern, *House of Ngo*, 16.
28. Ahern, *House of Ngo*, 23 (citing "FVSA 633, 21 May 1954"), 25, 24.
29. Ahern, *House of Ngo*, 16–17, 23, 25 (citing "FVSA 688, 23 June 1954"), 24.
30. Thomas L. Ahern, Jr., *CIA and Rural Pacification in South Vietnam* (Washington, DC: CIA, Center for the Study of Intelligence, 2001), xiii, declassified 2009, available online at https://www.cia.gov/library/readingroom/docs/3_CIA_AND_RURAL_PACIFICATION.pdf; George W. Allen, *None So Blind: A Personal Account of the Intelligence Failure in Vietnam* (Chicago: Ivan R. Dee, 2001), 78.
31. Miller, *Misalliance*, 53, 3–4.
32. Kahin, *Intervention*, 89; Ngô, "From Polarisation to Integration," 296–97.
33. Lien-Hang T. Nguyen, *Hanoi's War: An International History of the War for Peace in Vietnam* (Chapel Hill: University of North Carolina Press, 2012), 24–27.
34. Pierre Asselin, *Hanoi's Road to the Vietnam War, 1954–1965* (Berkeley: University of California Press, 2013), 194.
35. Thayer, *War by Other Means*, 15–19; Hickey, *Free in the Forest*, 12–16; Fall, *Two Viet-Nams*, 152, 358, 281; Ben Kiernan, *How Pol Pot Came to Power: Colonialism, Nationalism, and Communism in Cambodia, 1930–1975* (London: Verso, 1985), 154–55.
36. A May 1968 State Department study, quoted in Noam Chomsky, *Towards a New Cold War: Essays on the Current Crisis and How We Got There* (New York: Pantheon, 1982), 161.
37. Nguyen, *Hanoi's War*, 31, 34, 38, 43, 45; Thayer, *War by Other Means*, 15, 130.
38. Goscha, *Historical Dictionary of the Indochina War*, 260–61.
39. Thayer, *War by Other Means*, 11–14, 18, 84, 14–15; Jeffrey Race, *War Comes to Long An: Revolutionary Conflict in a Vietnamese Province* (Berkeley: University of California Press, 1972), 35–36.
40. Thayer, *War by Other Means*, 19, 105, 150, 184–85; Kahin, *Intervention*, 109; Asselin, *Hanoi's Road*, 59–66, 166–69; Nguyen, *Hanoi's War*, 46–47; Merle Pribbenow, trans., *Victory in Vietnam: The Official History of the People's Army of Vietnam, 1954–1975* (Lawrence: University of Kansas Press, 2002), 446. For Cambodian communist usage of these graduated terms in the 1960s, see Kiernan, *How Pol Pot*, 271.
41. Brocheux and Hémery, *Indochina*, 371, map 8.3; Jayne S. Werner, *Peasant Politics and Religious Sectarianism: Peasant and Priest in the Cao Dai in Viet Nam* (New Haven, CT: Yale Southeast Asia Studies, 1981), 120–21.
42. Thayer, *War by Other Means*, 4; Fall, *Viet-Nam Witness*, 143; Kahin and Lewis, *United States in Vietnam*, 34; Miller, *Misalliance*, 106–107, 109–10.
43. Miller, *Misalliance*, 97, 99, 179; Ahern, *House of Ngo*, 118–19.

44. Ahern, *House of Ngo*, 118; Miller, *Misalliance*, 105, 109, 225–26; Thayer, *War by Other Means*, 123–24, table 6.5.
45. Miller, *Misalliance*, 94–95, 103, 47, 348n84, 110. On Trần Quốc Bửu and the Ngôs, see Edmund F. Wehrle, "The Paradox of Western-Style Trade Unionism in South Vietnam," in *Vietnam and the West*, ed. Wynn Wilcox (Ithaca, NY: Cornell University Press, 2010), 143–54, esp. 150–54.
46. Ahern, *House of Ngo*, 39–40; Fall, *Two Viet-Nams*, 290–91; Miller, *Misalliance*, 97–98, 192, 377n20; Seth Jacobs, *Cold War Mandarin: Ngo Dinh Diem and the Origins of America's War in Vietnam, 1950–1953* (Lanham, MD: Rowman & Littlefield, 2006), 43–53; Peter Hansen, "Bắc Đi Cư: Catholic Refugees from the North of Vietnam, and Their Role in the Southern Republic, 1954–1959," *Journal of Vietnamese Studies* 4, no. 3 (Fall 2009): 180, 190.
47. Miller, *Misalliance*, 166, 170; Thayer, *War by Other Means*, 119; Hansen, "Bắc Đi Cư," 195–96.
48. Miller, *Misalliance*, 152–53.
49. John C. Donnell, "Politics in South Vietnam: Doctrines of Authority in Conflict" (PhD diss., University of California, Berkeley, 1964), 48–49, 67–68; Huỳnh Sanh Thông, "Greatest Little Man in Asia," *The Nation*, Feb. 18, 1961, 141; Fall, *Two Viet-Nams*, 272.
50. Ahern, *Rural Pacification*, 65.
51. Miller, *Misalliance*, 103–7, 111–13.
52. Miller, *Misalliance*, 120–23, 126; Fall, *Viet-Nam Witness*, 157–59; Thayer, *War by Other Means*, 48.
53. Pierre Bernardini, "L'implantation caodaiste au Cambodge en 1969," *Actes du XXIXe Congrès international des Orientalistes: Asie du Sud-Est continentale* (Paris: L'Asiathèque, 1976), 1:2; Thayer, *War by Other Means*, 39.
54. Thayer, *War by Other Means*, 53; Miller, *Misalliance*, 140–42, 144.
55. Letter to State Department from International Security Agency, April 22, 1955, excerpted in *Credibility Gap: A Digest of the Pentagon Papers*, comp. Len Ackland (Philadelphia: National Peace Literature Service, 1972), 35.
56. Franklin B. Weinstein, *Vietnam's Unheld Elections: The Failure to Carry Out the 1956 Reunification Elections and the Effect on Hanoi's Present Outlook* (Ithaca, NY: Cornell Southeast Asia Program, 1966), 32–33; Thayer, *War by Other Means*, 71, 75–79; Miller, *Misalliance*, 304; Ahern, *Rural Pacification*, 23; Robert Scigliano, *South Vietnam: Nation under Stress* (Boston: Houghton-Mifflin, 1963), 207.
57. Weinstein, *Vietnam's Unheld Elections*, 50–52; Race, *War Comes*, 18–19, 89; Miller, *Misalliance*, 144–45, 206.
58. Ahern, *Rural Pacification*, 17; Race, *War Comes*, 20–21; Miller, *Misalliance*, 154, 223, 236, 244.
59. Nguyen-Anh-Tuan, *Forces politiques*, 263–64; Eric M. Bergerud, *The Dynamics of Defeat: The Vietnam War in Hau Nghia Province* (Boulder, CO: Westview, 1991), 15.
60. Miller, *Misalliance*, 169.
61. Ahern, *Rural Pacification*, 24.
62. Nguyen-Anh-Tuan, *Forces politiques*, 264–65; Thayer, *War by Other Means*, 119–22; Miller, *Misalliance*, 168–70.
63. Bergerud, *Dynamics*, 56; Thayer, *War by Other Means*, 119.
64. Denis Warner, *The Last Confucian* (Sydney: Angus & Robertson, 1964); Anthony Bouscaren, *Last of the Mandarins: Diem of Vietnam* (Pittsburgh: Duquesne, 1965); Geoffrey Shaw, *The Lost Mandate of Heaven* (San Francisco: Ignatius, 2015), 17; Ahern, *Rural Pacification*, 22, 32.
65. Donnell, "Politics," 74, 58–59.

66. Miller, *Misalliance*, 43–44, 232–33; Donnell, "Politics," 78, 101–10.
67. Huỳnh Sanh Thông, "Greatest Little Man," 140.
68. See for example, Donnell, "Politics," 71–75a, and Ahern, *House of Ngo*, 31.
69. Miller, *Misalliance*, 46, 212; Donnell, "Politics," 67–68, 48; Ahern, *Rural Pacification*, 15–16.
70. Lansdale quoted in Kahin, *Intervention*, 96; Donnell, "Politics," 62, 56, 67–68, 48; Ahern, *Rural Pacification*, 27, 18.
71. Ahern, *Rural Pacification*, 27, 29.
72. Nhu, interview with Gerald C. Hickey, Aug. 1961, in John C. Donnell and Gerald C. Hickey, *The Vietnamese "Strategic Hamlets": A Preliminary Report*, Rand Corporation, Memorandum RM 3208-ARPA, Aug. 1962, 30.
73. Donnell, "Politics," 86–87, 89; Nhu quoted in Donnell and Hickey, *Vietnamese "Strategic Hamlets,"* 17.
74. Miller, *Misalliance*, 176–77, 181–83, 196, 206, 244; Donnell, "Politics," 72; Ahern, *Rural Pacification*, 55, 32, 83.
75. Ahern, *Rural Pacification*, 21; Donnell, "Politics," 92, 79.
76. Ahern, *Rural Pacification*, 17.
77. Thayer, *War by Other Means*, 49; Ahern, *Rural Pacification*, 18–19.
78. Kahin, *United States in Vietnam*, 100, 121; Thayer, *War by Other Means*, 81–82.
79. Thayer, *War by Other Means*, 116, 215n20; Kahin, *United States in Vietnam*, 100; Amnesty International, *Report of an Amnesty International Mission to the Socialist Republic of Viet Nam, 10–21 December, 1979* (London: Amnesty International Publications, 1981), 7; Race, *War Comes*, 101.
80. Thayer, *War by Other Means*, 118, 215n25.
81. Oscar Salemink, *The Ethnography of Vietnam's Central Highlanders* (Honolulu: University of Hawai'i Press, 2003), 200–201.
82. Lâm, *Story of Việt Nam*, 257–59; Jacobs, *Cold War Mandarin*, 86–89.
83. Ahern, *Rural Pacification*, 25, 32; Ronald H. Spector, *Advice and Support: The Early Years: The U.S. Army in Vietnam* (Washington, DC: Center of Military History, United States Army, 1985), 334–36.
84. Lâm, *Story of Việt Nam*, 260–61; Miller, *Misalliance*, 206, 322–23, 382n20.
85. Huỳnh Sanh Thông, "Greatest Little Man," 140.
86. Elliott, *Vietnamese War*, 1:219; Race, *War Comes*, 85–86, 75–81.
87. Thayer, *War by Other Means*, 105, 142–45; Race, *War Comes*, 82–84, 86–87.
88. Thayer, *War by Other Means*, 117, 143–45; Fall, *Viet-Nam Witness*, 185; Ahern, *Rural Pacification*, 66.
89. Thayer, *War by Other Means*, 15, 185; Race, *War Comes*, 97, 99–103, 110–11.
90. *Cách Mạng Quốc Gia*, Feb. 1959, quoted in *The Pentagon Papers*, Gravel ed., 1:337.
91. David G. Marr, *Vietnam: State, War and Revolution, 1945–1946* (Berkeley: University of California Press, 2013), 116; Nguyen, *Hanoi's War*, 46; Kahin, *Intervention*, 101–10.
92. Thayer, *War by Other Means*, 205n25, 87, 111, 64.
93. Elliott, *Vietnamese War*, 219; Ahern, *House of Ngo*, 118–19, 132.
94. Asselin, *Hanoi's Road*, 47; Nguyen, *Hanoi's War*, 30–31, 37–39, 46.
95. William Duiker, "Waging Revolutionary War: The Evolution of Hanoi's Strategy in the South, 1959–1965," in *The Vietnam War: Vietnamese and American Perspectives*, ed. Jayne S. Werner and Luu Doan Huynh (Armonk, NY: M. E. Sharpe, 1993), 28.
96. William J. Duiker, *The Communist Road to Power in Vietnam* (Boulder, CO: Westview, 1981), 187; R. B. Smith, *An International History of the Vietnam War*, Vol. 1, *Revolution versus Containment, 1955–61* (London: Macmillan, 1983), 166.

97. Trần Văn Trà, recollections at Columbia University conference on the History of the Vietnam War, Nov. 16, 1990; Asselin, *Hanoi's Road*, 51; Thayer, *War by Other Means*, 54.
98. Gareth Porter, *Vietnam: The Politics of Bureaucratic Socialism* (Ithaca, NY: Cornell University Press, 1993), 20; Asselin, *Hanoi's Road*, 53; Elliott, *Vietnamese War*, 1:228–29.
99. Asselin, *Hanoi's Road*, 59–60; Trần Văn Trà, recollections at Columbia University, Nov. 16, 1990.
100. Thayer, *War by Other Means*, 105; Asselin, *Hanoi's Road*, 60.
101. William S. Turley, *The Second Indochina War* (Lanham, MD: Rowman & Littlefield, 2009), 80, 39.
102. Thayer, *War by Other Means*, 185–87; Asselin, *Hanoi's Road*, 64–65; Elliott, *Vietnamese War*, 1:229.
103. Spector, *Early Years*, 330–32, cited in Ahern, *Rural Pacification*, 31; Lâm, *Story of Việt Nam*, 259.
104. Nguyễn Thị Định, *No Other Road to Take: Memoir of Mrs. Nguyen Thi Dinh*, trans. Mai Elliott (Ithaca, NY: Cornell Southeast Asia Program, 1976), 62.
105. Elliott, *Vietnamese War*, 1:229, 233–34.
106. Race, *War Comes*, 123; Carlyle A. Thayer, "The PRG and the Unification of Viet-Nam," *Dyason House Papers* 1, no. 5 (June 1975): 4.
107. Thayer, *War by Other Means*, 187.
108. Bernard B. Fall, cited in *Pentagon Papers*, 1:336; Fall, *Vietnam Witness, 1953–1966* (London: Pall Mall, 1966), 311; Neil Sheehan, *A Bright Shining Lie: John Paul Vann and America in Vietnam*, (New York: Vintage, 1989), 58.
109. Thayer, *War by Other Means*, 189.
110. Ahern, *Rural Pacification*, 36; Race, *War Comes*, 86–87.
111. David W. P. Elliott, *The Vietnamese War: Revolution and Social Change in the Mekong Delta 1930–1975*, concise ed. (Armonk, NY: M. E. Sharpe, 2007), 158.
112. Douglas E. Pike, *Viet Cong: The Organization and Techniques of the National Liberation Front of South Vietnam* (Cambridge, MA: MIT Press, 1966), 68, 435, 431, 202–3, 208; Werner, *Peasant Politics*, 67–69; Smith, *International History*, 1:228; Frost, *Australia's War*, 37, 49.
113. Vinh Sinh, ed., *Phan Châu Trinh and His Political Writings* (Ithaca, NY: Cornell Southeast Asia Program, 2009), 26n82; Pike, *Viet Cong*, 424.
114. Douglas Pike, *PAVN: People's Army of Vietnam* (Novato, CA: Presidio, 1986), 350; Duiker, "Waging Revolutionary War," 28; Elliott, "Hanoi's Strategy," 76, and *Vietnamese War*, concise ed., 158.
115. Samuel Adams, "Communism and Cambodia," U.S. CIA, Directorate of Intelligence, May 1972, declassified Feb. 19, 1987, 69.
116. Thayer, "PRG and the Unification," 4; William Duiker, *Historical Dictionary of Vietnam* (Lanham, MD: Scarecrow, 1998), 186; Goscha, *Historical Dictionary*, 336; Pike, *Viet Cong*, 421–36; Edith Lenart, "Coming Out of the Shadows to Rule," *Far Eastern Economic Review* (henceforth *FEER*), May 16, 1975, 18.
117. David Hunt, *Vietnam's Southern Revolution: From Peasant Insurrection to Total War* (Amherst: University of Massachusetts Press, 2009).
118. Miller, *Misalliance*, 222; Race, *War Comes*, 197.
119. *Aggression from the North: The Record of North Viet-Nam's Campaign to Conquer South Viet-Nam* (Washington, DC: Department of State, 1965), 6–11; Guenter Lewy, *America in Vietnam* (New York: Oxford University Press, 1978), 38.
120. Bergerud, *Dynamics*, 82–83; Elliott, *Vietnamese War*, 620.

121. Sheehan, *Bright Shining Lie*, 67–68.
122. Wilfred Burchett, *The Furtive War: The United States in Vietnam and Laos* (New York: International Publishers, 1963), 11–16; Denis Warner, *The Last Confucian* (Sydney: Angus and Robertson, 1964), 151–53; Michael Leifer, *Cambodia: The Search for Security* (New York: Praeger, 1967), 94–95.
123. Ahern, *Rural Pacification*, 104, 121–22.
124. Ahern, *Way We Do Things*; Gareth Porter, *Vietnam: The Politics of Bureaucratic Socialism* (Ithaca, NY: Cornell University Press, 1993), 172–73.
125. Lewy, *America in Vietnam*, 22, 24–25.
126. James P. Harrison, "History's Heaviest Bombing," in Werner and Huynh, *Vietnam War*, 132.
127. Ahern, *Rural Pacification*, 41, 73, 43–44, 64, 54, 59, 46–47.
128. J. P. Harris, "The Buon Enao Experiment and American Counterinsurgency," Royal Military Academy Sandhurst, Occasional Paper 8, 2013, 16–17.
129. Christopher K. Ives, *US Special Forces and Counterinsurgency in Vietnam: Military Innovation and Institutional Failure, 1961–1963* (New York: Routledge, 2007), 15.
130. Ahern, *Rural Pacification*, 46–47.
131. Ives, *US Special Forces*, 15–16; Harris, "Buon Enao," 15.
132. Ahern, *Rural Pacification*, 46–47.
133. Ahern, *Rural Pacification*, 47.
134. James C. Scott, *Weapons of the Weak: Everyday Forms of Peasant Resistance* (New Haven, CT: Yale University Press, 1985).
135. Harris, "Buon Enao," 15–17.
136. Ahern, *Rural Pacification*, 52–53, 58–59; Harris, "Buon Enao," 18.
137. Ahern, *Rural Pacification*, 53–54, 59; Ives, *US Special Forces*, 20, gives a total figure of 140,000 Rhadé in 1962, half of whom lived in Đắc Lắc province; Harris, "Buon Enao," 3.
138. Allen, *None So Blind*, 173–74.
139. Ahern, *Rural Pacification*, 109, 41, 66, 114; Harris, "Buon Enao," 29, 32–33; see also Salemink, *Ethnography of the Vietnamese Central Highlanders*, 202–3.
140. Salemink, *Ethnography*, 200–201; Hickey, *Free in the Forest*, 86.
141. Salemink, *Ethnography*, 184; Duiker, "Waging Revolutionary War," 29; Elliott, *Vietnamese War*, 614–16.
142. Fall, *Viet-Nam Witness*, 194; Harris, "Buon Enao," 32.
143. Barry Petersen, *Tiger Men: An Australian Soldier's Secret War in Vietnam* (Melbourne: Sun, 1989), 37.
144. Harris, "Buon Enao," 29; Salemink, *Ethnography*, 207–8.
145. Ahern, *Rural Pacification*, 105, 107.
146. Pike, *Viet Cong*, 115, 138; Elliott, *Vietnamese War*, concise ed., 152.
147. Scigliano, *South Vietnam*, 145, and epilogue, 8; Douglas Pike, *War, Peace, and the Viet Cong* (Cambridge, MA: MIT Press, 1969), 6. Young, *Vietnam Wars*, 73, cites figures for a South Vietnamese village in this period: "75% support for the Front, 20% trying to remain neutral, and 5% firmly pro-government." Her source is James Walker Trullinger, Jr., *Village at War: An Account of Revolution in Vietnam* (New York: Longman, 1980), 91.
148. Ahern, *Rural Pacification*, 421, 411.
149. Chomsky, *American Power*, 223n19, and *Towards a New Cold War*, 412n9, 141.
150. Robert K. Brigham, *ARVN: Life and Death in the South Vietnamese Army* (Lawrence: University Press of Kansas, 2006), 75–84; Sheehan, *Bright Shining Lie*, 203–65; Elliott, *Vietnamese War*, 403, 646.

151. Elliott, *Vietnamese War*, 610–11, 620–21, 659–61; Ahern, *Rural Pacification*, 411.
152. Allen, *None So Blind*, 175.
153. Author's interview with General Trần Văn Trà (ret.), Columbia University, Nov. 16–17, 1990; Pike, *Viet Cong*, 433; Werner and Huynh, *Vietnam War*, xiii; Nguyen, *Hanoi's War*, 71–72.
154. Race, *War Comes*, 184; Kahin, *Intervention*, 101.
155. Kahin, *Intervention*, 101; Miller, *Misalliance*, 264.
156. Robert J. Topmiller, *Lotus Unleashed: The Buddhist Peace Movement in South Vietnam, 1964–1966* (Lexington: University Press of Kentucky, 2002), 2.
157. Miller, *Misalliance*, 262–65.
158. Lâm, *Story of Việt Nam*, 263–64; Miller, *Misalliance*, 265–66, 260–61, 266–67.
159. Miller, *Misalliance*, 272–73.
160. Neil L. Jamieson, *Understanding Vietnam* (Berkeley: University of California Press, 1993), 241–44; Miller, *Misalliance*, 274.
161. Miller, *Misalliance*, 275; Ahern, *House of Ngo*, chs. 12–15, and *Rural Pacification*, 119; John Prados, "JFK and the Diem Coup," National Security Archive, Nov. 5, 2003, available online at http://www2.gwu.edu/~nsarchiv/NSAEBB/NSAEBB101 (accessed Jan. 25, 2015); Tim Weiner, "Lucien Conein, 79, Legendary Cold War Spy," *New York Times*, June 7, 1998.
162. Andrew Vickerman, *The Fate of the Peasantry: Premature "Transition to Socialism" in the Democratic Republic of Vietnam* (New Haven, CT: Yale Southeast Asia Studies, 1986), 82; Edwin Moise, "Land Reform and Land Reform Errors in North Vietnam," *Pacific Affairs* 49, no. 1 (Spring 1976): 84.
163. *Nhân Dân*, Oct. 10, 1953, cited in Vickerman, *Fate*, 79, 65; Moise, "Land Reform," 80.
164. *Học Tập* 1 (Feb. 1956): 22, cited in Moise, "Land Reform," 81n28, and Edwin Moise, "Class-ism in North Vietnam, 1953–56," in *Vietnamese Communism in Comparative Perspective*, ed. W. Turley (Boulder, CO: Westview, 1980) 93.
165. Vickerman, *Fate*, 107, 79.
166. Cited in Moise, "Land Reform," 76.
167. Moise, "Land Reform," 71, 78; Bui Tin, *Following Ho Chi Minh: Memoirs of a North Vietnamese Colonel* (Honolulu: University of Hawaii Press, 1995), 27; cf. D. Gareth Porter, *The Myth of the Bloodbath: North Vietnam's Land Reform Reconsidered*, Interim Report No. 2 (Ithaca, NY: Cornell International Relations of East Asia, 1972), 55–56.
168. Kim N. B. Ninh, *A World Transformed: The Politics of Culture in Revolutionary Vietnam, 1945–1965* (Ann Arbor: University of Michigan Press, 2002), 125–26.
169. Moise, "Land Reform," 75; Porter, *Myth*, 42.
170. Georges Boudarel, "Intellectual Dissidence in the 1950s: The *Nhân Văn Giai Phẩm* Affair," *Vietnam Forum* 13 (1990): 159; Peter Zinoman, "Nhân Văn Giai Phẩm and Vietnamese 'Reform Communism' in the 1950s," *Journal of Cold War Studies* 13, no. 1 (2011): 66.
171. Porter, *Myth*, 38; Fall, *Two Viet-Nams*, 156.
172. *Nhân Dân*, Oct. 31, 1956, translated in Porter, *Myth*, 44–46, and Moise, "Land Reform," 84–85.
173. *Nhân Dân*, Oct. 30, 1956, translated in Porter, *Myth*, 38; Asselin, *Hanoi's Road*, 39; Smith, *International History*, 1:94, 213; Moise, "Class-ism," 99.
174. Porter, *Myth*, 37; *Nhân Dân*, Nov. 2, 1956, quoted in Moise, "Land Reform," 84.
175. Fall, *Two Viet-Nams*, 156–57; Porter, *Myth*, 42.
176. Fall, *Two Viet-Nams*, 157.

177. *Thời Mới*, Dec. 4, 1956, cited in Porter, *Myth*, 49–50; Smith, *International History*, 1:213; Moise, "Class-ism," 99.
178. Asselin, *Hanoi's Road*, 39–40; Nguyen, *Hanoi's War*, 35, 53.
179. Duiker, *Communist Road*, 194; Peter Zinoman, *The Colonial Bastille: A History of Imprisonment in Vietnam, 1862–1940* (Berkeley: University of California Press, 2001), 229, 299–300. Duẩn had spent a decade on Poulo Condore (1931–36 and 1940–45); Thọ was there from 1930 to 1936, then in Tonkin jails from 1939 to 1944; Phạm Hùng had served time in both Saigon Prison (1931–34) and Poulo Condore (1934–36 and 1939–45). Duiker, *Historical Dictionary*, 200; Goscha, *Historical Dictionary*, 261, 369–70.
180. Goscha, *Historical Dictionary*, 318, 448; Kim Ninh, *World Transformed*, 130–31.
181. Asselin, *Hanoi's Road*, 87; Nguyen, *Hanoi's War*, 53–54.
182. Zinoman, "Nhân Văn Giai Phẩm," 72, 78; Boudarel, "Intellectual Dissidence," 158.
183. Ninh, *World Transformed*, 128–30; Boudarel, "Intellectual Dissidence," 157–58.
184. Ninh, *World Transformed*, 130–32, 138–43; Zinoman, "Nhân Văn Giai Phẩm," 72–74.
185. Ninh, *World Transformed*, 149–50; Vinh Sinh, *Phan Châu Trinh*, 21n67; Haydon Cherry, "Traffic in Translations: Đào Duy Anh and the Vocabulary of Vietnamese Marxism," paper presented at the Association for Asian Studies Annual Conference, San Diego, CA, March 21–24, 2013.
186. Zinoman, "Nhân Văn Giai Phẩm," 83ff.; Boudarel, "Intellectual Dissidence," 158.
187. Ninh, *World Transformed*, 149–50, 277n67; Zinoman, "Nhân Văn Giai Phẩm," 93.
188. Boudarel, "Intellectual Dissidence," 164.
189. Ninh, *World Transformed*, 154; Zinoman, "Nhân Văn Giai Phẩm," 60, 75.
190. Zinoman, "Nhân Văn Giai Phẩm," 77; Boudarel, "Intellectual Dissidence," 168–70.
191. Ninh, *World Transformed*, 162; Boudarel, "Intellectual Dissidence," 172–73; Vinh Sinh, *Phan Châu Trinh*, 21n67; Zinoman, "Nhân Văn Giai Phẩm," 82–83; Cherry, "Traffic in Translations."
192. Boudarel, "Intellectual Dissidence," 169.
193. "Nguyen Chi Thien," *The Viet Nam Literary Project*, http://vietnamlit.org/nguyenchithien; Margalit Fox, "Nguyen Chi Thien, Vietnamese Dissident Poet, Dies at 73," *New York Times*, Oct. 7, 2012.
194. "Nguyen Chi Thien," *Economist*, Oct.13, 2012, 114.
195. Fox, "Nguyen Chi Thien"; Porter, *Vietnam*, 172–73.
196. Vickerman, *Fate*, 111; Brocheux and Hémery, *Indochina*, 260; Moise, "Land Reform," 87, Table 4.
197. Moise, "Land Reform," 88–89; Benedict J. Tria Kerkvliet, *The Power of Everyday Politics: How Vietnamese Peasants Transformed National Policy* (Ithaca, NY: Cornell University Press, 2005), 42–43, 58, 70, 78.
198. Kerkvliet, *Power of Everyday Politics*, 58–60, 61, 78; Vickerman, *Fate*, 117.
199. Vickerman, *Fate*, 279, table 4.
200. Huỳnh Sanh Thông, "Greatest Little Man," 141.
201. Elliott, *Vietnamese War*, 611–14; Ahern, *Rural Pacification*, 162.
202. Pike, *PAVN*, 186, 350; Lenart, "Coming Out of the Shadows," 18; Nguyen, *Hanoi's War*, 65; Duiker, *Historical Dictionary*, 187.
203. Duiker, *Historical Dictionary*, 276–77.
204. Nguyen, *Hanoi's War*, 68–70; Asselin, *Hanoi's Road*, 169–72.
205. Huỳnh Kim Khánh, *Vietnamese Communism 1925–1945* (Ithaca, NY: Cornell University Press, 1982), 198, 204, 225; Daniel Hémery, *Révolutionnaires vietnamiens et pouvoir colonial en Indochine: Communistes, trotskystes, nationalistes à Saigon de*

1932 à 1937 (Paris: Maspero, 1975), 410–11; Martin Grossheim, "'Revisionism' in the Democratic Republic of Vietnam: New Evidence from the East German Archives," *Cold War History* 5, no. 4 (Nov. 2005): 451–77; see esp. 451–61.

206. Alexander B. Woodside, *Community and Revolution in Modern Vietnam* (Boston: Houghton Mifflin, 1976), 251.
207. Nguyen, *Hanoi's War*, 66–67, 79, 101–2, 56; Fox, "Nguyen Chi Thien."
208. *Aggression from the North*, 11–12; Kahin, *Intervention*, 307; Mark Philip Bradley, *Vietnam at War* (Oxford: Oxford University Press, 2009), 109; Asselin, *Hanoi's Road*, 200–201, 284n184.
209. Pike, *PAVN*, 350, and *Viet Cong*, 436.
210. Pike, *Viet Cong*, 115; Fall, *Viet-Nam Witness*, 316.
211. "Fighting between ARVN, Hoa Hao Results in 7 Killed," AFP, Saigon, Feb. 3, 1975; U.S. CIA, Foreign Broadcast Information Service, Daily Report, Asia and Pacific (henceforth FBIS-APA) 75-023, Feb. 3, 1975, p. L7.
212. Gerald C. Hickey, *Accommodation and Coalition in South Vietnam* (Santa Monica, CA: Rand Corporation, 1970), 17; Werner, *Peasant Politics*, 69.
213. Elliott, *Vietnamese War*, 617–18; James Wirtz, *The Tet Offensive: Intelligence Failure in War* (Ithaca, NY: Cornell University Press, 1991), 27; Harrison, "History's Heaviest Bombing," 132.
214. *Pentagon Papers*, Gravel ed., 2:304; Ann Blair, *Lodge in Vietnam: A Patriot Abroad* (New Haven, CT: Yale University Press, 1995), 104.
215. See, e.g., Kahin, *Intervention*, 182–87, 511nn27–28, and ch. 7; Ahern, *Rural Pacification*, 133.
216. Kahin, *Intervention*, 197–201; Khanh interview in *Stern* magazine, reprinted in *New Advocate*, April 1–15, 1972, quoted in Chomsky, *Towards a New Cold War*, 418–19.
217. *Pentagon Papers*, Gravel ed., 2:346ff.; Young, *Vietnam Wars*, 133; Kahin, *Intervention*, 256–57. See also Allen, *None So Blind*, 205–6.
218. Edwin E. Moise, *Tonkin Gulf and the Escalation of the Vietnam War* (Chapel Hill: University of North Carolina Press, 1996); Asselin, *Hanoi's Road*, 196–98.
219. *Kennan Diaries*, 431; John Lewis Gaddis, *George F. Kennan: An American Life* (New York: Penguin, 2011), 591.
220. Harrison, "History's Heaviest Bombing," 131–32.
221. W. S. Turley, "Urbanization in War: Hanoi, 1946–1973," *Pacific Affairs* 48, no. 3 (Autumn 1975): 380–88.
222. Ahern, *Rural Pacification*, 133; Bergerud, *Dynamics*, 73, 76; Young, *Vietnam Wars*, 146–48.
223. Ahern, *Rural Pacification*, 142, 147; Duiker, "Waging Revolutionary War," 32.
224. Asselin, *Hanoi's Road*, 198.
225. May 1968 State Department study cited in Chomsky, *Towards a New Cold War*, 161; Pribbenow, *Victory in Vietnam*, 126; Kahin, *Intervention*, 307; Ahern, *Rural Pacification*, 152; Lewy, *America in Vietnam*, 39–40; Asselin, *Hanoi's Road*, 200, 284n184.
226. Wirtz, *Tet Offensive*, 27; Robert K. Brigham, *ARVN: Life and Death in the South Vietnamese Army* (Lawrence: University Press of Kansas, 2006), 87–88; Elliott, *Vietnamese War*, 646.
227. Bruce Palmer, quoted in Wirtz, *Tet Offensive*, 28.
228. Lewy, *America in Vietnam*, 24; Kahin, *Intervention*, 263–64, 295–303.
229. Harrison, "History's Heaviest Bombing," 131.
230. Kahin, *Intervention*, 414, 416, 533n27.

231. Quoted in Michael Maclear, *Vietnam: The Ten Thousand Day War* (London: Methuen, 1981), 127–28.
232. Bergerud, *Dynamics*, 83; Ahern, *Rural Pacification*, 174; Frost, *Australia's War*, 37–38, 49, 52.
233. Bergerud, *Dynamics*, 82, 81, 47; Ahern, *Rural Pacification*, 152.
234. Ahern, *Rural Pacification*, 152, 394; Lewy, *America in Vietnam*, 39–40; Kahin, *Intervention*, 307–8; Maclear, *Vietnam*, 92, 119; Sam Adams, *War of Numbers: An Intelligence Memoir* (South Royalton, VT: Steerforth, 1994), 109.
235. Ahern, *Rural Pacification*, 180; Salemink, *Ethnography*, 203–204; Lewy, *America in Vietnam*, 110.
236. Bergerud, *Dynamics*, 197; Elliott, *Vietnamese War*, 613–16; Ahern, *Rural Pacification*, 241–42.
237. Race, *War Comes*, 64n; Bergerud, *Dynamics*, 93. For more provincial studies, see Elliott, *Vietnamese War*, and Hunt, *Vietnam's Southern Revolution*, on Mỹ Tho, and Frost, *Australia's War*, on Phước Tuy.
238. Elliott, *Vietnamese War*, 2:1323.
239. Bergerud, *Dynamics*, 197. On COSVN, see Young, *Vietnam Wars*, 72, 186; on the relationship between southern and northern communists, see Carlyle Thayer, "The PRG and the Reunification of Vietnam," *Dyason House Papers* 1, no. 5 (June 1975): 1–5.
240. Lewy, *America in Vietnam*, 75, 146–47.
241. Heonik Kwon, *After the Massacre: Commemoration and Consolation in Ha My and My Lai* (Berkeley: University of California Press, 2006), 196n53; Kahin, *Intervention*, 333–34.
242. Ahern, *Rural Pacification*, 413; Ives, *US Special Forces*, 115.
243. Ahern, *Rural Pacification*, 402.
244. Bergerud, *Dynamics*, 43; Elliott, *Vietnamese War*, 905–6.
245. Bernard B. Fall, *Last Reflections on a War* (New York: Doubleday, 1967), 28–29; Lewy, *America in Vietnam*, 69–73; Turse, *Kill Anything*, 76–79, 30–31.
246. Bergerud, *Dynamics*, 176, 89, 174, 277; Turse, *Kill Anything*, 56–57; Bernd Greiner, *War without Fronts: The USA in Vietnam* (New Haven, CT: Yale University Press, 2009), 68–74.
247. Lewy, *America in Vietnam*, 306; *Kennan Diaries*, 438.
248. *Réalités Cambodgiennes*, June 14, 1968, 19; see also July 7 and Aug. 18, 1967.
249. Quoted in Wilfred Burchett, *Vietnam Will Win!*, 2nd ed. (New York: Monthly Review Press, 1970), 111–13.
250. Adams, "Communism and Cambodia," 31, 22.
251. Bergerud, *Dynamics*, 99, 326, 306; Lewy, *America in Vietnam*, 72–73.
252. Elliott, *Vietnamese War*, 655–61.
253. William Fulbright, citing official Pentagon figures, quoted in Chomsky, *American Power*, 221n11; Maclear, *Vietnam*, 130, quotes another U.S. estimate, that 1965 guerrilla strength showed "an increase of thirty-three percent over 1964." Desertions from ARVN rose from 73,000 in 1964 to 113,000 in 1965; Young, *Vietnam Wars*, 142.
254. Pike, *Viet Cong*, 138; Adams, "Communism and Cambodia," 89.
255. Adams, *War of Numbers*, 84–86, 147, 152–53, 195, 66–67, 68–69, 82, xvi, 58, 148; Allen, *None So Blind*, ch. 12; C. Michael Hiam, *Who the Hell Are We Fighting? The Story of Sam Adams and the Vietnam Intelligence Wars* (Hanover, NH: Steerforth, 2006), 76, 81, 87–88, 100–101, 105, 113, 138, 248.
256. Wirtz, *Tet Offensive*, 119.

257. Nguyen, *Hanoi's War*, 79–80, 97–98.
258. Adams, *War of Numbers*, 101n; Adams, "Communism and Cambodia," 69n; Nguyen, *Hanoi's War*, 101–2.
259. Adams, "Communism and Cambodia," 31; Thayer, "PRG and the Unification," 4; Pike, *PAVN*, 186, and *Viet Cong*, 430; Bergerud, *Dynamics*, 197; Lenart, "Coming Out of the Shadows," 18.
260. Pike, *PAVN*, 207n6.
261. Brigham, *ARVN*, 24–25; Topmiller, *Lotus Unleashed*, 49, 71–90, 121–36; Kahin, *Intervention*, 418–32.
262. Topmiller, *Lotus Unleashed*, 135–36, 147, 129; Kahin, *Intervention*, 430.
263. *Pentagon Papers*, Gravel ed., 2:579–80, quoted in Bergerud, *Dynamics*, 112. Another U.S. official document proclaimed, "US influence over key decisions must be attained as quickly as possible" (*Pentagon Papers*, 2:580, 503), quoted in Cullen, "Document," 514. R. B. Smith describes the U.S. goal as "to ensure the survival of South Vietnam as an independent state: independent, that is, of North Vietnam—and also, in the long run, of the United States itself." Smith, *An International History of the Vietnam War*, vol. 3, *The Making of a Limited War, 1965–66* (New York: St. Martin's, 1991), 4.
264. Bergerud, *Dynamics*, 163; Kahin, *Intervention*, 412–13.
265. Bergerud, *Dynamics*, 73, 273, 76; Young, *Vietnam Wars*, 146–48.
266. Bergerud, *Dynamics*, 82, 326, 236–37, 161; Elliott, *Vietnamese War*, 614–15.
267. Bergerud, *Dynamics*, 274, 166, 172–73, 276, 114, 176, 277, 5; Turse, *Kill Anything*, 148–55, 160.
268. Jonathan Schell, *The Military Half: An Account of Destruction in Quảng Ngãi and Quảng Tin* (New York: Vintage, 1968); Greiner, *War without Fronts*, 143–238, 253–55; Turse, *Kill Anything*, 108–43; Earl Martin, *Reaching the Other Side* (New York: Crown, 1978), 161–66.
269. Bergerud, *Dynamics*, 236–37.
270. Turse, *Kill Anything*, 68–69, 74, 144–48.
271. Lewy, *America in Vietnam*, 75; Adams, *War of Numbers*, 117.
272. Adams, *War of Numbers*, 54–55, 71, 84, 86, 94, 132n, 147, 152–53; Adams, letter to the author, Sept. 26, 1976.
273. Don Oberdorfer, *Tet* (New York: Avon, 1971), 71, 134–35; Maclear, *Vietnam*, 195; Adams, *War of Numbers*, 149.
274. *New Republic*, Jan. 6, 1968, 29, citing an interview with Henry Brandon of the London *Sunday Times*, quoted in Chomsky, *American Power*, 188.
275. Robert L. Sansom, *The Economics of Insurgency in the Mekong Delta of Vietnam* (Cambridge, MA: MIT Press, 1970), 54–55.
276. Willbanks, *Tet Offensive*, 17–18.
277. Lewy, *America in Vietnam*, 67; Willbanks, *Tet Offensive*, 15–17.
278. Ronald H. Spector, "'How do you know if you're winning?' Perception and Reality in America's Military Performance in Vietnam, 1965–1970," in Werner and Huynh, *Vietnam War*, 154–55.
279. Willbanks, *Tet Offensive*, 19–25.
280. Willbanks, *Tet Offensive*, 39; Oberdorfer, *Tet*, 134; Allen, *None So Blind*, 258–60.
281. Ahern, *Rural Pacification*, 309; Greiner, *War without Fronts*, 68, 144.
282. Willbanks, *Tet Offensive*, 26–42, 98; Allen, *None So Blind*, 262.
283. *Kennan Diaries*, 450.
284. Sheehan, *Bright Shining Lie*, 719–20; Nhã Ca, *Mourning Headband for Hue: An Account of the Battle for Hue, Vietnam 1968*, trans. Olga Dror (Bloomington:

Indiana University Press, 2014); Dror's thoughtful introduction outlines varying U.S. and Vietnamese perspectives on the death toll and those responsible, xxiii–xxxi, xli–lvii. See also Stephen T. Hosmer, *Viet Cong Repression and Its Implications for the Future* (Lexington, MA: Heath, 1970), 48–51.

285. Lewy, *America in Vietnam*, 108; Bergerud, *Dynamics*, 213.
286. Greiner, *War without Fronts*, chs. 5–6; Michael Bilton and Kevin Sim, *Four Hours in My Lai* (New York: Viking, 1991; Kwon, *After the Massacre*; Turse, *Kill Anything*, 47, 60; Deborah Nelson, *The War Behind Me: Vietnam Veterans Confront the Truth about U.S. War Crimes* (New York: Basic Books, 2008); Michael Sallah and Mitch Weiss, *Tiger Force: A True Story of Men and War* (New York: Little, Brown, 2006); Gregory L. Vistica, *The Education of Lieutenant Kerrey* (New York: St. Martin's, 2003). For another view, see Gary Kulik and Peter Zinoman, "Misrepresenting Atrocities: *Kill Anything that Moves* and the Continuing Distortions of the War in Vietnam," *Cross-Currents* 12 (Sept. 2014): 162–98, available online at http://cross-currents.berkeley.edu/e-journal/issue-12/zinoman-and-kulik.
287. Ahern, *Rural Pacification*, 316.
288. Kennan, speech in Newark, New Jersey, Feb. 29, 1968, quoted in Frank Costigliola, "Is This George Kennan?," *New York Review of Books*, Dec. 8, 2011, available online at http://www.nybooks.com/articles/2011/12/08/is-this-george-kennan/ (accessed April 23, 2014).
289. Ahern, *Rural Pacification*, 317; *Kennan Diaries*, 454.
290. Ronald Spector, *After Tet: The Bloodiest Year in Vietnam* (New York: Free Press, 1993).
291. Lewy, *America in Vietnam*, 144.
292. Lewy, *America in Vietnam*, 142–44; Greiner, *War without Fronts*, 256–78; Turse, *Kill Anything*, 208–15, 248–56.
293. Greiner, *War without Fronts*, 73–74; Gibson, *Perfect War*, 229–30; see also Lewy, *America in Vietnam*, 444–45.
294. Barbara Harff and Ted Robert Gurr, "Towards Empirical Theory of Genocides and Politicides: Identification and Measurement of Cases since 1945," *International Studies Quarterly* 32, no. 3 (1988): 364–65; Harff and Gurr, "Victims of the State: Genocides, Politicides and Group Repression since 1945," *International Review of Victimology* 1 (1989): 26–27.
295. Hosmer, *Viet Cong Repression*, 42–45, 69–78; Kulik and Zinoman, "Misrepresenting Atrocities," 186.
296. Martin, *Reaching*, 132–35; Kwon, *After the Massacre*, ch. 2; Pham Xuan Sinh, "All My Ancestors are Buried Here," in Christian Appy, *Patriots: The Vietnam War Remembered from All Sides* (New York: Viking, 2003), 25–27; Charles Joiner, *The Politics of Massacre: Political Processes in South Vietnam* (Philadelphia, Temple University Press, 1974), 247, 291; Young, *Vietnam Wars*, 170.
297. Brigham, *ARVN*, 124, 48–49, 84–85, 88; Konrad Kellen, "1971 and Beyond: The View from Hanoi," in *Indochina in Conflict*, ed. J. J. Zasloff and A. E. Goodman (Lexington, MA: D.C. Heath, 1972), 103–7.
298. Elliott, *Vietnamese War*, 904–5; Ahern, *Rural Pacification*, 314, 387–88.
299. Donald Kirk, "Presidential Campaign Politics: the Uncontested 1971 Election," in *Electoral Politics in South Vietnam*, ed. John C. Donnell and Charles A. Joiner (Lexington, MA: D.C. Heath, 1974), 60.
300. Theresa A. Tull, "Broadening the Base: South Vietnamese Elections 1967–71," in Donnell, *Electoral Politics*, 37–38, 41–43.

301. Tull, "Broadening the Base," 43–45, 47–48, 50, 51; Kirk, "Presidential Campaign Politics," 67–68.
302. Dror, introduction to Nhã Ca, *Mourning Headband for Hue*, xvii, xx; K. W. Taylor, ed., *Voices from the Second Republic of South Vietnam, 1967–1975* (Ithaca, NY: Cornell Southeast Asia Program, 2014).
303. Ahern, *Rural Pacification*, 405.
304. Joiner, *Politics of Massacre*, 279.
305. Kirk, "Presidential Campaign Politics," 60, 68–69; Tull, "Broadening the Base," 38–39; Joiner, *Politics of Massacre*, 170–71.
306. Ta Van Tai and Jerry Mark Silverman, "Elections and Political Party Constraints Following the 1972 Offensive," in Donnell, *Electoral Politics*, 131, 137.
307. Ta and Silverman, "Elections and Political Party Constraints," 132; Tull, "Broadening the Base," 36.
308. Ahern, *Rural Pacification*, 350, 360, 334, 388, 329, 368, 386; Porter, *Vietnam*, 26.
309. Ahern, *Rural Pacification*, 330, 334.
310. Pike, *War, Peace and the Viet Cong*, 2, 6; Pike, *Viet Cong*, 115; Bergerud, *Dynamics*, 304, 254, 237.
311. Douglas Pike, *The Viet-Cong Strategy of Terror* (Saigon: U.S. Mission, 1970), 1, 11.
312. Bergerud, *Dynamics*, 314, 76; Young, *Vietnam Wars*, 146–48.
313. Bergerud, *Dynamics*, 273, 303, 314.
314. Ngo Vinh Long, "The Tet Offensive and Its Aftermath, Part 3," *Indochina Newsletter* 60 (Nov.-Dec. 1989): 7–10.
315. Bergerud, *Dynamics*, 317–18, 320, 328.
316. Ahern, *Rural Pacification*, 386; Elliott, *Vietnamese War*, 1291; Ngo, "Tet Offensive," 9–10.
317. Frost, *Australia's War in Vietnam*, 162; Ahern, *Rural Pacification*, 387–88.
318. Lewy, *America in Vietnam*, 410; *Kennan Diaries*, 473–74.
319. Maclear, *Vietnam*, 306, 310; Lewy, *America in Vietnam*, 410–12.
320. Maclear, *Vietnam*, 306.
321. Werner, *Peasant Politics*, 69; "'Big Minh' Statement," AFP, Saigon, Feb. 6, 1975, FBIS-APA-75-026, L4.
322. "Fighting between ARVN, Hoa Hao Results in 7 Killed," AFP, Saigon, FBIS-APA-75-023, Feb. 3, 1975, L7; "RVN Government Statement on Actions against Hoa Hao, Press," *Vietnam Press* (Saigon), Feb. 6, 1975, FBIS-APA-75-026, L1.
323. "Fighting between ARVN, Hoa Hao," L7; Edward Lansdale, "Hòa Hảo University" (June 1974), http://pghh-research.tripod.com/hoahaouniversity.html (accessed Oct. 4, 2014); Nguyễn Long Thành Nam, *Hoa Hao Buddhism in the Course of Vietnam's History* (New York: Nova, 2003), 144–45; "Two Hoa Hoa Leaders in RVN Sentenced to Hard Labor," AFP Saigon, April 6, 1975, FBIS-APA-75-071, L13.
324. "Fighting between ARVN, Hoa Hao," L7; "RVN Government Statement on Actions against Hoa Hao," L1.
325. *Repression of Montagnards: Conflicts over Land and Religion in Vietnam's Central Highlands* (New York: Human Rights Watch, 2002), 25; Salemink, *Ethnography*, 204, 254.
326. Martin, *Reaching*, 42ff.; Seth Lipsky, "Discounting Vietnam," *FEER*, May 9, 1975, 36.
327. Ahern, *Rural Pacification*, 413.
328. Ahern, *Rural Pacification*, 410; Gerald K. Haines, foreword to Ahern, *Rural Pacification*, x.
329. Turse, *Kill Anything*, 12–13.

CHAPTER 11

1. "'Big Minh' Statement," Agence France Press, Saigon, Feb. 6, 1975, FBIS-APA-75-026, L4.
2. Nayan Chanda, "When the Old Regime Bows Out," *FEER*, May 2, 1975, 15; Ben Kiernan, "Vietnamese Democracy: An Interview with Senator Vũ Văn Mẫu," *Tharunka*, March 26, 1975, 7; Bui Tin, *Following Ho Chi Minh: Memoirs of a Vietnamese Colonel* (Honolulu: University of Hawai'i Press, 1995), 85.
3. Peter Zinoman, "Vietnamese Americans and the Future of Vietnamese Studies in the United States," in *Southeast Asian Studies: Pacific Perspectives*, ed. Anthony Reid (Tempe: Arizona State University, 2003), 299–300.
4. Nayan Chanda, "The Last Word from Saigon," *FEER*, May 9, 1975, 10; Earl Martin, *Reaching the Other Side: The Journal of an American Who Stayed to Witness Vietnam's Postwar Transition* (New York: Crown, 1978); Nancy Viviani, *The Long Journey: Vietnamese Migration and Settlement in Australia* (Melbourne: Melbourne University Press, 1984), 20.
5. Bui, *Following Ho Chi Minh*, 84–86; Jonathan C. Randal, "Leading Vietnamese Communist, in West, Criticizes Government in Hanoi," *Washington Post*, Jan. 1, 1990.
6. Ngô Vĩnh Long, "From Polarisation to Integration in Vietnam," *Journal of Contemporary Asia* 39, no. 2 (May 2009): 302–4; Holmes Brown and Don Luce, *Hostages of War: Saigon's Political Prisoners* (Washington, DC: Indochina Mobile Education Project, 1973), iii; Nick Turse, *Kill Anything That Moves: The Real American War in Vietnam* (New York: Picador, 2013), 172–73, 178–82, 332n157; Vũ Văn Mẫu quoted in Kiernan, "Vietnamese Democracy," 7; George McT. Kahin, *Intervention: How America Became Involved in Vietnam* (New York: Knopf, 1986), 430; Donald Kirk, "Presidential Campaign Politics: The Uncontested 1971 Election," in *Electoral Politics in South Vietnam*, ed. John C. Donnell and Charles A. Joiner (Lexington, MA: D.C. Heath, 1974), 55.
7. Gareth Porter, *Vietnam: The Politics of Bureaucratic Socialism* (Ithaca, NY: Cornell University Press, 1993), 174. For examples, see U.S. Department of State, "Vietnam's Refugee Machine" (typescript), July 20, 1979, Doc. 1-100, "Interviews of Refugees by American Consul, Song Khla, Thailand, Mid-June 1979," 6, "Vietnamese Case Histories," B-3, B-4; Doan Van Toai, *Le goulag vietnamien* (Paris: Laffont, 1979).
8. *Report of an Amnesty International Mission to the Socialist Republic of Viet Nam, 10–21 December, 1979* (London: Amnesty International, 1981), 3, 17; Amnesty International, "Socialist Republic of Viet Nam: Amnesty International's Continuing Concerns Regarding Detention without Charge or Trial for the Purpose of 'Re-Education,'" London, April 1985, ASA 41/04/85, document 1, 6; Amnesty International, *Viet Nam: Arrests of Political Prisoners, 1990–1991*, London, June 1992, ASA 41/01/92, 1; Carlyle A. Thayer, "Political Development in Vietnam 1975–1985," in *Contemporary Vietnam: Perspectives from Australia*, ed. Colin Mackerras, Robert Cribb, and Allan Healy (Wollongong, Australia: University of Wollongong Press, 1988), 67; Porter, *Vietnam*, 175–76.
9. On July 12, 1975, Hanoi denounced the "Vietnamese traitors Lương Trọng Tường and Huỳnh Văn Nhiệm" and reported the dissolution of two Hòa Hảo "reactionary organizations," namely, "Lương Trọng Tường's central church, 1st mandate, and Huỳnh Văn Nhiệm's Hòa Hảo central committee, 4th mandate," which "they founded." FBIS-APA-75-135, July 14, 1975, L2. See also Nguyễn Long Thành Nam, *Hoa Hao Buddhism in the Course of Vietnam's History* (New York: Nova, 2003),

ch. 13; Melanie Beresford, *Vietnam: Politics, Economics and Society* (London: Frances Pinter, 1988), 126; Porter, *Vietnam*, 183–84.

10. Ngô Công Đức, "Statement," *New York Review of Books*, Nov. 5, 1970; Kirk, "Presidential Campaign Politics," 67–68; "Night Falls on *Morning News*," *FEER*, July 17, 1981, 20.
11. *Report of an Amnesty International Mission*, 7–8; Hue-Tam Ho Tai, pers. comm., Nov. 2, 2014.
12. *New York Times*, Oct. 7, 2012.
13. Porter, *Vietnam*, 175n100; Ben Kiernan, *The Pol Pot Regime: Race, Power and Genocide in Cambodia under the Khmer Rouge, 1975–1979* (New Haven, CT: Yale University Press, 1996), 1–3.
14. "Landmines Still Exacting a Heavy Toll on Vietnamese Civilians," *Guardian*, Sept. 18, 2012, available online at http://www.theguardian.com/world/2012/sep/18/vietnam-unexploded-landmines-bombs (accessed July 1, 2016); "Vietnamese Children Killed by Mortar Shell," *Guardian*, Dec. 3, 2012.
15. Edwin A. Martini, *Agent Orange: History, Science, and the Politics of Uncertainty* (Amherst: University of Massachusetts Press, 2012), 2, 198–99, 206.
16. Melanie Beresford, "Issues in Economic Unification: Overcoming the Legacies of Separation," in *Postwar Vietnam: Dilemmas in Socialist Development*, ed. David G. Marr and Christine P. White (Ithaca, NY: Cornell Southeast Asia Program, 1988), 99.
17. Douglas Beane, "On the Hanoi New Economic Zone" (typescript, Oct. 28, 1980, copy in possession of the author), 2–3, 6, 8; see also Andrew Hardy, *Red Hills: Migrants and the State in the Highlands of Vietnam* (Honolulu: University of Hawai'i Press, 2003), 218–19; Barry Wain, *The Refused: The Agony of the Indochina Refugees* (Hong Kong: Dow Jones, 1981), 40–42, 142–43,150; and Viviani, *Long Journey*, 26.
18. Hardy, *Red Hills*, 229; Li Tana, *Peasants on the Move: Rural-Urban Migration in the Hanoi Region* (Singapore: Institute of Southeast Asian Studies, 1996), 8.
19. U.S. Department of State, "Vietnam's Refugee Machine," Doc. 1-135, "Interview with a Former Religious Figure in Vietnam, July 20, 1979," 2–3.
20. Beresford, *Vietnam*, 151–52, 221n4; Li, *Peasants on the Move*, 8.
21. Stewart E. Fraser, "Vietnam's Exploding Population," in Mackerras, *Contemporary Vietnam*, 79; Pierre Brocheux and Daniel Hémery, *Indochina: an Ambiguous Colonization* (Berkeley: University of California Press, 2009), 261.
22. Bill Hayton, "The Paracels: Historical Evidence Must be Examined," RSIS Commentary 126/2014, July 3, 2014.
23. On the Vietnamese claim, see Trần Đức Anh Sơn, ed., *Tư liệu về chủ quyền của Việt Nam đối với quần đảo Hoàng Sa* (Hồ Chí Minh City: Nhà xuất bản Văn hóa-văn nghệ, 2014). On China's role in Southeast Asia, see Ben Kiernan, "The Inclusion of the Khmer Rouge in the Cambodian Peace Process: Causes and Consequences," in *Genocide and Democracy in Cambodia*, ed. Ben Kiernan (New Haven, CT: Yale Southeast Asia Studies, 1993), 199, 216–19.
24. Nayan Chanda, *Brother Enemy: The War after the War* (New York: Harcourt Brace Jovanovich, 1986), 19; *FEER*, "South China Sea: Dividing the Waters," Aug. 7, 1981, 30, 32.
25. Nayan Chanda, "A Massive Shock for Vietnam," *FEER*, Aug. 10, 1979, 89; Douglas Pike, *PAVN: People's Army of Vietnam* (Novato, CA: Presidio, 1986), 352–53; Carlyle A. Thayer, "The Regularization of Politics: Continuity and Change in the Party's Central Committee, 1951–1986," in Marr and White, *Postwar Vietnam*, 183–84.

26. Charles Benoit, "Viet Nam's 'Boat People,'" in *The Third Indochina Conflict*, ed. David W.P. Elliott (Boulder, CO: Westview, 1981), 143; Michael Godley, "A Summer Cruise to Nowhere: China and the Vietnamese Chinese in Perspective," *Australian Journal of Chinese Affairs* 4 (July 1980): 36, 49.
27. *FEER*, "South China Sea," 32.
28. Donald S. Zagoria, *Vietnam Triangle: Moscow, Peking, Hanoi* (New York: Pegasus, 1967); John C. Donnell and Melvin Gurtov, *North Vietnam: Left of Moscow, Right of Peking* (Santa Monica, CA, RAND, 1968).
29. Franklin B. Weinstein, "U.S.-Vietnam Relations and the Security of Southeast Asia," *Foreign Affairs*, July 1978, available online at http://www.foreignaffairs.com/articles/29531/franklin-b-weinstein/us-vietnam-relations-and-the-security-of-southeast-asia (accessed Oct. 24, 2014).
30. Kiernan, *Pol Pot Regime*, 103–7, 296; Chanda, *Brother Enemy*, 16.
31. Nayan Chanda, "Shake-up at the Bottom," *FEER*, April 16, 1982, 16.
32. Kiernan, *Pol Pot Regime*, 111ff., 1–3, 118–21; *Asiaweek*, Sept. 22, 1978: "Most intelligence analysts in Bangkok agree that Cambodian raids and land grabs escalated the ill-will... until peace was irretrievable." See also Ben Kiernan, "New Light on the Origins of the Vietnam-Kampuchea Conflict," *Bulletin of Concerned Asian Scholars* 12, no. 4 (1980): 61–65, esp. 64–65; Michael Vickery, *Cambodia 1975–82* (Boston: South End, 1984), 189–96; Kiernan, *How Pol Pot Came to Power* (London: Verso, 1985), 413–21.
33. Author's interviews with Vong Heng, Flers, France, Oct. 8, 1979, and Ly Veasna, Caen, France, Oct. 7, 1979. For more details, see Kiernan, *Pol Pot Regime*, 108–9, 359–60.
34. Richard Nations, "Inside the Bitter Border," *FEER*, Aug. 19, 1977, 10; Kiernan, *Pol Pot Regime*, 296–98, 423–25.
35. Ben Kiernan, *Cambodia: The Eastern Zone Massacres*, Columbia University, Center for the Study of Human Rights, Documentation Series No. 1, 1986.
36. On July 30, 1977, China's foreign minister, Huang Hua, in a private speech to Foreign Ministry cadres, clearly put the blame on Vietnam and said China's position had been communicated to the Indochinese states. King C. Chen, ed., *China and the Three Worlds* (White Plains, NY: M. E. Sharpe, 1979), 271–72.
37. Godley, "Summer Cruise," 48.
38. Richard Nations and Nayan Chanda, "The Bitter Border," *FEER*, Aug. 19, 1977, 9–12; Nayan Chanda, "The Bloody Border," *FEER*, April 21, 1978, 17–22; Kiernan, "New Light," 61–65.
39. Murray Hiebert, "Withdrawal Symptoms," *FEER*, July 14, 1988, 14.
40. Kiernan, *Pol Pot Regime*, 389; Wain, *Refused*, 42.
41. Godley, "Summer Cruise," 52, 41, 35; Benoit, "Viet Nam's 'Boat People,'" 151, and draft ms., 1–2.
42. Godley, "Summer Cruise," 37, 40; Wain, *Refused*, 66.
43. U.S. Department of State, "Vietnam's Refugee Machine," 5, 4.
44. *FEER*, May 30, 1985.
45. Benoit, "Viet Nam's 'Boat People,'" 140. See also Wain, *Refused*.
46. U.S. Department of State, "Vietnam's Refugee Machine," Introduction and Overview, 5, 1; Benoit, "Viet Nam's 'Boat People,'" 140; Patrick Smith, "Pull Factor Gets the Push," *FEER*, July 17, 1981, 26–31.
47. Benoit, "Viet Nam's 'Boat People,'" draft ms., 1.
48. Viviani, *Long Journey*, 68–69, 73–74, 85.

49. Alexander Barton Woodside, *Vietnam and the Chinese Model* (Cambridge, MA: Harvard University Press, 1971), 283.
50. Human Rights Watch, *Repression of Montagnards: Conflicts over Land and Religion in Vietnam's Central Highlands* (New York: Human Rights Watch, 2002), 25.
51. Author's interviews with Dega leaders Y Bhuat Eban and Sil Be, Site 2, Thailand, Jan. 21, 1986.
52. Barbara Crossette, "But Montagnards Still Wait in a Thai Camp," *New York Times*, Jan. 20, 1986.
53. Y Bhuat Eban and Sil Be interviews; Crossette, "But Montagnards Still Wait."
54. Y Bhuat Eban and Sil Be interviews; Crossette, "But Montagnards Still Wait."
55. Trường Chinh, Political Report of Vietnamese Communist Party, Hanoi Radio in English, Dec. 15, 1986.
56. Human Rights Watch, *Montagnard Christians in Vietnam: A Case Study in Religious Repression* (New York: Human Rights Watch, 2011), 3n4.
57. David W. P. Elliott, *The Vietnamese War: Revolution and Social Change in the Mekong Delta 1930–1975* (Armonk, NY: M. E. Sharpe, 2003), 1::4–5, 122–27, 483–521, 2:1235–44, 1380; Beresford, *Vietnam*, 149.
58. Ngo Vinh Long, "Some Aspects of Cooperativization in the Mekong Delta," in Marr and White, *Postwar Vietnam*, 169, citing a 1982 work by Le Minh Ngoc.
59. Christopher E. Goscha, *Historical Dictionary of the Indochina War, 1945–1954* (Honolulu: University of Hawai'i Press, 2012), 336; William J. Duiker, "The Legacy of History in Vietnam," *Current History*, Dec. 1984, 409–12, 432ff., 411n11.
60. William Duiker, *Historical Dictionary of Vietnam*, 2nd ed. (Lanham, MD: Scarecrow, 1998), 278.
61. "Night Falls on *Morning News*," *FEER*, July 17, 1981, 20; Duiker, *Historical Dictionary*, 241.
62. Duiker, *Historical Dictionary*, 187; "Biography of Nguyễn Văn Linh, General Secretary of the Communist Party of Vietnam" (Hanoi, 1987), 2; Samuel Adams, "Communism and Cambodia," U.S. CIA, Directorate of Intelligence, May 1972, declassified Feb. 19, 1987, 31n.; Carlyle A. Thayer, "The PRG and the Unification of Viet-Nam," *Dyason House Papers* 1, no. 5 (June 1975): 4.
63. Nguyễn Văn Linh, interview in *Đại đoàn kết*, Nov. 5, 1977, quoted in Nguyễn Văn Canh, *Vietnam under Communism, 1975–1982* (Stanford, CA, Hoover Institution Press, 1983), 26.
64. Adams, "Communism and Cambodia," 69; Goscha, *Historical Dictionary*, 336.
65. Thayer, "Political Development," 74. See also Benedict J. Tria Kerkvliet, *The Power of Everyday Politics: How Vietnamese Peasants Transformed National Policy* (Ithaca, NY: Cornell University Press, 2005).
66. Murray Hiebert, "The Compromise Candidate," *FEER*, July 7, 1988, 34.
67. Duiker, *Historical Dictionary*, 187, 278; Beresford, *Vietnam*, 153, 222n2; "Biography of Nguyễn Văn Linh," 2; Wain, *Refused*, 106.
68. Chanda, "Shake-up at the Bottom," 16.
69. Adams, "Communism and Cambodia," 23, 69, 41, 88, 69–80; Chanda, *Brother Enemy*, 14.
70. Kiernan, *Pol Pot Regime*, 389; Beresford, *Vietnam*, 152, 150, 134.
71. Carlyle A. Thayer, "Vietnam's New Pragmatism," *Current History*, April 1983, 158; Hiebert, "Compromise Candidate," 34; Duiker, "Legacy," 409; Beresford, *Vietnam*, 152.
72. Wain, *Refused*, 132; Benoit, "Viet Nam's 'Boat People,'" 140.
73. Thayer, "Political Development," 74; Beresford, *Vietnam*, 152–54.

74. Beresford, *Vietnam*, 160–61, dates the sixth plenum to August 1979; cf. Peggy Duff, "The Economic Decisions of the VIth Plenum of the Central Committee of the Vietnamese Communist Party, July, 1979," *Vietnam South East Asia International* 14, nos. 1–3 (Jan.–March 1980): appendix, 1–10; Thayer, "Vietnam's New Pragmatism," 158, dates the plenum to September 1979.
75. Thayer, "Vietnam's New Pragmatism," 158; Duff, "Economic Decisions," 3.
76. Duff, "Economic Decisions," 3–4.
77. Beresford, *Vietnam*, 124–25; "Night Falls on *Morning News*," *FEER*, July 17, 1981, 20; Porter, *Vietnam*, 167; Duiker, *Historical Dictionary*, 241.
78. Peter Woodrow, pers. comm., 1982.
79. Dương Thu Hương, *Paradise of the Blind* (New York: Perennial, 2002), "About the Author," 1; Nina McPherson, "Dương Thu Hương," *The Viet Nam Literature Project*, http://vietnamlit.org/wiki/index.php?title=Duong_Thu_Huong (accessed Sept. 29, 2014).
80. Paul Quinn-Judge, "A Vietnamese Cassandra," *FEER*, Feb. 26, 1982, 14–16.
81. Thayer, "Vietnam's New Pragmatism," 158.
82. "Biography of Nguyễn Văn Linh," 2.
83. Carlyle A. Thayer, "The Regularization of Politics: Continuity and Change in the Party's Central Committee, 1951–1986," in Marr and White, *Postwar Vietnam*, 189.
84. Thayer, "Vietnam's New Pragmatism," 159.
85. "Biography of Nguyễn Văn Linh," 2; Duiker, "Legacy," 410; Duiker, *Historical Dictionary*, 187; Kelvin Rowley, *After Lê Duẩn: Political Transition Underway in Hanoi* (Melbourne: Asian Bureau Australia, 1986), 5.
86. Beresford, *Vietnam*, 224n11.
87. Duiker, "Legacy," 411n11.
88. "The Man Behind Reform," *Asiaweek*, May 20, 1988, 29; Murray Hiebert, "Reforming Pains," *FEER*, March 17, 1988, 20.
89. Hiebert, "Cheer in Cholon," 21.
90. Thayer, "Vietnam's New Pragmatism," 158–60; Chanda, "Shake-up at the Bottom," 16–17.
91. Thayer, "Vietnam's New Pragmatism," 160.
92. Huynh Kim Khanh, "A Legend Demoted," *FEER*, April 9, 1982, 32–33; Chanda, "Shake-up at the Bottom," 16; Thayer, "Vietnam's New Pragmatism," 160, 161.
93. Duiker, *Historical Dictionary*, 278, 172, 202.
94. Thayer, "Regularization of Politics," 186–88.
95. Thayer, "Vietnam's New Pragmatism," 185; Beresford, *Vietnam*, 154.
96. Kerkvliet, *Power of Everyday Politics*, 143–45, 158–59, 168–70, 172, 196.
97. Kerkvliet, *Power of Everyday Politics*, 190, 234.
98. Porter, *Vietnam*, 161.
99. Thayer, "Vietnam's New Pragmatism," 158; Kerkvliet, *Power of Everyday Politics*, 177–78; *Tạp Chí Cộng Sản*, Feb. 1985, quoted in Ngo Vinh Long, "Cooperativization in the Mekong Delta," 165.
100. "Nguyen Van Linh Addresses Ho Chi Minh City Congress" (Oct. 23, 1986), Hanoi Radio, Oct. 25, 1986, translated in BBC *Summary of World Broadcasts*, Oct. 31, 1986, FE/8404 B/7.
101. "Nguyen Van Linh Addresses Ho Chi Minh City Congress," B/8; Duiker, "Legacy," 410–11.
102. Duiker, "Legacy," 411; Paul Quinn-Judge, "Hanoi's Liberal Experiment Slips Out of Control," *Guardian*, May 19, 1983; *FEER*, Dec. 15, 1983, 46–48.
103. Porter, *Vietnam*, 68, 139.

104. Duiker, "Legacy," 411.
105. Võ Văn Kiệt, "Transformation of Private Industry and Trade in South Vietnam—Some Practical Problems" (Dec. 1984), in *Việt Nam Social Sciences* 2 (1985): 47–48, 59, 60.
106. Barry Wain, "Vietnamese 'Club' Boldly Voices Dissent," *Asian Wall Street Journal*, April 27, 1989, 20; "Biography of Nguyễn Văn Linh," 2.
107. Murray Hiebert, "Cheer in Cholon," *FEER*, Aug. 4, 1988, 20–21.
108. Her short story "Miền Cỏ Tơ" (Land of the cotton grass) appeared in 1985 in the anthology *Chân Dung Người Hàng Xóm* (Portrait of my neighbors). McPherson, "Dương Thu Hương."
109. Nayan Chanda, "Back to Basics," *FEER*, Nov. 13, 1986, 108.
110. Bill Hayton, *Vietnam: Rising Dragon* (New Haven, CT: Yale University Press, 2010), 189.
111. Ben Kiernan, "Vietnam's New Broom Targets 'Economic Errors,'" *Guardian*, Feb. 13, 1987.
112. "Biography of Nguyễn Văn Linh," 2.
113. "Biography of Nguyễn Văn Linh," 2.
114. Bui, *Following Ho Chi Minh*, 145.
115. "Nguyen Van Linh Addresses Ho Chi Minh City Congress," B/11, 7.
116. "Nguyen Van Linh Addresses Ho Chi Minh City Congress," B/5, 14, 9–11.
117. "Nguyen Van Linh Addresses Ho Chi Minh City Congress," B/12.
118. "Nguyen Van Linh Addresses Ho Chi Minh City Congress," B/12.
119. "Nguyen Van Linh Addresses Ho Chi Minh City Congress," B/16.
120. Trường Chinh, "Summary of Political Report," speech at opening session of the VCP Sixth Congress, broadcast live on Hanoi Radio, Dec. 15, 1986, trans. Agence France Press, Hong Kong, 1.
121. Ben Kiernan, "In Vietnam, The Talk Is of Reform," *International Herald Tribune*, March 20, 1987.
122. Thayer, "Regularization of Politics," 187.
123. "Biography of Nguyễn Văn Linh," 1.
124. "A Firebrand Pen for Linh's Reforms," *Asiaweek*, June 28, 1987, 15.
125. Kiernan, "Vietnam's New Broom"; Barbara Crossette, "Vietnam Parley Ends," *New York Times*, Jan. 2, 1987.
126. Carlyle A. Thayer, "Vietnam: The South Must Manage the Economy," *International Herald Tribune*, Jan. 22, 1987.
127. Porter, *Vietnam*, 154, 97; Duiker, *Historical Dictionary*, 241.
128. Murray Hiebert, "Reform and Succession," *FEER*, March 31, 1988, 20.
129. Hiebert, "Cheer in Cholon," 20.
130. Li, *Peasants on the Move*, 4.
131. Huỳnh Kim Khánh, "Vietnam's Reforms: 'Renewal or Death,'" *Indochina Issues* 84 (Sept. 1988): 4.
132. Li, *Peasants on the Move*, 8.
133. Hiebert, "Withdrawal Symptoms," 14.
134. Kiernan, "Deferring Peace in Cambodia," 61; Kiernan, "Inclusion of the Khmer Rouge," 193–94; Hiebert, "Withdrawal Symptoms."
135. Porter, *Vietnam*, 53.
136. Bill Hayton, *The South China Sea: The Struggle for Power in Asia* (New Haven, CT: Yale University Press, 2014), 81–84.
137. *CIA World Factbook*, cited in Index Mundi, http://www.indexmundi.com/g/g.aspx?v=132&c=vm&l=en (accessed Oct. 24, 2014).

138. Bui, *Following Ho Chi Minh*, 145–46.
139. Murray Hiebert, "A Dragon-Year Blessing," *FEER*, Feb. 25, 1988, 22–23.
140. "Nguyễn Chí Thiện," *The Viet Nam Literature Project*, http://www.vietnamlit.org/nguyenchithien/ (accessed Nov. 14, 2014). See also Nguyễn Chí Thiện, "Autobiography of Nguyễn Chí Thiện," *The Viet Nam Literature Project*, http://www.vietnamlit.org/nguyenchithien/autobiography.html.
141. Huỳnh, "Vietnam's Reforms," 4–5.
142. FEER, *Asia 1990 Yearbook* (Hong Kong: Far Eastern Economic Review, 1990), 243.
143. Huỳnh, "Vietnam's Reforms," 2.
144. Wain, "Vietnamese 'Club' Boldly Voices Dissent," 1, 20.
145. Porter, *Vietnam*, 68.
146. Olga Dror, introduction to Nhã Ca, *Mourning Headband for Hue* (Bloomington: Indiana University Press, 2014), xlv–xlviii.
147. Hue-Tam Ho Tai, "Dương Thu Hương and the Literature of Disenchantment," *Việt Nam Forum* 14 (1993): 90.
148. Dương Thu Hương, *Beyond Illusions*, trans. Nina McPherson and Phan Huy Duong (New York: Hyperion, 2002), 17.
149. Dương, *Beyond Illusions*, 51.
150. Nina McPherson, "About the Author," in Dương, *Beyond Illusions*, 245–47; Bui, *Following Ho Chi Minh*, 145; McPherson, "Dương Thu Hương."
151. Bui, *Following Ho Chi Minh*, 146–47.
152. McPherson, "About the Author," 245–47; McPherson, "Dương Thu Hương."
153. McPherson, "About the Author," 247, and "Dương Thu Hương"; Nayan Chanda, "Indochina beyond the Cold War: The Chill from Eastern Europe," in *The Challenge of Reform in Indochina*, ed. Börje Ljunggren (Cambridge, MA: Harvard University Press, 1993), 27.
154. Murray Hiebert, "The Grim Reaper," *FEER*, May 26, 1988, 18–19, and "Socialist Stagnation," *FEER*, July 28, 1988, 20–21.
155. Huỳnh, "Vietnam's Reforms," 5.
156. FEER, *Asia 1990 Yearbook*, 242.
157. Chanda, "Indochina beyond the Cold War," 29.
158. Randal, "Leading Vietnamese Communist"; Peter Colm, "North Vietnamese Colonel Calls for Democracy, U.S.-Vietnam Trade," *Tenderloin Times*, San Francisco, Nov. 1991, 1, 12.
159. Nguyễn Khắc Viện, "Dear Respected Nguyễn Hữu Thọ," Jan. 6, 1991, trans. Indochina Project, Washington, DC.
160. Porter, *Vietnam*, 54.
161. Nayan Chanda, "Indochina Today: Reform and Paralysis," in *The Challenge of Indochina: An Examination of the U.S. Role*, ed. Dick Clark (Queenstown, MD: Aspen Institute, 1991), 19.
162. Porter, *Vietnam*, 54; Li, *Peasants on the Move*, 4, 9.
163. Beresford, *Vietnam*, 154; "Vietnam's Rice Output Faces Slide on Crop Switch," *Bloomberg News*, Sept. 11, 2013, http://www.bloomberg.com/news/2013-09-12/vietnam-s-rice-output-faces-slide-on-crop-switch-southeast-asia.html (accessed Oct. 24, 2014).
164. Florence Beaugé, "Determined to Succeed," *Guardian Weekly*, Feb. 7, 2010, 28–29 (from *Le Monde*).
165. *Institute of Southeast Asian Studies Monitor*, no. 5 (2014), 3; no. 6, 4; no. 2 (2015), 4, 12; no. 3, 14; no. 5, 17; no. 1 (2016), 4; no. 2 (2016), 4; "GDP Sees Biggest Increase in Five Years as NA's Ninth Session Opens," *Việt Nam News*, May 21,

2015, http://vietnamnews.vn/politics-laws/270619/gdp-sees-biggest-increase-in-five-years-as-nas-ninth-session-opens.html (accessed May 22, 2015). See also "Vietnam Economic Outlook," June 21, 2016, http://www.focus-economics.com/countries/vietnam (accessed June 21, 2016).

166. World Bank, "High-Technology Exports (Current US$)," http://data.worldbank.org/indicator/TX.VAL.TECH.CD/countries/VN?display=graph (accessed Oct. 24, 2014)

167. *CIA World Factbook*, cited in Index Mundi, http://www.indexmundi.com/g/g.aspx?v=118&c=vm&l=en (accessed Oct. 24, 2014).

168. Philip Taylor, "Apocalypse Now? Hoa Hao Buddhism Emerging from the Shadows of War," *Australian Journal of Anthropology* 12, no, 3 (2001): 350n15.

169. "Vietnam: Religious Freedom Denied," Human Rights Watch, May 9, 2008, http://www.hrw.org/en/news/2008/05/07/vietnam-religious-freedom-denied (accessed Oct. 31, 2014). See also Human Rights Watch, *On the Margins: Rights Abuses of Ethnic Khmer in Vietnam's Mekong Delta* (New York: Human Rights Watch, 2009), and Philip Taylor, "Losing the Waterways: The Displacement of Khmer Communities from the Freshwater Rivers of the Mekong Delta, 1945–2010," *Modern Asian Studies* 47, no. 2 (2013): 500–41.

170. Human Rights Watch, *Montagnard Christians in Vietnam*.

171. Cù Huy Hà Vũ, "Human Rights Suppression and Democracy Movement in Vietnam," presentation to the Yale Council on Southeast Asia Studies, Feb. 4, 2015. The *New York Times* later estimated there to be "more than 100" political prisoners. "Common Ground for Vietnam and the U.S.," editorial, *New York Times*, July 7, 2015, available online at http://www.nytimes.com/2015/07/08/opinion/common-ground-for-vietnam-and-the-us.html?ref=opinion&_r=0 (accessed July 9, 2015)

172. Carlyle A. Thayer, "The Trial of Lê Công Định: New Challenges to the Legitimacy of Vietnam's Party-State," *Journal of Vietnamese Studies* 5, no, 3 (Fall 2010): 207.

173. Lê Hồng Hiệp, *The One Party-State and Prospects for Democratization in Vietnam*, ISEAS Perspective 63 (Singapore: Institute of Southeast Asian Studies, 2013), 6–7.

174. Transparency International, https://www.transparency.org/country (accessed July 3, 2016).

175. Recent studies of outer urban areas include Erik Harms, *Saigon's Edge: On the Margins of Ho Chi Minh City* (Minneapolis: University of Minnesota Press, 2011), and Danielle Labbé, *Land Politics and Livelihoods on the Margins of Hanoi, 1920–2010* (Vancouver: UBC Press, 2014) (on corruption, see, e.g., 139–41).

176. Hi Hoang Hop, *The Oil Rig Incident*, ISEAS Perspective 61 (Singapore: Institute of Southeast Asian Studies, 2014), 3; Ian Storey, *The Sino-Vietnamese Oil Rig Crisis*, ISEAS Perspective 52 (Singapore: Institute of Southeast Asian Studies, 2014), 5.

177. Hi, "Oil Rig Incident," 3.

178. Storey, "Sino-Vietnamese Oil Rig Crisis," 5.

179. John Boudreau and Mai Ngoc Chau, "Vietnam Boat Attacked by Chinese Surveillance Ship," *Bloomberg News*, Oct. 23, 2014, http://www.bloomberg.com/news/2014-10-23/vietnam-boat-attacked-by-chinese-surveillance-ship.html (accessed Nov. 18, 2014).

180. Storey, "Sino-Vietnamese Oil Rig Crisis," 6.

181. "Beijing Places Missile Launchers on Disputed South China Sea Island," *Guardian*, Feb. 17, 2016, available online at http://www.theguardian.com/world/2016/feb/17/china-places-missiles-woody-south-china-sea-islands (accessed July 3, 2016).

182. Jason Morris-Jung, *Reflections on the Oil Rig Crisis: Vietnam's Domestic Opposition Grows*, ISEAS Perspective 43 (Singapore: Institute of Southeast Asian Studies, 2014).
183. Tania Branigan, "China Lambasts US over South China Sea Role," *Guardian*, Aug. 6, 2012, available online at http://www.theguardian.com/world/2012/aug/06/china-us-south-china-sea; Storey, "Sino-Vietnamese Oil Rig Crisis," 7–8.
184. Permanent Court of Arbitration, Case no. 2013-19, *In the Matter of the South China Sea*, Award of Arbitral Tribunal, July 12, 2016, available online at https://pca-cpa.org/wp-content/uploads/sites/175/2016/07/PH-CN-20160712-Award.pdf (accessed Sept. 26, 2016), 255.
185. Huong Le Thu, *Bumper Harvest in 2013 for Vietnamese Diplomacy*, ISEAS Perspective 4, (Singapore: Institute of Southeast Asian Studies, 2014), 4, 6–7.
186. Boudreau and Mai, "Vietnam Boat Attacked."
187. Kyle Mizokami, "The U.S. Is About to Sell Weapons to Vietnam," *The Week*, Oct. 23, 2014, available online at http://theweek.com/article/index/270307/the-us-is-about-to-sell-weapons-to-vietnam-thats-bad-news-for-china.
188. "Common Ground for Vietnam and the U.S.," editorial, *New York Times*, July 7, 2015.

EPILOGUE

1. Philip Taylor, *Goddess on the Rise: Pilgrimage and Popular Religion in Vietnam* (Honolulu: University of Hawai'i Press, 2004), 284, 91.
2. Olga Dror, *Cult, Culture, and Authority: Princess Liễu Hạnh in Vietnamese History* (Honolulu: University of Hawai'i Press, 2007), 188–89, 192.
3. Chung Van Hoang, "'Following Uncle Hồ to Save the Nation': Empowerment, Legitimacy, and Nationalistic Aspirations in a Vietnamese New Religious Movement," *Journal of Southeast Asian Studies* 47, no. 2 (June 2016): 235.
4. Taylor, *Goddess on the Rise*, 4–5, 252.
5. David Biggs, *Quagmire: Nation-Building and Nature in the Mekong Delta* (Seattle: University of Washington Press, 2010), 62.
6. Taylor, *Goddess*, 3–5, 59, 252.
7. Dror, *Cult, Culture, and Authority*, 195–96.
8. Nhung Tuyet Tran, "Gender, Property, and the 'Autonomy Thesis' in Southeast Asia: The Endowment of Local Succession in Early Modern Vietnam," *Journal of Asian Studies* 67, no. 1 (Feb. 2008): 43–72. See also Nhung Tuyet Tran, *Familial Properties: Gender, State, and Society in Early Modern Vietnam* (Honolulu: University of Hawai'i Press, forthcoming).
9. Anita Vandenbeld and Ha Hoa Ly, *Women's Representation in the National Assembly in Viet Nam—The Way Forward* (Hanoi: United Nations Development Programme, 2012), available online at http://www.un.org.vn/en/component/docman/doc_details/331-womens-representation-in-the-national-assembly-of-viet-nam-the-way-forward.html (accessed Nov. 17, 2014).
10. Vandenbeld and Ha, *Women's Representation*, 1, 4–5.
11. "Vietnam Adds US-educated Official to Party's Politburo," *Bloomberg News*, May 11, 2013, http://www.bloomberg.com/news/2013-05-11/vietnam-adds-u-s-educated-official-to-party-s-politburo.html (accessed Nov. 17, 2014); "11th Party Congress Announces CPVCC Members," *Vietnam+*, Jan. 18, 2011, http://en.vietnamplus.vn/Home/11th-Party-Congress-announces-CPVCC-members/20111/15511.vnplus

12. Jayne Werner, "Gender, Household and the State: Renovation (*Đổi Mới*) as Social Process in Việt Nam," in *Gender, Household, State: Đổi Mới in Việt Nam*, ed. Werner and Danièle Bélanger (Ithaca, NY: Cornell Southeast Asia Program, 2002), 29–47.
13. "Vietnam: Record Drought Threatens Livelihoods," *IRIN*, March 5, 2010, www.irinnews.org/report/88320/vietnam-record-drought-threatens-livelihoods (accessed Nov. 21, 2014).
14. "One Dam Thing After Another," *Economist*, Nov. 12, 2011, available online at http://www.economist.com/node/21538158 (accessed Nov. 18, 2014).
15. *Economist*, Feb. 16, 2016.
16. Võ Văn Kiệt, "Climate Change Could Submerge Mekong Delta," *Thanh Niên*, March 1, 2008; "Vietnam Mourns Reformist PM Vo Van Kiet," AFP, Ho Chi Minh City, June15,2008,availableonlineathttp://www.spacedaily.com/2006/080615053209.ux2vk9km.html (accessed April 17, 2016).
17. "Vietnam: Record Drought Threatens Livelihoods," and "Vietnam: From Rice to Shrimps and Ginger: Adapting to Saltwater Intrusion," *IRIN*, Dec. 28, 2011, http://www.irinnews.org/report/94552/vietnam-from-rice-to-shrimps-and-ginger-adapting-to-saltwater-intrusion (accessed Nov. 20, 2014).
18. "Vietnam: From Rice to Shrimps and Ginger."
19. "Salt of the Earth," *Economist*, April 30, 2016, 37. My estimate of a population of c. three million in 1930 is derived from Pierre Brocheux, *The Mekong Delta* (Madison: Center for Southeast Asian Studies, University of Wisconsin-Madison, 1995), 43, and Pierre Brocheux and Daniel Hémery, *Indochina: An Ambiguous Colonization, 1858–1954* (Berkeley: University of California Press, 2009), 254, table 6.1.
20. Laura E. Erban, Steven M. Gorelick, and Howard A. Zebker, "Groundwater Extraction, Land Subsidence, and Sea-Level Rise in the Mekong Delta, Vietnam," *Environmental Research Letters*, Aug. 15, 2014, 1–6, available online at http://iopscience.iop.org/1748-9326/9/8/084010/article;jsessionid=4E5F3817109266122563E28E9FB6E441.c1 (accessed Nov. 18, 2014).
21. "Vietnam: From Rice to Shrimps and Ginger."
22. "Salt of the Earth," *Economist*, April 30, 2016, 37.
23. Paul P. S. Teng, Mely Caballero-Anthony, and Jonatan Anderias, *The Future of Rice Security under Climate Change*, NTS Report no. 4 (Singapore: Centre for Non-Traditional Security Studies, Nanyang Technological University, 2016), 4, 59–62.
24. Hannah Beech and Alex Perry, "Rhinos at Risk: How Asia's Appetite for Rhino Horn Is Endangering One of Nature's Giants," *Time*, June 13, 2011 (European ed.), 40.
25. Beech and Perry, "Rhinos at Risk," 38–39.
26. Andrew Lam, "35 Years After War's End, Vietnamese Diaspora Finds Its Way Home," *New America Media*, Sept. 19, 2010, http://newamericamedia.org/2010/09/vietnamese-diaspora-slowing-returning-home.php (accessed May 20, 2016)
27. See for instance Janet A. Hoskins, *The Divine Eye and the Diaspora: Vietnamese Syncretism Becomes Transpacific Caodaism* (Honolulu: University of Hawai'i Press, 2015).
28. "Vietnam Arms Embargo to Be Fully Lifted, Obama Says in Hanoi," *New York Times*, May 23, 2016.

INDEX

Page numbers in italics refer to figures and tables.